'DRYDEN

THE DRAMATIC WORKS

SECRET LOVE · Sr MARTIN MAR-ALL · THE TEMPEST

AN EVENING'S LOVE · TYRANNICK LOVE

THE NOTES

IN SIX VOLUMES · VOLUME II

EDITED BY MONTAGUE SUMMERS

GORDIAN PRESS

NEW YORK

1968

Originally published 1932
by the Nonesuch Press
in an Edition of 1000 Sets
Reprinted 1968
by Gordian Press

Library of Congress Catalog Card Number 68-15208

THE CONTENTS

SECRET LOVE, or The Maiden Queen: P. 1

Sr MARTIN MAR-ALL, or The Feigned Innocence, a Comedy: P. 73

THE TEMPEST, or The Enchanted Island, A Comedy: P. 143

AN EVENING'S LOVE, or The Mock-Astrologer: P. 231

TYRANNICK LOVE, or The Royal Martyr, A Tragedy: P. 325

Textual Notes: P. 397

Explanatory Notes: P. 461

SECRET LOVE

OR THE MAIDEN QUEEN

————Vitiis nemo sine nascitur: optimus ille
Qui minimis urgetur.   Horace.

SOURCE

DRYDEN himself tells us that his "Play is founded on a story in the *Cyrus*, which he calls the Queen of *Corinth;* in whose Character, as it has been affirm'd to me, he represents that of the Famous *Christina*, Queen of *Sweden*." It must be remembered that *Artamène, ou le Grand Cyrus* by Madeleine de Scudéry was originally published under the name of her brother, Georges de Scudéry, hence "he calls." *Artamène, ou le Grand Cyrus* is the most famous as it is the longest of the de Scudéry romances. It was published Paris, 1649–53; and there are subsequent editions Paris, 1654, 1656, 1658; Leyde, 1655, 1656.

The Grand Cyrus was "Englished by F. G. Esq;", 2 vols., folio, London, 1653–4. *The Historie of Cleobuline* Queen of Corinth will be found in vol. II, pp. 108–136. It is related by Philocles, but Dryden's Philocles in de Scudéry is named Myrinthe. Lysimantes is Basilides. Asteria, the Queen's Confident, Stesilea; Candiope, Philimene. Dryden has merely used the outline of the story, and it is hardly exaggeration to say that all that is valuable is his own. Yet there is considerable charm in Madeleine de Scudéry's brocaded page, and in spite of all longueurs those who happily have the leisure to read her romances will find these old-time courtesies, high ideals, gallantries, outmoded perhaps in phrase but none the less of a quality almost lost to-day. At least here one can escape from the red-hot rush and mental pudder of the present age. In English the handiest edition is the duodecimos of 1691, where, so the publisher boasts, he has contracted *cumbersome Folio's into a far less Compass, chiefly for the conveni-ence of the Reader, by reducing them into so many smaller Divisions, as render them much more portable than before, and consequently less troublesome Companions for those that travel, or when their leisure hours invite 'em to delightful Conversation, under the pleasing Shades of Summer, with the Renowned* Artamenes.

Christina Alexandra, Queen of Sweden, daughter of Gustavus Adolphus II, was born at Stockholm, 8 December, 1626, and died at Rome, 19 April, 1689. When her father fell on the field of Lützen, 16 November, 1632, she was but six years of age. On 8 December, 1644, she assumed the supreme power, although she was not actually crowned until two years later. Her great delight was in the patronage of literature and science, and she has been called "the most accomplished woman of her time." The States and her ministers pressing her to marry, she prevailed upon them to name her cousin, Karl Gustav of Pfalz-Zweibrücken, who had sought her hand, her successor. She was, however, swayed by favourites, one of whom, Count Magnus Gabriel de la Gardie, is no doubt the Myrinthe of the romance and Philocles of the play. Queen Christina, indeed, actually married de la Gardie to the sister of Karl Gustav, just as Philocles is wedded to Candiope, the sister of Lysimantes. On 6 June, 1654, Christina solemnly transferred her regal authority to her cousin, and having thus abdicated, she set out on her travels. In Brussels she made private acknow-ledgement of her belief in the Catholic Church, whilst her public admittance took place, November, 1655, in the parish church of Innsbruck. For years

3

European scandal and gossip were very busy with her adventures, her eccentricities, her voyages, her dressing as an Amazon. In Rome, maugre her vagaries, her palace became the centre for the literary and artistic world. Her library, in particular, was very rich in rarest volumes. Her monument in S. Peter's is by Carlo Fontana.

The story of Pisistrate and Cerinthe, *Grand Cyrus*, Part IX, Book III (trans. F. G., folio, 1653–4, Vol. II, pp. 134–169), is amusingly told, but to seek for Celadon and Florimel, Olinda and Sabina, in Pisistrate, Cerinthe, Euridamie, Cleorante, is a mere carping flam. Celadon and Florimel are the lively creation of Dryden's genius.

On the other hand, as I have pointed out in the Introduction, Celadon has much of the spirit of Hylas in D'Urfe's *L'Astrée*, and the contract scene betwixt the two madcap lovers at the conclusion of *Secret Love* was certainly suggested by the thirteen articles agreed upon by Hylas and Stelle in the pastoral romance. Céladon is also the hero of *L'Astrée*, but he is an entirely different figure from Dryden's Celadon.

It is nugatory to compare the clever scene (Act IV, 1) where Melissa examines Olinda and Sabina as to their inclinations towards Celadon with the episode in Shirley's *The Changes, or Love in a Maze* (licensed 10 January, 1631–2, 4to, 1632), Act I, when Goldsworth, sounding his daughters Chrysolina and Aurelia, finds that they both affect Gerard. *The Changes* is certainly far from the best of Shirley's plays. The plot is involved without sufficient interest, the exposition thin. That this piece was received with great applause when revived after the Restoration seems due to the admirable acting of William Wintershal as Sir Gervase Simple and the excellent low comedy of Lacy as Thumpe. It was seen by Pepys on several occasions. Thursday, 22 May, 1662, he notes: "The play hath little in it, but Lacy's part of a country fellow which he did to admiration." Wednesday, 1 May, 1667, he thought it "but a sorry play, only Lacy clowne's part, which he did most admirably indeed." Saturday, 7 February, 1667–8, he writes of it "a dull, silly play, I think." Tuesday, 28 April, 1668, he remarked upon the "very good mirth of Lacy the clown, and Wintersell, the country-knight, his master." In truth, the judgement of Pepys seems very candid and just.

If there be any parallel at all between this episode of *Secret-Love* and the scene in *The Changes*, and at any rate it is negligible, Dryden both in character and contrivance is here infinitely superior to the older poet.

THEATRICAL HISTORY

SECRET *Love; or, The Maiden Queen* was produced at the Theatre Royal late in February, 1666–7. On Saturday, 2 March of that year Pepys notes: "After dinner, with my wife, to the King's house to see 'The Mayden Queene,' a new play of Dryden's, mightily commended for the regularity of it, and the strain and wit; and, the truth is, there is a comical part done by Nell, which is Florimell, that I never can hope ever to see the like done again, by man or woman. The King and Duke of York were at the play. But so great performance of a comical part was never, I believe, in the world before as Nell do this, both as a mad girle, then most and best of all when she comes in like a young gallant; and hath the motions and carriage of a spark the most that ever I saw any man have. It makes me, I confess, admire her."

Secret Love achieved a tremendous success, and was in particular among the favourite plays of Charles II, so that as Dryden himself tells us His Majesty "grac'd it with the Title of His Play," and thus then rescued it from the captious malice of a contemporary Zoilus, and the jaundiced sciomachia of a coetaneous St. John Ervine. The King, for example, saw the comedy again on Tuesday, 5 March, and it was performed at Court on Thursday, 18 April. Saturday, 4 January, 1667–8, Charles was at the Theatre Royal for *Secret Love*, and on Monday, 27 January it was commanded at Court. There are indeed continual performances recorded, both at the Theatre Royal and before the King at Court, of Dryden's brilliant and justly applauded scenes.

John Evelyn, who was very little given to visiting the playhouses, writes that on Thursday, 14 March, 1666–7, he "saw *The Virgin-Queen*, a play written by Mr. Dryden."

On Monday, 25 March, 1666–7, Pepys notes: "Sir W. Pen and I in the pit, and here saw 'The Maiden Queene' again; which indeed the more I see the more I like, and is an excellent play, and so done by Nell, her merry part, as cannot be better done in nature, I think." Friday, 25 May, 1667: "My wife and I and Sir W. Pen to the King's play house, and there saw 'The Mayden Queene,' which though I have often seen, yet pleases me infinitely, it being impossible, I think, ever to have the Queen's part, which is very good and passionate, and Florimel's part, which is the most comicall that ever was made for woman, ever done better than they two are by young Marshall and Nelly." Pepys further records visits to *Secret Love*, "which pleases us mightily," on Friday, 23 August, 1667, and on Friday, 24 January, 1667–8, when he "saw the best part of 'The Mayden Queen,' which, the more I see the more I love, and think one of the best plays I ever saw, and is certainly the best acted of any thing ever the House did, and particularly Becke Marshall, to admiration." On New Year's Day, 1 January, 1668–9, Pepys has, "My wife and I with our coach to the King's playhouse, and there in a box saw 'The Mayden Queene.' Knepp looked upon us, but I durst not shew her any countenance, and, as well as I could carry myself I found my wife uneasy there, poor wretch! therefore I shall avoid that house as much as I can." None the less on Wednesday, 13 January, 1668–9, we find: "To the King's playhouse, and there saw, I think, 'The Maiden Queene,' and so home."

It does not appear which actress undertook Florimel after the stage lost Nell Gwyn in 1671, but upon the Union of the two Companies, who opened at the Theatre Royal, 16 November, 1682, Celadon seems presently to have been assigned to William Mountfort, whose "Gaiety of Temper and Airy Disposition, which were very conspicuous, could not be easily restrain'd," and who was distinguished as "a Person of a great deal of good Nature, and perfectly well bred; He well understood Musick, could sing very agreeably, and he Danc'd finely." Mountfort, no doubt, played Celadon when *Secret Love* was given at Whitehall before James II on Friday, 15 December, 1686.

5

Secret Love maintained its place in the repertory of the theatre until well within the first decade of the eighteenth century. It is only played once in the 1703-4 season at Drury Lane, but in the following season it was given no less than half a dozen times.

At Drury Lane, 26 March, 1706, *Secret Love* was chosen for the benefit of the vivacious Mrs. Letitia Cross, who made an admirable Florimel.

Eventually Dryden's excellent comedy fell out of the list of acting plays shortly after Colley Cibber had conceived the extraordinary idea of hashing up the lighter episodes of *Secret Love* and *Marriage-à-la-Mode* into an olio, which he peppered with a gaming scene or two from *An Evening's Love*, spoiled by the admixture of his own savourless salt, and turned out on 4 February, 1707, upon the Haymarket (King's Theatre) boards as *The Comical Lovers*. Cibber himself was Celadon, who has become brother to Doralice from *Marriage À-la-Mode*, and Mrs. Oldfield, Florimel. Old Colley was an impudent vulgar dog, and nowhere has he shown his impudence more brazenly than by appropriating wholesale this exquisite wit, which has lost only too much by being strained through the colander of his cranium, and nowhere has he shown his vulgarity more blatantly than by the spiritless awkwardness with which he has concocted his ridiculous rifacimento. It is beyond the power of man to make Horace flat, and humble Maro's strains; to render Dryden dull and lumpish; but Cibber has had a brave essay.

The Comical Lovers, not infrequently as *Marriage À-la-Mode* and sometimes as *Court Gallantry*, appears at intervals until the latter half of the century.

On Tuesday afternoon, 19 January, 1886, *Secret Love* was revived for one matinée at the Court Theatre with the following cast: Lysimantes, W. T. Lovell; Philocles, Bernard Gould; Celadon, Hayden Coffin; Phormio, Cooper Cliffe; Queen of Sicily, Miss Webster, a granddaughter of Benjamin Webster; Candiope, Rose Dearing; Asteria, Alice Belmore; Florimel, Rose Norreys; Flavia, Miss Byron, a daughter of the Victorian dramatist; Melissa, Neva Bond; Olinda, Stephanie Baring; Sabina, Lilian Carr. The performance won warmest applause from the critics who were obviously surprised at the excellence of Dryden's play. Miss Webster was given "unstinted praise for the intelligent and really artistic way in which she came through no easy task." But "Mr. C. Hayden Coffin and Miss Norreys . . . carried away the chief honours. Mr. Coffin as an actor has never been seen to such advantage as in the part of Celadon. He . . . rattled through his work with a light and easy air, and with a buoyant humour which was very amusing and very enjoyable. Miss Norreys was even more successful as Florimel . . . she fairly took admiration by storm in every scene in which she appeared, and in that of Florimel's masquerading her acting was positively enchanting . . . she jigged away most lightly and merrily, Celadon looking on for a time, and then, being moved to emulation, himself joining in the dance, which moved the spectators to enthusiasm, and which had to be repeated in response to a demand that was not to be denied. This jig, indeed, was the big hit of the performance," as, in truth, had been Nelly's jig two hundred years before.

PREFACE

IT has been the ordinary practice of the French Poets, to dedicate their Works of this nature to their King, especially when they have had the least encouragement to it, by his approbation of them on the Stage. But I confess I want the confidence to follow their example, though perhaps I have as specious pretences to it for this Piece, as any they can boast of: it having been own'd in so particular a manner by His Majesty, that he has grac'd it with the Title of His Play, and thereby rescued it from the severity (that I may not say malice) of its Enemies. But, though a character so high and unde-serv'd, has not rais'd in me the presumption to offer such a trifle to his most serious view, yet I will own the vanity to say, that after this glory which it has receiv'd from a Soveraign Prince, I could not send it to seek protection from any Subject. Be this Poem then sacred to him without the tedious form of a Dedication, and without pre-suming to interrupt those hours which he is daily giving to the peace and settlement of his people.

For what else concerns this Play, I would tell the Reader that it is regular, according to the strictest of Dramatick Laws, but that it is a commendation which many of our Poets now despise, and a beauty which our common Audiences do not easily discern. Neither indeed do I value my self upon it, because with all that symmetry of parts, it may want an air and spirit (which consists in the writing) to set it off. 'Tis a question variously disputed, whether an Author may be al-lowed as a competent judg of his own works. As to the Fabrick and contrivance of them certainly he may, for that is properly the em-ployment of the judgment; which, as a Master-builder may deter-mine, and that without deception, whether the work be according to the exactness of the model; still granting him to have a perfect Idea of that pattern by which he works: and that he keeps himself always constant to the discourse of his judgment, without admitting self-love, which is the false Surveigher of his Fancy, to intermeddle in it. These Qualifications granted (being such as all sound Poets are pre-supposed to have within them) I think all Writers, of what kind so-ever, may infallibly judge of the frame and contexture of their Works. But for the ornament of Writing, which is greater, more various and bizarre in Poesie then in any other kind, as it is properly the Child of Fancy; so it can receive no measure, or at least but a very imperfect one of its own excellencies or faillures from the judgment.

7

Self-love (which enters but rarely into the offices of the judgment) here predominates. And Fancy (if I may so speak) judging of it self, can be no more certain or demonstrative of its own effects, then two crooked lines can be the adæquate measure of each other. What I have said on this subject, may, perhaps, give me some credit with my Readers, in my opinion of this Play, which I have ever valued above the rest of my Follies of this kind: yet not thereby in the least dissenting from their judgment, who have concluded the writing of this to be much inferior to my Indian Emperour. But the Argument of that was much more noble, not having the allay of Comedy to depress it: yet if this be more perfect, either in its kind, or in the general notion of a Play, 'tis as much as I desire to have granted for the vindication of my Opinion, and, what as nearly touches me, the sentence of a Royal Judg. Many have imagin'd the Character of *Philocles* to be faulty; some for not discovering the Queens love, others for his joining in her restraint. But though I am not of their number, who obstinately defend what they have once said, I may with modesty take up those answers which have been made for me by my Friends; namely, that *Philocles*, who was but a Gentleman of ordinary birth, had no reason to guess so soon at the Queens Passion, she being a person so much above him, and by the suffrages of all her People, already destin'd to *Lysimantes*: Besides, that he was prepossessed, (as the Queen somewhere hints it to him) with another inclination which rendred him less clear-sighted in it, since no man, at the same time, can distinctly view two different objects. And if this, with any shew of reason, may be defended I leave my Masters the Criticks to determine whether it be not much more conducing to the beauty of my Plot, that *Philocles* should be long ignorant of the Queens Love, then that with one leap he should have entred into the knowledge of it, and thereby freed himself, to the disgust of the Audience, from that pleasing Labyrinth of errors which was prepar'd for him. As for that other objection of his joyning in the Queens Imprisonment, it is indisputably that which every man, if he examines himself, would have done on the like occasion. If they answer that it takes from the height of his Character to do it; I would enquire of my over-wise Censors, who told them I intended him a perfect Character, or indeed what necessity was there he should be so, the variety of Images, being one great beauty of a Play? it was as much as I design'd, to show one great and absolute pattern of honour in my Poem, which I did in the Person of the Queen: All the defects of the other parts being set to show, the more to recommend that one character of Vertue to the Audience. But neither was the fault of *Philocles* so great, if the circumstances be

8

consider'd, which, as moral Philosophy assures us, make the essential differences of good and bad; He himself best explaining his own intentions in his last Act, which was the restauration of his Queen; and even before that, in the honesty of his expressions, when he was unavoidably led by the impulsion of his love to do it. That which with more reason was objected as an indecorum, is the management of the last Scene of the Play, where *Celadon* and *Florimell* are treating too lightly of their marriage in the presence of the Queen, who likewise seems to stand idle while the great action of the *Drama* is still depending. This I cannot otherwise defend, then by telling you I so design'd it on purpose to make my Play go off more smartly; that Scene, being in the opinion of the best judges, the most divertising of the whole Comedy. But though the Artifice succeeded, I am willing to acknowledge it as a fault, since it pleas'd His Majesty, the best Judg, to think it so. I have onely to add, that the Play is founded on a story in the *Cyrus*, which he calls the Queen of *Corinth*; in whose Character, as it has been affirm'd to me, he represents that of the famous *Christina*, Queen of *Sweden*. This is what I thought convenient to write by way of Preface, to the Maiden-Queen; in the reading of which, I fear you will not meet with that satisfaction which you have had in seeing it on the Stage; the chief parts of it, both serious and comick, being performed to that height of excellence, that nothing but a command, which I could not handsomely disobey, could have given me the courage to have made it publick.

PROLOGUE

I.

HE who writ this, not without pains and thought,
From French and English Theatres has brought,
Th' exactest Rules by which a Play is wrought.

II.

The Unities of Action, Place, and Time;
The Scenes unbroken; and a mingled chime
Of Johnson's Humour, with Corneilles rhyme.

III.

But while dead colours he with care did lay,
He fears his Wit, or Plot he did not weigh,
Which are the living Beauties of a Play.

IV.

Plays are like Towns, which howe're fortifi'd
By Engineers, have still some weaker side
By the o'reseen Defendant unespy'd.

V.

And with that Art you make approaches now;
Suck Skilful fury in Assaults you show,
That every Poet without shame may bow.

VI.

Ours therefore humbly would attend your doom,
If Souldier-like, he may have terms to come
With flying colours, and with beat of Drum.

The Prologue goes out, and stayes while a Tune is play'd, after
which he returnes again.

Second PROLOGUE

I *Had forgot one half I do protest,*
And now am sent again to speak the rest.
He bows to every great and noble Wit,
But to the little Hectors of the Pit
Our Poet's sturdy, and will not submit.
He'll be before-hand with 'em, and not stay
To see each peevish Critick stab his Play:
Each Puny Censor, who his skill to boast,
Is cheaply witty on the Poets cost.
No Criticks verdict, should, of right, stand good,
They are excepted all as men of blood:
And the same Law should shield them from their fury,
Which has excluded Butchers from a Jury.
You'd all be Wits———
But writing's tedious, and that way may fail;
The most compendious method is to rail:
Which you so like, you think your selves ill us'd,
When in smart Prologues you are not abus'd.
A civil Prologue is approv'd by no Man;
You hate it as you do a Civil woman:
Your Fancy's pall'd, and liberally you pay
To have it quicken'd, e're you see a Play.
Just as old Sinners worn from their delight,
Give money to be whip'd to appetite.
But what a Pox keep I so much ado
To save our Poet? he is one of you;
A Brother Judgment, and as I hear say,
A cursed Critick as e're damn'd a Play.
Good salvage Gentlemen your own kind spare,
He is, like you, a very Wolf or Bear;
Yet think not he'll your ancient rights invade,
Or stop the course of your free damning trade:
For he, (he vows) at no friends Play can sit,
But he must needs find fault to shew his Wit:
Then, for his sake, ne're stint your own delight;
Throw boldy, for he sets to all that write;
With such he ventures on an even lay,
For they bring ready money into Play.
Those who write not, and yet all Writers nick,
Are Bankrupt Gamesters, for they damn on Tick.

THE PERSONS

QUeen of *Sicily*   Mrs *Marshall.*
Candiope, Princess of the Blood   Mrs *Quin.*
Asteria, the Queens Confident   Mrs *Knep.*
Florimell, A Maid of Honour   Mrs *Ellen Guyn.*
Flavia, another Maid of Honour   Mrs *Frances Davenport.*
Olinda, ⎱ Sisters.   Mrs *Rutter.*
Sabina, ⎰   Mrs *Eliz. Davenport.*
Melissa, Mother to *Olinda* and *Sabina*   Mrs *Cory.*
Lysimantes, first Prince of the Blood   Mr *Burt.*
Philocles, the Queens favourite   Major *Mohun.*
Celadon, a Courtier   Mr *Hart.*
Guards.
Pages of Honour.
Souldiers.

The Scene *SICILY.*

SECRET-LOVE

OR, THE

Maiden Queen

ACT I. SCENE I.

The Scene is Walks, near the Court.

Enter Celadon, Asteria, *meeting each other: he in riding habit; they embrace.*

Celadon. DEar *Asteria!*
 Asteria. My dear Brother! welcome; a thousand welcomes: Me thinks this year you have been absent has been so tedious! I hope as you have made a pleasant Voyage, so you have brought your good humour back again to Court.

Cel. I never yet knew any Company I could not be merry in, except it were an old Womans.

Ast. Or at a Funeral;

Cel. Nay, for that you shall excuse me; for I was never merrier then I was at a Creditors of mine, whose Book perished with him. But what new Beauties have you at Court? How do *Melissa*'s two fair Daughters?

Ast. When you tell me which of 'em you are in love with, I'le answer you.

Cel. Which of 'em, naughty sister, what a question's there? With both of 'em, with each and singular of 'em.

Ast. Bless me! you are not serious!

Cel. You look as if it were a wonder to see a man in love: are they not handsome?

Ast. I, but both together———

Cel. I, and both asunder; why, I hope there are but two of 'em; the tall Singing and Dancing one, and the little Innocent one?

Ast. But you cannot marry both?

Cel. No, nor either of 'em I trust in Heaven; but I can keep them company, I can sing and dance with 'em, and treat 'em, and that, I take it, is somewhat better than musty marrying them: Marriage is poor folks pleasure, that cannot go to the cost of variety: but I am

13

out of danger of that with these two, for I love 'em so equally, I can never make choice between 'em: Had I but one mistress, I might go to her to be merry, and she, perhaps, be out of humour; there were a visit lost: But here, if one of 'em frown upon me, the other will be the more obliging, on purpose to recommend her own gayety, besides a thousand things that I could name.

Ast. And none of 'em to any purpose.

Cel. Well, if you will not be cruel to a poor Lover, you might oblige me by carrying me to their lodgings.

Ast. You know I am always busie about the Queen.

Cel. But once or twice onely, till I am a little flush'd in my acquaintance with other Ladies, and have learn'd to prey for my self: I promise you I'le make all the haste I can to end your trouble, by being in love somewhere else.

Ast. You would think it hard to be deny'd now.

Cel. And reason good: many a man hangs himself for the loss of one Mistris; How do you think then I should bear the loss of two; especially in a Court where I think Beauty is but thin sown.

Ast. There's one *Florimell* the Queen's Ward, a new Beauty, as wilde as you, and a vast Fortune.

Cel. I am for her before the world: bring me to her, and I'le release you of your promise for the other two.

Enter a Page. Madam, the Queen expects you.

Cel. I see you hold her favour: Adieu Sister, you have a little Emissary there, otherwise I would offer you my service.

Ast. Farewel Brother, think upon *Florimell.*

Cel. You may trust my memory for an handsome woman. I'le think upon her, and the rest too; I'le forget none of 'em.

Exit Asteria.

SCENE II.

Enter a Gentleman walking over the Stage hastily; after him Florimel, *and* Flavia *Masqued.*

Fla. Phormio, Phormio, you will not leave us——

Gent. In faith I have a little business——   *Exit Gentle.*

Cel. Cannot I serve you in the Gentlemans room, Ladies?

Fla. Which of us would you serve?

Cel. Either of you, or both of you.

Fla. Why, could you not be constant to one?

Cel. Constant to one! I have been a Courtier, a Souldier, and a

14

Traveller, to good purpose, if I must be constant to one; give me some Twenty, some Forty, some a Hundred Mistresses: I have more Love than any one woman can turn her to.

Flor. Bless us, let us be gone Cousin; we two are nothing in his hands.

Cel. Yet for my part, I can live with as few Mistresses as any man: I desire no superfluities, onely for necessary change, or so, as I shift my Linnen.

Flor. A pretty odd kind of fellow this: he fits my humour rarely:
[*aside.*

Fla. You are as unconstant as the Moon.

Flor. You wrong him: he's as constant as the Sun, he would see all the world round in 24 hours.

Cel. 'Tis very true, Madam, but, like him, I would visit and away.

Flor. For what an unreasonable thing it were to stay long, be troublesome, and hinder a Lady of a fresh Lover.

Cel. A rare Creature this!——besides, Madam, how like a fool a man looks, when after all his eagerness of two Minutes before, he shrinks into a faint kiss, and a cold complement.

Ladies both, into your hands I commit my selfe; share me betwixt you.

Fla. I'll have nothing to do with you, since you cannot be constant to one.

Cel. Nay, rather then loose either of you, I'll do more; I'll be Constant to an 100 of you: or, (if you will needs fetter me to one) agree the matter between your selves; and the most handsome take me.

Flor. Though I am not she, yet since my Masque's down, and you cannot convince me, have a good faith of my Beauty, and for once I take you for my servant.

Cel. And for once, I'll make a blind bargain with you: strike hands; i'st a Match Mistriss?

Flor. Done Servant:

Cel. Now I am sure I have the worst on't: for you see the worst of me, and that I do not of you, 'till you shew your face————

Yet now I think on't, you must be handsome————

Flor. What kind of Beauty do you like?

Cel. Just such a one as yours.

Flor. What's that?

Cel. Such an Ovall face, clear skin, hazle eyes, thick brown Eyebrowes, and Hair as you have for all the world.

Fla. But I can assure you she has nothing of all this.

Cel. Hold thy peace, Envy; nay, I can be constant, an' I set on't.

Flor. 'Tis true she tells you.

15

Cel. I, I, you may slander your self as you please: then you have —let me see.

Flor. I'll swear you shan'not see————

Cel. A turn'd up Nose, that gives an air to your face: Oh, I find I am more and more in love with you! A full neather-lip, an out-mouth, that makes mine water at it: the bottom of your cheeks a little blub, and two dimples when you smile: for your stature 'tis well; and for your wit, 'twas given you by one that knew it had been thrown away upon an ill face: come, you are handsome, there's no denying it:

Flor. Can you settle your spirits to see an ugly face, and not be frighted, I could find in my heart to lift up my Masque and dis-abuse you.

Cel. I defy your Masque; would you wou'd try the experiment.

Flor. No, I won'not; for your ignorance is the Mother of your devotion to me.

Cel. Since you will not take the pains to convert me, I'll make bold to keep my faith: a miserable man I am sure you have made me.

Fla. This is pleasant.

Cel. It may be so to you, but it is not to me; for ought I see I am going to the most constant *Maudlin.*——

Flor. 'Tis very well, *Celadon*, you can be constant to one you have never seen, and have forsaken all you have seen.

Cel. It seems you know me then: well, if thou shou'dst prove one of my cast Mistresses, I would use thee most damnably, for offering to make me Love thee twice.

Flor. You are i' th' right: an old Mistriss, or Servant, is an old Tune, the pleasure on't is past, when we have once learnt it.

Fla. But what woman in the world wou'd you wish her like?

Cel. I have heard of one *Florimel*, the Queens Ward, would she were as like her for Beauty, as she is for Humour.

Fla. Do you hear that Cousin?   [to *Flor.* aside.

Flor. *Florimell*'s not handsome: besides, she's unconstant, and only loves for some few days.

Cel. If she loves for shorter time than I, she must love by Winter daies and Summer nights i' faith.

Flor. When you see us together you shall judge: in the mean time adieu sweet servant.

Cel. Why you won'not be so inhumane to carry away my heart, and not so much as tell me where I may hear news on't?

Flor. I mean to keep it safe for you, for if you had it, you would bestow it worse: farwell, I must see a Lady.

16

Cel. So muſt I too, if I can pull off your Masque——
Flor. You will not be so rude, I hope.
Cel. By this light but I will.
Flor. By this leg but you shan' not. [*Ex.* Flor. & Fla. *running.*

SCENE III.

Enter Philocles, *and meets him going out.*

Cel. How! my Cousin, the new Favourite—— [*aside.*
Phil. Dear *Celadon!* moſt happily arriv'd.
I hear y' have been an Honour to your Country,
In the *Calabrian* Wars, and I am glad
I have some intereſt in't.
Cel. ——But in you,
I have a larger ſubjeƈt for my joyes.
To see so rare a thing as rising vertue,
And merit underſtood at Court.
Phil. Perhaps it is the onely aƈt that can
Accuse our Queen of weakness.

Enter *Lysimantes attended.*

Lys. O, my Lord *Philocles*, well overtaken!
I came to look you.
Phil. Had I known it sooner
My swift attendance, Sir, had spar'd your trouble.
——Cousin, you see Prince *Lysimantes*   *To Cel.*
Is pleas'd to favour me with his Commands:
I beg you'l be no ſtranger now at Court.
Cel. So long as there be Ladies there, you need
Not doubt me.   *Exit Celadon.*
Phil. Some of them will, I hope, make you a Convert.
Lys. My Lord *Philocles*, I am glad we are alone:
There is a business that concerns me nearly,
In which I beg your love,
Phil. Command my service.
Lys. I know your Intereſt with the Queen is great;
(I speak not this as envying your fortune,
For frankly I confess you have deserv'd it.)
Besides, my Birth, my Courage, and my Honour,
Are all above so base a Vice.

Phil. I know, my Lord, you are firſt Prince o' th' Blood;
Your Countries second hope;
And that the publick Vote, when the Queen weds,
Designes you for her choice.
    Lys. I am not worthy.
Except Love makes desert;
For doubtless she's the glory of her time;
Of faultless Beauty, blooming as the Spring,
In our *Sicilian* Groves; matchless in Vertue,
And largely sould, where ere her bounty gives,
As with each breath she could create new Indies.
    Phil. But jealous of her glory.
    Lys. You are a Courtier; and in other termes,
Would say she is averse from marriage,
Leſt it might lesson her authority.
But, whensoe're she does, I know the people
Will scarcely suffer her to match
With any neighb'ring Prince, whose power might bend
Our free *Sicilians* to a foreign Yoke.
    Phil. I love too well my Country to desire it.
    Lys. Then to proceed, (as you well know, my Lord)
The Provinces have sent their Deputies,
Humbly to move her she would choose at home:
And, for she seems averse from speaking with them
By my appointment, have design'd these walks,
Where well she cannot shun them. Now, if you
Assiſt their suit, by joining yours to it,
And by your mediation I prove happy,
I freely promise you.——
    Phil. Without a Bribe command my utmoſt in it:——
And yet, there is a thing, which time may give me
The confidence to name:——
    Lys. 'Tis yours whatever.
But tell me true; does she not entertain
Some deep, and setled thoughts againſt my person?
    Phil. I hope not so; but she, of late, is froward;
Reserv'd, and sad, and vex'd at little things;
Which her great Soul asham'd of, shakes them off,
And ſtraight composes.
    Lys. You are ſtill near the Queen, and all our Actions come to
Princes Eyes, as they are represented by them that hold the Mirour.
    Phil. Here she comes, and with her the Deputies;——
I fear all is not right.
18

*Enter Queen; Deputies after her; Asteria, Guard, Flavia, Olinda,
    Sabina.*

Queen turnes back to the Deputies, and speaks entring.

Qu. And I must tell you,
It is a sawcy boldness you assume
To press on my retirements.————
   1. *Dep.* Our business being of no less concern
Then is the peace and quiet of your Subjects————
And that delay'd————
   2. *Dep.* ————we humbly took this time
To represent your peoples fears and dangers.
   Qu. My peoples fears! who made them States-men?
They much mistake their business, if they think
It is to govern:————
The Rights of Subjects and of Sovereigns
Are things distinct in Nature: theirs, is to
Enjoy Propriety, not Empire.
   Lys. If they have err'd, 'twas but an over-care;
An ill-tim'd Duty.————
   Qu. Cousin, I expect
From your near Bloud, not to excuse, but check 'em.
By all the Gods they would impose a Ruler
Upon their Lawful Queen:
For what's an Husband else?
   Lys. Farr, Madam, be it from the thoughts
Of any who pretends to that high Honour,
To wish for more than to be reckon'd
As the most grac'd and first of all your servants.
   Qu. These are th' insinuating promises
Of those who aim at pow'r: but tell me Cousin;
(For you are unconcern'd and may be Judge)
Should that aspiring man
Compass his ends,
What pawn of his obedience could he give me,
When Kingly pow'r were once invested in him?
   Lys. What greater pledge than Love? when those fair eyes
Cast their commanding beams, he that cou'd be
A Rebel to your birth, must pay them homage.
   Qu. All eyes are fair
That sparkle with the Jewels of a Crown:
But now I see my Government is odious;

My people find I am not fit to Reign,
Else they would never——
    Lys. So far from that, we all acknowledge you
The bounty of the Gods to *Sicilie:*
More than they are you cannot make our Joyes;
Make them but lasting in a Successor.
    Phil. Your People seek not to impose a Prince;
But humbly offer one to your free choice:
And such a one as he is, (may I have leave
To speak some little of his great deserts.)
    Qu. I'le hear no more——
To the Dep. For you, attend to morrow at the Council,
There you shall have my firm resolves; mean time
My Cousin I am sure will welcome you.
    Lys. Still more and more mysterious: but I have gain'd one of her
women that shall unriddle it:—— Come Gentlemen.——
    All Dep. Heav'n preserve your Majesty.
                                [*Exeunt* Lysimantes *and* Deputies.
    Qu. *Philocles* you may stay.
    Phil. I humbly wait your Majesties commands.
    Qu. Yet now I better think on't, you may go.
    Phil. Madam!
    Qu. I have no Commands.——or, what's all one
You no obedience.
    Phil. How, no obedience, Madam?
I plead no other merit; 'tis the Charter
By which I hold your favour, and my fortunes.
    Qu. My favours are cheap blessings, like Rain and Sun-shine,
For which we scarcely thank the Gods, because
We daily have them.
    Phil. Madam, your Breath which rais'd me from the dust
May lay me there again:
But fate nor time can ever make me lose
The sense of your indulgent bounties to me.
    Qu. You are above them now; grown popular:
Ah *Philocles,* could I expect from you
That usage I have found! no tongue but yours
To move me to a marriage?——   [*weeps.*
The factious Deputies might have some end in't,
And my ambitious Cousin gain a Crown;
But what advantage could there come to you?
What could you hope from *Lysimantes's Reign*
That you can want in mine?
20

Phil. You your self clear me, Madam, had I sought
More pow'r, this Marriage sure was not the way.
But, when your safety was in question,
When all your people were unsatisfied,
Desir'd a King, nay more, design'd the Man,
It was my duty then.————
  Qy. Let me be judge of my own safety;
I am a woman,
But danger from my Subjects cannot fright me.
  Phil. But *Lysimantes*, Madam, is a person————
  Qy. I cannot love,——
Shall I, I who am born a Sovereign Queen,
Be barr'd of that which God and Nature gives
The meanest Slave, a freedom in my love?
——Leave me, good *Philocles*, to my own thoughts;
When next I need your counsel I'le send for you————
  Phil. I'm most unhappy in your high displeasure;
But, since I must not speak, Madam, be pleas'd
To peruse this, and therein, read my care.
  *He plucks out a paper, and presents it to her, But drops, unknown to
    him, a picture.*
  Queen reads.————   *Exit* Philocles.
A Catalogue of such Persons————
  Spies the box. What's this he has let fall? *Asteria?*
  Ast. Your Majesty——
  Qy. Take that up, it fell from *Philocles.*
                        She takes it up, looks on it, and smiles.
How now, what makes you merry?
  Ast. A small discovery I have made, Madam.
  Qy. Of what?
  Ast. Since first your Majesty grac'd *Philocles,*
I have not heard him nam'd for any Mistriss,
But now this picture has convinc'd me,——
  Qy. Ha! let me see it————   [*Snatches it from her.*
Candiope, Prince *Lysimantes* sister!
  Ast. Your favour Madam, may encourage him——
And yet he loves in a high place for him:
A Princess of the Blood, and what is more,
Beyond comparison the fairest Lady
Our Isle can boast.——
  Qy. How! she the fairest
Beyond comparison: 'tis false, you flatter her;
She is not fair.——

21

Ast. I humbly beg forgiveness on my knees,
If I offended you: But next yours, Madam,
Which all muſt yield to——
   Qu. I pretend to none.
   Ast. She passes for a beauty.
   Qu. I, She may pass.———But why do I speak of her?
Dear *Asteria* lead me, I am not well o' th' sudden.—— [*She faints.*
   Ast. Who's near there? help the Queen.   *The Guards are coming.*
   Qu. Bid 'em away, 'twas but a qualm,
And 'tis already going.——
   Ast. Dear Madam, what's the matter! y' are
Of late so alter'd I scarce know you.
You were gay humour'd, and you now are pensive,
Once calm, and now unquiet;
Pardon my boldness that I press thus far
Into your secret thoughts: I have at leaſt
A ſubjeects share in you.
   Qu. Thou haſt a greater,
That of a friend; but am I froward, saiſt thou!
   Ast. It ill becomes me, Madam, to say that.
   Qu. I know I am: prithee forgive me for it.
I cannot help it, but thou haſt
Not long to ſuffer it.
   Ast. Alas!
   Qu. I feel my ſtrength insensibly consume,
Like Lillies wasting in a Lymbecks heat.
Yet a few dayes——
And thou shalt see me lie all damp and cold,
Shrowded within some hollow Vault, among
My silent Anceſtors.
   Ast. O deareſt Madam!
Speak not of death, or think not, if you die
That I will ſtay behind.
   Qu. Thy love has mov'd me, I for once will have
The pleasure to be pitied; I'le unfold
A thing so ſtrange, so horrid of my self;——
   Ast. Bless me, sweet Heaven!
So horrid, said you, Madam?
   Qu. That Sun, who with one look surveys the Globe,
Sees not a wretch like me: and could the world
Take a right measure of my ſtate within,
Mankind muſt either pity me, or scorn me.
   Ast. Sure none could do the laſt.

22

Qu. Thou long'st to know't:
And I to tell thee, but shame stops my mouth.
First promise me thou wilt excuse my folly,
And next be secret.——

   Ast. ——Can you doubt it Madam!

   Qu. Yet you might spare my labour;
Can you not guess——

   Ast. Madam, please you, I'le try.

   Qu. Hold: *Asteria.*
I would not have you guess, for should you find it
I should imagine, that some other might,
And then, I were most wretched.
Therefore, though you should know it, flatter me:
And say you could not guess it——

   Ast. Madam, I need not flatter you, I cannot.——and yet,
Might not Ambition trouble your repose?

   Qu. My *Sicily* I thank the Gods, contents me.
But since I must reveal it, know 'tis love:
I who pretended so to glory, am
Become the slave of love.——

   Ast. I thought your Majesty had fram'd designes
To subvert all your Laws; become a Tyrant,
Or vex your neighbours with injurious wars;
Is this all? Madam?

   Qu. Is not this enough?
Then, know, I love below my self; a Subject;
Love one who loves another, and who knows not
That I love him.

   Ast. He must be told it, Madam.

   Qu. Not for the world: *Asteria:*
When ere he knows it I shall die for shame.

   Ast. What is it then that would content you?

   Qu. Nothing, but that I had not lov'd.

   Ast. May I not ask, without offence, who 'tis?

   Qu. Ev'n that confirms me, I have lov'd amiss;
Since thou canst know I love, and not imagine
It must be *Philocles.*

   Ast. My Cousin is indeed a most deserving person;
Valiant and wise; and handsome; and well born,

   Qu. But not of Royal bloud:
I know his fate unfit to be a King.
To be his wife I could forsake my Crown; but not my glory:
Yet,——would he did not love *Candiope*;

Would he lov'd me,——but knew not of my love,
Or ere durſt tell me his.
    Aſt. In all this Labyrinth,
I find one path conducing to your quiet.
    Qu. O tell me quickly then.
    Aſt. Candiope, as Princess of the Bloud,
Without your approbation cannot marry:
Firſt break his match with her, by vertue of
Your Sovereign Authority.
    Qu. I fear. That were to make him hate me.
Or, what's as bad, to let him know I love him:
Could you not do it of your self?
    Aſt. Ile not be wanting to my pow'r:
But if your Majeſty appears not in it;
The love of *Philocles* will soon surmount
All other difficulties.
    Qu. Then, as we walk, we'l think what means are beſt
Effeɛt but this, and thou shar'ſt halfe my breaſt.   *Exeunt.*

ACT II.

SCENE I. *The Queens appartments.*

Aſteria, Sola. NOthing thrives that I have plotted:
             For I have sounded *Philocles*, and find
He is too conſtant to *Candiope*:
Her too I have assaulted, but in vain,
Objeɛting want of quality in *Philocles*.
I'le to the Queen, and plainly tell her
She muſt make use of her Authority
To break the Match.

SCENE II.

Enter Celadon *looking about him.*

Brother! what make you here
About the Queens appartments?
Which of the Ladies are you watching for?

24

Cel. Any of 'em that will do me the good turn to make me soundly in love.

Ast. Then I'le bespeak you one; you will be desp'rately in love with *Florimel*: so soon as the Queen heard you were return'd, she gave you her for Miſtriss.

Cel. Thank her Majeſty; but to confess the truth my fancy lies partly another way.

Ast. That's ſtrange: *Florimel* vows you are already in love with her.

Cel. She wrongs me horribly, if ever I saw or spoke with this *Florimel*—

Ast. Well, take your fortune, I muſt leave you. [*Exit* Aſteria.

SCENE III.

Enter Florimel, *sees him, and is running back.*

Cel. Nay 'faith I am got betwixt you and home, you are my pris'ner, Lady bright, till you resolve me one queſtion.

She signs. She is dumb.

Pox; I think she's dumb: what a vengeance doſt thou at Court, with such a rare Face, without a tongue to answer to a kind queſtion. Art thou dumb indeed, then, thou canſt tell no tales,——*goes to kiss her.*

Flor. Hold, hold, you are not mad!

Cel. Oh, my miss in a Masque! have you found your tongue?

Flor. 'Twas time, I think; what had become of me, if I had not?

Cel. Methinks your lips had done as well.

Flor. I, if my Masque had been over 'em, as it was when you met me in the walks.

Cel. Well ; will you believe me another time? did not I say you were infinitely handsome: they may talk of *Florimel*, if they will, but i'faith she muſt come short of you.

Flor. Have you seen her, then?

Cel. I look'd a little that way, but I had soon enough of her, she is not to be seen twice without a surfeit.

Flor. However you are beholding to her, they say she loves you.

Cel. By fate she shan'not love me: I have told her a piece of my mind already: pox o' these coming women: they set a man to dinner before he has an appetite.   *Flavia at the door.*

Florimel you are call'd within.——   [*Exit.*

Cel. I hope in the Lord you are not *Florimel*.

Flor. Ev'n she at your service; the same kind and coming *Florimel* you have describ'd.

Cel. Why then we are agreed already, I am as kind and coming as you for the heart of you: I knew at first we two were good for nothing but one another.

Flor. But, without raillery, are you in Love?

Cel. So horribly much, that contrary to my own Maxims, I think in my conscience I could marry you.

Flor. No, no, 'tis not come to that yet: but if you are really in love, you have done me the greatest pleasure in the world.

Cel. That pleasure, and a better too, I have in store for you.

Flor. This Animal call'd a Lover I have long'd to see these two years.

Cel. Sure you walk'd with your mask on all the while, for if you had been seen, you could not have been without your wish.

Flor. I warrant you mean an ordinary whining Lover; but I must have other proofs of love ere I believe it.

Cel. You shall have the best that I can give you.

Flor. I would have a Lover, that if need be, should hang himself, drown himself, break his neck, or poyson himself, for very despair: he that will scruple this, is an impudent fellow if he sayes he is in love.

Cel. Pray, Madam, which of these four things would you have your Lover do? for a man's but a man, he cannot hang, and drown, and break his neck, and poyson himself, altogether.

Flor. Well then, because you are but a beginner, and I would not discourage you, any one of these shall serve your turn in a fair way.

Cel. I am much deceiv'd in those eyes of yours, if a Treat, a Song, and the Fiddles, be not more acceptable proof of love to you, then any of those Tragical ones you have mentioned.

Flor. However you will grant it is but decent you should be pale, and lean, and melancholick, to shew you are in love: and that I shall require of you when I see you next.

Cel. When you see me next? why you do not make a Rabbet of me, to be lean at 24 hours warning? in the mean while we burn daylight, loose time and love.

Flor. Would you marry me without consideration?

Cel. To choose, by heaven, for they that think on't, twenty to one would never do it, hang forecast; to make sure of one good night is as much in reason as a man should expect from this ill world.

Flor. Methinks a few more years and discretion would do well: I do not like this going to bed so early; it makes one so weary before morning.

26

Cel. That's much as your pillow is laid before you go to sleep.

Flor. Shall I make a proposition to you? I will give you a whole year of probation to love me in; to grow reserv'd, discreet, sober and faithful; and to pay me all the services of a Lover.————

Cel. And at the end of it you'll marry me?

Flor. If neither of us alter our minds before.——

Cel. By this light a necessary clause.————but if I pay in all the foresaid services before the day, you shall be obliged to take me sooner into mercy.

Flor. Provided if you prove unfaithful, then your time of a Twelve-month to be prolong'd; so many services I will bate you so many dayes or weeks; so many faults I will add more to your 'Prentiship, so much more: And of all this I onely to be Judg.

SCENE IV.

Enter Philocles *and* Lysimantes.

Lys. Is the Queen this way, Madam?

Flor. I'le see, so please your Highness: Follow me, Captive.

Cel. March on Conquerour————   [*She pulls him.*

Lys. You're sure her Majesty will not oppose it?

                              [*Exeunt Cel. Flor.*

Phil. Leave that to me my Lord.

Lys. Then, though perhaps my Sisters birth might challenge
An higher match,
I'le weigh your merits on the other side
To make the ballance even.

Phil. I go my Lord this minute.

Lys. My best wishes wait on you.   [*Exit Lysimantes.*

SCENE V.

Enter the Queen and Asteria.

Qu. Yonder he is; have I no other way?

Ast. O Madam, you must stand this brunt:
Deny him now, and leave the rest to me:
I'le to *Candiope*'s Mother,
And under the pretence of friendship, work

On her Ambition to put off a match
So mean as *Philocles*.

    Qu. to *Phil.*] You may approach, Sir,
We two discourse no secrets.

    Phil. I come, Madam, to weary out your royal bounty.

    Qu. Some suit I warrant for your Cousin *Celadon*.
Leave his advancement to my care.

    Phil. Your goodness ſtill prevents my wishes:—yet I have one
       requeſt
Might it not pass almoſt for madness, and
Extream Ambition in me.————

    Qu. You know you have a favourable Judg,
It lies in you not to ask any thing
I cannot grant.

    Phil. Madam, perhaps you think me too faulty:
But Love alone inspires me with ambition,
Though but to look on fair *Candiope*, were an excuse for both.

    Qu. Keep your Ambition, and let Love alone;
That I can cloy, but this I cannot cure.
I have some reasons (invincible to me) which muſt forbid
Your marriage with *Candiope*.

    Phil. I knew I was not worthy.

    Qu. Not for that, *Philocles*, you deserve all things,
And to show I think it, my Admiral I hear is dead,
His vacant place (the beſt in all my Kingdom,)
I here confer on you.

    Phil. Rather take back all you had giv'n before,
Then not give this.
For believe, Madam, nothing is so near
My soul, as the possession of *Candiope*.

    Qu. Since that belief would be your disadvantage,
I will not entertain it.

    Phil. Why, Madam, can you be thus cruel to me?
To give me all things which I did not ask,
And yet deny that onely thing I beg:
And so beg that I find I cannot live
Without the hope of it.

    Qu. Hope greater things;
But hope not this. Haſte to o'recome your love,
It is but putting a short liv'd passion to a violent death.

    Phil. I cannot live without *Candiope*.
But I can die without a murmur,
Having my doom pronounced from your fair mouth.

28

Qu. If I am to pronounce it, live my *Philocles*,
But live without (I was about to say
Without his love, but that I cannot do)   [*aside.*
Live *Philocles* without *Candiope*.
  Phil. Ah, Madam, could you give my doom so quickly,
And knew it was irrevocable!
'Tis too apparent
You who alone love glory, and whose soul
Is loosned from your senses cannot judg
What torments mine, of grosser mould, endures.
  Qu. I cannot suffer you
To give me praises which are not my own:
I love like you, and am yet much more wretched
Then you can think your self.
  Phil. Weak barrs they need muſt be that fortune puts
'Twixt Soveraign Power, and all it can desire.
When Princes love, they call themselves unhappy,
Only because the word sounds handsome in a Lovers mouth.
But you can cease to be so when you please,
By making *Lysimantes* fortunate.
  Qu. Were he indeed the man, you had some reason;
But 'tis another, more without my power,
And yet a subjeét too.
  Phil. O, Madam, say not so,
It cannot be a Subjeét if not he.
It were to be injurious to your self
To make another choice.
  Qu. Yet *Lysimantes*, set by him I love,
Is more obscur'd then Stars too near the Sun;
He has a brightness of his own,
Not borrow'd of his Fathers, but born with him.
  Phil. Pardon if I say, who'ere he be,
He has praétis'd some ill Aéts upon you, Madam:
For he, whom you describe, I see is born
But from the lees o' th' people.
  Qu. You offend me, *Philocles*.
Whence had you leave to use those insolent terms
Of him I please to love: one I muſt tell you,
(Since foolishly I have gone thus far)
Whom I eſteem your equal,
And far superiour to Prince *Lysimantes*;
One who deserves to wear a Crown.——
  Phil. Whirlwinds bear me hence before I live

To that detested day.———That frown assures me
I have offended, by my over freedom;
But yet methinks a heart so plain and honest
And zealous of your glory, might hope your pardon for it.
    Qu. I give it you; but
When you know him better
You'l alter your opinion; he's no ill friend of yours.
    Phil. I well perceive
He has supplanted me in your esteem;
But that's the least of ills this fatal wretch
Has practis'd.———Think, for Heavens sake, Madam, think
If you have drunk no Phylter.———
    Qu. Yes he has given me a Phylter;
But I have drunk it onely from his eyes.
    Phil. Hot Irons thank 'em for't.———
                              [*Softly or turning from her.*
    Qu. What's that you mutter?
Hence from my sight: I know not whether
I ever shall endure to see you more.
    Phil. But hear me, Madam:
    Qu. I say be gone.———See me no more this day.———
I will not hear one word in your excuse:
Now, Sir, be rude again; *And give Laws to your Queen.*
                     Exit Philocles *bowing.*

Asteria, come hither.
Was ever boldness like to this of *Philocles?*
Help me to reproach him; for I resolve
Henceforth no more to love him.
    Ast. Truth is, I wondred at your patience, Madam:
Did you not mark his words, his meen, his action,
How full of haughtiness, how small respect?
    Qu. And he to use me thus, he whom I favour'd,
Nay more, he whom I lov'd?
    Ast. A man, me thinks, of vulgar parts and presence!
    Qu. Or allow him something handsome, valiant, or so———
Yet this to me!———
    Ast. The workmanship of inconsiderate favour,
The Creature of rash love; one of those Meteors
Which Monarchs raise from earth,
And people wondring how they came so high,
Fear, from their influence, Plagues, and Wars, and Famine.
    Qu. Ha!
    Ast. One whom instead of banishing a day,

30

You should have plum'd of all his borrow'd honours:
And let him see what abject things they are
Whom Princes often love without desert.

    Qu. What has my *Philocles* deserv'd from thee,
That thou shouldſt use him thus?
Were he the baseſt of Mankind thou could'ſt not
Have given him ruder language.

    Aſt. Did not your Majeſty command me,
Did not your self begin?

    Qu. I grant I did, but I have right to do it;
I love him and may rail;——in you 'tis malice;
Malice in the moſt higheſt degree; for never man
Was more deserving than my *Philocles.*
Or, do you love him, ha! and plead that title?
Confess, and I'le forgive you.——
For none can look on him but needs muſt love.

    Aſt. I love him, Madam! I beseech your Majeſty
Have better thoughts of me.

    Qu. Doſt thou not love him then!
Good Heav'n, how ſtupid and how dull is she!
How moſt invincibly insensible!
No woman does deserve to live
That loves not *Philocles*——

    Aſt. Dear madam, recollect your self; alas
How much diſtracted are your thoughts, and how
Dis-jointed all your words;————
The Sybills leaves more orderly were laid.
Where is that harmony of mind, that prudence
Which guided all you did! that sense of glory
Which rais'd you, high above the reſt of Kings,
As Kings are o're the level of mankind!

    Qu. Gone, gone *Aſteria*, all is gone,
Or loſt within me far from any use.
Sometimes I ſtruggle like the Sun in Clouds,
But ſtraight I am o'recaſt.——

    Aſt. I grieve to see it.——

    Qu. Then thou haſt yet the goodness
To pardon what I said.——
Alas, I use my self much worse then thee.
Love rages in great souls,————
For there his pow'r moſt opposition finds;
High trees are shook, because they dare the winds.   [*Exeunt.*

ACT III.

SCENE of the Act. *The Court Gallery.*

Philocles, solus.

Phil. 'TIS true, she banish'd me but for a day;
　　　　But Favourites, once declining, sink apace.
Yet Fortune, stop,——this is the likeliest place
To meet *Asteria*, and by her convey,
My humble vows to my offended Queen.

Enter Queen and Asteria.

Ha! She comes her self; Unhappy man!
Where shall I hide?—— 　　　　　　　　　 [*is going out.*
　　Qu. Is not that *Philocles*
Who makes such haste away? *Philocles, Philocles*——
Philocles coming back.] I fear'd she saw me.
　　Qu. How now, Sir, am I such a Bugbear
That I scare people from me?
　　Phil. 'Tis true, I should more carefully have shun'd
The place where you might be; as, when it thunders
Men reverently quit the open Air,
Because the angry Gods are then abroad.
　　Qu. What does he mean, *Asteria!*
I do not understand him.
　　Ast. Your Majesty forgets you banish'd him
Your presence for this day.——— 　　　　　[*to her softly.*
　　Qu. Ha! banish'd him! 'tis true indeed;
But, as thou sayst, I had forgot it quite.—*to her.*
　　Ast. That's very strange, scarce half an hour ago.
　　Qu. But Love had drawn his pardon up so soon
That I forgot he e're offended me.
　　Phil. Pardon me, that I could not thank you sooner:
Your sudden grace, like some swift flood pour'd in on narrow
　　bancks
O'reflowed my spirits.
　　Qu. No; tis for me to ask your pardon, *Philocles,*
For the great injury I did you,
In not remembring I was angry with you.
But I'le repair my fault,
And rowze my anger up against you yet.

32

Phil. No, Madam, my forgiveness was your Act of grace,
And I lay hold of it.

Qu. Princes sometimes may pass,
Acts of Oblivion in their own wrong.

Phil. 'Tis true, but not recall them.

Qu. But, *Philocles*, since I have told you there is one I love.
I will go on; and let you know
What passed this day betwixt us; be you judg
Whether my servant have dealt well with me.

Phil. I beseech your Majesty excuse me:
Any thing more of him may make me
Relapse too soon, and forfeit my late pardon.

Qu. But you'l be glad to know it.

Phil. May I not hope then
You have some quarrel to him?

Qu. Yes, a great one.
But first to justifie my self,
Know, *Philocles*, I have conceal'd my passion
With such care from him, that he knows not yet
I love, but onely that I much esteem him.

Phil. O stupid wretch
That by a thousand tokens could not guess it!

Qu. He loves elsewhere, and that has blinded him.

Phil. He's blind indeed!
So the dull Beasts in the first Paradise
With levell'd eyes gaz'd each upon their kind;
There fix'd their love: and ne're look'd up to view
That glorious Creature man, their soveraign Lord.

Qu. Y'are too severe, on little faults, but he has crimes, untold,
Which will, I fear, move you much more against him.
He fell this day into a passion with me,
And boldly contradicted all I said.

Phil. And stands his head upon his Shoulders yet?
How long shall this most insolent——

Qu. Take heed you rail not,
You know you are but on your good behaviour.

Phil. Why then I will not call him Traytor—
But onely rude, audacious and impertinent,
To use his Soveraign so——I beg your leave
To wish you have, at least imprison'd him.

Qu. Some people may speak ill, and yet mean well:
Remember you were not confin'd; and yet
Your fault was great. In short, I love him,

And that excuses all; but be not jealous;
His rising shall not be your overthrow,
Nor will I ever marry him.
    Phil. That's some comfort yet,
He shall not be a King.
    Qu. He never shall. But you are discompos'd;
Stay here a little; I have somewhat for you
Shall shew you still are in my favour.   [*Exeunt* Queen *and* Asteria.

Enter to him Candiope *weeping*.

    Phil. How now, in tears, my fair *Candiope?*
So through a watry Clowd
The Sun at once seems both to weep and shine.
For what Forefathers sin do you afflict
Those precious Eyes? for sure you have
None of your own to weep.
    Can. My Crimes both great and many needs must show,
Since Heav'n will punish them with loosing you.
    Phil. Afflictions sent from Heav'n without a cause
Make bold Mankind enquire into its Laws.
But Heav'n, which moulding beauty takes such care,
Makes gentle fates on purpose for the fair:
And destiny that sees them so divine,
Spins all their fortunes in a silken twine:
No mortal hand so ignorant is found
To weave course work upon a precious ground.
    Can. Go preach this doctrine in my Mother's ears.
    Phil. Has her severity produc'd these tears:
    Can. She has recall'd those hopes she gave before,
And strictly bids me ne're to see you more.
    Phil. Changes in froward age are Natural;
Who hopes for constant weather in the fall?
'Tis in your pow'r your duty to transfer,
And place that right in me which was in her.
    Can. Reason, like foreign foes, would ne're o'recome,
But that I find I am betray'd at home.
You have a friend that fights for you within.
    Phil. Let Reason ever lose, so love may win.

Enter Queen *and* Asteria.
Queen with a Picture in her hand.

    Qu. See there, *Asteria,*
All we have done succeeds still to the worse;

34

We hindred him from seeing her at home,
Where I but onely heard they lov'd; and now
She comes to Court, and mads me with the sight on't.

    Ast. Dear Madam, overcome your self a little,
Or they'l perceive how much you are concern'd.

    Qu. I struggle with my heart,————but it will have some vent.
Cousin, you are a stranger at the Court.   [*To Cand.*

    Can. It was my duty I confess,
To attend oftner on your Majesty.

    Qu. *Asteria*, Mend my Cousins Handkerchief;
It sits too narrow there, and shows too much
The broadness of her Shoulders————Nay fie, *Asteria*,
Now you put it too much backward, and discover
The bigness of her breasts.

    Can. I beseech your Majesty
Give not your self this trouble.

    Qu. Sweet Cousin, you shall pardon me;
A beauty such as yours
Deserves a more then ordinary care,
To set it out.
Come hither, *Philocles*, do but observe,
She has but one gross fault in all her shape,
That is, she bears up here too much,
And the malicious Workman has left it open to your eye.

    Phil. Where, and, please your Majesty, methinks 'tis very well?

    Qu. Do not you see it, Oh how blind is love!

    Can. And how quick-sighted malice!   [*Aside.*

    Qu. But yet methinks, those knots of sky, do not
So well with the dead colour of her face.

    Ast. Your Majesty mistakes, she wants no red.
The Queen *here plucks out her Glass, and looks sometimes on her self,*
    sometimes on her Rival.

    Qu. How do I look to day, *Asteria!*
Methinks not well.

    Ast. Pardon me, Madam, most victoriously.

    Qu. What think you, *Philocles?* come do not flatter.

    Phil. *Paris* was a bold man who presum'd
To judg the beauty of a Goddess.

    Can. Your Majesty has given the reason why
He cannot judge; his Love has blinded him.

    Qu. Methinks a long patch here beneath her eye
Might hide that dismal hollowness, what think you *Philocles?*

    Can. Beseech you, Madam, aske not his opinion;

35

What my faults are it is no matter;
He loves me with them all.
    Qu. I, he may love, but when he marries you,
Your Bridal shall be kept in some dark Dungeon.
Farewel, and think of that, too easie Maid,
I blush, thou shar'st my bloud.   *[Exeunt* Queen, Asteria.
    Can. Inhumane Queen!
Thou canst not be more willing to resign
Thy part in me, then I to give up mine.
    Phil. Love, how few Subjects do thy Laws fulfil,
And yet those few, like us, thou usest ill!
    Can. The greatest slaves, in Monarchies, are they,
Whom Birth sets nearest to Imperial sway.
While jealous Pow'r does sullenly orespy,
We play like Deer within the Lions eye.
Would I for you some Shepherdess had been;
And, but each May, ne're heard the name of Queen.
    Phil. If you were so, might I some Monarch be,
Then, you should gain what now you loose by me:
Then, you in all my glories should have part,
And rule my Empire, as you rule my heart.
    Can. How much our golden wishes are in vain?
When they are past we are our selves again.

           Enter Queen *and* Asteria *above.*

    Qu. Look, look *Asteria*, yet they are not gone.
Hence, we may hear what they discourse alone.
    Phil. My Love inspires me with a gen'rous thought
Which you unknowing, in those wishes taught.
Since happiness may out of Courts be found,
Why stay we here on this enchanted ground?
And choose not rather with content to dwell
(If Love and we can find it) in a Cell?
    Can. Those who, like you, have once in Courts been great,
May think they wish, but wish not to retreat.
They seldom go but when they cannot stay;
As loosing Gamesters throw the Dice away:
Ev'n in that Cell, where you repose would find,
Visions of Court will haunt your restless mind;
And glorious dreams stand ready to restore
The pleasing shapes of all you had before.
    Phil. He, who with your possession once is blest,
On easie terms may part with all the rest.
36

All my Ambition will in you be crown'd;
And those white Arms shall all my wishes bound.
Our life shall be but one long Nuptial day,
And like chaf't Odours, melt in Sweets away;
Soft as the Night our Minutes shall be worn,
And chearful as the Birds that wake the Morn.

    Can. Thus hope misleads it self in pleasant way;
And takes more joyes on truſt then Love can pay!
But Love, with long possession, once decayd,
That face which now you Court, you will upbraid.

    Phil. False Lovers broach these tenets, to remove
The fault from them by placing it on Love.——

    Can. Yet grant in Youth you keep alive your Fire,
Old age will come, and then it muſt expire:
Youth but a while does at Loves Temple ſtay,
As some fair Inn to lodge it on the way.

    Phil. Your doubts are kind; but to be satisfy'd,
I can be true, I beg I may be try'd.

    Can. Tryals of love too dear the making coſt;
For, if successless, the whole venture's loſt.
What you propose, brings wants and care along.

    Phil. Love can bear both.

    Can. But is your love so ſtrong?

    Phil. They do not want, who wish not to have more;
Who ever said an Anchoret was poor?

    Can. To answer gen'rously as you have done,
I should not by your arguments be won:
I know I urge your ruine by consent;
Yet love too well that ruine to prevent.

    Phil. Like water giv'n to those whom Feavers fry,
You kill but him, who muſt without it die.

    Can. Secure me I may love without a Crime;
Then, for our flight, appoint both place and time.

    Phil. Th' ensuing hour my plighted vows shall be;
The time's not long; or onely long to me.

    Can. Then, let us go where we shall ne'r be seen
By my hard Mother.

    Phil. Or my cruel Queen.   [*Exeunt* Phil. Cand.

    Queen above.] O *Philocles* unkind to call me cruel!
So false *Æneas* did from *Dido* fly;
But never branded her with cruelty.
How I despise my self for loving so!

    Aſt. At once you hate your self and love him too.

Qu. No, his ingratitude has cur'd my wound:
A painful cure indeed!
Ast. And yet not sound.
His ignorance of your true thoughts
Excuses this; you did seem cruel, Madam.
Qu. But much of kindness still was mix'd with it.
Who could mistake so grosly not to know
A *Cupid* frowning when he draws his Bowe?
Ast. He's going now to smart for his offence.
Qu. Should he without my leave depart from hence?
Ast. No matter; since you hate him, let him go.
Qu. But I my hate by my revenge will show:
Besides, his head's a forfeit to the State.
Ast. When you take that I will believe you hate.
Let him possess, and then he'll soon repent:
And so his Crime will prove his punishment.
Qu. He may repent; but he will first possess:
Ast. O, Madam, now your hatred you confess:
If, his possessing her your rage does move,
'Tis jealousie the avarice of love.
Qu. No more, *Asteria.*
Seek *Lysimantes* out, bid him set his Guards through all the Court
    and City.
Prevent their marriage first; then stop their flight.
Some fitting punishments I will ordain,
But speak not you of *Philocles* again:
'Tis bold to search, and dangerous to find,
Too much of Heaven's, or of a Princes mind.
                              [Qu. *descends, and exit.*
    As the Queen has done speaking, Flavia *is going hastily over the Stage;*
                    Asteria *sees her.*
Ast. Flavia, Flavia, Whither so fast?
Fla. Did you call, *Asteria.*
Ast. The Queen has business with Prince *Lysimantes;*
Speak to any Gentleman that's next, to fetch him.
                              [*Exit* Asteria *from above.*
    Fla. I suspect somewhat, but I'le watch you close;
Prince *Lysimantes* has not chose in me,
The worst Spy of the Court.——*Celadon!* what makes he here!

Enter Celadon, Olinda, Sabina; *they walk over the Stage together, he*
                    seeming to court them.

    Olin. Nay sweet *Celadon.*——
38

Sab. Nay dear *Celadon*.

Fla. O-ho, I see his business now, 'tis with *Melissa*'s two Daughters: Look, look, how he peeps about to see if the Coaſt be clear; like an Hawk that will not plume if she be look'd on.————

[*Exeunt* Cel. Ol. Sab.

So————at laſt he has truss'd his quarry.————

Enter Florimel.

Flor. Did you see *Celadon* this way?

Fla. If you had not ask'd the queſtion, I should have thought you had come from watching him; he's juſt gone off with *Melissa*'s Daughters.

Flor. Melissa's Daughters! he did not Court 'em I hope?

Fla. So busily, he loſt no time: while he was teaching the one a tune, he was kissing the others hand.

Flor. O fine Gentleman!

Fla. And they so greedy of him! Did you never see two Fishes about a Bait, tugging it this way and t'other way; for my part, I look'd at leaſt he should have loſt a Leg or Arm i' th' service.———— Nay, never vex your self, but e'en resolve to break with him.

Flor. No no, 'tis not come to that, yet; I'le correct him firſt, and then hope the beſt from time.

Fla. From time! Believe me, there's little good to be expected from him. I never knew the old Gentleman with the Scythe and Hour-glass bring any thing but gray hair, thin cheeks, and loss of teeth: you see *Celadon* loves others.

Flor. There's the more hope he may love me among the reſt: hang't, I would not marry one of these solemn Fops; they are good for nothing but to make Cuckolds: Give me a servant that is an high Flier at all games, that is bounteous of himself to many women: and yet whenever I pleas'd to throw out the lure of Matrimony, should come down with a swing, and fly the better at his own quarry.

Fla. But are you sure you can take him down when you think good?

Flor. Nothing more certain.

Fla. What wager will you venture upon the Trial?

Flor. Any thing.

Fla. My Maydenhead to yours.

Flor. That'a good one, who shall take the forfeit?

Fla. I'le go and write a Letter as from these two Siſters, to summon him immediately; it shall be deliver'd before you. I warrant you see a ſtrange combat betwixt the Flesh and the Spirit: if he leaves you to go to them, you'l grant he loves them better?

39

Flor. Not a jot the more: a Bee may pick of many Flowers, and yet like some one better then all the rest.

Fla. But then your Bee must not leave his sting behind him.

Flor. Well; make the experiment however: I hear him coming, and a whole noise of Fiddles at his heels. Hey-day, what a mad Husband shall I have?——

Enter Celadon.

Flav. And what a mad wife will he have? Well I must goe a little way, but I'le return immediately and write it: You'l keep him in discourse the while? [*Exit* Flav.

Cel. Where are you, Madam? what do you mean to run away thus? pray stand to't, that we may dispatch this business.

Flor. I think you mean to watch me as they do Witches, to make me confess I love you. Lord, what a bustle have you kept this Afternoon? what with eating, singing and dancing, I am so wearied, that I shall not be in case to hear any more love this fortnight.

Cel. Nay, if you surfeit on't before Tryal, Lord have mercy upon you when I have married you.

Flor. But what Kings Revenue do you think will maintain this extravagant expence?

Cel. I have a damnable Father, a rich old Rogue, if he would once die! Lord, how long does he mean to make it ere he dies!

Flor. As long as ever he can, I'le pass my word for him.

Cel. I think then we had best consider him as an obstinate old fellow that is deaf to the news of a better world; and ne're stay for him.

Flor. But e'en marry; and get him Grandchildren in abundance, and great Grandchildren upon them, and so inch him, and shove him out of the World by the very force of new Generations:——If that be the way you must excuse me.

Cel. But dost thou know what it is to be an old Maid?

Flor. No, nor I hope I sha'n't these twenty years.

Cel. But when that time comes, in the first place thou wilt be condemn'd to tell Stories, how many men thou mightst have had; and none believe thee: Then thou growest froward, and impudently weariest all thy Friends to sollicite Man for thee.

Flor. Away with your old Common place-wit: I am resolved to grow fat, and look young till forty, and then slip out of the world with the first wrinckle, and the reputation of five and twenty.

Cel. Well, what think you now of a reckoning betwixt us?

Flor. How do you mean?

Cel. To discount for so many dayes of my years service, as I have paid in since morning.

40

Flor. With all my heart.

Cel. Inprimis, For a Treat.

Item. For my Glass Coach.

Item. For sitting bare and wagging your Fann.

And lastly, and principally, for my Fidelity to you this long hour and half.

Flor. For this I 'bate you three Weeks of your Service; now hear your Bill of Faults; for your comfort 'tis a short one.

Cel. I know it.

Flor. Inprimis, Item, and Sum totall, for keeping company with *Melissa*'s Daughters.

Cel. How the Pox came you to know of that: Gad I believe
The Devil plays booty against himself, and tels you of my sins.

[aside.

Flor. The offence being so small the punishment shall be but proportionable, I will set you back onely half a year.

Cel. You're most unconscionable: why then do you think we shall come together? there's none but the old Patriarchs could live long enough to marry you at this rate. What do you take me for some Cousin of *Methusalem*'s, that I must stay an hundred years before I come to beget Sons and Daughters?

Flor. Here's an impudent Lover, he complains of me without ever offering to excuse himself; *Item,* a fortnight more for that.

Cel. So ther's another puff in my voyage has blown me back to the North of *Scotland.*

Flo. All this is nothing to your excuse for the two Sisters.

Cel. 'Faith if ever I did more than kiss 'em, and that but once—

Flo. What could you have done more to me?

Cel. An hundred times more; as thou shalt know, dear Rogue, at time convenient.

Flo. You talk, you talk; Could you kiss 'em, though but once, and ne're think of me?

Cel. Nay if I had thought of thee, I had kiss'd 'em over a thousand times, with the very force of imagination.

Flo. The Gallants are mightily beholding to you, you have found 'em out a new way to kiss their Mistresses, upon other womens lips.

Cel. What would you have? You are my Sultana Queen, the rest are but in the nature of your Slaves; I may make some slight excursion into the Enemies Country for forage or so, but I ever return to my head quarters.

Enter one with a Letter.

Cel To me?

Mess. If your name be *Celadon.*   [Celad. *reads softly.*

41

Flo. He's swallowing the Pill; presently we shall see the opera-tion.

Cel. to the Page.] Child, come hither Child; here's money for thee: So, be gone quickly good Child, before any Body examines thee: Thou art in a dangerous place, Child.———[*Thrusts him out.* Very good, the Sisters send me word they will have the Fiddles this Afternoon, and invite me to sup there!———Now cannot I forbear and I should be damn'd, though I have scap'd a scouring so lately for it. Yet I love *Florimel* better than both of 'em together;—there's the Riddle on't: but onely for the sweet sake of variety.———[*Aside.* Well, we must all sin, and we must all repent, and there's an end on't.

Flo. What is it that makes you fidg up and down so?

Cel. 'Faith I am sent for by a very dear friend, and 'tis upon a business of life and death.

Flo. On my life some woman?

Cel. On my honour some man; Do you think I would lye to you?

Flo. But you engag'd to sup with me!

Cel. But I consider it may be scandalous to stay late in your Lodg-ings. Adieu Dear Miss if ever I am false to thee again. [*Exit* Cel.

Flo. See what constant metal you men are made of! He begins to vex me in good earnest. Hang him, let him go and take enough of 'em: and yet methinks I can't endure he should neither. Lord, that such a Mad-Cap as I should ever live to be jealous!
I must after him.
Some Ladies would discard him now, but I
   A fitter way for my revenge will find,
   I'le marry him, and serve him in his kind.   [*Exit* Florimel.

ACT IV.

SCENE, *The Walks.*

Melissa, *after her* Olinda *and* Sabina.

Melissa. I Must take this business up in time: this wild fellow be-gins to haunt my house again. Well, I'le be bold to say it, 'tis as easie to bring up a young Lyon, without mischief, as a Maidenhead of Fifteen, to make it tame for an Husbands bed. Not but that the young man is handsome, rich and young, and I could be content he should marry one of 'em but to seduce 'em both in this

42

manner.————Well, I'le examine 'em apart, and if I can find out which he loves, I'le offer him his choice.————*Olinda*. Come hither Child.————

Olin. Your pleasure, Madam?

Mel. Nothing but for your good, *Olinda*, what think you of *Celadon?*

Olin. Why I think he's a very mad fellow; but yet I have some obligements to him: he teaches me new ayres on the Guitarre, and talks wildely to me, and I to him.

Mel. But tell me in earneſt, do you think he loves you?

Olin. Can you doubt it? There were never two so cut out for one another; we both love Singing, Dancing, Treats and Musick. In short, we are each others counterpart.

Mel. But does he love you seriously?

Olin. Seriously! I know not that; if he did, perhaps I should not love him: but we sit and talk, and wrangle, and are friends; when we are together we never hold our tongues; and then we have always a noise of Fiddles at our heels, he hunts me merrily as the Hounds does the Hare; and either this is Love, or I know it not.

Mel. Well, go back, and call *Sabina* to me.   Olinda *goes behind.* This is a Riddle paſt my finding out: whether he loves her or no is the queſtion; but this I am sure of, she loves him:————O my little Favourite, I muſt ask you a queſtion concerning *Celadon*: is he in love with you?

Sab. I think indeed he does not hate me, at leaſt if a man's word may be taken for it.

Mel. But what expressions has he made you?

Sab. Truly the Man has done his part: he has spoken civilly to me, and I was not so young but I underſtood him.

Mel. And you could be content to marry him?

Sab. I have sworn never to marry; besides, he's a wild young man; yet to obey you, Mother, I would be content to be sacrific'd.

Mel. No, no, we wou'd but lead you to the Altar.

Sab. Not to put off the Gentleman neither; for if I have him not I am resolv'd to die a Maid, that's once, Mother.————

Mel. Both my Daughters are in love with him, and I cannot yet find he loves either of 'em.

Olin. Mother, mother, yonder's *Celadon* in the walks.

Mel. Peace, wanton; you had beſt ring the Bells for joy. Well, I'le not meet him, because I know not which to offer him; yet he seems to like the youngeſt beſt: I'le give him oportunity with her; *Olinda*, do you make haſte after me.

Olin. This is something hard though.   [*Exit* Mel.

43

Enter Celadon.

Cel. You see Ladies the least breath of yours brings me to you: I have been seeking you at your Lodgings, and from thence came hither after you.

Sab. 'Twas well you found us.

Cel. Found you! Half this brightness betwixt you two was enough to have lighted me; I could never miss my way: Here's fair *Olinda* has beauty enough for one Family; such a voice, such a wit, so noble a stature, so white a skin.

Olin. I thought he would be particular at last.   [*Aside.*

Cel. And young *Sabina,* so sweet an innocence,
Such a Rose-bud newly blown.
This is my goodly Pallace of Love, that my little withdrawing Room.
A word, Madam.———   [*To* Sab.

Olin. I like not this——[*aside.*] Sir, if you are not too busie with my Sister, I would speak with you.

Cel. I come, Madam.——

Sab. Time enough Sir; pray finish your Discourse.———and as you were asaying, Sir.——

Olin. Sweet Sir.——

Sab. Sister you forget, my Mother bid you make haste.

Olin. Well, go you and tell her I am coming.

Sab. I can never endure to be the Messenger of ill news; but if you please. I'le send her word you won't come.

Olin. Minion, Minion, remember this.——   [*Exit* Olinda.

Sab. She's horribly in love with you.

Cel. Lord who could love that walking Steeple: She's so high that every time She sings to me, I am looking up for the Bell that tolls to Church.——Ha! Give me my little Fifth-rate! that lies so snug.—— She, hang her, a Dutch built bottom; she's so tall, there's no boarding her. But we lose time—Madam, let me seal my love upon your mouth.   [*kiss.*

Soft and sweet by Heaven! sure you wear Rose-leaves between your lips.

Sab. Lord, Lord; What's the matter with me! my breath grows so short I can scarce speak to you.

Cel. No matter, give me thy lips again and I'le speak for thee.

Sab. You don't love me.——

Cel. I warrant thee; set down by me and kiss again——
She warms faster then *Pygmalion's* Image.   *aside.*
(*kiss.*)——I marry sir, this was the original use of lips; talking, eating and drinking came in bith' by.——

Sab. Nay pray be civil; will you be at quiet?

Cel. What would you have me sit ſtill and look upon you like a little Puppy dog that's taught to beg with his fore-leg up?

Enter Florimel.

Flor. Celadon the faithful! in good time, Sir.——

Cel. In very good time, *Florimel*; for Heavens sake help me quickly.

Flor. What's the matter?

Cel. Do you not see! here's a poor Gentlewoman in a swoon! (swoon away!) I have been rubbing her this half hour, and cannot bring her to her senses.

Flor. Alas, how came she so?

Cel. Oh barbarous! do you ſtay to ask queſtions, run for charity.

Flor. Help, help, alas poor Lady.——   [*Exit* Flor.

Sab. Is she gone?

Cel. I, thanks to my wit that helpt me at a pinch;
I thank Heaven, I never pumpt for a lye in all my life yet.

Sab. I am affraid you love her, *Celadon!*

Cel. Onely as a civil acquaintance or so, but however to avoid slander, you had beſt begone before she comes again.

Sab. I can find a tongue as well as she——

Cel. I, but the truth is, I am a kind of scandalous person, and for you to be seen in my company——Stay in the walks, by this kiss I'le be with you presently.   [*Exit* Sab.

Enter Florimel *running.*

Flor. Help, help, I can find no body.

Cel. 'Tis needless now my dear, she's recover'd, and gone off, but so wan and weakly.——

Flor. Umh! I begin to smell a ratt, what was your business here, *Celadon?*

Cel. Charity, Chriſtian Charity; you saw I was labouring for life with her.

Flor. But how came you hither; not that I care this,——but onely to be satisfied——   [*Sings.*

Cel. You are jealous in my Conscience.

Flor. Who I jealous! Then I wish this sigh may be the laſt that ever I may draw.——   [*Sighs.*

Cel. But why do you sigh then?

Flor. Nothing but a cold, I cannot fetch my breath well.——
But what will you say if I wrote the Letter you had, to try your faith?

45

Cel. Hey-day! This is juſt the Devil and the Sinner; you lay snares for me, and then punish me for being taken; there's trying a man's Faith indeed: What did you think I had the faith of a Stock, or of a Stone? Nay, and you go to tantalize a man,——'gad I love you upon the square, I can endure no tricks to be used to me.

Olinda and Sabina at the door Peeping.

Ol. Sab. Celadon, Celadon!

Flor. What voices are those?

Cel. Some Camerades of mine that call me to play;——
Pox on 'em they'l spoil all—— *Aside.*

Flor. Pray let's see 'em.

Cel. Hang 'em Tatterdemallions, they are not worth your sight; 'pray Gentlemen be gone, I'le be with you immediately.

Sab. No, we'll ſtay here for you.

Flor. Do your Gentlemen speak with Treble-voices? I am resolved to see what company you keep.

Cel. Nay, good my Dear.——

He lays hold of her to pull her back; she lays hold of Olinda, *by whom* Sabina *holds; so that he pulling they all come in.*

Flor. Are these your Comerades?
[*Sings*] 'Tis *Strephon* calls what would my love?
Why do not you roar out like a great Bass-vyal, Come follow to the *Myrtle-grove.* Pray Sir, which of these fair Ladies is it, for whom you were to do the courtesie, for it were unconscionable to leave you to 'em both: What a man's but a man you know.

Olin. The Gentleman may find an owner.

Sab. Though not of you.

Flor. Pray agree whose the loſt sheep is, and take him.

Cel. 'Slife they'l cry me anon, and tell my marks.

Flor. Troth I pity your Highness there, I perceive he has left you for the little one: Methinks he should have been affraid to break his neck when he fell so high as from you to her.

Sab. Well my drolling Lady, I may be even with you.—

Flor. Not this ten years by thy growth, yet.

Sab. Can flesh and blood endure this!

Flor. How now, my *Amazon in decimo sexto!*

Olin. Do you affront my Siſter?—

Flor. I, but thou art so tall, I think I shall never affront thee.——

Sab. Come away Siſter, we shall be jeer'd to Death else.

[*Exeunt* Olin. Sab.

Flor. Why do you look that way, you can'nt forbear leering after the forbidden Fruit.——But when e're I take a Wenchers word again!—

46

Cel. A Wenchers word, Why should you speak so contemptibly of the better half of Mankind? I'le ſtand up for the honour of my Vocation.

Flor. You are in no fault I warrant;—'ware my busk—

Cel. Not to give a fair Lady the lye, I am in fault;—but otherwise —Come let us be friends, and let me wait you to your Lodgings.

Flor. This Impudence shall not save you from my Table-Book. *Item.* A Month more for this fault.——   [*They walk to the door.*

1 *Souldier within.* Stand.

2 *Souldier.* Stand, give the word.

Cel. Now, what's the meaning of this trow, guards set.

1 *Souldier.* Give the word, or you cannot pass; these are they brother; let's in, and seize 'em.

The two Souldiers enter.

1 *Sold.* ———Down with him.

2 *Sold.* Disarm him.

Cel. How now Rascalls.——

Draws and beats one off, and catches the other.
Ask your life you villain.

2 *Sold.* Quarter, quarter.

Cel. Was ever such an Insolence?

Sold. We did but our duty; here we were set, to take a Gentleman and Lady, that would ſteal a marriage without the Queens consent, and we thought you had been they.   [*Exit* Sould.

Flor. Your Cousin *Philocles* and the Princess *Candiope* on my life! for I heard the Queen give private Orders to *Lysimantes*, and name them twice or thrice.

Cel. I know a score or two of Madcaps here hard by, whom I can pick up from Taverns and Gaming-Houses, and Bordells; those I'le bring to aid him: Now *Florimel*, there's an argument for wenching, where would you have had so many honeſt men together upon the sudden for a brave employment?

Flor. You'l leave me then to take my fortune?

Cel. No; if you will, I'le have you into the places aforesaid, and enter you into good company.

Flor. Thank you Sir, here's a key will let me through this back-door to my own Lodgings.

Cel. If I come off with Life, I'le see you this evening, if not—— Adieu *Florimel.*——

Flor. If you come not I shall conclude you are kill'd, or taken; to be hang'd for a Rebel to morrow morning—and then I'le honour your memory with a Lampoon inſtead of an Epitaph.

Cel. No, no, I truſt better in my Fate: I know I am reserv'd to do you a Courtesie.   [*Exit* Celadon.

As Florimel *is unlocking the door to go out,* Flavia *opens it againſt her, and enters to her, followed by a Page.*

Fla. Florimel, do you hear the News?

Flor. I guess they are in pursuit of *Philocles.*

Fla. When *Lysimantes* came with the Queens Orders,
He refused to render up *Candiope*;
And with some few brave Friends he had about him
Is forcing of his way through all the Guards.

Flor. A gallant Fellow: I'le in, will you with me.
Hark, the noise comes this way!

Fla. I have a Message from the Queen to *Lysimantes,*
I hope I may be safe among the Souldiers.

Flor. Oh very safe, perhaps some honeſt Fellow in the tumult may take pity of thy Maidenhead, or so——Adiew. [*Exit* Florimel.

Page. The noise comes nearer, Madam.

Fla. I am glad ont: this message gives me the opportunity of speaking privately with *Lysimantes.*

Enter Philocles *and* Candiope, *with three friends; pursued by* Lysimantes *and Souldiers.*

Lys. What is it renders you thus obſtinate? you have no hope of flight, and to resiſt is full as vain.

Phil. I'le die rather then yield her up.

Fla. My Lord!

Lys. How now, some new message from the Queen.

To Sould.] Retire a while to a convenient diſtance.
                                        Lys. *and* Fla. *whisper.*

Lys. O *Flavia* 'tis impossible! the Queen in love with *Philocles!*

Fla. I half suspeꝗed it before; but now,
My ears and eyes are witnesses,——
This hour I over-heard her to *Aſteria,*
Making such sad complaints of her hard fate!
For my part I believe you lead him back
But to his Coronation.

Lys. Hell take him firſt.

Fla. Presently after this she call'd for me.
And bid me run, and with ſtriꝗ care command you
On peril of your life he had no harm:
But, Sir, she spoke it with so great concernment,
Methought, I saw love, anger, and despair,
All combating at once upon her face.

48

Lys. Tell the Queen——I know not what, I am distracted so——
But go and leave me to my thoughts———   [*Exit* Flavia.
Was ever such amazing news
Told in so strange and critical a moment!
What shall I do!
Does she love *Philocles*, who loves not her,
And loves not *Lysimantes* who prefers her
Above his life! What rests but that I take
This opportunity, which she her self
Has given me, to kill this Happy Rival!
Assist me Souldiers.
    Phil. They shall buy me dearly.
    Cand. Ah me, unhappy maid!

Enter Celadon *with his Friends, unbutton'd and reeling.*

    Cel. Courage my noble Cousin, I have brought
A band of Blades, the bravest youths of *Syracuse*:
Some drunk, some sober, all resolv'd to run
Your fortune to the utmost. Fall on mad Boyes———
    Lys. Hold a little—
I'm not secur'd of victory against these desperate ruffins.
    Cel. No, but I'le secure you; they shall cut your throat for such
another word of 'em. Ruffins quoth a! call Gamesters, and Whore-
Masters, and Drunkards, Ruffins———
    Lys. Pray Gentlemen fall back a little———
    Cel. O ho, are they Gentlemen now with you!
Speak first to your Gentlemen Souldiers to retire; and then
I'le speak to my Gentlemen Ruffians.
There's your disciplin'd men now——— [*Cel. Signs to his Party.*]
         They Sign, and the Souldiers retire on both sides.
Come, Gentlemen, let's lose no time; while they are talking, let's
have one merry mayn before we die———for Mortality sake.
    1. Agreed, here's my Cloak for a Table.
    2. And my Hat for a Box.——   [*They lie down and throw.*
    Lys. Suppose I kill'd him!
'Twould but exasperate the Queen the more:
He loves not her, nor knows he she loves him:
A sudden thought is come into my head———
So to contrive it, that this *Philocles*,
And these his friends shall bring to pass that for me
Which I could never compass——True I strain
A point of honour; but then her usage to me! it shall be so———

Pray, *Philocles*, command your Souldiers off,
As I will mine: I've somewhat to propose
Which you perhaps may like.
    Cand. I will not leave him.
    Lys. —'Tis my desire you should not.
    Phil. —Cousin, lead off your friends.
    Cel. —One word in your ear Couz. Let me advise you; either
make your own conditions, or never agree with him: his men are
poor sober Rogues, they can never ſtand before us.
                            Exeunt omnes præter Lys. Phil. Cand.
    Lys. Suppose some Friend, e're night,
Should bring you to possess all you desire;
And not so onely, but secure forever
The Nations happiness————
    Phil. I would think of him
As some God or Angel.
    Lys. That God or Angel you or I may be to one another.
We have betwixt us
An hundred Men: The Cittadel you govern:
What were it now to seize the Queen!
    Phil. O Impiety! to seize the Queen!
To seize her, said you?
    Lys. The word might be too rough, I meant secure her.
    Phil. Was this your proposition,
And had you none to make it to but me?
    Lys. Pray hear me out e're you condemn me!
I would not the leaſt violence were offer'd
Her person; two small grants is all I ask,
To make me happy in her self, and you
In your *Candiope*.
    Cand. And will not you do this, my *Philocles*?
Nay, now my Brother speaks but reason.
    Phil. Int'reſt makes all seem reason that leads to it.
Int'reſt that does the zeal of Sects create,
To purge a Church, and to reform a State.
    Lys. In short, the Queen hath sent to part you two;
What more she means to her, I know not.
    Phil. To her! alas! why will not you protect her?
    Lys. With you I can: but where's my power alone?
    Cand. You know she loves me not: you lately heard her
How she insulted over me: how she
Despis'd that beauty which you say I have:
I see she purposes my death.
50

Phil. Why do you fright me with it?
'Tis in your Brother's pow'r to let us 'scape,
And then you run no danger.
 Lys. True, I may:
But then my head muſt pay the forfeit of it.
 Phil. O wretched *Philocles*, whither would Love
Hurry thee headlong!
 Lys. Cease these Exclamations.
Ther's no danger on your side: 'tis but
To live without my Siſter, resolve that
And you have shot the gulf.
 Phil. To live without her! is that nothing think you?
The damn'd in Hell endure no greater pain
Than seeing Heaven from far with hopeless eyes.
 Can. *Candiope* muſt die, and die for you;
See it not unreveng'd at leaſt.
 Phil. Ha, unreveng'd! on whom should I revenge it?
But yet she dies, and I may hinder it;
'Tis I then murder my *Candiope:*
And yet should I take armes againſt my Queen!
That favour'd me, rais'd me to what I am!
Alas it muſt not be.
 Lys. He cools again.————*aside.*] True; she once favour'd you
But now I am inform'd,
She is besotted on an upſtart wretch;
So far, that she intends to make him Maſter.
Both of her Crown and person.
 Phil. Knows he that!
Then, what I dreaded moſt is come to pass.—   [*aside.*
I am convinc'd of the necessity;
Let us make haſte to raze
That action from the Annals of her Reign:
No motive but her glory could have wrought me.
I am a Traytor to her, to preserve her
From Treason to her self; and yet Heav'n knows
With what a heavy heart
Philocles turns reformer: but have care
This fault of her ſtrange passion take no air.
Let not the vulgar blow upon her fame.
 Lys. I will be careful, shall we go my Lord:
 Phil. Time waſts apace; Each firſt prepare his men.
Come, my *Candiope*————   *Exeunt* Phil. Can.
 Lys. This ruines him forever with the Queen;

The odium's half his, the profit all my own.
Those who, like me, by others help would climb,
To make 'em sure, must dip 'em in their crime.   *Exit* Lys.

SCENE II. *The Queens appartments.*

Enter Queen *and* Asteria.

Qu. No more news yet from *Philocles?*

Ast. None, Madam, since *Flavia's* return!

Qu. O my *Asteria,* if you lov'd me, sure
You would say something to me of my *Philocles;*
I could speak ever of him.

Ast. Madam, you commanded me no more to name him to you.

Qu. Then I command you now to speak of nothing else:
I charge you here, on your allegiance, tell me
What I should do with him.

Ast. When you gave orders that he should be taken,
You seem'd resolv'd how to dispose of him.

Qu. Dull *Asteria* not to know,
Mad people never think the same thing twice.
Alas, I'm hurried restless up and down,
I was in anger once, and then I thought
I had put into shore!
But now a gust of love blows hard against me,
And bears me off again.

Ast. Shall I sing the Song you made of *Philocles,*
and call'd it *Secret-love?*

Qu. Do, for that's all kindness: and while thou sing'st it,
can think nothing but what pleases me.

SONG.

I Feed a flame within which so torments me
   That it both pains my heart, and yet contents me:
'Tis such a pleasing smart, and I so love it,
That I had rather die then once remove it.

Yet he for whom I grieve shall never know it,
My tongue does not betray, nor my eyes show it:
Not a sigh nor a tear my pain discloses,
But they fall silently like dew on Roses.

Thus to prevent my love from being cruel,
My heart's the sacrifice as 'tis the fuel;
And while I suffer this to give him quiet,
My faith rewards my love, though he deny it.

On his eyes will I gaze, and there delight me;
While I conceal my love, no frown can fright me:
To be more happy I dare not aspire;
Nor can I fall more low, mounting no higher.

Qu. Peace! Me thinks I hear the noise
Of clashing Swords, and clatt'ring Armes below.

Enter Flavia.

Now; what news, that you press in so rudely?
   Fla. Madam, the worst that can be;
Your Guards upon the sudden are surpris'd,
Disarm'd, some slain, all scatter'd.
   Qu. By whom?
   Fla. Prince *Lysimantes,* and Lord *Philocles.*
   Qu. It cannot be; *Philocles* is a Prisoner.
   Fla. What my eyes saw——
   Qu. Pull 'em out, they are false Spectacles.
   Ast. O vertue, impotent and blind as Fortune!
Who would be good, or pious, if this Queen
Thy great Example suffers!
   Qu. Peace, *Asteria,* accuse not vertue;
She has but given me a great occasion
Of showing what I am when Fortune leaves me.
   Ast. Philocles, to do this!
   Qu. I, *Philocles,* I must confess 'twas hard!
But there's a fate in kindness
Still, to be least return'd where most 'tis given.
Where's *Candiope?*
   Fla. Philocles was whispering to her.
   Qu. Hence Screech-Owl; call my Guards quickly there:
Put 'em apart in several Prisons.
Alas! I had forgot I have no Guards,
But those which are my Jaylors,
Never till now unhappy Queen:
The use of pow'r, till lost, is seldom known;
Now I would strike, I find my thunder gone.
               Exit Queen *and* Flavia.

Philocles *enters, and meets* Asteria *going out.*

Phil. *Asteria!* Where's the Queen?

Ast. Ah my Lord what have you done!
I came to seek you.

Phil. Is it from her you come?

Ast. No, but on her behalf: her heart's too great,
In this low ebb of Fortune, to intreat.

Phil. 'Tis but a short Ecclipse,
Which past, a glorious day will soon ensue:
But I would ask a favour too, from you.

Ast. When Conquerors petition, they command:
Those that can Captive Queens, who can withstand?

Phil. She, with her happiness, might mine create;
'Yet seems indulgent to her own ill fate:
But she, in secret, hates me sure; for why
If not, should she *Candiope* deny?

Ast. If you dare trust my knowledge of her mind,
She has no thoughts of you that are unkind.

Phil. I could my sorrows with some patience bear,
Did they proceed from any one but her:
But from the Queen! whose person I adore,
By Duty much, by inclination more.

Ast. He is inclin'd already, did he know
That she lov'd him, how would his Passion grow!   [*aside.*

Phil. That her fair hand with Destiny combines!
Fate ne're strikes deep, but when unkindness joynes!
For, to confess the secret of my mind,
Something so tender for the Queen I find,
That ev'n *Candiope* can scarce remove,
And, were she lower, I should call it love.

Ast. She charg'd me not this secret to betray,
But I best serve her if I disobey:
For, if he loves, 'twas for her int'rest done;
If not, he'll keep it secret for his own.   [*aside.*

Phil. Why are you in obliging me so slow?

Ast. The thing's of great importance you would know;
And you must first swear secresie to all.

Phil. I swear:

Ast. Yet hold; your oath's too general:
Swear that *Candiope* shall never know.

Phil. I swear:

Ast. No not the Queen her self:

Phil. I vow.

Ast. You wonder why I am so cautious grown
In telling what concerns your self alone:
But spare my Vow, and guess what it may be
That makes the Queen deny *Candiope:*
'Tis neither hate nor pride that moves her mind;
Methinks the Riddle is not hard to find.

   Phil. You seem so great a wonder to intend,
As were, in me, a crime to apprehend.

   Ast. 'Tis not a crime to know; but would be one
To prove ungrateful when your Duty's known.

   Phil. Why would you thus my easie faith abuse!
I cannot think the Queen so ill would chuse.
But stay, now your imposture will appear;
She has her self confess'd she lov'd elsewhere:
On some ignoble choice has plac'd her heart,
One who wants quality, and more, desert.

   Ast. This though unjust, you have most right to say,
For, if you'l rail against your self, you may.

   Phil. Dull that I was!
A thousand things now crowd my memory,
That makes me know it could be none but I.
Her Rage was Love: and its tempestuous flame,
Like Lightning, show'd the Heaven from whence it came.
But in her kindness my own shame I see;
Have I dethron'd her then, for loving me?
I hate my self for that which I have done,
Much more, discover'd, then I did unknown.
How does she brook her strange imprisonment?

   Ast. As great souls should, that make their own content.
The hardest term she for your act could find
Was onely this, O *Philocles*, unkind!
Then, setting free a sigh, from her fair eyes
She wip'd two pearls, the remnant of wild show'rs,
Which hung, like drops upon the bells of flowers:
And thank'd the Heav'ns,
Which better did, what she design'd, pursue,
Without her crime to give her pow'r to you.

   Phil. Hold, hold, you set my thoughts so near a Crown,
They mount above my reach to pull them down:
Here Constancy; Ambition there does move;
On each side Beauty, and on both sides Love.

   Ast. Me thinks the least you can is to receive
This love, with reverence, and your former leave.

Phil. Think but what difficulties come between!

Ast. 'Tis wond'rous difficult to love a Queen.

Phil, For pity cease more reasons to provide,
I am but too much yielding to your side;
And, were my heart but at my own dispose,
I should not make a scruple where to choose.

Ast. Then if the Queen will my advice approve,
Her hatred to you shall expel her love.

Phil. Not to be lov'd by her, as hard would be
As to be hated by *Candiope.*

Ast. I leave you to resolve while you have time;
You muſt be guilty, but may choose your crime.   *Exit* Aſteria.

Phil. One thing I have resolv'd; and that I'le do
Both for my love, and for my honour too.
But then, (Ingratitude and falshood weigh'd,)
I know not which would moſt my soul upbraid.
Fate shoves me headlong down, a rugged way;
Unsafe to run, and yet too ſteep to ſtay.   [*Exit* Phil.

ACT V.

SCENE *The Court.*

Florimel *in Mans Habit.*

Flor. 'TWill be rare now if I can go through with it, to out-do
this mad *Celadon* in all his tricks, and get both his Mis-
tresses from him; then I shall revenge my self upon all three, and
save my own ſtake into the bargain; for I find I love the Rogue in
spight of all his infidelities. Yonder they are, and this way they muſt
come.——If cloathes and a *bon meen* will take 'em, I shall do't.——
Save you *Monsieur Florimell*; Faith me thinks you are a very *janty*
fellow, *poudrè & ajuſtè* as well as the beſt of 'em. I can manage the
little Comb,—set my Hat, shake my Garniture, toss about my empty
Noddle, walk with a courant slurr, and at every ſtep peck down my
Head:——if I should be miſtaken for some Courtier now, pray
where's the difference?

Enter *to her* Celadon, Olinda, Sabina.

Olin. Never mince the matter!

Sab. You have left your heart behind with *Florimel;* we know it.

Cel. You know you wrong me; when I am with *Florimel* 'tis ſtill
your Prisoner, it only draws a longer chain after it.

56

Flor. Is it e'n so! then farewel poor *Florimel*, thy Maidenhead is condemn'd to die with thee——   [*aside.*

Cel. But let's leave the discourse; 'tis all digression that does not speak of your beauties.——

Flor. Now for me in the name of impudence!——

                           [*walks with them.*

They are the greatest beauties I confess that ever I beheld.——

Cel. How now, what's the meaning of this young fellow?

Flor. And therefore I cannot wonder that this Gentleman who has the honour to be known to you should admire you,——since I that am a stranger——

Cel. And a very impudent one, as I take it, Sir.——

Flor. Am so extreamly surpriz'd, that I admire, love, am wounded, and am dying all in a moment.

Cel. I have seen him somewhere, but where I know not! prithee my friend leave us, dost thou think we do not know our way in Court?

Flor. I pretend not to instruct you in your way; you see I do not go before you: but you cannot possibly deny me the happiness to wait upon these Ladies; me, who——

Cel. Thee, who shalt be beaten most unmercifully if thou dost follow them!

Flor. You will not draw in Court, I hope.

Cel. Pox on him, let's walk away faster, and be rid of him——

Flor. O take no care for me, Sir, you shall not lose me; I'le rather mend my pace, then not wait on you.

Olin. I begin to like this fellow——

Cel. You make very bold here in my Seraglio, and I shall find a time to tell you so, Sir.

Flor. When you find a time to tell me on't, I shall find a time to answer you: But pray what do you find in your self so extraordinary, that you should serve these Ladies better then I; let me know what 'tis you value your self upon, and let them Judg betwixt us.

Cel. I am somewhat more a man then you.

Flor. That is, you are so much older then I: Do you like a man ever the better for his age Ladies?

Sab. Well said, young Gentleman.

Cel. Pish, thee! a young raw Creature, thou hast ne're been under the Barbers hands yet.

Flor. No, nor under the Surgeons neither as you have been.

Cel. 'Slife what wouldst thou be at: I am madder then thou art?

Flor. The Devil you are: I'le Tope with you, I'le Sing with you, I'le Dance with you, I'le Swagger with you——

57

Cel. I'le fight with you.

Flor. Out upon fighting: 'tis grown so common a fashion, that a Modish man contemns it: A man of Garniture and Feather is above the dispensation of a Sword.

Olin. Uds my Life, here's the Queens Musick juſt going to us; you shall decide your quarrel by a Dance.

Sab. Who ſtops the Fiddles?

Cel. Bass and Trebble, by your leaves we arreſt you at these Ladies suits.

Flor. Come on Sirs, play me a Jigg:
You shall see how I'le baffle him.

Dance.

Flor. Your judgment, Ladies.

Olin. You sir, you sir: This is the rareſt Gentleman: I could live and die with him———

Sab. Lord, how he Sweats! Please you, Sir, make use of my Handkerchief?

Olind. You and I are merry, and juſt of an humour, Sir; therefore we two should love one another.

Sab. And you and I are juſt of an age, Sir, and therefore me thinks we should not hate one another.

Cel. Then I perceive Ladies, I am a Caſtaway, a Reprobate with you: why, faith this is hard luck now, that I should be no less then one whole hour in getting your affeſtions, and now muſt loose 'em in a quarter of it.

Olin. No matter, let him rail: does the loss affliſt you, Sir?

Cel. No, in faith does it not: for if you had not forsaken me, I had you: so the Willows may flourish for any branches I shall rob 'em of.

Sab. However, we have the advantage to have left you, not you us.

Cel. That's onely a certain nimbleness in Nature you women have to be first unconſtant: but if you had not made the more haſte, the wind was veering too upon my Weathercock: the beſt on't is, *Florimel* is worth both of you.

Flor. 'Tis like she'll accept of their leavings.

Cel. She will accept on't, and she shall accept on't: I think I know more than you of her mind Sir.

Enter Melissa.

Mel. Daughters there's a poor collation within that waits for you.

Flor. Will you walk muſty Sir?

58

Cel. No, merry Sir, I won'not: I have surfeited of that old womans face already.

Flor. Begin some frolick then; what will you do for her?

Cel. Faith I am no dog to show tricks for her; I cannot come aloft for an old Woman.

Flor. Dare you kiss her!

Cel. I was never dar'd by any man——by your leave old Madam ——   *[He plucks off her Ruff.*

Mel. Help, help, do you discover my nakedness?

Cel. Peace Tiffany! no harm.   *[He puts on the Ruff.* Now Sir here's *Florimels* health to you——   *[kisses her.*

Mel. Away sir——a sweet young man as you are to abuse the gift of Nature so.

Cel. Good Mother do not commend me so; I am flesh and blood, and you do not know what you may pluck upon that reverend person of yours——Come on, follow your leader.

        [Gives Florimel *the Ruff, she puts it on.*

Flor. Stand fair Mother——

Cel. What with your Hat on? Lie thou there——and thou too—— *[Plucks off her Hat and Perrucke, and discovers* Florimel.

Omnes. Florimel!

Flor. My kind Miſtresses how sorry I am I can do you no further service! I think I had beſt resign you to *Celadon* to make amends for me.

Cel. Lord what a misfortune it was Ladies, that the Gentleman could not hold forth to you.

Olin. We have loſt *Celadon* too.

Mel. Come away, this is paſt enduring.   *[Exeunt* Mel. Olin.

Sab. Well if ever I believe a man to be a man for the sake of a Perruks and Feather again——   *[Exit.*

Flor. Come, *Celadon*, shall we make accounts even? Lord what a hanging look was there: indeed if you had been recreant to your Miſtress, or had forsworn your love, that sinner's face had been but decent, but for the vertuous, the innocent, the conſtant *Celadon*——

Cel. This is not very heroick in you, now to insult over a man in his misfortunes; but take heed, you have rob'd me of my two Mistresses: I shall grow desperately conſtant, and all the tempeſt of my love will fall upon your head: I shall so pay you.

Flor. Who you, pay me! you are a banckrupt, caſt beyond all possibility of recovery.

Cel. If I am a banckrupt, I'le be a very honeſt one: when I cannot pay my debts, at leaſt, I'le give you up the possession of my body.

Flor. No, I'le deal better with you; since you are unable to pay, I'le give in your bond.

Enter Philocles *with a Commanders Staff in his hand, Attended*

Phil. Cousin, I am sorry I must take you from your company about an earnest business.

Flor. There needs no excuse, my Lord, we had dispatched our affairs, and were just parting.

Cel. Will you be going, Sir; sweet Sir, damn'd Sir, I have but one word more to say to you.

Flor. As I'm a man of Honour, I'le wait on you some other time——

Cel. By these Breeches——

Flor. Which if I marry you I am resolv'd to wear; put that into our Bargain, and so adieu, Sir——   [*Exit* Florimel.

Phil. Hark you Cousin——   [*They whisper.*
You'll see it exactly executed: I rely upon you.

Cel. I shall not fail, my Lord: may the conclusion of it prove happy to you.   [*Exit* Celadon.
                    Philocles *solus.*

Where're I cast about my wandring eyes,
Greatness lies ready in some shape to tempt me.
The royal furniture in every room,
The Guards, and the huge waving crowds of people,
All waiting for a sight of that fair Queen
Who makes a present of her love to me:
Now tell me, Stoique!
If all these with a wish might be made thine,
Would'st thou not truck thy ragged vertue for 'em?
If Glory was a bait that Angels swallow'd,
How then should souls ally'd to sence, resist it!

Enter Candiope.

Ah poor *Candiope!* I pity her,
But that is all.——

Cand. O my dear *Philocles!* A thousand blessings wait on thee!
The hope of being thine, I think will put
Me past my meat and sleep with extasie,
So I shall keep the fasts of Seraphim's,
And wake for joy like Nightingals in *May.*

Phil. Wake, *Philocles,* wake from thy dream of glory,

60

'Tis all but shadow to *Candiope*:
Canst thou betray a love so innocent!   [*Aside.*
   Cand. What makes you melancholick? I doubt
I have displeased you?
   Phil. No my love, I am not displeas'd with you,
But with my self when I consider
How little I deserve you.
   Cand. Say not so, my *Philocles*, a love so true as yours
That would have left a Court, and a Queens favour
To live in a poor Hermitage with me.——
   Phil. Ha! She has stung me to the quick!
As if she knew the falshood I intended:
But, I thank Heaven, it has recall'd my vertue;——   [*aside.*
O my dear, I love you, and you onely;   [*To her.*
Go in, I have some business for a while;
But I think minutes ages till we meet.
   Can. I knew you had; but yet I could not choose
But come and look upon you——   [*Exit* Candiope.
   Phil. What barbarous man could wrong so sweet a vertue!

   Enter the Queen in black with Asteria.

Madam, the States are straight to meet; but why
In these dark ornaments will you be seen?
   Qu. ——They fit the fortune of a Captive Queen.
   Phil. ——Deep shades are thus to heighten colours set;
So Stars in Night, and Diamonds shine in Jet.
   Qu. True friends should so, in dark afflictions shine,
But I have no great cause to boast of mine.
   Phil. You may have too much prejudice for some,
And think 'em false before their trial's come.
But, Madam, what determine you to do?
   Qu. I came not here to be advis'd by you:
But charge you by that pow'r which once you own'd,
And which is still my right, ev'n when unthron'd;
That whatsoe're the States resolve of me,
You never more think of *Candiope*.
   Phil. Not think of her! ah, how should I obey!
Her tyrant eyes have forc'd my heart away.
   Qu. By force retake it from those tyrant eyes,
I'le grant you out my Letters of Reprize.
   Phil. She has, too well, prevented that design,
By giving me her heart in change for mine.
   Qu. Thus foolish Indians Gold for Glass forgo,

61

'Twas to your loss you priz'd your heart so low.
I set its value when you were advanc'd,
And as my favours grew, its rate inhanc'd.

    Phil. The rate of Subjects hearts by yours must go,
And love in yours has set the value low.

    Qu. I stand corrected, and my self reprove,
You teach me to repent my low-plac'd love:
Help me this passion from my heart to tear,
Now rail on him, and I will sit and hear.

    Phil. Madam, like you, I have repented too,
And dare not rail on one I do not know.

    Qu. This, *Philocles,* like strange perverseness shows,
As if what e're I said, you would oppose;
How come you thus concern'd, for this unknown?

    Phil. I onely judg his actions by my own.

    Qu. I've heard too much, and you too much have said.
O Heav'ns, the secret of my soul's betray'd!
He knows my love, I read it in his face,
And blushes, conscious of his Queen's disgrace.——   [*aside.*
Hence quickly, hence, or I shall die with shame.   [*To him.*

    Phil. Now I love both, and both with equal flame.
Wretched I came, more wretched I retire,
When two winds blow it who can quench the fire!

                        Exit Philocles.

    Qu. O my *Asteria* I know not whom t' accuse;
But either my own eyes or you, have told
My love to *Philocles.*

    Ast. Is't possible that he should know it, Madam!

    Qu. Me thinks you ask'd that question guiltily.
Confess, for I will know, what was the subject of your long discourse
                  [*Her hand on* Asteria's *shoulder.*
I' th Antichamber with him.

    Ast. It was my business to convince him, Madam,
How ill he did, being so much oblig'd,
To joyn in your imprisonment.

    Qu. Nay, now I am confirm'd my thought was true;
For you could give him no such reason
Of his obligements as my love.

    Ast. Because I saw him much a Malecontent,
I thought to win him to your int'rest, Madam,
By telling him it was no want of kindness
Made your refusal of *Candiope.*
And he perhaps——

62

Qu. What of him now.

Ast. As Men are apt, interpreted my words
To all th' advantage he could wrest the sence,
As if I meant you Lov'd him.

Qu. Have I deposited within thy breast
The dearest treasure of my life, my glory,
And hast thou thus betray'd me!
But why do I accuse thy female weakness
And not my own for trusting thee!
Unhappy Queen, *Philocles* knows thy fondness,
And needs must think it done by thy Command.

Ast. Dear Madam, think not so.

Qu. Peace, peace, thou should'st for ever hold thy tongue.
For it has spoke too much for all thy life.——   *[To her.*
Then *Philocles* has told *Candiope,*
And courts her kindness with his scorn of me.
O whither am I fallen! But I must rouze my self, and give a stop
To all these ills by headlong passion caus'd;
In hearts resolv'd weak love is put to flight,
And onely conquers when we dare not fight.
But we indulge our harms, and while he gains
An entrance, please our selves into our pains.

Enter Lysimantes.

Ast. Prince *Lysimantes,* Madam!——

Qu. Come near you poor deluded criminal;
See how ambition cheats you:
You thought to find a Prisoner here,
But you behold a Queen.

Lys. And may you long be so: 'tis true this Act
May cause some wonder in your Majesty.

Qu. None, Cousin, none; I ever thought you
Ambitious, Proud, designing.

Lys. Yet all my Pride, Designs, and my Ambition
Were taught me by a Master
With whom you are not unacquainted, Madam.

Qu. Explain your self; dark purposes, like yours,
Need an Interpretation.

Lys. 'Tis love I mean.

Qu. Have my low fortunes giv'n thee
This insolence, to name it to thy Queen?

Lys. Yet you have heard love nam'd without offence,

As much below you as you think my passion,
I can look down on yours.——
    Qu. Does he know it too!
This is th' extreamest malice of my Stars!——   [*aside.*
    Lys. You see, that Princes faults,
(How e're they think 'em safe from publick view)
Fly out through the dark crannies of their Closets:
We know what the Sun does,
Ev'n when we see him not in t' other world.
    Qu. My actions, Cousin, never fear'd the light.
    Lys. Produce him then, your darling of the dark,
For such an one you have.
    Qu. I know no such.
    Lys. You know, but will not own him.
    Qu. Rebels ne're want pretence to blacken Kings,
And this, it seems, is yours: do you produce him,
Or ne're hereafter sully my Renown
With this aspersion:——Sure he dares not name him.——[*aside.*
    Lys. I am too tender of your fame; or else—
Nor are things brought to that extremity:
Provided you accept my passion,
I'le gladly yield to think I was deceiv'd.
    Qu. Keep in your error still; I will not buy
Your good opinion at so dear a rate,
As my own misery by being yours.
    Lys. Do not provoke my patience by such scornes.
For fear I break through all and name him to you.
    Qu. Hope not to fright me with your mighty looks;
Know I dare stem that tempest in your brow,
And dash it back upon you.
    Lys. Spight of prudence it will out: 'Tis *Philocles.*
Now judge, when I was made a property
To cheat my self by making him your Prisoner,
Whether I had not right to take up armes?
    Qu. Poor envious wretch!
Was this the venome that swell'd up thy brest?
My grace to *Philocles* mis-deem'd my love!
    Lys. 'Tis true, the Gentleman is innocent;
He ne're sinn'd up so high, not in his wishes;
You know he loves elsewhere.
    Qu. You mean your Sister.
    Lys. I wish some Sybil now would tell me
Why you refus'd her to him?

Qu. Perhaps I did not think him worthy of her.

Lys. Did you not think him too worthy, Madam?
This is too thin a vail to hinder your passion,
To prove you love him not, yet give her him,
And I'le engage my honour to lay down my Armes.

Qu. He is arriv'd were I would wish——   [*aside.*
Call in the company and you shall see what I will do.——

Lys. Who waits without there?——   [*Exit* Lys.

Qu. Now hold, my heart, for this one act of honour,
And I will never ask more courage of thee:
Once more I have the means to reinstate my self into my glory,
I feel my love to *Philocles* within me
Shrink, and pull back my heart from this hard tryal,
But it must be when glory says it must,
As children wading from some Rivers bank
First try the water with their tender feet;
Then shruddring up with cold, step back again,
And streight a little further venture on,
Till at the last they plunge into the deep,
And pass at once, what they were doubting long:
I'le make the same experiment; it shall be done in haste,
Because I'le put it past my pow'r t' undo.

Enter at one Door Lysimantes, *at the other* Philocles, Celadon, Candiope, Florimel, Flavia, Olinda, Sabina; *the three Deputies, and Soldiers.*

Lys. In Armes! is all well, *Philocles?*

Phil. No, but it shall be.

Qu. He comes, and with him
The fevour of my love returns to shake me.
I see love is not banish'd from my soul
He is still there, but is chain'd up by glory.

Ast. You've made a noble conquest, Madam.

Qu. Come hither, *Philocles*: I am first to tell you
I and my Cousin are agreed, he has
Engag'd to lay down Armes.

Phil. 'Tis well for him he has; for all his party,
By my command already are surpriz'd,
While I was talking with your Majesty.

Cel. Yes 'Faith I have done him that courtesie;
I brought his followers, under pretence of guarding it, to a straight place where they are all coupt up without use of their Armes, and may be pelted to death by the small infantry o' the town.

Qu. 'Twas more then I expected, or could hope;
Yet still I thought your meaning honest.
  Phil. My fault was rashness, but 'twas full of zeal:
Nor had I e're been led to that attempt,
Had I not seen it would be done without me:
But by compliance I preserv'd the pow'r
Which I have since made use of for your service.
  Qu. And which I purpose so to recompence.——
  Lys. With her Crown she means; I knew 'twould come to't.
                                                        [*aside.*

  Phil. O Heav'ns, she'll own her love!
Then I must lose *Candiope* for ever,
And floating in a vast abyss of glory,
Seek and not find my self!—   [*aside.*
  Qu. Take your *Candiope*; and be as happy
As love can make you both:—how pleas'd I am
That I can force my tongue,
To speak words so far distant from my heart!——   [*aside.*
  Can. My happiness is more then I can utter!
  Lys. Methinks I could do violence on my self for taking Armes
Against a Queen so good, so bountiful:
Give me leave, Madam, in my extasie
Of joy, to give you thanks for *Philocles*,
You have preserv'd my friend, and now he owes not
His fortunes onely to your favour; but
What's more, his life, and more then that, his love.
I am convinc'd, she never lov'd him now;
Since by her free consent, all force remov'd
She gives him to my Sister.
Flavia was an Impostor and deceiv'd me.——   [*aside.*
  Phil. As for me, Madam, I can onely say
That I beg respit for my thanks; for on the sudden,
The benefit's so great it overwhelmes me.
  Ast. Mark but th' faintness of th' acknowledgment.
                                            [*To the* Queen *aside.*
  Qu. to *Ast.*] I have observ'd it with you, and am pleas'd
He seems not satisfi'd; for I still wish
That he may love me.
  Phil. I see *Asteria* deluded me
With flattering hopes of the Queens love
Only to draw me off from *Lysimantes*:
But I will think no more on't.
I'm going to possess *Candiope*,
66

And I am ravish'd with the joy on't! ha!
Not ravish'd neither.
For what can be more charming then that Queen!
Behold how night sits lovely on her eye-brows,
While day breaks from her eyes! then, a Crown too!
Loſt, loſt, for ever loſt, and now 'tis gone
'Tis beautifull.———   *aside.*

   Aſt. How he eyes you ſtill!   *to the Queen.*
   Phil. Sure I had one of the fallen Angels Dreams;
All Heav'n within this hour was mine!   *aside.*
   Can. What is it that diſturbs you Dear?
   Phil. Onely the greatness of my joy:
I've ta'ne too ſtrong a Cordial, love,
And cannot yet digeſt it.
   Qu. 'Tis done! but this pang more; [*Clapping her hand on* Aſteria.
And then a glorious birth.
The Tumults of this day, my loyal Subjeſts
Have setled in my heart a resolution,
Happy for you, and glorious too for me.
Firſt for my Cousin, though attempting on my person,
He has incurr'd the danger of the Laws,
I will not punish him.
   Lys. You bind me ever to my loyalty.
   Qu. Then, that I may oblige you more to it.
I here declare you rightful successor,
And heir immediate to my Crown:
This, Gentlemen.———   [*to the Deputies.*
I hope will ſtill my subjeſts discontents,
When they behold succession firmly setled.
   Deputies. Heav'n preserve your Majeſty.
   Qu. As for my self, I have resolv'd
Still to continue as I am, unmarried:
The cares, observances, and all the duties
Which I should pay an Husband, I will place
Upon my people; and our mutual love
Shall make a blessing more then Conjugal.
And this the States shall ratifie.
   Lys. Heav'n bear me witness that I take no joy
In the succession of a Crown
Which muſt descend to me so sad a way.
   Qu. Cousin, no more; my resolution's paſt,
Which fate shall never alter.
   Phil. Then, I am once more happy!

For since none possess her, I am pleas'd
With my own choice, and will desire no more.
For multiplying wishes is a curse
That keep the mind ſtill painfully awake.
     Qu. Celadon!
Your care and loyalty have this day obliged me;
But how to be acknowledging I know not,
Unless you give the means.

Cel. I was in hope your Majeſty had forgot me; therefore if you please, Madam, I onely beg a pardon for having taken up armes once to day againſt you; for I have a foolish kind of Conscience, which I wish many of your Subjeƈts had, that will not let me ask a recompence for my loyalty, when I know I have been a Rebel.

Qu. Your modeſty shall not serve the turn: Ask something.

Cel. Then I beg, Madam, you will command *Florimel* never to be friends with me.

Flor. Ask again; I grant that without the Queen: But why are you affraid on't?

Cel. Because I am sure as soon as ever you are, you'l marry me.

Flor. Do you fear it?

Cel. No, 'twill come with a fear.

Flor. If you do, I will not ſtick with you for an Oath.

Cel. I require no Oath 'till we come to Church; and then after the Prieſt, I hope; for I find it will be my deſtiny to marry thee.

Flor. If ever I say a word after the black Gentleman for thee, *Celadon——*

Cel. Then, I hope, you'l give me leave to beſtow a faithful heart elsewhere.

Flor. I but if you would have one you muſt bespeak it, for I am sure you have none ready made.

Cel. What say you, shall I marry *Flavia?*

Flor. No, she'll be too cunning for you.

Cel. What say you to *Olinda* then? she's tall, and fair, and bonny.

Flor. And foolish, and apish, and fickle.

Cel. But *Sabina,* there's pretty, and young, and loving, and innocent.

Flor. And dwarfish, and childish, and fond, and flippant: if you marry her Siſter, you will get May-poles; and if you marry her, you will get Fayries to dance about them.

Cel. Nay, then the case is clear, *Florimel:* if you take 'em all from me, 'tis because you reserve me for your self.

Flor. But this Marriage is such a Bugbear to me; much might be if we could invent but any way to make it easie.

68

Cel. Some foolish people have made it uneasie, by drawing the knot faſter then they need; but we that are wiser will loosen it a little.

Flor. 'Tis true, indeed, there's some difference betwixt a Girdle and an Halter.

Cel. As for the firſt year, according to the laudable cuſtome of new married people, we shall follow one another up into Chambers, and down into Gardens, and think we shall never have enough of one another——So far 'tis pleasant enough, I hope.

Flor. But after that, when we begin to live like Husband and Wife, and never come near one another——what then, Sir?

Cel. Why then our onely happiness muſt be to have one mind, and one will, *Florimel*.

Flor. One mind if thou wilt, but prithee let us have two wills; for I find one will be little enough for me alone; But how if those wills should meet and clash, *Celadon?*

Cel. I warrant thee for that: Husbands and Wives keep their wills far enough asunder for ever meeting: one thing let us be sure to agree on, that is, never to be jealous.

Flor. No, but e'en love one another as long as we can; and confess the truth when we can love no longer.

Cel. When I have been at play, you shall never ask me what money I have loſt.

Flor. When I have been abroad you shall never enquire who treated me.

Cel. Item, I will have the liberty to sleep all night, without your interrupting my repose for any evil design whatsoever.

Flor. Item, Then you shall bid me good night before you sleep.

Cel. Provided always, that whatever liberties we take with other people, we continue very honeſt to one another.

Flor. As far as will consiſt with a pleasant life.

Cel. Laſtly, Whereas the names of Husband and Wife hold forth nothing but clashing and cloying, and dulness and faintness in their signification; they shall be abolish'd for ever betwixt us.

Flor. And inſtead of those, we will be married by the more agreeable names of Miſtress and Gallant.

Cel. None of my priviledges to be infring'd by thee *Florimel*, under the penalty of a month of Faſting-nights.

Flor. None of my priviledges to be infring'd by thee *Celadon*, under the penalty of Cuckoldom.

Cel. Well, if it be my fortune to be made a Cuckold, I had rather thou shouldſt make me one then any one in *Sicily:* and for my comfort I shall have thee oftner then any of thy servants.

Flor. La ye now, is not such a marriage as good as wenching, *Celadon?*

Cel. This is very good, but not so good, *Florimel.*

Qu. Now set me forward to th' Assembly.
You promise Cousin your consent?

Lys. But most unwillingly.

Qu. Philocles, I must beg your voice too.

Phil. Most joyfully I give it.

Lys. Madam but one word more; since you are so resolv'd,
That you may see, bold as my passion was,
'Twas onely for your person, not your Crown;
I swear no second love
Shall violate the flame I had for you,
But in strict imitation of your Oath
I vow a single life.

Qu. to *Asteria.*] Now, my *Asteria,* my joys are full;
The pow'rs above that see
The innocent love I bear to *Philocles,*
Have giv'n its due reward; for by this means
The right of *Lysimantes* will devolve
Upon *Candiope;* and I shall have
This great content, to think, when I am dead,
My Crown may fall on *Philocles* his head.   *Exeunt omnes.*

EPILOGUE

Written by a Person of Honour.

OUR *Poet something doubtful of his Fate*
   Made choice of me to be his Advocate,
Relying on my Knowledg in the Laws,
And I as boldly undertook the Cause.
I left my Client yonder in a rant
Against the envious, and the ignorant,
Who are, he sayes, his onely Enemies:
But he contemns their malice, and defies
The sharpest of his Censurers to say
Where there is one gross fault in all his Play.
The language is so fitted for each part,
The Plot according to the Rules of Art;
And twenty other things he bid me tell you,
But I cry'd, e'en go do't your self for Nelly.
Reason, with Judges, urg'd in the defence
Of those they would condemn, is insolence;
I therefore wave the merits of his Play,
And think it fit to plead this safer way.
If, when too many in the purchase share
Robbing's not worth the danger nor the care;
The men of business must, in Policy,   ⎫
Cherish a little harmless Poetry;   ⎬
All Wit wou'd else grow up to Knavery. ⎭
Wit is a Bird of Musick, or of Prey,
Mounting she strikes at all things in her way;
But if this Birdlime once but touch her wings,
On the next bush she sits her down, and sings.
I have but one word more; tell me I pray
What you will get by damning of our Play?
A whipt Fanatick who does not recant
Is by his Brethren call'd a suff'ring Saint;
And by your hands shou'd this poor Poet die
Before he does renounce his Poetry,
His death must needs confirm the Party more
Then all his scribling life could do before.

Where so much zeal does in a Sect appear,
'Tis to no purpose, 'faith, to be severe.
But 'tother day I heard this rhyming Fop
Say Criticks were the Whips, and he the Top;
For, as a Top spins best the more you baste her,
So every lash you give, he writes the faster.

FINIS

S^R

MARTIN
MAR-ALL

OR

THE FEIGN'D
INNOCENCE

A COMEDY

SOURCE

"SIR MARTIN MARALL was originally a mere translation from the French, made by William, Duke of Newcastle, and by him presented to our author, who revised and adapted it to the stage; but it was entered at Stationers' Hall, June 24, 1668, as the Duke's play, without any mention of Dryden, either from respect to that nobleman, (on which account, perhaps, it was published anonymously,) or lest, were it delivered to the publick as the Laureate's performance, the giving it away from the King's Servants, with whom he was in a kind of partnership, might be considered as a breach of his contract." Thus Malone, *The Life of Dryden* (*Prose Works of John Dryden*, London, 1800, Vol. I, Part I, p. 93); and it seems that this pretty well sums up the case. Pepys, who was present at the second performance of this comedy at the Duke's house on Friday, 16 August, 1668, describes it as "a play made by my Lord Duke of Newcastle, but, as every body says, corrected by Dryden." Downes in the *Roscius Anglicanus* notes: "Sir *Martin Marral*, The Duke of *New-Castle*, giving Mr. *Dryden* a bare Translation of it, out of a Comedy of the Famous *French* Poet *Monseur Moleire*: He Adapted the Part purposely for the Mouth of Mr. *Nokes*, and curiously Polishing the whole."

Molière's *L'Étourdi; ou, Les Contre-Temps*, a comedy in verse and in five acts, is adapted from a piece by Nicolò Barbieri entitled *L'Inavvertito, overo Scappino Disturbato e Mezzettino Travagliato*, 1629. *L'Étourdi*, the scene of which is at Messina, with its imbroglio of meshed intrigue directed by Mascarille, retains much of its Italian origin. It was produced at Lyons in 1653, and then given at Béziers before the Prince de Conti. It was first seen in Paris on the stage of the Théâtre du Petit-Bourbon on 3 November, 1658, but not printed until 1663. (Bibliographers mention an edition of 1658, but no copy is known, and the statement is considered suspect. Lélie, l'étourdi, is maugre all his faults a gallant figure, and whilst we laugh at his blunders we hope for his ultimate success. This perhaps is one of the chief differences between Molière and the English play, where Sir Martin is inept and gross in his clumsiness. He does not deserve the lady, nor are we concerned that he should achieve a victory.

Yet if *Sr Martin Mar-all* owes something to Molière, it owes far more to *L'amant indiscret* of Quinault.

L'Amant indiscret, ou le Maître étourdi, a comedy in five acts, in verse, by Philippe Quinault (1635–1688), who perhaps to-day is better known owing to the sarcasms of Boileau than from his writings ("Zoile de Quinault"), was produced at the hôtel de Bourgogne in 1654, but not printed until ten years later, *A Rouen et se vend à Paris*, 12 mo. 1664. It is true the Soleinnes catalogue speaks of an edition "chez Toussaint Quinet" of 1656, but this does not appear to be traced. *L'Amant indiscret* is hardly to be compared with *L'Étourdi*, although in both cases the theme of a blundering lover is the same. It is disputed,

75

indeed, which comedy is the earliest. Molière, as we have noted, derived his incidents from *L'Inavvertito* (1629) of Nicolò Barbieri, and it is not impossible Quinault was indebted to the same source. Each play shows us the silliness of a master, who continually upsets the plans and devices which his servant is at no small pains to construct to gain their ends. *L'Amant indiscret* has met with some harsh judgement from critics. Auger extravagantly declared that Quinault's comedy "est denouée de toute espéce de mérite," which is absurd. The valet Philipin is a very lively character, full of wit and resource, whilst Lucresse is far from lacking charm. Carpalin and Courcaillet, the two hosts, one vaunting the "Teste-Noire" the other "l'Espée-Royale" are not unamusing. Amongst Dryden's debts to Quinault may be reckoned the scene where Sir Martin confides the tale of his meeting with Mrs. Millisent at Canterbury to Sir John in spite of Warner's interruptions. So Cleandre relates to Lisipe his passion for Lucresse, whilst Philipin vainly tries to close his mouth. Sir Martin's complaints of his ill-luck at the gaming-tables are exactly from the French. "Le jeu n'est pas plaisant lorsque l'on perd aussi," says Lisipe. "The pleasure of Play is lost, when one loses at that unreasonable Rate," says Sir John. Lucresse sends Lisipe off to the place Royal; Mrs. Millisent dispatches Sir John to Gray's Inn Walks. Carpalin, the host of the "Teste-Noire," appears disguised as a peasant bearing a letter to Lisipe from his uncle Albiron "Feu votre père est mort, c'est tout ce qu'on vous mande." First he fumbles for the letter and hands Lisipe a paper, "A Monsieur Paul Grimaud, apprenty savatier." So the Landlord disguised like a Carrier brings from old Uncle Anthony a letter to Sir John wherein the news of his father's death is related. But first the Landlord plucks out the wrong missive: "To Mr. *Paul Grimbard*—Apprentice to—No, that not for you, Sir." This stratagem to send a rival to a distance occurs in several plays, as in Boursault's *Le Mort vivant*. In Hauteroche's *Le Deuil*, and in *L'Etourdi*, the sons, in order to get money, pretend their fathers are dead. This is taken from XVI of Noel du Fail's *Contes d'Eutrapel*. In *L'Inavvertito* Scapin employs a feigned courier and a pretended letter.

Philipin next advises Rosette, Lucresse's maid, to hide the bag in which are important legal papers belonging to Lisipe. So Rose gives Warner the Writings entrusted to her by Sir John, and when asked for them protests that they have been left behind at Canterbury. Yet even if Dryden takes more than one hint from Quinault, he has vastly improved the original. In *L'Amant indiscret* eventually Cléandre is united to Lucresse, and Philipin takes Rosette.

It may be noted that the scene (Act IV) when Warner in order to dissuade Sir John from marrying Mrs. Millisent throws doubts upon the lady's virtue is not unlike the episode in *Monsieur de Pourceaugnac*, II, 4, where Sbrigani describes Julie as a "coquette achevée" and Monsieur de Pourceaugnac recoils from cuckoldom. But Molière's farce was first played at Chambord in September, 1669. Did Molière borrow from Dryden?

The famous incident when Sir Martin to serenade his mistress pretends to play upon the lute whilst Warner concealed performs his part is taken from the picaresque romance of *La vraie Histoire Comique de Francion* (1622), by Charles Sorel, 1599–1674. *Francion* was translated into German and into English. The first English version appeared in 1655; and was more than once

76

reprinted, notably in 1703. The passage in question which occurs in Book VII, and concerns the adventures of an amorous count who solicits a physician's daughter, is as follows: "De fortune il y avoit avec lui un gentilhomme qui touchoit fort bïen un luth, il le priste en prendre un, et le fit cacher derrière lui, pour jouer quelques pièces dessus, tandis qu'il en tiendroit un autre avec lequel on croiroit que ce fût lui qui jouât, ayant opinion qu'il enteroit d'autant plus aux bonnes grâces de sa maîtresse s'il lui faisoit paroître qu'il étoit donné de cette gentile perfection. Mais le grand malheur pour lui fut qu'il y avoit une des compagnons de la fille du médecin qui sçavoit bien jouer de cet instrument, et voyant qu'il ne faisoit que couler les doigts sur les touches du sien elle reconnut que n'étoit pas lui qui faisoit produire l'harmonie. Même elle en fut plus certaine apres avoir monté un étage plus haut d'où elle aperçut l'autre qui jouoit."

The Frolick of the Altitudes by which old Moody and Sir John Swallow are finally choused is borrowed from an incident, IV, 1, in Shackerley Marmion's *A Fine Companion*, acted in 1633 and printed the same year. Careless, Lackwit, the Captain, the Lieutenant, with four Wenches are carousing in a tavern. They dance, and anon the Captain asks: "What's to pay?" "You have built a sconce since you came in of thirty pounds," he is answered. The revels continue, and the Captain bids "Reach three Ioynt stooles hither Drawer." As part of their pranks Lackwit is bidden ascend "and be Captaine of this Fort." He does so, and the rest incontinently rub off leaving the gull as a pawn.

THEATRICAL HISTORY

Sᴿ *Martin Mar-all; or, The Feignd Innocence*, was produced at the Duke's House on Thursday, 15 August, 1667. Pepys, who was minded to be present, found "The King and Court there: the house full, and an act begun." Accordingly he saw at the Theatre Royal *The Merry Wives of Windsor*, which (he notes) "did not please me at all, in no part of it." On the following day after dinner "My wife and I to the Duke's playhouse, where we saw the new play acted yesterday 'The Feign Innocence, or Sir Martin Marr-all'; a play made by my Lord Duke of Newcastle, but, as every body says, corrected by Dryden. It is the most entire piece of mirth, a complete farce from one end to the other, that certainly was ever writ. I never laughed so in all my life. I laughed till my head [ached] all the evening and night with the laughing; and at very good wit therein, not fooling. The house full, and in all things of mighty content to me."

On Monday, 19 August, Pepys "took coach and to the Duke of York's house, all alone, and there saw 'Sir Martin Marr-all' again, though I saw him but two days since, and do find it the most comical play that ever I saw in my life." The next day he again went to the Duke's Playhouse "and there saw 'Sir Martin Marr-all' again, which I have now seen three times, and it hath been acted but four times, and still find it a very ingenious play, and full of variety."

Downes has the following account of this comedy. "Sir *Martin Marral*, The

Duke of *New-Castle*, giving Mr. *Dryden* a bare Translation of it, out of a Comedy of the Famous *French* Poet *Monseur Moleire:* He Adapted the Part purposely for the Mouth of Mr. *Nokes*, and curiously Polishing the whole; Mr. *Smith*, Acting Sir *John Swallow;* Mr. *Young*, Lord *Dartmouth;* Mr. *Underhill*, Old *Moody;* Mr. *Harris, Warner;* Mrs. *Norris*, Lady *Dupe;* Mrs. *Millisent*, Madam *Davies*. All the Parts being very Just and Exactly perform'd, 'specially Sir *Martin* and his Man, Mr. *Smith*, and several others since have come very near him, but none Equall'd, nor yet Mr. *Nokes* in Sir *Martin:* This Comedy was Crown'd with an Excellent Entry: In the last Act at the Mask, by Mr. *Priest* and Madam *Davies;* This, and Love in a Tub, got the Company more Money than any preceding Comedy."

Josias Priest, who acted the small part of the Landlord, was a famous dancer. It was he who invited Purcell to compose a musical entertainment for the young ladies of his school at Chelsea, and accordingly the great musician wrote for them in 1689, or the early part of 1690, his opera *Dido and Aeneas*.

Flecknoe's lines on Madam Davies for "*her excellent Dancing and Singing*" are well known. They may be found in *Euterpe Reviv'd*, 1675 (p. 64), commencing thus:

> How I admire thee, *Davies!*
> Who would not say, to see thee *dance* so *light*,
> Thou wert all *air*, or else all *flame* and spright——

Sr Martin Mar-all was a favourite play with Pepys, who on Saturday, 28 September, 1667, records that he saw "a piece" of it "with great delight, though I have seen it so often." On Monday, 14 October, following, he "went in for nothing into the pit, at the last act, to see Sir Martin Marr-all, . . . still being pleased with the humour of the play, almost above all that ever I saw." He was able to obtain free admittance into the theatre owing to the fact that the play was nearly done. On Wednesday, 1 January, 1667–8, he went "after dinner to the Duke of York's playhouse, and there saw 'Sir Martin Mar-all'; which I have seen so often, and yet am mightily pleased with it, and think it mighty witty, and the fullest of proper matter for mirth that ever was writ; and I do clearly see that they do improve in their acting of it. Here a mighty company of citizens, 'prentices, and others." On Saturday, 25 April, 1668, he notes: "to the Duke of York's playhouse, and there saw 'Sir Martin Marr-all,' which the more I see, the more I like." On Friday, 22 May, following, he is still enthusiastic: "to the Duke of York's house to a play, and saw Sir Martin Marr-all, where the house is full; and though I have seen it, I think, ten times, yet the pleasure I have is yet as great as ever, and is undoubtedly the best comedy ever was wrote." It may be remarked that the encomiums of the good diarist are amply deserved, for indeed the comedy, which is so exquisitely pleasant in the reading, upon the boards must have been irresistible.

Sr Martin Mar-all was one of the most popular plays of the day, and there are continual records of performances. James Nokes, whose appearances towards the end of his career had grown less and less frequent, died 8 September, 1696. Henry Harris had retired from the stage a little before the union of 1682. William Smith died in December, 1695. We know from Downes that Smith succeeded Harris in the rôle of Warner; but it is very uncertain which actors followed Nokes and Smith as the foolish knight and Billy his man.

At Drury Lane, 18 August, 1704, *Sr Martin Mar-all* was announced as "Not acted 5 years"; and at the same house it was twice given during the ensuing season, for the first time on 4 October, 1704, when it was followed by *The School-Boy; or, The Comical Rivals*, a farce first produced at Drury Lane, 26 October, 1702, and being nothing else than an adaptation of the lighter scenes from Cibber's *Womans Wit; or, The Lady in Fashion*, which had been damned some half a dozen years before.

At the Haymarket during the summer season, 26 July, 1707, Bullock, "the best Comedian that has trod the stage since Nokes and Leigh," appeared as Sir Martin; Booth, who occasionally "would condescend to some Parts in Comedy," Warner; Ben Johnson, "a true Copy of Mr. *Underhill*," who "arrived to as great a Perfection in Acting, as his great Namesake did in Poetry," Old Moody; Mills, Sir John Swallow; Mrs. Porter, Mrs. Millisent; and Mrs. Bradshaw, the original Corinna in *The Confederacy*, Dorinda in *The Beaux Stratagem*, and Arabella Zeal in *The Fair Quaker*, who was much applauded as Anne Page, Charlotte Welldon, Estifania, the Woman Captain, Elvira, Madam Fickle, and a very wide variety of characters, Rose.

On 24 June, 1708, at Drury Lane the summer Company gave Dryden's comedy, probably with the same cast as of the previous year.

At the Haymarket, 16 June, 1710, Mills played Warner, a part in which he was not suited, to the Sir Martin of Bullock.

At Drury Lane on 4 December of the same year George Powell, whose loose and libertine genius easily topped the rôle, was the Warner to Bullock's knight. Johnson and Mrs. Porter assumed their former characters; Mrs. Saunders, Anne Oldfield's friend and confidante, and always esteemed a very good actress, Rose; and Miss Willis, "a most excellent actress in low humour," Mrs. Christian.

Sr Martin Mar-all, although performed at rarer and rarer intervals, continues in the repertory. Thus we find it is given at Drury Lane, 17 October, 1712, followed by *The School-Boy*; 7 December, 1713, and 19 October, 1714.

At the same house 2 July, 1717, Joe Miller the jester appeared as Sir Martin. Mills played Warner; and Johnson, Old Moody. *The County Wake* was added as a *bonne bouche* with Bickerstaffe as Hob.

On 13 April, 1719, again at Drury Lane, *Sr Martin Mar-all* was performed, being the only time this comedy was acted that season.

At Drury Lane on 15 August, 1721, the summer Company played *Sr Martin Mar-all* with Miller in the title-rôle. This appears to have been one of the latest productions of Dryden's comedy, which it is scarcely hazardous to say did not survive beyond the first quarter of the eighteenth century. It may be that in some sense the place of *Sr Martin Mar-all* was being taken by Mrs. Centlivre's popular but immeasurably inferior play, *The Busie Body*, originally produced at Drury Lane in May, 1709. That Mrs. Centlivre borrowed from Dryden does not appear; in any case her scenes are merest shoddy compared to the rich full flavour of the greater dramatist.

Exquisitely humorous in the reading, *Sʳ Martin Mar-all*, given by actors with a true vein of comedy, would indeed be rare fun upon the stage. It was one of the plays a revival of which I constantly urged during my directorship of The Phœnix, but as it was not easily to be found in some cheap modern edition, it proved beyond the purview of the committee.

PROLOGUE

FOols, which each man meets in his Dish each day,
  Are yet the great Regalio's of a Play;
In which to Poets you but just appear,
To prize that highest which costs them so dear:
Fops in the Town more easily will pass;
One story makes a statutable Ass:
But such in Plays must be much thicker sown,
Like yolks of Eggs, a dozen beat to one.
Observing Poets all their walks invade,
As men watch Woodcocks gliding through a Glade:
And when they have enough for Comedy,
They stow their several Bodies in a Pye:
The Poet's but the Cook to fashion it,
For, Gallants, you your selves have found the Wit.
To bid you welcome would your Bounty wrong,
None welcome those who bring their Chear along.

EPILOGUE

AS Country Vicars, when the Sermon's done,
  Run hudling to the Benediction;
Well knowing, though the better sort may stay,
The Vulgar Rout will run unblest away:
So we, when once our Play is done, make haste
With a short Epilogue to close your taste.
In thus withdrawing we seem mannerly,
But when the Curtain's down we peep, and see
A Jury of the Wits who still stay late,
And in their Club decree the poor Plays fate;
Their Verdict back is to the Boxes brought,
Thence all the Town pronounces it their thought.
Thus, Gallants, we like Lilly can foresee,
But if you ask us what our doom will be,
We by to morrow will our Fortune cast,
As he tell all things when the Year is past.

THE NAMES OF THE PERSONS.

*L*Ord *Dartmouth.*	In love with Mrs. *Christian.*
Mr. Moody.	The Swash-Buckler.
Sir Martin Marr-all.	A Fool.
Warner.	His Man.
Sir John Swallow.	A Kentish Knight.
Lady Dupe.	The old Lady.
Mrs. Christian.	Her young Niece.
Mrs. Millisent.	The Swash-Bucklers Daughter.
Rose.	Her Maid.
Mrs. Preparation.	Woman to the old Lady.

Other Servants, Men and Women.
A Carrier.
Bayliffs.

The SCENE Covent-Garden.

The Feign'd Innocence

OR,

Sir Martin Marrall

ACT I.

Enter Warner *Solus.*

Warn. WHere the Devil is this Master of mine? he is ever out of the way when he should do himself good. This 'tis to serve a Coxcomb, one that has no more Brains than just those I carry for him. Well! of all Fopps commend me to him for the greatest; he's so opinion'd of his own Abilities, that he is ever designing somewhat, and yet he sows his Stratagems so shallow, that every Daw can pick 'em up: from a plotting Fool the Lord deliver me. Here he comes, O! it seems his Cousin's with him, then it is not so bad as I imagin'd.

Enter Sir Martin Marral, *Lady* Dupe.

La. Dupe. I think 'twas well contriv'd for your access to lodge her in the same House with you.

Sir Mart. 'Tis pretty well, I must confess.

Warn. Had he plotted it himself, it had been admirable. [*Aside.*

La. Dupe. For when her Father *Moody* writ to me to take him Lodgings, I so order'd it, the choice seem'd his, not mine.

Sir Mart. I have hit of a thing my self sometimes, when wiser Heads have miss'd it.———But that might be meer luck.

La. Dupe. Fortune does more than Wisdom.

Sir Mart. Nay, for that you shall excuse me;
I will not value any mans Fortune at a rush,
Except he have Wit and Parts to bear him out.
But when do you expect 'em?

La. Dupe. This Tide will bring them from *Gravesend.*
You had best let your man go as from me,
And wait them at the Stairs in *Durham*-yard.

Sir Mart. Lord, Cousin, what a do is here with your Counsel!
As though I could not have thought of that my self.

I could find in my heart not to send him now—stay a little
—I could soon find out some other way.

Warn. A minute's stay may lose your business.

Sir Mart. Well, go then,——but you must grant, if he had stay'd,
I could have found a better way,——you grant it.

La. Dupe. For once I will not stand with you.— [*Exit Warner.*
'Tis a sweet Gentlewoman this Mrs. *Millisent*, if you can get her.

Sir Mart. Let me alone for plotting.

La. Dupe. But by your favour, Sir, 'tis not so easie,
Her Father has already promis'd her:
And the young Gentleman comes up with 'em:
I partly know the Man,——but the old Squire is humoursome,
He's stout, and plain in speech and in behaviour;
He loves none of the fine Town-tricks of breeding,
But stands up for the old *Elizabeth* way in all things.
This we must work upon.

Sir Mart. Sure! you think you have to deal with a Fool, Cousin?

Enter Mrs. Christian.

La. Dupe. O my dear Neice, I have some business with you.
[*Whispers.*

Sir Mart. Well, Madam, I'le take one turn here i' th' *Piazza*'s;
A thousand things are hammering in this head;
'Tis a fruitful Noddle, though I say it.   [*Exit Sir Martin.*

La. Dupe. Go thy ways, for a most conceited Fool——
But to our Business, Cousin: you are young, but I am old, and have
had all the Love-experience, that a discreet Lady ought to have: and
therefore let me instruct you about the Love this rich Lord makes
to you.

Chr. You know, Madam, he's married, so that we cannot work
upon that ground of Matrimony.

La. Dupe. But there are advantages enough for you, if you will
be wise, and follow my advice.

Chr. Madam, my Friends left me to your care, therefore I will
wholly follow your Counsel with secrecy and obedience.

La. Dupe. Sweet-heart, it shall be the better for you another day:
well then, this Lord that pretends to you, is crafty and false, as most
men are, especially in Love——therefore we must be subtle to
meet with all his Plots, and have Countermines against his Works
to blow him up.

Chr. As how, Madam?

La. Dupe. Why, Girl, hee'l make fierce Love to you, but you
must not suffer him to ruffle you, or steal a kiss: but you must weep

and sigh, and say you'll tell me on't, and that you will not be us'd so; and play the innocent just like a Child, and seem ignorant of all.

Chr. I warrant you I'le be very ignorant, Madam.

La. Dupe. And be sure when he has tows'd you, not to appear at Supper that night, that you may fright him.

Chr. No, Madam.

La. Dupe. That he may think you have told me.

Chr. I, Madam.

La. Dupe. And keep your Chamber, and say your head akes.

Chr. O most extreamly, Madam.

La. Dupe. And lock the Door, and admit of no night-visits: at Supper I'le ask, where's my Cousin; and being told you are not well, I'le start from the Table to visit you, desiring his Lordship not to incommode himself; for I will presently wait on him agen.

Chr. But how, when you are return'd, Madam?

La. Dupe. Then somewhat discompos'd, I'le say I doubt the Meazles or Small-pox will seize on you, and then the Girl is spoil'd; saying, Poor thing, her Portion is her Beauty and her Vertue: and often send to see how you do, by whispers in my Servants ears, and have those whispers of your health return'd to mine: if his Lordship thereupon askes how you do, I will pretend it was some other thing.

Chr. Right, Madam, for that will bring him farther in suspence.

La. Dupe. A hopeful Girl! then will I eat nothing that Night, feigning my grief for you: but keep his Lordship Company at Meal, and seem to strive to put my passion off, yet shew it still by small mistakes.

Chr. And broken Sentences.

La. Dupe. A dainty Girl! And after Supper visit you again, with promise to return strait to his Lordship: but after I am gone send an Excuse, that I have given you a Cordial, and mean to watch that night in person with you.

Chr. His Lordship then will find the Prologue of his trouble, doubting I have told you of his ruffling.

La. Dupe. And more than that, fearing his Father should know of it, and his Wife, who is a Termagant Lady: but when he finds the Coast is clear, and his late ruffling known to none but you, he will be drunk with joy.

Chr. Finding my simple innocence, which will inflame him more.

La. Dupe. Then what the Lyon's skin has fail'd him in, the Foxes sublety must next supply, and that is just, Sweet-heart, as I would have it; for crafty Folks treaties are their advantage: especially when his passion must be satisfi'd at any rate, and you keep Shop to set the price of Love: so now you see the Market is your own.

85

Chr. Truly, Madam, this is very rational; and by the blessing of Heav'n upon my poor endeavours, I do not doubt to play my part.

La. Dupe. My blessing and my pray'rs go along with thee.

Enter Sir John Swallow, *Mrs.* Millisent, *and* Rose *her Maid.*

Chr. I believe, Madam, here is the young Heiress you expect, and with her he who is to marry her.

La. Dupe. Howe're I am Sir *Martin's* Friend, I must now seem his Enemy.

Sir John. Madam, this fair young Lady begs the honour to be known to you.

Mill. My Father made me hope it, Madam.

La. Dupe. Sweet Lady, I believe you have brought all the Freshness of the Country up to Town with you.   [*They salute.*

Mill. I came up, Madam, as we Country-Gentlewomen use, at an *Easter-*Term, to the destruction of Tarts and Cheese-cakes, to see a New Play, buy a new Gown, take a Turn in the Park, and so down agen to sleep with my Fore-fathers.

Sir John. Rather, Madam, you are come up to the breaking of many a poor Heart, that like mine, will languish for you.

Chr. I doubt, Madam, you are indispos'd with your Voyage; will you please to see the Lodgings your Father has provided for you?

Mill. To wait upon you, Madam.

La. Dupe. This is the door,——there is a Gentleman will wait on you immediately in your Lodging, if he might presume on your Commands.   [*In whisper.*

Mill. You mean Sir *Martin Marral:* I am glad he has entrusted his Passion with so discreet a Person.

[*In whisper.*

Mill. Sir *John,* let me intreat you to stay here, that my Father may have Intelligence where to find us.

Sir John. I shall obey you, Madam.   [*Exeunt Women.*

Enter Sir Martin.

Sir John. Sir *Martin Marral!* most happily encounter'd! how long have you been come to Town?

Sir Mart. Some three days since, or thereabouts: but I thank God I am very weary on't already.

Sir John. Why what's the matter, man?

Sir Mart. My villainous old luck still follows me in gaming, I never throw the Dice out of my hand, but my Gold goes after 'em: if I go to Picquet, though it be but with a Novice in't, he will picque

and repicque, and Capot me twenty times together: and, which
moſt mads me, I lose all my Sets, when I want but one of up.

Sir John. The pleasure of play is loſt, when one loses at that un-
reasonable rate.

Sir Mart. But I have sworn not to touch either Cards or Dice this
half year.

Sir John. The Oaths of losing Gameſters are moſt minded; they
forswear play as an angry Servant does his Miſtress, because he
loves her but too well.

Sir Mart. But I am now taken up with thoughts of another
nature: I am in love, Sir.

Sir John. That's the worſt Game you could have play'd at, scarce
one Woman in an hundred will play with you upon the Square: you
venture at more uncertainty than at a Lottery: for you set your
heart to a whole Sex of Blanks. But is your Miſtress Widow, Wife,
or Maid?

Sir Mart. I can assure you, Sir, mine is a Maid;
The Heiress of a wealthy Family,
Fair to a Miracle.

Sir John. Does she accept your service?

Sir Mart. I am the only person in her favour.   [*Enter* Warner.

Sir John. Is she of Town or Country?

Warn. aside. How's this?

Sir Mart. She is of *Kent*, near *Canterbury*.

Warn. What does he mean? this is his Rival——   [*Aside.*

Sir John. Near *Canterbury*, say you? I have a small Eſtate lies
thereabouts, and more concernments than one besides.

Sir Mart. I'le tell you then; being at *Canterbury*,
It was my Fortune once in the Cathedral Church——

Warn. What do you mean, Sir, to intruſt this man with your
Affairs thus?——

Sir Mart. Truſt him? why he's a friend of mine.

Warn. No matter for that; hark you a Word, Sir——

Sir Mart. Prethee leave fooling:——and, as I was saying——I
was in the Church when I firſt saw this fair one.

Sir John. Her Name, Sir, I beseech you.

Warn. For Heaven's sake, Sir, have a care!

Sir Mart. Thou art such a Coxcomb————Her name's *Millisent.*

Warn. Now, the Pox take you, Sir, what do you mean?

Sir John. Millisent say you? that's the name of my miſtress.

Sir Mart. Lord! what luck is that now! well Sir, it happen'd, one
of her Gloves fell down, I ſtoop'd to take it up; And in the ſtooping
made her a Complement.——

87

Warn. The Devil cannot hold him, now will this thick skull'd Master of mine, tell the whole story to his Rival.——

Sir Mart. You'l say, 'twas strange, Sir; but at the first glance we cast on one another, both our hearts leap'd within us, our souls met at our Eyes, and with a tickling kind of pain slid to each others breast, and in one moment settled as close and warm as if they long had been acquainted with their lodging. I follow'd her somewhat at a distance, because her Father was with her.

Warn. Yet hold, Sir——

Sir Mart. Sawcy Rascal, avoid my sight; must you tutor me? So Sir, not to trouble you, I enquir'd out her Father's House, without whose knowledge I did Court the Daughter, and both then and often since coming to *Canterbury*, I receiv'd many proofs of her kindness to me.

Warn. You had best tell him too, that I am acquainted with her Maid, and manage your love under-hand with her.

Sir Mart. Well remember'd i'faith, I thank thee for that, I had forgot it I protest! my *Valet de Chambre*, whom you see here with me, grows me acquainted with her Woman——

Warn. O the Devil.——

Sir Mart. In fine, Sir, this Maid being much in her Mistresses favour, so well sollicited my Cause, that in fine I gain'd from fair Mistress *Millisent* an assurance of her kindness, and an ingagement to marry none but me.

Warn. 'Tis very well! you've made a fair discovery!——

Sir John. A most pleasant Relation I assure you: you are a happy man, Sir! but what occasion brought you now to *London?*

Sir Mart. That was in expectation to meet my Mistress here; she writ me word from *Canterbury*, she and her Father shortly would be here.

Sir John. She and her Father, said you, Sir?

Warn. Tell him, Sir, for Heaven sake tell him all——

Sir Mart. So I will, Sir, without your bidding: her Father and she are come up already, that's the truth ont, and are to lodge, by my Contrivance, in yon House; the Master of which is a cunning Rascal as any in Town——him I have made my own, for I lodge there.

Warn. You do ill Sir to speak so scandalously of my Landlord.

Sir Mart. Peace, or I'le break your Fools Head——So that by his means I shall have free egress and regress when I please, Sir—— without her Fathers knowledge.

Warn. I am out of patience to hear this.——

88

Sir John. Methinks you might do well, Sir, to speak openly to her Father.

Sir Mart. Thank you for that i'faith, in speaking to old *Moody* I may soon spoil all.

Warn. So now he has told her Father's name, 'tis past recovery.

Sir John. Is her Father's name *Moody* say you?

Sir Mart. Is he of your acquaintance?

Sir John. Yes Sir, I know him for a man
Who is too wise for you to over-reach;
I am certain he will never marry his Daughter
To you.

Sir Mart. Why, there's the jest on't:
He shall never know it: 'tis but your
Keeping of my Counsel; I'le do as much for you,
mun.——

Sir John. No Sir, I'le give you better; trouble not your self about this Lady; her affections are otherwise engag'd to my knowledge ——hark in your Ear——her Father hates a Gamester like the Devil: I'le keep your Counsel for that too.

Sir Mart. Nay but this is not all dear Sir *John.*

Sir John. This is all I assure you: only I will make bold
To seek your Mistress out another Lodging.—   [*Ex.* Sir John.

Warn. Your Affairs are now put into an excellent posture, Thank your incomparable discretion——this was a Stratagem my shallow wit could ner'e have reach'd, to make a Confident of my Rival.

Sir Mart. I hope thou art not in earnest man! is he my Rival?

Warn. 'Slife he has not found it out all this while! well,
Sir, for a quick apprehension let you alone.

Sir Mart. How the Devil cam'st thou to know ont? and
Why the Devil didst thou not tell me on't?

Warn. To the first of your Devil's I answer, her Maid *Rose* told me on't: to the second I wish a thousand Devils take him that would not hear me.

Sir Mart. O unparallell'd Misfortune!

Warn. O unparallell'd ignorance! why he left her Father at the water-side, while he lead the Daughter to her lodging, whither I directed him; so that if you had not laboured to the contrary, Fortune had plac'd you in the same House with your Mistress, without the least suspition of your Rival, or of her Father: but 'tis well, you have satisfi'd your talkative humour; I hope you have some new project of your own to set all right agen: for my part I confess all my designs for you are wholly ruin'd; the very foundations of 'em are blown up.

Sir Mart. Prethee insult not over the Destiny of a poor undone Lover, I am punish'd enough for my indiscretion in my despair, and have nothing to hope for now but death.

Warn. Death is a Bug-word, things are not brought to that extremity, I'le cast about to save all yet.

Enter Lady Dupe.

La. Dupe. O, Sir *Martin!* yonder has been such a stir within, Sir *John*, I fear, smoaks your design, and by all means would have the old man remove his Lodging; pray God your man has not play'd false.

Warn. Like enough I have: I am Coxcomb sufficient to do it, my Master knows that none but such a great Calf as I could have done it, such an overgrown Ass, a self-conceited Ideot as I.——

Sir Mart. Nay, *Warner.*——

Warn. Pray, Sir, let me alone:——what is it to you if I rail upon my self? now could I break my own Loggar-head.

Sir Mart. Nay, sweet *Warner.*

Warn. What a good Master have I, and I to ruine him: O Beast!——

La. Dupe. Not to discourage you wholly, Sir *Martin*, this storm is partly over.

Sir Mart. As how? dear Cousin.

La. Dupe. When I heard Sir *John* complain of the Landlord, I took the first hint of it, and joyn'd with him, saying, if he were such an one, I would have nothing to do with him: in short, I rattled him so well, that Sir *John* was the first who did desire they might be lodg'd with me, not knowing that I was your Kinswoman.

Sir Mart. Pox on't, now I think on't, I could have found out this my self.——

Warn. Are you there agen, Sir?——now as I have a Soul.——

Sir Mart. Mum, good *Warner*, I did but forget my self a little, I leave my self wholly to you, and my Cousin; get but my Mistress for me, and claim what e're reward you can desire.

Warn. Hope of reward will diligence beget,
    Find you the money, and I'le find the wit.   [*Exeunt.*

ACT II.

Enter Lady Dupe, *and Mrs*. Christian.

Chr. IT happen'd, Madam, juſt as you said it would,
But was he so concern'd for my feign'd sickness?

La. Dupe. So much, that *Moody* and his Daughter, our new
Gueſts, took notice of the trouble, but the Cause was kept too close
for Strangers to divine.

Chr. Heav'n grant he be but deep enough in love, and then——

La. Dupe. And then thou shalt diſtill him into Gold my Girl.
Yonder he comes, I'le not be seen:——you know
Your Lesson, Child.   [*Exit.*

Chr. I warrant you.

Enter Lord Dartmouth.

Lord. Pretty Miſtress *Chriſtian*,
How glad am I to meet you thus alone!

Chr. O the Father! what will become of me now?

Lord. No harm, I warrant you, but why are you so 'fraid?

Chr. A poor weak innocent Creature as I am, Heav'n of his
mercy, how I quake and tremble! I have not yet claw'd off your laſt
ill usage, and now I feel my old fit come again, my Ears tingle al-
ready, and my back shuts and opens; I, juſt so it began before.

Lord. Nay, my sweet Miſtress, be not so unjuſt,
To suspeɕt any new attempt.
I am too penitent for my laſt fault,
So soon to sin again——
I hope you did not tell it to your Aunt.

Chr. The more Fool I, I did not.

Lord. You never shall repent your goodness to me:
But may not I presume there was some little
Kindness in it, which mov'd you to conceal my
Crime?

Chr. Methought I would not have mine Aunt angry with you,
For all this earthly good;
But yet I'le never be alone with you agen.

Lord. Pretty Innocence! let me sit nearer to you:
You do not underſtand what love I bear you.
I vow it is so pure——
My Soul's not sullied with one spot of sin:
Were you a Daughter, or a Siſter to me,
With a more holy Flame I could not burn.

91

Chr. Nay, now you speak high words——I cannot underſtand you.

Lord. The business of my life shall be but how to make your Fortune, and my care and ſtudy to advance and see you settled in the World.

Chr. I humbly thank your Lordship.

Lord. Thus I would sacrifice my Life and Fortunes,
And in return you cruelly deſtroy me.

Chr. I never meant you any harm, not I.

Lord. Then what does this white Enemy so near me?

Touching her hand glov'd.

Sure 'tis your Champion, and you arm it thus to bid defiance to me.

Chr. Nay fye my Lord, in faith you are too blame.

[*Pulling her hand away.*

Lord. But I am for fair Wars, an Enemy muſt firſt be search'd for privy Armour, e're we do ingage.   [*Pulls at her glove.*

Chr. What does your Lordship mean?

Lord. I fear you bear some Spells and Charms about you,
And, Madam, that's againſt the Laws of Arms.

Chr. My Aunt charg'd me not to pull off my Glove for fear of Sun-burning my hand.

Lord. She did well to keep it from your Eyes, but I will thus preserve it.   [*hugging her bare hand.*

Chr. Why do you crush it so? nay, now you hurt me; nay——if you squeeze it ne're so hard——there's nothing to come out on't ——fye——is this loving one?——
What makes you take your breath so short?

Lord. The Devil take me if I can answer her a word,
All my Sences are quite imploy'd another way.

Chr. Ne're ſtir, my Lord, I muſt cry out——

Lord. Then I muſt ſtop your mouth——this Ruby for a Kiss ——that is but one Ruby for another.

Chr. This is worse and worse.

Lady within. Why, Neece, where are you, Neece?

Lord. Pox of her old mouldy Chops.

Chr. Do you hear, my Aunt calls? I shall be hang'd for ſtaying with you——let me go, my Lord.   [*Gets from him.*

Enter Lady Dupe.

La. Dupe. My Lord, Heaven bless me, what makes your Lordship here?

Lord. I was juſt wishing for you, Madam, your Neece and I have been so laughing at the blunt humour of your Country Gentleman ——I muſt go pass an hour with him.   [*Ex.* Lord.

Chr. You made a little too much haste;
I was just exchanging a Kiss for a Ruby.

La. Dupe. No harm done; it will make him come on the faster:
Never full-gorge an Hawk you mean to fly:
The next will be a Neck-lace of Pearl, I warrant you.

Chr. But what must I do next?

La. Dupe. Tell him I grew suspitious, and examin'd you
Whether he made not love, which you deny'd.
Then tell him how my Maids and Daughters watch you;
So that you tremble when you see his Lordship.

Chr. And that your Daughters are so envious, that they would
raise a false report to ruine me.

La. Dupe. Therefore you desire his Lordship,
As he loves you, of which you are confident,
Hence-forward to forbear his Visits to you.

Chr. But how if he should take me at my word?

La. Dupe. Why, if the worst come to the worst, he leaves you an
honest woman, and there's an end on't: but fear not that, hold out
his messages, and then he'll write, and that is it my Bird which you
must drive it to: then all his Letters will be such Extacies, such
Vows and Promises, which you must answer short and simply, yet
still ply out of 'em your advantages.

Chr. But, Madam! he's i' th' house, he will not write.

La. Dupe. You Fool——he'll write from the next Chamber to
you. And, rather than fail, send his Page Post with it upon a Hobby-
horse:——then grant a meeting, but tell me of it, and I'le prevent
him, by my being there; hee'l curse me, but I care not. When you
are alone hee'l urge his lust, which answer you with scorn and
anger.——

Chr. As thus, an't please you, Madam?
What? does he think I will be damn'd for him?
Defame my Family, ruine my Name,
To satisfie his pleasure?

La. Dupe. Then he will be prophane in's Arguments,
Urge Natures Laws to you.

Chr. By'r Lady, and those are shrewd Arguments;
But I'm resolv'd I'le stop my Ears.

La. Dupe. Then when he sees no other thing will move you,
Hee'l sign a Portion to you before hand:
Take hold of that, and then of what you will.   [*Exeunt*.

Enter Sir John, *Mrs*. Millisent, *and* Rose.

Sir John. Now, fair Mrs. *Millisent*, you see your Chamber,

93

Your Father will be busie a few minutes, and in the mean time permits me the happiness to wait on you—

Mill. Methinks you might have chose us better Lodgings,
This house is full; the other, we saw first, was more convenient.

Sir John. For you perhaps, but not for me:
You might have met a Lover there, but I a Rival.

Mill. What Rival?

Sir John. You know Sir *Martin*, I need not name him to you.

Mill. I know more men besides him.

Sir John. But you love none besides him, can you deny your affection to him?

Mill. You have vex'd me so, I will not satisfie you.

Sir John. Then, I perceive, I am not likely to be so much oblig'd to you as I was to him.

Mill. This is Romance——I'le not believe a word on't——

Sir John. That's as you please: however 'tis believ'd
His wit will not much credit your choice.
Madam, do justice to us both; pay his ingratitude and folly with your scorn; my service with your Love.
By this time your Father stays for me: I shall be discreet enough to keep
This fault of yours from him.
The Lawyers wait for us to draw your Joynture:
And I would beg your pardon for my absence,
But that my Crime is punish'd in it self. [*Exit.*

Mill. Could I suspect this usage from a favour'd Servant!

Rose First hear Sir *Martin* ere you quite condemn him.
Consider, 'tis a Rival who accus'd him.

Mill. Speak not a word in his behalf——
Methought too, Sir *John* call'd him Fool.

Rose. Indeed he has a rare way of acting a Fool, and does it so naturally, it can be scarce distinguish'd.

Mill. Nay, he has wit enough, that's certain.

Rose. How blind Love is!

Enter Warner.

Mill. How now, what's his business?
I wonder, after such a Crime,
If his Master has the face to send him to me!

Rose. How durst you venture hither;
If either Sir *John* or my old Master see you.

Warn. Pish! they are both gone out.

Rose. They went but to the next ſtreet; ten to one but they return and catch you here.

Warn. Twenty to one I am gone before, and save 'um a labour

Mill. What says that Fellow to you? what business can he have here?

Warn. Lord, that your Ladiſhip should ask that queſtion, Knowing whom I serve!

Mill. I'le hear nothing from your Maſter.

Warn. Never breathe, but this anger becomes your Ladiſhip moſt admirably; but though you'l hear nothing from him, I hope I may speak a word or two to you from my self, Madam.

Rose. 'Twas a sweet Prank your Maſter play'd us: a Lady's well helpt up that truſts her Honour in such a persons hands: to tell all so ——and to his Rival too. Excuse him if thou canſt.   [*Aside.*

Warn. How the Devil should I excuse him! thou knoweſt he is the greateſt Fop in Nature——   [*Aside to* Rose.

Rose. But my Lady does not know it; if she did——

Mill. I'le have no whispering.

Warn. Alas, Madam, I have not the confidence to speak out, Unless you can take mercy on me.

Mill. For what?

Warn. For telling Sir *John* you lov'd my Maſter, Madam. But sure I little thought he was his Rival.

Rose. The witty Rogue has taken't on himself.   [*Aside.*

Mill. Your Maſter then is innocent?

Warn. Why, could your Ladiſhip suspeċt him guilty? Pray tell me, do you think him Ungrateful, or a Fool?

Mill. I think him neither.

Warn. Take it from me, you see not the depth of him. But when he knows what thoughts you harbour of him, As I am faithful, and muſt tell him—— I wish he does not take some pet, and leave you.

Mill. Thou art not mad I hope, to tell him on't; If thou doſt, I'le be sworn, I'le foreswear it to him.

Warn. Upon condition then you'l pardon me, I'le see what I can do to hold my tongue.

Mill. This Evening, in St. *James*'s Park, I'le meet him.
    [*Knock within.*

Warn. He shall not fail you, Madam.

Rose. Some body knocks——Oh, Madam, what shall we do! 'Tis Sir *John*, I hear his Voice.

Warn. What will become of me?
Mill. Step quickly behind that Door.   [*He goes out.*

To them Sir John.

Mill. You've made a quick dispatch, Sir.
Sir John. We have done nothing, Madam, our man of Law was not within—but I muſt look some Writings.
Mill. Where are they laid!
Sir John. In the Portmanteau in the Drawing-Room.
                                        [*Is going to the Door.*
Mill. Pray ſtay a little, Sir——
Warn. at the Door. He muſt pass juſt by me; and if he sees me, I am but a dead man.
Sir John. Why are you thus concern'd? why do you hold me.
Mill. Only a word or two I have to tell you.
'Tis of Importance to you——
Sir John. Give me leave——
Mill. I muſt not before I discover the Plot to you.
Sir John. What Plot?
Mill. Sir *Martin*'s Servant, like a Rogue, comes hither
To tempt me from his Maſter, to have met him.
Warn. at the Door. Now would I had a good Bag of Gun-powder at my Breech, to ram me into some hole.
Mill. For my part, I was so ſtartled at the Message,
That I shall scarcely be my self these two days.
Sir John. Oh, that I had the Rascal! I would teach him
To come upon such Errands.
Warn. Oh, for a gentle Composition now!
An Arm or Leg I would give willingly.
Sir John. What Answer did you make the Villain?
Mill. I over-reach'd him clearly, by a promise
Of an appointment of a place I nam'd,
Where I ne're meant to come: but would have had
The pleasure firſt to tell you how I serv'd him.
Sir John. And then to chide your mean suspition of me,
Indeed I wonder'd you should love a Fool.
But where did you appoint to meet him?
Mill. In *Grayes*-Inn Walks.
Warn. By this light, she has put the change upon him!
O sweet Woman-kind! How I love thee for that heavenly gift of
    lying!
Sir John. For this Evening I will be his Miſtress;
He shall meet another *Penelope* then he suspeĉts.

Mill. But ſtay not long away.

Sir John. You over-joy me, Madam.   [*Exit.*

Warn. entring. Is he gone, Madam?

Mill. As far as *Grayes*-Inn Walks: now I have time
To walk the other way, and see thy Maſter.

Warn. Rather let him come hither: I have laid
A Plot shall send his Rival far enough from watching him e're long.

Mill. Art thou in earneſt?

Warn. 'Tis so design'd, Fate cannot hinder it.
Our Landlord, where we lye, vex'd that his Lodgings should be so
left by Sir *John*, is resolv'd to be revenged, and I have found the
Way.
You'l see the' effeſt on't presently.

Rose. O Heavens! the door opens agen, and Sir *John* is return'd
once more.

Enter Sir John.

Sir John. Half my business was forgot; you did not tell me when
you were to meet him. Ho! What makes this Rascal here?

Warn. 'Tis well you're come, Sir, else I muſt have left untold a
Message I have for you.

Sir John. Well, what's your business, Sirrah?

Warn. We muſt be private firſt; 'tis only for your ear.

Rose. I shall admire his wit, if in this plunge he can get off.

Warn. I came hither, Sir, by my Maſters order——

Sir John. I'le reward you for it, Sirrah, immediately.

Warn. When you know all, I shall deserve it, Sir;
I came to sound the Vertue of your Miſtress; which I have done so
cunningly, I have at laſt obtain'd the promise of a meeting.
But my good Maſter, whom I muſt confess more generous than
wise, knowing you had a Passion for her, is resolv'd to quit:
And, Sir, that you may see how much he loves you, sent me in pri-
vate to advise you ſtill to have an eye upon her aſtions.

Sir John. Take this Diamond for thy good news;
And give thy Maſter my acknowledgments.

Warn. Thus the world goes, my Maſters, he that will cozen you,
commonly gets your good will into the bargain.   [*Aside.*

Sir John. Madam, I am now satisfi'd of all sides; firſt of your
truth, then of Sir *Martin*'s friendship.
In short, I find you two cheated each other,
Both to be true to me.

Mill. Warner is got off, as I would wish, and the Knight over-
reach'd.

Enter to them the Landlord *disguis'd like a Carrier.*

Rose. How now! what would this Carrier have?

Warn. This is our Landlord, whom I told you of; but keep your Countenance—— *[Aside to her.*

Landl. I was looking here-away for one Sir *John Swallow*; they told me I might hear news of him in this house.

Sir John. Friend, I am the man: what have you to say to me?

Landl. Nay, 'faith, Sir, I am not so good a Schollard to say much, But I have a Letter for you in my Pouch:
There's plaguy news in't, I can tell you that.

Sir John. From whom is your Letter?

Landl. From your old Uncle *Anthony.*

Sir John. Give me your Letter quickly.

Landl. Nay, soft and fair goes far—Hold you, hold you.
It is not in this Pocket.

Sir John. Search in the other then; I ſtand on Thorns.

Landl. I think I feel it now; this shou'd be who?

Sir John. Pluck it out then.

Landl. I'll pluck out my Spectacles, and see firſt. *[Reads.*
To Mr. *Paul Grimbard*——Apprentice to——
No, that's not for you, Sir—that's for the Son of the Brother of the Nephew of the Cousin of my Gossip *Dobson.*

Sir John. Prithee dispatch; doſt thou not know the Contents on't?

Landl. Yes, as well as I do my *Pater noſter.*

Sir John. Well, what's the business on't?

Landl. Nay, no great business; 'tis but only that your Worship's Father's dead.

Sir John. My Loss is beyond expression! how dy'd he?

Landl. He went to bed as well to see to as any man in *England,* And when he awaken'd the next morning——

Sir John. What then?

Landl. He found himself ſtark dead.

Sir John. Well, I muſt of necessity take orders for my Father's Funeral, and my Eſtate; Heaven knows with what regret I leave you, Madam.

Mill. But are you in such haſte, Sir? I see you take all occasions to be from me.

Sir John. Dear Madam, say not so, a few days will, I hope, return me to you.

To them Sir Martin.

Noble Sir *Martin,* the welcomeſt man alive!
Let me embrace my friend.

98

Rose. How untowardly he returns the salute? *Warner* will be
found out.   [*aside.*

Sir John. Well, friend, you have oblig'd me to you eternally.

Sir Mart. How have I oblig'd you, Sir? I would have you to know
I scorn your words; and I would I were hang'd if it be not the
farthest of my thoughts.

Mill. O cunning Youth, he acts the Fool most naturally.
Were we alone, how would we laugh together?   [*aside.*

Sir John. This is a double generosity,
To do me favours and conceal 'um from me;
But honest *Warner* here has told me all.

Sir Mart. What has the Rascal told you?

Sir John. Your plot to try my Mistress for me———you under-
stand me, concerning your appointment.

Warn. Sir, I desire to speak in private with you.

Sir Mart. This impertinent Rascal, when I am most busie, I am
ever troubled with him.

Warn. But it concerns you I should speak with you, good Sir.

Sir Mart. That's a good one i'faith, thou knowest breeding well,
that I should whisper with a Serving-man before company.

Warn. Remember, Sir, last time it had been better———

Sir Mart. Peace, or I'le make you feel my double Fists;
If I don't fright him, the sawcy Rogue will call me Fool before the
Company.

Mill. That was acted most naturally again.   [*aside.*

Sir John to him. But what needs this dissembling, since you are
resolv'd to quit my Mistress to me?

Sir Mart. I quit my Mistress! that'a good one i'faith.

Mill. Tell him you have forsaken me.   [*aside.*

Sir Mart. I understand you, Madam, you would save
A quarrel; but i'faith I am not so base:
I'le see him hang'd first.

Warn. Madam, my Master is convinc'd in prudence
He should say so; but Love o'remasters him:
When you are gone perhaps he may.

Mill. I'le go then: Gentlemen, your Servant;
I see my presence brings constraint to the Company.
         Exeunt Mill. Rose.

Sir John. I'm glad she's gone, now we may talk more freely;
For if you have not quitted her, you must.

Warn. Pray, Sir, remember your self; did not you send me of a
message to Sir *John*, that for his friendship you had left Mistress
Millisent?

Sir Mart. Why, what an impudent lying Rogue art thou!

Sir John. How's this! has *Warner* cheated me?

Warn. Do not suspect it in the least: you know, Sir,
It was not generous before a Lady,
To say he quitted her.

Sir John. O! was that it?

Warn. That was all: say, Yes, good Sir *John*———or I'le swindge
you.   [*aside.*

Sir Mart. Yes, good Sir *John.*

Warn. That's well; once in his life he has heard good counsel.
                                                   [*aside.*

Sir Mart. Heigh, Heigh, what makes my Landlord here? he has
put on a Fool's Coat, I think, to make us laugh.

Warn. The Devil's in him; he's at it again; his folly's like a sore
in a surfeited Horse, cure it in one place, and it breaks out in
another.   [*aside.*

Sir Mart. Honest Landlord, i'faith, and what makes you here?

Sir John. Are you acquainted with this honest man?

Landl. Take heed what you say, Sir.   [*To Sir* Martin *softly.*

Sir Mart. Take heed what I say, Sir, why? who should I be afraid
of? of you, Sir? I say, Sir, I know him, Sir; and I have reason to
know him, Sir, for I am sure I lodge in his House, Sir———nay,
never think to terrifie me, Sir; 'tis my Landlord here in *Charles*
Street, Sir.

Landl. Now I expect to be paid for the News I brought him.

Sir John. Sirrah! Did not you tell me that my Father———

Landl. Is in very good health, for ought I know, Sir; I beseech
you to trouble your self no farther concerning him.

Sir John. Who set you on to tell this lye?

Sir Mart. I, who set you on, Sirrah? this was a Rogue that would
cozen us both; he thought I did not know him: down on your
marribones, and confess the truth: Have you no Tongue, you
Rascal?

Sir John. Sure 'tis some silenc'd Minister: he's grown so fat, he
cannot speak.

Landl. Why, Sir, if you would know, 'twas for your sake I did it.

Warn. For my Master's sake! why, you impudent Varlet, do you
think to 'scape us with a lye?

Sir John. How! was it for his sake?

Warn. 'Twas for his own, Sir; he heard you were th' occasion the
Lady lodg'd not at his House, and so he invented this lye; partly to
revenge himself of you; and partly, I believe, in hope to get her once
again, when you were gone.

100

Sir John. Fetch me a Cudgel prithee.

Landl. O good Sir! if you beat me, I shall run into oyl immediately.

Warn. Hang him, Rogue, he's below your anger: I'le maul him for you——the Rogue's so big, I think 'twill ask two days to beat him all over. [*Beats him.*

Landl. O Rogue, O Villain *Warner*, bid him hold,
And I'le confess, Sir.

Warn. Get you gone without replying: muſt such as you be prating? [*Beats him out.*

Enter Rose. Sir, Dinner waits you on the Table.

Sir John. Friend, will you go along, and take part of a bad Repaſt?

Sir Mart. Thank you; but I am juſt risen from Table.

Warn. Now he might sit with his Miſtress, and has not the wit to find it out.

Sir John. You shall be very welcome.

Sir Mart. I have no ſtomack, Sir.

Warn. Get you in with a vengeance: You have a better ſtomack than you think you have. [*Pushes him.*

Sir Mart. This hungry *Diego* Rogue would shame me;
He thinks a Gentleman can eat like a Servingman.

Sir John. If you will not, adieu dear Sir;
In anything command me. [*Exit.*

Sir Mart. Now we are alone; han't I carry'd matters bravely, Sirrah.

Warn. O yes, yes, you deserve Sugar-Plums; firſt, for
Your quarrelling with Sir *John*; then for discovering your
Landlord: and laſtly, for refusing to dine with your Miſtress:
All this is since the laſt reckoning was wip'd out.

Sir Mart. Then why did my Landlord disguise himself, to make a Fool of us?

Warn. You have so little Brains, that a Penn'orth of Butter melted under 'um, would set 'um afloat: he put on that disguise to rid you of your Rival.

Sir Mart. Why was not I worthy to keep your counsel then?

Warn. It had been much at one: you would but have drunk the secret down, and piss'd it out to the next company.

Sir Mart. Well, I find I am a miserable man: I have loſt my Miſtress, and may thank my self for't.

Warn. You'l not confess you are a Fool, I warrant.

Sir Mart. Well I am a Fool, if that will satisfie you:
But what am I the neerer for being one?

Warn. O yes much the neerer; for now Fortune's bound to provide for you; As Hospitals are built for lame people, because they cannot help themselves.

Well; I have yet a project in my pate.

Sir Mart. Dear Rogue, what is't?

Warn. Excuse me for that: but while 'tis set a working, You would do well to scrue your self into her Fathers good Opinion.

Sir Mart. If you will not tell me, my mind gives me I shall discover it again.

Warn. I'le lay it as far out of your reach as I can possible.

————For Secrets are edg'd Tools,

And must be kept from Children, and from Fools. [*Exeunt.*

ACT III.

Enter Rose *and* Warner *meeting.*

Rose. YOur Worship's most happily encounter'd.

 Warn. Your Ladiship's most fortunately met.

Rose. I was going to your Lodging.

Warn. My Business was to yours.

Rose. I have something to say to you, that——

Warn. I have that to tell you——

Rose. Understand then——

Warn. If you'l hear me——

Rose. I believe that——

Warn. I am of opinion that——

Rose. Prithee hold thy peace a little till I have done.

Warn. Cry you mercy, Mrs. *Rose,* I'le not dispute your antient priviledges of talking.

Rose. My Mistress knowing Sir *John* was to be abroad upon business this Afternoon, has asked leave to see a Play: and Sir *John* has so great a confidence of your Master, that he will trust no body with her, but him.

Warn. If my Master gets her out, I warrant her he shall show her a better Play than any is at either of the Houses——here they are: I'le run and prepare him to wait upon her.   [*Exit.*

Enter Old Moody, *Mistress* Millesent, *and Lady* Dupe.

Mill. My Hoods and Scarfs there, quickly.

La. Dupe. Send to call a Coach there.

Mood. But what kind of man is this Sir *Martin*, with whom you are to go?

La. Dupe. A plain downright Country Gentleman, I assure you.

Moody. I like him much the better for't.
For I hate one of those you call a man o'th' Town.
One of those empty fellows of meer outside:
They've nothing of the true old English manliness.

Rose. I confess, Sir, a Woman's in a sad condition, that has nothing to trust to, but a Perriwig above, and a well trim'd shoe below.

To them Sir Martin.

Mill. This, Sir, is Sir *John's* Friend; he is for your humour, Sir; He is no man o' th' Town, but bred up in the old *Elizabeth* way of Plainness.

Sir Mart. I, Madam, your Ladiship may say your pleasure of me.

To them Warner.

Warn. How the Devil got he here before me! 'tis very unlucky I could not see him first——

Sir Mart. But as for Painting, Musick, Poetry, and the like, I'le say this of my self——

Warn. I'le say that for him, my Master understands none of 'um, I assure you, Sir.

Sir Mart. You impudent Rascal, hold your tongue: I must rid my hands of this fellow; the Rogue is ever discrediting me before Company.

Moody. Never trouble your self about it, Sir, for I like a man that——

Sir Mart. I know you do, Sir, and therefore I hope you'll think never the worse of me for his prating: for, though I do not boast of my own good parts——

Warn. He has none to boast of, upon my faith, Sir.

Sir Mart. Give him not the hearing, Sir; for, if I may believe my friends, they have flatter'd me with an opinion of more———

Warn. Of more than their flattery can make good, Sir——'tis true he tells you they have flatter'd him; but, in my Conscience, he is the most downright simple natur'd creature in the world.

Sir Mart. I shall consider you hereafter, Sirrah; but I am sure, in all Companies I pass for a *Vertuoso*.

Moody. *Vertuoso!* what's that too? is not *Vertue* enough, without *oso?*

Sir Mart. You have Reason, Sir!

Moody. There he is again too; the Town Phrase, a great Compliment I wiss; you have Reason, Sir; that is, you are no beaſt, Sir.

Warn. A word in private, Sir; You miſtake this old man; he loves neither Painting, Musick, nor Poetry; yet recover your Self, if you have any brains.   [*aside to him.*

Sir Mart. Say you so? I'le bring all about again, I warrant you ——I beg your pardon a thousand times, Sir; I vow to Gad I am not Maſter of any of those perfections; for in fine,
Sir, I am wholly ignorant of Painting, Musick, and Poetry;
Only some rude escapes————but, in fine, they are such, that,
In fine, Sir——

Warn. This is worse than all the reſt.   [*aside.*

Moody. By Coxbones, one word more of all this Gibberish, and old Madge shall fly about your ears: what is this *in fine,* he keeps such a coil with too?

Mill. 'Tis a Phrase *a-la-mode,* Sir, and is us'd in conversation now, as a whiff of Tobacco was formerly, in the midſt of a discourse, for a thinking while.

La. Dupe. In plain English, in fine, is, in the end, Sir.

Mood. But, by Coxbones, there is no end on't methinks: if thou wilt have a foolish word to lard thy lean discourse with, take an English one when thou speakeſt English; as So Sir, and, Then Sir; and so forth: 'tis a more manly kind of nonsense: and a Pox of in fine, for I'le hear no more on't.

Warn. He's gravell'd, and I muſt help him out.   [*aside.*
Madam there's a Coach at Door to carry you to the Play.

Sir Mart. Which House do you mean to go to?

Mill. The Dukes, I think.

Sir Mart. It is a damn'd Play, and has nothing in't.

Mill. Then let us to the Kings.

Sir Mart. That's e'ne as bad.

Warn. This is paſt enduring.   [*aside.*
There was an ill Play set up, Sir, on the Poſts, but I can assure you the Bills are altered since you saw 'um, and now there are two admirable Comedies at both Houses.

Moody. But my Daughter loves serious Plays.

Warn. They are Tragi-Comedies, Sir, for both.

Sir Mart. I have heard her say she loves none but Tragedies.

Moody. Where have you heard her say so, Sir?

Warn. Sir, you forget your self, you never saw her in your life before.

Sir Mart. What, not at *Canterbury,* in the Cathedral Church there? This is the impudenteſt Rascal——

Warn. Mum, Sir——

Sir Mart. Ah Lord, what have I done! as I hope to be sav'd, Sir, it was before I was aware; for if ever I set Eyes on her before this day——I wish——

Moody. This fellow is not so much fool, as he makes one believe he is.

Mill. I thought he would be discover'd for a wit: this 'tis to over-act ones part!   *[aside.*

Moody. Come away, Daughter, I will not trust you in his hands; there's more in't than I imagin'd. *Exeunt* Moody, Mill. Lady, Rose.

Sir Mart. Why do you frown upon me so, when you know your looks go to the heart of me? what have I done besides a little *lapsus linguæ?*

Warn. Why, who says you have done any thing? you a meer Innocent.

Sir Mart. As the Child that's to be born, in my intentions; if I know how I have offended my self any more than in one word——

Warn. But don't follow me however—I have nothing to say to you.

Sir Mart. I'll follow you to the worlds end, till you forgive me.

Warn. I am resolv'd to lead you a Dance then.   *[Exit running.*

Sir Mart. The Rogue has no mercy in him, but I must mollifie him with money.   *[Exit.*

Enter old La. Truly my little Cousin's the aptest Scholar, and takes out love's lessons so exactly, that I joy to see it: she has got already the Bond of two thousand Pounds seal'd for her Portion, which I keep for her; a pretty good beginning: 'tis true, I believe he has enjoy'd her, and so let him: *Mark Anthony* woed not at so dear a price.

To her Chr. O Madam! I fear I am a breeding!

La. Dupe. A taking Wench! but 'tis no matter; have you told any body?

Chr. I have been venturing upon your foundations, a little to dissemble.

La. Dupe. That's a good Child, I hope it will thrive with thee, as it has with me: Heaven has a blessing in store upon our en-deavours.

Chr. I feign'd my self sick, and kept my bed; my Lord he came to visit me, and in the end, I disclos'd it to him in the saddest passion.

La. Dupe. This frighted him, I hope, into a study how to cloak your disgrace, lest it should have vent to his Lady.

Chr. 'Tis true, but all the while I subt'ly drove it, that he should name you to me, as the fitteſt inſtrument of the concealment; but how to break it to you, ſtrangely does perplex him: he has been seeking you all o're the house; therefore I'll leave your Ladiſhip; for fear we should be seen together.　　　　　　　　　[*Exit.*

　La. Dupe. Now I muſt play my part;
Nature, in Women, teaches more than Art.

Enter Lord.

　Lord. Madam, I have a Secret to impart;
A sad one too, and have no Friend to truſt but only you.
　La. Your Lady, or your Children sick?
　Lord. Not that I know.
　La. You seem to be in health.
　Lord. In body, not in mind.
　La. Some scruple of Conscience, I warrant; my Chaplain shall resolve you.
　Lord. Madam, my Soul's tormented.
　La. O take heed of despair, my Lord!
　Lord. Madam, there's no Medicine for this sickness, but only you; your friendship's my safe Haven, else I am loſt and ship-wrack'd.
　La. Pray tell me what it is.
　Lord. Could I express it by sad sighs and groans,
Or drown it with my self in Seas of Tears,
I should be happy, would, and would not tell.
　La. Command whatever I can serve you in,
I will be faithful ſtill to all your ends, provided they be juſt and vertuous.
　Lord. That word has ſtopt me.
　La. Dupe. Speak out, my Lord, and boldly tell what 'tis.
　Lord. Then, in obedience to your Commands, your Cousin is with Child.
　La. Dupe. Which Cousin?
　Lord. Your Cousin *Chriſtian* here i' the house.
　La. Dupe. Alas! then she has ſtoln a Marriage, and undone her self:
Some young Fellow, on my Conscience, that's a Beggar!
Youth will not be advis'd; well, I'le never meddle more with Girls;
One is no more assur'd of 'um than Grooms of Mules, they'l ſtrike when leaſt one thinks on't: but, pray your Lordship, what is her choice then for an Husband?
　Lord. She is not married that I know of, Madam.
　La. Dupe. Not married! 'tis impossible, the Girl does sure abuse

you. I know her Education has been such, the flesh could not prevail; therefore she does abuse you, it muſt be so.

Lord. Madam, not to abuse you longer, she is with Child, and I the unfortunate man, who did this moſt unlucky act.

La. Dupe. You! I'le never believe it.

Lord. Madam, 'tis too true; believe it, and be serious how to hide her shame: I beg it here upon my knees.

La. Dupe. Oh, oh, oh———   *[She faints away.*

Lord. Who's there? who's there? help, help, help.

Enter two *Women*, Rose, Penelope.

1 *Wom.* O merciful God, my Lady's gone!

2 *Wom.* Whither?

1 *Wom.* To Heaven, God knows, to Heaven.

Rose. Rub her, rub her; fetch warm Cloaths.

2 *Wom.* I say, run to the Cabinet of Quintessence; *Gilberts* Water, *Gilberts* Water.

1 *Wom.* Now all the good Folks of Heaven look down upon her.

Mill. Set her in the Chair.

Rose. Open her mouth with a Dagger, or a Key; pour, pour; where's the Spoon?

2 *Wom.* She ſtirs, she revives, merciful to us all; what a thing was this! speak, Lady, speak.

La. Dupe. So, so, so.

Mill. Alas, my Lord, How came this fit?

Lord. With Sorrow, Madam.

La Dupe. Now I am better: *Bess,* you have not seen me thus.

1 *Wom.* Heav'n forefend! that I should live to see you so agen

La. Dupe. Go, go, I'm pretty well; withdraw into the next Room, but be near, I pray, for fear of the worſt.   *[They go out.*

———My Lord, sit down near me, I pray, I'le ſtrive to speak a few words to you, and then to bed———nearer———my voice is faint——— My Lord, Heav'n knows how I have ever lov'd you, and is this my reward? had you none to abuse but me in that unfortunate fond Girl, that you know was dearer to me than my life? this was not Love to her, but an inveterate malice to poor me.

Oh, oh———   *[Faints again.*

Lord. Help, help, help.

All the *Women* again.

1 *Wom.* This fit will carry her: Alass! It is a Lechery!

2 *Wom.* The Balsom, the Balsom!

1 *Wom.* No, no, the Chymiſtry Oyl of Rosemary: Hold her up, and give her Air.

Mill. Feel whether she breathes, with your hand before her Mouth.

Rose. No, Madam, 'tis Key-cold.

1 *Wom.* Look up, dear Madam, if you have any Hope of Salvation!

2 *Wom.* Hold up your finger, Madam, if you have any hope of Fraternity. O the blessed Saints that hear me not, take her Mortality to them.

La. Dupe. Enough; so, 'tis well————withdraw, and let me reſt a while, only my dear Lord remain.

1 *Wom.* Pray your Lordship keep her from swebbing.

[Exeunt Women.

Lord. Here humbly once again, I beg your pardon and your help.

La. Dupe. Heaven forgive you, and I do: Stand up, my Lord, and sit close by me:
O this naughty girl! but did your Lordship win her soon?

Lord. No, Madam, but with much difficulty.

La. Dupe. I'm glad on't; it shew'd the Girl had some Religion in her, all my Precepts were not in vain: but you men are ſtrange tempters: good, my Lord, where was this wicked aċt then firſt committed?

Lord. In an out-room upon a Trunk.

La. Dupe. Poor Heart, what shift Love makes! Oh she does love you dearly, though to her ruine! and then what place, my Lord?

Lord. An old waſte room, with a decay'd Bed in't.

La. Dupe. Out upon that dark Room for deeds of darkness! and that rotten Bed! I wonder it did hold your Lordship's vigour: but you dealt gently with the Girl. Well, you shall see I love you, for I will manage this business to both your advantages, by the assiſtance of Heaven I will: good, my Lord, help, lead me out.   *[Exeunt.*

Warner, Rose.

Rose. A mischief upon all Fools! do you think your Maſter has not done wisely? firſt to miſtake our old man's humour, then to dispraise the Plays: and laſtly, to discover his Acquaintance with my Miſtress. my old Maſter has taken such a Jealousie of him, that he will never admit him into his sight again.

Warn. Thou mak'ſt thy self a greater Fool than he, by being angry at what he cannot help————I have been angry with him too, but these friends have taken up the quarrel————[*Shews gold.*] Look you, he has sent these Mediators to mitigate your wrath: here are
108

twenty of 'um have made a long Voyage from *Guinny* to kiss your hands: and when the Match is made, there are an hundred more in readiness to be your humble Servants.

Rose. Rather then fall out with you, I'le take 'um; but I confess it troubles me to see so loyal a Lover have the heart of an Emperour, and yet scarce the brains of a Cobler.

Warn. Well, what device can we two beget betwixt us, to separate Sir *John Swallow* and thy Mistress?

Rose. I cannot on the sudden tell; but I hate him worse than foul weather without a Coach.

Warn. Then I'le see if my project will be luckier than thine. Where are the Papers concerning the Joynture I have heard you speak of?

Rose. They lye within in three great Bags, some twenty Reams of Paper in each Bundle, with six lines in a sheet: but there is a little Paper where all the business lyes.

Warn. Where is it? canst thou help me to it?

Rose. By good chance he gave it to my custody before he set out for *London.* You came in good time, here it is, I was carrying it to him; just now he sent for it.

Warn. So, this I will secure in my Pocket: when thou art ask'd for it, make two or three bad faces, and say 'twas left behind: by this means he must of necessity leave the Town, to see for it in *Kent.*

Enter Sir John, *Sir* Martin, *Mrs.* Mill.

Sir John. 'Tis no matter, though the old man be suspicious; I knew the story all before-hand; and since then you have fully satisfi'd me of your true friendship to me————Where are the Writings?

[*To* Rose.

Rose. Sir, I beg your pardon; I thought I had put 'um up amongst my Ladys things, and, it seems, in my haste I quite forgot 'um, and left 'um at *Canterbury.*

Sir John. This is horribly unlucky! where do you think you left 'um?

Rose. Upon the great Box in my Ladys Chamber; they are safe enough I'me sure.

Sir John. It must be so————I must take Post immediately:
Madam, for some few days I must be absent;
And to confirm you, friend, how much I trust you,
I leave the dearest Pledge I have on Earth,
My Mistress, to your care.

Mill. If you lov'd me, you would not take all occasions to leave me thus!

Warn. [*aside.*] Do, go to *Kent,* and when you come again,
Here they are ready for you.   [*Shows the Paper.*

Sir Mart. What's that you have in your hand there, Sirrah?

Warn. [*Aside.*] Pox, what ill luck was this! what shall I say?

Sir Mart. Sometimes you've tongue enough, what are you silent?

Warn. 'Tis an Accompt, Sir, of what Money you have lost since you came to Town.

Sir Mart. I'm very glad on't: now I'l make you all see the severity of my Fortune——give me the Paper.

Warn. Heaven! what does he mean to do, it is not fair writ out, Sir.

Sir John. Besides, I am in haste, another time, Sir——

Sir Mart. Pray, oblige me, Sir—'tis but one minute: all people love to be pity'd in their Misfortunes, and so do I: will you produce it, Sirrah?

Warn. Dear Master!

Sir Mart. Dear Rascal! am I Master or you? you Rogue!

Warn. Hold yet, Sir, and let me read it:—you cannot read my hand.

Sir Mart. This is ever his way to be disparaging me—but I'le let you see, Sirrah, that I can read your hand better than you your self can.

Warn. You'l repent it, there's a trick in't, Sir——

Sir Mart. Is there so, Sirrah? But I'le bring you out of all your Tricks with a Vengeance to you——   [*Reads.*
How now! What's this? A true particular of the Estate of Sir *John Swallow,* Knight; lying, and scituate in, &c.

Sir John. This is the very Paper I had lost: [*Takes the Paper.*
I'm very glad on't, it has sav'd me a most unwelcome Journey——
but I will not thank you for the Courtesie, which now I find you never did intend me—this is Confederacy, I smoak it now——
Come, Madam, let me wait on you to your Father.

Mill. Well, of a witty man, this was the foolishest part that ever I beheld.   [*Exeunt Sir* John, Millisent, *and* Rose.

Sir Mart. I am a Fool, I must confess, and I am the most miserable one without thy help——but yet it was such a mistake, as any man might have made.

Warn. No doubt on't.

Sir Mart. Prethee chide me! this indifference of thine wounds me to the heart.

Warn. I care not.

Sir Mart. Wilt thou not help me for this once?

Warn. Sir, I kiss your hands, I have other business.

Sir Mart. Dear *Warner!*

Warn. I am inflexible.

Sir Mart. Then I am resolv'd I'le kill my self.

Warn. You are Maſter of your own Body.

Sir Mart. Will you let me damn my Soul?

Warn. At your pleasure, as the Devil and you can agree about it.

Sir Mart. D'ye see, the points ready? Will you do nothing to save my Life?

Warn. Not in the leaſt.

Sir Mart. Farewel, hard-hearted *Warner.*

Warn. Adieu, soft headed Sir *Martin.*

Sir Mart. Is it possible?

Warn. Why don't you dispatch, Sir? why all these Preambles?

Sir Mart. I'le see thee hang'd firſt: I know thou would'ſt have me kill'd, to get my Cloaths.

Warn. I knew it was but a Copy of your Countenance; people in this Age are not so apt to kill themselves.

Sir Mart. Here are yet ten pieces in my Pocket, take 'em, and let's be Friends.

Warn. You know the Eas'ness of my Nature, and that makes you work upon it so. Well, Sir——for this once I caſt an Eye of pity on you——but I muſt have ten more in hand, before I can ſtir a foot.

Sir Mart. As I am a true Gameſter, I have loſt all but these, ————but if thou't lend me them, I'le give 'em thee agen.

Warn. I'le rather truſt you till to morrow;
Once more look up, I bid you hope the beſt.
  Why should your folly make your Love miscarry,
  Since men firſt play the Fools, and then they marry? [*Exeunt.*

ACT IV.

Enter Sir Martin *and* Warner.

Sir Mart. BUT are they to be married this day in private, say you?

Warn. 'Tis so concluded, Sir, I dare assure you.

Sir Mart. But why so soon, and in private?

Warn. So soon, to prevent the designs upon her; and in private, to save the effusion of Chriſtian Money.

Sir Mart. It ſtrikes to my heart already; in fine, I am a dead man —*Warner.*

Warn. Well, go your ways, I'le try what may be done. Look, if he will ſtir now; your Rival and the Old man will see us together, we are juſt below the Window.

Sir Mart. Thou can'ſt not do't.

Warn. On the peril of my twenty pieces be it.

Sir Mart. But I have found a way to help thee out, truſt to my wit but once.

Warn. Name your wit, or think you have the leaſt grain of wit once more, and I'le lay it down for ever.

Sir Mart. You are a sawcy maſterly Companion, and so I leave you,   [*Exit.*

Warn. Help, help, good People, Murther, Murther!

Enter Sir John *and* Moody.

Sir John & Mood. How now, what's the matter?

Warn. I am abus'd, I am beaten, I am lam'd for ever.

Mood. Who has us'd thee so?

Warn. The Rogue my Maſter.

Sir John. What was the Offence?

Warn. A trifle, juſt nothing.

Sir John. That's very ſtrange.

Warn. It was for telling him he loſt too much at Play; I meant him nothing but well, Heav'n knows, and he in a cursed damn'd humour would needs revenge his losses upon me: A' kick'd me, took away my money, and turn'd me off; but if I take it at his hands——

Mood. By Cox nowns it was an ill-natur'd part; nay, I thought no better could come on't, when I heard him at his Vow to Gads, and in fines.

Warn. But if I live, I'le cry quittance with him: he had engag'd me to get Mrs. *Millisent* your Daughter, for him; but if I do not all that ever I can to make her hate him, a great Booby, an over-grown Oafe, a conceited *Bartlemew*——

Sir John. Prethee leave off thy Choler, and hear me a little: I have had a great mind to thee a long time, if thou think'ſt my Service better than his, from this minute I entertain thee.

Warn. With all my heart, Sir, and so much the rather, that I may spight him with it——This was the moſt propitious Fate——

Mood. Propitious! and Fate! What a damn'd Scander-bag-Rogue art thou to talk at this rate? hark you, Sirrah, one word more of this Gibberish, and I'le set you packing from your new Service: I'le have neither Propitious nor Fate, come within my doors——

Sir John. Nay, pray Father.

Warn. Good old Sir be pacified: I was pouring out a little of the dregs that I had left in me of my former Service, and now they are gone, my stomach's clear of 'em.

Sir John. This Fellow is come in a happy hour; for now, Sir, you and I may go to prepare the Licence, and in the mean time he may have an Eye upon your Daughter.

Warn. If you please I'le wait upon her till she's ready, and then bring her to what Church you shall appoint.

Mood. But, Friend, you'l find she'l hang an Arse, and be very loth to come along with you; and therefore I had best stay behind and bring her my self.

Warn. I warrant you, I have a Trick for that, Sir: she knows nothing of my being turn'd away: so I'le come to her as from Sir *Martin,* and under pretence of carrying her to him, conduct her to you.

Sir John. My better Angel———

Mood. By th' mess 'twas well thought on; well Son, go you before, I'le speak but one Word for a Dish or two at Dinner, and follow you to the Licence-Office. Sirrah———stay you here———till my return.   [*Ex. Sir* John *and* Moody.

Warn. solus. Was there ever such a lucky Rogue as I! I had always a good opinion of my wit, but could never think I had so much as now I find. I have now gained an opportunity to carry away Mrs. *Millisent* for my Master, to get his Mistress by means of his Rival, to receive all his happiness, where he could expect nothing but misery: After this exploit I will have *Lilly* draw me in the Habit of a Hero, with a Lawrel on my Temples, and an Inscription below it, *This is* Warner *the flower of Serving-men.*

Enter Messenger.

Mess. Pray do me the favour to help me to the speech of Mr. *Moody.*

Warn. What's your business?

Mess. I have a Letter to deliver him.

Warn. Here he comes, you may deliver it your self to him.

                              [*Re-enter* Moody.

Mess. Sir, a Gentleman met me at the corner of the next Street, and bid me give this into your own hands.

Moody. Stay friend, till I have read it.

Mess. He told me, Sir, it required no Answer.   [*Ex.* Mess.

Moody reads. *Sir, permit me, though a stranger, to give you counsel; some young Gallants have had intelligence, that this day you intend privately to marry your Daughter, the rich Heiress; and, in fine,*

above twenty of them have dispersed themselves to watch her going out:
therefore put it off, if you will avoid mischief, and be advised by

Your unknown Servant.

Moody. By the Mackings, I thought there was no good in't, when,
I saw *in fine* there; there are some Papishes, I'le warrant, that lie in
wait for my Daughter, or else they are no English-men, but some of
your French Outalian-Rogues; I owe him thanks however, this un-
known Friend of mine, that told me on't.

Warner, no Wedding to day, *Warner*.

Warn. Why, what's the matter, Sir?

Moody. I say no more, but some wiser than some, I'le keep my
Daughter at home this Afternoon, and a fig for all these Outalians.
                                                    [*Exit* Moody.

Warn. So here's another Trick of Fortune, as unexpected for
bad, as the other was for good. Nothing vexes me, but that I had
made my Game Cock-sure, and then to be back-gammon'd: it must
needs be the Devil that writ this Letter; he ow'd my Master a
spight, and has paid him to the purpose: and here he comes as
merry too, he little thinks what misfortune has befal'n him.
and for my part I am asham'd to tell him.   [*Enter Sir* Martin
                                                        laughing.

Sir Mart. Warner, such a Jest, *Warner*.   [*Laughs agen.*

Warn. What a Murrain is the matter, Sir?
Where lyes this Jest that tickles you?

Sir Mart. Let me laugh out my Laugh, and I'le tell thee?
                                                    [*Laughs agen.*

Warn. I wish you may have cause for all this mirth.

Sir Mart. Hereafter, *Warner*, be it known unto thee, I will
endure no more to be thy May-game: thou shalt no more dare to
tell me, I spoil thy projects, and discover thy designs: for I have
play'd such a Prize, without thy help, of my own Mother-wit,
('tis true, I am hasty sometimes, and so do harm; but when I have
a mind to shew my self, there's no man in *England*, though I say't,
comes near me, as to a point of imagination) I'le make thee acknow-
ledge I have laid a Plot that has a soul in't.

Warn. Pray, Sir, keep me no longer in ignorance of this rare
Invention.

Sir Mart. Know then, *Warner*, that when I left thee, I was pos-
sest with a terrible fear, that my Mistress should be married: well,
thought I to my self, and must'ring up all the Forces of my Wit,
I did produce such a Stratagem.

Warn. But what was it?

Sir Mart. I feign'd a Letter, as from an unknown Friend to

Moody, wherein I gave him to underſtand, that if his Daughter went out this Afternoon, she would infallibly be snapt by some young Fellows that lay in wait for her.

Warn. Very good.

Sir Mart. That which follows is yet better; for he I sent assures me, that in that very Nick of time my Letter came, her Father was juſt sending her abroad with a very foolish rascally fellow that was with him.

Warn. And did you perform all this a' god's name? could you do this wonderful miracle, without giving your soul to the Devil for his help?

Sir Mart. I tell thee man I did it, and it was done by the help of no Devil, but this familiar of my own brain; how long would it have been, e're thou could'ſt have thought of such a projeƈt? *Martin* said to his man, *Who's the fool now?*

Warn. Who's the fool? why, who us'd to be the fool? he that ever was, since I knew him, and will ever be so!

Sir Mart. What a Pox? I think thou art grown envious; not one word in my commendations?

Warn. Faith, Sir, my skill is too little to praise you, as you deserve; but if you would have it according to my poor ability, you're one that had a knock in your Cradle, a conceited lack-wit, a designing Ass, a hair-brain'd Fop, a confounded busie-brain, with an eternal Wind-mil in it; this, in short, Sir, is the Contents of your Panegyrick.

Sir Mart. But what the Devil have I done, to set you thus againſt me?

Warn. Only this, Sir, I was the foolish rascally fellow that was with *Moody*, and your Worship was he to whom I was to bring his Daughter.

Sir Mart. But how could I know this? I am no witch.

Warn. No, I'le be sworn for you, you are no conjurer.
Will you go Sir?

Sir Mart. Will you hear my juſtifications?

Warn. Shall I see the back of you? speak not a word in your defence.   [*Shoves him.*

Sir Mart. This is the ſtrangeſt luck now——   [*Exit.*

Warn. I'm resolv'd this Devil of his shall never weary me, I will overcome him; I will invent something that shall ſtand good, in spight of his folly. Let me see——

Enter Lord.

Lord. Here he is——I muſt venture on him, for the tyranny of this old Lady is unsupportable, since I have made her my confident, there passes not an hour, but she passes a pull at my Purse-ſtrings; I shall be ruin'd if I do not quit my self of her suddenly: I find now, by sad experience, that a Miſtress is much more chargeable than a Wife, and after a little time too, grows full as dull and insignificant. Mr. *Warner*! have you a mind to do your self a courtesie, and me another?

Warn. I think, my Lord, the Queſtion need not be much disputed, for I have always had a great service for your Lordship, and some little kindness for my self.

Lord. What, if you should propose Miſtress *Chriſtian* as a Wife to your Maſter? you know he's never like to compass t' other.

Warn. I cannot tell that my Lord——

Lord. 500 *l.* are yours at day of marriage.

Warn. 500 *l.* 'tis true, the temptation is very sweet, and powerful; the Devil, I confess, has done his part, and many a good Murder and Treason have been committed at a cheaper rate; but yet——

Lord. What yet——

Warn. To confess the truth, I am resolv'd to beſtow my Maſter upon that other Lady (as difficult as your Lordship thinks it) for the honour of my wit is ingag'd in it: will it not be the same to your Lordship, were she married to any other?

Lord. The very same.

Warn. Come, my Lord, not to dissemble with you any longer, I know where it is that your Shoe wrings you: I have observ'd something in the House, betwixt some parties that shall be nameless: and know that you have been taking up Linnen at a much dearer rate, than you might have had it at any Drapers in Town.

Lord. I see I have not danc'd in a Net before you.

Warn. As for that old Lady, whom Hell confound, she is the greateſt Jilt in Nature, cheat is her ſtudy, all her joy to cosen, she loves nothing but her self, and draws all lines to that corrupted centre.

Lord. I have found her out, though late: first, I'le undertake I n'ere enjoy'd her Neice under the rate of 500 *l.* a time; never was womans flesh held up so high: every night I find out for a new maidenhead, and she has sold it me as often as ever mother *Temple*, *Bennet*, or *Gifford*, have put off boil'd Capons for Quails and Partridges.

Warn. This is nothing to what Bills you'l have, when she's brought to bed, after her hard bargain, as they call it: then cram'd Capons, Pea-hens, Chickens in the grease, Pottages, and Frigacies, Wine from *Shatling*, and *La-fronds*, with New-River, clearer by sixpence the pound than ever God Almighty made it; then Midwife—Dry-Nurse——Wet-Nurse——and all the reſt of their Accomplices, with Cradle, Baby-Clouts, and Bearing-Cloaths——

116

Possets, Cawdels, Broth, Jellies and Gravies; and behind all these, Glisters, Suppositers, and a barbarous Pothecary's Bill, more in-humane than a Taylors.

Lord. I sweat to think on't.

Warn. Well, my Lord! chear up! I have found a way to rid you of it all, within a short time you shall know more; yonder appears a young Lady, whom I must needs speak with, please you go in and prepare the old Lady, and your Mistress.

Lord. Good luck, and 500 *l.* attend thee.   [*Exit.*

Enter Millisent *and* Rose *above.*

Mill. I am resolv'd I'le never marry him!

Rose. So far you are right, Madam.

Mill. But how to hinder it, I cannot possibly tell! for my Father presses me to it, and will take no denial: wou'd I knew some way—

Warn. Madam, I'le teach you the very nearest, for I have just now found it out.

Rose. Are you there, Mr. Littleplot?

Warn. Studying to deserve thee, *Rose,* by my diligence for thy Lady; I stand here, methinks, just like a wooden Mercury, to point her out the way to Matrimony.

Rose. Or, Serving-man-like, ready to carry up the hot meat for your Master, and then to fall upon the cold your self.

Warn. I know not what you call the cold, but I believe I shall find warm work on't: in the first place, then I must acquaint you, that I have seemingly put off my Master, and entred my self into Sir *John's* Service.

Mill. Most excellent!

Warn. And thereupon, but base——

Mill. Something he would tell us, but see what luck's here!

Enter Moody.

Moody. How now, Sirrah? are you so great there already?

Mill. I find my Father's jealous of him still!

Warn. Sir, I was only teaching my young Lady a new Song, and if you please you shall hear it.

SINGS.

Make ready, fair Lady, to night,
And stand at the Door below,
For I will be there
To receive you with Care,
And to your true Love you shall go.

117

Moody. Ods Bobs this is very pretty.

Mill. I, so is the Lady's Answer too, if I could but hit on't.

SINGS.

And when the Stars twinckle so bright,
Then down to the Door will I creep,
To my Love will I flye,
E're the jealous can spye,
And leave my old daddy asleep.

Moody. Bodikins, I like not that so well, to cosen her old Father; it may be my own case another time.

Rose. Oh, Madam! yonder's your Persecutor return'd.

Enter Sir John.

Mill. I'le into my Chamber, to avoid the sight of him, as long as I can; Lord! that my old doting Father should throw me away upon such an Ignoramus, and deny me to such a Wit as Sir *Martin.*

[*Ex.* Mill. *and* Rose *from above.*

Moody. O Son! here has been the moſt villainous Tragedy againſt you.

Sir John. What Tragedy? has there been any blood shed since I went?

Moody. No blood shed, but, as I told you, a moſt damnable Tragedy.

Warn. A Tragedy! I'le be hang'd if he does not mean a Strata-gem.

Moody. Jack Sawce! if I say it is a Tragedy, it shall be a Tragedy in spight of you; teach your Grandham how to piss——what—— I hope I am old enough how to spought English with you, Sir?

Sir John. But what was the reason you came not after me?

Moody. 'Twas well I did not, I'le promise you, there were those would have made bold with Miſtress Bride; an' if she had ſtir'd out of doors, there were Whipſters abroad, i'faith, Padders of Maiden-heads, that would have truss'd her up, and pick'd the lock of her affeċtions, e're a man could have said, what's this: But, by good luck, I had warning of it by a friends Letter.

Sir John. The remedy for all such dangers is easie; you may send for a Parson, and have the business dispatch'd at home.

Moody. A match, i'faith, do you provide a *Domine,* and I'le go tell her our resolutions, and hearten her up againſt the day of battel.

[*Ex.*

Sir John. Now I think on't, this Letter muſt needs come from Sir *Martin*; a Plot of his, upon my life, to hinder our marriage.

Warn. I see, Sir, you'l ſtill miſtake him for a Wit; but I am much deceiv'd, if that Letter came not from another hand.

Sir John. From whom I prithee?

Warn. Nay, for that you shall excuse me, Sir: I do not love to make a breach betwixt persons that are to be so near related.

Sir John. Thou seemſt to imply that my Miſtress was in the Plot.

Warn. Can you make a doubt on't? do you not know she ever lov'd him, and can you hope she has so soon forsaken him? you may make your self miserable, if you please, by such a marriage.

Sir John. When she is once mine, her Vertue will secure me.

Warn. Her Vertue!

Sir John. What, do you make a mock on't?

Warn. Not I, I assure you, I think it no such jeſting matter.

Sir John. Why, is she not honeſt?

Warn. Yes in my Conscience is she, for Sir *Martin*'s Tongue's no slander.

Sir John. But does he say to the contrary?

Warn. If one would believe him, which for my part I do not, he has in a manner, confess'd it to me.

Sir John. Hell and Damnation!

Warn. Courage, Sir, never vex your self, I'le warrant you 'tis all a Lye.

Sir John. But how shall I be 'sur'd 'tis so?

Warn. When you are married, you'l soon make tryal, whether she be a Maid or no?

Sir John. I do not love to make that Experiment at my own coſt.

Warn. Then you muſt never marry.

Sir John. I, but they have so many tricks to cheat a man, which are entayl'd from Mother to Daughter through all Generations, there's no keeping a Lock for that Door for which every one has a Key.

Warn. As for Example, their drawing up their breaths with Oh! you hurt me, can you be so cruel? then the next day she ſteals a Visit to her Lover, that did you the Courtesie before hand, and in private tells him how she cozened you twenty to one; but she takes out another Lesson with him to practise the next night.

Sir John. All this while miserable I muſt be their May-game.

Warn. 'Tis well if you escape so; for commonly he ſtrikes in with you, and becomes your friend.

Sir John. Deliver me from such a friend that ſtays behind with my Wife, when I gird on my Sword to go abroad.

Warn. I, there's your man, Sir; besides, he will be sure to watch your haunts, and tell her of them, that if occasion be, she may have wherewithal to recriminate: at least she will seem to be jealous of you, and who would suspect a jealous Wife?

Sir John. All manner of ways I am most miserable

Warn. But if she be not a Maid when you marry her, she may make a good Wife afterwards, 'tis but imagining you have taken such a mans Widow.

Sir John. If that were all; but the man will come and claim her again.

Warn. Examples have been frequent of those that have been wanton, and yet afterwards take up.

Sir John. I, the same thing they took up before.

Warn. The truth is, an honest simple Girl that's ignorant of all things, maketh the best Matrimony; there is such a pleasure in instructing her, the best is, there's not one Dunce in all the Sex; such a one with a good Fortune——

Sir John. I, but where is she, *Warner?*

Warn. Near enough, but that you are too far engag'd.

Sir John. Engag'd to one that hath given me the earnest of Cuckoldom before-hand?

Warn. What think you then of Mrs. *Christian* here in the house? There's 5000 *l.* and a better penny.

Sir John. I, but is she Fool enough?

Warn. She's none of the wise Virgins, I can assure you.

Sir John. Dear *Warner*, step in the next Room, and inveigle her out this way, that I may speak to her.

Warn. Remember, above all things, you keep this Wooing secret; if it takes the least wind, old *Moody* will be sure to hinder it.

Sir John. Dost thou think I shall get her Aunts Consent?

Warn. Leave that to me.   [*Exit* Warner.

Sir John. How happy a man shall I be, if I can but compass this! and what a Precipice have I avoided! then the revenge too is sweet, to steal a Wife under her Fathers nose, and leave 'um in the lurch who has abus'd me: well, such a Servant, as this *Warner*, is a Jewel.

Enter Warner *and* Mrs. Christian *to him.*

Warn. There she is, Sir, now I'le go to prepare her Aunt.

Sir John. Sweet Mistress, I am come to wait upon you.

Chr. Truly you are too good to wait on me.

Sir John. And in the Condition of a Suitor.

Chr. As how, forsooth?

Sir John. To be so happy as to marry you.

Chr. O Lord, I would not marry for any thing!

Sir John. Why? 'tis the honest end of Woman-kind.

Chr. Twenty years hence, forsooth: I would not lye in bed with a man for a world, their beards it will so prickle one.

Sir John. Pah,——what an innocent Girl it is, and very child! I like a Colt that was never yet back'd, for so I shall make her what I list, and mould her as I will; Lord! her innocency makes me laugh; my Cheeks all wet,——Sweet Lady——   [*Aside.*

Chr. I'm but a Gentlewoman, forsooth.

Sir John. Well then, sweet Mistress, if I get your Friends consent, shall I have yours?

Chr. My old Lady may do what she will, forsooth, but by my truly, I hope she will have more care of me, then to marry me yet; Lord bless me, what should I do with a Husband?

Sir John. Well, sweet Heart, then instead of wooing you, I must wooe my old Lady.

Chr. Indeed, Gentleman, my old Lady is married already: cry you mercy, forsooth, I think you are a Knight.

Sir John. Happy in that Title only to make you a Lady.

Chr. Believe me, Mr. Knight, I would not be a Lady, it makes Folks proud, and so humerous, and so ill Huswifes, forsooth.

Sir John. Pah,——she's a Baby, the simplest thing that ever yet I knew; the happiest man I shall be in the world; for should I have my wish, it should be to keep School, and teach the bigger Girls, and here in one my wish it is absolv'd.

Enter Lady Dupe.

La. Dupe. By your leave, Sir: I hope this noble Knight will make you happy, and you make him.

Chr. What shall I make him?   [*Sighing.*

La. Dupe. Marry, you shall make him happy in a good Wife.

Chr. I will not marry, Madam.

La. Dupe. You Fool!

Sir John. Pray, Madam, let me speak with you; on my Soul 'tis the pretti'st, innocent'st thing in the world.

La. Dupe. Indeed, Sir, she knows little besides her Work, and her Prayers; but I'le talk with the Fool.

Sir John. Deal gently with her, dear Madam.

La. Dupe. Come, *Christian*, will not you marry this noble Knight?

Chr. Yes, yes, yes——   [*Sobbingly.*

La. Dupe. Sir, it shall be to night.

Sir John. This Innocence is a Dowry beyond all price.

[*Exeunt Old Lady and Mrs.* Christian.

Enter Sir Martin *and Sir* John, *musing.*

Sir Mart. You are very Melancholy, methinks, Sir.

Sir John. You are mistaken, Sir.

Sir Mart. You may dissemble as you please, but Mrs. *Millisent* lyes at the bottom of your Heart.

Sir John. My Heart, I assure you, has no room for so poor a Trifle.

Sir Mart. Sure you think to wheadle me, would you have me imagine you do not love her?

Sir John. Love her! why should you think me such a Sot? Love a Prostitute, and infamous person!

Sir Mart. Fair and soft, good Sir *John.*

Sir John. You see I am no very obstinate Rival, I leave the field free to you: go on, Sir, and pursue your good Fortune, and be as happy as such a common Creature can make thee.

Sir Mart. This is Hebrew-Greek to me; But I must tell you, Sir, I will not suffer my Divinity to be prophan'd by such a Tongue as yours.

Sir John. Believe it; whate're I say, I can quote my Author for.

Sir Mart. Then, Sir, whoever told it you, ly'd in his Throat, d' you see, and deeper than that d' ye see, in his stomach, and his guts d' ye see: tell me she's a common person! he's a Son of a Whore that said it, and I'll make him eat his words, though he spoke 'em in a privy-house.

Sir John. What if *Warner* told me so? I hope you'l grant him to be a competent Judge in such a business.

Sir Mart. Did that precious Rascal say it?—Now I think on't, I'le not believe you: in fine, Sir, I'le hold you an even Wager he denies it.

Sir John. I'le lay you ten to one, he justifies it to your face.

Sir Mart. I'le make him give up the Ghost under my fist, if he does not deny it.

Sir John. I'le cut off his Ears upon the Spot, if he does not stand to't.

Enter Warner.

Sir Mart. Here he comes in Pudding-time to resolve the question: come hither, you lying Varlet, hold up your hand at the Bar of Justice, and answer to what I shall demand.

Warn. What a Goodier is the matter, Sir?

Sir Mart. Thou Spawn of the old Serpent, fruitful in nothing but in Lyes!

Warn. A very fair beginning this.

122

Sir Mart. Did'st thou dare to cast thy Venom upon such a Saint as Mrs. *Millisent*, to traduce her Vertue, and say it was adulterate?

Warn. Not guilty, my Lord.

Sir Mart. I told you so.

Sir John. How, Mr. Rascal! have you forgot what you said but now concerning Sir *Martin* and Mrs. *Millisent?* I'le stop the Lye down your Throat, if you dare deny't.

Sir Mart. Say you so! are you there agen i'faith?

Warn. Pray pacifie your self, Sir, 'twas a Plot of my own devising.

Sir Mart. Leave off your winking and your pinking, with a Horse-Pox t' ye, I'le understand none of it; tell me in plain English the truth of the business; for an' you were my own Brother, you should pay for it: belye my Mistress! what a Pox d' ye think I have no sense of Honour?

Warn. What the Devil's the matter w'ye? either be at quiet, or I'le resolve to take my heels and be gone.

Sir Mart. Stop Thief there! What did you think to scape the hand of Justice?   [*Lays hold on him.* The best on't is, Sirrah, your heels are not altogether so nimble as your tongue.   [*Beats him.*

Warn. Help! Murder! Murder!

Sir Mart. Confess, you Rogue, then.

Warn. Hold your Hands, I think the Devil's in you——I tell you, 'tis a device of mine.

Sir Mart. And have you no body to devise it on but my Mistress, the very Map of Innocence?

Sir John. Moderate your anger, good Sir *Martin*.

Sir Mart. By your patience, Sir, I'le chastise him abundantly.

Sir John. That's a little too much, Sir, by your favour, to beat him in my presence.

Sir Mart. That's a good one i'faith, your presence shall hinder me from beating my own Servant?

Warn. O Traytor to all sense and reason! he's going to discover that too.

Sir Mart. An' I had a mind to beat him to Mummy, he's my own, I hope.

Sir John. At present I must tell you he's mine, Sir.

Sir Mart. Hey-day! here's fine Jugling!

Warn. Stop yet, Sir, you are just upon the brink of a Precipice.

Sir Mart. What is't thou meanest now—a Lord! my mind misgives me, I have done some fault, but would I were hang'd if I can find it out.   [*Aside.*

Warn. There's no making him understand me.

123

Sir Mart. Pox on't, come what will, I'le not be fac'd down with a Lye; I say he is my man.

Sir John. Pray remember your self better; did not you turn him away for some fault lately, and laid a Livery of black and blew on his Back before he went?

Sir Mart. The Devil of any fault, or any black and blew that I remember: either the Rascal put some Trick upon you, or you would upon me.

Sir John. O, ho, then it seems the cudgelling and turning away were pure invention; I am glad I underſtand it.

◆*Sir Mart. In fine*, it's all so damn'd a Lye.————

Warn. Alas! he has forgot it, Sir, good Wits, you know, have bad Memories.

Sir John. No, no, Sir, that shall not serve your turn, you may return when you please to your old Maſter, I give you a fair discharge, and a glad man I am to be so rid of you: were you thereabouts i'faith? what a Snake I had entertain'd into my bosom? fare you well, Sir, and lay your next Plot better between you.   [*Exit Sir* John.

Warn. Lord, Sir, how you ſtand! as you were nip'd i' th' head; have you done any new piece of Folly, that makes you look so like an Ass?

Sir Mart. Here's three pieces of Gold yet, if I had the heart to offer it thee.   [*Holds the Gold afar off trembling.*

Warn. Noble Sir, what have I done to deserve so great a Liberality. I confess if you had beaten me for my own fault, if you had utterly deſtroy'd all my projeɕts, then it might ha' bin expeɕted that ten or twenty pieces should have been offer'd by way of recompence or satisfaɕtion.

Sir Mart. Nay, on' you be so full of your Flowts, your Friend and Servant; who the Devil could tell the meaning of your signs and tokens, an' you go to that?

Warn. You are no Ass then?

Sir Mart. Well, Sir, to do you Service, d'ye see, I am an Ass in a fair way; will that satisfie you?

Warn. For this once produce those three pieces, I am contented to receive that inconsiderable tribute: or make 'em six, and I'le take the fault upon my self.

Sir Mart. Are we Friends then? if we are let me advise you.————

Warn. Yet advising————

Sir Mart. For no harm, good *Warner*: but pray next time make me of your Counsel, let me enter into the business, inſtruɕt me in every point, and then if I discover all, I am resolv'd to give over affairs, and retire from the world.

124

Warn. Agreed, it shall be so; but let us now take breath awhile, then on agen.

> For though we had the worſt, those heats were paſt,
> Wee'l whip and spur, and fetch him up at laſt.   [*Exeunt.*

ACT V.

Enter Lord, *Lady* Dupe, *Miſtress* Chriſtian, Rose, *and* Warner.

Lord. YOur promise is admirably made good to me, that Sir *John Swallow* should be this night married to Mrs. *Chriſtian*; inſtead of that, he is more deeply engag'd than ever with old *Moody.*

Warn. I cannot help these ebbs and flows of fortune.

La. Dupe. I am sure my Neice suffers moſt in't, he's come off to her with a cold Complement of a miſtake in his Miſtress's Vertue, which he has now found out, by your Maſter's folly, to be a Plot of yours to separate them.

Chr. To be forsaken when a woman has given her consent!

Lord. 'Tis the same Scorn, as to have a Town render'd up, and afterwards slighted.

Rose. You are a sweet youth, Sir, to use my Lady so, when she depended on you; is this the faith of a *Valet de Chambre*? I would be asham'd to be such a dishonour to my profession; it will reflect upon us in time, we shall be ruin'd by your good example.

Warn. As how, my dear Lady Embassadress?

Rose. Why, they say the women govern their Ladies, and you govern us: So if you play faſt and loose, not a Gallant will bribe us for our good wills; the gentle *Guiny* will now go to the Ordinary, which us'd as duly to ſteal into our hands at the ſtair-foot, as into Mr. Doctors at parting.

Lord. Night's come, and I expect your promise.

La. Dupe. Fail with me if you think good, Sir.

Chr. I give no more time.

Rose. And if my Miſtress go to bed a Maid to night—

Warn. Hey day! You are dealing with me, as they do with the Banquers, call in all your debts together; there's no possibility of payment at this rate, but I'le coin for you all as faſt as I can, I assure you.

La. Dupe. But you muſt not think to pay us with false Money, as you have done hitherto.

125

Rose. Leave off your Mountebank tricks with us, and fall to your business in good earneſt.

Warn. Faith, and I will, *Rose*; for to confess the truth, I am a kind of a Mountebank, I have but one Cure for all your Diseases; that is, that my Mr. may marry Mrs. *Millisent*, for then Sir *John Swallow* will of himself return to Mrs. *Chriſtian*.

Lord. He says true, and therefore we muſt all be helping to that design.

Warn. I'le put you upon something, give me but a thinking-time in the firſt place, get a Warrant and Bailifs to arreſt Sir *John Swallow*, upon a promise of marriage to Miſtress *Chriſtian*.

Lord. Very good.

La. Dupe. We'll all swear it.

Warn. I never doubted your Ladiship in the leaſt, Madam—— for the reſt we will consider hereafter.

Lord. Leave this to us.   [*Ex.* Lord, La. Dupe, Chr.

Warn. Rose where's thy Lady?

Mill. What have you to say to her?

Warn. Only to tell you, Madam, I am going forward in the great work of projeċtion.

Mill. I know not whether you will deserve my thanks when the work's done.

Warn. Madam, I hope you are not become indifferent to my Maſter.

Mill. If he should prove a fool after all your crying up his wit, I shall be a miserable woman.

Warn. A fool! that were a good jeſt i'faith: but how comes your Ladiship to suspeċt it?

Rose. I have heard, Madam, your greateſt wits have ever a touch of madness and extravagance in them, so perhaps has he.

Warn. There's nothing more diſtant than wit and folly, yet like Eaſt and Weſt, they may meet in a point, and produce aċtions that are but a hairsbreadth from one another.

Rose. I'le undertake he has wit enough to make one laugh at him a whole day together; He's a moſt Comical person.

Mill. For all this I will not swear he is no fool; he has ſtill discover'd all your plots.

Warn. O Madam, that's the common fate of your Machivilians, they draw their Designs so subtile, that their very fineness breaks them.

Mill. However I'm resolv'd to be on the sure side, I will have certain proof of his wit before I marry him.

Warn. Madam, I'le give you one, he wears his cloaths like a great

126

sloven, and that's a sure sign of wit, he neglects his outward parts; besides, he speaks French, sings, dances, plays upon the Lute.

Mill. Does he do all this, say you?

Warn. Most divinely, Madam.

Mill. I ask no more; then let him give me a Serenade immediately: but let him stand in the view; I'le not be cheated.

Warn. He shall do't, Madam: but how, the Devil knows——
for he sings like a Scritch-Owle, and never touch'd the Lute. [*Aside.*

Mill. You'le see't perform'd?

Warn. Now I think on't, Madam; this will but retard our enterprize.

Mill. Either let him do't, or see me no more.

Warn. Well, it shall be done, Madam; but where's your Father? will not he over-hear it?

Mill. As good hap is, he's below stairs, talking with a Seaman, that has brought him news from the *East-Indies.*

Warn. What concernment can he have there?

Mill. He had a Bastard-Son there, whom he loved extreamly: but not having any news from him these many years, concluded him dead; this Son he expects within these three days.

Warn. When did he see him last?

Mill. Not since he was seven years old.

Warn. A sudden thought comes into my head, to make him appear before his time; let my Master pass for him, and by that means he may come into the House unsuspected by your Father, or his Rival.

Mill. According as he performs his Serenade, I'le talk with you ——make haste——I must retire a little.   [*Ex.* Mill. *from above.*

Rose. I'le instruct him most rarely, he shall never be found out; but in the mean time, what wilt thou do with a Serenade?

Warn. Faith, I am a little non-plus'd on the sudden, but a warm consolation from thy lips, *Rose,* would set my wits a working again.

Rose. Adieu, *Warner.*

Warn. Inhumane *Rose,* adieu.   [*Exit* Rose.
Blockhead *Warner,* into what a premunire hast thou brought thy self! this 'tis to be so forward to promise for another——but to be Godfather to a Fool, to promise and vow he should do anything like a Christian——

Enter Sir Martin.

Sir Mart. Why, how now Bully, in a Brown Study? for my good I warrant it; there's five shillings for thee, what, we must encourage good wits sometimes.

127

Warn. Hang your white pelf: sure, Sir, by your largess you mistake me for *Martin Parker*, the Ballad-Maker, your covetousness has offended my Muse, and quite dull'd her.

Sir Mart. How angry the poor Devil is! in fine, thou art as cholerick as a Cook by a Fire-side.

Warn. I am over-heated, like a Gun, with continual discharging my wit: 'slife, Sir, I have rarified my brains for you, till they are evaporated; but come, Sir, do something for your self like a man, I have engag'd you shall give to your Miſtress a Serenade, in your proper person: I'le borrow a Lute for you.

Sir Mart. I'le warrant thee, I'le do't, man.

Warn. You never learn't; I don't think you know one ſtop.

Sir Mart. 'Tis no matter for that, Sir, I'le play as faſt as I can, and never ſtop at all.

Warn. Go to, you are an invincible Fool I see; get up into your Window, and set two Candles by you, take my Land-lord's Lute in your hand, and fumble on't, and make grimmaces with your mouth, as if you sung; in the mean time, I'le play in the next Room in the dark, and consequently your Miſtress, who will come to her Balcone over againſt you, will think it to be you; and at the end of every Tune, I'le ring the Bell that hangs between your Chamber and mine, that you may know when to have done.

Sir Mart. Why, this is fair Play now, to tell a man before-hand what he muſt do; Gramercy, i'faith, Boy, now if I fail thee————

Warn. About your business then, your Miſtress and her Maid appear already: I'le give you the sign with the Bell, when I am prepar'd, for my Lute is at hand in the Barbers Shop.   [*Exeunt.*

Enter Millisent, Rose, *with a Candle by 'em above.*

Rose. We shall have rare Musick.

Mill. I wish it prove so; for I suspeᶜt the Knight can neither play nor sing.

Rose. But if he does, you're bound to pay the Musick, Madam.

Mill. I'le not believe it, except both my Ears and Eyes are Witnesses.

Rose. But 'tis night, Madam, and you cannot see 'em; yet he may play admirably in the dark.

Mill. Where's my Father?

Rose. You need not fear him, he's ſtill employ'd with that same Sea-man, and I have set Mrs. *Chriſtian* to watch their discourse, that betwixt her and me *Warner* may have wherewithal to inſtruᶜt his Maſter.

Mill. But yet there's fear my Father will find out the Plot.

128

Rose. Not in the least, for my old Lady has provided two rare disguises for the Master and the Man.

Mill. Peace, I hear them beginning to tune the Lute.

Rose. And see, Madam, where your true Knight, Sir *Martin*, is plac'd yonder like *Apollo*, with his Lute in his hand, and his Rays about his head.

Sir Martin *appears at the adverse window, a Tune play'd; when it is done,* Warner *rings, and Sir* Martin *holds.*

Did he not play most excellently, Madam?

Mill. He play'd well; and yet methinks he held his Lute but untowardly.

Rose. Dear Madam, peace; now for the Song.

The SONG.

BLind Love to this hour,
    Had never like me, a slave under his power.
  Then blest be the dart
  That he threw at my heart,
    For nothing can prove
A joy so great as to be wounded with love.

My Days and my Nights
Are fill'd to the purpose with sorrows and frights;
  From my heart still I sigh,
  And my Eyes are ne're dry,
    So that, Cupid *be prais'd,*
I am to the top of Love's happiness rais'd.

My Soul's all on fire,
So that I have the pleasure to doat and desire,
  Such a pretty soft pain,
  That it tickles each vein,
    'Tis the dream of a smart,
Which makes me breathe short when it beats at my heart.

Sometimes in a Pet,
When I am despis'd, I my freedom would get;
  But streight a sweet smile
  Does my anger beguile,
    And my heart does recall,
Then the more I do struggle, the lower I fall.

Heaven does not impart
Such a grace as to love unto ev'ry ones heart;
　For many may wish
　To be wounded, and miss:
　　Then blest be loves Fire,
And more blest her Eyes that first taught me desire.

The Song being done, Warner *rings agen; but Sir* Martin *continues fumbling, and gazing on his Mistress.*

Mill. A pretty humour'd Song——but stay, methinks he plays and sings still, and yet we cannot hear him——Play louder, Sir *Martin,* that we may have the fruits on't.

Warn. peeping. Death! this abominable Fool will spoil all agen. Dam him, he stands making his Grimaces yonder, and he looks so earnestly upon his Mistress, that he hears me not.　　[*Rings agen.*

Mill. Ah, ah! have I found you out, Sir? now, as I live and breathe, this is pleasant, *Rose,*—his man play'd and sung for him, and he, it seems, did not know when he should give over.

[Millisent *and* Rose *laugh.*

Warn. They have found him out, and laugh yonder, as if they would split their sides. Why, Mr. Fool, Oafe, Coxcomb, will you hear none of your names?

Mill. Sir *Martin,* Sir *Martin,* take your mans counsel, and keep time with your Musick.

Sir Mart. peeping. Ha! what do you say, Madam? how does your Ladiship like my Musick?

Mill. O most heavenly! just like the Harmony of the Spheres, that is to be admired, and never heard.

Warn. You have ruin'd all by your not leaving off in time.

Sir Mart. What the Devil would you have a man do when my hand is in! well, o'my conscience, I think there is a Fate upon me.

[*Noise within.*

Mill. Look, *Rose,* what's the matter?

Rose. 'Tis Sir *John Swallow,* pursu'd by the Bailiffs, Madam, according to our plot; it seems they have dog'd him thus late to his Lodging.

Mill. That's well! for though I begin not to love this Fool; yet I am glad I shall be rid on him.　　[*Ex.* Millisent, Rose.

Enter Sir John, *pursu'd by three Bailiffs over the Stage.*

Sir Mart. Now I'le redeem all agen, my Mistress shall see my Valour, I'm resolv'd on't; Villains, Rogues, Poultroons! what? three upon one? in fine, I'le be with you immediately.　　[*Exit.*

130

Warn. Why, Sir, are you ſtark mad? have you no grain of sense left? he's gone! now is he as earneſt in the quarrel, as Cokes among the Poppits; 'tis to no purpose whatever I do for him.

Exit Warner.

Enter Sir John *and Sir* Martin (*having driven away the Bailiffs*) *Sir* Martin *flourisheth his Sword.*

Sir Mart. Victoria! Victoria! what heart, Sir *John*, you have received no harm, I hope?

Sir John. Not the leaſt, I thank you, Sir, for your timely assistance which I will requite with anything but the resigning of my Mrs.—Dear Sir *Martin*, a good night.

Sir Mart. Pray let me wait upon you in, Sir *John*.

Sir John. I can find my way to Mrs. *Millisent* without you, Sir, I thank you.

Sir Mart. But pray, what were you to be arreſted for?

Sir John. I know no more than you; some little debts, perhaps, I left unpaid by my negligence: once more good night, Sir. [*Exit.*

Sir Mart. He's an ungrateful Fellow; and so, in fine, I shall tell him, when I see him next—Monsieur——   [*Enter* Warner.
Warner, A propos! I hope you'l applaud me now, I have defeated the Enemy, and that in sight of my Miſtress; Boy, I have charm'd her, i'faith, with my Valour.

Warn. I, juſt as much as you did e'ne now with your Musick; go, you are so beaſtly a Fool, that a Chiding is thrown away upon you.

Sir Mart. Fool in your Face, Sir; call a man of Honour, Fool, when I have juſt atchieved such an Enterprise—Gad now my blood's up, I am a dangerous person, I can tell you that, *Warner*.

Warn. Poor Animal, I pity thee.

Sir Mart. I grant I am no Musician, but you muſt allow me for a Sword-man, I have beat 'em bravely; and in fine, I am come off unhurt, save only a little scratch i'th'head.

Warn. That's impossible, thou haſt a Scull so thick, no Sword can pierce it: but much good may't d'ye, Sir, with the fruits of your Valour: you rescu'd your Rival when he was to be arreſted, on purpose to take him off from your Miſtress.

Sir Mart. Why, this is ever the Fate of ingenious men; nothing thrives they take in hand.

Enter Rose.

Rose. Sir *Martin*, you have done your business with my Lady, she'l never look upon you more; she says, she's so well satisfied of your Wit and Courage, that she will not put you to any farther tryal.

Sir Mart. *Warner*, is there no hopes, *Warner?*

Warn. None that I know.

Sir Mart. Let's have but one civil plot more before we part.

Warn. 'Tis to no purpose.

Rose. Yet if he had some golden Friends that would engage for him the next time——

Sir Mart. Here's a Jacobus and a Carolus will enter into Bonds for me.

Rose. I'le take their Royal words for once.

[She fetches two disguises.

Warn. The meaning of this, dear *Rose.*

Rose. 'Tis in pursuance of thy own invention, *Warner*; a child which thy wit hath begot upon me: but let us lose no time, Help! Help! dress thy Master, that he may be *Anthony*, old *Moody's* Bastard, and thou his, come from the *East Indies.*

Sir Mart. Hey-tarockit——now we shall have *Roses* device too, I long to be at it, pray let's hear more on't.

Rose. Old *Moody* you must know in his younger years, when he was a *Cambridge*-Scholar, made bold with a Towns-man's Daughter there, by whom he had a Bastard whose name was *Anthony*, whom you, Sir *Martin*, are to represent.

Sir Mart. I warrant you, let me alone for *Tony:* but pray go on, *Rose.*

Rose. This Child in his Fathers time, he durst not own, but bred him privately in the Isle of *Ely*, till he was seven years old, and from thence sent him with one *Bonaventure* a Merchant for the *East-Indies.*

Warn. But will not this over-burden your memory, Sir?

Sir Mart. There's no answering thee any thing, thou think'st I am good for nothing.

Rose. Bonaventure dy'd at *Surat* within two Years, and this *Anthony* has liv'd up and down in the *Moguls* Country unheard of by his Father till this night, and is expected within these three days: now if you can pass for him, you may have admittance into the house, and make an end of all the business before the other *Anthony* arrives.

Warn. But hold, *Rose*, there's one considerable Point omitted; what was his Mother's name.

Rose. That indeed I had forgot; her name was *Dorothy*, Daughter to one *Draw-water* a Vintner at the *Rose.*

Warn. Come, Sir, are you perfect in your Lesson? *Anthony Moody*, born in *Cambridge*, bred in the Isle of *Ely*, sent into the *Moguls* Country at seven years old with one *Bonaventure* a Merchant, who dy'd within two years; your Mother's name *Dorothy Draw-water* the Vintners Daughter at the *Rose.*

Sir Mart. I have it all *ad unguem*——what, dost think I'm a Sot? but stay a little; how have I liv'd all this while in that same Country?

Warn. What Country?——Pox, he has forgot already——

Rose. The *Moguls* Country.

Sir Mart. I, I, the *Moguls* Country! what a Devil, any man may mistake a little, but now I have it perfect: but what have I been doing all this while in the *Moguls* Country? He's a Heathen Rogue, I am afraid I shall never hit upon his name.

Warn. Why, you have been passing your time there, no matter how.

Rose. Well, if this passes upon the Old man, I'le bring your business about agen with my Mistress, never fear it; stay you here at the door, I'll go tell the Old man of your arrival.

Warn. Well, Sir, now play your part exactly, and I'le forgive all your former errours——

Sir Mart. Hang 'em, they were only slips of Youth——how peremptory and domineering this Rogue is! now he sees I have need of his service: would I were out of his power agen, I would make him lye at my feet like any Spaniel.

Enter Moody, *Sir* John, *Lord, Lady* Dupe, Millisent,
Christian, Rose.

Moody. Is he here already, say'st thou? which is he?

Rose. That Sun-burn'd Gentleman.

Moody. My dear Boy *Anthony*, do I see thee agen before I dye? welcome, welcome.

Sir Mart. My dear Father, I know it is you by instinct, for methinks I am as like you as if I were spit out of your mouth.

Rose. Keep it up I beseech your Lordship.   [*Aside to the Lord.*

Lord. He's wond'rous like indeed.

La. Dupe. The very image of him.

Moody. Anthony you must salute all this Company: this is my Lord *Dartmouth*, this is my Lady *Dupe*, this her Niece Mrs. *Christian.*   [*He salutes them.*

Sir Mart. And that's my Sister, methinks I have a good resemblance of her too: honest Sister, I must needs kiss you, Sister.

Warn. This fool will discover himself; I foresee it already, by his carriage to her.

Moody. And now, *Anthony*, pray tell's a little of your Travels.

Sir Mart. Time enough for that, forsooth Father, but I have such a natural affection for my Sister, that methinks I could live and dye with her: give me thy hand, sweet Sister.

Sir John. She's beholding to you, Sir.

Sir Mart. What if she be, Sir, what's that to you, Sir?

Sir John. I hope, Sir, I have not offended you?

Sir Mart. It may be you have, and it may be you have not, Sir; you see I have no mind to satisfie you, Sir: what a Devil! a man cannot talk a little to his own flesh and blood, but you must be interposing, with a murrain to you.

Moody. Enough of this, good *Anthony*; this Gentleman is to marry your Sister.

Sir Mart. He marry my Sister! ods foot, Sir, there are some Bastards, that shall be nameless, that are as well worthy to marry her, as any man, and have as good blood in their veins.

Sir John. I do not question it in the least, Sir.

Sir Mart. 'Tis not your best course, Sir; you may marry my Sister; what have you seen of the world, Sir; I have seen your Hurricanoes, and your Calentures, and your Eclipticks, and your Tropick Lines, Sir, an' you go to that, Sir.

Warn. You must excuse my Master, the Sea's a little working in his brain, Sir.

Sir Mart. And your *Prestor Johns* o' th' *East-Indies*, and your Great Turk of *Rome* and *Persia*.

Moody. Lord, what a thing it is to be Learned, and a Traveller! Bodikins, it makes me weep for joy; but, *Anthony*, you must not bear your self too much upon your Learning, Child.

Mill. Pray Brother be civil to this Gentleman for my sake.

Sir Mart. For your sake, Sister *Millisent*, much may be done, and here I kiss your hand on't.

Warn. Yet again stupidity?

Mill. Nay, pray Brother, hands off, now you are too rude——

Sir Mart. Dear Sister, as I am a true *East-India* Gentleman——

Moody. But pray, Son *Anthony*, let's talk of other Matters, and tell me truly, had you not quite forgot me? and yet I made woundy much of you when you were young.

Sir Mart. I remember you as well as if I saw you but yesterday: A fine grey-headed——grey-bearded old Gentleman, as ever I saw in all my life.

Warn. aside. Grey-bearded old Gentleman! when he was a Scholar at *Cambridge*.

Moody. But do you remember where you were bred up?

Sir Mart. O yes, Sir, most perfectly; in the Isle——stay——let me see; oh——now I have it——in the Isle of *Silly*.

Moody. In the Isle of *Ely*, sure you mean?

Warn. Without doubt he did, Sir; but this damn'd Isle of *Silly* runs in's head ever since his Sea-Voyage.

Moody. And your Mother's name was——come, pray let me examine you——for that I'm sure you cannot forget.

Sir Mart. Warner! what was it, *Warner?*

Warn. Poor Mrs. *Dorothy Draw-water*, if she were now alive, what a joyful day would this be to her?

Moody. Who the Devil bid you speak, Sirrah?

Sir Mart. Her name, Sir, was Mrs. *Dorothy Draw-water*.

Sir John. I'le be hang'd if this be not some Cheat.

Mill. He makes so many ſtumbles, he muſt needs fall at laſt.

Moody. But you remember, I hope, where you were born?

Warn. Well, they may talk what they will of *Oxford* for an University, but *Cambridge* for my Money.

Moody. Hold your tongue, you scanderbag Rogue you, this is the second time you have been talking when you should not.

Sir Mart. I was born at *Cambridge*, I remember it as perfeſtly as if it were but yeſterday.

Warn. How I sweat for him! he's remembering ever since he was born.

Moody. And who did you go over withall to the *Eaſt-Indies?*

Sir Mart. Warner!

Warn. 'Twas a happy thing, Sir, you lighted upon so honeſt a Merchant, as Mr. *Bonaventure*, to take care of him.

Moody. Sawcy Rascal! this is paſt all sufferance.

Rose. We are undone *Warner*, if this discourse go on any farther.

Lord. Pray, Sir, take pity o' th' poor Gentleman, he has more need of a good Supper, than to be ask'd so many Queſtions.

Sir John. These are Rogues, Sir, I plainly perceive it; pray let me ask him one queſtion——which way did you come home Sir?

Sir Mart. We came home by Land, Sir.

Warn. That is, from *India* to *Persia*, from *Persia* to *Turkey*, from *Turkey* to *Germany*, from *Germany* to *France.*

Sir John. And from thence, over the narrow Seas on Horse-back?

Moody. 'Tis so, I discern it now; but some shall smoke for't. Stay a little, *Anthony*, I'le be with you presently.　　　[*Ex.* Mood.

Warn. That wicked old Man is gone for no good, I am afraid, would I were fairly quit of him.　　　　　　　　　　　[*Aside.*

Mill. aside. Tell me no more of Sir *Martin, Rose*; he wants natural sence, to talk after this rate; but for this *Warner*, I am ſtrangely taken with him, how handsomly he brought him off!

Enter Moody *with two Cudgels.*

Moody. Among half a score tough Cudgels I had in my Chamber I have made choice of these two, as beſt able to hold out.

135

Mill. Alas! poor *Warner* muſt be beaten now for all his wit, would I could bear it for him.

Warn. But to what end is all this preparation, Sir?

Moody. In the firſt place, for your Worship, and in the next, for this *Eaſt-Indian* Apoſtle, that will needs be my Son *Anthony.*

Warn. Why, d'ye think he is not?

Moody. No, thou wicked Accomplice in his designs, I know he is not.

Warn. Who, I his Accomplice? I beseech you, Sir, what is it to me, if he should prove a Counterfeit; I assure you he has cozen'd me in the firſt place.

Sir John. That's likely, i'faith, cozen his own Servant?

Warn. As I hope for mercy, Sir, I am an utter ſtranger to him, he took me up but yeſterday, and told me the ſtory word for word as he told it you.

Sir Mart. What will become of us two now? I truſt to the Rogue's wit to bring me off.

Moody. If thou would'ſt have me believe thee, take one of these two Cudgels, and help me to lay it on soundly.

Warn. With all my heart.

Moody. Out, you Cheat, you Hypocrite, you Impoſter! do you come hither to cozen an honeſt man?   [*Beats him.*

Sir Mart. Hold, hold, Sir.

Warn. Do you come hither with a lye to get a Father, Mr. *Anthony* of *Eaſt-India?*

Sir Mart. Hold, you inhumane Butcher.

Warn. I'le teach you to counterfeit again, Sir.

Sir Mart. The Rogue will murder me.   [*Ex. Sir* Mart.

Moody. A fair riddance of 'em both; let's in and laugh at 'em.
[*Exeunt.*

Re-enter *Sir* Martin, *and* Warner.

Sir Mart. Was there ever such an affront put upon a man, to be beaten by his Servant?

Warn. After my hearty salutations upon your back-side, Sir, may a man have leave to ask you, what news from the *Moguls* Country?

Sir Mart. I wonder where thou hadſt the impudence to move such a queſtion to me, knowing how thou haſt us'd me.

Warn. Now, Sir, you may see what comes of your indiscretion and ſtupidity: I always gave you warning of it, but for this time I am content to pass it by without more words; partly, because I have already correⅽted you, though not so much as you deserve.

136

Sir Mart. Do&t thou think to carry it off at this rate, after such an injury?

Warn. You may thank your self for't; nay, 'twas very well I found out that way, otherwise I had been suspe&ted as your Accomplice.

Sir Mart. But you laid it on with such a vengeance, as if you were beating of a Stock-fish.

Warn. To confess the truth on't, you had anger'd me, and I was willing to evaporate my choler; if you will pass it by so, I may chance to help you to your Mi&tress: no more words of this business, I advise you, but go home and grease your back.

Sir Mart. In fine, I mu&t suffer it at his hands; for if my shoulders had not paid for this fault, my purse mu&t have sweat blood for't: the Rogue has got such a hank upon me———

Warn. So, so; here's another of our Vessels come in,

[*Enter* Rose.

after the Storm that parted us: what comfort, *Rose*, no Harbour near?

Rose. My Lady, as you may well imagine, is mo&t extreamly incens'd again&t Sir *Martin*, but she applauds your ingenuity to the Skies. I'le say no more, but thereby hangs a Tale.

Sir Mart. I am considering with my self about a Plot, to bring all about again.

Rose. Yet again plotting! if you have such a mind to't, I know no way so proper for you as to turn Poet to *Pugenello*.   [*Musick Plays.*

Warn. Hark! is not that Musick in your house?

Rose. Yes, Sir *John* has given my Mi&tress the Fiddles, and our Old man is as jocund yonder, and does so hug himself, to think how he has been reveng'd upon you.

Warn. Why, he does not know 'twas we, I hope?

Rose. 'Tis all one for that.

Sir Mart. I have such a Plot; I care not, I will speak an' I were to be hang'd for't———shall I speak, dear *Warner?* let me now; it does so wamble within me, ju&t like a Cly&ter, i'faith law, and I can keep it no longer for my heart.

Warn. Well, I am indulgent to you; out with it boldly, in the name of Non-sense.

Sir Mart. We two will put on Vizards, and with the help of my Landlord, who shall be of the party, go a Mumming there, and by some device of dancing get my Mi&tress away unsuspe&ted by 'em all.

Rose. What if this should hit now, when all your proje&ts have fail'd, *Warner*.

137

Warn. Would I were hang'd if it be not somewhat probable: nay, now I consider better on't—exceeding probable: it must take, 'tis not in Nature to be avoided.

Sir Mart. O must it so, Sir! and who may you thank for't?

Warn. Now am I so mad he should be the Author of this device. How the Devil, Sir, came you to stumble on't?

Sir Mart. Why should not my brains be as fruitful as yours, or any mans?

Warn. This is so good, it shall not be your Plot, Sir; either disown it, or I will proceed no farther.

Sir Mart. I would not lose the credit of my Plot to gain my Mistress: the Plot's a good one, and I'le justifie it upon any ground of *England*; an' you will not work upon't, it shall be done without you.

Rose. I think the Knight has reason.

Warn. Well, I'le order it however to the best advantage: hark you, *Rose.*   [*whispers.*

Sir Mart. If it miscarry by your ordering, take notice, 'tis your fault, 'tis well invented I'le take my Oath on't.

Rose. I must in to 'em, for fear I should be suspected; but I'le acquaint my Lord, my old Lady, and all the rest who ought to know it, with your design.

Warn. We'll be with you in a twinkling: you and I, *Rose*, are to follow our Leaders, and be pair'd to night——

Rose. To have, and to hold, are dreadful words, *Warner*; but for your sake I'le venture on 'em.   [*Exeunt.*

Enter Lord, *Lady* Dupe, *and* Christian.

La. Dupe. Nay! good my Lord, be patient.

Lord. Does he think to give Fiddles and Treatments in a house where he has wrong'd a Lady? I'le never suffer it.

La. Dupe. But upon what ground will you raise your quarrel?

Lord. A very just one, as I am her Kinsman.

La. Dupe. He does not know yet why he was to be arrested; try that way agen.

Lord. I'le hear of nothing but revenge.   [*Enter* Rose.

Rose. Yes, pray hear me one word, my Lord, Sir *Martin* himself has made a Plot.

Chr. That's like to be a good one.

Rose. A Fool's Plot may be as lucky as a Fool's Handsel; 'tis a very likely one, and requires nothing for your part, but to get a Parson in the next Room, we'll find work for him.

La. Dupe. That shall be done immediately; *Christian*, make haste

138

and send for Mr. *Ball*, the Non-conformiſt, tell him here are two or three Angels to be earn'd.

Chr. And two or three Possets to be eaten: may I not put in that, Madam?

La. Dupe. Surely you may.   [*Exit* Christian.

Rose. Then for the reſt——'tis only this——Oh! they are here! pray take it in a whisper: my Lady knows of it already.

Enter Moody, *Sir* John, Millisent.

Mill. Strike up agen, Fiddle, I'le have a French Dance.

Sir John. Let's have the Brawls.

Moody. No, good Sir *John*, no quarrelling among Friends.

La. Dupe. Your Company is like to be increas'd, Sir; some Neighbors that heard your Fiddles, are come a mumming to you.

Mood. Let 'em come in, and we'l be Jovy: an' I had but my Hobby-horse at home——

Sir John. What, are they Men or Women?

La. Dupe. I believe some Prentices broke loose.

Mill. Rose! Go and fetch me down two Indian-gowns and Vizard-masks——you and I will disguise too, and be as good a Mummery to them, as they to us.   [*Exit* Rose.

Moody. That will be moſt rare.

Enter Sir Martin, Warner, Landlord *disguised like a Tony*.

Moody. O, here they come! Gentlemen Maskers, you are welcome —— [Warner *signs to the musick for a Dance*. He signs for a Dance I believe; you are welcome, Mr. Musick, ſtrike up, I'le make one as old as I am.

Sir John. And I'le not be out.   [*Dance*.

Lord. Gentlemen Maskers, you have had the Frolick, the next turn is mine; bring two Flute-glasses, and some stools, Ho, we'll have the Ladies health.

Sir John. But why ſtools, my Lord?

Lord. That you shall see: the humour is, that two men at a time are hoyſted up; when they are above, they name their Ladies, and the reſt of the Company dance about them while they drink: this they call the Frolick of the Altitudes.

Moody. Some High-lander's invention, I'le warrant it.

Lord. Gentlemen Maskers, you shall begin.

[*They hoyſt Sir* Martin *and* Warner.

Sir John. Name the Ladies.

Lord. They point to Mrs. *Millisent*, and Mrs. *Chriſtian*. A Lou's Touche! Touche!

139

Moody. A rare toping health this: come Sir *John*, now you and I will be in our altitudes.

While they drink, the Company dances and sings: they are taken down.

Sir John. What new device is this tro?
Moody. I know not what to make on't.

When they are up, the Company dances about 'em: then dance off.
Tony dances a Jig.

Sir John to Tony. Pray, Mr. Fool, where's the rest o' your Company? I would fain see 'em again.
Landl. Come down and tell 'em so, *Cudden.*
Sir John. I'le be hang'd if there be not some plot in't, and this Fool is set here to spin out the time.
Moody. Like enough: undone! undone! my Daughter's gone; let me down, Sirrah.
Landl. Yes, *Cudden.*
Sir John. My Mistress is gone, let me down first.
[*He offers to pull down the stools.*
Landl. This is the quickest way, *Cudden.*
Sir John. Hold! hold! or thou wilt break my neck.
Landl. An you will not come down, you may stay there, *Cudden.*
[*Exit Landlord, dancing.*
Moody. O Scanderbag Villains!
Sir John. Is there no getting down?
Moody. All this was long of you Sir *Jack.*
Sir John. 'Twas long of your self to invite them hither.
Moody. O you young Coxcombs, to be drawn in thus!
Sir John. You old Sot you, to be caught so sillily!
Moody. Come but an inch nearer, and I'le so claw thee.
Sir John. I hope I shall reach to thee.
Moody. And 'twere not for thy wooden breast-work there.
Sir John. I hope to push thee down from *Babylon.*

Enter Lord, *Lady* Dupe, *Sir* Martin, Warner, Rose, Millisent *vail'd,* Landlord.

Lord. How, Gentlemen! what quarrelling among your selves!
Moody. Coxnowns! help me down, and let me have fair play, he shall never marry my Daughter.
Sir Martin leading Rose. No I'le be sworn that he shall not, therefore never repine, Sir, for Marriages you know are made in Heaven; in fine, Sir, we are joyn'd together in spight of Fortune.
Rose pulling off her mask. That we are indeed, Sir *Martin,* & these

are Witnesses; therefore in fine never repine, Sir, for marriages, you know are made in Heaven.

Omnes. *Rose!*

Warn. What, is *Rose* split in two? sure I ha' got one *Rose!*

Mill. I, the beſt *Rose* you ever got in all your Life.

Pulls off her Mask.

Warn. This amazeth me so much, I know not what to say or think.

Moody. My Daughter married to *Warner!*

Sir Mart. Well, I thought it impossible any man in *England* should have over-reach'd me: sure, *Warner* there was some miſtake in this: prithee *Billy*, let's go to the Parson to set all right again, that every man may have his own before the matter go too far.

Warn. Well, Sir! for my part I will have nothing farther to do with these Women, for I find they will be too hard for us, but e'ne sit down by the loss, and content my self with my hard fortune: But, Madam, do you ever think I will forgive you this, to cheat me into an Eſtate of 2000 *l.* a year?

Sir Mart. And I were as thee, I would not be so serv'd *Warner!*

Mill. I have serv'd him but right for the cheat he put upon me, when he perswaded me you were a Wit——now there's a trick for your trick, Sir.

Warn. Nay, I confess you have out-witted me.

Sir John. Let me down, and I'le forgive all freely.

[They let him down.

Mood. What am I kept here for?

Warn. I might in policy keep you there, till your Daughter and I had been in private, for a little consummation; But for once, Sir, I'le truſt your good nature. *[Takes him down too.*

Mood. And thou wert a Gentleman, it would not grieve me!

Mill. That I was assur'd of before I married him, by my Lord here.

Lord. I cannot refuse to own him for my Kinsman, though his Father's sufferings in the late times have ruin'd his Fortunes.

Mood. But yet he has been a Serving-man.

Warn. You are miſtaken, Sir, I have been a Maſter; and besides, there's an Eſtate of 800 *l.* a year, only it is mortgaged for 6000 *l.*

Mood. Well, we'll bring it off, and for my part, I am glad my Daughter has miss'd *in fine*, there.

Sir John. I will not be the only man that muſt sleep without a Bedfellow to night, if this Lady will once again receive me.

La. Dupe. She's yours, Sir.

Lord. And the same Parson, that did the former execution, is ſtill

141

in the next Chamber; what with Cawdels, Wine, and Quidding, which he has taken in abundance, I think he will be able to wheadle two more of you into matrimony.

Mill. Poor Sir *Martin* looks melancholly! I am half afraid he is in love.

Warn. Not with the Lady that took him for a wit, I hope.

Rose. At least, Sir *Martin* can do more than you Mr. *Warner*, for he can make me a Lady, which you cannot my Mistress.

Sir Mart. I have lost nothing but my man, and in fine, I shall get another.

Mill. You'll do very well, Sir *Martin*, for you'll never be your own man, I assure you.

Warn. For my part I had lov'd you before if I had follow'd my inclination.

Mill. But now I am afraid you begin of the latest, except your love can grow up like a Mushroom at a nights warning.

Warn. For that matter never trouble your self, I can love as fast as any man, when I am nigh possession; my love falls heavy, and never moves quick till it comes near the Centre; he's an ill Falconer that will unhood before the quarry be in sight.

> Love's an high mettal'd Hawk that beats the Air,
> But soon grows weary when the Game's not near.

FINIS.

THE TEMPEST

OR THE ENCHANTED ISLAND

A COMEDY

SOURCE

TIECK pointed out the resemblance between Shakespeare's *The Tempest* and the German play *Comedia von der schönen Sidea* by Jakob Ayrer, where the parallels are indeed so striking that it almost seems there must have been some common original, unless perchance Shakespeare knew of the play from the English comedians who visited Nürnburg, Ayrer's native town, in 1604 and 1606. Moreover, English actors performed a *Sidea* "in good German" in 1613. Jakob Ayrer died 26 March, 1605, so he cannot in any case have been the borrower. Yet even if Shakespeare did thus glean certain incidents from theatrical gossip of *Sidea*, that bare hint cannot have been his main source for *The Tempest*. The poet Collins gave a misleading clue when he spoke of *Aurelio and Isabella*, but none the less I am inclined to believe that Shakespeare was indeed indebted to some lost romance. This seems to me supported by the fact that there are several loose threads in *The Tempest* such as might well be left in a play founded upon a romance, and, although they have been remarked, in my opinion the significance of these has been overlooked. For example, we are never told what was the one thing Sycorax did for which they would not take her life—it was assuredly not the fact of her pregnancy; the whole business of the marriage of Claribel to the King of Tunis is insufficiently introduced, either some other motive for the voyage should have been suggested or more should have been made of this episode,—Dryden, it will be noted, represents Alonzo as returning from Portugal, where he has very Christianly fought the Barbary foe. These are slight, but significant, points.

There is some faint trace of such a romance in a Spanish tale by Antonio de Eslava, which forms part of the collection *Las noches de invierno*, published at Madrid in 1609.

Here we have a dispossessed king, Dardanus, who is a beneficent magician, who raises an ensorcelled palace amid the seas, and provides his daughter, Seraphina, with a royal bridegroom. A tempest helps to unravel the plot of the story, and Sirens, Dryads, Nymphs, Tritons, minister the will of the kindly thaumaturge.

No doubt various records of Jacobean voyaging and adventure, relations of the expedition of Sir Thomas Gates and Sir George Somers, published in 1610, supplied Shakespeare with suggestions of which he made most excellent use. To endeavour to locate the enchanted isle seems the crassest folly, an ineptitude of that kind well-beloved of many Shakespearean commentators.

Since the Masque of Iris, Ceres, and Juno does not appear in the comedy of Davenant and Dryden, it were impertinent to discuss it here. There are certain pseudo-editors that would deny *The Tempest* to be Shakespeare's writing. As an ox tumbles hay, so a fool threshes his folly.

Some of Shakespeare's names, Ferdinand, Alonzo, Sebastian, Gonzalo, were probably suggested by Eden's *History of Travaile*, 1577, whence was also taken the name *Setebos*, a great devil.

Caliban is generally considered to be a metathesis of Canibal, *i.e.* Caribee; and Shakespeare's source here was indisputably Florio's *Montaigne*, published 1603, Book I, c. 30 *Of the Caniballes*.

Various ingenious, but hardly satisfactory, derivatives have been advanced for the name Sycorax, in whose figure at least one ingenious editor, with more historical perception of truth than fact and gallantry, sees an allegorization of that "bright Occidental star" Queen Elizabeth.

In his preface to *The Tempest* Dryden explicitly states that the character of Hippolito is due to Davenant. Herman Grimm, *Fünfzehn Essays*, Berlin, 8vo, 1785, once made a futile, and indeed ridiculous, attempt to show that Hippolito is borrowed from Calderon's *En esta vida todo es verdad, y todo mentira*. H. H. Furness in his very faulty edition of *The Tempest*, *Variorum Shakespeare*, 1892, jumped at the suggestion, and absurdly wrote that "the mutilations, or rather the additions, for which Dryden took to himself credit as the author, are wholesale 'conveyances' from a play of Calderon." It is obvious that Furness had no acquaintance with the play in question, which has absolutely nothing in common with *The Tempest*. The error, however, was unfortunately repeated by Strunk.

Calderon's drama, *En esta vida todo es verdad, y todo mentira*, is a play of strange and beautiful fantasy detailing in exquisite poetry knightly adventure, which, however, to the unimaginative English taste must almost inevitably seem conceited and extravagant, if not altogether too whimsical and grotesquely bizarre. Nevertheless, the whole is informed and irradiated with such grace and lordliness of diction that not even the most regular critic could deny his applause. The drama cannot be earlier than 1637, and it is quoted in a romance printed in 1641; we are able to date it within these. The plot may be roughly outlined thus: Astolfo, the ambassador of Mauricio, Emperor of Constantinople, after a battle in which Mauricio was slain by Focas, fled to the caverns of Mount Etna carrying with him Eraclio, the infant son of the dead Emperor. Irifile, a maiden beloved by Focas and by him left pregnant on his departure for the war, tried to follow him. In the wild mountain passes she was delivered of a son, Leonido. The mother expired, but the babe being found by Astolfo is brought up with Eraclio far from the haunts of men. Many years after, the First Day (Jornada Prima) commences with the solemn triumph of Focas, who to the sound of sweet-stringed instruments is received in state by Cintia, Queen of Sicily. Presently Libia, daughter of the famous magician Lisippo, appears in great alarm. Among the lonely dells of Etna she has been frightened by the apparition of "a man like a beast." This proves to be Astolfo in search of Eraclio and Leonido. Contrary to his stern precepts they have left their caves to wander abroad. When the long processions and tuneful choirs have passed from the stage, three strange figures, tanned, clad in skins, uncouth and unkempt, make their entrance. The old man is severely blaming the youths for having disobeyed his injunctions, but they excuse themselves, saying that the music and voices irresistibly attracted them from their seclusion. Astolfo replies that in tracking them he has met a woman who will, he declares, ruin them all. Eraclio and Leonido have never seen a woman, and Astolfo warns them of

146

impending disaster should they once set eyes upon a fair female form. Soon, however, Eraclio is left alone, and in a few moments Cintia appears. They gaze at each other in wonderment and perplexity. There is also an encounter between Libia and Leonido. Astolfo interrupts, but he is met and recognized by Focas, to whom the old man announces that one of the two savage lads is the Emperor Mauricio's son, but which he refuses to reveal. Focas threatens Astolfo, and the two youths stoutly defend their foster-father against the royal guards. Much tumult and confusion ensues, when suddenly the wizard Lisippo appears. By his incantations he raises a terrific storm, and amid the crash of thunder and lightning's blaze the First Day closes.

The Second Day is occupied with the myriad difficulties and entanglements which have arisen owing to the secret Astolfo jealously holds.

In the Third Day Libia proclaims that Eraclio is Mauricio's son. This she has learned from her father, the mage. Leonido wishes to kill Focas sleeping, but he is prevented by Eraclio. Focas awakes and sees the two youths with naked swords, whereupon Leonido asserts he drew to defend the King against Eraclio. This Eraclio denies, and during their contention news is brought that Fedrico, Prince of Calabria, has landed with a hostile force. A battle ensues between the invaders and the army of Focas, who is slain on the field by Eraclio, and the play ends with cries of "Viva Eraclio, Eraclio viva!"

It is true that there are in Calderon half a dozen verses which bear some resemblance to as many lines in *The Tempest; or, The Enchanted Island*, but given the situation, the coincidence in thought is almost inevitable.

It should be noted that Pierre Corneille's tragedy, *Heraclius, Empereur d'Orient*, with "Heraclius, Fils de l'Empereur Maurice, crû Martian Fils de Phocas, Amant d'Eudoxe" and "Martian, Fils de Phocas, crû Léonce Fils de Léontine, Amant de Pulchérie" is wholly different from Calderon's drama. The critics, however, discussed which was the original, and this gave occasion to Voltaire's apt remark: "Le lecteur comparera le Théâtre espagnol avec le français, et il découvrira au premier coup d'œil quel est l'original. Si après cela il reste des disputes ce ne sera pas contre les personnes éclairées."

THEATRICAL HISTORY

THE Davenant-Dryden *The Tempest; or, The Enchanted Island*, was produced on Thursday, 7 November, 1667. Pepys, who was present, found himself among "a great many great ones. The house mighty full; the King and Court there: and the most innocent play that ever I saw; and a curious piece of musique is an echo of half-sentences, the echo repeating the former half, whilst the man goes on to the latter; which is mighty pretty." This is the song sung by Ferdinand in Act III, 3, where Ariel echoes *Go thy way*. It was set by Banister, who with Pelham Humphreys supplied the music in 1667. All, Pepys tells us, "were mightily pleased with the play." The diarist saw the comedy several times, and on one occasion was admitted behind the scenes, and "had the pleasure to see the actors in their several dresses, especially the seamen, and monster, which were very droll."

No list of actors was printed with the quarto, but we know that Henry Harris played Ferdinand; Edward Angel, "an incomparable Comedian," Stephano; Cave Underhill, Trincalo. Moll Davis was also in the original cast, her rôle perhaps being Hippolito, for the "right Heir of the Dukedom of *Mantua*" was assigned to a woman, and little Miss Davies in breeches parts had already proved an irresistible attraction. After she left the stage she was succeeded in *The Tempest* by Mrs. Gosnell, who, according to Pepys, was a sorry substitute. Betterton himself did not appear in the play.

The Davenant-Dryden comedy was printed quarto, 1670, the preface by Dryden being dated 1 December, 1669. It was for the first time edited by myself in my volume *Shakespeare Adaptations*, 1922. Downes records: "In 1673 [rather 1674] *The Tempest; or Inchanted Island;* made into an Opera by Mr. *Shadwell:* having all new in it; as Scenes, Machines; particularly, one scene painted with myriads of *Ariel* Spirits; and another flying away with a table, furnisht out with fruits, sweet-meats, and all sorts of viands, just when Duke *Trincalo* and his companions were going to dinner; all things perform'd in it so admirably well, that not any succeeding opera got more money." Mr. W. J. Lawrence in his *Did Thomas Shadwell write an Opera on "The Tempest"* (*Elizabethan Playhouse*, I, p. 203) fixes "the date of production of the Shadwell *Tempest* at circa 30 April, 1674, probably a sound approximation." This operatic version was printed quarto, 1674; 1676 (*bis*); 1690; 1695; and 1701. With the exception of the folio Dryden, 1701, this is the text which has been given in all editions of Dryden's work.

The first alteration of *The Tempest* seems immediately to have been absorbed in the opera, which was extraordinarily popular, indeed few pieces upon the Restoration stage proved so great and so continued an attraction. The Opera was seen by the King on Tuesday, 17 November, 1674; upon the following day, upon Saturday, 28 of that month; upon Monday, 5 November, 1677; and apparently again ten days later.

There are innumerable contemporary allusions to *The Tempest*, to the elaborate *mise-en-scène* and effects; to Duke Trincalo and the sailors; to Caliban and Sycorax; to the singing and dancing; to the spirits and devils; to the Terminal Masque; all of these having fairly ensorcelled the Town.

For the Opera new instrumental music was written by Matthew Lock, and new vocal music by Pietro Reggio and J. Hart. The dances were composed by Giovanni Battista Draghi. In a private letter to myself the late Mr. W. Barclay Squire wrote (1922): "Excepting Draghi's dances I think we now have the whole of the music for Shadwell's version." The song *Arise, arise! ye subterranean winds*, at the end of the second act, will be found, duly ascribed to Shadwell, "A Song in The Tempest. The Words by Mr. Shadwell," in the work advertised in the *London Gazette*, 1680, as "A choice collection of Songs set by Signior Pietro Reggio to be engraved on copper in an extraordinary manner in very large folio, most of them out of Mr. A. Cowley's excellent Poems." A MS. copy of the same setting is ascribed to Grabu, but this is obviously an error, for a second MS. copy, corrected, bears Reggio's name.

The Operatic *The Tempest*, as being one of the most splendid spectacles known to the London stage, took the chief place of the three magnificent productions seen by the Morocco Ambassador at Dorset Garden early in 1682. His Excellency declared himself "extreamly pleased" at the performances.

Edward Angel had died in the spring or early summer of 1673, and it is doubtful if Henry Harris was acting in 1682, but Cave Underhill played Trincalo, his original part, it was in fact one of his most eminent rôles.

There were special revivals of *The Tempest* in 1690 and 1691, and it was probably for these that the opera, with additions, was wholly re-set by Henry Purcell. Towards the close of 1695 a song for Dorinda, "Dear Pretty Youth," not to be found in the quarto, was published in Book III of *Deliciæ Musicæ* as "A New Song in *The Tempest*, sung by Miss *Cross* to her Lover who is supposed Dead. Set by Mr. Henry Purcell."

A performance of *The Tempest* with "all the original Flyings and Musick" is announced in the *Daily Courant*, 13 February, 1707–8, "Dorinda by Mrs. *Cross* with the Song of 'Dear Pretty Youth.'"

It is, of course, only possible to chronicle a very few performances of *The Tempest*, which, it is interesting to note, we find frequently advertised in *The Spectator*. At Drury Lane, 4 June, 1714, Powell played Prospero; Johnson, Caliban; Ryan, Ferdinand; Mrs. Mountfort, Hippolito; Mrs. Santlow, Dorinda; whilst Bullock had succeeded Underhill as Trincalo.

2 January, 1729, at the same theatre, John Mills was Prospero; Wilks, Ferdinand; Joe Miller, Trincalo; Mrs. Cibber, Hippolito; Mrs. Booth, Miranda; Miss Robinson, Ariel; and Kitty Raftor, a young nymph of seventeen, who afterwards became Kitty Clive, Dorinda.

31 January, 1746, Garrick revived *The Tempest* as by Shakespeare. Luke Sparks acted Prospero; Macklin, Stephano; and Kitty Clive, Ariel. None the less the Masque of *Neptune and Amphitrite*, for which Arne had written new music, was appended.

In December of the following year *The Tempest*, loosely announced as "Not acted 7 years," was given at Drury Lane with Berry as Prospero; Macklin, Trincalo; Isaac Sparks, Caliban; Taswell, a great farceur, Sycorax; Peg Woffington, Hippolito; Mrs. Mozeen, Miranda; Kitty Clive, Ariel; and Mrs. Green, Dorinda. The whole concluded with the Masque.

There is an interesting and detailed account of the production of *The Tempest* at Dublin on 13 January, 1748–9, at the Theatre Royal, Smock-alley.

Sheridan had got together for the season of 1748–9 an exceptionally strong company, including Mr. and Mrs. Macklin, Mrs. Bland, Mr. and Mrs. Lampe, Mr. Sullivan, Mrs. Mozeen, Mrs. Storer, Mr. Howard, and Signor Pasquali. In the Dublin papers he announced that, in order to do full justice to the musical plays and operas, he had engaged an orchestra consisting of ten violins, a tenor, a 'cello, two hautbois, two bassoons, two double-basses, two French horns, a trumpet, and a harpsichord. At the request of several patrons, in December, the Drury Lane revival of *The Tempest* was put in rehearsal by Macklin, who played Trincalo, and was duly produced on Friday, 13 January, 1749.

The *Dublin Courant* of 3–7 January, 1748–9, announced that on Friday, 13 January, would be revived *The Tempest*, with the original songs "and Musick, compos'd by Mr. Purcell." This advertisement was repeated in the issue of 7–10 January, and the play was given to a crowded house. Its success was assured, and the second performance followed on 19 January. The advertisement for this repeat performance contains the announcement that the play was now performed "for the second time in the present Manner in this Kingdom." A later advertisement, in the issue for 14–17 January, informs the public that the original "Musick by the celebrated Purcell" would be given, and that the whole was to conclude with "a Grand Masque of Neptune and Amphitrite." In the announcement of the third performance, which took place on 25 January, the advertisement held out as a lure "the original Musick composed by Purcell," as well as "Sinkings, Flyings, and other Decorations," and "an extraordinary Piece of Machinery representing the Rising Sun."

On 11 February, 1756, Garrick put on an operatic version of *The Tempest* prepared by himself. Hippolito and Dorinda, it is true, have disappeared; but there were wholesale conveyances from *Tyrannick Love*; Trincalo, Stephano, and Ventoso indulge in a trio; and there are many other impertinent interpolations, whilst Shadwell's *Arise, arise! ye subterranean winds* is sung by Milcha. New music had been composed by John Christopher Smith. With not unmerited sarcasm did Theophilus Cibber write of "*The Tempest* castrated into an opera. Oh! what an agreeable Lullaby might it have prov'd to our Beaus and Belles to have heard Caliban, Sycorax, and one of the Devils, trilling of trios."

Shakespeare's *The Tempest* without adulteration was revived by Garrick on 20 October, 1757, and announced as "Not acted 14 years."

Bell's acting edition of Shakespeare "regulated from the prompt-books by permission of the managers" (1773–1775) supplies a "pure and unmixed," if greatly abridged, text of *The Tempest*, and Shakespeare alone held the stage until 13 October, 1787, when Kemble at Drury Lane restored Hippolito, played by the lovely Mrs. Goodall, and Dorinda, Miss Farren.

31 October, 1812, Young attempted Prospero at Covent Garden, but it is said that the performance, though intelligent and correct, suffered by comparison with Kemble. Mrs. Henry Johnston was the Hippolito, and Miss Booth, Dorinda.

Hippolito and Dorinda did not, indeed, finally disappear from the London theatre until 13 October, 1838, when at Covent Garden Macready gave his sumptuous and extremely successful production of *The Tempest* "from the text of Shakespeare." This ran for fifty-five nights. The music was "selected from the works of Purcell, Linley, and Dr. Arne, and arranged by Mr. T. Cooke." Macready appeared as Prospero; Anderson, Ferdinand; Phelps, Antonio; G. Bennett, Caliban; Harley, Trincalo; Bartley, Stephano; Miss Faucit, Miranda; and Priscilla Horton, Ariel. On 29 November and 1 and 4 December Miss Vanderhoff was the Miranda.

Professor Dent in his *Foundations of English Opera*, 1928, p. 147, writes: "I am indebted to the kindness of Mr. W. Bridges Adams for a copy of a playbill dated 23 July, 1845, announcing a performance of *The Tempest*, in the Theatre at Southwell, in which not only Hypolito (*sic*) and Dorinda appeared in the list of characters, but also Rosebud and Bluebell, two spirits whose names suggest that they belonged to the same century as the performance."

Probably Shadwell's songs have not been heard in *The Tempest* since 1756, and it must be remembered that Hippolito and Dorinda wholly belong to Sir William Davenant and Dryden.

PREFACE to the *Enchanted Island*.

THE *writing of Prefaces to Plays was probably invented by some very ambitious Poet, who never thought he had done enough: Perhaps by some Ape of the French Eloquence, who uses to make a business of a Letter of gallantry, an examen of a Farce; and in short, a great pomp and ostentation of words on every trifle. This is certainly the talent of that Nation, and ought not to be invaded by any other. They do that out of gayety which would be an imposition upon us.*

We may satisfie our selves with surmounting them in the Scene, and safely leave them those trappings of writing, and flourishes of the Pen, with which they adorn the borders of their Plays, and which are indeed no more than good Landskips to a very indifferent Picture. I must proceed no farther in this argument, lest I run my self beyond my excuse for writing this. Give me leave therefore to tell you, Reader, that I do it not to set a value on any thing I have written in this Play, but out of gratitude to the memory of Sir William Davenant, *who did me the honour to joyn me with him in the alteration of it.*

It was originally Shakespear's: *a Poet for whom he had particularly a high veneration, and whom he first taught me to admire. The Play it self had formerly been acted with success in the* Black-Fryers: *and our excellent* Fletcher *had so great a value for it, that he thought fit to make use of the same Design, not much varied, a second time. Those who have seen his* Sea-Voyage, *may easily discern that it was a Copy of* Shakespear's Tempest: *the Storm, the desart Island, and the Woman who had never seen a Man, are all sufficient testimonies of it. But* Fletcher *was not the only Poet who made use of* Shakespear's *Plot: Sir* John Suckling, *a profess'd admirer of our Author, has follow'd his footsteps in his* Goblins; *his* Regmella *being an open imitation of* Shakespear's Miranda; *and his Spirits, though counterfeit, yet are copied from* Ariel. *But Sir* William Davenant, *as he was a Man of quick and piercing imagination, soon found that somewhat might be added to the Design of* Shakespear, *of which neither* Fletcher *nor* Suckling *had ever thought: and therefore to put the last hand to it, he design'd the Counterpart to* Shakespear's *Plot, namely, that of a Man who had never seen a Woman; that by this means those two Characters of Innocence and Love might the more illustrate and commend each other. This excellent contrivance he was pleas'd to communicate to me, and to desire my assistance in it. I confess that from the very first moment it so pleas'd me, that I never writ any thing with more delight. I must likewise do him that justice to acknowledge, that my writing*

152

received daily his amendments, and that is the reason why it is not so faulty, as the rest which I have done without the help or correction of so judicious a friend. The Comical parts of the Saylors were also his Invention, and for the most part his writing, as you will easily discover by the Style. In the time I writ with him, I had the opportunity to observe somewhat more neerly of him, than I had formerly done, when I had only a bare acquaintance with him: I found him then of so quick a fancy, that nothing was propos'd to him, on which he could not suddenly produce a thought extremely pleasant and surprizing: and those first thoughts of his, contrary to the old Latine Proverb, were not always the least happy. And as his fancy was quick, so likewise were the products of it remote and new. He borrowed not of any other; and his imaginations were such as could not easily enter into any other man. His corrections were sober and judicious: and he corrected his own writings much more severely than those of another man; bestowing twice the time and labour in polishing which he us'd in invention. It had perhaps been easie enough for me to have arrogated more to my self than was my due in the writing of this Play, and to have pass'd by his name with silence in the publication of it, with the same ingratitude which others have us'd to him, whose Writings he hath not only corrected, as he has done this, but has had a greater inspection over them, and sometimes added whole Scenes together, which may as easily be distinguish'd from the rest, as true Gold from counterfeit by the weight. But besides the unworthiness of the action which deterred me from it (there being nothing so base as to rob the dead of his reputation) I am satisfi'd I could never have receiv'd so much honour in being thought the Author of any Poem, how excellent soever, as I shall from the joining my imperfections with the merit and name of Shakespear and Sir William D'avenant.

JOHN DRIDEN.

Decemb. 1.
  1669.

Prologue to the *Tempest*, or the *Enchanted Island*.

AS when a Tree's cut down the secret root
   Lives under ground, and thence new Branches shoot;
So, from old Shakespear's honour'd dust, this day
Springs up and buds a new reviving Play.
Shakespear, who (taught by none) did first impart
To Fletcher Wit, to labouring Johnson Art.
He Monarch-like gave those his subjects law,
And is that Nature which they paint and draw.
Fletcher reach'd that which on his heights did grow,
Whilst Johnson crept and gather'd all below.
This did his Love, and this his Mirth digest:
One imitates him most, the other best.
If they have since out-writ all other Men,
'Tis with the drops which fell from Shakespear's Pen.
The Storm which vanish'd on the Neighb'ring shore,
Was taught by Shakespear's Tempest first to roar.
That Innocence and Beauty which did smile
In Fletcher, grew on this Enchanted Isle.
But Shakespear's Magick could not copy'd be,
Within that Circle none durst walk but he.
I must confess 'twas bold, nor would you now,
That liberty to vulgar Wits allow,
Which works by Magick supernatural things:
But Shakespear's Pow'r is sacred as a King's.
Those Legends from old Priest-hood were receiv'd,
And he then writ, as people then believ'd.
But, if for Shakespear we your grace implore,
We for our Theatre shall want it more:
Who by our dearth of Youths are forc'd t' employ
One of our Women to present a Boy.
And that's a transformation you will say
Exceeding all the Magick in the Play.
Let none expect in the last Act to find,
Her Sex transform'd from man to Woman-kind.
What e're she was before the Play began,
All you shall see of her is perfect man.
Or if your fancy will be farther led,
To find her Woman, it must be abed.

DRAMATIS PERSONÆ.

A *Lonzo* Duke of *Savoy*, and Usurper of the Dukedom of *Mantua*.
Ferdinand his Son.
Prospero right Duke of *Millain*.
Antonio his Brother, Usurper of the Dukedom.
Gonzalo a Nobleman of *Savoy*.
Hippolito, one that never saw Woman, right Heir of the Dukedom
    of *Mantua*.
Stephano Master of the Ship.
Mustacho his Mate.
Trincalo Boatswain.
Ventoso a Mariner.
Several Mariners.
A Cabbin-Boy.
Miranda
   and   (Daughters to *Prospero*) that never saw Man.
Dorinda
Ariel an aiery Spirit, attendant on *Prospero*.
Several Spirits Guards to *Prospero*.
Caliban
   and   Two Monsters of the Isle.
Sycorax his Sister

THE TEMPEST

OR, THE

Enchanted Island.

ACT I.

Enter Mustacho *and* Ventoso.

Vent. WHat a Sea comes in?
    Must. A hoaming Sea! we shall have foul weather.

Enter Trincalo.

Trinc. The Scud comes against the Wind, 'twill blow hard.

Enter Stephano.

Steph. Bosen!
Trinc. Here, Master what cheer?
Steph. Ill weather! let's off to Sea.
Must. Let's have Sea-room enough, and then let it blow the Devils head off.
Steph. Boy!

Enter Cabin-Boy.

Boy. Yaw, yaw, here Master.
Steph. Give the Pilot a dram of the Bottle.

                              [Exeunt Stephano *and* Boy.

Enter Mariners and pass over the Stage.

Trinc. Heigh, my hearts, chearly, chearly, my hearts, yare, yare.

Enter Alonzo, Antonio, Gonzalo.

Alon. Good Bosen have a care; where's the Master? Play the men.
Trinc. Pray keep below.
Ant. Where's the Master, Bosen?
Trinc. Do you not hear him? you mar our labour: keep your Cabins, you help the storm.
Gonz. Nay, good friend be patient.

Trinc. I, when the Sea is hence; what care these Roarers for the name of Duke? to Cabin; silence; trouble us not.

Gonz. Good friend, remember whom thou haſt aboard.

Trinc. None that I love more than my self: you are a Counsellour, if you can advise these Elements to silence: use your Wisdom: if you cannot, make your self ready in the Cabin for the ill hour. Cheerly good hearts! out of our way, Sirs.   [*Exeunt* Trincalo *and Mariners.*

Gonz. I have great comfort from this Fellow; methinks his Complexion is perfeĉt Gallows; ſtand faſt, good fate, to his hanging; make the Rope of his deſtiny our Cable, for our own does little advantage us; if he be not born to be hang'd we shall be drown'd.
                                                                                                    [*Exit.*

Enter Trincalo *and* Stephano.

Trinc. Up aloft Lads. Come, reef both Top-sails.

Steph. Let's weigh, Let's weigh, and off to Sea.   [*Ex.* Stephano.

Enter two Mariners and pass over the Stage.

Trinc. Hands down! man your main-Capſtorm.

Enter Muſtacho *and* Ventoso *at the other door.*

Muſt. Up aloft! and man your seere-Capſtorm.

Vent. My Lads, my hearts of Gold, get in your Capſtorm-Bar. Hoa up, hoa up, &c.   [*Exeunt* Muſtacho *and* Ventoso.

Enter Stephano.

Steph. Hold on well! hold on well! nip well there; Quarter-Maſter, get's more Nippers.   [*Exit* Stephano.

Enter two Mariners and pass over again.

Trinc. Turn out, turn out all hands to Capſtorm?
You dogs, is this a time to sleep?
Heave together Lads.   [Trincalo *whiſtles.*
                                                                    [*Exeunt* Muſtacho *and* Ventoso.

Muſt. within. Our Viall's broke.

Vent. within. 'Tis but our Vial-block has given way. Come heave Lads! we are fix'd again. Heave together Bullyes.

Enter Stephano.

Steph. Cut off the Hamocks! cut off the Hamocks, come my Lads: Come *Bullys*, chear up! heave luſtily.
The Anchor's a peek.

Trinc. Is the Anchor a peek?

Steph. Is a weigh! Is a weigh!

Trinc. Up aloft my Lads upon the Fore-Castle!
Cut the Anchor, cut him.

All within. Haul Catt, Haul Catt, &c. Haul Catt, haul:
haul, Catt, haul. Below.

Steph. Aft, Aft! and loose the Misen!

Trinc. Get the Misen-tack aboard. Haul Aft Misen-sheet!

Enter Mustacho.

Must. Loose the main Top-sail!

Steph. Furle him again, there's too much Wind.

Trinc. Loose Foresail! Haul Aft both sheats! trim her right afore
the Wind. Aft! Aft! Lads, and hale up the Misen here.

Must. A Mackrel-Gale, Master.

Steph. within. Port hard, port! the Wind grows scant, bring the
Tack aboard Port is. Star-board, star-board, a little steady; now
steady, keep her thus, no neerer you cannot come.

Enter Ventoso.

Vent. Some hands down: the Guns are loose.   [*Ex.* Must.

Trinc. Try the Pump, try the Pump!   [*Exit* Ventoso.

Enter Mustacho *at the other door.*

Must. O Master! six foot Water in Hold.

Steph. Clap the Helm hard aboard! Flat, flat, flat in the Fore-
sheat there.

Trinc. Over-haul your fore-boling.

Steph. Brace in the Lar-board.   [*Exit.*

Trinc. A Curse upon this howling,   [*A great cry within.*
They are louder than the weather.   [*Enter* Antonio *and* Gonzalo.
Yet again, what do you here! shall we give o're, and drown? ha' you
a mind to sink?

Gonz. A Pox o' your throat, you bawling, blasphemous, un-
charitable Dog.

Trinc. Work you then.

Ant. Hang, Cur, hang, you whorson insolent noise-maker, we
are less afraid to be drown'd than thou art.

Trinc. Brace off the Fore-yard.   [*Exit.*

Gonz. I'll warrant him for drowning, though the Ship were no
stronger than a Nut-shell, and as leaky as an unstanch'd Wench.

Enter Alonzo *and* Ferdinand.

Ferd. For my self I care not, but your loss brings a thousand
Deaths to me.

Alonzo. O name not me, I am grown old, my Son; I now am tedious to the World, and that, by use, is so to me: but, *Ferdinand,* I grieve my subjects loss in thee: Alas! I suffer justly for my crimes, but why thou shouldest——O Heaven! Hark, farewel my Son! a long farewel!   *[A cry within.*

Ferd. Some lucky Plank, when we are lost by Shipwrack, waft hither, and submit it self beneath you.
Your blessing, and I dye contented.   *[Embrace and Exeunt.*

Enter Trincalo, Mustacho, *and* Ventoso.

Trinc. What must our mouths be cold then?
Vent. All's lost. To prayers, to prayers.
Gonz. The Duke and Prince are gone within to prayers. Let's assist them.
Must. Nay, we may e'ne pray too; our case is now alike.
Ant. We are meerly cheated of our lives by Drunkards.
This wide chopt Rascal: would thou might'st lye drowning
The long washing of ten Tides. *[Exeunt* Trincalo, Mustacho, *and*
                                          Ventoso.

Gonz. He'll be hang'd yet, though every drop of water swears against it; now would I give ten thousand Furlongs of Sea for one Acre of barren ground, Long-heath, Broom-furs, or any thing. The wills above be done, but I would fain dye a dry death.
          [A confused noise within.

Ant. Mercy upon us! we split, we split.
Gonz. Let's all sink with the Duke, and the young Prince.
          [Exeunt.

Enter Stephano, Trincalo.

Trinc. The Ship is sinking.   *[A new cry within.*
Steph. Run her ashore!
Trinc. Luffe! luffe! or we are all lost! there's a Rock upon the Star-board Bow.
Steph. She strikes, she strikes! All shift for themselves. *[Exeunt.*

Enter Prospero *and* Miranda.

Prosp. Miranda! where's your Sister?
Mir. I left her looking from the pointed Rock, at the walks end, on the huge beat of Waters.
Prosp. It is a dreadful object.
Mir. If by your Art, my dearest Father, you have put them in this roar, allay 'em quickly.
Had I been any God of power, I would have sunk the Sea into the Earth, before it should the Vessel so have swallowed.
160

THE TEMPEST

Prosp. Collect your self, and tell your piteous heart,
There's no harm done.

Mir. O woe the day!

Prosp. There is no harm:
I have done nothing but in care of thee,
My Daughter, and thy pretty Sister:
You both are ignorant of what you are,
Not knowing whence I am, nor that I'm more
Than *Prospero*, Master of a narrow Cell,
And thy unhappy Father.

Mir. I ne're indeavour'd to know more than you were pleas'd
to tell me.

Prosp. I should inform thee farther: wipe thou thine Eyes, have
comfort; the direful spectacle of the wrack, which touch'd the very
virtue of compassion in thee, I have with such a pity safely order'd,
that not one Creature in the Ship is lost.

Mir. You often, Sir, began to tell me what I am,
But then you stopt.

Prosp. The hour's now come;
Obey, and be attentive, Canst thou remember a time before we came
into this Cell? I do not think thou canst, for then thou wert not full
three years old.

Mir. Certainly I can, Sir.

Prosp. Tell me the image then of any thing which thou dost keep
in thy remembrance still.

Mir. Sir, had I not four or five Women once that tended
me?

Prosp. Thou hadst, and more, *Miranda:* what see'st thou else in
the dark back-ward, and abyss of Time?
If thou remembrest ought e're thou cam'st here, then, how thou
cam'st thou may'st remember too.

Mir. Sir, that I do not.

Prosp. Fifteen Years since, *Miranda*, thy Father was the Duke of
Millan, and a Prince of power.

Mir. Sir, are not you my Father?

Prosp. Thy Mother was all Virtue, and she said, thou wast my
Daughter, and thy Sister too.

Mir. O Heavens! what foul play had we, that we hither came, or
was't a blessing that we did?

Prosp. Both, both, my Girl.

Mir. How my heart bleeds to think what you have suffer'd. But,
Sir, I pray proceed.

Prosp. My Brother, and thy Uncle, call'd *Antonio*, to whom I

VOL. II.—M   161

trusted then the manage of my State, while I was wrap'd with secret
Studies: That false Uncle (do'st thou attend me Child?)

Mir. Sir, most heedfully.

Prosp. Having attain'd the craft of granting Suits, and of denying
them; whom to advance, or lop, for over-toping, soon was grown the
Ivy which did hide my Princely Trunck, and suckt my verdure out:
thou attend'st not.

Mir. O good Sir, I do.

Prosp. I thus neglecting worldly ends, and bent to closeness, and
the bettering of my mind, wak'd in my false Brother an evil Nature:
He did believe
He was indeed the Duke, because he then did execute the outward
face of Soveraignty. Do'st thou still mark me?

Mir. Your story would cure deafness.

Prosp. To have no screen between the part he plaid, and whom he
plaid it for; he needs would be Absolute *Millan*, and Confederates
(so dry he was for Sway) with *Savoy*'s Duke, to give him Tribute,
and to do him homage.

Mir. False man!

Prosp. This Duke of *Savoy* being an Enemy,
To me inveterate, strait grants my Brother's Suit,
And on a night
Mated to his design, *Antonio* opened the Gates of *Millan*, and i' th'
dead of darkness, hurri'd me thence with thy young Sister, and thy
crying self.

Mir. But wherefore did they not that hour destroy us?

Prosp. They durst not, Girl, in *Millan*, For the love my people
bore me; in short, they hurri'd us away to *Savoy*, and thence aboard
a Bark at *Nissa*'s Port: bore us some Leagues to Sea, where they
prepar'd a rotten Carkass of a Boat, not rigg'd, no Tackle, Sail, nor
Mast; the very Rats instinctively had quit it: they hoisted us, to
cry to Seas which roar'd to us; to sigh to Winds, whose pity sighing
back again, did seem to do us loving wrong.

Mir. Alack! what trouble was I then to you?

Prosp. Thou and thy Sister were two Cherubins, which did
preserve me: you both did smile, infus'd with fortitude from
Heaven.

Mir. How came we ashore?

Prosp. By Providence Divine,
Some food we had, and some fresh Water, which a Noble man of
Savoy, called *Gonzalo*, appointed Master of that black design, gave
us; with rich Garments, and all necessaries, which since have
steaded much: and of his gentleness (knowing I lov'd my Books) he

furnisht me from mine own Library, with Volumes which I prize above my Dukedom.

Mir. Would I might see that man.

Prosp. Here in this Island we arriv'd, and here have I your Tutor been. But by my skill I find that my mid-Heaven doth depend on a moſt happy Star, whose influence if I now court not, but omit, my Fortunes will ever after droop: here cease more queſtion, thou art inclin'd to ſleep: 'tis a good dullness, and give it way; I know thou canſt not chuse.   [*She falls asleep.*
Come away my Spirit: I am ready now, approach
My *Ariel*, Come.   *Enter* Ariel.

Ariel. All hail great Maſter, grave Sir, hail, I come to answer thy beſt pleasure, be it to fly, to swim, to shoot into the fire, to ride on the curl'd Clouds; to thy ſtrong bidding, task *Ariel* and all his qualities.

Prosp. Haſt thou, Spirit, perform'd to point the Tempeſt that I bad thee?

Ariel. To every Article.
I boarded the Duke's Ship, now on the Beak, now in the Waſte, the Deck, in every Cabin; I flam'd amazement, and sometimes I seem'd to burn in many places on the Top-Maſt, the Yards and Bore-sprit; I did flame diſtinctly.

Prosp. My brave Spirit!
Who was so firm, so conſtant, that this coil did not infect his Reason?

Ariel. Not a Soul
But felt a Feaver of the Mind, and play'd some tricks of desperation: all, but Mariners, plung'd in the foaming brine, and quit the Vessel; the Duke's Son, *Ferdinand*, with hair upſtairing (more like Reeds than Hair) was the firſt Man that leap'd; cry'd, Hell is empty, and all the Devils are here.

Prosp. Why that's my Spirit;
But was not this nigh Shore?

Ariel. Close by, my Maſter.

Pros. But, *Ariel*, are they safe?

Ariel. Not a hair perisht.
In Troops I have disper'd them round this Isle.
The Duke's Son I have landed by himself, whom I have left warming the air with sighs, in an odde angle of the Isle, and sitting, his arms he folded in this sad knot.

Prosp. Say how thou haſt dispos'd the Mariners of the Duke's Ship, and all the reſt of the Fleet.

Ariel. Safely in Harbour
Is the Duke's Ship, in the deep Nook, where once thou call'dſt
Me up at Midnight to fetch Dew from the
Still vext *Bermoothes*, there she's hid,
The Mariners all under hatches ſtow'd,
Whom, with a charm, join'd to their suffer'd labour,
I have left asleep, and for the reſt o' th' Fleet
(Which I disperſt) they all have met again,
And are upon the *Mediterranean* Float,
Bound sadly home for *Italy*;
Supposing that they saw the Duke's Ship wrackt,
And his great person perish.
 Prosp. Ariel, thy charge
Exactly is perform'd, but there's more work:
What is the time o' th' day?
 Ariel. Paſt the mid-season.
 Prosp. At leaſt two Glasses: the time 'tween six and now muſt
by us both be spent moſt preciously.
 Ariel. Is there more toyl? since thou doſt give me pains, let me
remember thee what thou haſt promis'd, which is not yet perform'd
me.
 Prosp. How now, *Moodie?*
What is't thou canſt demand?
 Ariel. My liberty.
 Prosp. Before the time be out? no more.
 Ariel. I prethee!
Remember I have done thee faithful service,
Told thee no lyes, made thee no miſtakings,
Serv'd without or grudge, or grumblings:
Thou didſt promise to bate me a full year.
 Prosp. Doſt thou forget
From what a torment I did free thee?
 Ariel. No.
 Prosp. Thou doſt, and think'ſt it much to tread the Ooze
Of the salt deep:
To run againſt the sharp wind of the North,
To do my business in the Veins of the Earth,
When it is bak'd with Froſt.
 Ariel. I do not, Sir.
 Prosp. Thou ly'ſt, malignant thing! haſt thou forgot the foul
Witch *Sycorax*, who with Age and Envy was grown into a Hoop?
haſt thou forgot her?
 Ariel. No, Sir!

164

Prosp. Thou haſt; where was she born? speak, tell me.

Ariel. Sir, in *Argier*.

Prosp. Oh, was she so! I muſt
Once every Month recount what thou haſt been, which thou for-
getteſt. This damn'd Witch *Sycorax* for mischiefs manifold, and
sorceries too terrible to enter humane hearing, from *Argier* thou
knowſt was banisht: but for one thing she did, they would not take
her life: is not this true?

Ariel. I Sir.

Prosp. This blew-ey'd Hag was hither brought with child,
And here was left by th' Saylors, thou, my slave,
As thou report'ſt thy self, waſt then her servant,
And 'cause thou waſt a spirit too delicate
To aʦt her earthy and abhorr'd commands;
Refusing her grand Heſts, she did confine thee,
By help of her more potent Miniſters,
(In her unmitigable rage) into a cloven Pine,
Within whose rift imprison'd, thou didſt painfully
Remain a dozen years; within which space she dy'd,
And left thee there; where thou didſt vent thy
Groans, as faſt as Mill-wheels ſtrike.
Then was this Isle (save for two Brats, which she did
Litter here, the brutish *Caliban*, and his twin Siſter,
Two freckel'd-hag-born Whelps) not honour'd with
A humane shape.

Ariel. Yes! *Caliban* her Son, and *Sycorax* his Siſter.

Prosp. Dull thing, I say so; he, that *Caliban*, and she that *Sycorax*,
whom I now keep in service. Thou beſt knowſt what torment I did
find thee in, thy groans did make Wolves howl, and penetrate the
breaſts of ever angry Bears, it was a torment to lay upon the damn'd,
which *Sycorax* could ne're again undo: It was my Art, when I arriv'd,
and heard thee, that made the Pine to gape and let thee out.

Ariel. I thank thee, Maſter.

Prosp. If thou more murmureſt, I will rend an Oak,
And peg thee in his knotty Entrails, till thou
Haſt howld away twelve Winters more.

Ariel. Pardon, Maſter.
I will be correspondent to command, and be
A gentle spirit.

Prosp. Do so, and after two days I'll discharge thee.

Ariel. That's my noble Maſter.
What shall I do? say? what? what shall I do?

Prosp. Be subjeʦt to no sight but mine; invisible to

Every eye-ball else: hence with diligence.
My Daughter wakes. Anon thou shalt know more.   [*Ex*. Ariel.
Thou haſt slept well my child.

Mir. The sadness of your ſtory put heaviness in me.

Prosp. Shake it off; come on, I'le now call *Caliban*, my Slave,
Who never yields us a kind answer.

Mir. 'Tis a creature, Sir, I do not love to look on.

Prosp. But as 'tis, we cannot miss him; he does make our Fire,
fetch in our Wood, and serve in Offices that profit us: What hoa!
Slave! *Caliban!* thou Earth thou, speak.

Calib. *within*. There's Wood enough within.

Prosp. Come forth, I say there's other business for thee.
Come thou Tortoise, when?   [*Enter* Ariel.
Fine apparition, my quaint *Ariel*,
Hark in thy ear.

Ariel. My Lord it shall be done.   [*Exit*.

Prosp. Thou poisonous Slave, got by the Devil himself upon thy
wicked Dam, come forth.   [*Enter* Caliban.

Calib. As wicked Dew, as e're my Mother brush'd with Raven's
Feather from unwholsome Fens, drop on you both: A South-weſt
blow on you, and bliſter you all o're.

Prosp. For this besure, to night thou shalt have Cramps, side-
ſtitches, that shall pen thy breath up; Urchins shall prick thee till
thou bleed'ſt: thou shalt be pinch'd as thick as Honey-Combs, each
pinch more ſtinging than the Bees which made 'em.

Calib. I muſt eat my dinner: this Island's mine by *Sycorax* my
Mother, which thou took'ſt from me. When thou cam'ſt first, thou
ſtroak'ſt me, and mad'ſt much of me, would'ſt give me Water with
Berries in't, and teach me how to name the bigger Light, and how
the less, that burn by day and night; and then I lov'd thee, and
shew'd thee all the qualities of the Isle, the fresh-Springs, brine-
Pits, barren places, and fertil. Curs'd be I, that I did so: All the
Charms of *Sycorax*, Toads, Beetles, Batts, light on thee, for I am all
the Subjeĉts that thou haſt. I first was mine own Lord; and here
thou ſtay'ſt me in this hard Rock, whiles thou doſt keep me from the
reſt o' th' Island.

Prosp. Thou moſt lying Slave, whom ſtripes may move, not
kindness: I have us'd thee (filth that thou art) with humane care,
and lodg'd thee in mine own Cell, till thou didſt seek to violate the
honour of my Children.

Calib. Oh ho, Oh ho, would t'had been done: thou did'ſt prevent
me, I had peopl'd else this Isle with *Calibans*.

Prosp. Abhor'd Slave!

Who ne're would any print of goodness take, being capable of all
ill: I pity'd thee, took pains to make thee speak, taught thee each
hour one thing or other; when thou didst not (Savage) know thy own
meaning, but would'st gabble, like a thing most brutish, I endow'd
thy purposes with words which made them known: But thy wild
race (though thou did'st learn) had that in't, which good Natures
could not abide to be with: therefore wast thou deservedly pent up
into this Rock.

    Calib. You taught me language, and my profit by it is, that I
know to curse: the red botch rid you for learning me your language.

    Prosp. Hag-seed hence!
Fetch us in fewel, and be quick
To answer other business: shrugst thou (malice)
If thou neglectest or dost unwillingly what I command,
I'll wrack thee with old Cramps, fill all thy bones with
Aches, make thee roar, that Beasts shall tremble
At thy Din.

    Calib. No prethee!
I must obey. His Art is of such power,
It would control my Dam's God, *Setebos,*
And make a Vassal of him.

    Prosp. So Slave, hence. [*Exeunt* Prospero *and* Caliban *severally.*

                Enter Dorinda.

    Dor. Oh Sister! what have I beheld?
    Mir. What is it moves you so?
    Dor. From yonder Rock,
As I my Eyes cast down upon the Seas,
The whistling winds blew rudely on my face,
And the waves roar'd; at first I thought the War
Had been between themselves, but strait I spy'd
A huge great Creature.
    Mir. O you mean the Ship.
    Dor. Is't not a Creature then? it seem'd alive.
    Mir. But what of it?
    Dor. This floating Ram did bear his Horns above;
All ty'd with Ribbands, ruffling in the wind,
Sometimes he nodded down his head a while,
And then the Waves did heave him to the Moon;
He clamb'ring to the top of all the Billows,
And then again he curtsy'd down so low,
I could not see him: till, at last, all side long
With a great crack his belly burst in pieces.

Mir. There all had perisht
Had not my Father's magick Art reliev'd them.
But, Sifter, I have ftranger news to tell you;
In this great Creature there were other Creatures,
And shortly we may chance to see that thing,
Which you have heard my Father call, a man.
  Dor. But what is that? for yet he never told me.
  Mir. I know no more than you: but I have heard
My Father say we Women were made for him.
  Dor. What, that he should eat us, sifter?
  Mir. No sure, you see my Father is a man, and yet
He does us good. I would he were not old.
  Dor. Methinks indeed it would be finer, if we two
Had two young Fathers.
  Mir. No Sifter, no, if they were young, my Father
Said that we muft call them Brothers.
  Dor. But pray how does it come that we two are not Brothers
then, and have not Beards like him?
  Mir. Now I confess you pose me.
  Dor. How did he come to be our Father too?
  Mir. I think he found us when we both were little, and grew
within the ground.
  Dor. Why could he not find more of us? Pray sifter let you and I
look up and down one day, to find some little ones for us to play
with.
  Mir. Agreed; but now we muft go in. This is the hour
Wherein my Father's Charm will work,
Which seizes all who are in open Air:
Th' effect of his great Art I long to see,
Which will perform as much as Magick can.
  Dor. And I, methinks, more long to see a Man.   [*Exeunt.*

ACT II.

Enter Alonzo, Antonio, Gonzalo, *Attendants.*

Gonz. **B**Eseech your Grace be merry; you have cause, so have
we all, of joy for our ftrange scape: then wisely, good
Sir, weigh our sorrow with our comfort.
  Alonzo. Prithee peace! you cram these words into my Ears
againft my ftomack, how can I rejoyce, when my dear Son, perhaps
this very moment, is made a meal to some ftrange Fish?

Ant. Sir, he may live,
I saw him beat the billows under him, and ride upon their backs;
he trod the Water, whose enmity he flung aside, and breasted the
most swoln surge that met him, his bold head 'bove the contentious
waves he kept, and oar'd himself with his strong arms to shore, I do
not doubt he came alive to land.

Alonz. No, no, he's gone, and you and I, *Antonio*, were those who
caus'd his death.

Ant. How could we help it?

Alonz. Then, then, we should have helpt it, when thou betrayedst
thy Brother *Prospero*, and *Mantua's* Infant, Sovereign to my power:
And when I, too ambitious, took by force another's right; then lost
we *Ferdinand*, then forfeited our Navy to this Tempest.

Ant. Indeed we first broke truce with Heav'n;
You to the waves an Infant Prince expos'd,
And on the waves have lost an only Son;
I did usurp my Brother's fertile lands, and now
Am cast upon this desert Isle.

Gonz. These, Sir, 'tis true, were crimes of a black Dye,
But both of you have made amends to Heav'n,
By your late Voyage into *Portugal*,
Where, in defence of Christianity,
Your Valour has repuls'd the *Moors* of *Spain*.

Alonz. O name it not, *Gonzalo*.
No act but penitence can expiate guilt,
Must we teach Heaven what prize to set on Murthers?
What rate on lawless power, and wild ambition?
Or dare we traffick with the Powers above,
And sell by weight a good deed for a bad?   [*Musick within.*

Gonz. Musick! and in the air! sure we are shipwrackt on the
Dominions of some merry Devil.

Ant. This Isle's inchanted ground, for I have heard
Swift voices flying by my Ear, and groans
Of lamenting Ghosts.

Alonz. I pull'd a Tree, and Blood pursu'd my hand; O Heaven!
deliver me from this dire place, and all the after actions of my Life
shall mark my penitence and my bounty.
Heark!   [*A Dialogue within sung in parts.*
The sounds approach us.

   1. *D.* Where does proud Ambition dwell?
   2.   In the lowest Rooms of Hell.
   1.   Of the damn'd who leads the Host?
   2.   He who did oppress the most.

169

1.   Who such Troops of damned brings?

2.   Moſt are led by fighting Kings.
Kings who did Crowns unjuſtly get,
Here on burning Thrones are set.

Chor. Kings who did Crowns, *&c.*

Ant. Do you hear, Sir, how they lay our Crimes before us?

Gonz. Do evil Spirits imitate the good,
In shewing men their sins?

Alonz. But in a different way,
Those warn from doing, these upbraid 'em done.

1.   Who are the Pillars of Ambition's Court?

2.   Grim Deaths and Scarlet Murthers it support.

1.   What lyes beneath her Feet?

2.   Her footſteps tread,
On Orphans tender breaſts, and Brothers dead.

1.   Can Heaven permit such Crimes should be
Rewarded with felicity?

2.   Oh no! uneasily their Crowns they wear,
And their own guilt amidſt their Guards they fear.
Cares when they wake their Minds unquiet keep,
And we in visions lord it o're their sleep.

Cho. Oh no! uneasily their Crowns, *&c.*

Alonz. See where they come in horrid shapes!

Enter the two that sung, in the shape of Devils, placing themselves at two corners of the Stage.

Ant. Sure Hell is open to devour us quick.

1. *D.* Say Brother, shall we bear these mortals hence?

2.   Firſt let us shew the shapes of their offence.

1.   We'll muſter then their crimes on either side:
Appear! appear! their firſt begotten, Pride.   *[Enter Pride.*

Pride. Lo! I am here, who led their hearts aſtray,
And to Ambition did their minds betray.   *[Enter Fraud.*

Fraud. And guileful Fraud does next appear,
Their wandring ſteps who led,
When they from virtue fled,
And in my crooked paths their course did ſteer.   *[Enter Rapine.*

Rap. From Fraud to Force they soon arrive,
Where Rapine did their actions drive.   *[Enter Murther.*

Murd. There long they cannot ſtay,
Down the deep precipice they run,
And to secure what they have done,
To murder bend their way.

170

After which they fall into a round encompassing the Duke, &c. Singing.

> *Around, around, we pace*
> *About this cursed place,*
> *Whilst thus we compass in*
> *These mortals and their sin.*   *Dance.*

                                                    [*All the spirits vanish.*

Ant. Heav'n has heard me! they are vanish'd.

Alonz. But they have left me all unman'd;
I feel my Sinews slacken'd with the fright,
And a cold sweat trills down o're all my Limbs,
As if I were dissolving into Water.
  O *Prospero!* my crimes 'gainst thee sit heavy on my heart.

Ant. And mine, 'gainst him and young *Hippolito.*

Gonz. Heav'n have mercy on the penitent!

Alonz. Lead from this cursed ground;
The Seas, in all their rage, are not so dreadful.
This is the Region of despair and death.

Gonz. Shall we not seek some food?

Alonz. Beware all fruit but what the birds have peid,
The shadows of the Trees are poisonous too:
A secret venom slides from every branch.
My conscience doth distract me, O my Son!
Why do I speak of eating or repose,
Before I know thy fortune?   [*Exeunt.*

Enter Ferdinand, *and Ariel, invisible, playing and singing.*

Ariel's *Song.*

> *Come unto these yellow sands*
> *And then take hands.*
> *Curtsy'd when you have and kiss'd,*
> *The wild waves whist.*
> *Foot it featly here and there, and sweet sprights bear*
> *the Burthen.*   [*Burthen dispersedly.*
> *Hark! hark! Bow-waugh; the watch-dogs bark,*
> *Bow-waugh.*

Ariel. Hark! hark! I hear the strain of strutting Chanticleer
> *Cry Cock a doodle do.*

Ferd. Where should this Musick be? i' th' Air, or th' Earth?
It sounds no more, and sure it waits upon some God
O' th' Island, sitting on a Bank, weeping against the Duke
My Father's wrack. This musick hover'd o're me

On the waters, allaying both their fury and my passion
With charming Airs; thence I have follow'd it (or it
Hath drawn me rather) but 'tis gone;
No, it begins again.

Ariel. Song.

> *Full Fathoms five thy Father lyes,*
> *   Of his bones is Coral made:*
> *Those are Pearls that were his eyes,*
> *   Nothing of him that does fade:*
> *But does suffer a Sea-change*
> *Into something rich and strange:*
> *Sea-Nymphs hourly ring his [knell,]*
> *Hark now I hear 'em, Ding dong Bell.*

[Burthen, Ding dong.

Ferd. The mournful Ditty mentions my drown'd Father,
This is no mortal business, nor a sound which the
Earth owns: I hear it now before me,
However I will on and follow it.   [*Ex.* Ferd. *and* Ariel.

Enter Stephano, Mustacho, Ventoso.

Vent. The Runlet of Brandy was a loving Runlet, and floated after us out of pure pity.

Must. This kind Bottle, like an old acquaintance, swam after it. And this Scollop-shell is all our Plate now.

Vent. 'Tis well we have found something since we landed. I prethee fill a soop, and let it go round. Where hast thou laid the Runlet?

Must. I' th' hollow of an old Tree.

Vent. Fill apace, We cannot live long in this barren Island, and we may Take a soop before death, as well as others drink At our Funerals.

Must. This is prize-Brandy, we steal Custom, and it costs nothing. Let's have two rounds more.

Vent. Master, what have you sav'd?

Steph. Just nothing but my self.

Vent. This works comfortably on a cold stomach.

Steph. Fill's another round.

Vent. Look! *Mustacho* weeps. Hang losses as long as we have Brandy left. Prithee leave weeping.

Steph. He sheds his Brandy out of his eyes: he shall drink no more.

Must. This will be a doleful day with old *Bess*. She gave me a gilt Nutmeg at parting. That's lost too. But as you say, hang losses. Prithee fill agen.

Vent. Beshrew thy heart for putting me in mind of thy Wife, I had not thought of mine else, Nature will shew it self, I must melt. I prithee fill agen, my Wife's a good old jade, And has but one eye left: but she'll weep out that too, When she hears that I am dead.

Steph. Would you were both hang'd for putting me in thought of mine. But well, If I return not in seven years to my own Country, she may marry agen: and 'tis from this Island thither at least seven Years swimming.

Must. O at least, having no help of Boat nor Bladders.

Steph. Whoe'er she marries, poor Soul, she'll weep a nights when she thinks of *Stephano*.

Vent. But Master, sorrow is dry! there's for you agen.

Steph. A Mariner had e'en as good be a Fish as a Man, but for the comfort we get ashore: O for any old dry Wench now I am wet.

Must. Poor heart! that would soon make you dry agen: but all is barren in this Isle: here we may lye at Hull till the Wind blow Nore and by South, e're we can cry a Sail, a Sail, at sight of a white Apron. And therefore here's another soop to comfort us.

Vent. This Isle's our own, that's our comfort, for the Duke, the Prince, and all their train are perished.

Must. Our Ship is sunk, and we can never get home agen: we must e'en turn Salvages, and the next that catches his fellow may eat him.

Vent. No, no, let us have a Government; for if we live well and orderly, Heav'n will drive the Shipwracks ashore to make us all rich, therefore let us carry good Consciences, and not eat one another.

Steph. Whoever eats any of my subjects, I'le break out his Teeth with my Scepter: for I was Master at Sea, and will be Duke on Land: you *Mustacho* have been my Mate, and shall be my Vice-Roy.

Vent. When you are Duke you may chuse your Vice-Roy; but I am a free Subject in a new Plantation, and will have no Duke without my voice. And so fill me the other soop.

Steph. whispering. Ventoso, dost thou hear, I will advance thee, prithee give me thy voice.

Vent. I'le have no whisperings to corrupt the Election; and to show that I have no private ends, I declare aloud, that I will be Vice-Roy, or I'le keep my voice for my self.

Must. Stephano, hear me, I will speak for the people, because they are few, or rather none in the Isle to speak for themselves. Know then, that to prevent the farther shedding of Christian blood, we are all content *Ventoso* shall be Vice-Roy, upon condition I may be Vice-Roy over him. Speak good people, are you all agreed? What, no man answer? Well, you may take their silence for consent.

Vent. You speak for the people, *Mustacho?* I'le speak for 'em, and declare generally with one voice, one word and all; That there shall be no Vice-Roy but the Duke, unless I be he.

Must. You declare for the people, who never saw your face! Cold Iron shall decide it.   [*Both draw.*

Steph. Hold, loving Subjects: we will have no Civil War during our Reign: I do hereby appoint you both to be my Vice-Roys over the whole Island.

Both. Agreed! agreed!

Enter Trincalo *with a great bottle, half drunk.*

Vent. How! *Trincalo* our brave Bosen!

Must. He reels: can he be drunk with Sea-water?

Trinc. sings. I shall no more to Sea, to Sea,
        Here I shall dye ashore.
This is a very scurvy Tune to sing at a man's funeral,
But here's my comfort.   [*Drinks.*

Sings. The Master, the Swabber, the Gunner, and I,
        The Surgeon, and his Mate,
    Lov'd *Mall, Meg,* and *Marrian,* and *Margery,*
        But none of us car'd for *Kate.*
    For she had a tongue with a tang,
    Wou'd cry to a Saylor, go hang:
    She lov'd not the favour of Tar nor of Pitch,
    Yet a Taylor might scratch her where e're she did itch.

This is a scurvy Tune too, but here's my comfort agen.   [*Drinks.*

Steph. We have got another subject now; welcome, Welcome into our Dominions!

Trinc. What Subject, or what Dominions? here's old Sack Boys: the King of good fellows can be no subject. I will be Old *Simon* the King.

Must. Hah, old Boy! how didst thou scape?

Trinc. Upon a Butt of Sack, Boys, which the Saylors Threw overboard: but are you alive, hoa! for I will Tipple with no Ghosts till I'm dead: thy hand *Mustacho,* And thine *Ventoso;* the storm has done its worst: *Stephano* alive too! give thy Bosen thy hand, Master.

Vent. You muſt kiss it then, for, I muſt tell you, we have chosen him Duke in a full Assembly.

Trinc. A Duke! where? what's he Duke of?

Muſt. Of this Island, Man. Oh *Trincalo* we are all made, the Island's empty; all's our own, Boy; and we will speak to his Grace for thee, that thou may'ſt be as great as we are.

Trinc. You great? what the Devil are you?

Vent. We two are Vice-Roys over all the Island; and when we are weary of Governing thou shalt succeed us.

Trinc. Do you hear, *Ventoso*, I will succeed you in both your places before you enter into 'em.

Steph. *Trincalo*, sleep and be sober; and make no more uproars in my Country.

Trinc. Why, what are you, Sir, what are you?

Steph. What I am, I am by free election, and you *Trincalo* are not your self; but we pardon your firſt fault,
Because it is the firſt day of our Reign.

Trinc. Umph, were matters carried so swimmingly againſt me, whilſt I was swimming, and saving my self for the good of the People of this Island.

Muſt. Art thou mad, *Trincalo*, wilt thou diſturb a setled Government?

Trinc. I say this Island shall be under *Trincalo*, or it shall be a Common-wealth; and so my Bottle is my Buckler, and so I draw my Sword.   [*Draws.*

Vent. Ah *Trincalo*, I thought thou hadſt had more grace,
Than to rebel againſt thy old Maſter,
And thy two lawful Vice-Roys.

Muſt. Wilt not thou take advice of two that ſtand
For old Counsellors here, where thou art a meer ſtranger
To the Laws of the Country.

Trinc. I'll have no Laws.

Vent. Then Civil-War begins.   [*Vent. Muſt.* draw.

Steph. Hold, hold, I'le have no blood shed,
My Subjects are but few: let him make a rebellion
By himself; and a Rebel, I Duke *Stephano* declare him:
Vice-Roys, come away.

Trinc. And Duke *Trincalo* declares, that he will make open War wherever he meets thee or thy Vice-Roys. [*Ex.* Steph. Muſt. Vent.

Enter Caliban *with wood upon his Back.*

Trinc. Hah! who have we here?

Calib. All the infections that the Sun sucks up from Fogs, Fens,

Flats, on *Prospero* fall; and make him by inch-meal a Disease: his spirits hear me, and yet I needs muſt curse, but they'l not pinch, fright me with Urchin shows, pitch me i' th' mire, nor lead me in the dark out of my way, unless he bid 'em: but for every trifle he sets them on me; sometimes like Baboons they mow and chatter at me, and often bite me; like Hedge-hogs then they mount their prickles at me, tumbling before me in my barefoot way. Sometimes I am all wound about with Adders, who with their cloven tongues hiss me to madness. Hah! yonder ſtands one of his spirits sent to torment me.

Trinc. What have we here, a man, or a fish?
This is some Monſter of the Isle, were I in *England*,
As once I was, and had him painted;
Not a Holy-day fool there but would give me
Six-pence for the sight of him; well, if I could make
Him tame, he were a present for an Emperour.
Come hither pretty Monſter, I'le do thee no harm.
Come hither!

Calib. Torment me not;
I'le bring thee Wood home faſter.

Trinc. He talks none of the wiseſt, but I'le give him
A dram o' th' Bottle, that will clear his underſtanding.
Come on your ways Maſter Monſter, open your mouth.
How now, you perverse Moon-calf! what,
I think you cannot tell who is your friend!
Open your chops, I say.   [*Pours Wine down his throat.*

Calib. This is a brave God, and bears cœleſtial Liquor,
I'le kneel to him.

Trinc. He is a very hopeful Monſter; Monſter what say'ſt thou, art thou content to turn civil and sober, as I am? for then thou shalt be my subjeĉt.

Calib. I'le swear upon that Bottle to be true; for the liquor is not Earthly: didſt thou not drop from Heaven?

Trinc. Only out of the Moon, I was the man in her when time was. By this light, a very shallow Monſter.

Calib. I'll shew thee every fertile inch i' th' Isle, and kiss thy foot:
I prithee be my God, and let me drink.   [*Drinks agen.*

Trinc. Well drawn, Monſter, in good faith.

Calib. I'le shew thee the beſt Springs, I'le pluck thee Berrıes,
I'le fish for thee, and get thee wood enough:
A curse upon the Tyrant whom I serve, I'le bear him
No more ſticks, but follow thee.

Trinc. The poor Monſter is loving in his drink.

Calib. I prithee let me bring thee where Crabs grow,

And I, with my long Nails, will dig thee Pig-nuts,
Shew thee a Jay's Nest, and instruct thee how to snare
The Marmazet; I'le bring thee to cluster'd Filberds;
Wilt thou go with me?

    Trinc. This Monster comes of a good natur'd Race;
Is there no more of thy Kin in this Island?

    Calib. Divine, here is but one besides my self;
My Lovely Sister, beautiful and bright as the full Moon.

    Trinc. Where is she?

    Calib. I left her clambring up a hollow Oak,
And plucking thence the droping Honey-Combs.
Say my King, shall I call her to thee?

    Trinc. She shall swear upon the Bottle too.
If she proves handsome she is mine: here Monster,
Drink again for thy good news; thou shalt speak
A good word for me.   [*Gives him the Bottle.*

    Calib. Farewel, Old Master, farewel, farewel.

    Sings. No more Damms I'le make for Fish,
             Nor fetch in firing at requiring,
             Nor scrape Trencher, nor wash Dish;
             Ban, ban, *Cackaliban*
             Has a new Master, get a new man.
             Heigh-day, Freedom, freedom!

    Trinc. Here's two Subjects got already, the Monster,
And his Sister: Well, Duke *Stephano*, I say, and say agen,
Wars will ensue, and so I drink.   [*Drinks.*
From this worshipful Monster, and Mistriss,
Monster his Sister,
I'le lay claim to his Island by Alliance:
Monster, I say thy Sister shall be my Spouse:
Come away Brother Monster, I'le lead thee to my Butt
And drink her health.   [*Exeunt.*

             Enter Prospero *alone.*

    Prosp. 'Tis not yet fit to let my Daughters know I kept
The Infant Duke of *Mantua* so near them in this Isle,
Whose Father dying bequeath'd him to my care,
Till my false Brother (when he design'd t' Usurp
My Dukedome from me) expos'd him to that fate
He meant for me. By calculation of his birth
I saw death threat'ning him, if, till some time were
Past, he should behold the face of any Woman:
And now the danger's nigh: *Hippolito!*   [*Enter* Hippolito.

Hip. Sir, I attend your pleasure.

Prosp. How I have lov'd thee from thy infancy,
Heav'n knows, and thou thy self canſt bear me witness,
Therefore accuse not me for thy reſtraint.

Hip. Since I knew life, you've kept me in a Rock,
And you this day have hurry'd me from thence,
Only to change my Prison, not to free me.
I murmur not, but I may wonder at it.

Prosp. O gentle youth, Fate waits for thee abroad,
A black Star threatens thee, and death unseen
Stands ready to devour thee.

Hip. You taught me not to fear him in any of his shapes:
Let me meet death rather than be a Prisoner.

Prosp. 'Tis pity he should seize thy tender youth.

Hip. Sir, I have often heard you say, no creature liv'd
Within this Isle, but those which Man was Lord of,
Why then should I fear?

Prosp. But here are creatures which I nam'd not to thee,
Who share man's sovereignty by Natures Laws,
And oft depose him from it.

Hip. What are those Creatures, Sir?

Prosp. Those dangerous enemies of men call'd women.

Hip. Women! I never heard of them before.
But have I Enemies within this Isle, and do you
Keep me from them? Do you think that I want
Courage to encounter them?

Prosp. No courage can resiſt 'em.

Hip. How then have you, Sir,
Liv'd so long unharm'd among them?

Prosp. O they despise old age, and spare it for that reason:
It is below their conqueſt, their fury falls
Alone upon the young.

Hip. Why then the fury of the young shall fall on them again.
Pray turn me loose upon 'em: but, good Sir,
What are women like?

Prosp. Imagine something between young men and Angels:
Fatally beauteous, and have killing Eyes;
Their voices charm beyond the Nightingales;
They are all enchantment; those who once behold 'em,
Are made their slaves for ever.

Hip. Then I will wink and fight with 'em.

Prosp. 'Tis but in vain, for when your eyes are shut,
They through the lids will shine, and pierce your soul:
178

Absent, they will be present to you.
They'll haunt you in your very sleep.
    Hip. Then I'le revenge it on them when I wake.
    Prosp. You are without all possibility of revenge;
They are so beautiful that you can ne're attempt,
Nor wish to hurt them.
    Hip. Are they so beautiful?
    Prosp. Calm sleep is not so soft, nor Winter Suns,
Nor Summer Shades so pleasant.
    Hip. Can they be fairer than the Plumes of Swans?
Or more delightful than the Peacocks Feathers?
Or than the gloss upon the necks of Doves?
Or have more various beauty than the Rain-bow?
These I have seen, and without danger wondered at.
    Prosp. All these are far below 'em: Nature made
Nothing but Woman dangerous and fair:
Therefore if you should chance to see 'em,
Avoid 'em ſtreight, I charge you.
    Hip. Well, since you say they are so dangerous.
I'le so far shun 'em as I may with safety of the
Unblemish'd honour which you taught me.
But let 'em not provoke me, for I'm sure I shall
Not then forbear them.
    Prosp. Go in and read the Book I gave you laſt.
To morrow I may bring you better news.
    Hip. I shall obey you, Sir.   [*Exit* Hippolito.
    Prosp. So, so; I hope this lesson has secur'd him,
For I have been conſtrain'd to change his Lodging
From yonder Rock where firſt I bred him up,
And here have brought him home to my own Cell,
Because the Shipwrack happen'd near his Mansion.
I hope he will not ſtir beyond his limits,
For hitherto he has been all obedience:
The Planets seem to smile on my designs,
And yet there is one sullen Cloud behind,
I would it were disperſt.   [*Enter* Miranda *and* Dorinda.
How, my daughters! I thought I had inſtructed
Them enough: Children! retire;
Why do you walk this way?
    Mir. It is within our bounds, Sir.
    Prosp. But both take heed, that path is very dangerous.
Remember what I told you.
    Dor. Is the man that way, Sir?

179

Prosp. All that you can imagine ill is there:
The curled Lyon, and the rugged Bear
Are not so dreadful as that man.
    Mir. Oh me, why ſtay we here then?
    Dor. I'le keep far enough from his Den, I warrant him.
    Mir. But you have told me, Sir, you are a man,
And yet you are not dreadful.
    Prosp. I child! But I am a tame man: old men are tame
By Nature, but all the danger lies in a wild
Young man.
    Dor. Do they run wild about the woods?
    Prosp. No, they are wild within Doors, in Chambers,
And in Closets.
    Dor. But Father, I would ſtroak 'em, and make 'em gentle,
Then sure they would not hurt me.
    Prosp. You muſt not truſt them, Child: no woman can come
Near 'em but she feels a pain full nine Months:
Well I muſt in, for new affairs require my
Presence: Be you, *Miranda*, your Siſter's Guardian. [*Exit* Prospero.
    Dor. Come, Siſter, shall we walk the other way,
The man will catch us else, we have but two legs,
And he perhaps has four.
    Mir. Well, Siſter, though he have, yet look about you
And we shall spy him e're he comes too near us.
    Dor. Come back, that way is towards his Den.
    Mir. Let me alone: I'le venture firſt, for sure he can
Devour but one of us at once.
    Dor. How dare you venture?
    Mir. We'll find him sitting like a Hare in's Form
And he shall not see us.
    Dor. I, but you know my Father charg'd us both.
    Mir. But who shall tell him on't? We'll keep each
Others Counsel.
    Dor. I dare not for the world.
    Mir. But how shall we hereafter shun him, if we do not
Know him firſt?
    Dor. Nay I confess I would fain see him too. I find it in my
Nature, because my Father has forbidden me.
    Mir. I, there's it, Siſter, if he had said nothing I had been quiet.
Go softly, and if you see him firſt, be quick and becken me away.
    Dor. Well, if he does catch me, I'le humble my self to him,
And ask him pardon, as I do my Father,
When I have done a fault.
180

THE TEMPEST

Mir. And if I can but scape with life, I had rather be in pain
nine Months, as my Father threatn'd, than loose my longing.

[*Exeunt.*

The Scene changes, and discovers Hippolito *in a Cave walking:
his face from the Audience*

Hip. Prospero has often said that Nature makes
Nothing in vain: Why then are women made?
Are they to suck the poyson of the Earth,
As gaudy colour'd Serpents are? I'le ask that
Question, when next I see him here.

Enter Miranda *and* Dorinda *peeping*

Dor. O Sister, there it is; it walks about like one of us.
Mir. I, just so; and has legs as we have too.
Hip. It strangely puzzles me: yet 'tis most likely
Women are somewhat between men and spirits.
Dor. Heark! it talks, sure this is not it my Father meant,
For this is just like one of us: methinks I am not half
So much afraid on't as I was: see, now it turns this way.
Mir. Heav'n! what a goodly thing it is?
Dor. I'le go nearer it.
Mir. O no, 'tis dangerous, Sister! I'le go to it.
I would not for the world that you should venture.
My Father charg'd me to secure you from it.
Dor. I warrant you this is a tame man, dear Sister,
He'll not hurt me, I see it by his looks.
Mir. Indeed he will! but go back, and he shall eat me first:
Fye, are you not asham'd to be so much inquisitive?
Dor. You chide me for't, and wou'd give your self.
Mir. Come back, or I will tell my Father.
Observe how he begins to stare already.
I'll meet the danger first, and then call you.
Dor. Nay, Sister, you shall never vanquish me in kindness.
I'le venture you, no more than you will me.
Prosp. [*Within.*] Miranda, Child, where are you?
Mir. Do you not hear my Father call? Go in.
Dor. 'Twas you he nam'd, not me: I will but say my Prayers,
And follow you immediately.
Mr. Well, Sister, you'l repent it.   [*Exit* Miranda.
Dor. Though I dye for't, I must have th' other peep.
Hip. [*Seeing her.*] What thing is that? sure 'tis some Infant of the
Sun, dress'd in its Father's gayest Beams, and comes to play with

Birds: my sight is dazl'd, and yet I find I'm loth to shut my Eyes.
I must go nearer it—but stay a while,
May it not be that beauteous murderer, Woman,
Which I was charg'd to shun? Speak, what art thou?
Thou shining Vision!

Dor. Alass! I know not: but I'm told I am a Woman.
Do not hurt me, pray, fair thing.

Hip. I'd sooner tear my eyes out, than consent to do you any harm; though I was told a Woman was my Enemy.

Dor. I never knew what 'twas to be an Enemy, nor can I e're prove so to that which looks like you: for though I have been charg'd by him (whom yet I never disobey'd) to shun your presence, yet I'd rather dye than loose it; therefore, I hope, you will not have the heart to hurt me: though I fear you are a man, that dangerous Thing of which I have been warn'd: pray tell me what you are?

Hip. I must confess, I was inform'd I am a man,
But if I fright you, I shall wish I were some other Creature.
I was bid to fear you too.

Dor. Ay me! Heav'n grant we be not poyson to each other!
Alass! can we not meet but we must die?

Hip. I hope not so! for when two poysonous Creatures,
Both of the same kind, meet, yet neither dies.
I've seen two Serpents harmless to each other,
Though they have twin'd into a mutual Knot:
If we have any venome in us, sure, we cannot be more
Poysonous, when we meet, than Serpents are.
You have a hand like mine, may I not gently touch it?
                                                    [*Takes her hand.*

Dor. I've touch'd my Father's and my Sister's hands
And felt no pain; but now, alas! there's something,
When I touch yours, which makes me sigh: just so
I've seen two Turtles mourning when they met;
Yet mine's a pleasing grief; and so methought was theirs;
For still they mourn'd, and still they seem'd to murmur too,
And yet they often met.

Hip. Oh Heavens! I have the same sense too; your hand
Methinks goes through me; I feel at my heart,
And find it pleases, though it pains me.

Prosp. within. Dorinda!

Dor. My Father calls agen, ah, I must leave you.

Hip. Alas, I'm subject to the same command.

Dor. This is my first offence against my Father,
Which he, by severing us, too cruelly does punish.

182

Hip. And this is my first trespass too: but he hath more
Offended truth than we have him:
　He said our meeting would destructive be,
　But I no death but in our parting see.　　*[Exeunt several ways.*

ACT III.

Enter Prospero *and* Miranda.

Prosp. EXcuse it not, *Miranda*, for to you (the elder, and, I
　　thought the more discreet) I gave the conduct of your
Sister's actions.

　Mir. Sir, when you call'd me thence, I did not fail to mind her of
her duty to depart.

　Prosp. How can I think you did remember ners, when you forgot
your own? did you not see the man whom I commanded you to shun?

　Mir. I must confess I saw him at a distance.

　Prosp. Did not his Eyes infect and poyson you?
What alteration found you in your self?

　Mir. I only wondred at a sight so new.

　Prosp. But have you no desire once more to see him?
Come, tell me truly what you think of him?

　Mir. As of the gayest thing I ever saw, so fine, that it appear'd
more fit to be belov'd than fear'd, and seem'd so near my kind, that
I did think I might have call'd it Sister.

　Prosp. You do not love it?

　Mir. How is it likely that I should, except the thing had first
lov'd me?

　Prosp. Cherish those thoughts: you have a gen'rous soul;
And since I see your Mind not apt to take the light
Impressions of a sudden love, I will unfold
A secret to your knowledge.
That Creature which you saw, is of a kind which
Nature made a prop and guide to yours.

　Mir. Why did you then propose him as an object of terrour to my
mind? you never us'd to teach me anything but God-like truths, and
what you said I did believe as sacred.

　Prosp. I fear'd the pleasing form of this young man
Might unawares possess your tender breast,
Which for a nobler Guest I had design'd;
For shortly, my *Miranda*, you shall see another of his kind,

The full blown flower, of which this youth was but the
Op'ning-bud. Go in, and send your Sister to me.
    Mir. Heav'n still preserve you, Sir.   [*Ex.* Miranda.
    Prosp. And make thee fortunate.
Dordina now must be examin'd too concerning this
Late interview. I'm sure unartful truth lies open
In her mind, as Crystal streams their sandy bottom show.
I must take care her love grow not too fast,
For innocence is Love's most fertile soil,
Wherein he soon shoots up and widely spreads,
Nor is that danger which attends *Hippolito* yet overpast.
                            [*Enter* Dorinda.
    Prosp. O, come hither, you have seen a man to day,
Against my strict command.
    Dor. Who I? indeed I saw him but a little, Sir.
    Prosp. Come, come, be clear. your Sister told me all.
    Dor. Did she? truly she would have seen him more than I,
But that I would not let her.
    Prosp. Why so?
    Dor. Because, methought, he would have hurt me less
Than he would her. But if I knew you'd not be angry
With him, I could tell you, Sir, that he was much too blame.
    Prosp.   Hah! was he too blame?
Tell me, with that sincerity I taught you, how you became so bold
to see the man?
    Dor. I hope you will forgive me, Sir, because I did not see him
much till he saw me. Sir, he would needs come in my way, and
star'd, and star'd upon my face; and so I thought I would be re-
veng'd of him, and therefore I gaz'd on him as long; but if I e'er
come near a man again——
    Prosp. I told you he was dangerous; but you would not be
warn'd.
    Dor. Pray be not angry, Sir, if I tell you, you are mistaken in him;
for he did me no great hurt.
    Prosp. But he may do you more harm hereafter.
    Dor. No, Sir, I'm as well as e're I was in all my life,
But that I cannot eat nor drink for thought of him.
That dangerous man runs ever in my mind.
    Prosp. The way to cure you, is no more to see him.
    Dor. Nay pray, Sir, say not so, I promis'd him
To see him once again; and you know, Sir,
You charg'd me I shou'd never break my promise.
    Prosp. Wou'd you see him who did you so much mischief?

Dor. I warrant you I did him as much harm as he did me,
For when I left him, Sir, he sigh'd so as it griev'd
My heart to hear him.

Prosp. Those sighs were poysonous, they infected you:
You say they griev'd you to the heart.

Dor. 'Tis true; but yet his looks and words were gentle.

Prosp. These are the Day-dreams of a maid in love,
But still I fear the worst.

Dor. O fear not him, Sir,
I know he will not hurt you for my sake;
I'll undertake to tye him to a hair,
And lead him hither as my Pris'ner to you.

Prosp. Take heed, *Dorinda*, you may be deceiv'd;
This Creature is of such a Salvage race,
That no mild usage can reclaim his wildness;
But, like a Lyon's whelp bred up by hand,
When least you look for't, Nature will present
The Image of his Fathers bloody Paws,
Wherewith he purvey'd for his couching Queen;
And he will leap into his native fury.

Dor. He cannot change from what I left him, Sir.

Prosp. You speak of him with too much passion; tell me
(And on your duty tell me true, *Dorinda*)
What past betwixt you and that horrid creature?

Dor. How, horrid, Sir? if any else but you should call it so, in-
deed I should be angry.

Prosp. Go too! you are a foolish Girl; but answer to what I ask,
what thought you when you saw it?

Dor. At first it star'd upon me and seem'd wild,
And then I trembled, yet it look'd so lovely, that when
I would have fled away, my feet seem'd fasten'd to the ground,
Then it drew near, and with amazement askt
To touch my hand; which, as a ransom for my life,
I gave: but when he had it, with a furious gripe
He put it to his mouth so eagerly, I was afraid he
Would have swallow'd it.

Prosp. Well, what was his behaviour afterwards?

Dor. He on a sudden grew so tame and gentle,
That he became more kind to me than you are;
Then, Sir, I grew I know not how, and touching his hand
Again, my heart did beat so strong as I lackt breath
To answer what he ask'd.

Prosp. You have been too fond, and I should chide you for it.

Dor. Then send me to that creature to be punisht.

Prosp. Poor Child! thy passion like a lazy Ague
Has seiz'd thy blood, instead of striving thou humour'st
And feed'st thy languishing disease: thou fight'st
The Battels of thy Enemy, and 'tis one part of what
I threatn'd thee, not to perceive thy danger.

Dor. Danger, Sir?
If he would hurt me, yet he knows not how:
He hath no Claws, nor Teeth, nor Horns to hurt me,
But looks about him like a Callow-Bird
Just straggl'd from the Nest: pray trust me, Sir,
To go to him agen.

Prosp. Since you will venture,
I charge you bear your self reserv'dly to him,
Let him not dare to touch your naked hand,
But keep at distance from him.

Dor. This is hard.

Prosp. It is the way to make him love you more;
He will despise you if you grow too kind.

Dor. I'le struggle with my heart to follow this,
But if I lose him by it, will you promise
To bring him back agen?

Prosp. Fear not, *Dorinda*;
But use him ill and he'l be yours for ever.

Dor. I hope you have not couzen'd me agen.   [*Exit* Dorinda.

Prosp. Now my designs are gathering to a head.
My spirits are obedient to my charms.
What, *Ariel!* my servant *Ariel*, where art thou?

Enter Ariel.

Ariel. What wou'd my potent Master? here I am.

Prosp. Thou and thy meaner fellows your last service
Did worthily perform, and I must use you in such another
Work: how goes the day?

Ariel. On the fourth, my Lord, and on the sixth
You said our work should cease.

Prosp. And so it shall;
And thou shalt have the open air at freedom.

Ariel. Thanks my great Lord.

Prosp. But tell me first, my spirit,
How fares the Duke, my Brother, and their followers?

Ariel. Confin'd together, as you gave me order,

186

In the Lime-Grove which weather-fends your Cell;
Within that Circuit up and down they wander,
But cannot ſtir one ſtep beyond their compass.

    Prosp. How do they bear their sorrows?

    Ariel. The two Dukes appear like Men diſtraćted, their
Attendants brim-ful of sorrow mourning over 'em;
But chiefly, he you term'd the good *Gonzalo:*
His tears run down his Beard, like Winter-drops
From Eaves of Reeds, your Vision did so work 'em,
That if you now beheld 'em, your affećtions
Would become tender.

    Prosp. Doſt thou think so, Spirit?

    Ariel. Mine would, Sir, were I humane.

    Prosp. And mine shall:
Haſt thou, who art but air, a touch, a feeling of their
Afflićtions, and shall not I (a man like them, one
Who as sharply relish passions as they) be kindlier
Mov'd than thou art? though they have pierc'd
Me to the quick with injuries, yet with my nobler
Reason 'gainſt my fury I will take part;
The rarer aćtion is in virtue than in vengeance.
Go, my *Ariel*, refresh with needful food their
Famish'd Bodies. With shows and cheerful
Musick comfort 'em.

    Ariel. Presently, Maſter.

    Prosp. With a twinckle, *Ariel.*

    Ariel. Before you can say come and go,
And breath twice, and cry so; so.
Each spirit tripping on his toe,
Shall bring 'em meat with mop and moe,
Do you love me, Maſter, 1 or no?

    Prosp. Dearly, my dainty *Ariel*, but ſtay, spirit;
What is become of my Slave *Caliban*,
And *Sycorax* his Siſter?

    Ariel. Potent Sir!
They have caſt off your service, and revolted
To the wrack'd Mariners, who have already
Parcell'd your Island into Governments.

    Pros. No matter, I have now no need of 'em;
But, spirit, now I ſtay thee on the Wing;
Haſte to perform what I have given in charge:
But see they keep within the bounds I set 'em.

    Ariel. I'll keep 'em in with Walls of Adamant,

Invisible as air to mortal Eyes,
But yet unpassable.
    Prosp. Make haſt then.   *[Exeunt severally.*

                Enter Alonzo, Antonio, Gonzalo.

    Gonz. I am weary, and can go no farther, Sir,
My old Bones ake, here's a Maze trod indeed
Through forth-rights and Meanders, by your Patience
I needs muſt reſt.
    Alonz. Old Lord, I cannot blame thee, who am my self seiz'd
With a weariness to the dulling of my Spirits:
Sit and reſt.   *[They sit.*
Even here I will put off my hope, and keep it no longer
For my Flatterers: he is drown'd whom thus we
Stray to find, and the Sea mocks our fruſtrate
Search on Land: well! let him go.
    Ant. Do not for one repulse forego the purpose
Which you resolv'd t' effeﬅ.
    Alonz. I'm faint with hunger, and muſt despair
Of food, Heav'n hath incens'd the Seas and
Shores againſt us for our crimes.   *[Musick.*
What! Harmony agen, my good Friends, hark!
    Ant. I fear some other horrid apparition.
Give us kind Keepers, Heaven I beseech thee!
    Gonz. 'Tis chearful Musick, this, unlike the firſt;
And seems as 'twere meant t' unbend our cares,
And calm your troubled thoughts.

                Ariel *invisible Sings.*

        Dry those eyes which are o'reflowing,
        All your ſtorms are over-blowing:
        While you in this Isle are bideing,
        You shall feaſt without providing:
        Every dainty you can think of,
        Ev'ry Wine which you would drink of,
        Shall be yours; all want shall shun you,
        Ceres *Blessing so is on you.*

    Alonz. This voice speaks comfort to us.
    Ant. Wou'd 'twere come; there is no Musick in a Song
To me, my ſtomack being empty.
    Gonz. O for a heavenly Vision of Boyl'd,
Bak'd, and Roaſted!
188

Enter eight fat Spirits, with Cornu-Copia *in their hands.*

Alonz. Are these plump shapes sent to deride our hunger?

Gonz. No, no: it is a Masque of fatten'd Devils, the
Burgo-Masters of the lower Region.   [*Dance and vanish.*
O for a Collop of that large-haunch'd Devil
Who went out last!

Ant. going to the door. My Lord, the Duke, see yonder.
A Table, as I live, set out and furnisht
With all varieties of Meats and fruits.

Alonz. 'Tis so indeed, but who dares tast this feast,
Which Fiends provide, perhaps, to poyson us?

Gonz. Why that dare I; if the black Gentleman be so ill-natur'd,
he may do his pleasure.

Ant. 'Tis certain we must either eat or famish,
I will encounter it, and feed.

Alonz. If both resolve, I will adventure too.

Gonz. Then good my Lord, make haste,
And say no Grace before it, I beseech you,
Because the meat will vanish strait, if, as I fear,
An evil Spirit be our Cook.   [*Exeunt.*

Enter Trincalo *and* Caliban.

Trinc. Brother Monster, welcome to my private Palace.
But where's thy Sister, is she so brave a Lass?

Calib. In all this Isle there are but two more, the Daughters of
the Tyrant *Prospero*; and she is bigger than 'em both. O here she
comes; now thou may'st judge thy self, my Lord.   [*Enter* Sycorax.

Trinc. She's monstrous fair indeed. Is this to be my Spouse?
Well she's Heir of all this Isle (for I will geld Monster). The *Trin-
calo*'s, like other wise men, have anciently us'd to marry for Estate
more than for Beauty.

Sycorax. I prithee let me have the gay thing about thy neck, and
that which dangles at thy wrist.
          [Sycorax *points to his Bosens Whistle, and his Bottle.*

Trinc. My dear Blobber-lips; this, observe my Chuck, is a badge
of my Sea-Office; my fair Fuss, thou dost not know it.

Syc. No, my dread Lord.

Trinc. It shall be a Whistle for our first Babe, and when the next
Shipwrack puts me again to swimming, I'le dive to get a Coral to it.

Syc. I'le be thy pretty child, and wear it first.

Trinc. I prithee sweet Babby do not play the wanton, and cry for
my goods e're I'm dead. When thou art my Widow, thou shalt have
the Devil and all.

189

Syc. May I not have the other fine thing?

Trinc. This is a sucking-Bottle for young *Trincalo*.

Calib. This is a God a mighty liquor, I did but drink thrice of it, and it hath made me glad e're since.

Syc. He is the bravest God I ever saw.

Calib. You must be kind to him, and he will love you.
I prithee speak to her, my Lord, and come neerer her.

Trinc. By this light, I dare not till I have drank: I must
Fortifie my stomack first.

Syc. I shall have all his fine things when I'm a Widow.

[*Pointing to his Bottle, and Bosens Whistle.*

Calib. I, but you must be kind and kiss him then.

Trinc. My Brother Monster is a rare Pimp.

Syc. I'le hug thee in my Arms, my Brother's God.

Trinc. Think o' thy soul, *Trincalo*, thou art a dead man if this kindness continue.

Calib. And he shall get thee a young *Sycorax*, wilt thou not, my Lord?

Trinc. Indeed I know not how, they do no such thing in my Country.

Syc. I'le shew thee how: thou shalt get me twenty *Sycoraxes*; and I'le get thee twenty *Calibans*.

Trinc. Nay, if they are got, she must do't all her self, that's certain.

Syc. And we will tumble in cool Plashes, and the soft Fens, where we will make us Pillows of Flags and Bull-rushes.

Calib. My Lord, she would be loving to thee, and thou wilt not let her.

Trinc. Ev'ry thing in its season, Brother Monster; but you must counsel her; fair Maids must not be too forward.

Syc. My Brother's God, I love thee; prithee let me come to thee.

Trinc. Subject Monster, I charge thee keep the Peace between us.

Calib. Shall she not taste of that Immortal Liquor?

Trinc. Umph! that's another question: for if she be thus flipant in her Water, what will she be in her Wine?

[*Enter* Ariel (*invisible*) *and changes the Bottle which stands upon the ground.*

Ariel. There's Water for your Wine. [*Exit Ariel.*

Trinc. Well! since it must be so. [*Gives her the Bottle.*
How do you like it now, my Queen that [*She drinks.*
Must be?

Syc. Is this your heavenly liquor? I'le bring you to a River of the same.

Trinc. Wilt thou so, Madam Monster? what a mighty Prince shall I be then? I would not change my Dukedom to be great Turk *Trincalo.*

Syc. This is the drink of Frogs.

Trinc. Nay, if the Frogs of this Island drink such, they are the merryest Frogs in Christendom.

Calib. She does not know the virtue of this liquor: I prithee let me drink for her.

Trinc. Well said, Subject Monster.   [Caliban *drinks.*

Calib. My Lord, this is meer water.

Trinc. 'Tis thou hast chang'd the Wine then, and drunk it up, Like a debauch'd Fish as thou art. Let me see't, I'le taste it my self. Element! meer Element! as I live. It was a cold gulp, such as this, which kill'd my famous Predecessor old *Simon* the King.

Calib. How does thy honour? prithee be not angry, and I will lick thy shoe.

Trinc. I could find in my heart to turn thee out of my Dominions for a liquorish Monster.

Calib. O my Lord, I have found it out; this must be done by one of *Prospero*'s spirits.

Trinc. There's nothing but malice in these Devils, I never lov'd 'em from my Childhood. The Devil take 'em, I would it had bin holy-water for their sakes.

Syc. Will not thy mightiness revenge our wrongs, on this great Sorcerer? I know thou wilt, for thou art valiant.

Trinc. In my Sack, Madam Monster, as any flesh alive.

Syc. Then I will cleave to thee.

Trinc. Lovingly said, in troth: now cannot I hold out against her. This Wife-like Vertue of hers, has overcome me.

Syc. Shall I have thee in my arms?

Trinc. Thou shalt have Duke *Trincalo* in thy arms: But prithee be not too boistrous with me at first; Do not discourage a young beginner.   [*They embrace.*
Stand to your Arms, my Spouse,
And Subject Monster;   [*Enter* Steph. Must. Vent.
The Enemy is come to surprise us in our Quarters.
You shall know Rebels that I am Marry'd to a Witch,
And we have a thousand Spirits of our Party.

Steph. Hold! I ask a truce; I and my Vice-Roys
(Finding no food, and but a small remainder of Brandy)

Are come to treat a peace betwixt us,
Which may be for the good of both Armies,
Therefore *Trincalo* disband.

Trinc. Plain *Trincalo*, methinks I might have been a Duke in your
mouth, I'le not accept of your Embassy without my title.

Steph. A title shall break no squares betwixt us:
Vice-Roys, give him his ſtile of Duke, and treat with him,
Whilſt I walk by in ſtate.

[*Ventoso and* Muſtacho *bow whilſt* Trincalo *puts on his Cap.*

Muſt. Our Lord and Maſter, Duke *Stephano*, has sent us
In the firſt place to demand of you, upon what
Ground you make war againſt him, having no right
To Govern here, as being elected only by
Your own voice.

Trinc. To this I answer, that having in the face of the world
Espous'd the lawful Inheritrix of this Island,
Queen *Blouze* the firſt, and having homage done me,
By this hectoring Spark her Brother, from these two
I claim a lawful Title to this Island.

Muſt. Who, that Monſter? he a Hector?

Calib. Lo! how he mocks me, wilt thou let him, my Lord?

Vent. Lord! quoth he: the Monſter's a very natural.

Syc. Lo! lo! again; bite him to death I prithee.

Trinc. Vice-Roys! keep good tongues in your Heads
I advise you, and proceed to your business, for I have
Other affairs to dispatch of more importance betwixt
Queen Slobber-Chops and my self.

Muſt. Firſt and foremoſt, as to your claim that you have an-
swer'd.

Vent. But second and foremoſt, we demand of you,
That if we make a Peace, the Butt also may be
Comprehended in the Treaty.

Muſt. Is the Butt safe, Duke *Trincalo?*

Trinc. The Butt is partly safe: but to comprehend it in the Treaty,
or indeed to make any Treaty, I cannot, with my honour, without
your submission. These two, and the Spirits under me, ſtand like-
wise upon their honours.

Calib. Keep the liquor for us, my Lord, and let them drink Brine,
for I will not show 'em the quick freshes of the Island.

Steph. I underſtand, being present, from my Embassadors what
your resolution is, and ask an hours time of deliberation, and so I
take our leave; but firſt I desire to be entertain'd at your Butt, as
becomes a Prince, and his Embassadors.

192

Trinc. That I refuse, till acts of Hostility be ceas'd.
These Rogues are rather Spies than Embassadors;
I must take heed of my Butt. They come to pry
Into the secrets of my Dukedom.
    Vent. *Trincalo* you are a barbarous Prince, and so farewel.
                                      [*Exeunt* Steph. Must. Vent.
    Trinc. Subject Monster! stand you Sentry before my Cellar; my
Queen and I will enter and feast our selves within.
    Syc. May I not marry that other King and his two subjects, to
help you a nights?
    Trinc. What a careful Spouse have I? Well! if she does Cornute
me, the care is taken.
When underneath my power my foes have truckl'd,
To be a Prince, who would not be a Cuckold?   [*Exeunt.*

        Enter Ferdinand, *and* Ariel (*invisible.*)

    Ferd. How far will this invisible Musician conduct
My steps? he hovers still about me, whether
For good or ill I cannot tell, nor care I much;
For I have been so long a slave to chance, that
I'm as weary of her flatteries as her frowns,
But here I am——
    Ariel. Here I am.
    Ferd. Hah! art thou so? the Spirit's turn'd an Eccho:
This might seem pleasant, could the burthen of my
Griefs accord with any thing but sighs.
And my last words, like those of dying men
Need no reply. Fain I would go to shades, where
Few would wish to follow me.
    Ariel. Follow me.
    Ferd. This evil Spirit grows importunate,
But I'le not take his counsel.
    Ariel. Take his counsel.
    Ferd. It may be the Devil's counsel. I'le never take it.
    Ariel. Take it.
    Ferd. I will discourse no more with thee,
Nor follow one step further.
    Ariel. One step further.
    Ferd. This must have more importance than an Eccho.
Some Spirit tempts to a precipice.
I'le try if it will answer when I sing
My sorrows to the murmurs of this Brook.

He Sings.

	Go thy way.
Ariel.	*Go thy way.*
Ferd.	*Why should'st thou stay?*
Ariel.	*Why should'st thou stay?*
Ferd.	*Where the Winds whistle, and where the Streams creep,*
	Under yond Willow-tree, fain would I sleep.
	Then let me alone,
	For 'tis time to be gone.
Ariel.	*For 'tis time to be gone.*
Ferd.	*What cares or pleasures can be in this Isle?*
	Within this desart place
	There lives no humane race;
	Fate cannot frown here, nor kind fortune smile.
Ariel.	*Kind Fortune smiles, and she*
	Has yet in store for thee
	Some strange felicity.
	Follow me, follow me,
	And thou shalt see.

Ferd. I'le take thy word for once;
Lead on Musician.   [*Exeunt and return.*

Scene changes, and discovers Prospero *and* Miranda.

Prosp. Advance the fringed Curtains of thine Eyes, and say what thou seest yonder.

Mir. Is it a Spirit?
Lord! how it looks about! Sir, I confess it carries a brave form. But 'tis a Spirit.

Prosp. No Girl, it eats and sleeps, and has such senses as we have. This young Gallant, whom thou see'st, was in the wrack; were he not somewhat stain'd with grief (beauty's worst Cancker) thou might'st call him a goodly person; he has lost his company, and strays about to find 'em.

Mir. I might call him a thing divine, for nothing natural I ever saw so noble.

Prosp. It goes on as my Soul prompts it: Spirit, fine Spirit. I'le free thee within two days for this.

Ferd. She's sure the Mistress, on whom these Airs attend. Fair Excellence, if, as your form declares, you are divine, be pleas'd to instruct me how you will be worshiped; so bright a beauty cannot sure belong to humane kind.

Mir. I am, like you, a mortal, if such you are.

Ferd. My language too! O Heavens! I am the best of them who speak this Speech, when I'm in my own Country.

Prosp. How, the best? what wert thou if the Duke of *Savoy* heard thee?

Ferd. As I am now, who wonders to here thee speak of *Savoy*: he does hear me, and that he does I weep, my self am *Savoy*, whose fatal Eyes (e're since at ebbe) beheld the Duke my Father wrackt.

Mir. Alack! for pity.

Prosp. At the first sight they have chang'd Eyes, dear *Ariel*, I'le set thee free for this——young Sir, a word. With hazard of your self you do me wrong.

Mir. Why speaks my Father so urgently? This is the third man that e're I saw, the first whom E're I sigh'd for, sweet Heaven move my Father To be inclin'd my way.

Ferd. O! if a Virgin! and your affection not gone forth, I'le make you Mistress of *Savoy*.

Prosp. Soft, Sir! one word more. They are in each others powers, but this swift Bus'ness I must uneasie make, lest too light Winning make the prize light—one word more. Thou usurp'st the name not due to thee, and hast Put thy self upon this Island as a spy to get the Government from me, the Lord of it.

Ferd. No, as I'm a man.

Mir. There's nothing ill can dwell in such a Temple, If th' Evil Spirit hath so fair a house, Good things will strive to dwell with it.

Prosp. No more. Speak not you for him, he's a Traytor, Come! thou art my Pris'ner and shalt be in Bonds. Sea-water shalt thou drink, thy food Shall be the fresh-Brook-Muscles, wither'd Roots, And Husks, wherein the Acorn crawl'd; follow.

Ferd. No, I will resist such entertainment Till my Enemy has more power.

                    [*He draws, and is charm'd from moving.*

Mir. O dear Father! make not too rash a tryal Of him, for he's gentle and not fearful.

Prosp. My child my Tutor! put thy Sword up Traytor, Who mak'st a show, but dar'st not strike: thy Conscience is possest with guilt. Come from Thy Ward, for I can here disarm thee with This Wand, and make thy Weapon drop.

Mir. 'Beseech you Father.

Prosp. Hence: hang not on my Garment.

Mir. Sir, have pity,
I'le be his Surety.

Prosp. Silence! one word more shall make me chide thee,
If not hate thee: what, an advocate for an
Impoſtor? sure thou think'ſt there are no more
Such shapes as his?
To the moſt of men this is a *Caliban*,
And they to him are Angels.

Mir. My affeƈtions are then moſt humble,
I have no ambition to see a goodlier man.

Prosp. Come on, obey:
Thy Nerves are in their Infancy agen, and have
No vigour in them.

Ferd. So they are:
My Spirits, as in a Dream, are all bound up:
My Father's loss, the weakness which I feel,
The wrack of all my friends, and this man's threats,
To whom I am subdu'd, would seem light to me,
Might I but once a day through my Prison behold this maid:
All corners else o' th' Earth let liberty make use of:
I have space enough in such a Prison.

Prosp. It works: come on:
Thou haſt done well, fine *Ariel:* follow me.
Hark what thou shalt more do for me   [*Whispers* Ariel.

Mir. Be of comfort!
My Father's of a better nature, Sir,
Than he appears by speech: this is unwonted
Which now came from him.

Prosp. Thou shalt be as free as Mountain Winds:
But then exaƈtly do all points of my command.

Ariel. To a Syllable.   [*Exit* Ariel.

Prosp. to Mir. Go in that way, speak not a word for him:
I'le separate you.   [*Exit* Miranda.

Ferd. As soon thou may'ſt divide the waters
When thou ſtrik'ſt 'em, which pursue thy bootless blow,
And meet when 'tis paſt.

Prosp. Go praƈtise your Philosophy within,
And if you are the same you speak your self,
Bear your affliƈtions like a Prince——That Door
Shews you your Lodging.

Ferd. 'Tis in vain to ſtrive, I muſt obey.   [*Exit* Ferd.

196

Prosp. This goes as I would wish it.
Now for my second care, *Hippolito.*
I shall not need to chide him for his fault,
His passion is become his punishment.
Come forth, *Hippolito.*   [*Enter* Hippolito.

Hip. entring. 'Tis *Prospero*'s Voice.

Prosp. Hippolito! I know you now expect I should severely chide
you: you have seen a woman in contempt of my commands.

Hip. But, Sir, you see I am come off unharm'd;
I told you, that you need not doubt my Courage.

Prosp. You think you have receiv'd no hurt.

Hip. No, none Sir.
Try me agen, when e're you please I'm ready:
I think I cannot fear an Army of 'em.

Prosp. How much in vain it is to bridle Nature!   [*Aside.*
Well! what was the success of your encounter?

Hip. Sir, we had none, we yielded both at first,
For I took her to mercy, and she me.

Prosp. But are you not much chang'd from what you were?

Hip. Methinks I wish and wish! for what I know not,
But still I wish——yet if I had that woman,
She, I believe, could tell me what I wish for.

Prosp. What wou'd you do to make that Woman yours?

Hip. I'd quit the rest o' th' World that I might live alone with
Her, she never should be from me.
We two would sit and look till our Eyes ak'd.

Prosp. You'd soon be weary of her.

Hip. O, Sir, never.

Prosp. But you'l grow old and wrinckl'd, as you see me now,
And then you will not care for her.

Hip. You may do what you please, but, Sir, we two can
Never possibly grow old.

Prosp. You must, *Hippolito.*

Hip. Whether we will or no, Sir, who shall make us?

Prosp. Nature, which made me so.

Hip. But you have told me her works are various;
She made you old, but she has made us young.

Prosp. Time will convince you,
Mean while be sure you tread in honours paths,
That you may merit her, and that you may not want
Fit occasions to employ your Virtue, in this next
Cave there is a stranger lodg'd, one of your kind,
Young, of a noble presence, and as he says himself,

Of Princely birth, he is my Pris'ner and in deep
Affliction, visit, and comfort him; it will become you.
    Hip. It is my duty, Sir.   [*Exit* Hippolito.
    Prosp. True, he has seen a woman, yet he lives, perhaps I took
the moment of his birth amiss, perhaps my Art it self is false: on
what strange grounds we build our hopes and fears, mans life is all a
mist, and in the dark, our fortunes meet us.
If Fate be not, then what can we foresee,
Or how can we avoid it, if it be?
If by free-will in our own paths we move
How are we bounded by Decrees above?
Whether we drive, or whether we are driven,
If ill 'tis ours, if good the act of Heaven.   [*Exit* Prospero.

SCENE, *A Cave.*

Enter Hippolito *and* Ferdinand.

    Ferd. Your pity, noble youth, doth much oblige me,
Indeed 'twas sad to lose a Father so.
    Hip. I, and an only Father too, for sure you said
You had but one.
    Ferd. But one Father! he's wondrous simple!   [*Aside.*
    Hip. Are such misfortunes frequent in your World,
Where many men live?
    Ferd. Such we are born to.
But gentle youth, as you have question'd me,
So give me leave to ask you, what you are?
    Hip. Do not you know?
    Ferd. How should I?
    Hip. I well hop'd I was a man, but by your ignorance
Of what I am, I fear it is not so:
Well, *Prospero!* this is now the second time
You have deceiv'd me.
    Ferd. Sir, there is no doubt you are a man:
But I would know of whence?
    Hip. Why, of this world, I never was in yours.
    Ferd. Have you a Father?
    Hip. I was told I had one, and that he was a man, yet I have bin
so much deceived, I dare not tell't you for a truth; but I have still
been kept a Prisoner for fear of women.
198

Ferd. They indeed are dangerous, for since I came I have beheld
one here, whose beauty pierc'd my heart.

Hip. How did she pierce? you seem not hurt.

Ferd. Alas! the wound was made by her bright eyes,
And festers by her absence.
But to speak plainer to you, Sir, I love her.

Hip. Now I suspect that love's the very thing, that I feel too!
pray tell me truly, Sir, are you not grown unquiet since you saw her?

Ferd. I take no rest.

Hip. Just, just my disease.
Do you not wish you do not know for what?

Ferd. O no! I know too well for what I wish.

Hip. There, I confess, I differ from you, Sir:
But you desire she may be always with you?

Ferd. I can have no felicity without her.

Hip. Just my condition! alas, gentle Sir,
I'le pity you, and you shall pity me.

Ferd. I love so much, that if I have her not,
I find I cannot live.

Hip. How! do you love her?
And would you have her too? that must not be:
For none but I must have her.

Ferd. But perhaps, we do not love the same:
All beauties are not pleasing alike to all.

Hip. Why are there more fair Women, Sir,
Besides that one I love?

Ferd. That's a strange question. There are many more besides
that beauty which you love.

Hip. I will have all of that kind, if there be a hundred of 'em.

Ferd. But noble youth, you know not what you say.

Hip. Sir, they are things I love, I cannot be without 'em:
O, how I rejoyce! more women!

Ferd. Sir, if you love you must be ty'd to one.

Hip. Ty'd! how ty'd to her?

Ferd. To love none but her.

Hip. But, Sir, I find it is against my Nature.
I must love where I like, and I believe I may like all,
All that are fair: come! bring me to this Woman,
For I must have her.

Ferd. His simplicity
Is such that I can scarce be angry with him.   [*Aside.*
Perhaps, sweet youth, when you behold her,
You will find you do not love her.

Hip. I find already I love, because she is another Woman.

Ferd. You cannot love two women, both at once.

Hip. Sure 'tis my duty to lovè all who do resemble
Her whom I've already seen. I'le have as many as I can,
That are so good, and Angel-like, as she I love.
And will have yours.

Ferd. Pretty youth, you cannot.

Hip. I can do any thing for that I love.

Ferd. I may, perhaps, by force reſtrain you from it.

Hip. Why do so if you can. But either promise me
To love no Woman, or you muſt try your force.

Ferd. I cannot help it, I muſt love.

Hip. Well you may love, for *Prospero* taught me friendship too:
you shall love me and other men if you can find 'em, but all the
Angel-women shall be mine.

Ferd. I muſt break off this conference, or he will
Urge me else beyond what I can bear.
Sweet youth! some other time we will speak
Farther concerning both our loves; at present
I am indispos'd with weariness and grief,
And would, if you were pleas'd, retire a while.

Hip. Some other time be it; but, Sir, remember
That I both seek and much intreat your friendship,
For next to Women, I find I can love you.

Ferd. I thank you, Sir, I will consider of it.   [*Exit* Ferdinand.

Hip. This Stranger does insult and comes into my
World to take those heavenly beauties from me,
Which I believe I am inspir'd to love,
And yet he said he did desire but one.
He would be poor in love, but I'le be rich:
I now perceive that *Prospero* was cunning;
　For when he frighted me from woman-kind,
　Those precious things he for himself design'd.   [*Exit.*

ACT IV.

Enter Prospero, *and* Miranda.

Prosp. YOur suit has pity in't, and has prevail'd.
　　Within this Cave he lies, and you may see him:
But yet take heed; let Prudence be your Guide;
You muſt not ſtay, your visit muſt be short.   [*She's going.*

One thing I had forgot; insinuate into his mind
A kindness to that youth, whom first you saw;
I would have Friendship grow betwixt 'em.

Mir. You shall be obey'd in all things.

Prosp. Be earnest to unite their very souls.

Mir. I shall endeavour it.

Prosp. This may secure *Hippolito* from that dark danger which
my art forebodes; for friendship does provide a double strength t'
oppose th' assaults of fortune.   [*Exit* Prospero.

Enter Ferdinand.

Ferd. To be a Pris'ner where I dearly love, is but a double tye; a
Link of fortune joyn'd to the chain of love; but not to see her, and
yet to be so near her, there's the hardship; I feel my self as on a
Rack, stretch'd out, and nigh the ground, on which I might have
ease, yet cannot reach it.

Mir. Sir! my Lord? where are you?

Ferd. Is it your voice, my Love? or do I dream?

Mir. Speak softly, it is I.

Ferd. O heavenly Creature! ten times more gentle, than your
Father's cruel; how on a sudden all my griefs are vanish'd!

Mir. I come to help you to support your griefs.

Ferd. While I stand gazing thus, and thus have leave to touch
your hand, I do not envy freedom.

Mir. Hark! hark! is't not my Father's voice I hear? I fear he calls
me back again too soon.

Ferd. Leave fear to guilty minds: 'tis scarce a virtue when it is
paid to Heaven.

Mir. But there 'tis mix'd with love, and so is mine; yet I may fear,
for I am guilty when I disobey my Fathers will in loving you too
much.

Ferd. But you please Heav'n in disobeying him,
Heav'n bids you succour Captives in distress.

Mir. How do you bear your Prison?

Ferd. 'Tis my Palace while you are here, and love and silence wait
upon our wishes; do but think we chuse it, and 'tis what we would
chuse.

Mir. I'm sure what I would.
But how can I be certain that you love me?
Look to't; for I will dye when you are false.
I've heard my Father tell of Maids, who dy'd,
And haunted their false Lovers with their Ghosts.

Ferd. Your Ghost must take another form to fright me,

This shape will be too pleasing: do I love you?
O Heav'n! O Earth! bear witness to this sound,
If I prove false——
 Mir. Oh hold, you shall not swear;
For Heav'n will hate you if you prove forsworn.
 Ferd. Did I not love, I could no more endure this undeserved captivity, than I could wish to gain my freedom with the loss of you.
 Mir. I am a fool to weep at what I'm glad of: but I have a suit to you, and that, Sir, shall be now the only tryal of your love.
 Ferd. Y'ave said enough, never to be deny'd, were it my life; for you have far o'rebid the price of all that humane life is worth.
 Mir. Sir, 'tis to love one for my sake, who for his own deserves all the respect which you can ever pay him.
 Ferd. You mean your Father: do not think his usage can make me hate him; when he gave you being, he then did that which cancell'd all these wrongs.
 Mir. I meant not him, for that was a request, which if you love I should not need to urge.
 Ferd. Is there another whom I ought to love?
And love him for your sake?
 Mir. Yes such a one, who for his sweetness and his goodly shape, (if I, who am unskill'd in forms, may judge) I think can scarce be equall'd: 'Tis a youth, a Stranger too as you are.
 Ferd. Of such a graceful feature, and must I for your sake love?
 Mir. Yes, Sir, do you scruple to grant the first request I ever made? he's wholly unacquainted with the world, and wants your conversation. You should have compassion on so meer a stranger.
 Ferd. Those need compassion whom you discommend, not whom you praise.
 Mir. I only ask this easie tryal of you.
 Ferd. Perhaps it might have easier bin
If you had never ask'd it.
 Mir. I cannot understand you; and methinks am loth
To be more knowing.
 Ferd. He has his freedom, and may get access, when my
Confinement makes me want that blessing.
I his compassion need, and not he mine.
 Mir. If that be all you doubt, trust me for him.
He has a melting heart, and soft to all the Seals.
Of kindness; I will undertake for his compassion.
 Ferd. O Heavens! would I were sure I did not need it.
 Mir. Come, you must love him for my sake: you shall.
 Ferd. Must I for yours, and cannot for my own?

Either you do not love, or think that I do not:
But when you bid me love him, I muſt hate him.

 Mir. Have I so far offended you already,
That he offends you only for my sake?
Yet sure you would not hate him, if you saw
Him as I have done, so full of youth and beauty.

 Ferd. O poyson to my hopes!   [*Aside.*
When he did visit me, and I did mention this
Beauteous Creature to him, he did then tell me
He would have her.

 Mir. Alas, what mean you?

 Ferd. It is too plain: like moſt of her frail Sex, she's false,
But has not learnt the art to hide it;
Nature has done her part, she loves variety:
Why did I think that any Woman could be innocent,
Because she's young? No, no, their Nurses teach them
Change, when with two Nipples they divide their
Liking.

 Mir. I fear I have offended you, and yet I meant no harm:
But if you please to hear me—   [*A noise within.*
Hark! Sir! now I am sure my Father comes, I know
His ſteps; dear Love retire a while, I fear
I've ſtay'd too long.

 Ferd. Too long indeed, and yet not long enough: Oh jealousie!
Oh Love! how you diſtract me?   [*Exit* Ferdinand.

 Mir. He appears displeas'd with that young man, I know
Not why: but, till I find from whence his hate proceeds,
I muſt conceal it from my Father's knowledge,
For he will think that guiltless I have caus'd it;
And suffer me no more to see my Love.

Enter Prospero.

 Prosp. Now I have been indulgent to your wish,
You have seen the Prisoner?

 Mir. Yes.

 Prosp. And he spake to you?

 Mir. He spoke; but he receiv'd short answers from me.

 Prosp. How like you his converse?

 Mir. At second sight
A man does not appear so rare a Creature.

 Prosp. aside. I find she loves him much because she hides it.
Love teaches cunning even to innocence,
And where he gets possession, his firſt work is to

Dig deep within a heart, and there lie hid,
And like a Miser in the dark to feaſt alone.
But tell me, dear *Miranda*, how does he suffer
His imprisonment?

    Mir. I think he seems displeas'd.

    Prosp. O then 'tis plain his temper is not noble,
For the brave with equal minds bear good
And evil Fortune.

    Mir. O, Sir, but he's pleas'd again so soon
That 'tis not worth your noting.

    Prosp. To be soon displeas'd and pleas'd so suddenly again,
Does shew him of a various froward Nature.

    Mir. The truth is, Sir, he was not vex'd at all, but only
Seem'd to be so.

    Prosp. If he be not and yet seems angry, he is a dissembler,
Which shews the worſt of Natures.

    Mir. Truly, Sir, the man has faults enough; but in my conscience
that's none of 'em. He can be no dissembler.

    Prosp. aside. How she excuses him, and yet desires that I should
judge her heart indifferent to him? well, since his faults are many, I
am glad you love him not.

    Mir. 'Tis like, Sir, they are many,
But I know none he has, yet let me often see him,
And I shall find 'em all in time.

    Prosp. I'le think on't.
Go in, this is your hour of Orizons.

    Mir. aside. Forgive me, truth, for thus disguising thee; if I can
make him think I do not love the ſtranger much, he'll let me see him
oftner.   [*Exit* Miranda.

    Prosp. Stay! ſtay——I had forgot to ask her what she has said
Of young *Hippolito:* Oh! here he comes! and with him
My *Dorinda.* I'le not be seen, let   [*Enter* Hippolito *and* Dorinda.
Their loves grow in secret.   [*Exit* Prospero.

    Hip. But why are you so sad?

    Dor. But why are you so joyful?

    Hip. I have within me all, all the various Musick of
The Woods. Since laſt I saw you I have heard brave news!
I'll tell you, and make you joyful for me.

    Dor. Sir, when I saw you firſt, I through my eyes drew
Something in, I know not what it is;
But ſtill it entertains me with such thoughts
As makes me doubtful whether joy becomes me.

    Hip. Pray believe me;

As I'm a man, I'le tell you blessed news.
I have heard there are more Women in the World,
As fair as you are too.
    Dor. Is this your news? you see it moves not me.
    Hip. And I'le have 'em all.
    Dor. What will become of me then?
    Hip. I'le have you too.
But are not you acquainted with these Women?
    Dor. I never saw but one.
    Hip. Is there but one here?
This is a base poor world, I'le go to th' other;
I've heard men have abundance of 'em there.
But pray where is that one Woman?
    Dor. Who, my Sister?
    Hip. Is she your Sister? I'm glad o' that: you shall help me to her,
and I'll love you for't.   *[Offers to take her hand.*
    Dor. Away! I will not have you touch my hand.
My Father's counsel which enjoyn'd reservedness,   *[Aside.*
Was not in vain I see.
    Hip. What makes you shun me?
    Dor. You need not care, you'l have my Sisters hand.
    Hip. Why, must not he who touches hers touch yours?
    Dor. You mean to love her too.
    Hip. Do not you love her?
Then why should not I do so?
    Dor. She is my Sister, and therefore I must love her:
But you cannot love both of us.
    Hip. I warrant you I can:
Oh that you had more Sisters!
    Dor. You may love her, but then I'le not love you.
    Hip. O but you must;
One is enough for you, but not for me.
    Dor. My Sister told me she had seen another;
A man like you, and she lik'd only him;
Therefore if one must be enough for her,
He is that one, and then you cannot have her.
    Hip. If she like him, she may like both of us.
    Dor. But how if I should change and like that man?
Would you be willing to permit that change?
    Hip. No, for you lik'd me first.
    Dor. So you did me.
    Hip. But I would never have you see that man;
I cannot bear it.

Dor. I'le see neither of you.

Hip. Yes, me you may, for we are now acquainted;
But he's the man of whom your Father warn'd you:
O! he's a terrible, huge, monstrous creature,
I am but a Woman to him.

Dor. I will see him,
Except you'l promise not to see my Sister.

Hip. Yes for your sake I needs must see your Sister.

Dor. But she's a terrible, huge Creature too; if I were not
Her Sister she would eat me; therefore take heed.

Hip. I heard that she was fair, and like you.

Dor. No, indeed, she's like my Father, with a great Beard,
'Twould fright you to look on her,
Therefore that man and she may go together,
They are fit for no body but one another.

Hip. looking in. Yonder he comes with glaring eyes, fly! fly!
Before he sees you.

Dor. Must we part so soon?

Hip. Y'are a lost Woman if you see him.

Dor. I would not willingly be lost, for fear you
Should not find me. I'le avoid him.   [*Exit* Dorinda.

Hip. She fain would have deceived me, but I know her
Sister must be fair, for she's a Woman;
All of a Kind that I have seen are like to one
Another: all the Creatures of the Rivers and
The Woods are so.

Enter Ferdinand.

Ferd. O! well encounter'd, you are the happy man!
Y' have got the hearts of both the beauteous Women.

Hip. How! Sir? pray, are you sure on't?

Ferd. One of 'em charg'd me to love you for her sake.

Hip. Then I must have her.

Ferd. No, not till I am dead

Hip. How dead? what's that? but whatsoe'er it be
I long to have her.

Ferd. Time and my grief may make me dye.

Hip. But for a friend you should make haste; I ne're ask'd
Any thing of you before.

Ferd. I see your ignorance;
And therefore will instruct you in my meaning.
The Woman, whom I love, saw you and lov'd you.
Now, Sir, if you love her you'l cause my death.

Hip. Be sure I'll do't then.

Ferd. But I am your friend;
And I request you that you would not love her.

Hip. When friends request unreasonable things,
Sure th' are to be deny'd: you say she's fair,
And I must love all who are fair; for, to tell
You a secret, Sir, which I have lately found
Within my self; they all are made for me.

Ferd. That's but a fond conceit: you are made for one, and one
for you.

Hip. You cannot tell me, Sir.
I know I'm made for twenty hundred Women.
(I mean if there so many be i' th' World)
So that if once I see her I shall love her.

Ferd. Then do not see her.

Hip. Yes, Sir, I must see her.
For I wou'd fain have my heart beat again,
Just as it did when I first saw her Sister.

Ferd. I find I must not let you see her then.

Hip. How will you hinder me?

Ferd. By force of Arms?

Hip. By force of Arms?
My Arms perhaps may be as strong as yours.

Ferd. He's still so ignorant that I pity him, and fain
Would avoid force: pray, do not see her, she was
Mine first; you have no right to her.

Hip. I have not yet consider'd what is right, but, Sir,
I know my inclinations are to love all Women:
And I have been taught that to dissemble what I
Think is base. In honour then of truth, I must
Declare that I do love, and I will see your Woman.

Ferd. Wou'd you be willing I should see and Love your
Woman, and endeavour to seduce her from that
Affection which She vow'd to you?

Hip. I wou'd not you should do it, but if she should
Love you best, I cannot hinder her.
But, Sir, for fear she shou'd, I will provide against
The worst, and try to get your Woman.

Ferd. But I pretend no claim at all to yours;
Besides you are more beautiful than I,
And fitter to allure unpractis'd hearts.
Therefore I once more beg you will not see her.

Hip. I'm glad you let me know I have such beauty.

If that will get me Women, they shall have it
As far as e're 'twill go: I'le never want 'em.
    Ferd. Then since you have refused this act of friendship,
Provide your self a Sword; for we must fight.
    Hip. A Sword, what's that?
    Ferd. Why such a thing as this.
    Hip. What should I do with it?
    Ferd. You must stand thus, and push against me,
While I push at you, till one of us fall dead.
    Hip. This is brave sport,
But we have no Swords growing in our World.
    Ferd. What shall we do then to decide our quarrel?
    Hip. We'll take the Sword by turns, and fight with it.
    Ferd. Strange ignorance! you must defend your Life,
And so must I: but since you have no Sword
Take this; for in a corner of my Cave   [*Gives him his Sword.*
I found a rusty one, perhaps 'twas his who keeps
Me Pris'ner here: that I will fit:
When next we meet prepare your self to fight.
    Hip. Make haste then, this shall ne're be yours agen.
I mean to fight with all the men I meet, and
When they are dead, their Women shall be mine.
    Ferd. I see you are unskilful; I desire not to take
Your Life, but if you please we'll fight on
These conditions; He who first draws bloud,
Or who can take the others Weapon from him,
Shall be acknowledg'd as the Conquerour,
And both the Women shall be his.
    Hip. Agreed: And ev'ry day I'le fight for two more with you.
    Ferd. But win these first.
    Hip. I'le warrant you I'll push you.   [*Exeunt severally.*

Enter Trincalo, Caliban, Sycorax.

    Calib. My Lord, I see 'em coming yonder.
    Trinc. Who?
    Calib. The starv'd Prince, and his two thirsty Subjects,
That would have our Liquor.
    Trinc. If thou wert a Monster of parts I would make thee
My Master of Ceremonies, to conduct 'em in.
The Devil take all Dunces, thou hast lost a brave
Employment by not being a Linguist, and for want
Of behaviour.

Syc. My Lord, shall I go meet 'em? I'le be kind to all of 'em,
Juſt as I am to thee.

Trinc. No, that's againſt the fundamental Laws of my Dukedom:
you are in a high place, Spouse, and muſt give good Example. Here
they come, we'll put on the gravity of Statesmen, and be very dull,
that we may be held wise.

Enter Stephano, Ventoso, Muſtacho.

Vent. Duke *Trincalo*, we have consider'd.

Trinc. Peace, or War?

Muſt. Peace, and the Butt.

Steph. I come now as a private person, and promise to live peace-
ably under your Government.

Trinc. You shall enjoy the benefits of Peace; and the firſt Fruits
of it, amongſt all civil Nations, is to be drunk for joy: *Caliban* skink
about.

Steph. I long to have a Rowse to her Graces health, and to the
Haunse in Kelder, or rather Haddock in *Kelder*, for I guess it will be
half Fish.   [*Aside.*

Trinc. Subjeċt *Stephano* here's to thee; and let old quarrels be
drown'd in this draught.   [*Drinks.*

Steph. Great Magiſtrate, here's thy Siſters health to thee.
                                                          [*Drinks to* Caliban.

Syc. He shall not drink of that immortal liquor,
My Lord, let him drink water.

Trinc. O sweet heart, you muſt not shame your self to day.
Gentlemen Subjeċts, pray bear with her good Huswifry:
She wants a little breeding, but she's hearty.

Muſt. *Ventoso* here's to thee. Is it not better to pierce the Butt,
than to quarrel and pierce one anothers Bellies?

Vent. Let it come Boy.

Trinc. Now wou'd I lay greatness aside, and shake my heels, if I
had but Musick.

Calib. O my Lord! my Mother left us in her Will a hundred
Spirits to attend us, Devils of all sorts, some great roaring Devils,
and some little singing Sprights.

Syc. Shall we call? and thou shalt hear them in the Air.

Trinc. I accept the motion: let us have our Mother-in-Law's
Legacy immediately.

Calib. sings. We want Musick, we want Mirth,
        Up Dam and cleave the Earth,
        We have now no Lords that wrong us,
        Send thy merry Sprights among us. [*Musick heard.*

Trinc. What a merry Tyrant am I, to have my
Musick and pay nothing for't? come, hands, hands,
Let's lose no time while the Devil's in the Humour,   *[A Dance.*
    Trinc. Enough, enough: now to our Sack agen.
    Vent. The Bottle's drunk.
    Must. Then the Bottle's a weak shallow fellow if it be drunk first.
    Trinc. Caliban, give Bottle the belly full agen.
    Steph. May I ask your Grace a question? pray is that hectoring
Spark, as you call'd him, flesh or fish?
    Trinc. Subject I know not, but he drinks like a fish.
                                                    [Enter Caliban.

    Steph. O here's the Bottle agen; he has made a good voyage,
Come, who begins a Brindis to the Duke?
    Trinc. I'le begin it my self: give me the Bottle; 'tis my
Prerogative to drink first; *Stephano,* give me thy hand,
Thou hast been a Rebel, but here's to thee,   *[Drinks.*
Prithee why should we quarrel? shall I swear
Two Oaths? by Bottle, and by Butt I love thee:
In witness whereof I drink soundly.
    Steph. Your Grace shall find there's no love lost,
For I will pledge you soundly.
    Trinc. Thou hast been a false Rebel, but that's all one;
Pledge my Grace faithfully.
    Steph. I will pledge your Grace Up se Dutch.
    Trinc. But thou shalt not pledge me before I have drunk agen,
would'st thou take the Liquor of Life out of my hands; I see thou
art a piece of a Rebel still, but here's to thee, now thou shalt have it.
                                                    [Stephano drinks.
    Vent. We loyal Subjects may be choak'd for any drink we can get.
    Trinc. Have patience good people, you are unreasonable, you'd
be drunk as soon as I. *Ventoso* you shall have your time, but you must
give place to *Stephano.*
    Must. Brother *Ventoso,* I am afraid we shall loose our Places.
The Duke grows fond of *Stephano,* and will declare him
Vice-Roy.
    Steph. I ha' done my worst at your Graces Bottle.
    Trinc. Then the Folks may have it. *Caliban*
Go to the Butt, and tell me how it sounds:
Peer *Stephano,* dost thou love me?
    Steph. I Love your Grace and all your Princely Family.
    Trinc. 'Tis no matter if thou lov'st me; hang my Family:
Thou art my Friend, prithee tell me what
Thou think'st of my Princess.

Steph. I look on her as a very noble Princess.

Trinc. Noble! Indeed she had a Witch to her Mother, and the Witches are of great Families in *Lapland*, but the Devil was her Father, and I have heard of the Mounsor *De-Viles* in *France*; but look on her beauty, is she a fit Wife for Duke *Trincalo*? mark her behaviour too, she's tippling yonder with the serving-men.

Steph. An please your Grace she's somewhat homely, but that's no blemish in a Princess. She is Virtuous.

Trinc. Umph! virtuous! I am loth to disparage her:
But thou art my Friend, can'ſt thou be close?

Steph. As a ſtopt Bottle, an't please your Grace.

[*Enter* Caliban *agen with a Bottle.*

Trinc. Why then I'le tell thee, I found her an hour ago under and Elder-Tree, upon a sweet Bed of Nettles, singing Tory, Rory, and Ranthum, Scantum, with her own natural Brother.

Steph. O Jew! make love in her own Tribe!

Trinc. But 'tis no matter, to tell thee true, I marry'd her to be a great man and so forth: but make no words on't, for I care not who knows it, and so here's to thee agen, give me the Bottle, *Caliban!* did you knock the Butt? How does it sound?

Calib. It sounds as though it had a noise within.

Trinc. I fear the Butt begins to rattle in the throat, and is departing: give me the Bottle.   [*Drinks.*

Muſt. A short Life and a merry, I say.   [*Steph. whispers* Sycorax.

Syc. But did he tell you so?

Steph. He said you were as ugly as your Mother, and that he Marry'd you only to get possession of the Island.

Syc. My Mothers Devils fetch him for't.

Steph. And your Father's too, hem! skink about his Graces health agen. O if you would but caſt an eye of pity upon me————

Syc. I will caſt two eyes of pity on thee, I love thee more than Haws, or Black-Berries, I have a hoard of Wildings in the Moss, my Brother knows not of 'em, but I'le bring thee where they are.

Steph. Trincalo was but my man when time was.

Syc. Wert thou his God, and didſt thou give him Liquor?

Steph. I gave him Brandy, and drunk Sack my self; wilt thou leave him, and thou shalt be my Princess?

Sic. If thou canſt make me glad with this Liquor.

Steph. I warrant thee we'll ride into the Country whcre it grows.

Syc. How wilt thou carry me thither?

Steph. Upon a Hackney-Devil of thy Mothers.

Trinc. What's that you will do? hah! I hope you have not betray'd me? How does my Pigs-nye?   [*To* Sycorax.

211

Syc. Be gone! Thou shalt not be my Lord, thou say'ſt
I'm ugly.

Trinc. Did you tell her so—hah! he's a Rogue, do not believe him
chuck.

Steph. The foul words were yours: I will not eat 'em for you.

Trinc. I see if once a Rebel, then ever a Rebel. Did I receive thee
into grace for this? I will correct thee with my Royal Hand.

                                             [Strikes Stephano.

Syc. Doſt thou hurt my love?   *[Flies at* Trincalo.

Trinc. Where are our Guards? Treason, Treason!

                               [Vent. Muſt. Calib. *run betwixt.*

Vent. Who took up Arms firſt, the Prince or the People?

Trinc. This false Traytor has corrupted the Wife of my Bosom.

                               [Whispers Muſtacho *haſtily.*

Muſtacho ſtrike on my side, and thou shalt be my Vice-Roy.

Muſt. I'm againſt Rebels! *Ventoso,* obey your Vice-Roy.

Vent. You a Vice-Roy?   *[They two fight off from the reſt.*

Steph. Hah! Hector Monſter! do you ſtand neuter?

Calib. Thou would'ſt drink my Liquor, I will not help thee.

Syc. 'Twas his doing that I had such a Husband, but I'le claw
him.

               *[*Syc. *and* Calib. *Fight,* Syc. *beating him off the Stage.*

Trinc. The whole Nation is up in Arms, and shall I ſtand idle?

               *[Trincalo *beats off* Stephano *to the door. Exit* Stephano.

I'le not pursue too far,

For fear the Enemy should rally agen and surprise my Butt in the
Cittadel; well, I muſt be rid of my Lady *Trincalo,* she will be in the
fashion else; firſt Cuckold her Husband, and then sue for a separa-
tion, to get Alimony.   *[Exit.*

       Enter Ferdinand, Hippolito, *(with their swords drawn.)*

Ferd. Come, Sir, our Cave affords no choice of place,
But the ground's firm and even: are you ready?

Hip. As ready as your self, Sir.

Ferd. You remember on what conditions we muſt fight?
Who firſt receives a Wound is to submit.

Hip. Come, come, this loses time, now for the
Women, Sir.   *[They fight a little,* Ferdinand *hurts him.*

Ferd. Sir, you are wounded.

Hip. No.

Ferd. Believe your blood.

Hip. I feel no hurt, no matter for my blood.

Ferd. Remember our Conditions.

Hip. I'le not leave, till my Sword hits you too.
                    [Hip. *presses on*, Ferd. *retires and wards.*
Ferd. I'm loth to kill you, you are unskilful, Sir.
Hip. You beat aside my Sword, but let it come as near
As yours, and you shall see my skill.
Ferd. You faint for loss of blood, I see you ſtagger,
Pray, Sir, retire.
Hip. No! I will ne're go back——
Methinks the Cave turns round, I cannot find——
Ferd. Your eyes begin to dazle.
Hip. Why do you swim so, and dance about me?
Stand but ſtill till I have made one thruſt.
                    [Hippolito *thruſts and falls.*
Ferd. O help, help, help!
Unhappy man! what have I done?
Hip. I'm going to a cold sleep, but when I wake
I'le fight agen. Pray ſtay for me.   [*Swounds.*
Ferd. He's gone! he's gone! O ſtay sweet lovely Youth!
Help, help!

                    Enter Prospero.

Prosp. What dismal noise is that?
Ferd. O see, Sir, see!
What mischief my unhappy hand has wrought.
Prosp. Alas! how much in vain doth feeble Art endeavour
To resiſt the will of Heaven?   [*Rubs* Hippolito.
He's gone for ever; O thou cruel Son of an
Inhumane Father! all my designs are ruin'd
And unravell'd by this blow.
No pleasure now is left me but Revenge.
Ferd. Sir, if you knew my Innocence——
Prosp. Peace, peace.
Can thy excuses give me back his life?
What *Ariel!* sluggish spirit, where art thou?

                    Enter Ariel.

Ariel. Here, at thy beck, my Lord.
Prosp. I, now thou com'ſt, when Fate is paſt and not to be
Recall'd. Look there, and glut the malice of
Thy Nature, for as thou art thy ſelf, thou
Canſt not be but glad to see young Virtue
Nipt i' th' Blossom.
Ariel. My Lord, the Being high above can witness

I am not glad, we Airy Spirits are not of temper
So malicious as the Earthy,
But of a Nature more approaching good.
For which we meet in swarms, and often combat
Betwixt the Confines of the Air and Earth.

 Prosp. Why did'st thou not prevent, at least foretel,
This fatal action then?

 Ariel. Pardon, great Sir,
I meant to do it, but I was forbidden
By the ill Genius of *Hippolito*,
Who came and threatn'd me if I disclos'd it,
To bind me in the bottom of the Sea,
Far from the lightsome Regions of the Air,
(My native fields) above a hundred years.

 Prosp. I'le chain thee in the North for thy neglect,
Within the burning Bowels of Mount *Heila*,
I'll singe thy airy wings with sulph'rous flames,
And choak thy tender nostrils with blew smoak,
At ev'ry Hick-up of the belching Mountain
Thou shalt be lifted up to taste fresh Air,
And then fall down agen.

 Ariel. Pardon, dread Lord.

 Prosp. No more of pardon than just Heav'n intends thee,
Shalt thou e're find from me: hence! flye with speed,
Unbind the Charms which hold this Murtherer's
Father, and bring him with my Brother streight
Before me.

 Ariel. Mercy, my potent Lord, and I'le outfly thy thought.
               [*Exit* Ariel.

 Ferd. O Heavens! what words are those I heard?
Yet cannot see who spoke 'em: sure the Woman
Whom I lov'd was like this, some aiery Vision.

 Prosp. No, Murd'rer, she's, like thee, of mortal mould,
But much too pure to mix with thy black Crimes;
Yet she had faults and must be punish'd for 'em.
Miranda and *Dorinda!* where are ye?
The will of Heaven's accomplish'd: I have
Now no more to fear, and nothing left to hope,
Now you may enter.

    Enter Miranda *and* Dorinda.

 Mir. My Love! is it permitted me to see you once again?
 Prosp. You come to look your last; I will

214

For ever take him from your Eyes.
But, on my blessing, speak not, nor approach him.
 Dor. Pray, Father, is not this my Sisters man?
He has a noble form; but yet he's not so excellent
As my *Hippolito.*
 Prosp. Alas poor Girl, thou hast no man: look yonder;
There's all of him that's left.
 Dor. Why was there ever any more of him?
He lies asleep, Sir, shall I waken him?

> [*She kneels by* Hippolito, *and jogs him.*

 Ferd. Alas! he's never to be wak'd agen.
 Dor. My Love, my Love! will you not speak to me?
I fear you have displeas'd him, Sir, and now
He will not answer me, he's dumb and cold too,
But I'le run streight, and make a fire to warm him.

> [*Exit* Dorinda *running.*

Enter Alonzo, Gonzalo, Antonio. Ariel (*invisible.*)

 Alonz. Never were Beasts so hunted into toyls,
As we have been pursu'd by dreadful shapes.
But is not that my Son? O *Ferdinand!*
If thou art not a Ghost, let me embrace thee.
 Ferd. My Father! O sinister happiness! Is it
Decreed I should recover you alive, just in that
Fatal hour when this brave Youth is lost in Death,
And by my hand?
 Ant. Heaven! what new wonder's this?
 Gonz. This Isle is full of nothing else.
 Alonz. I thought to dye, and in the walks above,
Wand'ring by Star-light, to have sought thee out;
But now I should have gone to Heaven in vain,
Whilst thou art here behind.
 Ferd. You must indeed in vain have gone thither
To look for me. Those who are stain'd with such black
Crimes as mine, come seldom there.
 Prosp. And those who are, like him, all foul with guilt,
More seldom upward go. You stare upon me as
You n'ere had seen me; have fifteen years
So lost me to your Knowledge, that you retain
No memory of *Prospero?*
 Gonz. The good old Duke of *Millain!*
 Prosp. I wonder less, that thou *Antonio* know'st me not,

215

Because thou did'st long since forget I was thy Brother,
Else I never had bin here.

    Ant. Shame choaks my words.

    Alonz. And wonder mine.

    Pros. For you, usurping Prince,   *[To* Alonzo.
Know, by my Art, you shipwrackt on this Isle,
Where, after I a while had punish'd you, my vengeance
Wou'd have ended, I design'd to match that Son
Of yours with this my Daughter.

    Alonz. Pursue it still, I am most willing to't.

    Prosp. So am not I. No Marriages can prosper
Which are with Murd'rers made; look on that Corps,
This, whilst he liv'd, was young *Hippolito,* that
Infant Duke of *Mantua,* Sir, whom you expos'd
With me: and here I bred him up till that blood-thirsty
Man, that *Ferdinand*——
But why do I exclaim on him, when Justice calls
To unsheath her Sword against his guilt?

    Alonz. What do you mean?

    Prosp. To execute Heav'ns Laws.
Here I am plac'd by Heav'n, here I am Prince,
Though you have dispossess'd me of my *Millain.*
Blood calls for blood; your *Ferdinand* shall dye,
And I in bitterness have sent for you
To have the sudden joy of seeing him alive,
And then the greater grief to see him dye.

    Alonz. And think'st thou I or these will tamely stand
To view the execution?   *[Lays hand upon his Sword.*

    Ferd. Hold, dear Father! I cannot suffer you
T' attempt against his life who gave her being
Whom I love.

    Prosp. Nay then appear my Guards——I thought no more to
Use their aids; (I am curs'd because I us'd it)
                  [He stamps, and many Spirits appear.
But they are now the Ministers of Heaven,
Whilst I revenge this murder.

    Alonz. Have I for this found thee my Son, so soon agen
To lose thee? *Antonio, Gonzalo,* speak for pity:
He may hear you.

    Ant. I dare not draw that blood upon my self, by
Interceeding for him.

    Gonz. You drew this judgment down when you usurp'd
That Dukedom which was this dead Prince's right.

216

Alonz. Is this a time t' upbraid me with my sins, when
Grief lies heavy on me? y'are no more my friends,
But crueller than he, whose sentence has
Doom'd my Son to death.
    Ant. You did unworthily t' upbraid him.
    Gonz. And you do worse t' endure his crimes.
    Ant. Gonzalo we'll meet no more as friends.
    Gonz. Agreed *Antonio:* and we agree in discord.
    Ferd. to *Mir.* Adieu my faireſt Miſtress.
    Mir. Now I can hold no longer; I muſt speak.
Though I am loth to disobey you, Sir,
Be not so cruel to the man I love,
Or be so kind to let me suffer with him.
    Ferd. Recal that Pray'r, or I shall wish to live,
Though death be all the mends that I can make.
    Prosp. This night I will allow you, *Ferdinand*, to fit
You for your Death, that Cave's your Prison.
    Alonz. Ah, *Prospero!* hear me speak. You are a Father,
Look on my age, and look upon his youth.
    Prosp. No more! all you can say is urg'd in vain,
I have no room for pity left within me.
Do you refuse! help *Ariel* with your fellows
To drive 'em in; *Alonzo* and his Son beſtow in
Yonder Cave, and here *Gonzalo* shall with
Antonio lodge.   *[Spirits drive 'em in, as they are appointed.*

Enter Dorinda.

    Dor. Sir, I have made a fire, shall he be warm'd?
    Prosp. He's dead, and vital warmth will ne're return.
    Dor. Dead, Sir, what's that?
    Prosp. His soul has left his body.
    Dor. When will it come agen?
    Prosp. O never, never!
He muſt be laid in Earth, and there consume.
    Dor. He shall not lye in earth, you do not know
How well he loves me: indeed he'll come agen;
He told me he would go a little while,
But promis'd me he would not tarry long.
    Prosp. He's murder'd by the man who lov'd your Siſter.
Now both of you may see what 'tis to break
A Father's precept; you would needs see men, and by
That sight are made for ever wretched.

Hippolito is dead, and *Ferdinand* must die
For murdering him.
 Mir. Have you no pity?
 Prosp. Your disobedience has so much incens'd me, that
I this night can leave no blessing with you.
Help to convey the body to my Couch,
Then leave me to mourn over it alone.

           [*They bear off the Body of* Hippolito.

   Enter Miranda, *and* Dorinda *again.* Ariel *behind 'em.*

 Ariel. I've bin so chid for my neglect by *Prospero,*
That I must now watch all and be unseen.
 Mir. Sister, I say agen, 'twas long of you
That all this mischief happen'd.
 Dor. Blame not me for your own fault, your
Curiosity brought me to see the man.
 Mir. You safely might have seen him and retir'd, but
You wou'd needs go near him and converse, you may
Remember my Father call'd me thence, and I call'd you.
 Dor. That was your envy, Sister, not your love;
You call'd me thence, because you could not be
Alone with him your self; but I am sure my
Man had never gone to Heaven so soon, but
That yours made him go.   [*Crying.*
 Mir. Sister I could not wish that either of 'em shou'd
Go to Heaven without us, but it was his fortune,
And you must be satisfi'd?
 Dor. I'le not be satisfi'd: My Father says he'l make
Your man as cold as mine is now, and when he
Is made cold, my Father will not let you strive
To make him warm agen.
 Mir. In spight of you mine never shall be cold.
 Dor. I'm sure 'twas he that made me miserable,
And I will be reveng'd. Perhaps you think 'tis
Nothing to lose a man.
 Mir. Yes, but there is some difference betwixt
My *Ferdinand,* and your *Hippolito.*
 Dor. I, there's your judgment. Your's is the oldest
Man I ever saw, except it were my Father.
 Mir. Sister, no more. It is not comely in a Daughter,
When she says her Father's old.
 Dor. But why do I stay here, whilst my cold Love
218

Perhaps may want me?
I'le pray my Father to make yours cold too.
 Mir. Sister, I'le never sleep with you agen.
 Dor. I'le never more meet in a bed with you,
But lodge on the bare ground, and watch my Love.
 Mir. And at the entrance of that Cave I'le lye,
And eccho to each blaſt of wind a sigh.
    [Exeunt severally, looking discontentedly on one another.
 Ariel. Harsh discord reigns throughout this fatal Isle,
At which good Angels mourn, ill Spirits smile;
Old *Prospero,* by his Daughters rob'd of reſt,
Has in displeasure left 'em both unbleſt.
Unkindly they abjure each others bed,
To save the Living, and revenge the dead.
Alonzo and his Son are Pris'ners made,
And good *Gonzalo* does their crimes upbraid.
Antonio and *Gonzalo* disagree,
And wou'd, though in one Cave, at diſtance be.
The Seamen all that cursed Wine have spent,
Which ſtill renew'd their thirſt of Government;
And, wanting subjeꝏs for the food of Pow'r,
Each wou'd to rule alone the reſt devour.
The Monſters *Sycorax* and *Caliban*
More monſtrous grow by passions learn'd from man.
Even I not fram'd of warring Elements,
Partake and suffer in these discontents.
Why shou'd a mortal by Enchantments hold
In chains a spirit of ætherial mould?
Accursed Magick we our selves have taught,
And our own pow'r has our subjeꝏion wrought!   *[Exit.*

ACT V.

Enter Prospero *and* Miranda.

Prosp. YOU beg in vain; I cannot pardon him,
    He has offended Heaven.
 Mir. Then let Heaven punish him.
 Prosp. It will by me.
 Mir. Grant him at leaſt some respite for my sake.
 Prosp. I by deferring Juſtice should incense the Deity
Againſt my self and you.

Mir. Yet I have heard you say, The Powers above are slow
In punishing, and shou'd not you resemble them?
Prosp. The Powers above may pardon or reprieve,
As Sovereign Princes may dispense with Laws,
Which we, as Officers, must execute. Our Acts of grace
To Criminals are Treason to Heavens prerogative.
Mir. Do you condemn him for shedding blood?
Prosp. Why do you ask that question? you know I do.
Mir. Then you must be condemn'd for shedding his,
And he who condemns you, must dye for shedding
Yours, and that's the way at last to leave none living.
Prosp. The Argument is weak, but I want time
To let you see your errours; retire, and, if you love him,
Pray for him.   [*He's going.*
Mir. O stay, Sir, I have yet more Arguments.
Prosp. But none of any weight.
Mir. Have you not said you are his Judge?
Prosp. 'Tis true, I am; what then?
Mir. And can you be his Executioner?
If that be so, then all men may declare their
Enemies in fault; and Pow'r without the Sword
Of Justice, will presume to punish what e're
It calls a crime.
Prosp. I cannot force *Gonzalo* or my Brother, much
Less the Father to destroy the Son, it must
Be then the Monster *Caliban*, and he's not here,
But *Ariel* strait shall fetch him.

Enter Ariel.

Ariel. My potent Lord, before thou call'st, I come,
To serve thy will.
Prosp. Then Spirit fetch me here my salvage Slave.
Ariel. My Lord, it does not need.
Prosp. Art thou then prone to mischief, wilt thou be thy self the
Executioner?
Ariel. Think better of thy aiery Minister, who
For thy sake, unbid, this night has flown
O're almost all the habitable World.
Prosp. But to what purpose was all thy diligence?
Ariel. When I was chidden by my mighty Lord for my
Neglect of young *Hippolito*, I went to view
His body, and soon found his soul was but retir'd,

Not sally'd out, and frighted lay at skulk in
Th' inmoſt corner of his scarce-beating heart.

Prosp. Is he not dead?

Ariel. Hear me my Lord! I prun'd my wings, and, fitted for a journey, from the next Isles of our *Hesperides*, I gather'd Moly firſt, thence shot my self to *Paleſtine*, and watch'd the trickling Balm, which caught, I glided to the British Isles, and there the purple Panacea found.

Prosp. All this to night?

Ariel. All this, my Lord, I did,
Nor was *Hippolito*'s good Angel wanting, who
Climbing up the circle of the Moon,
While I below got Simples for the Cure, went to
Each Planet which o're-rul'd those Herbs,
And drew it's virtue to increase their pow'r:
Long e're this hour had I been back again,
But that a Storm took me returning back
And flag'd my tender Wings.

Prosp. Thou shalt have reſt my spirit,
But haſt thou search'd the wound?

Ariel. My Lord I have, and 'twas in time I did it; for
The soul ſtood almoſt at life's door, all bare
And naked, shivering like Boys upon a Rivers
Bank, and loth to tempt the cold air, but I took
Her and ſtop'd her in; and pour'd into his mouth
The healing juice of vulnerary Herbs.

Prosp. Thou art my faithful servant.

Ariel. His only danger was his loss of blood, but now
He's wak'd, my Lord, and juſt this hour
He muſt be dress'd again, as I have done it.
Anoint the Sword which pierc'd him with this
Weapon-Salve, and wrap it close from air till
I have time to visit him again.

Prosp. It shall be done, be it your task, *Miranda*, because your
Siſter is not present here, while I go visit your
Dear *Ferdinand*, from whom I will a while conceal
This News, that it may be more welcome.

Mir. I obey you, and with a double duty, Sir: for now
You twice have given me life.

Prosp. My *Ariel*, follow me.   [*Exeunt severally.*
            Hippolito *discovered on a Couch*, Dorinda *by him.*

Dor. How do you find your self?

Hip. I'm somewhat cold, can you not draw me nearer
To the Sun, I am too weak to walk?

Dor. My Love, I'le try.

                      [She draws the chair nearer to the Audience.

I thought you never would have walk'd agen,
They told me you were gone away to Heaven;
Have you bin there?

Hip. I know not where I was.

Dor. I will not leave you till you promise me you
Will not dye agen.

Hip. Indeed I will not.

Dor. You must not go to Heav'n unless we go together;
For I've heard my Father say that we must strive
To be each others Guide, the way to it will else
Be difficult, especially to those who are so young.
But I much wonder what it is to dye.

Hip. Sure 'tis to dream, a kind of breathless sleep
When once the Soul's gone out.

Dor. What is the Soul?

Hip. A small blew thing that runs about within us.

Dor. Then I have seen it in a frosty morning run
Smoaking from my mouth.

Hip. But if my soul had gone, it should have walk'd upon
A Cloud just over you, and peep'd, and thence I would have
Call'd you.

Dor. But I should not have heard you, 'tis so far.

Hip. Why then I would have rain'd and snow'd upon you,
And thrown down Hail-Stones gently till I hit you,
And make you look at least. But Dear *Dorinda*
What is become of him who fought with me?

Dor. O, I can tell you joyful news of him,
My Father means to make him dye to day,
For what he did to you.

Hip. That must not be, my dear *Dorinda*; go and beg your
Father he may not dye, it was my fault he hurt me,
I urg'd him to it first.

Dor. But if he live, he'll never leave killing you.

Hip. O no! I just remember when I fell asleep, I heard
Him calling me a great way off, and crying over me as
You wou'd do, besides we have no cause of quarrel now.

Dor. Pray how began your difference first?

Hip. I fought with him for all the Women in the World.

Dor. That hurt you had was justly sent from Heaven,
For wishing to have any more but me.

Hip. Indeed I think it was, but I repent it, the fault
Was only in my blood, for now 'tis gone, I find
I do not love so many.

Dor. In confidence of this, I'le beg my Father, that he
May live, I'm glad the naughty blood, that made
You Love so many, is gone out.

Hip. My Dear, go quickly, least you come too late.   [*Exit* Dor.

Enter Miranda *at the other Door, with* Hippolito's *Sword
wrap'd up.*

Hip. Who's this who looks so fair and beautiful, as
Nothing but *Dorinda* can surpass her? O!
I believe it is that Angel, Woman,
Whom she calls Sister

Mir. Sir, I am sent hither to dress your wound,
How do you find your strength?

Hip. Fair Creature, I am Faint with loss of blood.

Mir. I'm sorry for't.

Hip. Indeed so am I, for if I had that blood, I then
Should find a great delight in loving you.

Mir. But, Sir, I am anothers, and your love is given
Already to my Sister.

Hip. Yet I find that if you please I can love still a little.

Mir. I cannot be unconstant, nor shou'd you.

Hip. O my wound pains me.

Mir. I am come to ease you.   [*She unwraps the Sword.*

Hip. Alas! I feel the cold air come to me,
My wound shoots worse than ever.

                              [*She wipes and anoints the Sword.*

Mir. Does it still grieve you?

Hip. Now methinks there's something laid just upon it.

Mir. Do you find no ease?

Hip. Yes, yes, upon the sudden all the pain
Is leaving me, sweet Heaven how am I eas'd!

Enter Ferdinand *and* Dorinda *to them.*

Ferd. to Dor. Madam, I must confess my life is yours,
I owe it to your generosity.

Dor. I am o'rejoy'd my Father lets you live, and proud
Of my good fortune, that he gave your life to me,

Mir. How? gave his life to her!

Hip. Alas! I think she said so, and he said he ow'd it
To her generosity.

Ferd. But is not that your Sister with *Hippolito*?

Dor. So kind already?

Ferd. I came to welcome life, and I have met the
Cruellest of deaths.

Hip. My dear *Dorinda* with another man?

Dor. Sister, what bus'ness have you here?

Mir. You see I dress *Hippolito*.

Dor. Y'are very charitable to a Stranger.

Mir. You are not much behind in charity, to beg a pardon
For a man, whom you scarce ever saw before.

Dor. Henceforward let your Surgery alone, for I had
Rather he should dye, than you should cure his wound.

Mir. And I wish *Ferdinand* had dy'd before
He ow'd his life to your entreaty.

Ferd. to Hip. Sir, I'm glad you are so well recover'd, you
Keep your humour still to have all Women.

Hip. Not all, Sir, you except one of the number,
Your new Love there, *Dorinda*.

Mir. Ah *Ferdinand!* can you become inconstant?
If I must lose you, I had rather death should take
You from me than you take your self.

Ferd. And if I might have chose, I would have wish'd
That death from *Prospero*, and not this from you.

Dor. I, now I find why I was sent away.
That you might have my Sisters company.

Hip. Dorinda, kill me not with your unkindness,
This is too much, first to be false your self,
And then accuse me too.

Ferd. We all accuse each other, and each one denys their guilt,
I should be glad it were a mutual errour.
And therefore first to clear my self from fault,
Madam, I beg your pardon, while I say I only love
Your Sister.   [*to* Dorinda.

Mir. O blest Word!
I'm sure I love no man but *Ferdinand*.

Dor. Nor I, Heav'n knows, but my *Hippolito*.

Hip. I never knew I lov'd so much, before I fear'd
Dorinda's constancy; but now I am convinc'd that
I lov'd none but her, because none else can
Recompence her loss.

224

Ferd. 'Twas happy then you had this little tryal.
But how we all so much mistook, I know not.
 Mir. I have only this to say in my defence: my Father sent
Me hither, to attend the wounded Stranger.
 Dor. And *Hippolito* sent me to beg the life of *Ferdinand.*
 Ferd. From such small errours, left at first unheeded,
Have often sprung sad accidents in love:
But see, our Fathers and our friends are come
To mix their joys with ours.

   Enter Prospero, Alonzo, Antonio, Gonzalo.

 Alon. to Prosp. Let it no more be thought of, your purpose
Though it was severe was just. In losing *Ferdinand*
I should have mourn'd, but could not have complain'd.
 Prosp. Sir, I am glad kind Heaven decree'd it otherwise.
 Dor. O wonder!
How many goodly Creatures are there here!
How beauteous mankind is!
 Hip. O brave new World that has such people in't!
 Alon. to Ferd. Now all the blessings of a glad Father
Compass thee about,
And make thee happy in thy beauteous choice.
 Gonz. I've inward wept, or should have spoke e're this.
Look down sweet Heav'n, and on this Couple drop
A blessed Crown, for it is you chalk'd out the
Way which brought us hither
 Ant. Though penitence forc'd by necessity can scarce
Seem real, yet dearest Brother I have hope
My blood may plead for pardon with you, I resign
Dominion, which 'tis true I could not keep,
But Heaven knows too I would not.
 Prosp. All past crimes I bury in the joy of this
Blessed day.
 Alonz. And that I may not be behind in justice, to this
Young Prince I render back his Dukedom,
And as the Duke of *Mantua* thus salute him.
 Hip. What is it that you render back, methinks
You give me nothing.
 Prosp. You are to be Lord of a great people,
And o're Towns and Cities.
 Hip. And shall these people be all Men and Women?
 Gonz. Yes, and shall call you Lord.

Hip. Why then I'le live no longer in a Prison, but
Have a whole Cave to my self hereafter.

Prosp. And that your happiness may be compleat,
I give you my *Dorinda* for your Wife, she shall
Be yours for ever, when the Prieſt has made you one.

Hip. How shall he make us one, shall I grow to her?

Prosp. By saying holy words you shall be joyn'd in marriage
To each other.

Dor. I warrant you those holy words are charms.
My Father means to conjure us together.

Prosp. to his } My *Ariel* told me, when laſt night you quarrel'd,
daughter.   } You said you would for ever part your beds,
But what you threaten'd in your anger, Heaven
Has turn'd to Prophecy.
For you, *Miranda*, muſt with *Ferdinand*,
And you, *Dorinda*, with *Hippolito* lye in
One Bed hereafter.

Alonz. And Heaven make those Beds ſtill fruitful in
Producing Children to bless their Parents
Youth, and Grandsires age.

Mir. to Dor. If Children come by lying in a Bed, I wonder you
And I had none between us.

Dor. Siſter it was our fault, we meant like fools
To look 'em in the fields, and they it seems
Are only found in Beds.

Hip. I am o'rejoy'd that I shall have *Dorinda* in a Bed,
We'll lye all night and day together there,
And never rise again.

Ferd. aside to him. Hippolito! you are ignorant of your great
Happiness, but there is somewhat which for
Your own and fair *Dorinda*'s sake I muſt inſtruct
You in.

Hip. Pray teach me quickly how Men and Women in your
World make love, I shall soon learn
I warrant you.

Enter Ariel *driving in* Steph. Trinc. Muſt. Vent.
Calib. Syc.

Prosp. Why that's my dainty *Ariel*, I shall miss thee,
But yet thou shalt have freedom.

Gonz. O look, Sir, look the Maſter and the Saylors——
The Bosen too——my Prophecy is out, that if

226

A Gallows were on land, that Man could ne're
Be drown'd.

Alonz. to *Trinc.* Now Blasphemy, what not one Oath ashore?
Hast thou no mouth by land? why star'st thou so?

Trinc. What more Dukes yet, I must resign my Dukedom,
But 'tis no matter, I was almost starv'd in't.

Must. Here's nothing but wild Sallads without Oyl or
Vinegar.

Steph. The Duke and Prince alive! would I had now our gallant
Ship agen, and were her Master, I'd willingly give all my Island
for her.

Vent. And I my Vice-Roy-ship.

Trinc. I shall need no hangman, for I shall e'en hang
My self, now my friend Butt has shed his
Last drop of life. Poor Butt is quite departed.

Ant. They talk like mad men.

Prosp. No matter, time will bring 'em to themselves, and
Now their Wine is gone they will not quarrel.
Your Ship is safe and tight, and bravely rigg'd,
As when you first set Sail.

Alonz. This news is wonderful.

Ariel. Was it well done, my Lord?

Prosp. Rarely, my diligence.

Gonz. But pray, Sir, what are those mishapen Creatures?

Prosp. Their Mother was a Witch, and one so strong
She would control the Moon, make Flows
And Ebbs, and deal in her command without
Her power.

Syc. O *Setebos!* these be brave Sprights indeed.

Prosp. to *Calib.* Go Sirrah to my Cell, and as you hope for Pardon, trim it up.

Calib. Most carefully. I will be wise hereafter.
What a dull fool was I to take those Drunkards
For Gods, when such as these were in the world?

Prosp. Sir, I invite your Highness and your Train
To my poor Cave this night; a part of which
I will imploy in telling you my story.

Alonz. No doubt it must be strangely taking, Sir.

Prosp. When the morn dawns I'le bring you to your Ship,
And promise you calm Seas and happy Gales.
My *Ariel*, that's thy charge: then to the Elements
Be free, and fare thee well.

Ariel. I'le do it Master.

Sings. *Where the Bee sucks there suck I,*
In a Cowslips Bell, I lye,
There I couch when Owls do cry,
On the Swallows wing I flye
After Summer merrily.
Merrily, merrily shall I live now
Under the Blossom that hangs on the Bough.

Syc. I'le to Sea with thee, and keep thee warm in thy Cabin.
Trinc. No my dainty Dy-dapper, you have a tender conſtitution, and will be sick a Ship-board. You are partly Fish and may swim after me. I wish you a good Voyage.
Prosp. Now to this Royal Company, my servant, be visible, And entertain them with a Dance before they part.
Ariel. I have a gentle Spirit for my Love, Who twice seven years hath waited for my Freedom, It shall appear and foot it featly with me.
Milcha, my Love, thy *Ariel* calls thee.

Enter Milcha.

Milcha. Here!   [*They dance a Saraband.*
Prosp. Henceforth this Isle to the afflicted be
A place of Refuge as it was to me;
The Promises of blooming Spring live here,
And all the Blessings of the rip'ning year;
On my retreat let Heaven and Nature smile,
And ever flourish the *Enchanted Isle*.   [*Exeunt.*

EPILOGUE

GAllants, by all good signs it does appear,
That Sixty Seven's a very damning year,
For Knaves abroad, and for ill Poets here.

Among the Muses there's a gen'ral rot,
The Rhyming Monsieur and the Spanish Plot:
Defie or Court, all's one, they go to Pot.

The Ghosts of Poets walk within this place,
And haunt us Actors wheresoe're we pass,
In Visions bloodier than King Richard's was.

For this poor wretch he has not much to say,
But quietly brings in his part o' th' Play,
And begs the favour to be damn'd to day.

He sends me only like a Sh'riffs man here
To let you know the Malefactor's neer;
And that he means to dye, en Cavalier.

For if you shou'd be gracious to his Pen,
Th' Example will prove ill to other men,
And you'll be troubled with 'em all agen.

AN EVENING'S LOVE
OR THE
MOCK ASTROLOGER

Mallem Convivis quàm placuisse Cocis. Mart.

SOURCE

A^S Dryden very amply acknowledges in his Preface, "the Walk of the Astrologer" is originally taken from Calderon's *El Astrologo Fingido.* This delightful comedy which may be found in the First Volume (No. XXII, pp. 495–517) of Keil's *Las Comedias de D. Pedro Calderon,* Leipzig, 1827, may be deemed to have more poetry and refinement than, but it certainly does not display the humour, verve, and gaiety of *An Evening's Love.* The play is, as usual, divided into three Jornadas, the characters being Don Juan; Don Antonio; Don Diego; Don Carlos; Leonardo, *viejo;* Moron; Otañez, *Escudero;* Doña Maria; Doña Violante; Beatriz and Quiteria, *criadas.* Don Diego is the feigned astrologer. Doña Maria proclaims:

> Que el señor Don Diego es
> El astrólogo mejor,
> Que se conoce.

Don Juan de Medrano, who is supposed to be in Flanders, is lurking clandestinely in the house of Don Carlos. Accordingly he is able to visit Doña Violante and Quiteria rushes in, exclaiming:

> Jesus mil veces!
> Señora, verdad es clara
> El encanto; (muerta vengo!)
> Don Juan era el que llamaba
> A nuestra puerta.

In 1646 D'Ouville wrote *Jodelet astrologue,* much of which is derived from Calderon. In this piece the valet, Jodelet, plays the rôle of the astrologer.

Two years later Thomas Corneille produced *Le Feint Astrologue,* which was received with much applause and frequently represented. *Le Feint Astrologue* was printed quarto, 1651, Rouen, L. Meurry, and Paris, C. de Serey. In his Preface Corneille makes no mention of D'Ouville's comedy, which he must have known, but he gives all due to Calderon, and he declares that he would not perhaps have so confidently drawn on the Spanish "si je n'avois eû pour moi l'éxemple d'un de nos plus illustres Auteurs qui ayant accomodé le sujet de cette agréable Comédie dans son Illustre Bassa, au Galantines du Marquis François."

Ibrahim, ou l'Illustre Bassa, one of the favourite romances of Mlle de Scudéry, was published under the name of her brother, Georges de Scudéry, who in fact contributed not a little to the composition of these pages. Segrais says that *Ibrahim* appeared in 1635; but the earliest edition known to bibliographers seems to be that of 1641. The work was englished by Henry Cogan, London, folio, 1652. *The History of the feigned Astrologer* is related by the Marquis at the commencement of the Second Book of Part II. It may be remarked that when Pepys on Saturday, 20 June, 1668, saw *An Evening's Love* he records, "my wife tells me wholly (which he confesses a little in the epilogue) taken out of the 'Illustre Bassa.' " Mrs. Pepys was a great reader of de Scudéry, but "wholly" is too gross an exaggeration.

Corneille's *Le Feint Astrologue* is esteemed a good comedy, and although the poet himself says that what was applauded upon the stage may prove but cold and indifferent heavy in the script, the play may yet be read with pleasure. Corneille has also some slight borrowings from *L'Esprit Folet* of D'Ouville which appeared in 1641, and which is in its turn a pretty conveyance from Calderon's *La Dame Duende*. Corneille has cleverly put into dialogue the long scene with which *El Astrologo Fingido* commences, and his Philipin is undoubtedly more amusing than the Spanish Moron. Philipin boasts he is "demy Sorcier" and gulls old Mendoce with a trick of an aerial voyage. This scene is extremely amusing. In the same way Moron promises to transport Otañez to distant mountains. This is originally from Lope de Vega's *Entremos de la Hechizara*.

In 1668 was published quarto *The Feign'd Astrologer*, London: *Printed for Thomas Thorneycroft at the Eagle and Child near Worcester-house on the Strand*. The scene is laid in London, but this piece is little other than a somewhat jejune translation from Corneille. It is not recorded whether this version was ever given in the theatre, but I am disposed to think it was unacted.

A few slight hints for the character of Donna Aurelia may be traced to *Les Précieuses Ridicules*. Thus in Act III, scene 1, she demands "The Counsellor of the Graces." This is Madelon's "Vite, venez nous tendre ici dedans le conseiller des graces."

The brief but clever scene in Act IV where Don Alonzo and Don Melchor talk at cross purposes concerning the diamond ring recalls the confession of Lyconides to Euclio, who misinterprets his meaning in the *Aulularia*, a play which Plautus almost certainly borrowed from a lost comedy by Menander. Molière very closely follows this in *L'Avare* (produced at the Théâtre du Palais-Royal, 9 September, 1668), V, 3, where Valère acknowledges his love for Élise to Harpagon—"Brûlé pour ma cassette!" Obviously Dryden took his hint from Plautus, as *L'Avare* was not given until after *An Evening's Love*. Shadwell reproduces Molière fairly closely in *The Miser*, acted at the Theatre Royal in January, 1672. The amusing dialogue between Don Alonzo and Don Lopez in Act III was no doubt suggested by the episode in *Le Dépit Amoureux*, II, vii, where Albert consults Métaphraste. The love-quarrel of Wildblood and Jacinta, Maskall and Beatrix intervening, is copied, but with all the dexterity of a master, from Act IV, scenes 3 and 4, of the same comedy of Molière, who himself is here indebted to Italian sources. It is interesting to note how infinitely superior in every turn, in wit and literary grace, is Dryden to Vanbrugh who nearly forty years later presented his none too happy version of *Le Dépit Amoureux* as *The Mistake*, produced at Vanbrugh's own theatre in the Haymarket and under his proper management on Thursday, 27 December, 1705.

The incident towards the conclusion of the comedy where Don Alonzo (all being in the dark) catches Wildblood, who escapes owing to Maskall stepping between them and crying, "'Tis *Maskall* you have caught, Sir"; but immediately when Aurelia falls into Don Alonzo's arms and attempts to evade him by the same device he recognizes the trick, is from Quinault's *L'Amant Indiscret, ou, Le Maiſtre Eſtourdi*, V, 4:

Lidame, attrapant Cléandre. Il eſt pris le galant!
Cléandre.   Que le sort m'eſt contraire!
Philipin. Vous tenez Philipin, ne vous abusez pas,
            Peſte que rudement vous me serrez le bras!
Lidame. Quoy c'eſt toy Philipin! ce succez m'embarresse:
            Je croyois avoir pris notre fourbe en ta place.
Philipin. Pleuſt à Dieu qu'il fuſt vray que le Cid par bôheur
            Euſt en vos mains livré ce lache suborneur!
Lidame, prenant la main de Cleandre une seconde fois:
            Ha c'eſt douce à ce coup, je le tiens que je pense.
Cléandre. Vous tenez Philipin.
Philipin.   Dieu, quelle impertinence!
Lidame. L'artifice eſt grosse, je connoy bien sa voix.
Philipin. Ouy, vous tenez Cléandre, il eſt pris cette fois.
Lidame. Au voleur, au voleur, viſte de la chandelle.

Langbaine suggeſts that *An Evening's Love* also has "little Hints borrow'd from *Shakespear, Petronius Arbiter*, &c.," but this is plagiary-hunting run ſtark wood.

THEATRICAL HISTORY

A*N Evening's Love; or, The Mock-Aſtrologer*, was probably produced at the Theatre Royal, Bridges Street, on Friday, 12 June, 1668, when the King and Queen were present in the house. On Friday, 19 June, Pepys notes: "By and by comes my wife and Deb. home, have been at the King's playhouse to-day, thinking to spy me there; and saw the new play 'Evening Love' of Dryden's, which, though the world commends, she likes not." It may be remarked that Mrs. Pepys was indulging "a melancholy, fuſty humour." On the next day, Saturday, Pepys accompanied her "to the King's house, and there I saw this new play my wife saw yeſterday, and do not like it, it being very smutty, and nothing so good as 'The Maiden Queen' or 'The Indian Emperour,' of his making, that I was troubled at it." His wife also drew his attention to the parallel episode in the *Illuſtre Bassa*, and accordingly on Sunday afternoon "after dinner she to read in the 'Illuſtre Bassa' the plot of yeſterday's play, which is almoſt exactly the same."

On Monday, 8 March, 1668–9, Pepys has: "after dinner with my wife alone to the King's playhouse, and there saw 'The Mocke Aſtrologer,' which I have often seen and but an ordinary play."

On Friday, 19 June, 1668, Evelyn records: "To a new play with several of my relations, *The Evening Lover*, a foolish plot and very profane; it afflicted me to see how the ſtage was degenerated and polluted by the licentious times."

It is difficult to understand how so excellent and lively a comedy as *An Evening's Love* should thus be visited with the censures of Pepys and Evelyna like. Unless indeed the text has been much chastised in the printing—for it was not published until 1671—"smutty" and "profane" are singularly inapplicable to these scenes.

Downes by some curious error lists *The Mock-Astrologer* among the "Principal Old Stock Plays." He assigns the rôle of Theodosia to Mrs. Hughes, who doubtless created the part and was succeeded by Mrs. Boutell, just as Mrs. Marshall (Anne or Rebecca?) followed Mrs. Anne Quin in Donna Aurelia.

As it so well deserved, *An Evening's Love* was received with great applause; it remained in the theatrical repertory; and Downes tells us that there was a particular revival after the Union of the Two Companies in 1682. Betterton then appeared as Bellamy.

An Evening's Love was performed at Whitehall on 6 February, 1685–6; and the King and Queen again saw the play at the theatre on 13 October, 1686.

On 21 April, 1705, at Drury Lane, *An Evening's Love* is announced as "Not acted 6 years." No cast is recorded. It was again performed on the following 9 June for the benefit of the fair Letitia Cross, the original Miss Hoyden, Altisidora, Mrs. Sago, Lady Sadlife, and famous for her arch delivery of a saucy prologue or epilogue. Miss Cross played Jacinta, of which rôle her talents and her beauty must have made her an admirable exponent.

On 9 October, 1705, *An Evening's Love* was given at Drury Lane, but in subsequent seasons Dryden's comedy appears at less frequent intervals, and on 14 October, 1713, at the same house, it was announced as "Not acted 6 years."

On 30 May, 1716, at Drury Lane, *An Evening's Love* was followed by Dogget's *The Country Wake*, this farce probably being the altered version of one act as played at Drury Lane on 6 October, 1711.

On 18 October, 1717, again at Drury Lane, *An Evening's Love* was performed, but no cast is assigned. It was about this time that Dryden's comedy fell out of the theatrical repertory, and no revival of more recent date has been recorded.

To his GRACE

WILLIAM

DUKE OF *NEWCASTLE*,

One of His Majestie's most Honourable Privy Council;

and of the noble Order of

the Garter, &c.

Amongst those few persons of Wit and Honour, whose favourable opinion I have desir'd, your own vertue and my great obligations to your Grace, have justly given you the precedence. For what could be more glorious to me, than to have acquir'd some part of your esteem, who are admir'd and honour'd by all good men; who have been, for so many years together, the Pattern and Standard of Honor to the Nation: and whose whole life has been so great an example of Heroick vertue, that we might wonder how it happen'd into an Age so corrupt as ours, if it had not likewise been a part of the former? as you came into the world with all the advantages of a noble Birth and Education, so you have rendred both, yet more conspicuous by your vertue. Fortune, indeed, has perpetually crown'd your undertakings with success, but she has only waited on your valour, not conducted it. She has ministred to your glory like a slave, and has been led in triumph by it, or at most, while Honour led you by the hand to greatness, fortune only follow'd to keep you from sliding back in the ascent. That which Plutarch *accounted her favour to* Cymon *and* Lucullus, *was but her justice to your Grace: and, never to have been overcome where you led in person, as it was more than* Hannibal *could boast; so it was all that providence could do for that party which it had resolv'd to ruine Thus, my Lord, the last smiles of victory were on your armes: and, every where else, declaring for the Rebels, she seem'd to suspend her self, and to doubt, before she took her flight, whether she were able wholly to abandon that Cause for which you fought.*

But the greatest tryals of your Courage and Constancy were yet to come: many had ventur'd their fortunes, and expos'd their lives to the utmost dangers for their King and Country, who ended their loyalty with the War: and submitting to the iniquity of the times, chose rather to redeem

237

their former plenty by acknowledging an Usurper, then to suffer with an unprofitable fidelity (as those meaner spirits call'd it) for their lawful Soveraign. But, as I dare not accuse so many of our Nobility, who were content to accept their Patrimonies from the Clemency of the Conquerour, *and to retain only a secret veneration for their Prince, amidst the open worship which they were forc'd to pay to the Usurper, who had dethron'd him; so, I hope, I may have leave to extoll that vertue which acted more generously; and which was not satisfi'd with an inward devotion to Monarchy, but produc'd it self to view, and asserted the cause by open Martyrdome. Of these rare Patterns of loyalty your Grace was chief: those examples you cou'd not find, you made. Some few* Cato's *there were with you, whose invincible resolution could not be conquer'd by* that usurping Cæsar: *your vertue oppos'd it self to his fortune, and overcame it, by not submitting to it. The last and most difficult Enterprize he had to effect, when he had conquer'd three Nations, was to subdue your spirits: and he dy'd weary of that War, and unable to finish it.*

In the mean time you liv'd more happily in your exile then the other on his Throne: your loyalty made you friends and servants amongst Forreigners: and you liv'd plentifully without a fortune; for you liv'd on your own desert and reputation. The glorious Name of the valiant and faithful Newcastle, *was a Patrimony which cou'd never be exhausted.*

Thus, my Lord, the morning of your life was clear, and calm; and though it was afterwards overcast; yet, in that general Storm, you were never without a shelter. And now you are happily arriv'd to the evening of a day as serene, as the dawn of it was glorious: but such an evening as, I hope, and almost prophesie, is far from night: 'Tis the Evening of a Summer's Sun, *which keeps the day-light long within the skies. The health of your body is maintain'd by the vigour of your mind: neither does the one shrink from the fatigue of exercise, nor the other bend under the pains of study. Methinks I behold in you another* Caius Marius, *who in the extremity of his age, excercis'd himself almost every morning in the* Campus Martius, *amongst the youthful Nobility of* Rome. *And afterwards in your retirements, when you do honour to poetrie, by employing part of your leisure in it, I regard you as another* Silius Italicus, *who having pass'd over his Consulship with applause, dismiss'd himself from business, and from the Gown, and employ'd his age, amongst the shades, in the reading and imitation of* Virgil.

In which, least any thing should be wanting to your happiness, you have by a rare effect of Fortune, found in the person of your excellent Lady, not only a Lover, *but a Partner of your studies. A Lady whom our Age may justly equal with the* Sappho *of the* Greeks, *or the* Sulpitia *of the* Romans. *Who, by being taken into your bosome, seems to be enspir'd with your Genius: And by writing the History of your life, in so masculine a*

*style, has already plac'd you in the Number of the Heroes. She has antici-
pated the great portion of Fame which envy often hinders a living vertue
from possessing: which wou'd, indeed, have been given to your ashes, but
with a latter payment: and, of which you could have no present use, ex-
cept it were by a secret presage of that which was to come, when you were
no longer in a possibility of knowing it. So that if that were a praise, or
satisfaction to the greatest of Emperors, which the most judicious of Poets
gives him,*

Præsenti tibi maturos largimur honores, &c.

That the adoration which was not allowed to Hercules *and* Romulus
till after death, was given to Augustus *living; then certainly it cannot be
deny'd but that your Grace has receiv'd a double satisfaction: the one, to
see your self consecrated to immortality while you are yet alive; the other,
to have your praises celebrated by so dear, so just, and so pious an His-
torian.*

*'Tis the consideration of this that stops my pen: though I am loath to
leave so fair a subject, which gives me as much field as Poetry cou'd wish,
and yet no more than truth can justifie. But to attempt any thing of a
Panegyrick, were to enterprize on your Lady's right; and to seem to effect
those praises, which none but the* Dutchess *of* Newcastle *can deserve,
when she writes the actions of her Lord. I shall therefore leave that wider
space, and contract my self to those narrow bounds which best become my*
Fortune and Employment.

*I am oblig'd, my Lord, to return you not only my own acknowledgements,
but to thank you in the names of former Poets. The* manes *of* Johnson *and*
D'avenant *seem to require it from me, that those favours which you plac'd
on them, and which they wanted opportunity to own in publick, yet might
not be lost to the knowledge of Posterity, with a forgetfulness unbecoming
of the Muses, who are the Daughters of Memory. And give me leave, my
Lord, to avow so much of vanity, as to say, I am proud to be their Remem-
brancer: for, by relating how gracious you have been to them, and are to
me, I, in some measure, joyn my name with theirs: and the continu'd de-
scent of your favours to me is the best title which I can plead for my succes-
sion. I only wish, that I had as great reason to be satisfi'd with my self, in
the return of our common acknowledgements, as your Grace may justly take
in the confering them: for I cannot but be very sensible that the present of
an ill Comedy, which I here make you, is a very unsuitable way of giving
thanks for them, who, themselves have written so many better. This
pretends to nothing more than to be a foyl to those Scenes, which are compos'd
by the most noble Poet of our Age, and Nation: And to be set as a water-
mark of the lowest ebb, to which the wit of my Predecessors has sunk and
run down in me: but, though all of them have surpass'd me in the Scene;*

there is one part of glory in which I will not yield to any of them. I mean, my Lord, that honour and veneration which they had for you in their lives; and which I preserve after them, more holily than the Vestal fires were maintain'd from Age to Age; but with a greater degree of heat, and of devotion than theirs, as being with more respect and passion than they ever were,

Your GRACES most obliged, most

humble, and most obedient Servant

John Dryden.

PREFACE

I Had thought, Reader, in this Preface to have written somewhat concerning the difference betwixt the Playes of our Age, and those of our *Predecessors, on the* English *Stage: to have shewn in what parts of Dramatick Poesie we were excell'd by* Ben. Johnson, *I mean, humour, and contrivance of Comedy; and in what we may justly claim precedence of* Shakespear *and* Fletcher, *namely in Heroick Playes: but this design I have wav'd on second considerations; at least deferr'd it till I publish the Conquest of* Granada, *where the discourse will be more proper. I had also prepar'd to Treat of the improvement of our Language since* Fletcher's *and* Johnson's *dayes, and consequently of our refining the Courtship, Raillery, and Conversation of Playes: but as I am willing to decline that envy which I shou'd draw on my self from some old Opiniatre judges of the Stage; so likewise I am prest in time so much that I have not leisure, at present, to go thorough with it. Neither, indeed, do I value a reputation gain'd from Comedy, so far as to concern my self about it any more than I needs must in my own defence: for I think it, in its own nature, inferiour to all sorts of Dramatick writing. Low Comedy especially requires, on the Writers part, much of conversation with the vulgar: and much of ill nature in the observation of their follies. But let all men please themselves according to their several tastes: that which is not pleasant to me, may be to others who judge better: and, to prevent an accusation from my enemies, I am sometimes ready to imagine that my disgust of low Comedy proceeds not so much from my judgement as from my temper; which is the reason why I so seldom write it; and that when I succeed in it, (I mean so far as to please the Audience) yet I am nothing satisfi'd with what I have done; but am often vex'd to hear the people laugh, and clap, as they perpetually*

240

do, where I intended 'em no jest; while they let pass the better things without taking notice of them. Yet, even this confirms me in my opinion of slighting popular applause, and of contemning that approbation which those very people give, equally with me, to the Zany of a Mountebank; or to the appearance of an Antick on the Theatre, without wit on the Poets part, or any occasion of laughter from the Actor, besides the ridiculousness of his habit and his Grimaces.

But I have descended before I was aware, from Comedy to Farce; which consists principally of Grimaces. That I admire not any Comedy equally with Tragedy, is, perhaps, from the sullenness of my humor; but that I detest those Farces, which are now the most frequent entertainments of the Stage, I am sure I have reason on my side. Comedy consists, though of low persons, yet of natural actions, and characters; I mean some humours, adventures, and designs, as are to be found and met with in the world. Farce, on the other side, consists of forc'd humours, and unnatural events: Comedy presents us with the imperfections of humane nature. Farce entertains us with what is monstrous and chimerical: the one causes laughter in those who can judge of men and manners; by the lively representation of their folly or corruption; the other produces the same effect in those who can judge of neither, and that only by its extravagances. The first works on the judgment and fancy; the latter on the fancy only: There is more of satisfaction in the former kind of laughter, and in the latter more of scorn. But, how it happens, that an impossible adventure should cause our mirth, I cannot so easily imagine. Something there may be in the oddness of it, because on the Stage it is the common effect of things unexpected to surprize us into a delight: and that is to be ascrib'd to the strange appetite, as I may call it, of the fancy; which, like that of a longing Woman, often runs out into the most extravagant desires; and is better satisfy'd sometimes with Loam, or with the Rinds of Trees, than with the wholesome nourishments of life. In short, there is the same difference betwixt Farce and Comedy, as betwixt an Empirique and a true Physitian: both of them may attain their ends; but what the one performs by hazard, the other does by skill. And as the Artist is often unsuccessful, while the Mountebank succeeds; so Farces more commonly take the people than Comedies. For to write unnatural things, is the most probable way of pleasing them, who understand not Nature. And a true Poet often misses of applause, because he cannot debase himself to write so ill as to please his Audience.

After all, it is to be acknowledg'd, that most of those Comedies, which have been lately written, have been ally'd too much to Farce: and this must of necessity fall out till we forbear the translation of French Plays: for their Poets wanting judgement to make, or to maintain true characters, strive to cover their defects with ridiculous Figures and Grimaces. While I *say this, I accuse my self as well as others: and this very play would rise up in judgment against me, if I would defend all things I have written to be natural: but I confess I have given too much to the people in it, and am asham'd for them as well as for my self, that I have pleas'd them at so cheap a rate: not that there is any thing here which I would not defend to an ill-natur'd judge: (for I despise their censures, who I am sure wou'd write worse on the same subject:) but because I love to deal clearly and plainly, and to speak of my own faults with more criticism, than I would of another Poets. Yet I think it no vanity to say that this Comedy has as much of entertainment in it as many other which have been lately written: and, if I find my own errors in it, I am able at the same time, to arraign all my Contemporaries for greater. As I pretend not that I can write humour, so none of them can reasonably pretend to have written it as they ought.* Johnson *was the only man of all Ages and Nations, who has perform'd it well; and that but in three or four of his Comedies: the rest are but a* Crambe bis cocta; *the same humours a little vary'd and written worse: neither was it more allowable in him, than it is in our present Poets, to represent the follies of particular persons; of which many have accus'd him.* Parcere personis dicere de vitiis *is the rule of Plays. And* Horace *tells you, that the old Comedy amongst the* Grecians *was silenc'd for the too great liberties of the Poets.*

> ——In vitium libertas excidit & vim
> Dignam lege regi: lex est accepta chorusque
> Turpiter obticuit, sublato jure nocendi.

Of which he gives you the reason in another place: where having given the precept.

> Neve immunda crepent; ignominiosaque dicta:

He immediately subjoyns,

> Offenduntur enim, quibus est equus, & pater, & res.

But Ben. Johnson *is to be admir'd for many excellencies; and can be tax'd with fewer failings than any* English *Poet. I know I have been accus'd as an enemy of his writings; but without any other reason than that I do not admire him blindly, and without looking into his imperfections. For why should he only be exempted from those frailties, from which* Homer *and* Virgil *are not free? Or why should there be any* ipse dixit *in our Poetry, any more than there is in our Philosophy, I admire and applaud him where I ought: those who do more do but value themselves in their admiration of him: and by telling you they extoll* Ben. Johnson's *way, would insinuate to you that they can practice it. For my part I declare that I want judgement to imitate him: and should think it a great impudence in my self to attempt it. To make men appear pleasantly ridiculous on the Stage was, as I have said, his talent: and in this he needed not the acumen of wit, but that of judgement. For the characters and representation of folly are only the effects of observation; and observation is an effect of judgment. Some ingenious men, for whom I have a particular esteem, have thought I have much injur'd* Ben. Johnson, *when I have not allow'd his wit to be extraordinary: but they confound the notion of what is witty, with what is pleasant. That* Ben. Johnson's *Playes were pleasant, he must want reason who denyes: But that pleasantness was not properly wit, or the sharpness of conceit; but the natural imitation of folly: which I confess to be excellent in it's kind, but not to be of that kind which they pretend. Yet if we will believe* Quintilian *in his Chapter* de Movendo risu, *he gives his opinion of both in these following words,* Stulta reprehendere facillimum est; nam per se sunt ridicula: & a derisu non procul abest risus: sed rem urbanam facit aliqua ex nobis adjectio.

And some perhaps, would be apt to say of Johnson, *as it was said of* Demosthenes; Non displicuisse illi jocos, sed non contigisse, *I will not deny but that I approve most the mixt way of Comedy; that which is neither all wit, nor all humour, but the result of both. Neither so little of humour as* Fletcher *shews, nor so little of love and wit, as* Johnson. *Neither all cheat, with which the best Playes of the one are fill'd, nor all adventure, which is the common practice of the other. I would have the characters well chosen, and kept distant from interfaring with each other; which is more than* Fletcher *or* Shakespear *did: but I would have more of the* Urbana, venusta, salsa, faceta, *and the rest which* Quintilian *reckons up as the ornaments of wit; and these are extremely wanting in* Ben. Johnson. *As for repartie in particular, as it is the very soul of conversation, so it is the greatest grace of Comedy, where it is proper to the Characters: there may be much of acuteness in a thing well said; but there is more in a quick reply:* sunt, enim, longè venustiora omnia in respondendo quàm in provocando. *Of one thing I am sure, that no man ever will decry wit, but he who despairs of it himself; and who has no other quarrel to it but that which the Fox had to the Grapes. Yet, as Mr.* Cowley, *(who had a greater portion of it than any man I know) tells us in his Character of Wit, rather than all wit let there be none; I think there's no folly so great in any Poet of our Age as the superfluity and waste of Wit was in some of our predecessors: particularly we may say of* Fletcher *and of* Shakespear, *what was said of* Ovid, In omni ejus ingenio, facilius quod rejici, quàm quod adjici potest, invenies. *The contrary of which was true in* Virgil, *and our incomparable* Johnson.

Some enemies of Repartie have observ'd to us, that there is a great latitude

*in their Characters, which are made to speak it: And that it is easier
to write wit than humour; because in the characters of humour, the Poet
is confin'd to make the person speak what is only proper to it. Whereas all
kind of wit is proper in the Character of a witty person. But, by their
favour, there are as different Characters in wit as in folly. Neither is all
kind of wit proper in the mouth of every ingenious person. A witty Coward
and a witty Brave, must speak differently.* Falstaffe *and the* Lyar, *speak
not like* Don John *in the* Chances, *and* Valentine *in* Wit without
Money, *and* Johnson's Truwit *in the* Silent Woman, *is a Character
different from all of them. Yet it appears that this one Character of Wit
was more difficult to the Author, than all his images of humour in the
Play: For those he could describe and manage from his observation of
men; this he has taken, at least a part of it, from books: witness the
Speeches in the first Act, translated* verbatim *out of* Ovid de Arte
Amandi. *To omit what afterwards he borrowed from the sixth Satyre of*
Juvenal *against Women.*

*However, if I should grant, that there were a greater latitude in
Characters of Wit, than in those of Humour; yet that latitude would be of
small advantage to such Poets who have too narrow an imagination to
write it. And to entertain an Audience perpetually with Humour, is to
carry them from the conversation of Gentlemen, and treat them with the
follies and extravagances of* Bedlam.

*I find I have launch'd out farther than I intended in the beginning of
this Preface. And that in the heat of writing, I have touch'd at something,
which I thought to have avoided. 'Tis time now to draw homeward: and
to think rather of defending my self, than assaulting others. I have already
acknowledg'd that this Play is far from perfect: but I do not think my self
oblig'd to discover the imperfections of it to my Adversaries, any more than
a guilty person is bound to accuse himself before his Judges. 'Tis charg'd
upon me that I make debauch'd persons (such as they say my Astrologer
and Gamester are) my Protagonists, or the chief persons of the* Drama;
*and that I make them happy in the conclusion of my Play; against the
Law of Comedy, which is to reward virtue, and punish vice. I answer
first, that I know no such Law to have been constantly observ'd in
Comedy, either by the Ancient or Modern Poets.* Chœrea *is made happy
in the* Eunuch, *after having deflour'd a Virgin: and* Terence *generally
does the same through all his Plays, where you perpetually see, not only
debauch'd young men enjoy their Mistresses, but even the Courtezans
themselves rewarded and honour'd in the Catastrophe. The same may be
observ'd in* Plautus *almost every where.* Ben. Johnson *himself, after
whom I may be proud to erre, has given me more than once the example
of it. That in the* Alchemist *is notorious, where* Face, *after having con-
triv'd and carried on the great cozenage of the Play, and continued in it,*

244

without repentance, to the last, is not only forgiven by his Master, but inrich'd by his consent, with the spoils of those whom he had cheated. And, which is more, his Master himself, a grave man, and a Widower, is introduc'd taking his Man's counsel, debauching the Widow first, in hope to marry her afterward. In the Silent Woman, Dauphine (*who with the other two Gentlemen, is of the same Character with my* Celadon *in the* Maiden Queen, *and with* Wildblood *in this*) *professes himself in love with all the Collegiate Ladies: and they likewise are all of the same Character with each other, excepting only Madam* Otter, *who has something singular:*) *yet this naughty* Dauphine, *is crown'd in the end with the possession of his Uncles Estate, and with the hopes of enjoying all his Mistresses. And his friend Mr.* Truwit (*the best Character of a Gentleman which* Ben. Johnson *ever made*) *is not asham'd to pimp for him. As for* Beaumont *and* Fletcher, *I need not alledge examples out of them; for that were to quote almost all their Comedies. But now it will be objected that I patronize vice by the authority of former Poets, and extenuate my own faults by recrimination. I answer, that as I defend my self by their example; so that example I defend by reason, and by the end of all Dramatique Poesie. In the first place therefore give me leave to shew you their mistake who have accus'd me. They have not distinguish'd as they ought, betwixt the rules of Tragedy and Comedy. In Tragedy, where the Actions and Persons are great, and the crimes horrid, the laws of justice are more strictly to be observ'd: and examples of punishment to be made to deterre mankind from the pursuit of vice. Faults of this kind have been rare amongst the Ancient Poets: for they have punish'd in* Oedipus, *and in his posterity, the sinne which he knew not he had committed.* Medea *is the only example I remember, at present, who escapes from punishment after murder. Thus Tragedy fulfils one great part of its institution; which is by example to instruct. But in Comedy it is not so; for the chief end of it is divertisement and delight: and that so much, that it is disputed, I think, by* Heinsius, *before* Horace *his art of Poetry, whether instruction be any part of its employment. At least I am sure it can be but its secondary end: for the business of the Poet is to make you laugh: when he writes humour, he makes folly ridiculous; when wit, he moves you, if not always to laughter, yet to a pleasure that is more noble. And if he works a cure on folly, and the small imperfections in mankind, by exposing them to publick view, that cure is not perform'd by an immediate operation. For it works first on the ill nature of the Audience; they are mov'd to laugh by the representation of deformity; and the shame of that laughter, teaches us to amend what is ridiculous in our manners. This being then establish'd, that the first end of Comedie is delight, and instruction only the second; it may reasonably be inferr'd, that Comedy is not so much oblig'd to the punishment of the faults which it represents, as Tragedy. For the persons*

245

in Comedy are of a lower quality, the action is little, and the faults and vices are but the sallies of youth, and the frailties of humane nature, and not premeditated crimes: such to which all men are obnoxious, not such as are attempted only by few, and those abandonn'd to all sense of vertue: such as move pity and commiseration; not detestation and horror; such, in short, as may be forgiven, not such as must of necessity be punish'd. But, lest any man should think that I write this to make libertinism amiable; or that I car'd not to debase the end and institution of Comedy, so I might thereby maintain my own errors, and those of better Poets; I must farther declare, both for them and for my self, that we make not vicious persons happy, but only as heaven makes sinners so: that is by reclaiming them first from vice. For so 'tis to be suppos'd they are, when they resolve to marry; for then enjoying what they desire in one, they cease to pursue the love of many. So Chærea is made happy by Terence, *in marrying her whom he had deflour'd: And so are* Wildblood, *and the Astrologer in this Play.*

There is another crime with which I am charg'd, at which I am yet much less concern'd, because it does not relate to my manners, as the former did, but only to my reputation as a Poet: A name of which I assure the Reader I am nothing proud; and therefore cannot be very sollicitous to defend it. I am tax'd with stealing all my Playes, and that by some who should be the last men from whom I would steal any part of 'em. There is one answer which I will not make; but it has been made for me by him to whose Grace and Patronage I owe all things,

Et spes & ratio studiorum, in *Cæsare* tantum.

And without whose command they shou'd no longer be troubl'd with any thing of mine, that he only desir'd that they who accus'd me of theft, would always steal him Playes like mine. But though I have reason to be proud of this defence, yet I should wave it, because I have a worse opinion of my own Comedies than any of my Enemies can have. 'Tis true, that where ever I have lik'd any story in a Romance, Novel, or forreign Play, I have made no difficulty, nor ever shall, to take the foundation of it, to build it up, and to make it proper for the English Stage. *And I will be so vain to say it has lost nothing in my hands: But it always cost me so much trouble to heighten it; for our Theatre (which is incomparably more curious in all the ornaments of Dramatick Poesie, than the* French, *or* Spanish) *that when I had finish'd my Play, it was like the hulk of Sir* Francis Drake, *so strangely alter'd, that there scarce remain'd any Plank of the Timber which first built it. To witness this I need go no farther than this Play: It was first* Spanish, *and call'd* El Astrologo fingido; *then made* French *by the younger* Corneille: *and is now translated into* English, *and in Print, under the name of the* Feign'd Astrologer. *What I* have perform'd in this, will best appear, by comparing it with those: you will see that I have rejected some adventures which I judg'd were not divertising: that I have heightned those which I have chosen, and that I have added others which were neither in the French nor Spanish. And besides you will easily discover that the Walk of the Astrologer is the least considerable in my Play: for the design of it turns more on the parts of Wildblood and Jacinta, who are the chief persons in it. I have farther to add, that I seldome use the wit and language of any Romance, or Play which I undertake to alter; because my own invention (as bad as it is) can furnish me with nothing so dull as what is there. Those who have call'd Virgil, Terence, and Tasso Plagiaries (though they much injur'd them,) had yet a better colour for their accusation; For Virgil has evidently translated Theocritus, Hesiod, and Homer, in many places; besides what he has taken from Ennius in his own Language. Terence was not only known to translate Menander, (which he avows also in his Prologues) but was said also to be help't in those Translations by Scipio the African, and Lælius. And Tasso, the most excellent of modern Poets, and whom I reverence next to Virgil, has taken both from Homer many admirable things which were left untouch'd by Virgil, and from Virgil himself where Homer cou'd not furnish him. Yet the bodies of Virgil's and Tasso's Poems were their own: and so are all the Ornaments of language and elocution in them. The same (if there were any thing commendable in this Play) I could say for it. But I will come nearer to our own Countrymen. Most of Shakespear's Plays, I mean the Stories of them, are to be found in the Hecatommuthi, or hundred Novels of Cinthio. I have, my self, read in his Italian, that of Romeo, and Juliet, the Moor of Venice, and many others of them. Beaumont and Fletcher had most of theirs from Spanish Novels: witness the Chances, the Spanish Curate, Rule a Wife and have a Wife, the Little French Lawyer, and so many others of them, as compose the greatest part of their Volume in folio. Ben. Johnson, indeed, has design'd his Plots himself; but no man has borrow'd so much from the Ancients as he has done: And he did well in it, for he has thereby beautifi'd our language.

But these little Criticks do not well consider what is the work of a Poet, and what the Graces of a Poem: The Story is the least part of either: I mean the foundation of it, before it is modell'd by the art of him who writes it; who formes it with more care, by exposing only the beautiful parts of it to view, than a skilful Lapidary sets a Jewel. On this foundation of the Story the Characters are rais'd: and, since no Story can afford Characters enough for the variety of the English Stage, it follows that it is to be alter'd, and inlarg'd, with new persons, accidents and designs, which will almost make it new. When this is done, the forming it into Acts, and Scenes, disposing of actions and passions into their proper places, and beautifying both with descriptions, similitudes, and propriety of language, is the principall employment of the Poet; as being the largest field of fancy which is the principall quality requir'd in him: For so much the word ποιητὴς imployes. Judgement, indeed, is necessary in him; but 'tis fancy that gives the life touches, and the secret graces to it; especially in serious Plays, which depend not much on observation. For to write humour in Comedy (which is the theft of Poets from mankind) little of fancy is requir'd; the Poet observes only what is ridiculous, and pleasant folly, and by judging exactly what is so, he pleases in the representation of it.

But in general, the employment of a Poet, is like that of a curious Gunsmith or Watchmaker: the Iron or Silver is not his own; but they are the least part of that which gives the value: The price lies wholly in the workmanship. And he who works dully on a Story, without moving laughter in a Comedy, or raising concernments in a serious Play, is no more to be counted a good Poet, than a Gunsmith of the Minories is to be compar'd with the best workman of the Town.

But I have said more of this than I intended; and more, perhaps, than I needed to have done: I shall but laugh at them hereafter, who accuse me with so little reason; and withall contemn their dulness, who, if they could ruine that little reputation I have got, and which I value not, yet would want both wit and learning to establish their own, or to be rememberd in after ages for any thing, but only that which makes them ridiculous in this.

PROLOGUE

WHen first our Poet set himself to write,
  Like a young Bridegroom on his Wedding-night
He laid about him, and did so bestir him,
His Muse could never lye in quiet for him:
But now his Hony-moon is gone and past,
Yet the ungrateful drudgery must last:
And he is bound, as civil Husbands do,
To strain himself, in complaisance to you:
To write in pain, and counterfeit a bliss,
Like the faint smackings of an after kiss.
But you, like Wives ill pleas'd, supply his want;
Each Writing Monsieur is a fresh Gallant:
And though, perhaps, 'twas done as well before,
Yet still there's something in a new amour.
Your several Poets work with several tools,
One gets you wits, another gets you fools:
This pleases you with some by-stroke of wit,
This finds some cranny, that was never hit.
But should these janty Lovers daily come
To do your work, like your good man at home,
Their fine small-timber'd wits would soon decay;
These are Gallants but for a Holiday.
Others you had who oftner have appear'd,
Whom, for meer impotence you have cashier'd:
Such as at first came on with pomp and glory,
But, over-straining, soon fell flat before yee.
Their useless weight, with patience long was born,
But at the last you threw 'em off with scorn.
As for the Poet of this present night,
Though now he claims in you a Husbands right, }
He will not hinder you of fresh delight.
He, like a Seaman, seldom will appear;
And means to trouble home but thrice a year:
That only time from your Gallants he'll borrow;
Be kind to day, and Cuckold him to morrow.

PERSONS REPRESENTED

MEN

		By
Wildblood, *Bellamy,* } TWO young English Gentlemen.		{ Mr. *Hart.* Mr. *Mohun.*
Maskall, Their Servant.		Mr. *Shatterel.*
Don *Alonzo de Ribera,* an old Spanish Gentleman.		Mr. *Wintershall.*
Don *Lopez de Gamboa,* a young Noble Spaniard.		Mr. *Burt.*
Don *Melchor de Guzman,* A Gentleman of a great Family; but of a decay'd fortune.		Mr. *Lydall.*

WOMEN

		By
Donna Theodosia, *Donna Jacintha,* } Daughters to *Don Alonzo.*		{ Mrs. *Bowtell.* Mrs. *Ellen Guynn.*
Donna Aurelia, Their Cousin.		Mrs. *Marshal*; and formerly by Mrs. *Quin.*
Beatrix, Woman and Confident to the two Sisters.		Mrs. *Knepp.*
Camilla, Woman to *Aurelia.*		Mrs. *Betty Slate.*

Servants to Don *Lopez,* and Don *Alonzo.*

The Scene *Madrid,* in the Year 1665.

The Time, the last evening of the Carnival.

AN EVENING'S LOVE
OR,
The Mock-Astrologer.

ACT I. SCENE I.

Don Lopez, *and a Servant, walking over the Stage.*
Enter another Servant, and follows him.

Ser. **D**On *Lopez?*
    Lop. Any new business?
  Ser. My Master had forgot this Letter.
Which he conjures you, as you are his friend,
To give *Aurelia* from him.
    Lop. Tell Don *Melchor* 'tis a hard task which he enjoyns me:
He knows I love her, and much more than he;
For I love her alone, but he divides
His passion betwixt two: Did he consider
How great a pain 'tis to dissemble love,
He would never practise it.
    Sir. He knows his fault; but cannot mend it.
    Lop. To make the poor *Aurelia* believe
He's gone for *Flanders*, whiles he lies conceal'd,
And every night makes visits to her Cousin.
When will he leave this strange extravagance?
    Ser. When he can love one more, or t'other less.
    Lop. Before I lov'd my self, I promis'd him
To serve him in his love; and I'll perform it,
How e're repugnant to my own concernments.
    Serv. You are a noble Cavalier.   *Exit Servant.*

Enter Bellamy, Wildblood, Maskall.

  2^{d.} *Serv.* Sir, your Guests of the *English* Embassador's Retinue.
  Lop. Cavaliers, will you please to command my Coach to take the air this Evening?
  Bell. We have not yet resolv'd how to dispose of our selves; but however we are highly acknowledging to you, for your civility.

251

Lop. You cannot more oblige me then by laying your commands on me.

Wild. We kiss your hands.   *Exit* Lopez *cum Servo.*

Bell. Give the Don his due, he entertain'd us nobly this Carnival.

Wild. Give the Devil the Don, for anything I lik'd in his Entertainment.

Bell. I hope we had variety enough.

Wild. I, it look'd like variety, till we came to taste it; there were twenty several dishes to the eye, but in the pallat nothing but Spices. I had a mind to eat of a Pheasant, and as soon as I got it into my mouth, I found I was chawing a limb of Cinamon; then I went to cut a piece of Kid, and no sooner it had touch'd my lips, but it turn'd to red Pepper: at last I began to think my self another kind of *Midas*, that every thing I touch'd should be turn'd to Spice.

Bell. And for my part, I imagin'd his Catholick Majesty had invited us to eat his Indies. But prethee let's leave the discourse of it, and contrive together how we may spend the Evening; for in this hot Country, 'tis as in the Creation, the Evening and the Morning make the day.

Wild. I have a little serious business.

Bell. Put it off till a fitter season: for the truth is, business is then only tolerable, when the world and the flesh have no baits to set before us for the day.

Wild. But mine perhaps is publick business.

Bell. Why is any business more publick than drinking and wenching? Look on those grave plodding fellows, that pass by us, as though they were meditating the reconquest of *Flanders:* fly 'em to a Mark, and I'll undertake three parts of four are going to their Courtezans. I tell thee *Jack*, the whisking of a Silk Gown, and the rash of a Tabby-Petticoat, are as comfortable sounds to one of these rich Citizens, as the chink of their Pieces of Eight.

Wild. This being granted to be the common design of humane kind, 'tis more than probable 'tis yours; therefore I'll leave you to the prosecution of it.

Bell. Nay, good *Jack*, mine is but a Mistress in Embrio; the possession of her is at least some ten dayes off, and till that time, thy company will be pleasant, and may be profitable to carry on the work. I would use thee like an under kind of Chymist, to blow the coals; 'twill be time enough for me to be alone when I come to projection.

Wild. You must excuse me, *Franck*; I have made an appointment at the Gameing-house.

Bell. What to do there I prithee? to mis-spend that money, which kind fortune intended for a Miſtress? or to learn new Oaths and Curses to carry into *England*? that is not it———I heard you were to marry when you left home: perhaps that may be ſtill running in your head, and keep you vertuous.

Wild. Marriage quoth a! what doſt thou think I have been bred in the Desarts of *Africk*, or among the Savages of *America*? nay, if I had, I muſt needs have known better things than so; the light of Nature would not have let me gone so far aſtray.

Bell. Well! what think you of the *Prado* this Evening?

Wild. Pox upon't, 'tis worse than our contemplative *Hide-Park*.

Bell. O! but we muſt submit to the Cuſtom of the Country for courtship: whatever the means are, we are sure the end is ſtill the same in all places. But who are these?

Enter Don Alonzo de Ribera, *with his two Daughters* Theodosia *and* Jacinta, *and* Beatrix *their Woman, passing by.*

Theo. Do you see those ſtrangers, Siſter, that eye us so earneſtly?

Jac. Yes, and I guess 'em to be feathers of the English Embassa-dor's Train; for I think I saw 'em at the grand Audience———And have the ſtrangeſt temptation in the world to talk to 'em: A mis-chief on this modeſty.

Beat. A mischief of this Father of yours that haunts you so.

Jac. 'Tis very true *Beatrix*; for though I am the younger Siſter, I should have the grace to lay modeſty firſt aside: however, Siſter, let us pull up our Vails, and give 'em an Essay of our faces.

They pull up their Vails, and pull 'em down agen.

Wild. Ah *Bellamy!* undone, undone! doſt thou see those Beauties?

Bell. Prithee *Wildblood* hold thy tongue, and do not spoil my contemplation; I am undoing my self as faſt as e're I can too.

Wild. I muſt go to 'em.

Bell. Hold Madman; doſt thou not see their father? haſt thou a mind to have our throats cut?

Wild. By a Hector of fourscore? Hang our throats, what a Lover and cautious? *Is going towards them.*

Alon. Come away Daughters, we shall be late else.

Bell. Look, you, they are on the wing already.

Wild. Prithee, dear *Frank*, let's follow 'em: I long to know who they are.

Mask. Let me alone, I'll dog 'em for you.

Bell. I am glad on't, for my shooes so pinch me, I can scarce go a ſtep farther.

253

Wild. Cross the way there lives a Shoomaker: away quickly, that we may not spoil our man's design.   *Exit* Bell. Wild.

Alon. *offers to go off—* Now friend! what's your business to follow us?

Mask. Noble *Don*; 'tis only to recommend my service to you: A certain violent passion I have had for your worship since the first moment that I saw you.

Alon. I never saw thee before to my remembrance.

Mask. No matter, Sir, true love never stands upon ceremony.

Alon. Prithee be gone my sawcie companion, I'll clap an Alguazile upon thy heels; I tell thee I have no need of thy service.

Mask. Having no servant of your own, I cannot in good manners leave you destitute.

Alon. I'll beat thee if thou follow'st me.

Mask. I am your Spaniel, Sir, the more you beat me, the better I'll wait on you.

Alon. Let me intreat thee to be gone; the boyes will hoot at me to see me follow'd thus against my will.

Mask. Shall you and I concern our selves for what the Boyes do, Sir? Pray do you hear the news at Court?

Alon. Prithee what's the news to thee or me?

Mask. Will you be at the next *Juego de cannas*?

Alon. If I think good.

Mask. Pray go on Sir, we can discourse as we walk together: And whither were you now a going, Sir?

Alon. To the Devil I think.

Mask. O! not this year or two, Sir, by your age.

Jac. My Father was never so match'd for talking in all his life before; he who loves to hear nothing but himself: Prethee, *Beatrix*, stay behind, and see what this impudent Englishman would have.

Beat. Sir! if you'll not let my Master go, I'll be his pawn.

Mask. Well, Sir, I kiss your hand, in hope to wait on you another time.

Alon. Let us mend our pace to get clear of him.

Theo. If you do not, he'll be with you agen, like *Atalanta* in the fable, and make you drop another of your golden Apples.

Exit Alon. Theod. Jacinta.
Maskal *whispers* Beatrix *the while*.

Beat. How much good language is here thrown away to make me betray my Ladies?

Mask. If you will discover nothing of 'em, let me discourse with you a little.

Beat. As little as you please.

Mask. They are rich I suppose.

Beat. Now you are talking of them agen: but they are as rich, as they are fair.

Mask. Then they have the *Indies:* well, but their Names my sweet Mistress.

Beat. Sweet Servant, their names are——

Mask. Their Names are——out with it boldly——

Beat. A secret not to be disclos'd.

Mask. A secret say you? Nay, then I conjure you as you are a Woman, tell it me.

Beat. Not a syllable.

Mask. Why then as you are a Waiting-woman, as you are the Sieve of all your Ladies Secrets tell it me.

Beat. You lose your labour: nothing will strain through me.

Mask. Are you so well stop'd i'th' bottom?

Beat. It was enjoyn'd me strictly as a Secret.

Mask. Was it enjoyn'd thee strictly, and canst thou hold it? Nay then thou art invincible: but, by that face, that more than ugly face, which I suspect to be under thy Vaile, disclose it to me.

Beat. By that Face of thine which is a Natural Visor: I will not tell thee.

Mask. By thy——

Beat. No more Swearing I beseech you.

Mask. That Woman's worth little, that is not worth an Oath: well, get thee gone, now I think on't thou shalt not tell me.

Beat. Shall I not? Who shall hinder me? They are Don *Alonzo de Ribera's* Daughters.

Mask. Out, out: I'le stop my Ears.

Beat. ——They live hard by, in the *Calle maior.*

Mask. O infernal Tongue——

Beat. And are going to the next Chappel with their Father.

Mask. Wilt thou never have done tormenting me? in my Conscience anon thou wilt blab out their Names too.

Beat. Their Names are *Theodosia* and *Jacinta.*

Mask. And where's your great Secret now?

Beat. Now I think I am reveng'd on you for running down my poor old Master.

Mask. Thou art not fully reveng'd till thou hast told me thy own Name too.

Beat. 'Tis *Beatrix,* at your service, Sir, pray remember I wait on 'em.

Mask. Now I have enough, I must be going.

Beat. I perceive you are juſt like other Men; when you have got your ends, you care not how soon you are going.———
———Farewel,———you'l be conſtant to me———

Mask. If thy face, when I see it, do not give me occasion to be otherwise.

Beat. You shall take a Sample that you may praise it when you see it next.   (*She pulls up her Vail.*)

Enter Wildblood *and* Bellamy.

Wild. Look, there's your Dog with a Duck in's mouth———
Oh she's got loose and div'd again———   [*Exit* Beatrix.

Bell. Well *Maskall*, what newes of the Ladies of the Lake?

Mask. I have learn'd enough to embarque you in an Adventure; they are Daughters to one Don *Alonzo de Ribera* in the *Calle major*, their Names *Theodosia* and *Jacinta*, and they are going to their Devotions in the next Chappel.

Wild. Away then, let us lose no time, I thank Heaven I never found my self better enclin'd to Godliness than at this present.———

Exeunt.

SCENE II. *A Chappel.*

Enter Alonzo, Theodosia, Jacinta, Beatrix, *other* Ladies *and* Cavaliers *as at their Devotion.*

Alon. By that time you have told your Beads I'll be agen with you.

Exit.

Jac. Do you think the *English* Men will come after us?

Beat. Do you think they can ſtay from you?

Jac. For my part I feel a certain qualm upon my heart, which makes me believe I am breeding Love to one of 'em.

Theo. How, Love, *Jacinta*, in so short a time? *Cupid's* Arrow was well feather'd to reach you so suddenly.

Jac. Faith as good at firſt as at laſt Siſter, 'tis a thing that muſt be done, and therefore 'tis beſt dispatching it out o' th' way.

Theo. But you do not mean to tell him so whom you love?

Jac. Why should I keep my Self and Servant in pain, for that which may be cur'd at a dayes warning?

Beat. My Lady tells you true, Madam, long tedious Courtship may be proper for cold Countries, where their Froſts are long a thawing; but Heaven be prais'd we live in a warm Climate.

Theo. The truth is, in other Countries they have opportunities for Courtship, which we have not, they are not mew'd up with double Locks and Grated Windows; but may receive Addresses at their leisure.

Jac. But our Love here is like our Grass; if it be not mow'd quickly 'tis burnt up.

Enter Bellamy, Wildblood, Maskall: *they look about 'em.*

Theo. Yonder are your Gallants, send you comfort of 'em: I am for my Devotions.

Jac. Now for my heart can I think of no other Prayer, but only that they may not mistake us——Why Sister, Sister,——will you Pray? What injury have I ever done you, that you should Pray in my company? If your servant Don *Melchor* were here, we should have you mind Heaven as little as the best on's.

Beat. They are at a loss, Madam, shall I put up my Vail that they may take aime?

Jac. No, let 'em take their Fortune in the dark: we shall see what Archers these *English* are.

Bell. Which are they think'st thou?

Wild. There's no knowing them, they are all Children of darkness.

Bell. I'll be sworn they have one sign of Godliness among 'em, there's no distinction of persons here.

Wild. Pox o' this blind-mans-buffe; they may be asham'd to provoke a man thus by their keeping themselves so close.

Bell. You are for the youngest you say; 'tis the eldest has smitten me. And here I fix, if I am right——happy man be his dole.

By Theodosia.

Wild. I'll take my fortune here. *By* Jacinta.
Madam I hope a stranger may take the libertie without offence to offer his devotions by you.

Jac. That, Sir, would interrupt mine, without being any advantage to your own.

Wild. My advantage, Madam, is very evident; for the kind Saint to whom you pray, may by the neighbourhood mistake my devotions for yours.

Jac. O Sir! our Saints can better distinguish between the prayers of a Catholick and a Lutheran.

Wild. I beseech you Madam, trouble not your self for my Religion; for though I am a Heretick to the men of your Country, to your Ladies I am a very zealous Catholick: and for fornication and adulterie, I assure you I hold with both Churches.

Theo. to *Bell.* Sir, if you will not be more devout, be at least more civil, you see you are observ'd.

Bell. And pray, Madam what do you think the lookers on imagine I am imploy'd about?

Theo. I will not trouble my self to guess.

Bell. Why, by all circumſtances, they muſt conclude that I am making love to you: and methinks it were scarce civil to give the opinion of so much good company the lye.

Theo. If this were true, you would have little reason to thank 'em for their Divination.

Bell. Meaning I should not be lov'd again.

Theo. You have interpreted my riddle, and may take it for your pains.

Enter Alonzo, (*and goes apart to his devotion*)

Beat. Madam, your Father is return'd.

Bell. She has netled me, would I could be reveng'd on her.

Wild. Do you see their Father: let us make as though we talk'd to one another, that we may not be suspeƈted.

Beat. You have loſt your Englishmen.

Jac. No, no, 'tis but design I warrant you: you shall see these Island Cocks wheel about immediately.

Beat. Perhaps they thought they were observ'd.

The English gather up close to them.

Wild to *Bell.* Talk not of our Countrie Ladies: I declare my self for the Spanish Beauties.

Bell. Prithee tell me what thou canſt find to dote on in these *Caſtilians*.

Wild. Their wit and beauty.

Theo. Now for our Champion St. *Jago* for *Spain* there.

Bell. Faith, I can speak no such miracles of either; for their beauty 'tis much as the *Moores* left it; not altogether so deep a black as the true *Æthiopian*: A kind of beautie that is too civil to the lookers on to do them any mischief.

Jac. This was your forwardness that provok'd him, Siſter.

Theo. But they shall not carry it off so.

Bell. As for their wit, you may judge it by their breeding, which is commonly in a Nunnerie; where the want of mankind while they are there, makes them value the blessing ever after.

Theo. Prethee dear *Jacinta* tell me, what kind of creatures were those we saw yeſterday at the Audience? Those I mean, that look'd so like *Frenchmen* in their habits, but only became their Apishness so much worse.

Jac. Englishmen I think they call 'em.

Theo. Crie you mercy; they were of your wild *English* indeed, that is a kind of Northern Beaſt, that is taught its feats of aƈtivity in

258

Monsieurland, and for doing 'em too lubberly, is laugh'd at all the world over.

Bell. Wildblood, I perceive the women underſtand little of discourse; their Gallants do not use them to it: they get upon their Gennits, and prance before their Ladies windows; there the Palfray curvets and bounds, and in short, entertains 'em for his Maſter.

Wild. And this horse-play they call making love,

Beat. Your Father Madam.————

Alon. Daughters! what Cavaliers are those which were talking by you?

Jac. Englishmen, I believe Sir, at their devotions: Cavalier, would you would try to pray a little better then you have railly'd.
aside to Wildblood.

Wild. Hang me if I put all my devotions out of order for you: I remember I pray'd but on Tuesday laſt, and my time comes not till Tuesday next.

Mask. You had as good pray, Sir; she will not ſtir till you have: Say any thing.

Wild. Fair Lady, though I am not worthy of the leaſt of your favours, yet give me the happiness this Evening to see you at your fathers door, that I may acquaint you with part of my sufferings.
aside to Jacinta.

Alon. Come Daughters, have you done?

Jac. Immediately, Sir,——————Cavalier, I will not fail to be there at the time appointed, if it be but to teach you more wit, henceforward, then to engage your heart so lightly.
aside to Wildblood.

Wild. I have engag'd my heart with so much zeal and true devotion to your divine beauty, that————

Alon. What means this Cavalier?

Jac. Some zealous ejaculation.

Alon. May the Saint hear him.

Jac. I'll answer for her.   *Ex. Father and Daughters.*

Wild. Now *Bellamy*, what success?

Bell. I pray'd to a more Marble Saint than that was in the Shrine, but you, it seems, have been successful.

Wild. And so shalt thou; let me alone for both.

Bell. If you'll undertake it, I will make bold to indulge my love; and within this two hours be a desperate Inamorado. I feel I am coming apace to it.

Wild. Faith I can love at any time with a wish at my rate: I give my heart according to the old law of pawns, to be return'd me before sun-set.

Bell. I love only that I may keep my heart warm; for a man's a pool if love ſtir him not; and to bring him to that pass, I firſt resolve whom to love, and presently after imagine I am in love; for a ſtrong imagination is requir'd in a Lover, as much as in a Witch.

Wild. And is this all your Receipt?

Bell. These are my principal ingredients; as for Piques, Jealousies, Duels, Daggers, and Halters, I let 'em alone to the vulgar.

Wild. Prithee let's round the ſtreet a little; till *Maskall* watches for their Woman.

Bell. That's well thought on: he shall about it immediately.

We will attempt the Miſtress by the Maid:

Women by women ſtill are beſt betray'd.   *Exeunt.*

ACT II.

Wildblood, Bellamy, Maskall.

Wild. **D**Id you speak with her Woman?

Mask. Yes, but she was in haſt, and bid me wait her hereabouts when she return'd.

Bell. Then you have discover'd nothing more?

Mask. Only, in general, that *Donna Theodosia* is engag'd else-where; so that all your Courtship will be to no purpose.

To Wild.] But for your Miſtress, Sir, she is waded out of her depth in love to you already.

Wild. That's very hard, when I am scarce knee-deep with her: 'tis true, I have given her hold of my heart, but if she take not heed, it will slip through her fingers.

Bell. You are Prince of the Soil, Sir, and may take your pleasure when you please; but I am the Eve to your Holy-day, and muſt faſt for being joyn'd to you.

Wild. Were I as thou art, I would content my self with having had one fair flight at her, without wearying my self on the wing for a retrieve; for when all's done the Quarry is but woman.

Bell. Thank you, Sir, you would fly 'em both your self, and while I turn tail, we should have you come gingling with your bells in the neck of my Patridge; do you remember who incourag'd me to love, and promis'd me his assiſtance?

Wild. I, while there was hope *Frank*, while there was hope; but there's no contending with one's deſtiny.

Bell. Nay, it may be I care as little for her as another man; but while she flyes before me I muſt follow: I can leave a woman firſt with ease, but if she begins to fly before me, I grow opiniatre as the Devil.

Wild. What a secret have you found out? why 'tis the nature of all mankind; we love to get our Miſtresses, and purr over 'em, as Cats do over Mice, and then let 'em go a little way; and all the pleasure is, to pat 'em back again: But yours, I take it, *Frank*, is gone too far; prithee how long doſt thou intend to love at this rate?

Bell. Till the evil conſtellation be paſt over me: yet I believe it would haſten my recovery, if I knew whom she lov'd.

Mask. You shall not be long without that satisfaction.

Wild. 'St, the door opens; and two women are coming out.

Bell. By this ſtature they should be thy gracious Miſtress and *Beatrix*.

Wild. Methinks you should know your Q. then and withdraw.

Bell. Well, I'll leave you to your fortune; but if you come to close fighting, I shall make bold to run in and part you.

Bellamy *and* Maskall *withdraw*.

Wild. Yonder she comes with full sails y' faith; I'll hail her a-main for *England*.

Enter Jacinta *and* Beatrix *at the other end of the Stage*.

Beat. You do love him then?

Jac. Yes, moſt vehemently.

Beat. But set some bounds to your affection.

Jac. None but fools confine their pleasure: what Usurer ever thought his Coffers held too much? No, I'll give my self the swinge, and love without reserve. If I'll keep a passion, I'll never ſtarve it in my service.

Beat. But are you sure he will deserve this kindness?

Jac. I never trouble my self so long before hand: Jealousies and disquiets are the dregs of an amour; but I'll leave mine before I have drawn it off so low: when it once grows troubled, I'll give vent to a fresh draught.

Beat. Yet it is but prudence to try him firſt; no Pilot ventures on an unknown Coaſt without sounding.

Jac. Well, to satisfie thee I am content; partly too because I find a kind of pleasure in laying baits for him.

Beat. The two great virtues of a Lover are conſtancy and liberality; if he profess those two, you may be happy in him.

Jac. Nay, if he be not Lord and Maſter of both those qualities, I disown him—But who goes there?

Beat. He, I warrant you, Madam; for his Servant told me, he was waiting hereabout.

261

Jac. Watch the door, give me notice if any come.

Beat. I'll secure you, Madam.——   *Exit* Beatrix.

Jac. to *Wild.* What have you laid an ambush for me?

Wild. Only to make a Reprisal of my heart.

Jac. 'Tis so wild, that the Lady who has it in her keeping, would be glad she were rid on't: it does so flutter about the Cage. 'Tis a meer *Bajazet*; and if it be not let out the sooner, will beat out the brains against the Grates.

Wild. I am afraid the Lady has not fed it, and 'tis wild for hunger.

Jac. Or perhaps it wants company; shall she put another to it?

Wild. I; but then 'twere best to trust 'em out of the Cage together; let 'em hop about at libertie.

Jac. But if they should lose one another in the wide world!

Wild. They'll meet at night I warrant 'em.

Jac. But is not your heart of the nature of those Birds, that breed in one Countrie, and goe to winter in another?

Wild. Suppose it does so; yet I take my Mate along with me. And now to leave our parables, and speak in the language of the vulgar, what think you of a voyage to merry *England*?

Jac. Just as *Æsop's* Frog did, of leaping into a deep Well in a drought: if he ventur'd the leap, there might be water; but if there were no water, how should he get out again?

Wild. Faith we live in a good honest Country, where we are content with our old vices, partly because we want wit to invent more new. A Colonie of *Spaniards*, or spiritual *Italians* planted among us, would make us much more racy. 'Tis true, our variety is not much; but to speak nobly of our way of living, 'tis like that of the Sun, which rises and looks upon the same things he saw yesterday, and goes to bed again.

Jac. But I hear your women live most blessedly; ther's no such thing as jealousie among the Husbands; if any man has horns, he bears them as loftily as a Stag, and as inoffensively.

Wild. All this I hope, gives you no ill Character of the Country.

Jac. But what need we go into another Climate; as our love was born here; so let it live and dye here, and be honestly buried in its native Country.

Wild. Faith agreed with all my heart. For I am none of those unreasonable lovers, that propose to themselves the loving to eternity; the truth is, a month is commonly my stint; but in that month I love so dreadfully, that it is after a twelvemonths rate of common love.

Jac. Or would not a fortnight serve our turn? for in troth a month looks somewhat dismally; 'tis a whole *Ægyptian* year, if a Moon changes in my love I shall think my *Cupid* grown dull, or fallen into an Apoplexie.

Wild. Well, I pray heaven we both get off as clear as we imagine; for my part, I like your humour so damnably well, that I fear I am in for a week longer than I propos'd; I am half afraid your *Spanish* Planet, and my *English* one have been acquainted, and have found out some by-room or other in the 12 houses: I wish they have been honourable.

Jac. The best way for both were to take up in time; yet I am afraid our forces are engag'd so far, that we must make a battel on't. What think you of disobliging one another from this day forward; and shewing all our ill humours at the first; which Lovers use to keep as a reserve till they are married?

Wild. Or let us encourage one another to a breach by the dangers of possession: I have a Song to that purpose.

Jac. Pray let me hear it: I hope it will go to the tune of one of our *Passa-calles*.

SONG.

> *You charm'd me not with that fair face*
>   *Though it was all divine:*
> *To be anothers is the Grace,*
>   *That makes me wish you mine.*
> *The God's and Fortune take their part*
>   *Who like young Monarchs fight;*
> *And boldly dare invade that heart*
>   *Which is anothers right.*
> *First mad with hope we undertake*
>   *To pull up every barr;*
> *But once possess'd, we faintly make*
>   *A dull defensive warr.*
> *Now every friend is turn'd a foe*
>   *In hope to get our store:*
> *And passion makes us Cowards grow,*
>   *Which made us brave before.*

Jac. Believe it, Cavalier, you are a dangerous person: do you hold forth your gifts in hopes to make me love you less?

Wild. They would signifie little, if we were once married: those gayeties are all nipt, and frost-bitten in the Marriage-bed i'faith.

Jack. I am sorry to hear 'tis so cold a place: but 'tis all one to us, who do not mean to trouble it: the truth is, your humor pleases me exceedingly; how long it will do so, I know not; but so long as it does, I am resolv'd to give my self the content of seeing you. For if I should once constrain my self, I might fall in love in good earnest, but I have stay'd too long with you, and would be loth to surfeit you at first.

Wild. Surfet me, Madam, why you have but Tantaliz'd me all this while.

Jac. What would you have?

Wild. A hand or lip, or any thing that you can spare; when you have Conjur'd up a Spirit he must have some employment, or he'll tear you a pieces.

Jac. Well, Here's my Picture; to help your contemplation in my absence.

Wild. You have already the Original of mine: but some revenge you must allow me: a Locket of Diamonds, or some such a trifle, the next time I kiss your hand.

Jac. Fie, fie; you do not think me mercinary! yet now I think on't, I'll put you into our *Spanish* Mode of Love: our Ladies here use to be the Banquiers of their Servants, and to have their Gold in keeping.

Wild. This is the least trial you could have made of me: I have some 300 Pistols by me; those I'll send you by my servant.

Jac. Confess freely; you mistrust me: but if you find the least qualme about your Gold, pray keep it for a Cordial.

Wild. The Cordial must be apply'd to the heart, and mine's with you Madam: Well; I say no more; but these are dangerous beginnings for holding on: I find my moneth will have more then one and thirty dayes in't.

Enter Beatrix *running.*

Beat. Madam, your Father calls in hast for you; and is looking you about the house.

Jac. Adieu servant, be a good manager of your stock of Love, that it may hold out your Moneth; I am afraid you'll waste so much of it before to morrow night that you'll shine but with a quarter Moon upon me.

Wild. It shall be a Crescent.   *Exit* Wild. Jacinta, *severally.*
Beatrix *is going, and* Maskal *runs and stops her.*

Mask. Pay your ransome; you are my Prisoner.

Beat. What do fight after the *French* Fashion; take Towns before you declare a Warr?

Mask. I should be glad to imitate them so far, to be in the middle of the Country before you could resist me.

Beat. Well, what composition Monsieur?

Mask. Deliver up your Lady's secret; what makes her so cruel to my Master?

Beat. Which of my Ladies, and which of your Masters? For I suppose we are Factors for both of them.

Mask. Your eldest Lady *Theodosia.*

Beat. How dare you press your Mistress to an inconvenience?

Mask. My Mistress? I understand not that language; the fortune of the Valet, ever follows that of the Master; and his is desperate; if his fate were alter'd for the better, I should not care if I ventur'd upon you for the worse.

Beat. I have told you already *Donna Theodosia* loves another.

Mask. Has he no name?

Beat. Let it suffice, he is born noble, though without a fortune. His povertie makes him conceal his love from her Father; but she sees him every night in private: and to blind the world about a fortnight agoe, he took a solemn leave of her, as if he were going into *Flanders:* in the mean time he lodges at the house of Don *Lopez de Gamboa,* and is himself call'd *Don Melchor de Guzman.*

Mask. Don Melchor de Guzman! O heavens!

Beat. What amazes you!

Theo. within. Why, *Beatrix,* where are you?

Beat. You hear I am call'd; Adieu; and be sure you keep my Counsel.

Mask. Come, Sir, you see the Coast is clear.   *Ex.* Beatrix.

Enter Bellamy.

Bell. Clear, dost thou say? no, 'tis full of Rocks and Quicksands: yet nothing vexes me so much as that she is in love with such a poor Rogue.

Mask. But that he should lodge privately in the same house with us! 'twas odly contriv'd of fortune.

Bell. Hang him Rogue, methinks I see him perching like an Owle by day, and not daring to flutter out till Moon-light. The Rascal invents love, and brews his complements all day, and broaches 'em at night; just as some of our dry wits do their stories before they come into company: well, if I could be reveng'd on either of 'em.

Mask. Here she comes again with *Beatrix;* but good Sir moderate your passion.

Enter Theodosia *and* Beatrix.

Bell. Nay, Madam, you are known; and must not pass till I have spoke with you.   Bellamy *lifts up* Theodosia's *Vail.*

Theo. This rudeness to a person of my quality may cost you dear. Pray when did I give you encouragement for so much familiarity?

265

Bell. When you scorn'd me in the Chappel.

Theo. The truth is, I deny'd you as heartily as I could; that I might not be twice troubled with you.

Bell. Yet you have not this aversion for all the world: however I was in hope though the day frown'd, the night might prove as propitious to me as it is to others.

Theo. I have now a quarrell both to the Sun and Moon, because I have seen you by both their lights.

Bell. Spare the Moon I beseech you, Madam, she is a very trusty Planet to you.

Beat. O *Maskal* you have ruin'd me.

Mask. Dear Sir, hold yet.

Bell. Away.

Theo. Pray, Sir, expound your meaning; for I confess I am in the dark.

Bell. Methinks you should discover it by Moon-light. Or if you would have me speak clearer to you, give me leave to wait on you at a midnight assignation; and that it may not be discover'd, I'll feign a voyage beyond sea, as if I were gone a Captaining to *Flanders*.

Mask. A pox on's memory, he has not forgot one syllable.

Theo. Ah *Beatrix*, you have betray'd and sold me.

Beat. You have betray'd and sold your self, Madam, by your own rashness to confess it; Heaven knows I have serv'd you but too faithfully.

Theo. Peace, impudence; and see my face no more.

Mask. Do you know what work you have made, Sir?

Bell. Let her see what she has got by slighting me.

Mask. You had best let *Beatrix* be turn'd away for me to keep: if you do, I know whose purse shall pay for't.

Bell. That's a curse I never thought on: cast about quickly and save all yet. Range, quest, and spring a lie immediately.

Theo. to Beat. Never importune me farther; you shall go, there's no removing me.

Beat. Well; this is ever the reward of innocence——   (*going*)

Mask. Stay, guiltless Virgin, stay; thou shalt not go.

Theo. Why, who should hinder it?

Mask. That will I, in the name of truth, (If this hard-bound lie would but come from me:) Madam, I must tell you it lies in my power to appease this tempest with one word.

Beat. Would it were come once.

Mask. Nay, Sir, 'tis all one to me, if you turn me away upon't; I can hold no longer.

Theo. What does the fellow mean?

266

Mask. For all your noddings, and your Mathematical grimaces, in short, Madam, my Master has been conversing with the Planets; and from them has had the knowledge of your affairs.

Bell. This Rogue amazes me.

Mask. I care not, Sir, I am for truth; that will shame you and all your Devils: in short, Madam, this Master of mine that stands before you, without a word to say for himself, so like an Oph, as I may say with reverence to him——

Bell. The Raskal makes me mad.

Mask. Is the greatest *Astrologer* in Christendome.

Theo. Your Master an *Astrologer?*

Mask. A most profound one.

Bell. Why you Dog, do you consider what an improbable lie this is; which you know I can never make good: disgorge it you Cormorant, or I'll pinch your throat out——   *Takes him by the throat.*

Mask. 'Tis all in vain, Sir, you are and shall be an *Astrologer* what e're I suffer: you know all things, see into all things, foretell all things; and if you pinch more truth out of me, I will confess you are a Conjurer.

Bell. How, sirrah, a Conjurer?

Mask. I mean, Sir, the Devil is in your fingers: own it you had best, Sir, and do not provoke me farther; what did not I see you an hour ago, turning over a great Folio with strange figures in it, and
               While he is speaking Bellamy *stops his mouth by fits.*
then muttering to your self like any Poet, and then naming *Theodosia*, and then staring up in the skie, and then poring upon the ground; so that betwixt God and the Devil, Madam, he came to know your love.

Bell. Madam, if ever I knew the least term in Astrologie, I am the arrantest Son of a whore breathing.

Beat. O, Sir, for that matter you shall excuse my Lady: Nay hide your tallents if you can, Sir.

Theo. The more you pretend ignorance, the more we are resolv'd to believe you skilfull.

Bell. You'll hold your tongue yet.

Mask. You shall never make me to hold my tongue, except you conjure me to silence: what did you not call me to look into a Chrystal, and there shew'd me a fair Garden, and a *Spaniard* stalking in his narrow breeches, and walking underneath a window; I should know him agen amongst a thousand.

Beat. Don *Melchor*, in my conscience, Madam.

Bell. This Rogue will invent more stories of me, than e're were father'd upon *Lilly*.

Mask. Will you confess then; do you think I'll ſtain my honour to swallow a lie for you?

Bell. Well, a pox on you, I am an Aſtrologer.

Beat. O, are you so, Sir?

Theo. I hope then, learned Sir, as you have been curious in enquiring into my secrets, you will be so much a Cavalier as to conceal 'em.

Bell. You need not doubt me, Madam; I am more in your power than you can be in mine: besides, if I were once known in Town, the next thing, for ought I know, would be to bring me before the fathers of the Inquisition.

Beat. Well, Madam, what do you think of me now; I have betray'd you, I have sold you; how can you ever make me amends for this imputation? I did not think you could have us'd me so.———

(Cries and claps her hands at her.)

Theo. Nay, prethee *Beatrix* do not crie; I'll leave off my new Gown to morrow, and thou shalt have it.

Beat. No, I'll crie eternally; you have taken away my good name from me; and you can never make me recompence—except you give me your new Gorget too.

Theo. No more words; thou shalt have it Girle.

Beat. O, Madam, your Father has surpriz'd us!

Enter Don Alonzo, *and frowns.*

Bell. Then I'll begone to avoid suspicion.

Theo. By your favour, Sir, you shall ſtay a little; the happiness of so rare an acquaintance, ought to be cherish'd on my side by a longer conversation.

Alon. Theodosia, what business have you with this Cavalier?

Theo. That, Sir, which will make you as ambitious of being known to him, as I have been: under the habit of a Gallant he conceals the greateſt *Aſtrologer* this day living.

Alon. You amaze me Daughter.

Theo. For my own part I have been consulting with him about some particulars of my fortunes paſt and future; both which he has resolv'd me with that admirable knowledge.———

Bell. Yes, faith, Sir, I was foretelling her of a disaſter, that severely threaten'd her: and (one thing I foresee already by my ſtarrs, that I muſt bear up boldly, or I am loſt.)

Mask. to Bellamy. Never fear him, Sir; he's an ignorant fellow, and credulous I warrant him.

Alon. Daughter be not too confident in your belief; there's nothing more uncertain than the cold Prophecies of these *Noſtradamusses*; but of what nature was the queſtion which you ask'd him?

268

Theo. What should be my fortune in marriage.

Alon. And, pray, what did you answer, Sir?

Bell. I answer'd her the truth, that she is in danger of marrying a Gentleman without a fortune.

Theo. And this, Sir, has put me into such a fright——

Alon. Never trouble your self about it, Daughter; follow my advice and I warrant you a rich Husband.

Bell. But the ſtarrs say she shall not follow your advice: if it happens otherwise I'll burn my folio Volumes, and my Manuscripts too, I assure you that, Sir.

Alon. Be not too confident, young man; I know somewhat in *Aſtrologie* my self; for in my younger years I ſtudy'd it; and though I say it, made some small proficience in it.

Bell. Marry Heaven forbid.——   [*aside.*

Alon. And I could only find it was no way demonſtrative, but altogether fallacious.

Mask. On what a Rock have we split our selves!

Bell. Now my ignorance will certainly come out!

Beat. Sir, remember you are old and crazie, Sir; and if the Evening Air should take you——beseech you Sir retire.

Alon. Knowledge is to be prefer'd before health; I muſt needs discusse a point with this learned Cavalier, concerning a difficult queſtion in that Art, which almoſt gravels me.

Mask. How I sweat for him, *Beatrix*, and my self too, who have brought him into this *Præmunire!*

Beat. You muſt be impudent; for our old man will ſtick like a burre to you, now he's in a dispute.

Alon. What Judgment may a man reasonably form from the trine Aſpeƈt of the two Infortunes in Angular houses?

Bell. That's a matter of nothing, Sir; I'll turn my man loose to you for such a queſtion.   (*Puts* Maskal *forward.*)

Alon. Come on, Sir, I am the quærent.

Mask. Meaning me, Sir! I vow to God, and your Worship knows it, I never made that Science my ſtudy in the leaſt, Sir.

Bell. The gleanings of mine are enough for that: why, you impudent rogue you, hold forth your gifts, or I'll—— What a devil muſt I be peſter'd with every trivial queſtion, when there's not a Maſter in Town of any Science, but has his Usher for these mean offices?

Theo. Trie him in some deeper queſtion, Sir; you see he will not put himself forth for this.

Alon. Then I'll be more abſtruse with him: what think you, Sir, of the taking *Hyleg?* or of the beſt way of reƈtification for a Nativity?

have you been conversant in the *Centiloquium* of *Trismegiſtus:* What think you of *Mars* in the tenth, when 'tis his own House, or of *Jupiter* configurated with malevolent Planets?

Bell. I thought what your skill was! to answer your queſtion in two words, *Mars* rules over the Martial, and *Jupiter* over the Jovial; and so of the reſt, Sir.

Alon. This every School-boy could have told me.

Bell. Why then you muſt not ask such School-boyes queſtions. (But your Carkase, Sirrah, shall pay for this.)   *Aside to* Maskal.

Alon. You seem not to underſtand the Terms, Sir?

Bell. By your favour, Sir, I know there are five of 'em; do not I know your Michaelmas, your Hillary, your Eaſter, your Trinity, and your Long Vacation Term, Sir?

Alon. I do not underſtand a word of this *Jargon.*

Bell. It may be not, Sir; I believe the terms are not the same in *Spain* they are in *England.*

Mask. Did one ever hear so impudent an Ignorance?

Alon. The terms of Art are the same every where.

Bell. Tell me that! you are an old man, and they are alter'd since you ſtudied them.

Alon. That may be I muſt confess; however, if you please to discourse something of the Art to me, you shall find me an apt Scholar.

Enter a Servant to Alonzo.

Ser. Sir.————(*whispers.*)

Alon. Sir, I am sorry a business of importance calls me hence; but I'll wait on you some other time, to discourse more at large of *Aſtrologie.*

Bell. Is your business very pressing?

Alon. It is, I assure you, Sir.

Bell. I am very sorry, for I should have inſtrucſted you in such rare secrets; I have no fault, but that I am too communicative.

Alon. I'll dispatch my business, and return immediately; come away Daughter.   *Exeunt Alonzo, Theodosia, Beatrix, Servus.*

Bell. A Devil on's learning; he had brought me to my laſt legs; I was fighting as low as ever was Squire *Widdrington.*

Mask. Who would have suspecſted it from that wicked Elder?

Bell. Suspecſted it? why 'twas palpable from his very Physnomy; he looks like *Haly*, and the spirit *Fircu* in the Fortune-book.

Enter Wildblood.

Wild. How now *Bellamy*, in wrath? prethee, what's the matter?

Bell. The ſtory is too long to tell you; but this Rogue here has made me pass for an errant Fortune-teller.

270

Mask. If I had not, I'm sure he muſt have pass'd for an errant Mad-man; he had discovered, in a rage, all that *Beatrix* had confess'd to me concerning her Miſtresse's love; and I had no other way to bring him off, but to say he knew it by the Planets.

Wild. And art thou such an Oph to be vext at this? as the adventure may be manag'd it may make the moſt pleasant one in all the Carnival.

Bell. Death! I shall have all *Madrid* about me within these two dayes.

Wild. Nay, all *Spain*, i'faith, as faſt as I can divulge thee: not a Ship shall pass out from any Port, but shall ask thee for a wind; thou shalt have all the trade of *Lapland* within a Month.

Bell. And do you think it reasonable for me to ſtand defendant to all the impertinent queſtions that the Town can ask me.

Wild. Thou shalt do't boy: pox on thee, thou doſt not know thine own happiness; thou wilt have the Ladies come to thee; and if thou doſt not fit them with fortunes, thou art bewitch'd.

Mask. Sir, 'tis the easieſt thing in Nature; you need but speak doubtfully, or keep your self in general terms, and for the moſt part tell good rather than bad fortune.

Wild. And if at any time thou ventur'ſt at particulars, have an evasion ready like *Lilly*; as thus, it will infallibly happen if our sins hinder not. I would undertake, with one of his Almanacks to give very good content to all Chriſtendom, and what good luck fell not out in one Kingdom, should in another.

Mask. The pleasure on't will be to see how all his Cuſtomers will contribute to their own deceiving; and verily believe he told them that, which they told him.

Bell. Umh! now I begin to taſte it; I am like the drunken Tinker in the Play, a great Prince, and never knew it.

Wild. A great Prince, a great Turk; we shall have thee within these two days, do grace to the Ladies, by throwing out a handkerchief; 'lif, I could feaſt upon thy fragments.

Bell. If the women come, you shall be sure to help me to undergo the burden; for though you make me an *Aſtronomer* I am no *Atlas*, to bear all upon my back.

But who are these?

Enter Musicians with disguises; and some in their hands.

Wild. You know the men if their Masquing habits were off; they are the Musick of our Embassadors Retinue; my proje&ct is to give our Miſtresses a Serenade; this being the laſt Evening of the Carnival; and to prevent discovery, here are disguises for us too.——

271

Bell. 'Tis very well; come *Maskall* help on with 'em, while they tune their Instruments.

Wild. Strike up Gentlemen; we'll entertain 'em with a song *al' Angloise*, pray be ready with your *Chorus*.

SONG.

After the pangs of a desperate Lover,
When day and night I have sigh'd all in vain,
Ah what a pleasure it is to discover
In her eyes pity, who causes my pain!

2.

When with unkindness our love at a stand is,
And both have punish'd our selves with the pain,
Ah what a pleasure the touch of her hand is,
Ah what a pleasure to press it again!

3.

When the denyal comes fainter and fainter,
And her eyes give what her tongue does deny,
Ah what a trembling I feel when I venture,
Ah what a trembling does usher my joy!

4.

When, with a Sigh, she accords me the blessing,
And her eyes twinkle 'twixt pleasure and pain;
Ah what a joy 'tis, beyond all expressing,
Ah what a joy to hear, shall we again!

Theodosia and Jacinta above.

Jacinta *throws down her handkerchief with a Favour ty'd to it.*
Jac. Ill Musicians must be rewarded; there, Cavalier, 'tis to buy your silence.——   *Exeunt women from above.*
Wild. By this light, which at present is scarce an oath, an handkerchief and a favour.

Musick and Guittars tuning on the other side of the Stage.

Bell. Hark *Wildblood*, do you hear; there's more melody; on my life some *Spaniards* have taken up this Post for the same design.
Wild. I'll be with their Cats-guts immediately.
Bell. Prithee be patient; we shall lose the sport else.

Don Lopez *and* Don Melchor *disguis'd, with Servants and Musicians on the other side.*

Wild. 'Tis some Rival of yours or mine, *Bellamy*: for he addresses to this window.

Bell. Damn him, let's fall on then.

The two Spaniards *and the* English *fight: the* Spaniards *are beaten off the Stage; the Musicians on both sides and Servants fall confusedly one over the other. They all get off, only* Maskal *remains upon the ground.*

Mask. rising. So, all's past, and I am safe: a pox on these fighting Masters of mine, to bring me into this danger with their valours and magnanimities. When I go a Serenading again with 'em, I'll give 'em leave to make Fiddle-strings of my small-guts

To him Don Lopez.

Lop. Who goes there?

Mask. 'Tis Don *Lopez* by his voice.

Lop. The same; and by yours you should belong to my two English Ghests. Did you hear no tumult hereabouts?

Mask. I heard a clashing of swords, and men a fighting.

Lop. I had my share in't; but how came you here?

Mask. I came hither by my Masters order, to see if you were in any danger.

Lop. But how could he imagine I was in any?

Mask. 'Tis all one for that, Sir, he knew it, by—Heaven, what was I a going to say, I had like to have discover'd all!

Lop. I find there is some secret in't; and you dare not trust me.

Mask. If you will swear on your honor to be very secret, I will tell you.

Lop. As I am a Cavalier, and by my Beard, I will.

Mask. Then, in few words, he knew it by *Astrologie*, or Magick.

Lop. You amaze me! Is he conversant in the occult Sciences?

Mask. Most profoundly.

Lop. I always thought him an extraordinary person; but I could never imagine his head lay that way.

Mask. He shew'd me yesterday in a glass a Ladies Maid at *London*, whom I well knew; and with whom I used to converse on a Pallet in a drawing-room, while he was paying his devotions to her Lady in the Bed-chamber.

Lop. Lord, what a treasure for a State were here! and how much might we save by this man, in Forreign Intelligence!

Mask. And juſt now he shew'd me how you were assaulted in the dark by Foreigners.

Lop. Could you guess what Countrymen?

Mask. I imagin'd them to be *Italians.*

Lop. Not unlikely; for they pla y'dmoſt furiously at our back-sides.

Mask. I will return to my Maſter with the good news of your safety; but once again be secret; or disclose it to none but friends. So there's one Wood-cock more in the Springe.   [*Exit.*

Lop. Yes, I will be very secret; for I will tell it only to one person; but she is a woman. I will to *Aurelia*, and acquaint her with the skill of this rare Artiſt: she is curious as all women are; and 'tis probable, will desire to look into the Glass to see *Don Melchor*, whom she believes absent. So that by this means, without breaking my oath to him, he will be discover'd to be in Town. Then his intrigue with *Theodosia* will come to light too, for which *Aurelia* will, I hope, discard him, and receive me. I will about it inſtantly:

Success, in love, on diligence depends;
No lazie Lover e're attain'd his ends.   *Exit.*

ACT III.

Enter Bellamy, Maskall.

Bell. THen they were certainly *Don Lopez* and *Don Melchor* with whom we fought!

Mask. Yes, Sir.

Bell. And when you met *Lopez* he swallow'd all you told him?

Mask. As greedily, as if it had been a new Saints miracle.

Bell. I see 'twill spread.

Mask. And the fame of it will be of use to you in your next amour; for the women you know run mad after Fortune-tellers and Preachers.

Bell. But for all my bragging, this amour is not yet worn off. I find conſtancy, and once a night come naturally upon a man towards thirty; only we set a face on't; and call our selves unconſtant for our reputation.

Mask. But, What say the Starrs, Sir?

Bell. They move faſter than you imagine; for I have got me an *Argol*, and an *English-Almanack*; by help of which, in one half hour, I have learnt to Cant with an indifferent good grace: *Conjunction, Opposition, Trine, Square,* and *Sextile,* are now no longer Bug-bears to me, I thank my Starrs for't.

Enter Wildblood.

——Monsieur *Wildblood*, in good time! What, you have been taking pains too, to divulge my Tallent?

Wild. So successfully, that shortly there will be no talk in Town but of you only; another Miracle or two, and a sharp Sword, and you ftand fair for a New Prophet.

Bell. But where did you begin to blow the Trumpet?

Wild. In the Gaming-house; where I found moft of the Town-wits; the Prose-wits playing, and the Verse-wits rooking.

Bell. All sorts of Gamefters are so superftitious, that I need not doubt of my reception there.

Wild. From thence I went to the latter end of a Comedy, and there whisper'd it to the next Man I knew who had a Woman by him.

Mask. Nay, then it went like a Train of Powder, if once they had it by the end.

Wild. Like a Squib upon a Line, 'ifaith, it ran through one row, and came back upon me in the next: at my going out, I met a knot of *Spaniards*, who were formally liftening to one who was relating it: but he told the ftory so ridiculously, with his Marginal Notes upon it, that I was forc'd to contradiƈt him.

Bell. 'Twas discreetly done.

Wild. I, for you, but not for me: What, sayes he, muft such Boracho's as you, take upon you to villifie a Man of Science? I tell you, he's of my intimate acquaintance, and I have known him long, for a prodigious person——When I saw my *Don* so fierce, I thought it not wisdom to quarrel for so slight a matter as your Reputation, and so withdrew.

Bell. A pox of your success! now shall I have my Chamber be-sieg'd to morrow morning: there will be no ftirring out for me; but I muft be fain to take up their Queftions in a cleft-Cane, or a Beg-ging-box, as they do Charity in Prisons.

Wild. Faith, I cannot help what your Learning has brought you to: Go in and ftudy; I foresee you will have but few Holy-dayes; in the mean time, I'll not fail to give the World an account of your in-dowments. Fare-well: I'll to the Gaming house. *Exit* Wildblood.

Mask. O, Sir, here is the rareft adventure, and which is more, come home to you.

Bell. What is it?

Mask. A fair Lady and her Woman, wait in the outer Room to speak with you.

Bell. But how know you she is fair?

275

Mask. Her Woman pluck'd up her Vaile when she spake to me; so that having seen her this evening, I know her Mistress to be *Donna Aurelia*, Cousin to your Mistress *Theodosia*, and who lodges in the same House with her: she wants a Starr or two, I warrant you.

Bell. My whole Constellation is at her service: but what is she for a Woman?

Mask. Fair enough, as *Beatrix* has told me; but sufficiently impertinent. She is one of those Ladies who make ten Visits in an afternoon; and entertain her they see, with speaking ill of the last from whom they parted: in few words, she is one of the greatest Coquette's in *Madrid*: and to shew she is one, she cannot speak ten words without some affected phrase that is in fashion.

Bell. For my part I can suffer any impertinence from a woman, provided she be handsome; my business is with her Beauty, not with her Morals: let her Confessor look to them.

Mask. I wonder what she has to say to you?

Bell. I know not; but I sweat for fear I should be gravell'd.

Mask. Venture out of your depth, and plunge boldly, Sir; I warrant you will swimm.

Bell. Do not leave me I charge you; but when I look mornfully upon you help me out.

Enter Aurelia *and* Camilla.

Mask. Here they are already.   [Aurelia *plucks up her vail.*

Aur. How am I drest to night, *Camilla*? is nothing disorder'd in my head?

Cam. Not the least hair, Madam.

Aur. No? let me see: give me the Counsellor of the Graces.

Cam. The Counsellor of the Graces, Madam?

Aur. My Glass I mean: what will you never be so spiritual as to understand refin'd language?

Cam. Madam!

Aur. Madam me no Madam, but learn to retrench your words; and say Mam; as yes Mam, and no Mam, as other Ladies Women do. Madam! 'tis a year in pronouncing.

Cam. Pardon me, Madam.

Aur. Yet again ignorance: par-don Madam, fie, fie, what a superfluity is there, and how much sweeter the Cadence is, parn me Mam! And for your Ladyship, your Laship.————Out upon't, what a furious indigence of Ribands is here upon my head! This dress is a Libel to my beauty; a meer Lampoon. Would any one that had the least revenue of common sense have done this?

Cam. Mam the Cavalier approaches your Laship.

276

Bell. to *Mask. Maskall,* pump the woman; and see if you can discover any thing to save my credit.

Aur. Out upon't; now I should speak I want assurance.

Bell. Madam, I was told you meant to honor me with your commands.

Aur. I believe, Sir, you wonder at my confidence in this visit: but I may be excus'd for waving a little modesty to know the only person of the Age.

Bell. I wish my skill were more to serve you, Madam.

Aur. Sir, you are an unfit judge of your own merits: for my own part I confess I have a furious inclination for the occult Sciences; but at present 'tis my misfortune——   [*sighs.*

Bell. But why that sigh, Madam?

Aur. You might spare me the shame of telling you; since I am sure you can divine my thoughts: I will therefore tell you nothing.

Bell. What the Devil will become of me now!——   [*Aside.*

Aur. You may give me an Essay of your Science, by declaring to me the secret of my thoughts.

Bell. If I know your thoughts, Madam, 'tis in vain for you to disguise them to me: therefore as you tender your own satisfaction, lay them open without bashfulness.

Aur. I beseech you let us pass over that chapter, for I am shame-fac'd to the last point: Since therefore I cannot put off my modesty, succour it, and tell me what I think.

Bell. Madam, Madam, that bashfulness must be laid aside: not but that I know your business perfectly; and will, if you please, unfold it to you all, immediately.

Aur. Favour me so far, I beseech you, Sir; for I furiously desire it.

Bell. But then I must call up before you a most dreadful Spirit, with head upon head, and horns upon horns: therefore consider how you can endure it.

Aur. This is furiously furious; but rather than fail of my expectances, I'll try my assurance.

Bell. Well then, I find you will force me to this unlawful, and abominable act of Conjuration: remember the sin is yours too.

Aur. I espouse the crime also.

Bell. I see when a woman has a mind to't, she'll never boggle at a sin. Pox on her, what shall I do?—Well, I'll tell you your thoughts, Madam; but after that expect no farther service from me; for 'tis your confidence must make my Art successful:———Well, you are obstinate then; I must tell you your thoughts?

Aur. Hold, hold, Sir, I am content to pass over that chapter, rather than be depriv'd of your assistance.

277

Bell. 'Tis very well; what need these circumſtances between us two? Confess freely, is not love your business?

Aur. You have touch'd me to the quick, Sir.

Bell. La you there; you see I knew it; nay, I'll tell you more, 'tis a man you love.

Aur. O prodigious Science! I confess I love a man moſt furiously, to the laſt point, Sir.

Bell. Now proceed Lady, your way is open; I am resolv'd I'll not tell you a word farther.

Aur. Well then, since I muſt acquaint you with what you know much better than my self; I will tell you I lov'd a Cavalier, who was noble, young, and handsome; this Gentleman is since gone for *Flanders*; now whether he has preserv'd his passion inviolate or not, is that which causes my inquietude.

Bell. Trouble not your self, Madam; he's as conſtant as a Romance Heros.

Aur. Sir, your good news has ravish'd moſt furiously; but that I may have a confirmation of it, I beg only, that you would lay your commands upon his *Genius*, or *Idea*, to appear to me this night, that I may have my sentence from his mouth. This, Sir, I know is a slight effeſt of your Science, and yet will infinitely oblige me.

Bell. What the Devil does she call a slight effeſt! (*aside.*) Why Lady, do you consider what you say? you desire me to shew you a man whom your self confess to be in *Flanders*.

Aur. To view him in a glass is nothing, I would speak with him in person, I mean his *Idea*, Sir.

Bell. I but Madam, there is a vaſt sea betwixt us and *Flanders*; and water is an enemy to Conjuration: A witches horse you know, when he enters into water, returns into a bottle of hay again.

Aur. But, Sir, I am not so ill a *Geographer*, or to speak more properly, a *Chorographer*, as not to know there is a passage by land from hence to *Flanders*.

Bell. That's true, Madam, but Magick works in a direſt line. Why should you think the Devil such an Ass to goe about? 'gad he'll not ſtir a ſtep out of his road for you or any man.

Aur. Yes, for a Lady, Sir; I hope he's a person that wants not that civility for a Lady: especially a spirit that has the honor to belong to you, Sir.

Bell. For that matter he's your Servant, Madam; but his education has been in the fire, and he's naturally an enemy to water I assure you.

Aur. I beg his pardon for forgetting his Antipathy; but it imports not much, Sir; for I have lately receiv'd a Letter from

278

my Servant, that he is yet in *Spain*; and ſtays for a wind in *St. Sebaſtians.*

Bell. Now I am loſt paſt all redemption—*Maskall*—muſt you be smickering after Wenches while I am in calamity?   [*aside.*

Mask. It muſt be he, I'll venture on't. [*aside.*] Alas Sir, I was complaining to my self of the condition of poor Don *Melchor,* who you know is windbound at *St. Sebaſtians.*

Bell. Why you impudent Villain, muſt you offer to name him publickly, when I have taken so much care to conceal him all this while?

Aur. Mitigate your displeasure I beseech you; and, without making farther teſtimony of it, gratifie my expeċtances.

Bell. Well, Madam, since the Sea hinders not, you shall have your desire. Look upon me with a fix'd eye—so—or a little more amorously if you please.—Good. Now favour me with your hand.

Aur. Is it absolutely necessary you should press my hand thus?

Bell. Furiously necessary, I assure you, Madam; for now I take possession of it in the name of the *Idea* of *Don Melchor.* Now, Madam, I am farther to desire of you, to write a Note to his Genius, wherein you desire him to appear, and this, we Men of Art, call a Compaċt with the *Idea's.*

Aur. I tremble furiously.

Bell. Give me your hand, I'll guide it.   [*They write.*

Mask. to *Cam.* Now, Lady mine, what think you of my Maſter?

Cam. I think I would not serve him for the world; nay, if he can know our thoughts by looking on us, we women are hypocrites to little purpose.

Mask. He can do that and more; for by caſting his eyes but once upon them, he knows whether they are Maids, bettcr than a whole Jury of Midwives.

Cam. Now Heaven defend me from him.

Mask. He has a certain small Familiar which he carries ſtill about him, that never fails to make discovery.

Cam. See, they have done writing; not a word more, for fear he knows my voice.

Bell. One thing I had forgot, Madam, you muſt subscribe your name to't.

Aur. There 'tis; farewell Cavalier, keep your promise, for I expeċt it furiously.

Cam. If he sees me I am undone.   [*Hiding her face.*

Bell. Camilla!

Cam. ſtarts and schreeks. Ah he has found me; I am ruin'd!

279

Bell. You hide your face in vain; for I see into your heart.

Cam. Then, sweet Sir, have pity on my frailty; for if my Lady has the least inkling of what we did last night, the poor Coachman will be turn'd away. *Exit after her Lady.*

Mask. Well, Sir, how like you your New Profession?

Bell. Would I were well quit on't; I sweat all over.

Mask. But what faint-hearted Devils yours are that will not go by water? Are they all *Lancashire* Devils, of the Brood of *Tybert* and *Grimalkin,* that they dare not wet their feet?

Bell. Mine are honest land Devils, good plain foot Posts, that beat upon the hoof for me; but to save their labour, here take this, and in some disguise deliver it to *Don Melchor.*

Mask. I'll serve it upon him within this hour, when he sallyes out to his assignation with *Theodosia:* 'tis but counterfeiting my Voice a little; for he cannot know me in the dark. But let me see, what are the words? *Reads.*

Don Melchor, *if the Magique of love have any power upon your spirit, I conjure you to appear this night before me: you may guess the greatness of my passion, since it has forc'd me to have recourse to Art: but no shape which resembles you can fright*

Aurelia.

Bell. Well, I am glad there's one point gain'd; for by this means he will be hindred to night from entertaining *Theodosia.*——Pox on him, is he here again? *Enter*

Don Alonzo.

Alon. Cavalier *Ingles* I have been seeking you: I have a Present in my Pocket for you; read it by your Art and take it.

Bell. That I could do easily;——but to shew you I am generous, I'll none of your Present; do you think I am mercenary?

Alon. I know you will say now 'tis some Astrological question, and so 'tis perhaps.

Bell. I, 'tis the Devil of a question without dispute.

Alon. No 'tis within dispute; 'tis a certain difficulty in the Art; a Problem which you and I will discuss, with the arguments on both sides.

Bell. At this time I am not problematically given; I have a humour of complaisance upon me, and will contradict no man.

Alon. We'll but discuss a little.

Bell. By your favour I'll not discusse; for I see by the Stars, that if I Dispute to day, I am infallibly threatned to be thought ignorant all my life after.

Alon. Well, then, we'll but cast an eye together, upon my eldest Daughters Nativity.

Bell. Nativity!—

Alon. I know what you would say now, that there wants the Table of Direction for the five Hylegiacalls; the Ascendant, *Medium Cœli*, Sun, Moon, and Sors; but we'll take it as it is.

Bell. Never tell me that, Sir——

Alon. I know what you would say again, Sir——

Bell. 'Tis well you do, for I'll be sworn I do not——   [*Aside.*

Alon. You would say, Sir——

Bell. I say, Sir, there is no doing without the Sun and Moon, and all that, Sir. And so you may make use of your Paper for your occasions. Come to a man of Art without [*tears it*] the Sun and Moon, and all that, Sir——

Alon. 'Tis no matter; this shall break no squares betwixt us. [*Gathers up the Torne Papers.*] I know what you would say now, that Men of parts are always cholerick; I know it by my self, Sir.

                              [*He goes to match the Papers.*

Enter Don Lopez.

Lop. *Don Alonzo* in my house! this is a most happy opportunity to put my other design in execution; for if I can perswade him to bestow his Daughter on *Don Melchor*, I shall serve my Friend, though against his will: and when *Aurelia* sees she cannot be his, perhaps she will accept my Love.

Alon. I warrant you, Sir, 'tis all piec'd right, both top, sides and bottom; for, look you, Sir, here was *Aldeboran*, and there *Cor Scorpii*—

Lop. *Don Alonzo*, I am happy to see you under my Roof: and shall take it—

Alon. I know what you would say, Sir, that though I am your neighbour, this is the first time I have been here. [*to Bellamy.*—— But, come, Sir, by *Don Lopez* his permission let us return to our Nativity.

Bell. Would thou wert there in thy Mother's Belly again.
                                                    Aside.

Lop. But *Sennor*——to *Alonzo.*

Alon. It needs not *Sennor*; I'll suppose your Compliment; you would say that your house and all things in it are at my service: but let us proceed without his interruption.

Bell. By no means, Sir; this Cavalier is come on purpose to perform the civilities of his house to you.

Alon. But, good Sir——

Bell. I know what you would say, Sir.

Exeunt Bellamy *and* Maskal.

Lop. No matter, let him go, Sir; I have long desir'd this opportunity to move a Sute to you in the behalf of a Friend of mine: if you please to allow me the hearing of it.

Alon. With all my heart, Sir.

Lop. He is a person of worth and vertue, and is infinitely ambitious of the honour——

Alon. Of being known to me; I understand you, Sir.

Lop. If you will please to favour me with your patience, which I beg of you a second time.

Alon. I am dumb, Sir.

Lop. This Cavalier, of whom I was speaking, is in Love—

Alon. Satisfie your self, Sir, I'll not interrupt you.

Lop. Sir, I am satisfied of your promise.

Alon. If I speak one Syllable more the Devil take me: speak when you please.

Lop. I am going, Sir.

Alon. You need not speak twice to me to be silent; though I take it somewhat ill of you to be tutor'd——

Lop. This eternal old Man will make me mad. [*Aside.*

Alon. Why when do you begin, Sir? How long must a man wait for you? pray make an end of what you have to say quickly, that I may speak in my turn too.

Lop. This Cavalier is in Love—

Alon. You told me that before, Sir: Do you speak Oracles, that you require this strict attention? either let me share the talk with you, or I am gone.

Lop. Why, Sir, I am almost mad to tell you, and you will not suffer me.

Alon. Will you never have done, Sir; I must tell you, Sir, you have tatled long enough; and 'tis now good Manners to hear me speak. Here's a Torrent of words indeed; a very *impetus dicendi,* Will you never have done?

Lop. I will be heard in spight of you.

This next Speech of Lopez, *and the next of* Alonzo's, *with both their Replies, are to be spoken at one time; both raising their voices by little and little, till they baul, and come up close to shoulder one another.*

Lop. There's one Don *Melchor de Guzman,* a Friend and Acquaintance of mine, that is desperately in Love with your eldest Daughter *Donna Theodosia.*

282

Alon (at the same time.) 'Tis the sentence of a Philosopher, *Loquere ut te videam*; Speak that I may know thee; now if you take away the power of speaking from me—

Both pause a little, then speak together again.

Lop. I'll try the Language of the Law; sure the Devil cannot out-talke that Gibberish—For this *Don Melchor* of *Madrid* aforesaid, as premised, I requeſt, move, and supplicate, that you would give, beſtow, Marry, and give in Mariage, this your Daughter aforesaid, to the Cavalier aforesaid—not yet, thou Devil of a Man thou shalt be silent—   [*Exit* Lopez *running.*

Alon. at the same time with Lopez *his laſt speech, and after* Lopez *is run out.*

Oh, how I hate, abominate, deteſt and abhor, these perpetual Talkers, Disputants, Controverters, and Duellers of the Tongue! But, on the other side, if it be not permitted to prudent men to speak their minds, appositely, and to the purpose, and in few words—If, I say, the prudent muſt be Tongue-ty'd; then let Great Nature be deſtroy'd; let the order of all things be turn'd topsy-turvy; let the Goose devour the Fox; let the Infants preach to their Great Grand-sires; let the tender Lamb pursue the Wolfe; and the Sick prescribe to the Physician. Let Fishes live upon dry-Land, and the Beaſts of the Earth inhabit in the Water.—
Let the fearful Hare——

Enter Lopez *with a Bell, and rings it in his ears.*

Alon. Help, help, murder, murder, murder.   *Exit* Alonzo *running.* There was no way but this to be rid of him.

Enter a Servant.

Serv. Sir, there are some Women without in Masquerade; and, I believe, persons of Quality, who are come to Play here.
Lop. Bring 'em in with all respect.

Enter again the Servant, after him Jacinta, Beatrix, *and other Ladies and Gentlemen; all Masqued.*

Lop. Cavaliers, and Ladies, you are welcome: I wish I had more company to entertain you:—Oh, here comes one sooner then I expeſted.
                    Enter Wildblood *and* Maskal.

Wild. I have swept your Gaming-house, i'faith, *Ecce signum.*
                                                   [*Shows Gold.*

Lop. Well, here's more to be had of these Ladies, if it be your fortune.

Wild. The first Stakes I would play for, should be their Vailes, and Visor Masques.

Jac. to Beat. Do you think he will not know us?

Beat. If you keep your Design of passing for an *African*.

Jac. Well, now I shall make an absolute trial of him; for, being thus incognita, I shall discover if he make Love to any of you. As for the Gallantry of his Serenade, we will not be indebted to him, for we will make him another with our Guittars.

Beat. I'll whisper your intention to the Servant, who shall deliver it to *Don Lopez*.   [Beatrix *whispers to the* Servant.

Serv. to Lopez. Sir, the Ladies have commanded me to tell you, that they are willing, before they Play, to present you with a Dance; and to give you an Essay of their Guittars.

Lop. They much honor me.

A DANCE.

After the Dance the Cavaliers *take the* Ladies, *and Court them.* Wild-blood *takes* Jacinta.

Wild. While you have been Singing, Lady, I have been Praying: I mean, that your Face and Wit may not prove equal to your Dancing, for, if they be, there's an heart gone astray to my knowledge.

Jac. If you pray against me before you have seen me, you'll curse me when you have look'd on me.

Wild. I believe I shall have cause to do so, if your Beauty be as killing as I imagine it.

Jac. 'Tis true, I have been flatter'd in my own Country, with an opinion of a little handsomeness; but, how it will pass in *Spain* is a question.

Wild. Why, Madam, Are you not of *Spain?*

Jac. No, Sir, of *Marocco*: I onely came hither to see some of my Relations who are setled here, and turn'd *Christians*, since the expulsion of my Countrymen the *Moors.*

Wild. Are you then a *Mahometan?*

Jac. A *Mussulman* at your service.

Wild. A *Mussulwoman* say you? I protest by your voice I should have taken you for a *Christian* Lady of my acquaintance.

Jac. It seems you are in love then: if so, I have done with you. I dare not invade the Dominions of another Lady; especially in a Country where my Ancestors have been so unfortunate.

Wild. Some little liking I might have, but that was onely a morning-dew, 'tis drawn up by the Sun-shine of your Beauty: I find your *African-Cupid* is a much surer Archer, then ours of *Europe*. Yet would I could see you; one look would secure your victory.

Jac. I'll reserve my Face to gratifie your imagination with it, make what head you please, and set it on my Shoulders.

Wild. Well, Madam, an eye, a nose, or a lip shall break no squares; the Face is but a spans breadth of beauty; and where there is so much besides, I'll never stand with you for that.

Jac. But, in earnest, Do you love me?

Wild. I, by *Alha* do I, most extreamly: You have Wit in abundance, you Dance to a Miracle, you Sing like an Angel, and I believe you look like a Cherubim.

Jac. And can you be constant to me?

Wild. By *Mahomet*, can I.

Jac. You swear like a *Turk*, Sir: but, take heed; for our Prophet is a severe punisher of Promise-breakers.

Wild. Your Prophet's a Cavalier: I honour your Prophet and his Law, for providing so well for us Lovers in the other World, Black Eyes, and Fresh-Maidenheads every day: go thy way, little *Mahomet*, i'faith thou shalt have my good word. But, by his favour Lady, give me leave to tell you, that we of the Uncircumcised, in a civil way, as Lovers, have somewhat the advantage of your *Mussulman*.

Jac. The Company are rejoyn'd, and set to play; we must go to 'em: Adieu, and when you have a thought to throw away, bestow it on your Servant *Fatyma*.   [*She goes to the Company.*

Wild. This Lady *Fatyma* pleases me most infinitely; now am I got among the *Hamets*, the *Zegrys*, and the *Bencerrages*. Hey, What work will the *Wildboods* make among the *Cids*, and the *Bens* of the *Arabians*!

Beat. to *Jac.* False or true, Madam?

Jac. False, as Hell; but by Heaven I'll fit him for't: Have you the high-running Dice about you?

Beat. I got them on purpose, Madam.

Jac. You shall see me win all their Mony; and when I have done, I'll return in my own person, and ask him for the money, which he promised me.

Beat. 'Twill put him upon a streight to be so surpriz'd; but, let us to the Table, the Company stayes for us.   [*The Company sit.*

Wild. What is the Ladies Game, Sir?

Lop. Most commonly they use Raffle. That is, to throw with three Dice, till Duplets and a chance be thrown; and the highest Duplets wins except you throw *In* and *In*, which is call'd Raffle; and that wins all.

285

Wild. I underſtand it: Come, Lady, 'tis no matter what I lose; the greateſt ſtake, my heart, is gone already. (*To Jacinta.*)

They play; and the reſt by couples.

Wild. So, I have a good chance, two quarters and a sice.

Jac. Two sixes and a trey wins it. [*sweeps the money.*

Wild. No matter; I'll try my fortune once again; what have I here? two sixes and a quarter?——an hundred Piſtols on that throw.

Jac. I take you, Sir,—*Beatrix* the high running Dice.——

Beat. Here Madam——

Jac. Three fives: I have won you Sir.

Wild. I, the pox take me for't, you have won me; it would never have vex'd me to have loſt my money to a Christian; but to a Pagan, an Infidel.——

Mask. Pray, Sir, leave off while you have some money.

Wild. Pox of this Lady *Fatyma!* Raffle thrice together, I am out of patience.

Mask. *to him*. Sir, I beseech you, if you will lose, to lose *en Cavalier*.

Wild. Toldera, toldera—pox and curse—toldera, &c. What the Devil did I mean to play with this Brunet of *Afrique?*

The Ladies rise.

Wild. Will you be gone already Ladies?

Lop. You have won our money; but however we are acknowledging to you for the honor of your company.

Jacinta *makes a sign of farewel to* Wildblood.

Wild. Farewell Lady *Fatyma*. *Exeunt all but* Wild. *and* Mask.

Mask. All the company took notice of your concernment.

Wild. 'Tis no matter; I do not love to fret inwardly, as your silent losers do, and in the mean time be ready to choak for want of vent.

Mask. Pray consider your condition a little; a younger Brother in a foreign Country, living at a high rate, your money loſt, and without hope of a supply. Now curse if you think good.

Wild. No, now I will laugh at myself moſt unmercifully: for my condition is so ridiculous, that 'tis paſt cursing. The pleasanteſt part of the adventure is, that I have promis'd 300 piſtols to *Jacinta:* but there is no remedy, they are now fair *Fatyma*'s.

Mask. *Fatyma!*

Wild. I, I, a certain *African* Lady of my acquaintance whom you know not.

Mask. But who is here, Sir!

Enter Jacinta *and* Beatrix *in their own shapes.*

Wild. Madam, what happy ſtar has conducted you hither to
night! A thousand Devils of this fortune?   [*aside.*

Jac. I was told you had Ladies here and fiddles; so I came partly
for the divertisement, and partly out of jealousie.

Wild. Jealousie! why sure you do not think me a Pagan, an In-
fidel? But the company's broke up you see. Am I to wait upon you
home, or will you be so kind to take a hard lodging with me to
night?

Jac. You shall have the honor to lead me to my Father's.

Wild. No more words then, let's away to prevent discovery.

Beat. For my part I think he has a mind to be rid of you.

Wild. No; but if your Lady should want sleep, 'twould spoil the
luſtre of her eyes to morrow. There were a Conqueſt loſt.

Jac. I am a peaceable Princess, and content with my own; I mean
your heart, and purse; for the truth is, I have loſt my money to night
in *Masquerade*, and am come to claim your promise of supplying me.

Wild. You make me happy by commanding me: to morrow
morning my servant shall wait upon you with 300 piſtols.

Jac. But I left my company with promise to return to play.

Wild. Play on tick, and lose the *Indies*, I'll discharge it all to
morrow.

Jac. To night, if you'll oblige me.

Wild. Maskall, go and bring me 300 piſtols immediately.

Mask. Are you mad Sir?

Wild. Do you expoſtulate you raſcall! how he ſtares! I'll be
hang'd if he have not loſt my gold at play: if you have, confess you
had beſt, and perhaps I'll pardon you; but if you do not confess, I'll
have no mercy: did you lose it?

Mask. Sir, 'tis not for me to dispute with you.

Wild. Why then let me tell you, you did lose it.

Jac. I, as sure as e're he had it, I dare swear for him: but com-
mend me you for a kind Maſter, that can let your Servant play off
300 piſtols, without the leaſt sign of anger to him.

Beat. 'Tis a sign he has a greater banck in ſtore to comfort him.

Wild. Well, Madam, I muſt confess I have more then I will
speak of at this time; but till you have given me satisfaction——

Jac. Satisfaction; why are you offended, Sir?

Wild. Heaven! that you should not perceive it in me: I tell you,
I am mortally offended with you.

Jac. Sure 'tis impossible.

Wild. You have done nothing I warrant to make a man

287

jealous: going out a gaming in *Masquerade*, at unseasonable hours, and losing your money, at play; that loss above all, provokes me.

Beat. I believe you; because she comes to you for more. [*Aside.*

Jac. Is this the quarrel? I'll clear it immediately.

Wild. 'Tis impossible you should clear it; I'll ſtop my ears if you but offer it. There's no satisfaction in the point.

Jac. You'll hear me?——

Wild. To do this in the beginning of an amour, and to a jealous servant as I am, had I all the wealth of *Peru*, I would not let go one Maravedis to you.

Jac. To this I answer—

Wild. Answer nothing, for it will but enflame the quarrel betwixt us: I muſt come to my self by little and little; and when I am ready for satisfaction I will take it: but at present it is not for my honor to be friends.

Beat. Pray let us neighbour Princes interpose a little.

Wild. When I have conquer'd, you may interpose; but at present, the mediation of all Chriſtendome would be fruitless.

Jac. Though Chriſtendome can do nothing with you, yet I hope an *African* may prevail. Let me beg you for the sake of the Lady *Fatyma.*

Wild. I begin to suspect that Lady *Fatyma* is no better than she should be. If she be turn'd Chriſtian again I am undone.

Jac. By *Alha* I am afraid on't too: By *Mahomet* I am.

Wild. Well, well, Madam, any man may be overtaken with an oath; but I never meant to perform it with her: you know no oaths are to be kept with Infidels. But——

Jac. No, the love you made was certainly a design of the charity you had to reconcile the two Religions. There's scarce such another man in *Europe* to be sent Apoſtle to convert the *Moor* Ladies.

Wild. Faith I would rather widen their breaches then make 'em up.

Jac. I see there's no hope of a reconcilement with you; and therefore I give it o're as desperate.

Wild. You have gain'd your point, you have my money; and I was only angry because I did not know 'twas you who had it.

Jac. This will not serve your turn, Sir; what I have got I have conquer'd from you.

Wild. Indeed you use me like one that's conquer'd; for you have plunder'd me of all I had.

Jac. I only disarm'd you for fear you should rebell again; for if you had the sinews of warr I am sure you would be flying out.

Wild. Dare but to ſtay without a new Servant till I am flush again,

288

and I will love you, and treat you, and present you at that unreasonable rate; that I will make you an example to all unbelieving Mistresses.

Jac. Well, I will trie you once more; but you must make haste then, that we may be within our time; methinks our love is drawn out so subtle already, that 'tis near breaking.

Wild. I will have more care of it on my part, than the kindred of an old Pope have to preserve him.

Jac. Adieu; for this time I wipe off your score,
Till you're caught tripping in some new amour.   [*Ex. Women.*

Mask. You have us'd me very kindly, Sir, I thank you.

Wild. You deserv'd it, for not having a lye ready for my occasions. A good Servant should be no more without it, than a Souldier without his Armes. But prethee advise me what's to be done to get *Jacinta.*

Mask. You have lost her, or will lose her by your submitting: if we men could but learn to value our selves, we should soon take down our Mistresses from all their Altitudes, and make 'em dance after our Pipes, longer perhaps than we had a mind to't————But I must make haste, or I shall lose *Don Melchor.*————

Wild. Call *Bellamy*, we'll both be present at thy enterprise: then I'll once more to the Gaming-house with my small stock, for my last refuge: if I win, I have wherewithal to mollifie *Jacinta.*

If I throw out, I'll bear it off with huffing;
And snatch the money like a Bulli-Ruffin.   [*Exeunt.*

ACT IV.

Bellamy, Wildblood: Maskall in a visor.

Bell. **H**Ere comes one, and in all probability it must be *Don Melchor* going to *Theodosia.*

Mask. Stand close, and you shall see me serve the Writ upon him.

Enter Don Melchor.

Wild. Now, *Maskall.*

Mask. I stay'd here, Sir, by express order from the Lady *Aurelia,* to deliver you this Note; and to desire you from her, to meet her immediately in the Garden.

Mel. Do you hear friend!

Mask. Not a syllable more, Sir, I have perform'd my orders.

Maskal retires to his Masters.

Mel. He's gone; and 'tis in vain for me to look after him. What envious Devil has discover'd to *Aurelia* that I am in Town? it muſt be *Don Lopez*, who to advance his own pretensions to her, has endeavour'd to ruine mine.

Wild. It works rarely.

Mel. But I am resolv'd to see *Aurelia*; if it be but to defeat him.
Exit Melchor.

Wild. Let's make haſte after him; I long to see the end of this adventure.

Mask. Sir, I think I see some women coming yonder.

Bell. Well; I'll leave you to your adventures; while I prosecute my own.

Wild. I warrant you have made an assignation to inſtruct some Lady in the Mathematicks.

Bell. I'll not tell you my design; because if it does not succeed, you shall not laugh at me.
Exit Bellamy.

Enter Beatrix; *and* Jacinta *in the habit of a Mulatta.*

Wild. Let us withdraw a little, and see if they will come this way.

Beat. We are right, Madam, 'tis certainly your *Englishman*, and his Servant with him. But why this second triall, when you engag'd to break with him, if he fail'd in the firſt?

Jac. 'Tis true, he has been a little inconſtant; cholerick, or so.

Beat. And it seems you are not contented with those vices; but are searching him for more. This is the folly of a bleeding Gameſter, who will obſtinately pursue a losing hand.

Jac. On t'other side, you would have me throw up my Cards before the game be loſt; let me make this one more triall, when he has money whether he will give it me, and then if he fails—

Beat. You'l forgive him agen.

Jac. He's already in Purgatory; but the next offence shall put him in the pit paſt all redemption; prithee sing to draw him nearer: Sure he cannot know me in this disguise.

Beat. Make haſte then; for I have more Irons in the fire; when I have done with you I have another assignation of my Lady *Theodosia*'s to Don *Melchor*.

SONG.

C*Alm was the Even, and cleer was the Skie,*
  And the new budding flowers did spring,
When all alone went Amyntas *and I*
   To hear the sweet Nightingal sing;

I sate, and he laid him down by me;
  But scarcely his breath he could draw;
For when with a fear, he began to draw near,
  He was dash'd with A ha ha ha ha!

2.

He blush'd to himself, and lay still for a while,
  And his modesty curb'd his desire;
But streight I convinc'd all his fear with a smile,
  Which added new Flames to his Fire.
O Sylvia, said he, you are cruel,
  To keep your poor Lover in awe;
Then once more he prest with his hand to my brest,
  But was dash'd with A ha ha ha ha!

3.

I knew 'twas his passion that caus'd all his fear;
  And therefore I pity'd his case:
I whisper'd him softly there's no body near,
  And laid my cheek close to his face:
But as he grew bolder and bolder,
  A Shepherd came by us and saw;
And just as our bliss we began with a kiss,
  He laugh'd out with A ha ha ha ha!

Wild. If you dare be the *Sylvia,* Lady, I have brought you a more confident *Amyntas,* than that bashful Gentleman in your Song——
                    Goes to lay hold of her.

Jac. Hold, hold; Sir, I am only an Ambassadress sent you from a Lady, I hope you will not violate the Laws of Nations.

Wild. I was only searching for your Letters of Credence: but methinks with that beauty you look more like a Herauld, that comes to denounce war to all mankind——

Jac. One of the Ladies in the Masque to night has taken a liking to you; and sent you by me this purse of gold, in recompence of that she saw you lose.

Wild. And she expects in return of it, that I should wait on her; I'll do't, Where lives she? I am desperately in love with her.

Jac. Why, Can you love her unknown?

Wild. I have a Banque of Love, to supply every ones occasions; some for her, some for another, and some for you; charge what you will upon me, I pay all at sight, and without questioning who brought the Bill.

Jac. Heyday, You dispatch your Mistresses as fast, as if you meant to o're-run all Woman-kind: sure you aime at the Universal-Monarchy.

Wild. Now I think on't, I have a foolish fancy to send thy Lady a taste of my love by thee.

Jac. 'Tis impossible your love should be so humble, to descend to a *Mulatta*.

Wild. One would think so, but I cannot help it. Gad, I think the reason is, because there's something more of sin in thy colour then in ours. I know not what's the matter, but a *Turky-Cock* is not more provok'd at red, then I bristle at the sight of black. Come, be kinder to me. Young, and slip an opportunity? 'Tis an Evening lost out of your life.

Jac. These fine things you have said over a thousand times; your cold Compliment's the cold Pye of love, which you serve up to every new guest whom you invite.

Wild. Come, because thou art very moving, here's part of the Gold, which thou brought'st to corrupt me for thy Lady: truth is, I had promis'd a summ to a *Spanish* Lady—but thy eyes have allur'd it from me.

Jac. You'll repent to morrow.

Wild. Let to morrow starve: or provide for himself, as to night has done: to morrow is a cheat in love, and I will not trust it.

Jac. I, but Heaven that sees all things—

Wild. Heaven that sees all things, will say nothing; that is, all eyes, and no tongue; *Et la lune & les estoiles,*—you know the Song.

Jac. A poor slave as I am—

Wild. It has been always my humour to love downward. I love to stoop to my prey, and to have it in my power to Sowse at when I please. When a man comes to a great Lady, he is fain to approach her with fear and reverence; methinks there's something of Godliness in't.

Jac. Yet I cannot believe, but the meanness of my habit must needs scandalize you.

Wild. I'll tell thee my friend and so forth, that I exceedingly honour course Linnen; 'tis as proper sometimes in an under Garment, as a course Towel is to rub and scrub me.

Jac. Now I am altogether of the other side, I can love no where but above me: methinks the ratling of a coach and six, sounds more eloquently, than the best Harrangue a Wit could make me.

Wild. Do you make no more esteem of a Wit then?

Jac. His commendations serve onely to make others have a mind to me; He does but say Grace to me like a *Chaplain*; and like him is the laſt that shall fall on. He ought to get no more by it, then a poor Silk-weaver does by the Ribband which he workes, to make a Gallant fine.

Wild. Then what is a Gentleman to hope from you?

Jac. To be admitted to pass my time with, while a better comes: to be the loweſt ſtep in my Stair-case, for a Knight to mount upon him, and a Lord upon him, and a Marquess upon him, and a Duke upon him, till I get as high as I can climb.

Wild. For ought I see, the Great Ladies have the Appetites which you Slaves should have; and you Slaves the Pride which ought to be in Ladies. For, I observe, that all women of your condition are like the women of the Play-house, ſtill Piquing at each other, who shall go the beſt Dreſt, and in the Richeſt Habits: till you work up one another by your high flying, as the *Heron* and *Jerfalcon* do. If you cannot out-shine your fellow with one Lover, you fetch her up with another: and, in short, all you get by it is onely to put Finery out of countenance; and to make the Ladies of Quality go plain, because they will avoid the Scandal of your bravery.

Beat. running in. Madam, come away; I hear company in the Garden.

Wild. You are not going?

Jac. Yes, to cry out a Rape if you follow me.

Wild. However, I am glad you have left your treasure behind you: farewel Fairie.

Jac. Farewel Changeling—Come *Beatrix.*   [*Exeunt Women.*

Mask. Do you know how you came by this money, Sir? You think, I warrant, that it came by fortune.

Wild. No, Sirrah, I know it came by my own induſtry. Did not I come out diligently to meet this gold, in the very way it was to come? what could Fate do leſs for me? they are such thoughtless, and undesigning Rogues as you, that make a drudge of poor providence, and set it a shifting for you. Give me a brave fellow like my self; that if you throw him down into the world, lights every where upon his legs, and helps himself, without being beholding to Fate, that is the Hospital of fools.

Mask. But after all your jollity, what think you if it was *Jacinta* that gave it you in this disguise? I am sure I heard her call *Beatrix* as she went away.

Wild. Umh! thou awaken'ſt a moſt villainous apprehension in me! methought indeed I knew the voice; but the face was such an evidence againſt it! If it were so, she is loſt for ever.

Mask. And so is *Beatrix!*

Wild. Now could I cut my throat for madness.

Mask. Now could I break my neck for despair; if I could find a precipice absolutely to my liking.

Wild. 'Tis in vain to consider on't. There's but one way; go you *Maskal*, and find her out, and invent some excuse for me, and be sure to beg leave I may come and wait upon her with the gold before she sleeps.

Mask. In the mean time you'l be thinking at your lodging.

Wild. But make haste then to relieve me; for I think over all my thoughts in half an hour. *Exit Maskall*.

Wild. solus. Hang't, now I think on't, I shall be but melancho-lique at my Lodging, I'll go pass my hour at the Gaming-house, and make use of this money while I have tools, to win more to it. Stay, let me see, I have the box and throw. My *Don* he sets me ten pistols; I nick him; ten more, I sweep them too. Now in all reason he is nettled, and sets me twenty: I win them too. Now he kindles and butters me with forty. They are all my own: in fine, he is vehement, and bleeds on to fourscore or an hundred; and I not willing to tempt fortune, come away a moderate winner of 200 pistols.

The Scene opens and discovers Aurelia *and* Camilla: *behind them a Table and lights set on it.*

The Scene *is a Garden with an Arbour in it.*

The Garden dore opens! How now! *Aurelia* and *Camilla* in expectation of Don *Melchor* at the Garden door; I'll away lest I prevent the designe, and within this half hour come sailing back with full pockets, as wantonly as a laden Galleon from the *Indies*. *Exit*.

Aur. But dost thou think the *Englishman* can keep his promise? for I confess I furiously desire to see the *Idea* of *Don Melchor*.

Cam. But, Madam, if you should see him, it will not be he, but the Devil in his likeness; and then why should you desire it?

Aur. In effect 'tis a very dark *Enigma*; and one must be very spiritual to understand it. But be what it will, bodie or fantome, I am resolv'd to meet it.

Cam. Can you do it without fear?

Aur. No; I must avow it, I am furiously fearful; but yet I am re-solv'd to sacrifice all things to my love. Therefore let us pass over that Chapter. *Don Melchor without*.

Cam. Do your hear, Madam, there's one treading already; how if it be he?

Aur. If it be he; that is to say, his Specter, that is to say, his Fan-tome, that is to say his Idea; that is to say, He and not he.

294

Cam. crying out. Ah, Madam, 'tis he himself; but he's as big again as he us'd to be, with eyes like sawcers.——I'll save my self.

runs under the table.

Enter Don Melchor: *they both shreek.*

Aur. Oh heaven! humanitie is not able to support it.   [*running.*

Mel. Dear *Aurelia*, what mean you?

Aur. The Tempter has imitated his voice too; avoid, avoid Specter.

Cam. If he should find me under the table now!

Mel. Is it thus my Dear that you treat your Servant?

Aur. I am not thy Dear; I renounce thee, spirit of darkness.

Mel. This Spirit of darkness, is come to see an Angel of light, by her command; and to assure her of his constancy, that he will be hers eternally.

Aur. Away Infernal, 'tis not thee, 'tis the true *Don Melchor* that I would see.

Mel. Hell and Furies.

Aur. Heaven and Angels! Ah———   *runs out shreeking.*

Mel. This is a riddle past my finding out, to send for me, and then to shun me; but here's one shall resolve it for me: *Camilla*, what dost thou there?

Cam. Help, help, I shall be carried away, bodily.

She rises up, overthrows the Table and lights, and runs out.

The Scene shuts.

Mel. alone. Why *Aurelia, Camilla!* they are both run out of hearing! This amazes me; what can the meaning of it be? Sure she has heard of my unfaithfulness, and was resolv'd to punish me by this contrivance! to put an affront upon me by this abrupt departure, as I did on her by my seeming absence.

Enter Theodosia *and* Beatrix.

Theo. Don Melchor? is it you my Love that have frighted *Aurelia* so terribly?

Mel. Alas, Madam, I know not; but coming hither by your appointment, and thinking my self secure in the night without disguise, perhaps it might work upon her fancie, because she thought me absent.

Theo. Since 'tis so unluckily fallen out, that she knows you are at *Madrid*, it can no longer be kept a secret; therefore you must now pretend openly to me, and run the risque of a denial from my Father.

295

Mel. O, Madam, there's no question but he'll refuse me; for alas, what is it he can see in me worthy of that honor? or if he should be so partial to me, as some in the world are, to think me valiant, learned, and not altogether a fool, yet my want of fortune would weigh down all.

Theo. When he has refus'd you his consent, I may with Justice dispose of my self; and that, while you are constant, shall never be to any but your self: in witness of which, accept this Diamond as a Pledge of my hearts firmness to you.

Beat. Madam, Your Father is coming this way.

Theo. 'Tis no matter; do not stir; since he must know you are return'd, let him now see you.

Enter Don Alonzo.

Alon. Daughter, What make you here at this unseasonable hour?

Theo. Sir,——

Alon. I know what you would say, That you heard a noise, and ran hither to see what it might be—Bless us! Who is this with you?

Mel. 'Tis your servant, Don *Melchor*; just return'd from St. *Sebastians.*

Alon. But, Sir, I thought you had been upon the Sea for *Flanders.*

Mel. I had so design'd it.

Alon. But, why came you back from St. *Sebastians?*

Mel. As for that, Sir, 'tis not material——

Theo. An unexpected Law Sute has call'd him back from St. *Sebastians.*

Alon. And, how fares my Son-in-Law that lives there?

Mel. In Catholique health, Sir.

Alon. Have you brought no Letters from him?

Mel. I had, Sir, but I was set on by the way, by Pickerons; and, in spight of my resistance, rob'd, and my Portmantue taken from me.

Theo. And this was that which he was now desiring me to excuse to you.

Alon. If my Credit, Friends, or Counsel, can do you any service in your Sute, I hope you will command them freely.

Mel. When I have dispatch'd some private business I shall not fail to trouble you; till then, humbly kisses your hands, the most oblig'd of your servants——   *Exit* Melchor.

Alon. Daughter, now this Cavalier is gone, What occasion brought you out so late? I know what you would say, That it is Melancholy; a Tincture of the Hypochondriaque you mean: but, what cause have you for this Melancholy? give me your hand, and answer me without Ambages or Ambiguities.

296

Theo. He will find out I have given away my Ring—I muſt prevent him—Sir, I am asham'd to confess it to you; but, in hope of your indulgence, I have loſt the Table Diamond you gave me.

Alon. You would say, The fear of my displeasure has caus'd this perturbation in you; well, do not disquiet your self too much, you say 'tis gone; I say so too. 'Tis ſtollen; and that by some Thief I take it: but, I will go and consult the *Aſtrologer* immediately. [*He is going.*

Theo. What have I done? to avoid one inconvenience, I have run into another: this Devil of an *Aſtrologer* will discover that *Don Melchor* has it. [*Aside.*

Alon. When did you lose this Diamond? the minute and second I should know; but the hour will serve for the Degree ascending.

Theo. Sir, the precise time I know not; but, it was betwixt six and seven this evening, as near as I can guess.

Alon. 'Tis enough; by all the Stars I'll have it for you; Therefore go in, and suppose it on your finger.

Beat. I'll watch you at a diſtance, Sir, that my *Englishman* may have wherewithal to answer you—(*Aside*)   *Exit* Theo. Beat.

Alon. This melancholy wherewith my Daughter laboureth, is ——a——I know what I would say, is a certain species of the Hysterical Diseases; or a certain motion, caused by a certain appetite, which at a certain time heaveth in her like a certain motion of an Earthquake——

Enter Bellamy.

Bell. This is the place, and very near the time that *Theodosia* appoints her meeting with Don *Melchor.* He is this night otherwise dispos'd of with *Aurelia*: 'Tis but trying my Fortune to tell her of his Infidelity, and my love. If she yields she makes me happy; if not, I shall be sure Don *Melchor* has not planted the Armes of *Spain* in the Fort before me. However, I'll push my Fortune as sure as I am an *Englishman.*

Alon. Sennor *Ingles*, I know your voice, though I cannot perfeƈtly discern you.

Bell. How the Devil came he to cross me?

Alon. I was juſt coming to have ask'd another Favour of you.

Bell. Without Ceremony command me, Sir.

Alon. My Daughter *Theodosia* has loſt a fair Diamond from her finger, the time betwixt six and seven this evening; now I desire you, Sir, to ereƈt a Scheme for it, and if it be loſt, or ſtollen, to reſtore it to me——This is all, Sir.

Bell. There is no end of this old Fellow; thus will he baite me from day to day, till my ignorance be found out—— [*Aside.*

Alon. Now he is casting a Figure by the Art of Memory, and making a Judgment of it to himself. This *Astrology* is a very mysterious speculation———— [*Aside.*

Bell. 'Tis a madness for me to hope I can deceive him longer. Since then he must know I am no Astrologer, I'll discover it my self to him, and blush once for all———— [*Aside.*

Alon. Well, Sir, and what do the Stars hold forth? What sayes nimble Master *Mercury* to the matter?

Bell. Sir, not to keep you longer in ignorance, I must ingeniously declare to you, that I am not the man for whom you take me. Some smattering in *Astrology* I have; which my Friends, by their indiscretion, have blown abroad, beyond my intentions. But, you are not a person to be impos'd on like the vulgar: therefore, to satisfie you in one word, my skill goes not farr enough to give you knowledge of what you desire from me.

Alon. You have said enough, Sir, to perswade me of your Science, if Fame had not publish'd it, yet this very humility of yours, were enough to confirm me in the beliefe of it.

Bell. Death, you make me mad, Sir: Will you have me Swear? As I am a Gentleman, a man of the Town, one who wears good Cloathes, Eates, Drinks, and Wenches abundantly; I am a damn'd ignorant, and senceless Fellow.

Enter Beatrix.

Alon. How now, Gentlewoman———— What, Are you going to reliefe by Moonshine?

Beat. I was going on a very charitable Office, to help a Friend that was gravell'd in a very doubtful business.

Bell. Some good newes, Fortune, I beseech thee.

Beat. But now I have found this learned Gentleman, I shall make bold to propound a Question to him from a Lady.

Alon. I will have my own Question first resolv'd.

Bell. O, Sir, 'tis from a Lady————

Beat. If you please, Sir, I'll tell it in your eare————My Lady has given Don *Melchor* the Ring; in whose company her Father found her but just now at the Garden door. [*In whisper.*

Bell. aloud. Come to me to morrow, and you shall receive an answer————

Beat. Your Servant, Sir,— [*Exit* Beatrix.

Alon. Sir, I shall take it very unkindly if you satisfie any other, and leave me in this perplexity.

Bell. Sir, if my knowledge were according—

Alon. No more of that, Sir, I beseech you.

Bell. Perhaps I may know something by my Art concerning it; but, for your quiet, I wish you would not press me.

Alon. Do you think I am not Master of my Passions?

Bell. Since you will needs know what I would willingly have conceal'd, the person who has your Diamond, is he whom you saw last in your Daughters company.

Alon. You would say 'tis Don *Melchor de Guzman.* Who, the Devil would have suspected him of such an action? But he is of a decay'd Family, and poverty, it seems, has inforc'd him to it: now I think on't better he has e'en stoln it for a fee to bribe his Lawyer; to requite a lye with a Theft; I'll seek him out, and tell him part of my mind before I sleep. [*Exit* Alon.

Bell. So, once more I am at liberty: but this *Astrologie* is so troublesome a Science—would I were well rid on't.

Enter Don Lopez *and a* Servant.

Lop. *Astrologie* does he say? O Cavalier is it you; not finding you at home, I came on purpose to seek you out: I have a small request to the Stars by your mediation.

Bell. Sir, for pity let 'em shine in quiet a little; for what for Ladies and their Servants, and younger Brothers, they scarce get a Holy-day in a twelvemoneth.

Lop. Pray pardon me, if I am a little curious of my destiny, since all my happiness depends on your answer.

Bell. Well, Sir, what is it you expect?

Lop. To know whether my love to a Lady will be successful.

Bell. 'Tis *Aurelia* he means—(*aside*) Sir, in one word I answer you, that your Mistress loves another: one who is your friend; but comfort your self; the Dragon's tail is between him and home, he shall never enjoy her.

Lop. But what hope for me?

Bell. The Stars have partly assur'd me you shall be happy, if you acquaint her with your passion, and with the double dealing of your friend, who is false to her.

Lop. You speak like an Oracle. But I have engag'd my promise to that friend to serve him in his passion to my Mistress.

Bell. We *English* seldom make such scruples; Women are not compriz'd in our Laws of friendship: they are *feræ naturæ,* our common game, like Hare and Partridge; every man has equal right to them, as he has to the Sun and Elements.

Lop. Must I then betray my friend?

Bell. In that case my friend is a Turk to me, if he will be so barbarous as to retain two women to his private use; I will be factious

299

for all diſtressed Damsels; who would much rather have their cause try'd by a full Jury, than a single Judge.

Lop. Well, Sir, I will take your counsel; and if I erre, the fault be on love and you——   *Exit* Lopez.

Bell. Were it not for love, I would run out of the Town, that's the short on't; for I have engag'd my self in so many promises for the Sun and Moon, and those little minc'd-meats of 'em, that I muſt hide before my day of payment comes. In the mean time I forget *Theodosia*; but now I defie the Devil to hinder me.

As he is going out, he meets Aurelia, *and almoſt juſtles her down. With her* Camilla *enters.*

Aur. What rudeness is this?

Bell. Madam *Aurelia*, is it you?

Aur. Monsieur *Bellamy?*

Bell. The same, Madam.

Aur. My Unkle told me he left you here: and indeed I came hither to complain of you: for you have treated me so inhumanely, that I have some reason to resent it.

Bell. What occasion can I have given you for a complaint?

Aur. Don *Melchor*, as I am inform'd by my Uncle, is effectively at *Madrid*: so that it was not his Idea, but himself in person whom I saw: and since you knew this, why did you conceal it from me?

Bell. When I spoke with you I knew it not: but I discover'd it in the erecting of my figure. Yet if inſtead of his Idea I conſtrain'd himself to come, in spight of his resolution to remain conceal'd, I think I have shewn a greater effect of my art then what I promis'd.

Aur. I render myself to so convincing an argument: but by over-hearing a discourse juſt now betwixt my Cousin *Theodosia* and her Maid, I find that he has conceal'd himself upon her account, which has given me jealousie to the laſt point; for to avow an inconteſtable truth, my Cousin is furiously handsome.

Bell. Madam, Madam, truſt not your ears too far; she talk'd on purpose that you might hear her: but I assure you, the true cause of *Don Melchor*'s concealment, was not love of her, but jealousie of you: he ſtaid in private to observe actions: build upon't Madam, he is inviolably yours.

Aur. Then will he sacrifice my Cousin to me?

Bell. 'Tis furiously true Madam.

Aur. O moſt agreeable assurance!

Cam. Albricias Madam, for my good news; *Don Melchor* is coming this way; I know him by his voice; but he is in company with another person.

300

Aur. It will not be convenient to give him any umbrage by seeing me with another person; therefore I will go before; do you stay here and conduct him to my Appartment. Good night Sir.   *Exit.*

Bell. I have promised *Don Lopez* he shall possess her; and I have promis'd her she shall possess *Don Melchor*; 'tis a little difficult, I confess, as to the Matrimonial part of it: but if *Don Melchor* will be civil to her, and she be civil to *Don Lopez*, my credit is safe without the benefit of my Clergie. But all this is nothing to *Theodosia*.
                                        Exit Bellamy.

Enter Don Alonzo *and* Don Melchor.

Cam. *Don Melchor*, a Word in private.

Mel. Your pleasure, Lady; Sir, I will wait on you immediately.

Cam. I am sent to you from a fair Lady, who bears you no ill will. You may guess whom I mean.

Mel. Not by my own merits, but by knowing whom you serve: but I confess I wonder at her late strange usage when she fled from me.

Cam. That was only a mistake; but I have now, by her command, been in a thousand places in quest of you.

Mel. You overjoy me.

Cam. And where amongst the rest do you think I have been looking you?

Mel. Pray refresh my memory.

Cam. In that same street, by that same shop; you know where, by a good token.

Mel. By what token?

Cam. Just by that shop, where out of your nobleness, you promis'd me a new Silk Gown.

Mel. O, now I understand you.

Cam. Not that I press you to a performance——

Mel. Take this, and please your self in the choice of it——
                                Gives her money.]

Cam. Nay, dear Sir, now you make me blush; in faith I——am asham'd——I swear 'tis only because I would keep something for your sake——But my Lady expects you immediately in her Appartment.

Mel. I'll wait on her if I can possibly——*Exit* Camilla. But if I can prevail with *Don Alonzo* for his Daughter, then will I again consider, which of the Ladies best deserves me——   [*Aside.*

To Alonzo. Sir, I beg your pardon for this rudeness, in leaving you.

Alon. I cannot possibly resolve with my self to tell him openly he is a thief; but I'll guild the pill for him to swallow.   [*aside.*

Mel. I believe he has discover'd our amour: how he surveys me for a Son in law!

Alon. Sir, I am sorry for your sake, that true nobility is not always accompanied with riches to support it in its lustre.

Mel. You have a just exception against the Caprichiousness of destiny; yet if I were owner of any noble qualities, (which I am not) I should not much esteem the goods of fortune.

Alon. But pray conceive me, Sir, your father did not leave you flourishing in wealth.

Mel. Only a very fair Seat in *Andalusia*, with all the pleasures imaginable about it: that alone, were my poor deserts according, which I confess they are not, were enough to make a woman happy in it.

Alon. But give me leave to come to the point, I beseech you, Sir. I have lost a Jewel which I value infinitely, and I hear it is in your possession: but I accuse your wants, not you, for it.

Mel. Your Daughter is indeed a Jewel, but she were not lost, were she in possession of a man of parts.

Alon. A pretious Diamond, Sir——

Mel. But a man of honor, Sir.

Alon. I know what you would say, Sir, that a man of honor is not capable of an unworthy action; but therefore I do not accuse you of the theft, I suppose the Jewel was only put into your hands.

Mel. By honourable wayes I assure you, Sir.

Alon. Sir, Sir, will you restore my Jewel?

Mel. Will you please, Sir, to give me leave to be the unworthy possessor of her? I know how to use her with that respect——

Alon. I know what you would say, Sir, but if it belongs to our Family; otherwise I assure you it were at your service.

Mel. As it belongs to your Family I covet it; not that I plead my own deserts, Sir.

Alon. Sir, I know your deserts; but, I protest I cannot part with it: for I must tell you, this Diamond Ring was originally my Great Grandfathers.

Mel. A Diamond Ring, Sir, do you mean?——

Alon. By your patience, Sir, when I have done you may speak your pleasure. I onely lent it to my Daughter; but, how she lost it, and how it came upon your Finger, I am yet in tenebris.

Mel. Sir——

Alon. I know it, Sir; but spare your self the trouble, I'll speak for you; you would say you had it from some other hand; I believe it, Sir.

Mel. But, Sir——

Alon. I warrant you, Sir, I'le bring you off without your speaking;

from another hand you had it; and now Sir, as you say, Sir, and as I am saying for you, Sir, you are loath to part with it.

Mel. Good Sir,—let me——

Alon. I understand you already, Sir, that you have taken a fancy to it, and would buy it; but, to that I answer as I did before, that it is a Relique of my family: now, Sir, if you can urge ought farther, you have liberty to speak without interruption.

Mel. This Diamond you speak on I confess——

Alon. But, What need you confess, Sir, before you are accus'd?

Mel. You promis'd you would hear me in my turn, Sir, but——

Alon. But, as you were saying, it is needless, because I have already spoken for you.

Mel. The truth is, Sir, I was too presumptuous to take this Pledge from *Theodosia* without your knowledge; but, you will pardon the invincible necessity, when I tell you——

Alon. You need not tell me, I know your necessity was the reason of it, and that place and opportunity have caus'd your error.

Mel. This is the goodest old man I ever knew; he prevents me in my motion for his Daughter. Since, Sir, you know the cause of my errors, and are pleas'd to lay part of the blame upon Youth and Opportunity; I beseech you favour me so far, to accept me as fair *Theodosia* already has——

Alon. I conceive you, Sir, that I would accept of your excuse: why restore the Diamond and 'tis done.

Mel. More joyfully then I receiv'd it; and with it I beg the honour to be receiv'd by you as your Son in Law.

Alon. My Son in Law! this is the most pleasant Proposition I ever heard.

Mel. I am proud you think it so; but, I protest I think not I deserve this honor.

Alon. Nor I, I assure you, Sir; marry my daughter—ha, ha, ha.

Mel. But, Sir——

Alon. I know what you would say, Sir, that there is too much hazard in the Profession of a Thief, and therefore you would Marry my Daughter to become rich, without venturing your Neck for't. I beseech you, Sir, steal on, be apprehended, and if you please, be hang'd, it shall make no breach betwixt us. For my part, I'll keep your Counsel, and so good night, Sir. [*Exit* Alonzo.

Mel. Is the Devil in this old man, first, to give me occasion to confess my Love, and, when he knew it, to promise he would keep my Counsel? But, Who are these? I'll not be seen; but to my old appointment with *Theodosia*, and desire her to unriddle it——

[*Exit* Melchor.

303

Enter Maskal, Jacinta, Beatrix.

Mask. But, Madam, do you take me for a Man of Honour.

Jac. No.

Mask. Why there's it; if you had, I would have sworn that my Master has neither done nor intended you any injury; I suppose you'll grant he knew you in disguise?

Beat. Nay, to know her, and use her so, is an aggravation of his Crime.

Mask. Unconscionable *Beatrix!* Would you two have all the Carnival to your selves? He knew you, Madam, and was resolv'd to countermine you in all your Plots. But, when he saw you so much piqued, he was too good natur'd to let you sleep in wrath, and sent me to you to disabuse you: for, if the business had gone on till to morrow, when *Lent* begins, you would have grown so peevish (as all good Catholicks are with fasting) that the quarrel would never have been ended.

Jac. Well; this mollifies a little: I am content he shall see me.

Mask. But, that you may be sure he knew you, he will bring the Certificate of the Purse along with him.

Jac. I shall be glad to find him innocent.

Enter Wildblood *at the other end of the Stage.*

Wild. No mortal man ever threw out so often. It could not be me, it must be the Devil that did it: he took all the Chances, and chang'd 'em, after I had thrown 'em: but, I'le be even with him; for, I'll never throw one of his Dice more.

Mask. Madam, 'tis certainly my Master; and he is so zealous to make his peace, that he could not stay till I call'd him to you———— Sir.

Wild. Sirrah, I'll teach you more manners then to leave me another time; you Rogue, you have lost me two hundred Pistolls, you and the Devil your accomplice; you, by leaving me to my self, and he by tempting me to Play it off.

Mask. Is the wind in that door? here's like to be fine doings.

Wild. Oh mischiefe! am I fallen into her ambush? I must face it out with another quarrel.————   [*Aside.*

Jac. Your Man has been treating your Accommodation; 'tis half made already.

Wild. I, On your part it may be.

Jac. He sayes you knew me.

Wild. Yes, I do know you so well, that my poor heart akes for't:

I was going to bed without telling you my mind; but, upon consideration I am come.

Jac. To bring the Money with you.

Wild. To declare my grievances, which are great, and many.

Mask. Well, for impudence, let thee alone.

Wild. As in the firſt place——

Jac. I'll hear no Grievances; Where's the Money?

Beat. I; keep to that, Madam.

Wild. Do you think me a person to be so us'd?

Jac. We will not quarrel; Where's the Money?

Wild. By your favour we will quarrel.

Beat. Money, Money——

Wild. I am angry, and can hear nothing.

Beat. Money, Money, Money, Money.

Wild. Do you think it a reasonable thing to put on two disguises in a Night, to tempt a man? (Help me, *Maskal*, for I want Arguments abominably) I thank Heaven I was never so barbarously us'd in all my Life.

Jac. He begins to anger me in good earneſt.

Mask. A thing so much againſt the Rules of Modeſty: so undecent a thing.

Wild. I, so undecent a thing; nay, now I do not wonder at my self for being angry. And then to wonder I should love her in those disguises? to quarrel at the natural desires of humane kind, assaulted by powerful temptations; I am inrag'd at that——

Jac. Hey day! you had beſt quarrel too for my bringing you the Money!

Wild. I have a grudging to you for't: (*Maskall*, the Money, *Maskall*; now help or we are gone.)

Mask. Would she offer to bring Money to you? firſt to affront your poverty.——

Wild. I; to affront my poverty. But, that's no great matter; and then——

Mask. And then, to bring you Money (I ſtick faſt, Sir.)

Wild. (Forward, you Dog, and invent, or I'll cut your throat;) and then, as I was saying, to bring me Money——

Mask. Which is the greateſt and moſt sweet of all temptations; and to think you could resiſt it: being also aggravated by her handsomeness who brought it?

Wild. Resiſt it? no, I would she would underſtand it, I know better what belongs to flesh and blood then so.

Beat. to Jac. This is plain confederacie; I smoak it; he came on purpose to quarrel with you; break firſt with him and prevent it.

Jac. If it be come to that once, the Devil take the hindmost; I'll not be last in love; for that will be a dishonour to my Sex.

Wild. And then——

Jac. Hold, Sir, there needs no more: you shall fall out; and I'll gratifie you with a new occasion: I only try'd you in hope you would be false; and rather than fail of my design, brought gold to bribe you to't.

Beat. As people when they have an ill bargain, are content to lose by't, that they may get it off their hands.

Mask. Beatrix, while our principals are engag'd, I hold it not for our honor to stand idle.

Beat. With all my heart: please you let us draw off to some other ground.

Mask. I dare meet you on any Spot, but one.

Wild. I think we shall do well to put it to an issue; this is the last time you shall ever be troubled with my addresses.

Jac. The favour had been greater to have spar'd this too.

Mask. Beatrix, let us dispatch; or they'll break off before us.

Beat. Break as fast as thou wilt, I am as brittle as thou art for thy heart.

Wild. Because I will absolutely break off with you, I will keep nothing that belongs to you: therefore take back your Picture, and your Handkerchief.

Jac. I have nothing of yours to keep; therefore take back your liberal promises. Take 'em in imagination.

Wild. Not to be behind hand with you in your frumps, I give you back your Purse of Gold: take you that——in imagination.

Jac. To conclude with you, take back your oathes and protestations; they are never the worse for the wearing I assure you; therefore take 'em, spick and span new, for the use of your next Mistress.

Mask. Beatrix, follow your leader; here's the sixpenny whittle you gave me, with the Mutton haft: I can spare it, for knives are of little use in *Spain*.

Beat. There's your Cizars with the stinking brass chain to 'em: 'tis well there was no love betwixt us; for they had been too dull to cut it.

Mask. There's the dandriffe Comb you lent me.

Beat. There's your ferret Ribbaning for garters.

Mask. I would never have come so near as to have taken 'em from you.

Beat. For your Letter I have it not about me; but upon reputation I'll burn it.

Mask. And for yours, I have already put it to a fitting imployment.—Courage, Sir; how goes the battel on your wing?

306

Wild. Juſt drawing off on both sides. Adieu *Spain.*

Jac. Farewel old *England.*

Beat. Come away in Triumph; the day's your own Madam.

Mask. I'll bear you off upon my shoulders, Sir; we have broke their hearts.

Wild. Let her go firſt then; I'll ſtay and keep the honor of the Field.

Jac. I'll not retreat, if you ſtay till midnight.

Wild. Are you sure then we have done loving?

Jac. Yes, very sure; I think so.

Wild. 'Tis well you are; for otherwise I feel my ſtomack a little maukish. I should have doubted another fit of love were coming up.

Jac. No, no; your inconſtancy secures you enough for that.

Wild. That's it which makes me fear my own returning; nothing vexes me but that you should part with me so slightly, as though I were not worth your keeping; well, 'tis a sign you never lov'd me.

Jac. 'Tis the leaſt of your care whether I did or did not; it may be it had been more for the quiet of my self, if I—but 'tis no matter, I'll not give you that satisfaction.

Wild. But what's the reason you will not give it me?

Jac. For the reason that we are quite broke off.

Wild. Why, are we quite broke off.

Jac. Why, are we not?

Wild. Well, since 'tis paſt, 'tis paſt; but a pox of all foolish quarrelling for my part.

Jac. And a mischief of all foolish diguisements for my part.

Wild. But if it were to do again with another Miſtress, I would e'en plainly confess, I had loſt my money.

Jac. And if I had to deal with another Servant, I would learn more wit then to tempt him in disguises: for that's to throw a Venice-glass to the ground, to try if it would not break.

Wild. If it were not to please you, I see no necessity of our parting.

Jac. I proteſt I do it only out of complaisance to you.

Wild. But if I should play the fool and ask your pardon, you would refuse it.

Jac. No, never submit, for I should spoil you again with pardoning you.

Mask. Do you hear this, *Beatrix?* they are juſt upon the point of accommodation; we muſt make haſte, or they'll make a peace by themselves; and exclude us from the Treaty.

Beat. Declare your self the Aggressor then; and I'll take you into mercy.

Wild. The worst that you can say of me is that I have lov'd you thrice over.

Jac. The prime Articles between *Spain* and *England* are seal'd; for the rest, concerning a more strict alliance; if you please we'll dispute them in the Garden.

Wild. But in the first place, let us agree on the Article of Navigation I beseech you.

Beat. These Leagues offensive and defensive will be too strict for us, *Maskall*: a Treaty of commerce will serve our turn.

Mask. With all my heart; and when our loves are veering,
We'll make no words, but fall to privateering.

> Exeunt, *the men leading the women*.

ACT V.

Lopez, Aurelia, and Camilla.

Lop. 'TIS true, if he had continued constant to you, I should have thought my self oblig'd in honor to be his friend; but I could no longer suffer him to abuse a person of your worth and beauty with a feign'd affection.

Aur. But is it possible *Don Melchor* should be false to love? I'll be sworn I did not imagine such a treacherie could have been in nature; especially to a Lady who had so oblig'd him.

Lop. 'Twas this, Madam, which gave me the confidence to wait upon you at an hour which would be otherwise unseasonable.

Aur. You are the most obliging person in the world.

Lop. But to clear it to you that he is false; he is at this very minute at an assignation with your Cousin in the Garden; I am sure he was endeavouring it not an hour ago.

Aur. I swear this Evenings Air begins to incommode me extremely with a cold; but yet in hope of detecting this perjur'd man I am content to stay abroad.

Lop. But withal you must permit me to tell you, Madam, that it is but just I should have some share in a heart which I endeavour to redeem: in the Law of Arms you know that they who pay the ransome have right to dispose of the prisoner.

Aur. The prize is so very inconsiderable that 'tis not worth the claiming.

Lop. If I thought the boon were small, I would not importune my Princess with the asking it: but since my life depends upon the grant—

308

Cam. Mam, I muſt needs tell your Laſhip that *Don Lopez* has deserv'd you: for he has acted all along like a Cavalier; and more for your intereſt than his own; besides Mam *Don Melchor* is as poor as he is false: for my part, I shall ne're endure to call him Maſter.

Aur. Don *Lopez* go along with me, I can promise nothing, but I swear I will do my beſt to disingage my heart from this furious tender which I have for him.

Cam. If I had been a man I could never have forsaken you: Ah those languishing caſts, Mam; and that pouting lip of your Laſhip, like a Cherry-bough weigh'd down with the weight of fruit.

Aur. And that sigh too I think is not altogether disagreeable: but something *charmante* and *mignonne*.

Cam. Well, *Don Lopez*, you'l be but too happy.

Lop. If I were once possessor—

Enter Bellamy *and* Theodosia.

Theo. O we are surpriz'd.

Bell. Fear nothing, Madam, I think I know 'em: *Don Lopez?*

Lop. Our famous *Aſtrologer*, how came you here!

Bell. I am infinitely happy to have met you with *Donna Aurelia*, that you may do me the favour to satisfie this Lady of a truth which I can scarce perswade her to believe.

Lop. I am glad our concernments are so equal: for I have the like favour to ask from *Donna Theodosia*.

Theo. Don *Lopez* is too noble to be refus'd any thing within my power; and I am ready to do him any service after I have ask'd my Cousin if ever Don *Melchor* pretended to her?

Aur. 'Tis the very queſtion which I was furiously resolv'd to have ask'd of you.

Theo. I muſt confess he has made some professions to me: and withal I will acknowledge my own weakness so far as to tell you I have given way he should often visit me when the world believ'd him absent.

Aur. O Cavalier *Aſtrologer*; how have you betray'd me! did not you assure me, that *Don Melchor*'s tender and inclination was for me only?

Bell. I had it from his Star, Madam, I do assure you, and if that twinkled false, I cannot help it: The truth is, there's no truſting the Planet of an inconſtant man; his was moving to you when I look'd on't, and if since it has chang'd the course, I am not to be blam'd for't.

Lop. Now, Madam, the truth is evident. And for this Cavalier he might easily be deceiv'd in *Melchor*, for I dare affirm it to you both, he never knew to which of you he was moſt inclin'd: for he visited one, and writ letters to the other.

Bell. to *Theo.* Then, Madam, I muſt claim your promise, (since I have discover'd to you, that *Don Melchor* is unworthy of your favours) that you would make me happy, who amongſt my many imperfections can never be guilty of such a falsehood.

Theo. If I have been deceiv'd in *Melchor* whom I have known so long, you cannot reasonably expect I should truſt you at a dayes acquaintance.

Bell. For that, Madam, you may know as much of me in a day as you can in all your life: all my humours circulate like my blood, at fartheſt, within 24 hours. I am plain and true, like all my Country-men; you see to the bottom of me as easily as you do to the gravel of a clear ſtream in Autumn.

Lop. You plead so well, Sir, that I desire you would speak for me too: my cause is the same with yours, only it has not so good an Advocate.

Aur. Since I cannot make my self happy, I will have the glory to felicitate another: and therefore I declare I will reward the fidelity of *Don Lopez.*

Theo. All that I can say at present is, that I will never be *Don Melchor's*; the reſt, time and your service muſt make out.

Bell. I have all I can expect, to be admitted as eldeſt Servant; as preferment falls I hope you will remember my seniority.

Cam. Mam, *Don Melchor.*

Aur. Cavaliers retire a little; we shall see to which of us he will make his Court.   *The men withdraw.*

Enter Don Melchor.

Don Melchor, I thought you had been a bed before this time.

Mel. Fair *Aurelia,* this is a blessing beyond expectation to see you agen so soon.

Aur. What important business brought you hither?

Mel. Onely to make my peace with you before I slept. You know you are the Saint to whom I pay my devotions.

Aur. And yet it was beyond your expectances to meet me? This is furiously incongruous.

Theo. advancing. Don Melchor, whither were you bound so late?

Mel. What shall I say? I am so confounded that I know not to which of them I should excuse my self.   *Aside.*

Theo. Pray answer me truly to one queſtion: did you never make any addresses to my Cousin.

Mel. Fie, fie, Madam, there's a queſtion indeed.

310

Aur. How Monster of ingratitude, can you deny the Declaration of your passion to me?

Mel. I say nothing Madam.

Theo. Which of us is it for whom you are concern'd?

Mel. For that, Madam, you must excuse me: I have more discretion then to boast a Ladies favour.

Aur. Did you counterfeit an address to me?

Mel. Still I say nothing, Madam; but I will satisfie either of you in private; for these matters are too tender for publick discourse.

Enter Lopez *and* Bellamy *hastily with their swords drawn.*

Bellamy and *Lopez!* This is strange!

Lop. Ladies, we would not have disturb'd you, but as we were walking to the Garden door, it open'd suddenly against us, and we confusedly saw, by Moon-light, some persons entring, but who they were we know not.

Bell. You had best retire into the Garden-house, and leave us to take our fortunes, without prejudice to your reputations.

Enter Wildblood, Maskall, Jacinta, Beatrix.

Wild. (to *Jacinta entring.*) Do not fear, Madam, I think I heard my friends voice.

Bell. Marry hang you, is it you that have given us this hot alarme?

Wild. There's more in't than you imagine, the whole house is up: for seeing you two, and not knowing you after I had entred the Garden-door, I made too much haste to get out again, and have left the key broken in it. With the noise one of the Servants came running in, whom I forc'd back; and doubtless he is gone for company, for you may see lights running through every Chamber.

Theo. ⎱ What will become of us?
Jaci. ⎰

Bell. We must have recourse to our former resolution. Let the Ladies retire into the Garden-house. And now I think on't you Gentlemen shall go in with 'em, and leave me and *Maskall* to bear the brunt on't.

Mask. Me, Sir? I beseech you let me go in with the Ladies too; dear *Beatrix* speak a good word for me, I protest 'tis more out of love to thy company than for any fear I have.

Bell. You Dog I have need of your wit and counsel. We have no time to deliberate. Will you stay, Sir?   [*To Maskall.*

Mask. No, Sir, 'tis not for my safety.

Bell. Will you in Sir?   [*To Melchor.*

Mel. No Sir, 'tis not for my honor, to be assisting to you: I'll to *Don Alonzo*, and help to revenge the injury you are doing him.

Bell. Then we are lost, I can do nothing.

Wild. Nay, and you talk of honor, by your leave Sir. I hate your *Spanish* honor, ever since it spoil'd our *English* Playes, with faces about and t'other side.

[*Falls upon him, throws him down.*

Mel. What do you mean, you will not murder me?
Must valour be oppress'd by multitudes?

Wild. Come yarely my mates, every man to his share of the burthen. Come yarly hay.

The four men take him each by a limb, and carry him out, he crying murder.

Theo. If this *Englishman* save us now I shall admire his wit.

Beat. Good wits never think themselves admir'd till they are well rewarded: You must pay him in *specie*, Madam, give him love for his wit.

Enter the Men again.

Bell. Ladies fear nothing, but enter into the Garden-house with these Cavaliers——

Mask. Oh that I were a Cavalier too!   *Is going with them.*

Bell. Come you back Sirrah.   *Stops him.*
Think your selves as safe as in a Sanctuary, only keep quiet whatever happens.

Jac. Come away then, they are upon us.

Exeunt all but Bell. *and* Mask.

Mask. Hark, I hear the foe coming: methinks they threaten too, Sir; pray let me go in for a Guard to the Ladies, and poor *Beatrix*. I can fight much better when there is a wall betwixt me and danger.

Bell. Peace, I have occasion for your wit to help me lie.

Mask. Sir, upon the faith of a sinner you have had my last lye already; I have not one more to do me credit, as I hope to be sav'd, Sir.

Bell. Victore, victore; knock under you rogue, and confess me Conquerour, and you shall see I'll bring all off.

Enter Don Alonzo *and six Servants; with lights, and swords drawn.*

Alon. Search about there.

Bell. Fear nothing, do but vouch what I shall say.

312

Mask. For a passive lye I can yet do something.

Alon. Stand: who goes there?

Bell. Friends.

Alon. Friends? who are you?

Bell. Noble *Don Alonzo*, such as are watching for your good.

Alon. Is it you, Sennor *Ingles?* why all this noise and tumult? where are my Daughters and my Neece? But, in the first place, though last nam'd, how came you hither, Sir?

Bell. I came hither——————by Astrologie, Sir.

Mask. My Master's in, heavens send him good shipping with his lye, and all kind Devils stand his friends.

Alon. How, by Astrologie, Sir? meaning you came hither by Art Magick.

Bell. I say, by pure Astrologie, Sir, I foresaw by my Art a little after I had left you that your Neece and Daughters would this night run a risque of being carried away from this very Garden.

Alon. O the wonders of this speculation!

Bell. Thereupon I call'd immediately for my sword, and came in all haste to advertise you; but I see there's no resisting Destiny, for just as I was entring the Garden door I met the Women with their Gallants all under sail, and outward bound.

Mask. Thereupon what does me, he but draws by my advice.——

Bell. How now, Mr. Raskall? are you itching to be in?

Mask. Pray, Sir, let me go snip with you in this lye, and be not too covetous of honor? You know I never stood with you; now my courage is come to me, I cannot resist the temptation.

Bell. Content; tell on.

Mask. So, in short, Sir, we drew, first I, and then my Master; but, being overpower'd, they have escap'd us, so that I think you may go to bed and trouble your self no further, for gone they are.

Bell. You tell a lye! you have curtail'd my invention: you are not fit to invent a lye for a Bawd when she would whedle a young Squire.

Alon. Call up the Officers of Justice, I'll have the Town search'd immediately.

Bell. 'Tis in vain, Sir; I know, by my Art, you'll never recover 'em; besides, 'tis an affront to my friends the Stars, who have otherwise dispos'd of 'em.

Enter a Servant.

Ser. Sir, the key is broken in the Garden-door, and the door lock'd, so that of necessitie they must be in the Garden yet.

Alon. Disperse your selves, some into the Wilderness, some into the Allyes, and some into the Parterre: you, *Diego*, go trie to get out the key, and run to the Corigidore for his assistance: in the mean time I'll search the Garden-house my self.

Exeunt all the Servants but one.

Mask. I'll be unbetted again if you please Sir, and leave you all the honor of it. [*To* Bellamy *aside.*

Alon. Come Cavalier, let us in together.

Bell. holding him. Hold Sir for the love of heaven, you are not mad!

Alon. We must leave no place unsearch'd. A light there.

Bell. Hold, I say, do you know what you are undertaking? and have you arm'd your self with resolution for such an adventure?

Alon. What adventure?

Bell. A word in private—The place you would go into is full of enchantments; there are at this time, for ought I know, a Legion of spirits in it.

Alon. You confound me with wonder, Sir!

Bell. I have been making there my Magical operations, to know the event of your Daughters flight; and, to perform it rightly, have been forc'd to call up Spirits of several Orders: and there they are humming like a swarm of Bees, some stalking about upon the ground, some flying, and some sticking upon the walls like Rear-mice.

Mask. The Devil's in him, he's got off again.

Alon. Now, Sir, I shall trie the truth of your friendship to me. To confess the secret of my soul to you, I have all my life been curious to see a Devil: And to that purpose have con'd *Agrippa* through and through, and made experiment of all his Rules, *Pari die & incremento Lunæ,* and yet could never compass the sight of one of these *Dæmoniums*: if you will ever oblige me let it be on this occasion.

Mask. There's another storm arising.

Bell. You shall pardon me, Sir, I'll not expose you to that peril for the world without due preparations of ceremony.

Alon. For that, Sir, I always carry a Talisman about me; that will secure me; and therefore I will venture in a God's name, and defie 'em all at once. [*Going in.*

Mask. How the pox will he get off from this?

Bell. Well, Sir, since you are so resolv'd, send off your Servant that there may be no noise made on't, and we'll take our venture.

Alon. Pedro, leave your light, and help the fellows search the Garden. *Exit Servant*

Mask. What does my incomprehensible Master mean?

Bell. Now I must tell you, Sir, you will see that which will very much astonish you, if my Art fail me not. *Goes to the door.* You, Spirits and Intelligences, that are within there, stand close, and silent, at your perril, and fear nothing, but appear in your own shapes, boldly.——Maskal *open the door.*

> Maskal *goes to the one side of the Scene, which draws and discovers* Theo. Jac. Aur. Beat. Cam. Lop. Wild. *standing all without motion in a rank.*

Now Sir what think you?

Alon. They are here, they are here: we need search no farther. Ah, you ungratious baggages!   [*Going toward them.*

Bell. Stay, or you'll be torn in pieces: these are the very shapes I Conjur'd up, and truly represent to you in what company your Niece and Daughters are, this very moment.

Alon. Why are they not they? I durst have sworn that some of 'em had been my own flesh and blood——Look, one of them is just like that rogue your camrade.

> Wildblood *shakes his head and frowns at him.*

Bell. Do you see how you have provok'd that *English* Devil? take heed of him; if he gets you once into his clutches:— Wildblood *embracing* Jacinta.

Alon. He seems to have got possession of the Spirit of my *Jacinta,* by his hugging her.

Bell. Nay, I imagin'd as much: do but look upon his physiognomy, you have read *Baptista Porta:* has he not the leer of a very lewd debauch'd Spirit?

Alon. He has indeed: Then there's my Neece *Aurelia,* with the Spirit of *Don Lopez*; but that's well enough; and my Daughter *Theodosia* all alone: pray how comes that about?

Bell. She's provided for with a Familiar too; one that is in this very room with you, and by your Elbow; but I'll shew you him some other time.

Alon. And that Baggage, *Beatrix,* how I would swinge her, if I had her here; I lay my life she was in the Plot for the flight of her Mistresses.   [Beat. *Claps her hands at him.*

Bell. Sir you do ill to provoke her; for being the Spirit of a Woman, she is naturally mischievous: you see she can scarce hold her hands from you already.

Mask. Let me alone to revenge your quarrel upon *Beatrix*; if e're she come to light I'll take a course with her I warrant you Sir.

Bell. Now come away, Sir, you have seen enough: the Spirits are in pain whilst we are here: we keep 'em too long condens'd in bodies: if we were gone, they would rarifie into air immediately. *Maskall* shut the door.   Maskall *goes to the Scene, and it closes.*

Alon. Monstrum hominis! O prodigie of Science!

315

Enter two Servants with Don Melchor.

Bell. Now help me with a lye, *Maskall,* or we are lost.

Mask. Sir, I could never lie with man or woman in a fright.

Ser. Sir, we found this Gentleman bound and gagg'd, and he desir'd us to bring him to you with all haste imaginable.

Mel. O Sir, Sir, your two Daughters and your Niece—

Bell. They are gone he knows it: but are you mad Sir to set this pernicious wretch at libertie?

Mel. I endeavour'd all that I was able—

Mask. Now, Sir, I have it for you— *Aside to his Master.* He was endeavouring indeed to have got away with 'em; for your Daughter *Theodosia* was his Prize: but we prevented him, and left him in the condition in which you see him.

Alon. I thought somewhat was the matter that *Theodosia* had not a Spirit by her, as her Sister had.

Bell. This was he I meant to shew you.

Mel. Do you believe him Sir?

Bell. No, no, believe *him,* Sir: you know his truth ever since he stole your Daughters Diamond.

Mel. I swear to you by my honor.

Alon. Nay, a thief I knew him; and yet after that, he had the impudence to ask me for my Daughter.

Bell. Was he so impudent? The case is plain Sir, put him quickly into custody.

Mel. Hear me but one word Sir, and I'll discover all to you.

Bell. Hear him not, Sir: for my Art assures me if he speaks one syllable more, he will cause great mischief.

Alon. Will he so? I'll stop my ears; away with him.

Mel. Your Daughters are yet in the Garden, hidden by this fellow, and his accomplices.

Alon. at the same time drowning him. I'll stop my ears, I'll stop my ears.

Bell. Mask. at the same time also. A thief, a thief, away with him.

Servants carry Melchor *off struggling.*

Alon. He thought to have born us down with his confidence.

Enter another Servant.

Ser. Sir, with much ado we have got out the key and open'd the door.

Alon. Then, as I told you, run quickly to the Corigidor, and desire him to come hither in person to examine a malefactor.

Wildblood sneezes within.

Alon. Hark, what noise is that within? I think one sneezes.

Bell. One of the Devils I warrant you has got a cold with being so long out of the fire.

Alon. Bless his Devilship as I may say. Wildblood *sneezes again.*

Ser. to *Don Alonzo.* This is a mans voice, do not suffer your self to be deceiv'd so grossly, Sir.

Mask. A man's voice, that's a good one indeed! that you should live to these years, and yet be so silly, as not to know a man from a Devil.

Alon. There's more in't than I imagin'd: hold up your Torch and go in first, *Pedro*, and I'll follow you.

Mask. No let me have the honour to be your Usher.

Takes the Torch and goes in.

Mask. within. Help, help, help.

Alon. What's the matter?

Bell. Stir not upon your life Sir.

Enter Maskall *again without the Torch.*

Mask. I was no sooner entred, but a huge Giant seiz'd my Torch, and fell'd me along, with the very whiffe of his breath as he paſt by me.

Alon. Bless us!

Bell. at the door to them within. Pass out now while you have time in the dark: the Officers of Juſtice will be here immediately, the Garden-door is open for you.

Alon. What are you muttering there, Sir?

Bell. Only dismissing these Spirits of darkness, that they may trouble you no further: go out I say.

They all come out upon the Stage, groaping their way. Wildblood *falls into* Alonzo's *hands.*

Alon. I have caught some body: are these your Spirits? Another light quickly, *Pedro.*

Mask. slipping between Alonzo *and* Wildblood. 'Tis *Maskall* you have caught, Sir; do you mean to ſtrangle me that you press me so hard between your Arms?

Alon. letting Wildblood *go.* Is it thee *Maskall*? I durſt have sworn it had been another.

Bell. Make haſte now before the Candle comes.

Aurelia *falls into* Alonzo's *armes.*

Alon. Now I have another.

Aur. 'Tis *Maskall* you have caught, Sir.

Alon. No I thank you Niece, this artifice is too gross! I know your voice a little better. What ho bring lights there.

Bell. Her impertinence has ruin'd all.

Enter Servants with lights and swords drawn.

Ser. Sir, the Corigidor is coming according to your desire: in the mean time we have secur'd the Garden doors.

Alon. I am glad on't: I'll make some of 'em severe examples.

Wild. Nay then as we have liv'd merrily, so let us die together: but we'll shew the *Don* some sport first.

Theo. What will become of us!

Jac. We'll die for company: nothing vexes me but that I am not a man to have one thrust at that malicious old father of mine before I go.

Lop. Let us break our way through the Corigidor's band.

Jac. A match i'faith: we'll venture our bodies with you: you shall put the baggage in the middle.

Wild. He that pierces thee, I say no more, but I shall be somewhat angry with him: *(to Alonzo)* in the mean time I arrest you, Sir, in the behalf of this good company. As the Corigidor uses us, so we'll use you.

Alon, You do not mean to murder me!

Bell. You murder your self if you force us to it.

Wild. Give me a Razor there, that I may scrape his weeson, that the bristles may not hinder me when I come to cut it.

Bell. What need you bring matters to that extremity? you have your ransome in your hand: here are three men, and there are three women; you understand me.

Jac. If not, here's a sword and there's a throat: you understand me.

Alon. This is very hard!

Theo. The propositions are good, and marriage is as honorable as it us'd to be.

Beat. You had best let your Daughters live branded with the name of Strumpets: for what ever befals the men, that will be sure to be their share.

Alon. I can put them into a Nunnery.

All the Women. A Nunnery!

Jac. I would have thee to know, thou graceless old man, that I defie a Nunnery: name a Nunnery once more, and I disown thee for my Father.

Lop. You know the Custome of the Country, in this case, Sir: 'tis either death or marriage: the business will certainly be publick; and if they die, they have sworn you shall bear 'em company.

Alon. Since it muſt be so, run *Pedro* and ſtop the Corigidor; tell him it was only a Carnival merriment, which I miſtook for a Rape and Robbery.

Jac. Why now you are a dutiful Father again, and I receive you into grace.

Bell. Among the reſt of your miſtakes, Sir, I muſt desire you to let my *Aſtrologie* pass for one: my Mathematicks, and Art Magick werc only a Carnival device; and now that's ended, I have more mind to deal with the flesh than with the devil.

Alon. No Aſtrologer! 'tis impossible!

Mask. I have known him, Sir, this seven years, and dare take my oath he has been always an utter ſtranger to the Stars: and indeed to any thing that belongs to heaven.

Lop. Then I have been cozen'd among the reſt.

Theo. And I; but I forgive him.

Beat. I hope you will forgive me, Madam; who have been the cause on't; but what he wants in Aſtrologie he shall make up to you some other way, I'll pass my word for him.

Alon. I hope you are both Gentlemen?

Bell. As good as the Cid himself, Sir.

Alon. And for your Religion, right Romanes——

Wild. As ever was *Marc Anthony.*

Alon. For your fortunes and courages——

Mask. They are both desperate, Sir; especially their Fortunes.

Theo. to *Bell.* You should not have my consent so soon, but only to revenge my self upon the falseness of *Don Melchor.*

Aur. I muſt avow that gratitude, for *Don Lopez,* is as prevalent with me as revenge againſt *Don Melchor.*

Alon. Lent you know begins to morrow; when that's over marriage will be proper.

Jac. If I ſtay till after Lent, I shall be to marry when I have no love left: I'll not bate you an Ace of to night, Father: I mean to bury this man e're Lent be done, and get me another before Eaſter.

Alon. Well, make a night on't then.   [*Giving his Daughters.*

Wild. Jacinta Wildblood, welcome to me; since our Starres have doom'd it so, we cannot help it: but 'twas a meer trick of Fate, to catch us thus at unawares: to draw us in with a what do you lack as we pass'd by: had we once separated to night, we should have had more wit than ever to have met again to morrow.

Jac. 'Tis true, we shot each other flying: we were both upon wing I find; and had we pass'd this Critical minute, I should have gone for the *Indies,* and you for *Greenland* e're we had met in a bed upon consideration.

319

Mask. You have quarrell'd twice to night without bloodshed, 'ware the third time.

Jac. A propos! I have been retrieving an old Song of a Lover that was ever quarrelling with his Mistress: I think it will fit our amour so well, that if you please I'll give it you for an Epithalamium, and you shall sing it.   *Gives him a Paper.*

Wild. I never sung in all my life; nor ever durst trie when I was alone, for fear of braying.

Jac. Just me, up and down; but for a frolick let's sing together: for I am sure if we cannot sing now, we shall never have cause when we are married.

Wild. Begin then; give me my Key, and I'll set my voice to't.

Jac. Fa la, fa la, fa la.

Wild. Fala, fala, fala. Is this your best upon the faith of a Virgin?

Jac. I by the Muses, I am at my pitch.

Wild. Then do your worst: and let the company be judge who sings worst.

Jac. Upon condition the best singer shall wear the breeches: prepare to strip Sir; I shall put you into your drawers presently.

Wild. I shall be reveng'd with putting you into your smock anon; St. *George* for me.

Jac. St. *James* for me: come start, Sir.

SONG.

Damon.   *Celimena, of my heart,*
            None shall e're bereave you:
            If with your good leave I may
            Quarrel with you once a day.
            I will never leave you.

2.

Celimena.   *Passion's but an empty name*
            Where respect is wanting:
            Damon *you mistake your ayme;*
            Hang your heart, and burn your flame,
            If you must be ranting.

3.

Damon.   *Love as dull and muddy is,*
            As decaying liquor:
            Anger sets it on the lees,
            And refines it by degrees,
            Till it workes it quicker.

4.

Celimena. *Love by quarrels to beget*
Wisely you endeavour;
With a grave Physician's wit,
Who to cure an Ague fit
Put me in a Feavor.

5.

Damon. *Anger rouzes love to fight,*
And his only bayt is,
'Tis the spurre to dull delight,
And is but an eager bite,
When desire at height is.

6.

Celimena. *If such drops of heat can fall*
In our wooing weather;
If such drops of heat can fall,
We shall have the Devil and all
When we come together.

Wild. Your judgement, Gentlemen: a Man or a Maid?

Bell. And you make no better harmony after you are married then you have before, you are the miserablest couple in Christendome.

Wild. 'Tis no great matter; if I had had a good voice she would have spoil'd it before to morrow.

Bell. When *Maskall* has married *Beatrix*, you may learn of her.

Mask. You shall put her life into a Lease then.

Wild. Upon condition that when I drop into your house from hunting, I may set my slippers at your door, as a *Turk* does at a *Jews*, that you may not enter.

Beat. And while you refresh your self within, he shall wind the horn without.

Mask. I'll throw up my Lease first.

Bell. Why thou would'st not be so impudent, to marry *Beatrix*: for thy self only?

Beat. For all his ranting and tearing now, I'll pass my word he shall degenerate into as tame and peaceable a Husband as a civil Woman would wish to have.

Enter Don Melchor *with a Servant.*

Mel. Sir——

Alon. I know what you would say, but your discoverie comes too late now.

Mel. Why the Ladies are found.

Aur. But their inclinations are loſt I can assure you.

Jac. Look you Sir, there goes the game: your Plate-fleet is divided; half for *Spain*, and half for *England*.

Theo. You are juſtly punish'd for loving two.

Mel. Yet I have the comfort of a caſt Lover: I will think well of my self; and despise my Miſtresses.　　　　　　*Exit.*

DANCE.

Bell. Enough, enough; let's end the Carnival abed.

Wild. And for these Gentlemen, when e're they try,
　　May they all speed as soon, and well as I.

　　　　　　　　　　　　　　　　　　Exeunt Omnes.

EPILOGUE

M Y *part being small, I have had time to day,*
　To mark your various censures of our Play:
Firſt, looking for a Judgement or a Wit,
Like Jews *I saw 'em scatter'd through the Pit:*
And where a knot of Smilers lent an eare
To one that talk'd, I knew the foe was there.
The Club of jeſts went round; he who had none
Borrow'd o' th' next, and told it for his own:
Among the reſt they kept a fearfull ſtir,
In whisp'ring that he ſtole th' Aſtrologer;
And said, betwixt a French *and* English *Plot*
He eas'd his half-tir'd Muse, on pace and trot.
Up ſtarts a Monsieur new come o're; and warm
In the French *ſtoop; and the pull-back o' th' arm;*
Morbleu dit il, and cocks, I am a rogue
But he has quite spoil'd the feint Aſtrologue.

322

Pox, sayes another; here's so great a stir
With a son of a whore Farce that's regular,
A rule where nothing must decorum shock!
Dam' me 'ts as dull as dining by the clock.
An Evening! why the devil should we be vext,
Whither he gets the Wench this night or next?
When I heard this, I to the Poet went,
Told him the house was full of discontent,
And ask'd him what excuse he could invent.
He neither swore nor storm'd as Poets do,
But, most unlike an Author, vow'd 'twas true.
Yet said, he us'd the French *like Enemies,*
And did not steal their Plots, but made 'em prize.
But should he all the pains and charges count
Of taking 'em, the bill so high wou'd mount
That, like Prize-goods, which through the Office come,
He could have had 'em much more cheap at home.
He still must write; and Banquier-like, each day
Accept new Bills, and he must break, or pay.
When through his hands such sums must yearly run,
You cannot think the Stock is all his own.
His haste his other errors might excuse;
But there's no mercy for a guilty Muse:
For, like a Mistress, she must stand or fall,
And please you to a height, or not at all.

FINIS

TYRANNICK LOVE

OR THE

ROYAL MARTYR
A TRAGEDY

Non jam prima peto—neq ; vincere certo ;
Extremum rediisse pudet.   Virg.

SOURCE

"AS to the Plot of this Tragedy 'tis founded upon History," says Langbaine, and in the Preface Dryden refers to his reading in Herodian, Eusebius and Metaphrastes. Relevant and illustrative passages from these authors are cited in the Explanatory Notes, and here also is given some account of the *Sainte Catherine* of Desfontaines, from which tragedy Dryden was idly accused of having conveyed material, whereas he borrowed but one error, Act V, 5: "Fils d'un soldat Goth et d'une femme Alaine." *L'Amour Tyrannique* (acted in 1638) of Georges De Scudéry, whence some imagined Dryden had taken his design, will be seen by the description I have furnished in the Explanatory Notes to have nothing at all in common with *Tyrannick Love*.

It should perhaps be remarked that Adam of Saint-Victor wrote a fine poem in honour of Saint Catherine, "Vox sonora nostri chori . . .", and it was to her that Bossuet dedicated one of the most magnificent of his panegyrics. Modern scepticism has evilly, but with a complete futility, essayed to impugn the authenticity of the history of this great Saint, to whom in England alone are dedicated no less than three and sixty churches.

THEATRICAL HISTORY

TYRANNICK *Love; or, The Royal Martyr* was produced at the Theatre Royal, Bridges Street, during the last week of June, 1669; and achieved a signal success, being played to thronging houses for a fortnight together, in those days an extraordinary and exceptional run. The King expressed himself to Killigrew as vastly pleased with the new drama. The cast was indeed of the finest. Michael Mohun, who was very great as Cethegus full of rant and fire in *Catiline*, revived 18 December, 1668, won fresh laurels in the tyrant Maximin; Charles Hart, from whose performance Rymer averred "that the best tragedies on the English stage have received their lustre," acted Porphyrius; handsome Ned Kynaston, Placidius; Mrs. Marshall (Ann or Rebecca?), Berenice; Mrs. Hughes, S. Catherine; Nell Gwyn, Valeria, which rôle, although she hated serious parts, she must have sustained with charm and pathos, or Dryden would assuredly never have entrusted her with Almahide eighteen months after, whilst in any case her delivery of the Epilogue passed into theatrical tradition. Mrs. Mary Knepp doubled Felicia and the aetherial spirit, Nakar; whose companion soft Damilcar was Mrs. James. The small rôle of Erotion fell to Mrs. Susanna Uphill, the lovely but imperious mistress of Sir Robert Howard.

There was no little difficulty and delay about the original production of *Tyrannick Love*, and Mr. Hotson has printed some interesting particulars of a

327

Chancery suit which evolved therefrom (*Commonwealth and Restoration Stage*, pp. 250–53).

On behalf of the Theatre Royal, Killigrew, Hart, and Mohun, complained that the King's Company having to produce ". . . a new play or Tragedy called the Royal Martyr or St. Katherine about the latter end of April, 1669, and there being a necessity of making a new Scene of an Elysium to be presented in the said Tragedy. . . . and one Isaac Fuller being a Painter and one who sometimes did apply himself for painting of Scenes," an agreement was made with Fuller to paint this scene, it being particularly impressed upon the artist that he must use dispatch and have all ready within a fortnight. According to the actors this arrangement was concluded on 14 April, 1669, but according to Fuller not until "the latter end of April or the beginning of May."

However, not only was it painted "very meanly and inconsiderably" but it was not finished until the end of June, and on this account Killigrew "received very great blame from his said Majesty," whilst their audiences fell off and grew thin. Damages are claimed, especially in view of the fact that Fuller had recently taken legal action against Hart and Mohun and recovered £335 10s. for his work.

Fuller declared that he had never agreed to complete such a scene within a fortnight, a thing which was a practical impossibility. About the latter end of April or the beginning of May in the year . . . 1669, "One Mr. Dryden (a Poet as this Defendant hath heard that Sometimes makes Plays" for Killigrew's Company "and one Mr. Wright (a Joiner belonging to the said Company) by the order . . . of the said Company . . . did come unto this Defendant then lying sick at his own house and did propose unto him the painting of the said Scene of an Elysium." He avers that the scene was painted very quickly at great trouble to himself, and perfected "about the 23d of June." He is very certain that the tale about being blamed by the King is untrue, since a few days after the play was produced Killigrew thanked him personally for the pains he had taken, and told him that he "had very well pleased his Majesty and the whole house." Moreover, *Tyrannick Love* proved an exceptional success, inasmuch as it was acted "about 14 days together" and "their said House all the said 14 days was very full, the Pit Boxes and other Places thereof being thronged with Spectators." The receipts were doubled and even more than doubled. Fuller makes it very plain that he only took legal action as the last recourse as the Company repeatedly and with threats refused to pay him his fees. At the trial, held at the Guildhall in Easter term 1670, the jury had already found for Fuller and valued the painting at £335 10s.; of which only forty pounds had been recovered. It would appear that the artist was in the right since the actors did not proceed with their suit.

Tyrannick Love passed into the repertory of the Theatre Royal, it was seen by the King at the Theatre on 18 May, 1676; and there were particular revivals in 1677, 1686, 1694, and 1702.

After the union of the Two Companies in 1682 the rôle of Maximin was sustained by Betterton, but since the death of this great actor *Tyrannick Love* seems completely to have been laid aside.

To the most Illustrious and High-born Prince,

JAMES,

Duke *of Monmouth and Bucclugh,*

One of His Majesties most Honourable Privy-Council, and Knight

of the most Noble Order of the Garter, &c.

SIR,

THE favourable Reception which your Excellent Lady afforded to one of my former Plays, has encourag'd me to double my presumption, in addressing this to your Graces Patronage. So dangerous a thing it is to admit a Poet into your Family, that you can never afterwards be free from the chiming of ill Verses, perpetually sounding in your ears, and more troublesom than the neighbourhood of Steeples. I have been favourable to my self in this expression; a zealous Fanatick would have gone farther; and have called me the Serpent, who first presented the fruit of my Poetry to the Wife, and so gain'd the opportunity to seduce the Husband. Yet I am ready to avow a Crime so advantagious to me; but the World, which will condemn my boldness, I am sure will justifie and applaude my choice. All men will joyn with me in the adoration which I pay you, they would wish only I had brought you a more noble Sacrifice. Instead of an Heroick Play, you might justly expect an Heroick Poem, filled with the past Glories of your Ancestors, & the future certainties of your own. Heaven has already taken care to form you for an Heroe. You have all the advantages of Mind and Body, and an Illustrious Birth, conspiring to render you an extraordinary Person. The *Achilles* and *Rinaldo* are present in you, even above their Originals; you only want a *Homer* or a *Tasso,* to make you equal to them. Youth, Beauty and Courage, (all which you possess in the height of their perfection) are the most desirable gifts of Heaven: and Heaven is never prodigal of such Treasures, but to some uncommon purpose. So goodly a Fabrick was never framed by an Almighty Architect for a vulgar Guest. He shewed the value which he set upon your Mind, when he took care to have it so nobly and so beautifully lodg'd. To a graceful fashion and deportment of Body, you have joyned a win-ning Conversation, and an easie Greatness, derived to you from the

329

best, and best belov'd of Princes. And with a great power of obliging, the world has observed in you, a desire to oblige, even beyond your power. This, and all that I can say on so excellent and large a subject, is only History, in which Fiction has no part; I can employ nothing of Poetry in it, any more than I do in that humble protestation which I make, to continue ever

Your Graces most obedient
and most devoted Servant,
John Dryden.

PREFACE

I Was mov'd to write this Play by many reasons: amongst others, the Commands of some Persons of Honour, for whom I have a most particular respect, were daily sounding in my ears, that it would be of good example to undertake a Poem of this Nature. Neither was my own inclination wanting to second their desires. I consider that pleasure was not the only end of Poesie; and that even the instructions of Morality were not so wholly the business of a Poet, as that the Precepts and Examples of Piety were to be omitted. For to leave that employment altogether to the Clergie, were to forget that Religion was first taught in Verse (which the laziness or dulness of succeeding Priesthood turn'd afterwards into Prose:) and it were also to grant, which I never shall, that Representations of this kind may not as well be conducing to Holiness, as to good Manners. Yet far be it from me, to compare the use of Dramatique Poesie with that of Divinity: I only maintain, against the Enemies of the Stage, that patterns of piety, decently represented, and equally removed from the extremes of Superstition and Prophaneness, may be of excellent use to second the Precepts of our Religion. By the Harmony of words, we elevate the mind to a sense of Devotion, as our solemn Musick, which is inarticulate Poesie, does in Churches; and by the lively images of piety, adorned by action, through the senses, allure the Soul: which while it is charmed in a silent joy of what it sees and hears, is struck at the same time with a secret veneration of things Celestial, and is wound up insensibly into the practice of that which it admires. Now, if, instead of this, we sometimes see on our Theaters, the Examples of Vice rewarded, or at least unpunished, yet it ought not to be an Argument against the Art, any more than the Extravagances and Impieties of the Pulpit in the late times of Rebellion, can be against the Office and Dignity of the Clergie.

But many times it happens, that Poets are wrongfully accus'd; as it is

my own Case in this very Play, where I am charg'd by some ignorant or malicious persons, with no less Crimes than Prophaneness and Irreligion.

The part of Maximin, *against which these holy Criticks so much declaim, was designed by me to set off the Character of St.* Catharine. *And those who read the Roman History, may easily remember, that* Maximin *was not only a bloody Tyrant,* vastus corpore, animo ferus, *as* Herodian *describes him; but also a Persecutor of the Church, against which he raised the sixth Persecution. So that whatsoever he speaks or acts in this Tragedy, is no more than a Record of his life and manners; a Picture, as near as I could take it, from the Original. If, with much pains and some success I have drawn a deform'd piece, there is as much of Art, and as near an imitation of Nature, in a* Lazare *as in a* Venus. Maximin *was an Heathen, and what he speaks against Religion, is in contempt of that which he professed. He defies the Gods of* Rome, *which is no more than* S. Catharine *might with decency have done. If it be urged, that a person of such Principles, who scoffes at any Religion, ought not to be presented on the Stage; why then are the lives and sayings of so many wicked and prophane persons recorded in the Holy Scriptures? I know it will be answer'd, That a due use may be made of them; that they are remembred with a Brand of Infamy fixt upon them; and set as Sea-marks for those who behold them to avoid. And what other use have I made of* Maximin? *have I proposed him as a pattern to be imitated, whom even for his impiety to his false Gods I have so severely punish'd? Nay, as if I had foreseen this Objection I purposely remov'd the Scene of the Play which ought to have been at* Alexandria *in* Egypt, *(where* S. Catharine *suffered) and laid it under the Walls of* Aquileia *in* Italy, *where* Maximin *was slain; that the punishment of his Crime might immediately succeed its execution.*

This, Reader, is what I owed to my just defence, and the due reverence of that Religion which I profess, to which all men, who desire to be esteemed good or honest are obliged; I have neither leisure nor occasion to write more largely on this subject, because I am already justified by the sentence of the best and most discerning Prince in the World, by the suffrage of all unbiass'd Judges; and, above all, but the witness of my own Conscience, which ahbors the thought of such a Crime; to which I ask leave to add my outward Conversation, which shall never be justly taxed with the Note of Atheism or Prophaneness.

In what else concerns the Play, I shall be brief: for the faults of the writing and contrivance, I leave them to the mercy of the Reader. For I am as little apt to defend my Errours, as to find those of other Poets. Only I observe, that the great Censors of Wit and Poetry, either produce nothing of their own, or what is more ridiculous than any thing they reprehend.

331

Much of ill Nature, and a very little Judgment, go far in finding the mistakes of Writers.

I pretend not that any thing of mine can be Correct: This Poem, especially, which was contrived and written in seven weeks, though afterwards hindred by many accidents from a speedy representation, which would have been its just excuse.

Yet the Scenes are every where unbroken, and the unities of place and time more exactly kept, than perhaps is requisite in a Tragedy; or at least then I have since preserv'd them in the Conquest of Granada.

I have not every where observed the equality of numbers, in my Verse; partly by reason of my haste; but more especially because I would not have my sense a slave to Syllables.

'Tis easie to discover that I have been very bold in my alteration of the Story, which of it self was too barren for a Play: and that I have taken from the Church two Martyrs, in the persons of Porphyrius *and the Empress, who suffered for the Christian Faith, under the Tyranny of* Maximin.

I have seen a French Play, call'd the Martyrdom of S. Catharine; *but those who have read it, will soon clear me from stealing out of so dull an Author. I have only borrow'd a mistake from him, of one* Maximin *for another: for finding him in the French Poet, call'd the Son of a Thracian Herds-man, and an Alane Woman, I too easily believ'd him to have been the same* Maximin *mention'd in* Herodian. *Till afterwards consulting* Eusebius *and* Metaphrastes, *I found the French-man had betray'd me into an Errour (when it was too late to alter it) by mistaking that first* Maximin *for a second, the Contemporary of* Constantine *the Great, and one of the Usurpers of the Eastern Empire.*

But neither was the other name of my Play more fortunate: for as some, who had heard of a Tragedy of S. Catharine, *imagin'd I had taken my plot from thence; so others, who had heard of another Play, called* L'Amour Tyrannique, *with the same ignorance, accus'd me to have borrow'd my design from it, because I have accidentally given my Play the same Title, not having to this day seen it: and knowing only by report, that such a Comedy is extant in French, under the Name of Monsieur* Scudery.

As for what I have said of Astral or Aerial Spirits, it is no invention of mine, but taken from those who have written on that Subject. Whether there are such Beings or not, it concerns not me: 'tis sufficient for my purpose, that many have believ'd the affirmative: and that these Heroick Representations, which are of the same Nature with the Epick, are not limited, but with the extremest bounds of what is credible.

For the little Critiques who pleas'd themselves with thinking they have found a flaw in that line of the Prologue, (And he who servilely creeps after sence, is safe, &c.) *as if I patronized my own nonsense, I may*

reasonably suppose they have never read Horace. Serpit humi tutus,
*&c. are his words: He who creeps after plaine, dull, common sence, is safe
from committing absurdities; but can never reach any heighth, or excellence
of wit: and sure I could not meane that any excellence were to be found in
nonsence. With the same ignorance, or malice, they would accuse me for
useing,* empty Arms, *when I writ of a Ghost or shadow: which has onely
the appearance of a body or limbs; and is empty or voyd of flesh and blood;
and* vacuis amplectitur ulnis, *was an expression of* Ovid's *on the same
subject. Some foole before them, had charg'd me in the* Indian Emperour
with nonsence in these words, And follow fate which does too fast
pursue. *Which was borrow'd from* Virgil *in the XIth of his Æneids,*
Eludit gyro interior, sequiturque sequentem. *I quote not these to
prove that I never write Nonsence, but onely to shew that they are so
unfortunate as not to have found it.*

VALE

PROLOGUE

SElf-love (which never rightly understood)
Makes Poets still conclude their Plays are good:
*And malice in all Criticks raigns so high,
That for small Errors, they whole Plays decry;
So that to see this fondness, and that spite,
You'd think that none but Mad-men judge or write.
Therefore our Poet, as he thinks not fit
T'impose upon you, what he writes for Wit,
So hopes that leaving you your censures free,
You equal Judges of the whole will be:
They judge but half who only faults will see.
Poets like Lovers should be bold and dare,
They spoil their business with an over-care.
And he who servilely creeps after sence,
Is safe, but ne're will reach an Excellence.
Hence 'tis our Poet in his conjuring,
Allow'd his Fancy the full scope and swing.
But when a Tyrant for his Theme he had,
He loos'd the Reins, and bid his Muse run mad:
And though he stumbles in a full career;
Yet rashness is a better fault than fear.
He saw his way; but in so swift a pace,
To chuse the ground, might be to lose the race.
They then who of each trip th' advantage take,
Find but those Faults which they want Wit to make.*

333

Persons Represented.

Maximin, *Tyrant of* Rome,   By Major *Mohun.*

Porphyrius, *Captain of the Prætorian Bands,* }   Mr. *Hart.*

Charinus, *the Emperour's Son,*   Mr. *Harris.*

Placidius, *a great Officer,*   Mr. *Kynaston.*

Valerius,
Albinus, } *Tribunes of the Army,* }   Mr. *Lydall.*
     Mr. *Littlewood.*

Nigrinus, *a Tribune and Conjurer,*   Mr. *Beeston.*

Amariel, *Guardian Angel to S.* Catharine,   Mr. *Bell.*

Apollonius, *a Heathen Philosopher,*   Mr. *Cartwright.*

Berenice, *Wife to* Maximin,   By Mrs. *Marshall.*

Valeria, *Daughter to* Maximin,   Mrs. *Ellen Guyn.*

S. Catharine, *Princess of* Alexandria,   Mrs. *Hughes.*

Felicia, *her Mother,*   Mrs. *Knepp.*

Erotion,
Cydnon, } *Attendants,* }   Mrs. *Uphill.*
     Mrs. *Eastland.*

SCENE *The Camp of Maximin,* under the Walls of *Aquileia.*

TYRANNICK LOVE

OR THE

ROYAL MARTYR

ACT I. SCENE I.

A Camp or Pavillion Royal.

Maximin, Charinus, Placidius, Albinus, Valerius, Apollonius,
Guards.

Max. THUS far my Arms have with success been crown'd;
　　And found no ſtop, or vanquish'd what they found.
The German Lakes my Legions have o're-paſt,
With all the bars which Art or Nature caſt:
My Foes, in watry Faſtnesses inclos'd,
I sought, alone, to their whole War expos'd,
Did firſt the depth of trembling Marshes sound,
And fix'd my Eagles in unfaithful ground;
By force submitted to the Roman sway
Fierce Nations, and unknowing to obey:
And now, for my reward, ungrateful *Rome*,
For which I fought abroad, rebels at home.
　　Alb. Yet 'tis their fear which does this War maintain:
They cannot brook a Martial Monarchs Raign:
Your Valour would too much their sloth accuse;
And therefore, like themselves, they Princes chuse.
　　Placid. Two, tame, gown'd Princes, who at ease, debate
In lazy Chairs, the business of the State:
Who reign but while the People they can please,
And only know the little Arts of Peace.
　　Char. In fields they dare not fight where Honour calls;
But breath a faint defiance from their Walls:
The very noise of War their Souls does wound;
They quake, but hearing their own Trumpets sound.
　　Val. An casie Summons but for form they wait,
And to your Fame will open wide the gate.
　　Placid. I wish our Fame that swift success may find;
But Conqueſts, Sir, are easily design'd:

335

However soft within themselves they are,
To you they will be valiant by despair.
For having once been guilty, well they know
To a revengeful Prince they ſtill are so.
    Alb. 'Tis true, that since the Senates succours came,
They grow more bold.
    Max. ———That Senate's but a name;
Or they are Pageant Princes which they make;
That pow'r they give away, they would partake.
Two equal pow'rs, two different ways will draw,
While each may check, and give the other Law.
True, they secure propriety and peace;
But are not fit an Empire to increase.
When they should aid their Prince, the Slaves dispute;
And fear success should make him absolute.
They let Foes conquer, to secure the State,
And lend a Sword, whose edge themselves rebate.
    Char. When to increase the Gods you late are gone,
I'le swiftly chuse to dye, or reign alone:
But these half-Kings our courage cannot fright;
The thrifty State will bargain e're they fight:
Give juſt so much for every Victory;
And rather lose a fight, than over-buy.
    Max. Since all delays are dangerous in War,
Your men, *Albinus*, for assault prepare:
Crispinus and *Menephilus*, I hear
Two Consulars, these *Aquileians* chear;
By whom they may, if we protract the time,
Be taught the courage to defend their crime.
    Placid. Put off th' assault but only for this day;
No loss can come by such a small delay.
    Char. We are not sure to morrow will be ours:
Wars have, like Love, their favourable hours:
Let us use all; for if we lose one day,
That white one, in the crowd, may slip away.
    Max. Fates dark recesses we can never find;
But Fortune at some hours to all is kind;
The lucky have whole days, which ſtill they choose;
Th' unlucky have but hours, and those they lose.
    Placid. I have consulted one, who reads Heav'n's doom,
And sees at present, things which are to come.
'Tis that *Nigrinus*, made by your command
A Tribute in the new Panonian Band.

336

Him have I seen, (on *Ister*'s Banks he stood,
Where last we winter'd) bind the headlong Flood
In sudden ice; and where most swift it flows,
In chrystal nets, the wondring fishes close.
Then, with a moments thaw, the streams inlarge,
And from the Mesh the twinkling Guests discharge.
In a deep vale, or near some ruin'd wall
He would the Ghosts of slaughter'd Souldiers call;
Who slow, to wounded bodies did repair,
And loth to enter, shiver'd in the air;
These his dread Wand did to short Life compel,
And forc'd the Fates of Battels to foretel.

    Max. 'Tis wondrous strange! But, good *Placidius*, say,
What prophesies *Nigrinus* of this day?

    Placid. In a lone Tent, all hung with black, I saw,
Where in a Square he did a Circle draw:
Four Angles, made by that circumference,
Bore holy words inscrib'd, of mystick sence;
When first a hollow wind began to blow,
The Sky grew black, and belli'd down more low,
Around the fields did nimble Lightning play,
Which offer'd us by fits, and snatch'd the day.
'Midst this, was heard the shrill and tender cry
Of well-pleas'd Ghosts, which in the storm did fly;
Danc'd to and fro, and skim'd along the ground,
Till to the Magick Circle they were bound.
They coursing it, while we were fenc'd within,
We saw this dreadful Scene of Fate begin.

    Char. Speak without fear; what did the Vision shew?

    Placid. A Curtain drawn presented to our view
A Town besieg'd; and on the neighb'ring Plain
Lay heaps of visionary Souldiers slain.
A rising mist obscur'd the gloomy head
Of one, who in Imperial Robes lay dead.
Near this, in Fetters stood a Virgin, crown'd;
Whom many *Cupids* strove in vain to wound:
A voice to morrow, still to morrow rung:
Another *Iö*; *Iö*, *Pæan*, sung.

    Char. Visions and Oracles still doubtful are,
And ne're expounded till th' event of War.
The Gods fore-knowledge on our Swords will wait:
If we fight well, they must fore-show good Fate.

To them a Centurion.

Cent. A rising dust which troubles all the air,
And this way travels, shews some Army near.
    Char. I hear the sound of Trumpets from afar.   [*Exit* Albinus.
    Max. It seems the voice of Triumph, not of War.
                              To them Albinus *again.*
    Alb. Health and success our Emperour attends;
The Forces marching on the Plain, are friends.
Porphyrius, whom you *Ægypts* Prætor made,
Is come from *Alexandria* to your aid.
    Max. It well becomes the conduct and the care
Of one so fam'd and fortunate in War.
You must resign, *Placidius*, your Command,
To him I promis'd the Prætorian Band.
Your duty in your swift compliance show,
I will provide some other charge for you.
    Placid. May *Cæsar*'s pleasure ever be obey'd
With that submission, which by me is paid.
Now all the Curses envy ever knew,
Or could invent, *Porphyrius* pursue.   *Aside.*
    Alb. *Placidius* does too tamely bear his loss;   [*To* Charinus.
This new pretender will all pow'r ingross:
All things must now by his direction move;
And you, Sir, must resign your Father's love.
    Char. Yes; every name to his repute must bow;
There grow no Bayes for any other brow.
He blasts my early Honour in the bud,
Like some tall Tree the Monster of the Wood:
O're-shading all which under him would grow,
He sheds his venim on the Plants below.
    Alb. You must some noble action undertake;
Equal with his your own renown to make.
    Char. I am not for a slothful envy born;
I'll do't this day, in the dire Visions scorn.
He comes: We two, like the twin Stars appear;
Never to shine together in one Sphere.   *Exit cum* Alb.

Enter Porphyrius *attended.*

    Max. *Porphyrius*, welcome, welcome as the light
To cheerful Birds; or as to Lovers night.
Welcome as what thou bring'st me, Victory.
    Por. That waits, Sir, on your Arms, and not on me.

You left a Conquest more than half atchiev'd;
And for whose easiness I almost griev'd.
Yours only the *Ægyptian* Laurels are;
I bring you but the reliques of your War.
The Christian Princess to receive your doom,
Is from her Conquer'd *Alexandria* come.
Her Mother, in another Vessel sent,
A Storm surpriz'd; nor know I the event:
Both from your bounty must receive their state;
Or must on your triumphant Chariot wait.

Max. From me they can expect no grace, whose minds,
An execrable superstition blinds.

Apoll. The Gods who rais'd you to the Worlds Command,
Require these Victims from your grateful hand.

Por. To minds resolv'd, the threats of Death are vain;
They run to fires, and there enjoy their pain:
Not *Mucius* made more hast his hand t' expose
To greedy flames, than their whole bodies those.

Max. How, to their own destruction, they are blind!
Zeal is the pious madness of the mind.

Por. They all our fam'd Philosophers defy;
And would our Faith by force of reason try.

Apoll. I beg it, Sir, by all the pow'rs Divine,
That in their right, this Combat may be mine.

Max. It shall, and fifty Doctors of our Laws,
Be added to you, to maintain the cause.

Enter Berenice *the Empress,* Valeria *Daughter to the Emperour,*
Erotion.

Placid. The Empress and your Daughter, Sir, are here.

Por. What dangers in these charming Eyes appear!
Looking on the Empress.
How my old wounds are open'd at this view!
And in my murd'rers presence bleed anew!

Max. I did expect your coming to partake   *To the Ladies.*
The general gladness which my Triumphs make.
You did *Porphyrius* as a Courtier know,
But as a Conquerour behold him now.

Ber. You know (I read it in your blushing face)   *To* Por.
To merit, better than receive a grace:
And I know better silently to own,
Than with vain words to pay your service done.

339

Por. Princes, like Gods, reward e're we deserve;

> *Kneeling to kiss her hand.*

And pay us in permitting us to serve.

Oh might I still grow here, and never move!　　　　　*(lower.)*

　　Ber. How dangerous are these exſtasies of Love!

He shews his passion to a thousand Eyes!

He cannot ſtir, nor can I bid him rise.

That word my heart refuses to my tongue.　　　　　*Aside.*

　　Max. Madam, you let the General kneel too long.

　　Por. Too long, as if Eternity were so!　　　　　*Aside.*

　　Ber. Rise, good *Porphyrius*, (since it muſt be so.)　　　*Aside.*

　　Por. Like Hermits from a Vision I retire;　　　　　*rising.*

With Eyes too weak to see what I admire.　　　　　*Aside.*

　　Val. The Empress knows your worth; but, Sir, there be

> *To* Porphyrius, *who kisses her hand.*

Those who can value it as high as she.

And 'tis but juſt, (since in my Father's cause,

You fought) your Valour should have my applause.

　　Placid. O Jealousie, how art thou Eagle-ey'd!

She loves; and would her Love in praises hide:

How am I bound this Rival to pursue,

Who ravishes my Love and Fortune too!　　　　　*Aside.*

> *A dead march within, and Trumpets.*

　　Max. Somewhat of mournful, sure, my Ears does wound;

Like the hoarse murmurs of a Trumpets sound,

And Drums unbrac'd, with Souldiers broken cryes.

Enter Albinus.

Albinus, Whence proceeds this dismal noise?

　　Alb. Too soon you'l know what I want words to tell.

　　Max. How fares my Son? Is my *Charinus* well?

Not answer me! Oh my prophetique fear!

　　Alb. How can I speak; or how, Sir, can you hear?

Imagine that which you would moſt deplore,

And that which I would speak is it, or more.

　　Max. Thy mournful message in thy looks I read:

Is he (oh that I live to ask it) dead?

　　Alb. Sir ———

　　Max. Stay; if thou speak'ſt that word, thou speak'ſt thy laſt:

Some God now, if he dares, relate what's paſt:

Say but he's dead, that God shall mortal be.

　　Alb. Then what I dare not speak, look back and see.

> Charinus *born in dead by Souldiers.*

Max. See nothing, Eyes, henceforth, but Death and wo;
You've done me the worst office you can do.
You've shewn me Destiny's prepost'rous crime;
An unripe fate; disclos'd e're Nature's time.

Placid. Asswage, great Prince, your passion, lest you show
There's somewhat in your Soul which Fate can bow.

Por. Fortune should by your greatness be controul'd:
Arm your great mind, and let her take no hold.

Max. To tame Philosophers teach constancy;
There is no farther use of it in me.
Gods! (But why name I you!
All that was worth a pray'r to you, is gone:)
I ask not back my Vertue, but my Son.

Alb. His too great thirst of fame his ruine brought,
Though, Sir, beyond humanity he fought.

Placid. This was my Vision of this fatal day!

Alb. With a fierce hast he led our Troops the way:
While fiery show'rs of Sulphur on him rain'd;
Nor left he till the Battlements he gain'd:
There with a Forest of their Darts he strove;
And stood like *Capaneus* defying *Jove.*
With his broad Sword the boldest beating down,
While Fate grew pale lest he should win the Town,
And turn'd the Iron leafs of its dark Book,
To make new dooms; or mend what it mistook.
Till sought by many Deaths, he sunk though late,
And by his fall asserted doubtful Fate.

Valer. Oh my Dear Brother! whom Heav'n let us see,
And would no longer suffer him to be!

Max. And didst not thou a Death with Honour chuse,   *To* Alb.
But impudently liv'st to bring this news?
After his loss how didst thou dare to breath?
————But thy base Ghost shall follow him in death.
A decimation I will strictly make
Of all who my *Charinus* did forsake.
And of each Legion each Centurion
Shall dye:————*Placidius,* see my pleasure done.

Por. Sir, you will lose by this severity
Your Souldiers hearts.

Max. ————Why, they take Pay to dye.

Por. Then spare *Albinus* only.

Max. ————I consent
To leave his life to be his punishment.

Discharg'd from trust; branded with infamy,
Let him live on, till he ask leave to dye.

    Ber. Let me petition for him.

    Max. ————I have said:
And will not be intreated, but obey'd.
But, Empress, whence does your compassion grow?

    Ber. You need not ask it, since my birth you know.
The Race of *Antonin's* was nam'd the Good:
I draw my pity from my Royal Blood.

    Max. Still must I be upbraided with your Line?
I know you speak it in contempt of mine.
But your late Brother did not prize me less,
Because I could not boast of Images.
And the Gods own'd me more, when they decreed
A Thracian Shepherd should your Line succeed.

    Ber. The Gods! O do not name the pow'rs divine;
They never mingled their Decrees with thine.
My Brother gave me to thee for a Wife,
And for my Dowry thou didst take his life.

    Max. The Gods by many Victories have shown,
That they my merits and his death did own.

    Ber. Yes; they have own'd it; witness this just day;
When they begin thy mischiefs to repay.
See the reward of all thy wicked care,
Before thee thy succession ended there.
Yet but in part my Brothers Ghost is pleas'd:
Restless till all the groaning world be eas'd.
For me; no other happiness I owne,
Than to have born no Issue to thy Throne.

    Max. Provoke my rage no farther, lest I be
Reveng'd at once upon the Gods and thee.

    Por. aside.] What horrid tortures seize my lab'ring mind!
O, only excellent of all thy kind!
To hear thee threatned while I idle stand!
Heaven! was I born to fear a Tyrant's hand?

    Max. to Ber. Hence from my sight————thy blood, if thou dost
    stay————

    Ber. Tyrant! too well to that thou know'st the way.   *[going.*

    Por. Let baser Souls from falling Fortunes flye:
I'le pay my duty to her though I dye.   *Exit leading her.*

    Max. What made *Porphyrius* so officious be?
The action look'd as done in scorn of me.

342

Val. It did indeed some little freedom show;
But somewhat to his Services you owe.
    Max. Yet, if I thought it his presumption were——
    Placid. Perhaps he did not your displeasure hear.
    Max. My anger was too loud, not to be heard.
    Placid. I'm loth to think he did it not regard.
    Max. How, not regard!
    Val. Placidius, you foment,
On too light grounds, my Father's discontent.
But when an action does two faces wear,
'Tis Justice to believe what is most fair.
I think, that knowing what respect there rests
For her late Brother in the Souldiers breasts,
He went to serve the Emp'rour: and design'd
Only to calm the tempest in her mind,
Lest some Sedition in the Camp should rise.
    Max. I ever thought him loyal as he's wise.
Since therefore, all the Gods their spight have shown
To rob my Age of a successive Throne;
And you who now remain
The only Issue of my former bed
In Empire cannot by your Sex succeed:
To bind *Porphyrius* firmly to the State,
I will this day my *Cæsar* him create:
And, Daughter, I will give you him for Wife.
    Val. O day, the best and happiest of my life!
    Placid. O day, the most accurst I ever knew!   *Aside.*
    Max. See to my Son perform'd each Funeral due:
Then to the toyls of War we will return,
And make our Enemies our losses mourn.   *Exeunt.*

ACT II. SCENE I.

The Royal Camp.

Berenice, Porphyrius.

Ber. POrphyrius, you too far did tempt your Fate,
    In owning her the Emperour does hate.
'Tis true, your duty to me it became;
But, praising that, I must your conduct blame.
    Por. Not to have own'd my zeal at such a time,
Were to sin higher than your Tyrants crime.

Ber. 'Twas too much my disgrace t'accompany;
A silent wish had been enough for me.
   Por. Wishes are aids, faint Servants may supply,
Who ask Heav'n for you what themselves deny.
Could I do less than my respect to pay,
Where I before had giv'n my heart away?
   Ber. You fail in that respect you seem to bear,
When you speak words unfit for me to hear.
   Por. Yet you did once accept those vows I paid.
   Ber. Those vows were then to *Berenice* made;
But cannot now be heard without a sin,
When offer'd to the Wife of *Maximin*.
   Por. Has, then, the change of Fortune chang'd your will?
Ah! why are you not *Berenice* still?
To *Maximin* you once declar'd your hate;
Your Marriage was a Sacrifice to th' State:
Your Brother made it to secure his Throne,
Which this man made a step to mount it on.
   Ber. Whatever *Maximin* has been, or is,
I am to bear, since Heav'n has made me his.
For wives, who must themselves of pow'r devest,
When they love blindly, for their peace love best.
   Por. If mutual love be vow'd when faith you plight,
Then he, who forfeits first, has lost his right.
   Ber. Husbands a forfeiture of love may make;
But what avails the forfeit none can take?
As in a general wreck
The Pirate sinks with his ill-gotten gains,
And nothing to anothers use remains:
So, by his loss, no gain to you can fall:
The Sea, and vast destruction swallows all.
   Por. Yet he, who from the shore, the wreck descrys,
May lawfully inrich him with the prize.
   Ber. Who sees the wreck can yet no title plead,
Till he be sure the Owner first is dead.
   Por. If that be all the claim I want to love,
This Pirate of your heart I'le soon remove;
And, at one stroke, the world and you set free.
   Ber. Leave to the care of Heav'n that world and me.
   Por. Heav'n, as its instrument my courage sends.
   Ber. Heav'n ne'r sent those who fight for private ends.
We both are bound by trust, and must be true;
I to his Bed, and to his Empire you.
344

For he who to the bad betrays his trust,
Though he does good, becomes himself unjust.

Por. When *Brutus* did from *Cæsar Rome* redeem,
The Act was good.

Ber. ————But 'twas not good in him.
You see the Gods adjudg'd it Parricide,
By dooming the event on *Cæsar's* side.
'Tis vertue not to be oblig'd at all;
Or not conspire our Benefactors fall.

Por. You doom me then to suffer all this ill,
And yet I doom my self to love you still.

Ber. Dare not *Porphyrius* suffer then with me,
Since what for him I for my self decree?

Por. How can I bear those griefs you disapprove?

Ber. To ease 'em, I'le permit you still to love.

Por. That will but haste my death, if you think fit
Not to reward, but barely to permit.
Love without hope does like a torture wound,
Which makes me reach in pain, to touch the ground.

Ber. If hope, then, to your life so needful be,
Hope still.

Por. ————Blest News!

Ber. ——————But hope, in Heav'n, not me.

Por. Love is too noble such deceits to use.
Referring me to Heav'n, your gift I lose.
So Princes cheaply may our wants supply,
When they give that their Treasurers deny.

Ber. Love blinds my Vertue: If I longer stay,
It will grow dark, and I shall lose my way.

Por. One kiss from this fair hand can be no sin;
I ask not that you gave to *Maximin.*
In full reward of all the pains I've past,
Give me but one.

Ber. ————Then let it be your last.

Por. 'Tis gone!
Like Souldiers prodigal of their Arrears,
One minute spends the Pay of many years.
————Let but one more be added to the sum,
And pay at once for all my pains to come.

Ber. Unthrifts will starve if we before-hand give:
                                    [*Pulling back her hand.*
I'le see you shall have just enough to live.

Enter Erotion.

Ero. Madam, the Emperour is drawing near;
And comes, they say, to seek *Porphyrius* here.
    Ber. Alas!
    Por. ———I will not ask what he intends;
My life, or death, alone, on you depends.
    Ber. I muſt withdraw; but muſt not let him know   *Aside.*
How hard the precepts of my Vertue grow.
But what e're Fortune is for me design'd,
Sweet Heav'n, be ſtill to brave *Porphyrius* kind!   *Exit cum* Erotio.
    Por. She's gone unkindly, and refus'd to caſt
One glance to feed me for so long a faſt.

Enter Maximin, Placidius, *Guards.*

    Max. *Porphyrius*, since the Gods have ravish'd one,
I come in you to seek another Son.
Succeed him then in my Imperial ſtate;
Succeed in all, but his untimely fate.
If I adopt you with no better grace,
Pardon a fathers tears, upon my face.
And give 'em to *Charinus* memory:
May they not prove as ominous to thee.
    Por. With what misfortunes Heav'n torments me ſtill!
Why muſt I be oblig'd to one so ill?   [*Aside.*
    Max. Those offers which I made you, Sir, were such,
No private man should need to ballance much.
    Por. Who durſt his thought to such ambition lift?   [*Kneeling.*
The greatness of it made me doubt the gift.
The diſtance was so vaſt, that to my view
It made the objeƈt seem at firſt untrue;
And now 'tis near, the sudden excellence
Strikes through, and flashes on my tender sence.
    Max. Yet Heav'n and Earth, which so remote appear,
                                    [*raising him.*
Are by the Air, which flows betwixt 'em, near.
And 'twixt us two my Daughter be the chain;
One end with me, and one with you remain.
    Por. You press me down with such a glorious Fate,
                                    [*kneeling again.*
I cannot rise againſt the mighty weight.
Permit I may retire some little space,
And gather ſtrength to bear so great a grace.   [*Exit bowing.*

346

Placid. How Love and Fortune lavishly contend,
Which should *Porphyrius* wishes moſt befriend!
The mid-ſtream's his; I, creeping by the side,
Am shoulder'd off by his impetuous Tide.   [*Aside.*

Enter Valerius *haſtily.*

Val. I hope my business may my haſte excuse;
For, Sir, I bring you moſt surprizing news.
The Chriſtian Princess in her Tent confers
With fifty of your learn'd Philosophers;
Whom with such Eloquence she does perswade,
That they are Captives to her reasons made.
I left 'em yielding up their vanquish'd cause,
And all the Souldiers shouting her applause;
Ev'n *Apollonius* does but faintly speak,
Whose voice the murmers of th' assiſtants break.

Max. Conduct this Captive Chriſtian to my Tent;
She shall be brought to speedy punishment.
I muſt in time some remedy provide,   [*Exit* Valerius.
Leſt this contagious Errour spread too wide.

Placid. T'infected zeal you muſt no mercy show:
For, from Religion, all Rebellions grow.

Max. The silly crowd, by factious Teachers, brought
To think that Faith untrue their youth was taught,
Run on in new Opinions blindly bold;
Neglect, contemn, and then assault the old.
Th' infectious madness seizes every part,
And from the head diſtils upon the heart.
And firſt, they think their Princes faith not true,
And then presume to offer him a new;
Which if refus'd, all duty from 'em caſt,
To their new Faith they make new Kings at laſt.

Placid. Those ills by Male-contents are often wrought,
That by their Prince their duty may be bought.
They head those holy Factions which they hate,
To sell their duty at a dearer rate.
But, Sir, the Tribune is already here
With your fair Captive.

Max. ————————Bid 'em both appear.

Enter S. Catharine, Valerius, Apollonius, *Guards.*

See where she comes, with that high Air and meen,
Which marks in bonds, the greatness of a Queen.

What pity 'tis!———but I no charms muſt see
In her who to our Gods is enemy.———
Fair foe of Heav'n, whence comes this haughty pride,   *[To her.*
Or is it Frenzy does your mind misguide
To scorn our Worship, and new Gods to find?

   S. Cath. Nor pride, nor frenzy, but a setled mind,
Enlightned from above, my way does mark.

   Max. Tho' Heaven be clear, the way to it is dark.

   Cath. But where our Reason with our Faith does go,
We're both above enlightned, and below.
But Reason with your fond Religion fights;
For many Gods are many Infinites:
This to the firſt Philosophers was known,
Who, under various names, ador'd but one.
Though your vain Poets after did miſtake,
Who every Attribute a God did make.
And so obscene their Ceremonies be,
As good men loath, and *Cato* blush'd to see.

   Max. War is my Province; Prieſt, why ſtand you mute?
You gain by Heav'n, and therefore should dispute.

   Apol. In all Religions, as in ours, there are
Some solid truths, and some things popular.
The popular in pleasing Fables lye,
The truths, in precepts of Morality.
And these to humane life are of that use,
That no Religion can such Rules produce.

   S. Cath. Then let the whole Dispute concluded be
Betwixt these Rules and Chriſtianity.

   Apol. And what more noble can your Doſtrine preach,
Than Vertues which Philosophy does teach?
To keep the passions in severeſt awe,
To live to Reason, (Nature's greateſt Law)
To follow Vertue, as its own reward;
And good and ill, as things without, regard.

   S. Cath. Yet few could follow those ſtriſt Rules they gave;
For humane life will humane frailties have;
And love of Vertue is but barren praise,
Airy as Fame: nor ſtrong enough to raise
The aſtions of the Soul above the sence.
Vertue grows cold without a recompence.
We virtuous aſts as duty do regard;
Yet are permitted to expeſt reward.

Apoll. By how much more your Faith reward assures,
So much more frank our Virtue is than yours.

S. Cath. Blind men! you seek ev'n those rewards you blame:
But ours are solid; yours an empty name.
Either to open praise your Acts you guide,
Or else reward your selves with secret pride.

Apol. Yet still our Moral virtues you obey:
Ours are the Precepts though apply'd your way.

S. Cath. 'Tis true, your virtues are the same we teach;
But in our practice they much higher reach.
You but forbid to take anothers due;
But we forbid e'vn to desire it too.
Revenge of injuries you Virtue call;
But we forgiveness of our wrongs extoll:
Immodest deeds you hinder to be wrought,
But we proscribe the least immodest thought.
So much your Virtues are in ours refin'd,
That yours but reach the actions, ours the mind.

Max. Answer in short to what you heard her speak.   [*To* Apol.

Apol. Where Truth prevails, all arguments are weak.
To that convincing power I must give place:
And with that Truth that Faith I will embrace.

Max. O Traytor to our Gods; but more to me;
Dar'st thou of any Faith but of thy Princes be?
But sure thou rav'st; thy foolish Errour find:
Cast up the poyson that infects thy mind;
And shun the Torments thou art sure to feel.

Apol. Nor fire, nor torture, nor revenging Steel,
Can on my Soul the least impression make:
How gladly, Truth, I suffer for thy sake!
Once I was ignorant of what was so;
But never can abandon Truth I know:
My Martyrdom I to thy Crown prefer;
Truth is a Cause for a Philosopher.

S. Cath. Lose not that Courage which Heav'n does inspire;
                                        [*To* Apollonius.
But fearless go to be baptiz'd in fire.
Think 'tis a Triumph, not a danger near:
Give him your blood; but give him not a tear.
Go, and prepare my Seat: and hovering be
Near that bright space which is reserv'd for me.

Max. Hence with the Traytor; bear him to his Fate.

Apol. Tyrant, I fear thy pity, not thy hate:
A Life Eternal I by Death obtain.
   Max. Go, carry him, where he that Life may gain.
                     Ex. Apollonius, Valerius, *and Guards.*
   Placid. From this Enchantress all these ills are come
You are not safe till you pronounce her doom.
Each hour she lives a Legion sweeps away;
She'll make your Army Martyrs in a day.
   Max. 'Tis juſt: this Chriſtian Sorceress shall dy:
(Would I had never prov'd her Sorcery:)
Not that her charming Tongue this change has bred;
I fear 'tis something that her Eyes have fed.
I love: and am asham'd it should be seen.   *[Aside.*
   Placid. Sir, shall she dy?
   Max. ———Consider she's a Queen.
   Placid. Those claims in *Cleopatra* ended were.
   Max. How many *Cleopatra's* live in her?   *[Aside.*
   Placid. When you condemn'd her, Sir, she was a Queen.
   Max. No, Slave; she only was a Captive then,
   S. Cath. My joyful Sentence you defer too long.
   Max. I never knew that Life was such a wrong.
But if you needs will dy:———it shall be so.
———Yet think it does from your perverseness flow.
Men say, indeed, that I in Blood delight;
But you shall find———Haſte, take her from my sight.
———For *Maximin* I have too much confeſt:
And for a Lover not enough exprest.
Absent, I may her Martyrdom decree;
But one look more will make that Martyr me.
              [Exit S. Catherine *Guarded.*
   Placid. What is it, Sir, that shakes your mighty mind?
   Max. Somewhat I am asham'd that thou should'ſt find.
   Placid. If it be Love that does your Soul possess———
   Max. Are you my Rival that so soon you guess?
   Placid. Far, mighty Prince, be such a crime from me, *[Kneeling.*
Which, with the pride, includes impiety.
Could you forgive it, yet the Gods above
Would never pardon me a Chriſtian Love.
   Max. Thou ly'ſt:———there's not a God inhabits there,
But for this Chriſtian would all Heav'n forswear.
Ev'n *Jove* would try more shapes her Love to win: ⎫
And in new birds, and unknown beaſts would sin: ⎬
At leaſt, if *Jove* could love like *Maximin.*   ⎭
350

Placid. A Captive, Sir, who would a Martyr dye?
  Max. She courts not death, but shuns Captivity.
Great gifts, and greater promises I'le make;
And what Religion is't, but they can shake?
She shall live high:———Devotion in diſtress
Is born, but vanishes in happiness.   *Exit* Maximin.
  Placid. solus. His Son forgot, his Empress unappeas'd;
How soon the Tyrant with new Love is seiz'd!
Love various minds does variously inspire:
He ſtirs in gentle Natures gentle fire;
Like that of Incense on the Altars laid:
But raging flames tempeſtuous Souls invade.
A Fire which every windy passion blows;
With pride it mounts, and with revenge it glows.
But I, accurs'd, who servilely muſt move;
And smooth his passion for his Daughters Love!
Small hope, 'tis true, attends my mighty care.
But of all passions Love does laſt despair.   *Exit.*

ACT III. SCENE I. *The Royal Pavilion.*

Maximin, Placidius, *Guards and Attendants.*

Max. THis Love that never could my youth engage,
     Peeps out his coward head to dare my age.
Where haſt thou been thus long, thou sleeping form,
That wak'ſt like drowsie Sea-men in a ſtorm?
A sullen hour thou chuseſt for thy birth:
My Love shoots up in tempeſts, as the Earth
Is ſtirr'd and loosen'd in a bluſtring wind,
Whose blaſts to waiting flowers her womb unbind.
  Placid. Forgive me, if I say your passions are
So rough, as if in Love you would make War.
But Love is soft———
And with soft beauty tenderly complies;
In lips it laughs, and languishes in eyes.
  Max. There let it laugh; or like an Infant, weep:
I cannot such a supple passion keep.
Mine, ſtiff with age, and ſtubborn as my arms,
Walks upright; ſtoops not to, but meets her charms.
  Placid. Yet fierceness suits not with her gentle kind;
They brave assaults; but may be undermin'd.

Max. Till I in those mean Arts am better read,
Court thou, and fawn, and flatter in my ſtead.

Enter S. Catharine.

She comes; and now, methinks, I could obey:
Her form glides through me, and my heart gives way:
This Iron heart, which no impression took
From Wars, melts down, and runs, if she but look.   *Exit* Maximin.
  Placid. Madam, I from the Emperour am come
T'applaud your Vertue, and reverse your doom.
He thinks, whatever your Religion be,
This Palm is owing to your conſtancy.
  S. Cath. My conſtancy from him seeks no renown;
Heav'n, that propos'd the course, will give the Crown.
  Placid. But Monarchs are the Gods Vicegerents here;
Heav'n gives rewards; but what it gives they bear:
From Heav'n to you the Ægyptian Crown is sent,
Yet 'tis a Prince who does the gift present.
  S. Cath. The Deity I serve, had he thought fit,
Could have preserv'd my Crown unconquer'd yet:
But when his secret Providence design'd
To level that, he levell'd too my mind;
Which, by contraĉting its desires, is taught
The humble quiet of possessing nought.
  Placid. To Stoicks leave a happiness so mean:
Your Vertue does deserve a nobler Scene.
You are not for obscurity design'd:
But, like the Sun, muſt cheer all humane kind.
  S. Cath. No happiness can be where is no reſt:
Th' unknown, untalk'd of man is only bleſt.
He, as in some safe Cliff, his Cell does keep,
From thence he views the labours of the Deep:
The Gold-fraught Vessel which mad tempeſts beat,
He sees now vainly make to his retreat:
And, when from far, the tenth wave does appear,
Shrinks up in silent joy, that he's not there.
  Placid. You have a Pilot who your Ship secures;
The Monarch both of Earth and Seas is yours.
He who so freely gives a Crown away,
Yet asks no tribute but what you may pay.
One smile on him a greater wealth beſtows,
Than *Ægypt* yields, when *Nilus* overflows.
352

S. Cath. I cannot wholly innocent appear,
Since I have liv'd such words as these to hear.
O Heav'n, which dost of chastity take care!———
　Placid. Why do you lose an unregarded pray'r?
If happiness, as you believe, be rest,
That quiet sure is but the Gods possest:———
'Tis greatness to neglect, or not to know
The little business of the world below.
　S. Cath. This doctrine well befitted him who thought
A casual world was from wild Atoms wrought:
But such an order in each chance we see,
(Chain'd to its cause, as that to its decree,)
That none can think a workmanship so rare
Was built or kept without a Workman's care.

To them Maximin, Attendants and Guards.

　Max. Madam, you from *Placidius* may have heard
Some news, which will your happiness regard.
For what a greater happiness can be,
Than to be courted and be lov'd by me?
The Ægyptian Crown I to your hands remit; 　　*She turns aside.*
And, with it, take his heart who offers it.
Do you my person and my gift contemn?
　S. Cath. My hopes pursue a brighter Diadem.
　Max. Can any any brighter than the Roman be?
I find my proffer'd Love has cheapned me:
Since you neglect to answer my desires,
Know, Princess, you shall burn in other fires.
———Why should you urge me to so black a deed?
Think all my anger did from Love proceed.
　S. Cath. Nor threats nor promises my mind can move:
Your furious anger, nor your impious Love.
　Max. The Love of you can never impious be;
You are so pure———
That in the Act 'twou'd change th' impiety.
Heav'n would unmake it sin———
　S. Cath. I take my self from thy detested sight:
To my respect thou hast no longer right:
Such pow'r in bonds true piety can have,
That I command, and thou art but a Slave. 　　*Exit. S.* Cath.
　Max. To what a height of arrogance she swells!
Pride or ill nature still with Vertue dwells;
Her death shall set me free this very hour;
———But is her death within a Lovers pow'r?

Wild with my rage, more wild with my desire,
Like meeting tides—but mine are tides of fire.
What petty promise was't that caus'd this frown?
  Placid. You heard: no less than the Ægyptian Crown.
  Max. Throw *Ægypt*'s by, and offer in the ſtead;
Offer—the Crown on *Berenice's* head.
I am resolv'd to double till I win;
About it ſtraight, and send *Porphyrius* in.   *Exit* Placid.
We look like Eagles tow'ring in the Sky;
While her high flight ſtill raises mine more high.

To him Porphyrius.

  Por. I come, Sir, to expeƈt your great commands.
  Max. My happiness lyes only in thy hands.
And, since I have adopted thee my Son,
I'le keep no secret from thy breaſt unknown:
Led by the int'reſt of my rising Fate,
I did espouse this Empress whom I hate:
And therefore with less shame I may declare,
That I the Fetters of thy Captive wear.
  Por. Sir, you amaze me with so ſtrange a Love.
  Max. Pity, my Son, those flames you disapprove.
The cause of Love can never be assign'd;
'Tis in no face, but in the Lover's mind.
  Por. Yet there are Beauties which attraƈt all hearts;
And all mankind lyes open to their darts:
Whose Soveraignty, without dispute, we grant;
Such Graces, sure, your Empress does not want.
  Max. Beauty has bounds——
And can no more to every heart be so,
Than any Coin through every Land can go.
Some secret Grace, which is but so to me,
Though not so great, may yet more pow'rful be:
All guard themselves when ſtronger Foes invade;
Yet, by the weak, surprizes may be made:
But you, my Son, are not to judge, but aid.
  Por. What is it, Sir, you can require of me?
  Max. I would from *Berenice's* bonds be free,
This yoke of Marriage from us both remove,
Where two are bound to draw, tho neither love.
  Por. Neither the Gods nor man will give consent
To put in praƈtice your unjuſt intent.
  Max. Both muſt consent to that which I decree.
354

Por. The Souldiers love her Brother's memory;
And for her sake some Mutiny will ſtir.
    Max. Our parting therefore—shall be sought by her.
Go, bid her sue for a Divorce, or dye;
I'le cut the knot, if she will not untye:
Haſte to prepare her, and thy self return;
Thy *Hymen*'s Torch this day with mine shall burn.   *Exit.*
    Por. Rather my Funeral-torch;—for though I know
Valeria's fair, and that she loves me too,
Gainſt her my Soul is arm'd on every part:
Yet there are secret Rivets to my heart;
Where *Berenice's* Charms have found the way;
Subtile as Lightnings, but more fierce than they.
How shall I this avoid, or gain that Love!
So near the Rock I, to the Port muſt move.

          To him, Valeria *attended.*

Val. Porphyrius, now my joy I may express,
Nor longer hide the Love I muſt possess.
Should I have ſtaid till Marriage made us one,
You might have thought it was by duty done;
But of my heart I now a present make;
And give it you e're it be yours to take.
Accept it as when early fruit we send:
And let the rareness the small gift commend.
    Por. Great Monarchs, like your Father, often give
What is above a Subject to receive:
But faithful Officers should countermand,
And ſtop the gift that passes through their hand:
And to their Prince, that mass of wealth reſtore,
Which lavish'd thus, would make whole Nations poor.
    Val. But to this gift a double right you have:
My Father gives but what before I gave.
    Por. In vain you such unequal presents make,
Which I ſtill want capacity to take.
Such fatal bounty once the *Gaules* did shew;
They threw their Rings, but threw their Targets too.
Bounty so plac'd, does more like ruine look;
You pour the Ocean on a narrow Brook.
    Val. Yet, if your Love before prepares a Boat,
The ſtream so pour'd, drowns not, but makes it float.
    Por. But when the Vessel is on Quick-sands caſt,
The flowing tide does more the sinking haſt,

Val. And on what Quick-sands can your heart be thrown?
Can you a Love besides *Valeria's* own?

Por. If he who at your feet his heart would lay,
Be met with first, and robb'd upon the way,
You may indeed the Robbers strength accuse,
But pardon him who did the Present lose.

Val. Who is this Thief that does my right possess?
Name her, and then we of her strength may guess.———
From whence does your unwonted silence come?

Por. She bound and gag'd me, and has left me dumb.

Val. But of my wrongs I will aloud complain;
False man, thou would'st excuse thy self in vain:
For thee I did a Maidens blush forsake.
And own'd a Love thou hast refus'd to take.

Por. Refus'd it!———like a Miser midst his store,
Who grasps, and grasps, till he can hold no more;
And when his strength is wanting to his mind,
Looks back, and sighs on what he left behind.

Val. No, I resume that heart thou didst possess;
My Father shall my injuries redress:
With me thou losest his Imperial Crown,
And speedy death attends upon his frown.

Por. You may revenge your wrongs a nobler way;
Command my death, and I will soon obey:

Val. No, live; for on thy life my cure depends:
In Debters deaths all obligation ends.
'Twill be some ease Ungrateful thee to call;
And, Bankrupt-like, say, trusting him lost all.

Por. Upbraided thus, what gen'rous man would live!
But Fortune will revenge what you forgive.
When I refuse (as in few hours I must)
This offer'd grace, your Father will be just.

Val. Be just! say rather he will cruel prove,
To kill that only person I can love.
Yet so it is!———
Your int'rest in the Army is so high;
That he must make you his, or you must dye!
It is resolv'd! who e're my Rival be,   *Aside after a pause.*
I'le show that I deserve him more than she.
And if at last he does ingrateful prove,
My constancy it self rewards my Love.   *Exit.*

Por. She's gone, and gazing round about, I see
Nothing but death, or glorious misery;

Here Empire ſtands, if I could Love displace;
There, hopeless Love, with more Imperial Grace;
Thus, as a sinking Hero compass'd round,
Beckens his braveſt Foe for his laſt wound,
And him into his part of Fame does call,
I'le turn my Face to Love, and there I'le fall.

To him Berenice, Erotion.

Ber. I come, *Porphyrius,* to congratulate
This happy change of your exalted Fate:
You to the Empire are, I hear, design'd,
And fair *Valeria* muſt th'Alliance bind.
    Por. Would Heav'n had my succession so decreed,
That I in all might *Maximin* succeed!
He offers me th' Imperial Crown, 'tis true:
I would succeed him, but it is in you.
    Ber. In me! I never did accept your Love;
But You, I see, would handsomly remove.
And I can give you leave without a frown:
I always thought you merited a Crown.
    Por. I never sought that Crown but on your brow;
But you with such indifference would allow
My change, that you have kill'd me with that breath:
I feel your scorn cold as the hand of death.
    Ber. You'l come to Life in your *Valeria's* arms:
'Tis true, I cannot boaſt of equal charms;
Or if I could, I never did admit
Your Love to me, but only suffer'd it.
I am a Wife, and can make no return;
And 'twere but vain, in hopeless fires to burn.
    Por. Unkind! can you whom only I adore,
Set open to your Slave the Prison-door?
You use my heart juſt as you would afford
A fatal freedom to some harmless bird,
Whom, breeding, you ne're taught to seek its food,
And now let flye to perish in the Wood.
    Ber. Then, if you will love on, and disobey,
And lose an Empire for my sake, you may.
Will a kind look from me pay all this score,
For you well know you muſt expect no more?
    Por. All I deserve it will, not all I wish:
But I will brave the Tyrants rage, for this.

If I refuse, my death muſt needs ensue;
But you shall see that I dare dye for you.
    Ber. Would you for me,
A Beauty and an Empire too deny?
I love you now so well——that you shall dye,
Dye mine; 'tis all I can with honour give:
Nor should you dye, if after, I would live.
But when your Marriage and your Death I view,
That makes you false, but this will keep you true.
    Por. Unbind thy brows, and look abroad to see,
O mighty Love, thy mightieſt Victory!
    Ber. And yet——is there no other way to try?
'Tis hard to say I love, and let you dye.
    Por. Yes, there remains some help, which you might give,
If you, as I would dye for Love, would live.
    Ber. If death for Love be sweet, sure life is more:
Teach me the means your safety to reſtore.
    Por. Your Tyrant the Ægyptian Princess loves;
And to that height his swelling passion moves,
That, fearing in your death the Souldiers force,
He from your bed does ſtudy a Divorce.
    Ber. Th' Ægyptian Princess I disputing hard,
And as a Miracle her mind regard.
But yet I wish that this Divorce be true.   *Gives her hand.*
    Por. 'Tis, Madam, but it muſt be sought by you.
By this he will all Mutinies prevent;
And this, as well, secures your own content.
    Ber. I hate this Tyrant, and his bed I loath;
But, once submitting, I am ty'd to both:
Ty'd to that Honour, which all Women owe,
Though not their Husbands person, yet their vow.
Something so sacred in that bond there is,
That none should think there could be ought amiss:
And if there be, we should in silence hide
Those Faults, which blame our Choice when they are spy'd.
    Por. But, since to all the world his crimes are known,
And, by himself the Civil War's begun,
Would you th'advantage of the fight delay,
If, ſtriking firſt, you were to win the day?
    Ber. I would, like Jews, upon their Sabbath fall:
And rather than ſtrike firſt, not ſtrike at all.
    Por. Againſt your self you sadly prophesie:
You either this Divorce muſt seek, or dye.

Ber. Then death from all my griefs shall set me free.
Por. And would you rather chuse your death, than me?
Ber. My earthy part———
Which is my Tyrants right, death will remove,
I'le come all Soul and Spirit to your Love.
With silent steps I'le follow you all day;
Or else before you in the Sun-beams, play.
I'le lead you thence to melancholy Groves.
And there repeat the Scenes of our past Loves.
At night, I will within your Curtains peep;
With empty arms embrace you while you sleep.
In gentle dreams I often will be by;
And sweep along, before your closing eye.
All dangers from your bed I will remove;
But guard it most from any future Love.
And when at last, in pity, you will dye,
I'le watch your Birth of Immortality:
Then, Turtle-like, I'le to my Mate repair;
And teach you your first flight in open Air. *Exit* Berenice *cum* Erotio.
   Por. She has but done what Honour did require:
Nor can I blame that Love, which I admire.
But then her death!
I'le stand betwixt, it first shall pierce my heart:
We will be stuck together on his dart.
But yet the danger not so high does grow:
I'le charge death first, perhaps repulse him too.
But if o'repower'd, I must be overcome;
Forc'd back, I'le fight each inch into my Tomb.   *Exit.*

ACT IV. SCENE I. *Indian Cave.*

Placidius, Nigrinus. Nigrinus *with two drawn Swords, held upwards
in his hands.*

Placid. ALL other means have fail'd to move her heart;
    Our last recourse is, therefore, to your Art.
   Nig. Of Wars, and Bloodshed, and of dire Events,
Of Fates, and fighting Kings, their Instruments,
I could with greater certainty foretell;
Love only does in doubts and darkness dwell.
For, like a wind, it in no quarter stays;
But points and veers each hour a thousand ways.

On Women Love depends, and they on Will;
Chance turns their Orb while Destiny sits still.

Placid. Leave nothing unattempted in your pow'r;
Remember you oblige an Emperour.

Nig. An earthy Fiend by compact me obeys;
But him to light intents I must not raise.
Some Astral forms I must invoke by prayer,
Fram'd all of purest Atoms of the Air;
Not in their Natures simply good or ill,
But most subservient to bad Spirits will.
Nakar of those does lead the mighty Band,
For eighty Legions move at his Command:
Gentle to all, but, far above the rest,
Mild *Nakar* loves his soft *Damilcar* best.
In Aery Chariots they together ride,
And sip the dew as through the Clouds they glide:
These are the Spirits which in Love have pow'r.

Placid. Haste, and invoke 'em in a happy hour.

Nig. And so it proves: for, counting sev'n from Noon,
'Tis *Venus* hour, and in the wexing Moon.
With Chalk I first describe a Circle here,
Where these Ætherial Spirits must appear.
Come in, come in; for here they will be strait:
Around, around, the place I fumigate:
My fumigation is to *Venus*, just:
The Souls of Roses, and red Corals dust:
A lump of *Sperma Ceti*; and to these,
The stalks and chips of *Lignum Aloes*.
And, last, to make my fumigation good,
'Tis mix'd with Sparrows brains and Pigeons blood.

        Nigrinus *takes up the Swords.*

They come, they come, they come! I hear 'em now.

Placid. A death-like damp sits cold upon my brow:
And misty vapours swim before my sight.

Nig. They come not in a shape to cause your fright.

     Nakar *and* Damilcar *descend in Clouds, and sing.*

  Nak. *Hark, my* Damilcar, *we are call'd below!*

  Dam. *Let us go, let us go!*
Go to relieve the care
Of longing Lovers in despair!

  Nak. *Merry, merry, merry, we sail from the East*
Half tippled at a Rain-bow Feast.

Dam. In the bright Moon-shine while winds whistle loud,
Tivy, tivy, tivy, we mount and we fly,
All racking along in a downy white Cloud;
And lest our leap from the Skie should prove too far,
We slide on the back of a new-falling Star.
    Nak. *And drop from above,*
In a Gelly of Love!
    Dam. *But now the Sun's down, and the Element's red,*
The Spirits of Fire against us make head!
    Nak. *They muster, they muster, like Gnats in the Air:*
Alas! I must leave thee, my Fair;
And to my light Horse-men repair.
    Dam. *O stay, for you need not to fear 'em to night;*
The wind is for us, and blows full in their sight;
And o're the wide Ocean we fight!
Like leaves in the Autumn our Foes will fall down;
And hiss in the Water————
    Both. *And hiss in the Water and drown!*
    Nak. *But their men lye securely intrench'd in a Cloud:*
And a Trumpeter-Hornet to battel sounds loud.
    Dam. *Now Mortals that spie*
How we tilt in the Skie,
With wonder will gaze;
And fear such events as will ne're come to pass!
    Nak. *Stay you to perform what the man will have done.*
    Dam. *Then call me again when the Battel is won.*
    Both, *So ready and quick is a Spirit of Air*
To pity the Lover, and succour the fair,
That, silent and swift, that little soft God
Is here with a wish, and is gone with a nod.

> *The Clouds part,* Nakar *flies up, and* Damilcar *down.*

Nig. I charge thee, Spirit, stay; and by the pow'r [*To* Damilcar.
Of *Nakar's* Love, and of this holy Wand,
On the North quarter of my Circle stand:
(Sev'n foot around for my defence I take!)
To all my questions faithful answers make;
So may'st thou live thy thousand years in peace;
And see thy Aery progeny increase:
So may'st thou still continue young and fair,
Fed by the blast of pure Ætherial Air.
And, thy full term expir'd, without all pain,
Dissolve into thy Astral source again.

Dam. Name not my hated Rival *Gemory,*
And I'le speak true whate're thy questions be.
  Nig. Thy Rivals hated name I will refrain.
Speak, shall the Emperour his love obtain?
  Dam. Few hours shall pass before your Emperour shall be
Possess'd of that he loves, or from that love be free.
  Placid. Shall I enjoy that Beauty I adore?
  Dam. She, Suppliant-like, e're long, thy succour shall implore:
And thou with her thou lov'st in happiness may'st live,
If she not dies before, who all the joys can give.
  Nig. Say, what does the Ægyptian Princess now?
  Dam. A gentle slumber sits upon her brow.
  Nig. Go, stand before her in a golden dream:
Set all the pleasures of the world to show,
And in vain joys let her loose spirit flow.
  Dam. Twice fifty Tents remove her from your sight,
But I'll cut through e'm all with rays of light:
And covering other objects to your eyes,
Show where intranc'd in silent sleep she lies.

> *Damilcar stamps, and the Bed arises with S. Catharine in it.*

Dam. Singing.   *You pleasing dreams of Love and sweet delight,*
> *Appear before this slumb'ring Virgins sight:*
> *Soft visions set her free*
> *From mournful piety.*
> *Let her sad thoughts from Heav'n retire;*
> *And let the Melancholy Love*
> *Of those remoter joys above*
> *Give place to your more sprightly fire.*
> *Let purling streams be in her fancy seen;*
> *And flowry Meads, and Vales of chearful green:*
> *And in the midst of deathless Groves*
> *Soft sighing wishes ly,*
> *And smiling hopes fast by,*
> *And just beyond e'm ever laughing Loves.*

> *A Scene of a Paradise is discovered.*

  Placid. Some pleasing objects do her mind employ;
For on her face I read a wandring Joy.

SONG.

Dam.   *Ah how sweet it is to love,*
            Ah how gay is young desire!

And what pleasing pains we prove
When we first approach Loves fire!
Pains of Love be sweeter far
Than all other pleasures are.

Sighs which are from Lovers blown,
Do but gently heave the Heart:
Ev'n the tears they shed alone
Cure, like trickling Balm their smart.
Lovers when they lose their breath,
Bleed away in easie death.

Love and Time with reverence use,
Treat 'em like a parting friend:
Nor the golden gifts refuse
Which in youth sincere they send:
For each year their price is more,
And they less simple than before.

Love, like Spring-tides, full and high,
Swells in every youthful vein:
But each Tide does less supply,
Till they quite shrink in again:
If a flow in Age appear,
'Tis but rain, and runs not clear.

At the end of the Song a Dance of Spirits. After which Amariel, *the Guardian-Angel of S.* Catharine, *descends to soft Musick, with a flaming Sword. The Spirits crawl off the Stage amazedly, and* Damilcar *runs to a corner of it.*

Amar. From the bright Empire of Eternal day,
Where waiting minds for Heav'ns Commission stay,
Amariel flies: (a darted Mandate came
From that great will which moves this mighty Frame,
Bid me to thee, my Royal charge, repair,
To guard thee from the Dæmons of the Air;
My flaming Sword above 'em to display,
(All keen and ground upon the edge of day;)
The flat to sweep the Visions from thy mind,
The edge to cut 'em through that stay behind.)
Vain Spirits, you that shunning Heav'ns high noon,
Swarm here beneath the concave of the Moon,
What folly, or what rage your duty blinds,
To violate the sleep of holy minds?

Hence, to the task assign'd you here below:
Upon the Ocean make loud Tempests blow;
Into the wombs of hollow Clouds repair,
And crush out Thunder from the bladder'd Air.
From pointed Sun-beams take the Mists they drew,
And scatter them again in pearly dew:
And of the bigger drops they drain below,
Some mould in Hail, and others stamp in Snow.
 Dam. Mercy, bright Spirit, I already feel
The piercing edge of thy immortal steel:
Thou Prince of day, from Elements Art free;
And I all body when compar'd to thee.
Thou tread'st th' Abyss of light!
And where it streams with open eyes canst go:
We wander in the Fields of Air below:
Changlings and Fooles of Heav'n; and thence shut out,
Wildly we roam in discontent about:
Gross-heavy-fed, next man in ignorance and sin,
And spotted all without; and dusky all within.
Without thy Sword I perish by thy sight,
I reel, I stagger, and am drunk with light.
 Ama. If e're again thou on this place art found;
Full fifty years I'le chain thee under ground;
The damps of Earth shall be thy daily food;
All swoln and bloated like a dungeon toad:
And when thou shalt be freed, yet thou shalt ly
Gasping upon the ground, too faint to fly;
And lag below thy fellows in the sky.
 Dam. O pardon, pardon this accursed Deed,
And I no more on Magick fumes will feed;
Which drew me hither by their pow'rful steams.
 Ama. Go expiate thy guilt in holy dreams.   [*Ex.* Dam.
 To S. Cath.] But thou, sweet Saint, henceforth disturb'd no more
With dreams not thine, thy thoughts to Heav'n restore.
      The Angel ascends, and the Scene shuts.
 Nig. Some holy Being does invade this place,
And from their duty does my Spirits chase.
I dare no longer near it make abode:
No Charms prevail against the Christians God.   *Exit.*
 Placid. How doubtfully these Specters Fate foretell!
In double sense, and twi-light truth they dwell:
Like fawning Courtiers for success they wait,
And then come smiling and declare for Fate.

364

Enter Maximin *and* Porphyrius, *attended by* Valerius
and Guards.

But see, the Tyrant and my Rival come:
I, like the Fiends, will flatter in his doom:
None but a Fool diſtaſtful Truth will tell,
So it be new, and please, 'tis full as well.

          Placid. *whispers with the Emperour, who seems pleas'd.*

  Max. You charm me with your news, which I'le reward:
By hopes we are for coming joys prepar'd:
Possess her Love, or from that Love be free————
Heav'n speaks me fair: if she as kind can prove,
I shall possess, but never quit my Love.
Go, tell me when she wakes————   *Exit* Placidius.

          Porphyrius *seems to beg something of him,*

————————*Porphyrius,* no;
She has refus'd, and I will keep my vow.

  Por. For your own sake your cruel vow defer;.
The time's unsafe, your Enemies are near.
And to displease your men when they should fight————

  Max. My looks alone my Enemies will fright;
And o're my men I'le set my careful Spies,
To watch Rebellion in their very eyes.
No more, I cannot bear the leaſt reply.

  Por. Yet, Tyrant, thou shalt perish e're she dye.   *Aside.*

Enter Valeria.

Valeria here! How Fortune treats me ſtill
With various harms, magnificently ill?

  Max. Valeria, I was sending to your Tent,   *To* Valeria.
But my Commands your presence does prevent.
This is the hour wherein the Prieſt shall joyn
Your holy Loves, and make *Porphyrius* mine.

  Val. aside. Now hold, my Heart, and *Venus* I implore,
Be Judge if she he loves deserves him more.

  Por. aside. Paſt hope! and all in vain I would preserve
My life, not for my self, but her I serve.

  Val. I come, great Sir, your juſtice to demand.   *To the Emp.*

  Max. You cannot doubt it from a Father's hand.

  Por. Sir, I confess before her Suit be known;
And by my self condemn'd, my crime I own.
I have refus'd————

  Val. ————Peace, peace, while I confess
I have refus'd thee for unworthiness.

                                  365

Por. I am amaz'd.

Max. ——What Riddles do you use?
Dare either of you my Commands refuse?

Val. Yes, I dare owne how e're 'twas wisely done
T'adopt so mean a person for your Son:
So low you should not for your Daughter chuse:
And therefore, Sir, this Marriage I refuse.

Max. You lik'd the choice when first I thought it fit.

Val. I had not then enough consider'd it.

Max. And you have now consider'd it too much:
Secrets of Empire are not safe to touch.

Por. Let not your mighty anger rise too high:
'Tis not *Valeria* merits it, but I.
My own unworthiness so well I knew,
That from her Love I consciously withdrew.

Val. Thus rather than endure the little shame
To be refus'd, you blast a Virgins name.
You to refuse, and I to be deny'd!
Learn more discretion, or be taught less pride.

Por. O Heav'n, in what a Labyrinth am I led!
I could get out, but she detains the thred!
Now I must wander on till I can see,
Whether her pity or revenge it be!   *Aside.*

Max. With what child's anger do you think you play?
I'le punish both, if either disobey.

Val. Since all the fault was mine, I am content
Porphyrius should not share the punishment.

Por. Blind that I was till now, that could not see,
'Twas all th' effects of generosity.
She loves me, e'n to suffer for my sake;
And on her self would my refusal take.   *Aside.*
                                                       To Val.
Max. Children to serve their Parents int'rest, live.
Take heed what doom against your self you give.

Por. Since she must suffer, if I do not speak,
'Tis time the Laws of Decency to break.
She told me, Sir, that she your choice approv'd:
And (though I blush to owne it) said she lov'd.
Lov'd me desertless, who, with shame, confest
Another flame had seiz'd upon my brest.
Which, when, too late, the generous Princess knew,
And fear'd your justice would my crime pursue,
Upon her self she makes the Tempest fall,
And my refusal her contempt would call.

Val. He raves, Sir, and to cover my disdain,
Unhandsomly would his denial feign.
And all means failing him, at laſt would try
T'usurp the credit of a scorn, and dye.
But——let him live——his punishment shall be
The grief his pride will bring for losing me.

Max. You both obnoxious to my juſtice are;
And, Daughter, you have not deserv'd my care.
'Tis my Command you ſtrictly guarded be,
Till your fantaſtick quarrel you agree.

Por. Sir————

Max. I'le not hear you speak, her crime is plain,
She owns her pride which you perhaps may feign.
She shall be Prisoner till she bend her mind
To that which is for both of you design'd.

Val. You'l find it hard my free-born will to bound.

Max. I'le find that pow'r o're wills which Heav'n ne're found.
Free will's a cheat in any one but me:
In all but Kings 'tis willing slavery.
And unseen Fate which forces the desire,
The will of Puppets Danc'd upon a wyre.
A Monarch is
The Spirit of the World in every mind;
He may match Wolves to Lambs, and make it kind.
Mine is the business of your little Fates:
And though you war like petty wrangling States,
You're in my hand; and when I bid you cease,
You shall be crush'd together into peace.

Val. *aside.* Thus by the world my courage will be priz'd;
Seeming to scorn, who am, alas, despis'd:
Dying for Love's, fulfilling Honour's Laws;
A secret Martyr while I owne no cause.   *Exit* Valeria.

Max. Porphyrius, ſtay; there's something I would hear:
You said you lov'd, and you muſt tell me where.

Por. All Heav'n is to my sole deſtruction bent.   *Aside.*

Max. You would, it seems, have leisure to invent.

Por. Her name, in pity, Sir, I muſt forbear,
Leſt my offences you revenge on her.

Max. My promise for her life I do engage.

Por. Will that, Sir, be remember'd in your rage?

Max. Speak, or your silence more my rage will move;
'Twill argue, that you rival me in Love.

367

Por. Can you believe that my ambitious flame
Should mount so high as *Berenice's* name?
Max. Your guilt dares not approach what it would hide;
But draws me off (and Lapwing like) flies wide.
'Tis not my Wife, but Miſtress you adore:
Though that affronts, yet this offends me more.
Who courts my Wife————
Does to my Honour more injurious prove;
But he who courts my Miſtress, wrongs my Love.
Por. Th' *Ægyptian* Princess ne're could move my heart.
Max. You could not perish by a nobler Dart.
Por. Sir, I presume not beauties to compare:
But in my eye, my Princess is as fair.
Max. Your Princess! then it seems, though you deny
Her name you love, you owne her quality.
Por. Though not by Birth or Title so; yet she
Who rules my heart, a Princess is to me.
Max. No, no————
'Tis plain that word you unawares did use,
And told a truth, which now you would excuse.
Besides my Wife and Miſtress here are none
Who can the Title of a Princess owne.
Por. There is one more————
Your Daughter, Sir: let that your doubt remove.
Max. But she is not that Princess whom you love.
Por. I nam'd not Love, though it might doubtful seem;
She's fair; and is that Princess I eſteem.
Max. Go, and to passion your eſteem improve,
While I command her to receive your Love.   *Exit* Por.

Enter S. Catherine.

S. Cath. I come not now as Captive to your pow'r,
To beg; but as high Heav'ns Embassadour,
The Laws of my Religion to fulfill;
Heav'n sends me to return you good for ill.
Your Empress to your Love I would reſtore;
And to your mind the peace it had before.
Max. While in another's name you Peace declare,
Princess, you in your own proclaim a War.
Your too great pow'r does your design oppose;
You make those breaches which you ſtrive to close,
S. Cath. That little beauty which too much you prize
Seeks not to move your heart, or draw your eyes:

Your Love to *Berenice* is due alone:
Love, like that pow'r which I adore, is one.
When fixt to one, it safe at Anchor rides,
And dares the fury of the winds and tides:
But losing once that hold, to the wide Ocean born,
It drives away at will, to every wave a scorn.

Max. If to new persons I my Love apply,
The Stars and Nature are in fault, not I;
My Loves are like my old Prætorian bands,
Whose Arbitrary pow'r their Prince commands;
I can no more make passion come or go,
Than you can bid your *Nilus* ebb or flow.
'Tis lawless, and will love, and where it lift:
And that's no sin which no man can resift:
Those who impute it to me as a crime,
Would make a God of me before my time.

S. Cath. A God, indeed, after the *Roman* ftyle,
An Eagle mounting from a kindled Pile.
But you may make your self a God below:
For Kings who rule their own desires are so.
You roam about, and never are at reft;
By new desires, that is, new torments, ftill posseft.
Qualmish and loathing all you had before:
Yet with a sickly appetite to more.
As in a fev'rish dream you ftill drink on;
And wonder why your thirft is never gone.
Love, like a ghoftly Vision haunts your mind;
'Tis ftill before you, what you left behind.

Max. How can I help those faults which Nature made?
My appetite is sickly, and decay'd,
And you forbid me change (the sick mans ease)
Who cannot cure, muft humour his disease.

S. Cath. Your mind should first the remedy begin;
You seek without, the Cure that is within.
The vain experiments you make each day,
To find content, ftill finding it decay,
Without attempting more, should let you see
That you have sought it where it ne're could be.
But when you place your joys on things above,
You fix the wand'ring Planet of your Love:
Thence you may see
Poor humane kind all daz'd in open day,
Erre after bliss, and blindly miss their way:

The greatest happiness a Prince can know,
Is to love Heav'n above, do good below.

To them Berenice *and Attendants.*

Ber. That happiness may *Berenice* find,
Leaving these empty joys of Earth behind:
And this frail Being, where so short a while
Th' unfortunate lament, and prosp'rous smile.
Yet a few days, and those which now appear
In youth and beauty like the blooming year,
In life's swift Scene shall change; and cares shall come
And heavy age, and death's relentless doom.
   S. Cath. Yet man, by pleasures seeks that Fate which he would
     shun;
And, suck'd in by the stream, does to the Whirl-pool run.
   Max. How Madam, are you to new ways inclin'd?   *To* Ber.
I fear the Christian Sect perverts your mind.
   Ber. Yes, Tyrant, know that I their Faith embrace,
And owne it in the midst of my disgrace.
That Faith, which abject as it seems to thee,
Is nobler than thy Purple Pageantry:
A Faith, which still with Nature is at strife;
And looks beyond it to a future life.
A Faith which vitious Souls abhor and fear,
Because it shews Eternity too near,
And therefore every one————
With seeming scorn of it the rest deceives:
All joining not to own what each believes.
   S. Cath. O happy Queen! whom pow'r leads not astray,
Nor youth's more powerful blandishments betray.
   Ber. Your Arguments my reason first inclin'd,
And then your bright example fix'd my mind.
   Max. With what a holy Empress am I blest,
What scorn of Earth dwells in her heav'nly brest!
My Crown's too mean; but he whom you adore,
Has one more bright of Martyrdom in store.
She dyes, and I am from the envy freed: *Aside.*
She has, I thank her, her own death decreed.
No Souldier now will in her rescue stir;
Her death is but in complaisance to her.
I'le haste to gratifie her holy will;
Heav'n grant her zeal may but continue still.

370

To Val. Tribune, a Guard to seize the Empress ſtrait,
Secure her person Pris'ner to the State.　　　　*Exit* Maximin.
　　Val. *going to her.* Madam, believe 'tis with regret I come
To execute my angry Prince's doom.

Enter Porphyrius.

　　Por. What is it I behold! Tribune from whence
Proceeds this more than barbarous insolence?
　　Val. Sir, I perform the Emperour's Commands.
　　Por. Villain, hold off thy sacrilegious hands,
Or by the Gods——retire without reply:
And, if he asks who bid thee, say 'twas I. Valerius *retires to a diſtance.*
　　Ber. Too generously your safety you expose
To save one moment her whom you muſt lose.
　　Por. 'Twixt you and death ten thousand lives there ſtand;
Have courage, Madam, the Prætorian Band
Will all oppose your Tyrants cruelty.
　　S. Cath. And I have Heav'n implor'd she may not dye.
As some to witness truth Heav'ns call obey;
So some on Earth muſt, to confirm it, ſtay.
　　Por. What Faith, what Witness is it that you name?
　　Ber. Knowing what she believes, my Faith's the same.
　　Por. How am I cross'd what way so e're I go!
To the unlucky every thing is so.
Now, Fortune, thou haſt shewn thy utmoſt spight:
The Souldiers will not for a Chriſtian fight.
And, Madam, all that I can promise now,
Is but to dye before death reaches you.
　　Ber. Now death draws near, a ſtrange perplexity
Creeps coldly on me, like a fear to dye:
Courage uncertain dangers may abate;
But who can bear th' approach of certain Fate?
　　S. Cath. The wiseſt and the beſt some fear may show;
And wish to ſtay, though they resolve to go.
　　Ber. As some faint Pilgrim ſtanding on the shore,
Firſt views the Torrent he would venture o're;
And then his Inn upon the farther ground,
Loth to wade through, and lother to go round:
Then dipping in his ſtaff do's tryal make,
How deep it is; and, sighing, pulls it back;
Sometimes resolv'd to fetch his leap; and then
Runs to the Bank, but there ſtops short agen;

371

So I at once——————
Both heav'nly Faith, and humane fear obey;
And feel before me in an unknown way.
For this blest Voyage I with joy prepare;
Yet am asham'd to be a stranger there.
    S. Cath. You are not yet enough prepar'd to dye:
Earth hangs too heavy for your Soul to flye.
    Por. One way (and Heav'n I hope inspires my mind)
I for your safety in this straight can find:
But this fair Queen must farther my intent.
    S. Cath. Name any way your reason can invent.
    Por. to Ber. Though your Religion, (which I cannot blame,
Because my secret Soul avows the same)
Has made your life a forfeit to the Laws,
The Tyrants new-born passion is the cause.
Were this bright Princess once remov'd away,
Wanting the food, the flame would soon decay.
And I'le prepare a faithful Guard this night
T'attend her person, and secure her flight.
    Ber. to S. Cath. By this way I shall both from death be freed,
And you unforc'd to any wicked deed.
    S. Cath. Madam, my thoughts are with themselves at strife;
And Heav'n can witness how I prize your life:
But 'tis a doubtful conflict I must try.
Betwixt my pity and my piety,
Staying, your precious life I must expose:
Going, my Crown of Martyrdom I lose.
    Por. Your equal choice when Heav'n does thus divide,
You should, like Heav'n, still lean on mercy's side.
    S. Cath. The will of Heav'n, judg'd by a private brest,
Is often what's our private interest.
And therefore those who would that will obey,
Without their int'rest must their duty weigh.
As for my self, I do not life despise;
But as the greatest gift of Nature prize.
My Sex is weak, my fears of death are strong;
And whate're is, its Being would prolong.
Were there no sting in death, for me to dye
Would not be conquest, but stupidity.
But if vain Honour can confirm the Soul,
And sense of shame the fear of death controul,
How much more then should Faith uphold the mind,
Which, showing death, shews future life behind?

372

Ber. Of death's contempt Heroick proofs you give;
But, Madam, let my weaker Vertue live.
Your Faith may bid you, your own life resign;
But not when yours must be involv'd with mine.
Since, then, you do not think me fit to dye,
Ah, how can you that life I beg, deny!

    S. Cath. Heav'n does in this my greatest tryal make,
When I for it, the care of you forsake.
But I am plac'd as on a Theater,
Where all my Acts to all Mankind appear,   }
To imitate my constancy or fear.
Then, Madam, judge what course I should pursue,
When I must either Heav'n forsake, or you.

    Por. Were saving *Berenice's* life a sin,
Heav'n had shut up your flight from *Maximin.*

    S. Cath. Thus with short Plummets Heav'ns deep will we
       sound
That vast Abyss where humane Wit is drown'd!
In our small Skiff we must not launce too far;
We here but Coasters, not Discov'rers are.
Faith's necessary Rules are plain and few;
We, many, and those needless Rules pursue:
Faith from our hearts into our heads we drive;
And make Religion all Contemplative.
You, on Heav'ns will may witty glosses feign;
But that which I must practise here, is plain:
If the All-great decree her life to spare,
He will, the means, without my crime prepare.   *Exit S.* Cath.

    Por. Yet there is one way left! it is decreed,
To save your life that *Maximin* should bleed.
'Midst all his Guards I will his death pursue,
Or fall a Sacrifice to Love and you.

    Ber. So great a fear of death I have not shown,
That I would shed his blood to save my own.
My fear is but from humane frailty brought;
And never mingled with a wicked thought.

    Por. 'Tis not a Crime, since one of you must dye;
Or is excus'd by the necessity.

    Ber. I cannot to a Husband's death consent;
But, by revealing, will your crime prevent.
The horrour of this deed————
Against the fear of death has arm'd my mind;
And now less guilt in him than you I find:

373

If I a Tyrant did deteſt before,
I hate a Rebel and a Traitor more:
Ungrateful man————
Remember whose Succeſſor thou art made,
And then thy Benefactors life invade.
Guards to your charge I give your Pris'ner back:
And will from none but Heav'n my ſafety take.

Exit with Valerius *and Guards.*

    Por. ſolus. 'Tis true, what she has often urg'd before;
He's both my Father and my Emperour!
O Honour, how canſt thou invent a way
To ſave my Queen, and not my truſt betray!
Unhappy I, that e're he truſted me!
As well his Guardian-Angel may his Murd'rer be.
And yet————let Honour, Faith, and Vertue flye,
But let not Love in *Berenece* dye.
She lives!————
That's put beyond dispute, as firm as Fate:
Honour and Faith let Argument debate.

    Enter Maximin *and* Valerius *talking, and Guards.*

    Max. 'Tis said; but I am loth to think it true,   *To* Porphy.
That my late Orders were contemn'd by you:
That *Berenice* from her Guards you freed.
    Por. I did it, and I glory in the deed.
    Max. How, glory, my Commands to disobey!
    Por. When those Commands would your Renown betray.
    Max. Who should be Judge of that Renown you name
But I?
    Por. ————Yes I, and all who love your fame.
    Max. Porphyrius, your replies are insolent.
    Por. Sir, they are juſt, and for your service meant.
If, for Religion you our lives will take,
You do not the offenders find, but make.
All Faiths are to their own believers juſt;
For none believe, because they will, but muſt.
Faith is a force from which there's no defence;
Because the Reason it does firſt convince.
And Reason Conscience into fetters brings;
And Conscience is without the pow'r of Kings.
    Max. Then Conscience is a greater Prince than I;
At whose each erring call a King may dye.

Who Conscience leaves to its own free command,
Puts the worst Weapon in a Rebels hand.

Por. It's Empire, therefore, Sir, should bounded be;
And but in acts of it's Religion, free:
Those who ask Civil pow'r and Conscience too,
Their Monarch to his own destruction woo.
With needful Arms let him rescue his peace;
Then, that wild beast he safely may release.

Max. I can forgive these liberties you take,
While but my Counsellor your self you make:
But you first act your sense, and then advise:
That is, at my expence you will be wise.
My Wife, I for Religion do not kill;
But she shall dye————because it is my will.

Por. Sir, I acknowledge I too much have done;
And therefore merit not to be your Son:
I render back the Honours which you gave;
My liberty's the only gift I crave.

Max. You take too much:—but, e're you lay it down,
Consider what you part with, in a Crown:
Monarchs of cares in Policy complain,
Because they would be pity'd while they raign;
For still the greater troubles they confess,
They know their pleasures will be envy'd less.

Por. Those joys I neither envy nor admire;
But beg I from the troubles may retire.

Max. What Soul is this which Empire cannot stir!
Supine and tame as a Philosopher!
Know then, thou wert adopted to a Throne,
Not for thy sake so much as for my own.
My thoughts were once about thy death at strife;
And thy succession's thy reprieve for life.

Por. My life and death are still within your pow'r:
But your succession I renounce this hour.
Upon a bloody Throne I will not sit;
Nor share the guilt of Crimes which you commit.

Max. If you are not my *Cæsar*, you must dye.

Por. I take it as a nobler Destiny.

Max. I pity thee, and would thy faults forgive:
But thus presuming on, thou canst not live.

Por. Sir, with your Throne your pity I restore;
I am your Foe; nor will I use it more.

Now all my debts of gratitude are paid,
I cannot trusted be, nor you betray'd.   *Is going.*
    Max. Stay, stay! in threatning me to be my Foe,
You give me warning to conclude you so.
Thou to succeed a Monarch in his Seat!

                Enter Placidius.

No, Fool, thou art too honest to be great.
Placidius, on your life this Pris'ner keep:
Our enmity shall end before I sleep.
    Placid. I still am ready, Sir, when e're you please.   *To* Porphy.
To do you such small services as these.
    Max. The Sight with which my eyes shall first be fed,
Must be my Empress and this Traitors head.
    Por. Where e're thou stand'st I'le level at that place
My gushing blood, and spout it at thy face.
Thus, not by Marriage, we our blood will joyn:
Nay, more, my arms shall throw my head at thine.   *Exit guarded.*
    Max. There, go adoption:——I have now decreed
That *Maximin* shall *Maximin* succeed:
Old as I am, in pleasures I will try
To waste an Empire yet before I dye:
Since life is fugitive, and will not stay,
I'le make it flye more pleasantly away.   *Exit.*

ACT V. SCENE I.

Valeria, Placidius.

Val. IF, as you say, you silently have been
        So long my Lover, let my pow'r be seen:
One hours discourse before *Porphyrius* dye,
Is all I ask, and you too may be by.
    Placid. I must not break
The order, which the Emperour did sign.
    Val. Has then his hand more pow'r with you than mine?
    Placid. This hand if given would far more pow'rful be
Than all the Monarchs of the World to me:
But 'tis a bait which would my heart betray;
And, when I'm fast, will soon be snatcht away.
    Val. O say not so; for I shall ever be
Oblig'd to him who once obliges me.
376

Placid. Madam, I'le wink, and favour your deceit:
But know, fair Coz'ner, that I know the cheat:
Though to these eyes I nothing can refuse,
I'le not the merit of my ruine lose:
It is enough I see the hook, and bite:
But firſt I'll pay my death with my delight.   [*Kisses her hand, and*

Val. What can I hope from this sad interview!   *Exit.*
And yet my brave design I will pursue.
By many signs I have my Rival found:
But Fortune him, as deep as me does wound.
For, if he love the Empress, his sad Fate
More moves my pity, than his scorn my hate.

To her Placidius *with Porphyrius.*

Placid. I am, perhaps, the firſt
Who forc'd by Fate, and in his own despight,
Brought a lov'd Rival to his Miſtress sight.

Val. But, in revenge, let this your comfort be,
That you have brought a man who loves not me.
However, lay your causeless envy by;
He is a Rival who muſt quickly dye.

Por. And yet I could with less concernment bear
That death of which you speak, than see you here.
So much of guilt in my refusal lies,
That Debtor-like, I dare not meet your eyes.

Val. I do not blame you, if you love elsewhere:
And, would to Heav'n, I could your suff'rings bear;
Or once again could some new way invent
To take upon my self your punishment:
I sent for you to let you know that ſtill
(Though now I want the pow'r) I have the will.

Placid. Can all this Ocean of your kindness be
Pour'd upon him, and not one drop on me?

Val. 'Tis pour'd; but falls from this ungrateful man,
Like drops of water from a rising Swan.
Upon his breaſt no sign of wet remains;
He bears his Love more proudly than his Chains.

Por. This thankless man his death will soon remove,
And quickly end so undeserv'd a Love.

Val. Unthankful as you are, I know not why,
But ſtill I love too well to see you dye.
Placidius, can you love, and see my grief,
And for my sake not offer some relief?

377

Placid. Not all the Gods his ruine shall prevent;
Your kindness does but urge his punishment.
Besides——
What is it I can for his safety do?
He has declar'd himself your Father's Foe.
    Val. Give out he is escap'd, and set him free:
And, if you please, lay all the fault on me.
    Por. O do not on those terms my freedom name:
Freed by your danger I should dye with shame.
    Placid. I muſt not farther by your prayers be won: *To her.*
All I could do I have already done.
    Val. To bring *Porphyrius* only to my sight,
Was not to shew your pity, but your spight:
Would you but half oblige her you adore?
You should not have done this, or should do more.
    Placid. Alas, what hope can there be left for me
When I muſt sink into the Mine I see?
My heart will fall before you, if I ſtay;
Each word you speak saps part of it away.——
——Yet all my Fortune on his death is set:
And he may love her, though he loves not yet.
He muſt——and yet she says he muſt not dye:
O, if I could but wink, I could deny.

To them Albinus.

    Alb. The Emperour expeĉts your Pris'ner ſtrait;
And, with impatience, for his death does wait.
    Placid. Nay, then it is too late my Love to weigh.   *Exit* Alb.
Your pardon, Madam, if I muſt obey.
    Por. I am prepar'd, he shall not long attend.
    Val. Then hear my pray'rs, and my submissions end.
Placidius know, that hour in which he dyes,
My death (so well I love) shall wait on his.
    Placid. O, Madam, do not fright me with your death!
    Val. My life depends alone upon his breath.
But, if I live in him, you do not know
How far my gratitude to you may go.
I do not promise——but it so may prove,
That gratitude, in time, may turn to Love.
Try me——
    Placid. ——Now I consider it, I will: *Musing a little.*
'Tis in your pow'r to save him or to kill.
378

I'le run the hazard to preserve his life,
If, after that, you vow to be my Wife.
   Val. Nay, good *Placidius*, now you are too hard:
Would you do nothing but for meer reward?
Like Usurers to men in want you prove,
When you would take Extortion for my Love.
   Placid. You have concluded then that he must dye.
                           [*Going with* Porphy.
   Val. O stay, if no price else his life can buy,
My Love a ransom for his life I give:
              [*Holding her Handkerchief before her face.*
Let my *Porphyrius* for another live.
   Por. You too much value the small merchandise:
My life's o're-rated, when your Love's the price.

             Enter Albinus.

   Alb. I long have list'ned to your generous strife,
As much concern'd for brave *Porphyrius* life.
For mine, I to his favour ow'd this day;
Which with my future Service I will pay.
   Placid. Lest any your intended flight prevent,
I'le lead you first the back way to my Tent:
Thence, in disguise, you may the City gain,
While some excuse for your escape I feign.
   Val. Farewel, I must not see you when you part:
                      [*Turning her face away.*
For that last look would break my tender heart.
Yet—let it break—I must have one look more: [*Looking on him.*
Nay, now I'm less contented than before.
For that last look draws on another too;
Which sure I need not to remember you.
For ever—yet I must one glance repeat:
But quick and short as starving people eat.
So much humanity dwells in your brest,
Sometimes to think on her who loves you best.
             [*Going, he takes her hand and kisses it.*
   Por. My wandring steps where ever Fortune bear,
Your memory I in my breast will wear:
Which, as a precious Amulet, I still
Will carry, my defence and guard from ill.
Though to my former vows I must be true,
I'le ever keep one Love entire for you.

                               379

That Love which Brothers with chaſte Siſters make:
And by this Holy kiss, which now I take
From your fair hand———
This common Sun which absent both shall see,
Shall ne're behold a breach of Faith in me.
  Val. Go, go, my death will your short vows reſtore:
You've said enough, and I can hear no more.
                    Exit Valeria *one way, and* Porphy. *and* Alb. *another.*
  Placid. Love and good Nature, how do you betray!
Misleading those who see and know their way!
I, whom deep Arts of State could ne're beguile,
Have sold my self to ruine for a smile.
Nay, I am driv'n so low, that I muſt take
That smile, as Alms, giv'n for my Rivals sake.
He, like a secret Worm, has eat his way;
And, lodg'd within, does on the kernel prey:
I creep without; and hopeless to remove
Him thence, wait only for the husk of Love.

                Enter Maximin *talking with* Valerius.

  Max. And why was I not told of this before?
  Val. Sir, she this evening landed on the shore.
For with her Daughter being Pris'ner made,
She in another Vessel was convey'd.
  Max. Bring hither the Ægyptian Princess ſtrait.   *To* Placid.
And you, *Valerius,* on her Mother wait.   *Exit* Valerius.
  Placid. The Mother of th' Ægyptian Princess here!
  Max. Porphyrius death I will a while defer.
And this new opportunity improve
To make my laſt effort upon her Love———   *Exit* Placidius.
Those who have youth may long endure to court;
But he muſt quickly catch whose Race is short.
I in my Autumn do my Siege begin;
And muſt make haſte, e're Winter comes, to win.
This hour—no longer shall my pains endure:
Her Love shall ease me, or her death shall cure,

        Enter at one door Felicia *and* Valerius; *at the other* S. Catharine
                        and Placidius.

  S. Cath. O, my dear Mother!
  Fel. ———With what joy I see
My deareſt Daughter from the Tempeſt free.

S. Cath. Dearer than all the joys vain Empire yields,
Or then to youthful Monarchs conquer'd fields,
Before you came——my Soul
All fill'd with Heav'n, did earthly joys disdain,
But you pull back some part of me again.
    Placid. You see, Sir, she can owne a joy below.
    Max. It much imports me that this truth I know.
    Fel. How dreadful death does on the waves appear!
Where Seas we only see, and Tempest hear.
Such frightful Images did then pursue
My trembling Soul, that scarce I thought of you.
    Placid. All Circumstances to your wish combine:
Her fear of death advances your design.
    Fel. But to that only pow'r we serve I pray'd,
Till he, who bid it rise, the Tempest laid.
    Max. You are a Christian then!   *To* Felicia.
For death this very hour you must prepare:
I have decreed no Christians life to spare.
    Fel. For death! I hope you but my courage try:
What ever I believe, I dare not dye,
Heav'n does not, sure, that Seal of Faith require;
Or, if he did, would firmer thoughts inspire.
A Womans witness can no credit give
To Truths Divine, and therefore I would live.
    Max. I cannot give the life which you demand:
But that and mine are in your Daughter's hand:
Ask her, if she will yet her Love deny;
And bid a Monarch, and her Mother dye.
    Fel. Now, mighty Prince, you cancel all my fear:
My life is safe when it depends on her.
How can you let me languish thus in pain!   *To S.* Cath.
Make haste to cure those doubts which yet remain.
Speak quickly, speak, and ease me of my fear.
    S. Cath. Alas, I doubt it is not you I hear.
Some wicked Fiend assumes your voice and face,
To make frail Nature triumph over Grace.
It cannot be——
That she who taught my Childhood Piety,
Should bid my riper age my Faith deny:
That she who bid my hopes this Crown pursue,
Should snatch it from me when 'tis just in view.
    Fel. Peace, peace, too much my age's shame you show:
How easie 'tis to teach! how hard to do!

My lab'ring thoughts are with themselves at ſtrife:
I dare not dye, nor bid you save my life.
    Max. You muſt do one, and that without delay;
Too long already for your death I ſtay:
I cannot with your small concerns dispence;
For deaths of more importance call me hence.
Prepare to execute your office ſtrait.   *To his Guards.*
    Fel. O ſtay, and let 'em but one minute wait.
Such quick Commands for death you would not give,
(Ah) if you knew how sweet it were to live.
    Max. Then bid her love.
    Fel. ———Is duty grown so weak,   *To S.* Cath.
That Love's a harder word than Death to speak ?
    S. Cath. Oh!
    Fel. Miſtake me not, I never can approve [*privately to S.* Cath.
A thing so wicked as the Tyrants Love.
I ask you would but some false promise give,
Only to gain me so much time to live.
    S. Cath. That promise is a ſtep to greater sin:
The hold once loſt, we seldom take agen.
Each bound to Heav'n we fainter Essays make:
Still losing somewhat till we quite go back.
    Max. Away, I grant no longer a reprieve.
    Fel. O do but beg my life, and I may live.   *To S.* Cath.
Have you not so much pity in your breſt?
He ſtays to have you make it your requeſt.
    S. Cath. To beg your life———
Is not to ask a grace of *Maximin:*
It is a silent bargain for a sin.
Could we live always, life were worth our coſt;
But now we keep with care what muſt be loſt.
Here we ſtánd shiv'ring on the Bank, and cry,
When we should plunge into Eternity.
One moment ends our pain;
And yet the shock of death we dare not ſtand,
By thought scarce measur'd, and too swift for sand:
'Tis but because the Living death ne're knew,
They fear to prove it as a thing that's new.
Let me th'Experiment before you try,
I'le show you firſt how easie 'tis to dye.
    Max. Draw then that Curtain, and let death appear,
And let both see how easie 'twill be there.

TYRANNICK LOVE

The Scene opens, and shews the Wheel.

Fel. Alas, what torments I already feel!

Max. Go, bind her hand and foot beneath that Wheel:
Four of you turn the dreadful Engine round;
Four others hold her faſt'ned to the ground:
That by degrees her tender breaſts may feel,
Firſt the rough razings of the pointed ſteel:
Her Paps then let the bearded Tenters ſtake,
And on each hook a gory Gobbet take.
Till th' upper flesh by piece-meal torn away,
Her beating heart shall to the Sun display.

Fel. My deareſt Daughter at your feet I fall;   *Kneeling.*
Hear, O yet hear your wretched Mothers call.
Think, at your Birth, ah think what pains I bore,
And can your eyes behold me suffer more?
You were the Child which from your infancy
I ſtill lov'd beſt, and then you beſt lov'd me.
About my neck your little arms you spred,
Nor could you sleep without me in the bed.
But sought my bosom when you went to reſt,
And all night long would lie across my breſt.
Nor without cause did you that fondness show:
You may remember when our *Nile* did flow;
While on the Bank you innocently ſtood,
And with a Wand made Circles in the flood,
That rose, and juſt was hurrying you to death,
When I, from far, all pale and out of breath,
Ran and rusht in———
And from the waves my floating pledge did bear,
So much my Love was ſtronger than my fear.
But you———

Max. Woman, for these long tales your life's too short;
Go, bind her quickly, and begin the sport.

Fel. No, in her arms my Sanctuary's plac'd:
                                   [Running to her Daughter.
Thus I will cling for ever to her waſte.

Max. What muſt my will by women be control'd?
Haſte, draw your Weapons, and cut off her hold.

S. Cath. Thus my laſt duty to you let me pay: [*Kissing her Mother.*
Yet, Tyrant, I to thee will never pray.
Though hers to save I my own life would give,
Yet by my sin, my Mother shall not live.

To thy foul lust I never can consent;
Why dost thou then defer my punishment?
I scorn those Gods thou vainly dost adore:
Contemn thy Empire, but thy bed abhor.
If thou would'st yet a bloodier Tyrant be,
I will instruct thy rage, begin with me.
   Max. I thank thee that thou dost my anger move:
It is a Tempest that will wreck my Love.
I'le pull thee hence, close hidden as thou art,

                              [Claps his hand to his breast.

And stand with my drawn Sword before my heart.
Yes, you shall be obey'd, though I am loth;
Go, and while I can bid you, bind 'em both.
Go, bind 'em e're my fit of Love return:
Fire shall quench fire, and anger Love shall burn.
Thus I prevent those follies I should do;
And 'tis the nobler Fever of the two.
   Fel. Torn piece by piece, alas what horrid pains!
   S. Cath. Heav'n is all mercy, who that death ordains,
And that which Heav'n thinks best is surely so:
But bare and naked, shame to undergo,
'Tis somewhat more than death!
Expos'd to lawless eyes I dare not be,
My modesty is sacred, Heav'n to thee.
Let not my body be the Tyrant's spoil;
Nor hands nor eyes thy purity defile.
   Amariel *descends swiftly with a flaming Sword, and strikes at the*
       Wheel, which breaks in pieces, then he ascends again.
   Max. Is this th' effect of all your boasted skill?
These brittle toys to execute my will;
A Puppet-show of death I only find,
Where I a strong and sinewy pain design'd.
By what weak infant was this Engine wrought?
   Val. From *Bilbilis* the temper'd steel was brought:
Metall more tough the Anvil ne're did beat,
Nor from the Forge, did hissing waters heat.
   Placid. I saw a Youth descend all Heav'nly fair,
Who in his hand a flaming Sword did bear,
And Whirlwind-like, around him drove the Air.
At his rais'd arm the rigid Iron shook;
And, bending backwards, fled before the stroke.
   Max. What! Miracles, the tricks of Heav'n to me?
I'le try if she be wholly Iron free.

384

If not by Sword, then she shall dye by fire;
And, one by one, her Miracles I'le tire.
If proof againſt all kind of death she be,
My Love's immortal, and she's fit for me.

    S. Cath. No, Heav'n has shown its pow'r, and now thinks fit,
Thee to thy former fury to remit.
Had Providence my longer life decreed,
Thou from thy passion hadſt not yet been freed.
But Heav'n, which suffer'd that, my Faith to prove,
Now to it self does vindicate my Love.
A pow'r controls thee which thou doſt not see;
And that's a Miracle it works in thee.

    Max. The truth of this new Miracle we'll try;
To prove it, you muſt take the pains to dye.
Bring me their heads————

    Fel. That mercy, Tyrant, thou deny'ſt to me,
At thy laſt breath may Heav'n refuse to thee.
My fears are going, and I death can view:
I see, I see him there thy ſteps pursue,
And with a lifted arm and silent pace,
Stalk after thee, juſt aiming in his chace.

    S. Cath. No more, dear Mother, ill in death it shows
Your peace of mind by rage to discompose:
No ſtreak of blood (the reliques of the Earth)
Shall ſtain my Soul in her immortal birth;
But she shall mount all pure, a white, and Virgin mind;
And full of all that peace, which there she goes to find.

        Exeunt S. Catharine *and* Felicia, *with* Valerius *and Guards.*

        The Scene shuts.

    Max. She's gone, and pull'd my heart-ſtrings as she went.
Were penitence no shame, I could repent.
Yet 'tis of bad example she should live;
For I might get th'ill habit to forgive.
Thou soft Seducer of my heart, away————
Who lingring, would'ſt about its confines ſtay,
To watch when some Rebellion would begin;
And ready at each sigh to enter in.
In vain; for thou
Doſt on the outside of the body play,
And when drawn neareſt, shalt be whirl'd away.
What ails me, that I cannot lose thy thought!
Command the Empress hither to be brought;   *To* Placid.

I in her death shall some diversion find,
And rid my thoughts at once of woman-kind.
  Placid. 'Tis well he thinks not of *Porphyrius* yet.   *Aside. Exit.*
  Max. How hard it is this Beauty to forget!
My ſtormy rage has only shook my will:
She crept down lower, but she ſticks there ſtill.
Fool that I am to ſtruggle thus with Love!
Why should I that which pleases me remove?
True, she should dye were she concern'd alone;
But I love, not for her sake, but my own.
Our Gods are Gods 'cause they have pow'r and will;
Who can do all things, can do nothing ill.
Ill is Rebellion 'gainſt some higher pow'r,
The World may sin, but not its Emperour.
My Empress then shall dye, my Princess Live;
If this be ill, I do my self forgive.

To him Valerius.

  Val. Your will's obey'd; for, mighty Emperour,
The Princess and her Mother are no more.
  Max. She is not dead!
  Val. ——Great Sir, your will was so.
  Max. That was my will of half an hour ago.
But now 'tis alter'd; I have chang'd her Fate,
She shall not dye.
  Val. ————Your pity comes too late.
Betwixt her Guards she seem'd by Bride-men led,
Her cheeks with cheerful blushes were o'respred,   }
When, smiling, to the Ax she bow'd her head.
Juſt at the ſtroke————
Ætherial musick did her death prepare;
Like joyful sounds of Spousals in the Air.
A radiant Light did her crown'd Temples guild,
And all the place with fragrant scents was fill'd.
The Balmy miſt came thick'ning to the ground,
And sacred silence cover'd all around.
But when (its work perform'd) the Cloud withdrew,
And day reſtor'd us to each others view,
I sought her head to bring it on my Spear;
In vain I sought it, for it was not there.
No part remain'd; but from afar our sight
Discover'd in the Air long tracts of light;

386

Of charming notes we heard the laſt rebounds,
And Musick dying in remoter sounds.
   Max. And doſt thou think
This lame account fit for a Love-sick King?
Go——from the other World a better bring.
          [*Kills him, then sets his foot on him, and speaks on.*]
When in my breaſt two mighty passions ſtrove,
Thou hadſt err'd better in obeying Love.
'Tis true, that way thy death had follow'd too.
But I had then been less displeas'd than now.
Now I muſt live unquiet for thy sake;
And this poor recompence is all I take.   *Spurns the body.*

   Here the Scene opens and discovers Berenice *on a Scaffold, the
     Guards by her, and amongſt them* Porphyrius *and* Albinus,
     like Moors, as all the Guards are.* Placidius *enters, and whispers
     the Emperour whilſt* Porphyrius *speaks.*

   Por. From *Berenice* I cannot go away;
But, like a Ghoſt, muſt near my Treasure ſtay.
   Alb. Night and this shape secure us from their eyes.
   Por. Have courage then for our bold enterprise.
Duty and Faith no tye on me can have,
Since I renounc'd those Honours which he gave.
   Max. The time is come we did so long attend,   *To* Berenice.
Which muſt these discords of our Marriage end.
Yet *Berenice* remember you have been
An Empress, and the Wife of *Maximin.*
   Ber. I well remember I have been your Wife;
And therefore, dying, beg from Heav'n your life:
Be all the discords of our Bed forgot,
Which, Vertue witness, I did never spot.
What errors I have made, though while I live
You cannot pardon, to the dead forgive.
   Max. How much she is to piety inclin'd!
Behead her while she's in so good a mind.
   Por. Stand firm, *Albinus,* now the time is come
To free the Empress.
   Alb. ——And deliver *Rome.*
   Por. Within I feel my hot blood swell my heart,
And generous tremblings in each outward part.
'Tis done——Tyrant, this is thy lateſt hour.
   Porphyrius *and* Albinus *draw, and are making at the Emperour.*

Ber. Look to your self, my Lord the Emperour:
Treason, help, help, my Lord!

Maximin turns and defends himself, the Guards set on Porphyrius
and Albinus.

Max. Disarm 'em, but their lives I charge you spare.

After they are disarm'd.

Unmask 'em, and discover who they are.
Good Gods, is it *Porphyrius* whom I see!

Placid. I wonder how he gain'd his liberty.

Max. Traytor!

Por. ———Know, Tyrant, I can hear that name,
Rather than Son, and bear it with less shame.
Traytor's a name which were my arm yet free,
The *Roman* Senate would bestow on thee.

To Ber. Ah, Madam, you have ruin'd my design,
And lost your life; for I regard not mine.
Too ill a Mistress, and too good a Wife.

Ber. It was my duty to preserve his life.

Max. Now I perceive.   *To* Porphyrius.
In what close walks your mind so long did move:
You scorn'd my Throne, aspiring to her Love.

Ber. In Death I'le owne a Love to him so pure;
As will the test of Heav'n it self endure.
A Love so chast, as Conscience could not chide;
But cherisht it, and kept it by its side.
A Love which never knew a hot desire,
But flam'd as harmless as a lambent fire.
A Love which pure from Soul to Soul might pass,
As Light transmitted through a Crystal glass.
Which gave *Porphyrius* all without a sin;
Yet kept entire the Right of *Maximin.*

Max. The best return that I to both can make,
Shall be to suffer for each others sake.

Por. Barbarian, do not dare her blood to shed,
Who from my vengeance sav'd thy cursed head.
A flight no Honour ever reach'd before;
And which succeeding Ages will adore.

Ber. Porphyrius I must dye!
That common debt to Nature paid must be;
But I have left a debt unpaid to thee.
To *Maximin*———
I have perform'd the duty of a Wife;
But, saving his, I cast away thy life.

Ah, what ill Stars upon our Loves did shine,
That I am more thy Murd'rer than he mine.
   Max. Make haste.
   Por. So hasty none in execution are,
But they allow the dying time for pray'r.
Farewel, sweet Saint, my pray'r shall be to you:
My Love has been unhappy, but 'twas true.
Remember me! Alas What have I sed?
You must dye too!
But yet remember me when you are dead.
   Ber. If I dye first I will——
Stop short of Heav'n, and wait you in a Cloud;
For fear we lose each other in the crowd.
   Por. Love is the only Coyn in Heav'n will go.
Then take all with you, and leave none below.
   Ber. 'Tis want of knowledge, not of Love, I fear,
Lest we mistake when bodies are not there,
O as a mark that I could wear a Scroul,
With this Inscription, *Berenice's* Soul.
   Por. That needs not, sure, for none will be so bright,
So pure, or with so small allays of light.
   Max. From my full eyes fond tears begin to start;
Dispatch, they practise treason on my Heart.

                 Porphyrius *kisses his hand, and blows it to* Berenice *saying*
   Por. Adieu: this farewel sigh I as my last bequeath,
Catch it, 'tis Love expiring in a breath.

                     Berenice *kissing hers in the same manner.*
   Ber. This sigh of mine shall meet it half the way,
As pledges giv'n that each for other stay.

      Enter Valeria *and* Cydon *her Woman.*

   Val. What dismal Scene of Death is here prepar'd!
   Max. Now strike.
   Val. They shall not strike till I am heard.
   Max. From whence does this new impudence proceed,
That you dare alter that which I decreed?
   Val. Ah, Sir, to what strange courses do you fly,
To make your self abhorr'd for cruelty!
The Empire groans under your bloody Reign,
And its vast body bleeds in every vein.
Gasping and pale, and fearing more, it lyes;
And now you stab it in the very eyes:

Your *Cæsar* and the Partner of your Bed;
Ah who can wish to live when they are dead?
If ever gentle pity touch'd your breſt————
————I cannot speak—my tears shall speak the reſt.
Weeping and sobbing.

Por. She adds new grief to what I felt before,
And Fate has now no room to put in more.
Max. Away, thou shame and slander of my Blood.   *To* Val.
Who taught thee to be pitiful or good?
Val. What hope have I
The name of Vertue should prevail with him,
Who thinks ev'n it, for which I plead, a crime?
Yet Nature, sure, some Argument may be;
If them you cannot pity, pity me.
Max. I will, and all the World shall judge it so:
I will th' excess of pity to you show.
You ask to save
A dangerous Rebel, and disloyal Wife;
And I in mercy—will not take your life.
Val. You more than kill me by this cruelty,
And in their persons bid your Daughter dye.
I honour *Berenice's* Vertue much;
But for *Porphyrius* my Love is such,
I cannot, will not live when he is gone.
Max. I'le do that Cure for you which on my self is done.
You muſt, like me, your Lovers life remove;
Cut off your hope, and you deſtroy your Love.
If it were hard I would not bid you try
The Med'cine: but 'tis but to let him dye.
Yet since you are so soft, (which you call good)
And are not yet confirm'd enough in blood,
To see his death;
Your frailty shall be favour'd with this grace,
That they shall suffer in another place.
If after they are dead, their memory,
By any chance into your mind be brought,
Laugh, and divert it with some other thought.
Away with 'em.
          Exeunt Berenice, Porphyrius, Albinus, *carried off*
               by Guards.
Val. Since pray'rs nor tears can bend his cruel mind,
                    [*Looking after* Porphy.]
Farewel, the beſt and braveſt of Mankind;
390

How I have lov'd Heav'n knows; but there's a Fate,
Which hinders me from being fortunate.
My Father's Crimes hang heavy on my head,
And like a gloomy Cloud about me spread;
I would in vain be pious, that's a grace
Which Heav'n permits not to a Tyrant's race.

   Max. Hence to her Tent the foolish Girl convey.

   Val. Let me be juſt before I go away:
Placidius, I have vow'd to be your Wife;
Take then my hand, 'tis yours while I have life.
One moment here, I muſt anothers be:
But this, *Porphyrius*, gives me back to thee.

     Stabs her self twice, and then Placidius *wreſts the Dagger from her.*

   Placid. Help, help the Princess, help!

   Max. What rage has urg'd this act which thou haſt done?

   Val. Thou, Tyrant, and thy Crimes, have pull'd it on.
Thou who canſt death with such a pleasure see,
Now take thy fill, and glut thy sight in me.
But————I'le the occasion of my death forget;
Save him I love, and be my Father yet:
I can no more————*Porphyrius*, my dear————

   Cyd. Alas, she raves, and thinks *Porphyrius* here.

   Val. Have I not yet deserv'd thee now I dye?
Is *Berenice* ſtill more fair than I?
Porphyrius, do not swim before my sight;
Stand ſtill, and let me, let me aim aright.
Stand ſtill but while thy poor *Valeria* dyes,
And sighs her Soul into her Lovers Eyes.   *Dyes.*

   Placid. She's gone from Earth, and with her went away
All of the Tyrant that deserv'd to ſtay:
I've loſt in her all joys that life can give;
And only to revenge her death would live————   *Aside.*

   Cyd. The Gods have claim'd her, and we muſt resign.

   Max. What had the Gods to do with me or mine?
Did I moleſt your Heav'n?————
Why should you then make *Maximin* your Foe,
Who paid you Tribute, which he need not do?
Your Altars I with smoak of Gums did crown:
For which you lean'd your hungry noſtrils down.
All daily gaping for my Incense there,
More than your Sun could draw you in a year.
And you for this these Plagues on me have sent;
But by the Gods (by *Maximin* I meant)

Henceforth I and my World
Hostility with you and yours declare:
Look to it, Gods; for you th' Aggressors are.
Keep you your Rain and Sun-shine in your Skies,
And I'le keep back my flame and Sacrifice.
Your Trade of Heav'n shall soon be at a stand,
And all your Goods lie dead upon your hand.

    Placid. Thus, Tyrant, since the Gods th' Aggressors are,

                             [*Stabbing him.*

Thus by this stroke they have begun the War.

           Maximin *struggles with him, and gets the Dagger from him.*

    Max. Thus I return the strokes which they have given;

                           [*Stabbing* Placid.

Thus, Traytor, thus, and thus I would to Heav'n.

    Stabbing upward with his Dagger. Placidius *falls, and the Emperour*
        staggers after him, and sits down upon him; the Guards come
        to help the Emperour.

    Max. Stand off, and let me, e're my strength be gone,
Take my last pleasure of revenge alone.

                Enter a Centurion.

    Cen. Arm, arm, the Camp is in a mutiny:
For *Rome* and Liberty the Souldiers cry.
Porphyrius mov'd their pity as he went,
To rescue *Berenice* from punishment,
And now he heads their new attempted crime.

    Max. Now I am down, the Gods have watch'd their time.
You think————
To save your credit, feeble Deities;
But I will give my self the strength to Rise.

              He strives to get up, and being up, staggers

It wonnot be————   •
My body has not strength my mind to bear.
I must return again—and conquer here.   *Sits down upon the Body.*
My coward Body does my will controul;
Farwel thou base deserter of my Soul.
I'le shake this Carcass off, and be obey'd;
Reign an Imperial Ghost without its aid.
Go, Souldiers, take my Ensigns with you, fight,
And vanquish Rebels in your Soveraign's right:
Before I die————
Bring me *Porphyrius* and my Empress dead,
I would brave Heav'n, in my each hand a head.

Placid. Do not regard a dying Tyrants breath,   [*To the Souldiers.*
He can but look revenge on you in death.
   Max. Vanquish'd, and dar'ſt thou yet a Rebel be?
Thus—I can more than look revenge on thee.   [*Stabs him again.*
   Placid. Oh, I am gone!   *Dyes.*
   Max.   ——And after thee I go,
Revenging ſtill, and following ev'n to th' other world my blow.
                                 Stabs him again.
And shoving back this Earth on which I sit,
I'le mount—and scatter all the Gods I hit.   *Dyes.*

Enter Porphyrius, Berenice, Albinus, *Souldiers.* Porphyrius
      looks on the Bodies entring, and speaks.

   Por. 'Tis done before, (this mighty work of Fate!)
And I am glad your Swords are come too late.
He was my Prince, and though a bloody one,
I should have conquer'd, and have mercy shown.
Sheath all your Swords, and cease your enmity;
They are not Foes, but *Romans* whom you see.
   Ber. He was my Tyrant, but my Husband too;
And therefore duty will some tears allow.
   Por. Placidius here!
And fair *Valeria*, new depriv'd of breath?
Who can unriddle this dumb-show of death?
   Cyd. When, Sir, her Father did your life deny,
She kill'd her self, that she with you might dye.
Placidius made the Emp'rours death his crime;
Who, dying, did revenge his death on him.
                Porphyrius *kneels, and takes* Valeria's *hand.*
   Por. For thy dear sake I vow each week I live,
One day to faſting and juſt grief I'le give:
And what hard Fate did to thy life deny,
My gratitude shall pay thy memory.
   Cent. Mean time to you belongs the Imperial pow'r:
We with one voice salute you Emperour.
   Souldiers. Long live *Porphyrius* Emperour of the *Romans.*
   Por. Too much, my Country-men, your Love you show,
That you have thought me worthy to be so.
But, to requite that Love, I muſt take Care,
Not to engage you in a Civil War.
Two Emperours at *Rome* the Senate chose,
And whom they chuse no *Roman* should oppose.

In Peace or War, let Monarchs hope or fear;
All my ambition shall be bounded here.   *Kissing* Berenice's *hand*.
    Ber. I have too lately been a Prince's Wife,
And fear th'unlucky Omen of the life.
Like a rich Vessel beat by storms to shore,
'Twere madness should I venture out once more.
Of glorious troubles I will take no part,
And in no Empire reign, but of your heart.
    Por. Let to the winds your golden Eagles flye,   [*To the Souldiers.*
Your Trumpets sound a bloodless Victory:
Our Arms no more let *Aquileia* fear,
But to her Gates
Our peaceful Ensigns crown'd with Olives bear:
While I mix Cypress with my Myrtle Wreath:
Joy for your life, and mourn *Valeria's* Death.   *Exeunt omnes.*

EPILOGUE.

Spoken by Mrs. *Ellen*, when she was to be carried off
dead by the Bearers.

To the   *H*Old, are you mad? you damn'd confounded Dog,
Bearer.   *I am to rise and speak the Epilogue.*
To the Audience. *I come, kind Gentlemen, strange news to tell ye,*
I am the Ghost of poor departed Nelly.
Sweet Ladies, be not frighted, I'le be civil,
I'm what I was, a little harmless Devil.
For after Death, we Sprights have just such Natures,
We had for all the World, when humane Creatures;
And therefore I that was an Actress here,
Play all my Tricks in Hell, a Goblin there.
Gallant's look to't, you say there are no Sprights;
But I'le come dance about your Beds at nights.
And 'faith you'l be in a sweet kind of taking,
When I surprise you between sleep and waking.
To tell you true, I walk because I dye
Out of my Calling in a Tragedy.
O Poet! damn'd dull Poet, who could prove
So sensless! to make Nelly *dye for Love,*
Nay, what's yet worse, to kill me in the prime
Of Easter-Term, *in Tart and Cheese-cake time!*
I'le fit the Fopp; for I'le not one word say
T' excuse his godly out of fashion Play.
A Play which if you dare but twice sit out,
You'l all be slander'd, and be thought devout.
But, farewel Gentlemen, make haste to me,
I'm sure e're long to have your company.
As for my Epitaph, when I am gone,
I'le trust no Poet, but will write my own.

Here *Nelly* lies, who, though she liv'd a Slater'n,
Yet dy'd a Princess acting in S. *Cathar'n.*

FINIS.

TEXTUAL NOTES

SECRET-LOVE

Secret-Love, 4to 1, 1668. 4tos 1669, 1679, 1691, 1698. The British Museum copy of 4to 1 has a cancelled leaf, pp. 7 and 8. This presents some few variations which have been duly noted in order below. Of the Editio Princeps thus there are four diftinct varieties, some copies have the note of Errata on p. xii; some are without this note; some have a cancelled leaf pp. 7 and 8; some are without the cancelled leaf.

p. 7, l. 25. *competent judg.* 1669 and later, judge.
p. 7, l. 27. *judgment.* 1669, 1679, judgement.
p. 7, l. 32. *Surveigher.* 1669 and later, Surveyer.
p. 8, l. 14. *Judg.* 1669 and later, Judge.
p. 9, l. 12. *divertising.* Folio 1701, diverting.
p. 9, l. 15. *beft Judg.* So 1668, 1669. 1679, Judge.
p. 9, l. 15. *onely.* 1679 and later, only.
p. 11, l. 28. *Brother Judgment.* 1669, 1679, *Brother Judgement.* Folio 1701, wrongly, *Brother's Judgment.*
p. 11, l. 32. *he'll.* 1669, 1679, he'l.
p. 11, l. 41. *Tick.* 1669, 1679, *tick.*
p. 12, l. 3. *Mrs. Quin.* 1679, 1691, 1698, Mrs. Queen.
p. 12, l. 15. *Sicily.* Firft 4to, 1668 gives at the foot of page xii a lift of ten Errata, all of which have been severally corrected in this edition. Mr. Wise, *A Dryden Library*, notes: "Some copies, doubtless those earlieft ftruck off, are without the four lines of Errata."
p. 14, l. 12. *prey.* Folio 1701 misprints, pray.
p. 15, l. 11. *unconftant.* Folio 1701, Inconftant.
p. 17, l. 9. *Country.* 1669, Countrey.
p. 17, l. 21. *Phil. Had I known.* 1668, 1669, 1679 and later, "to look you (*Phil.*) had I known." An awkward arrangement.
p. 17, l. 30. *business.* 1668, busines.
p. 18, l. 10. *sould.* 1669, 1679, 1691, Folio 1701, sold. 1698, Sould.
p. 18, l. 13. *termes.* 1668, cancelled leaf, terms.
p. 18, l. 19. *Our free Sicilians.* 1668, Our *Sicilins.* But cancelled leaf as text.
p. 18, l. 27. *by joining.* 1668 cancelled leaf, joyning.
p. 18, l. 38. *Soul.* 1668 cancelled leaf, soul.
p. 18, l. 38. *shakes them off.* 1668 cancelled leaf, ftraight shakes off. 1669 and later, ftrait shakes off.
p. 18, l. 39. *And ftraight composes.* 1668 cancelled leaf, 1669 and later, And is compos'd again.
p. 18, l. 41. *Mirour.* 1669, Miror. 1679, Miroir. Folio 1701 has an extraordinary misprint, Miter.

p. 19, l. 5.   *you assume.* 1668 cancelled leaf, 1669 and later, thus to press.
p. 19, l. 11. *and dangers.* 1669 and later substitute, to you.
p. 19, l. 18. *Lys. If they.* 1668 cancelled leaf, *Lysim.* If they . . .
p. 19, l. 21. *Bloud.* 1668 cancelled leaf, Bloud.
p. 19, l. 22. *By all the Gods.* Only 1668. All later editions omit.
p. 19, l. 32. *aspiring man,*
                 Compass his ends. 1668 cancelled leaf joins as one line.
p. 19, l. 36. *than Love.* 1668 cancelled leaf, then Love.
p. 20, l. 11. *I'le.* 1669, 1679, I'l. 1691, 1698, I'll.
p. 20, l. 33. *me lose.* 1668, me loose.
p. 20, l. 37. *usage I have found.* All editions save 4to 1 omit "I have found."
                 1669, 1679, 1698, usuage.
p. 22, l. 11. *y'are.* 1668 misprints again, "You are" to commence next line.
p. 22, l. 25. *insensibly.* Only 4to 1. All later, each day and hour.
p. 24, l. 20. *appartments.* 1669, 1679, *Apartment.*
p. 25, l. 15. *'faith.* 1669, y'faith. 1679, i'faith.
p. 25, l. 20. *goes to kiss her.* 4to 1, 1668, gives this as part of Celadon's
                 speech, but it is obviously a stage-direction.
p. 26, l. 20. *neck, or poyson.* 1669, neck, poison. 1698, neck, and poyson.
p. 27, l. 12. *add more.* All quartos save the first omit "more."
p. 28, l. 17. *look on.* 4to 1 misprints, "look from."
p. 28, l. 42. *murmur.* 4to 1, murmure.
p. 32, l. 16. *from me.* "Me" has dropped out of 4to 1.
p. 33, l. 8.   *you judg.* 4to 2, 1669 and later, "our judge."
p. 33, l. 32. *I said.* 4to. 1, 1668: I sed.
p. 33, l. 33. *Shoulders.* 1669 misprints, Sholders.
p. 37, l. 4.   *Sweets away.* 1668 misprints, Sweats.
p. 37, l. 8.   *takes more joyes.* 1668 misprints, takes mores joyes.
p. 39, l. 6.   *truss'd.* 1668 misprints, truss'ed.
p. 39, l. 7.   *Enter Florimel.* 1668, Florimell.
p. 40, l. 5.   *noise of Fiddles.* 1668 and subsequent editions, Fidlers.
p. 41, l. 17. *why then.* 1679 and later, when then.
p. 42, l. 7.   *invite me.* 1668, invites.
p. 45, l. 40. *if I wrote.* 1668, write.
p. 48, l. 17. *Page. The noise.* 1668, 1669, 1679, 1691, 1698, *Page* 1. But
                 only one page accompanies Flavia.
p. 49, l. 21. *secure.* 1668, secur'd.
p. 49, l. 29. *They Sign.* All editions, *They Sing,* which is surely a misprint.
p. 50, l. 40. *you lately heard her.* Folio 1701 omits this, and the next line.
p. 51, l. 32. *from the Annals.* 1668 misprints, from Annals.
p. 56, l. 28. *Monsieur Florimell.* The 4tos vary between Florimel and
                 Florimell here and in many passages.
p. 58, l. 32. *unconstant.* Folio 1701, Inconstant.
p. 59, l. 8.   *plucks off her Ruff.* 1668, *plucks of.*
p. 59, l. 20. *Perrucke.* This is the reading of 1668.
p. 60, l. 20. *Where're.* 1668, Wheree're. 1691, Where'er. 1679 and folio
                 1701, VVhere'er. 1698, Where'ere.

400

p. 60, l. 20. *wandring.* 1669, wondring.
p. 61, l. 13. *recall'd.* 1669, recal'd.
p. 65, l. 26. *is all well.* 1669 misprints, is al! well.
p. 68, l. 43. *make it easie.* 1669 misprints, mak.

SIR MARTIN MARR-ALL

1691 has: Sir Martin Marr-all:/Or, The/Feign'd Innocence./———/. 1697 has: Sr Martin Marr-All:/Or, The/Feign'd Innocence/. Folio 1701 has Sir Martin Mar-all,/ Or, The/Feign'd Innocence./———/.

Mr. T. J. Wise in his *A Dryden Library*, 1930, pp. 14–15, points out that in 1668 "there were two distinct editions and not merely two 'issues' of the Comedy." "The setting differs throughout. In the First Quarto the Prologue and Epilogue are upon one leaf, recto and verso, p. i and p. ii following the Text of the Comedy pp. 1–70." I have ventured to place the Prologue and Epilogue together at the commencement of the play.

In the Second Quarto, 1668, which has been continually mistaken for the first edition, the Prologue is on p. iii; the text of the Comedy follows pp. 1–70, and this is followed by a leaf with the Epilogue on the recto, verso blank.

In the First Quarto between H4 and I1 an unsigned leaf, paged 57–58, carries the Song *Blind Love.* I1 continuing the numeration from H4 is also paged 57–58.

Upon the title-page of 4to 1 above the imprint is an ornamental rectangular block. On the title-page of 4to 2 this is replaced by a group of sixteen small printer's ornaments.

The title-page of 4to 1 in Mr. Wise's library reads "Feignd Innocence:" the title-page of 4to, Bodley shelf-mark 4° O.29 Art. (6), reads "Feign'd Innocence:". In the First Edition p. 70 concludes with "Finis." In the Second Edition this is deleted and replaced with the catch-word *Epilogue.*

In his *John Dryden Bibliographical Memoranda* (1922), p. 7, Mr. Percy Dobell has the following note upon the text of *Sr Martin Mar-all:* "Some alterations were evidently made while the play was passing through the press. The original leaves [of 4to 1668] C1, C2, and H4 were cancelled, and it may possibly have had two or three more leaves at the end than are at present known. I have a copy with the original leaf C2 (pp. 11–12), containing a page of conversation between Moody and Sir John Swallow, which does not appear in the play as known, and which shows that originally Moody appeared on the stage before the conclusion of the first act." As we now have the script Moody does not enter until early in Act III.

p. 83, l. 9. *Fopps.* 1691, 1697, and folio, Fops.
p. 83, l. 12. *plotting.* Folio, Plotting.
p. 83, l. 15. *Marral.* 1691, 1697, and folio, Marr-all.
p. 83, l. 26. *mans.* 1691, 1697, and folio, Man's.

p. 83, l. 31.   *Durham-yard.* Folio, *Durham-Yard.*
p. 84, l. 3.   *minute's.* Folio, Minute's.
p. 84, l. 6.   [*Exit Warner.* 1691, 1697, [*Ex.* Warner. Folio [*Exit* Warner.
p. 84, l. 8.   *plotting.* Folio, Plotting.
p. 84, l. 13.   *speech and in behaviour.* 1691, 1697, and folio, Speech and in Behaviour.
p. 84, l. 19.   *Neice.* 1691, 1697, and folio, Niece.
p. 84, l. 21.   *I'le.* 1678, I'l. 1691, 1697, and folio, I'll.
p. 84, l. 29.   *married.* 1678 and folio, Marry'd. 1691, 1697, marry'd.
p. 84, l. 30.   *ground.* 1691, 1697, and folio, Ground.
p. 84, l. 41.   *hee'l.* 1691, 1697, and folio, he'll.
p. 84, l. 42.   *kiss.* 1691, 1697, and folio, Kiss.
p. 85, l. 2.   *innocent.* 1691, 1697, and folio, Innocent.
p. 85, l. 3.   *I'le.* 1691, 1697, and folio, I'll.
p. 85, l. 5.   *night.* 1691, 1697, and folio, Night.
p. 85, l. 9.   *head.* 1691, 1697, and folio, Head.
p. 85, l. 10.   *extreamly.* folio, extremely.
p. 85, l. 11.   *night-visits.* 1691, 1697, and folio, Night-Visits.
p. 85, l. 12.   *I'le.* 1678, I'l. 1691, 1697, and folio, I'll.
p. 85, l. 12.   *where's.* 1691, 1697, and folio, Where's.
p. 85, l. 13.   *I'le.* 1678, I'l. 1691, 1697, and folio, I'll.
p. 85, l. 14.   *agen.* Folio, again.
p. 85, l. 16.   *I'le.* 1678, I'l. 1691, 1697, and folio, I'll.
p. 85, l. 17.   *Small-pox.* Folio, Small-Pox.
p. 85, l. 18.   *Poor.* 1691, 1697, and folio, poor.
p. 85, l. 19.   *ears.* 1691, 1697, and folio, Ears.
p. 85, l. 21.   *askes.* 1678, 1697, and folio, asks.
p. 85, l. 24.   *Meal.* Folio, Meals.
p. 85, l. 25.   *passion.* 1691, 1697, and folio, Passion.
p. 85, l. 29.   *ſtrait.* 1691, 1697, and folio, ſtraight.
p. 85, l. 31.   *night.* 1691, 1697, and folio, Night.
p. 85, l. 31.   *person.* 1691, 1697, and folio, Person.
p. 85, l. 37.   *joy.* 1691, 1697, and folio, Joy.
p. 85, l. 38.   *innocence.* 1691, 1697, and folio, Innocence.
p. 85, l. 39.   *skin.* 1691, 1697, and folio, Skin.
p. 85, l. 40.   *sublety.* 1691, 1697, and folio, Subtilty.
p. 85, l. 41.   *treaties.* 1691, 1697, and folio, Treaties.
p. 85, l. 41.   *advantage.* 1691, 1697, and folio, Advantage.
p. 85, l. 42.   *passion.* 1691, 1697, and folio, Passion.
p. 85, l. 42.   *rate.* 1691, 1697, and folio, Rate.
p. 85, l. 43.   *price.* 1691, 1697, and folio, Price.
p. 86, l. 2.   *endeavours.* 1691, 1697, and folio, Endeavours.
p. 86, l. 3.   *blessing.* 1691, 1697, and folio, Blessing.
p. 86, l. 3.   *pray'rs.* 1691, 1697, and folio, Prayers.
p. 86, l. 7.   *Howe're.* 1697, How e'er. Folio, Howe'er.
p. 86, l. 11.   *Mill. My Father.* Folio, *Mil.* My Father.
p. 86, l. 17.   *agen.* Folio, again.

p. 86, l. 28.   [*In whisper.* 1691, 1697, and folio, [*Whispers* (bis).
p. 86, l. 29.   *Mill. Sir John.* Although all editions give this speech to Lady Dupe, I have ventured to alter the speech-prefix as it is obviously Mrs. Millisent who speaks.
p. 86, l. 33.   *Marral.* 1691, 1697, and folio, *Marr-all.*
p. 86, l. 37.   *man.* 1691, 1697, and folio, Man.
p. 86, l. 38.   *luck.* 1691, 1697, and folio, Luck.
p. 86, l. 38.   *gaming.* 1691, 1697, and folio, Gaming.
p. 87, l. 2.   *one of up.* Folio, one up.
p. 87, l. 3.   *play is loſt.* 1691, 1697, and folio, Play is loſt.
p. 87, l. 8.   *play.* 1691, 1697, and folio, Play.
p. 87, l. 10.   *thoughts.* 1691, 1697, and folio, Thoughts.
p. 87, l. 11.   *love.* 1691, 1697, and folio, Love.
p. 87, l. 20.   *service.* 1691, 1697, and folio, Service.
p. 87, l. 21.   *favour.* 1691, 1697, and folio, Favour.
p. 87, l. 27.   *concernments.* 1691, 1697, and folio, Concernments.
p. 87, l. 29.   *Fortune once.* 1691, 1697, and folio, Fortune, once.
p. 87, l. 30.   *man.* 1691, 1697, and folio, Man.
p. 87, l. 32.   *friend.* 1691, 1697, and folio, Friend.
p. 87, l. 34.   *Prethee.* 1691, 1697, and folio, Prithee.
p. 87, l. 35.   *fair.* 1691, 1697, and folio, Fair.
p. 87, l. 38.   *name's.* 1691, 1697, and folio, Name's.
p. 87, l. 41.   *well.* 1691, 1697, and folio, Well.
p. 88, l. 3.   *You'l.* 1691, 1697, and folio, You'll.
p. 88, l. 4.   *hearts.* 1691, 1697, and folio, Hearts.
p. 88, l. 4.   *souls.* 1691, 1697, and folio, Souls.
p. 88, l. 6.   *breaſt.* Folio, Breaſt.
p. 88, l. 10.   *tutor.* Folio, Tutor.
p. 88, ll. 12–13.   *both then and often since coming.* 1697 and folio, both then, and often since, coming.
p. 88, l. 27.   *man.* 1691, 1697, and folio, Man.
p. 88, l. 32.   *Heaven sake.* 1678, 1697, and folio, Heavens sake.
p. 88, l. 34.   *ont.* 1691, 1697, and folio, on't.
p. 88, l. 40.   *I'le.* 1691, 1697, and folio, I'll.
p. 88, l. 43.   *patience.* 1691, 1697, and folio, Patience.
p. 89, l. 5.   *name.* 1691, 1697, and folio, Name.
p. 89, l. 7.   *acquaintance.* 1691, 1697, and folio, Acquaintance.
p. 89, l. 8.   *man.* 1691, 1697, and folio, Man.
p. 89, l. 9.   *wise.* Folio, Wise.
p. 89, l. 10.   *marry.* Folio, Marry.
p. 89, l. 12.   *jeſt.* 1691, 1697, and folio, Jeſt.
p. 89, l. 14.   *I'le.* 1691, 1697, and folio, I'll.
p. 89, l. 15.   *mun.* 1691, 1697, and folio, Mun.
p. 89, l. 16.   *I'le.* 1697 and folio, I'll.
p. 89, l. 17.   *affeĉtions.* 1691, 1697, and folio, Affeĉtions.
p. 89, l. 19.   *I'le.* 1691, 1697, and folio, I'll.
p. 89, l. 25.   *wit.* 1691, 1697, and folio, Wit.

p. 89, l. 25. *ner'e.* 1678, ne're. 1691, 1697, and folio ne'er.
p. 89, l. 35. *ignorance.* 1691, 1697, and folio, Ignorance.
p. 89, l. 36. *water-side.* Folio, Water-side.
p. 89, l. 36. *lodging.* 1691, 1697, and folio, Lodging.
p. 90, l. 2. *despair.* 1691, 1697, and folio, Despair.
p. 90, l. 3. *death.* 1691, 1697, and folio, Death.
p. 90, l. 4. *Bug-word.* Folio, Bug-bear-word. But 12mo, Tonson, 1735, "Bug-word."
p. 90, l. 9. *man.* 1691, 1697, and folio, Man.
p. 90, l. 9. *your man.* 1691, 1697, and folio, your Man.
p. 90, l. 24. *joyn'd.* 1691, 1697, and folio, join'd.
p. 90, l. 25. *rattled.* 1691 and folio, ratled.
p. 90, l. 35. *money.* 1691, 1697, and folio, Money.
p. 90, l. 35. *wit.* 1691, 1697, and folio, Wit.
p. 91, l. 4. *sickness.* 1691, 1697, and folio, Sickness.
p. 91, l. 9. *diſtill.* 1691, 1678, 1697, and folio, diſtil.
p. 91, l. 19. *mercy.* 1691, 1697, and folio, Mercy.
p. 91, l. 20. *usage.* 1691, 1697, and folio, Usage.
p. 91, l. 20. *fit.* 1691, 1697, and folio, Fit.
p. 91, l. 21. *back.* 1691, 1697, and folio, Back.
p. 91, l. 23. *attempt.* 1691, 1697, and folio, Attempt.
p. 91, l. 24. *fault.* 1691, 1697, and folio, Fault.
p. 91, l. 28. *goodness.* 1691, 1697, and folio, Goodness.
p. 91, l. 32. *mine Aunt.* 1691, 1697, and folio, my Aunt. 1668 misprints, mine Aunt an angry with you.
p. 91, l. 33. *earthly.* 1691, 1697, and folio, Earthly.
p. 91, l. 34. *I'le.* 1691, 1697, and folio, I'll.
p. 91, l. 34. *agen.* 1691, 1697, and folio, again.
p. 91, l. 36. *love.* 1691, 1697, and folio, Love.
p. 91, l. 38. *sin.* 1691, 1697, and folio, Sin.
p. 92, l. 2. *business.* 1691, 1697, and folio, Business.
p. 92, l. 2. *life.* 1691, 1697, and folio, Life.
p. 92, l. 3. *care.* 1691, 1697, and folio, Care.
p. 92, l. 3. *ſtudy.* 1691, 1697, and folio, Study.
p. 92, l. 6. *sacrifice.* 1691, 1697, and folio, Sacrifice.
p. 92, l. 10. *hand glov'd.* 1691, 1697, and folio, *Hand-glov'd.*
p. 92, l. 12. *fye.* 1691, 1697, and folio, fie.
p. 92, l. 12. *faith.* 1691, 1697, and folio, Faith.
p. 92, l. 13. *hand.* 1691, 1697, and folio, *Hand.*
p. 92, l. 15. *e're.* 1691, 1697, and folio, e'er.
p. 92, l. 15. *glove.* 1691, 1697, and folio, *Glove.*
p. 92, l. 18. *Laws.* Folio, Law.
p. 92, l. 22. *hugging.* 1691, 1697, and folio, Hugging.
p. 92, l. 22. *hand.* 1691, 1697, and folio, Hand.
p. 92, l. 23. *ne're.* 1691, 1697, and folio, ne'er.
p. 92, l. 26. *breath.* 1691, 1697, and folio, Breath.
p. 92, l. 28. *imploy'd.* 1691, 1697, and folio, employ'd.

p.	92, l. 29.	*Ne're ſtir.* 1678, Ne'r ſtir. 1691, 1697, and folio, Ne'er ſtir.
p.	92, l. 30.	*mouth.* 1691, 1697, and folio, Mouth.
p.	92, l. 33.	*Neece.* 1691, 1697, and folio, Niece (bis).
p.	92, l. 40.	*your Neece.* 1691, 1697, and folio, your Niece.
p.	92, l. 42.	*[Ex. Lord.* Folio, [*Exit* Lord.
p.	93, l. 8.	*love.* 1691, 1697, and folio, Love.
p.	93, l. 12.	*report.* 1691, 1697, and folio, Report.
p.	93, l. 15.	*Hence-forward.* Folio, Hence forward.
p.	93, l. 18.	*woman.* 1691, 1697, and folio, Woman.
p.	93, l. 19.	*messages.* 1691, 1697, and folio, Messages.
p.	93, l. 19.	*that is it.* Folio, that's it.
p.	93, l. 20.	*Extacies.* 1691, 1697, and folio, Ecſtasies.
p.	93, l. 22.	*advantages.* 1691, 1697, and folio, Advantages.
p.	93, l. 23.	*house.* 1691, 1697, and folio, House.
p.	93, l. 26.	*meeting.* 1691, 1697, and folio, Meeting.
p.	93, l. 26.	*I'le.* 1691, 1697, and folio, I'll.
p.	93, l. 27.	*hee'l.* 1691, 1697, and folio, he'll.
p.	93, l. 28.	*luſt.* 1691, 1697, and folio, Luſt.
p.	93, l. 31.	*does.* 1691, 1697, and folio, Does.
p.	93, l. 33.	*pleasure.* 1691, 1697, and folio, Pleasure.
p.	93, l. 37.	*I'le.* 1691, 1697, and folio, I'll.
p.	93, l. 39.	*Hee'l.* 1691, 1697, and folio, He'll.
p.	94, l. 1.	*minutes.* 1691, 1697, and folio, Minutes.
p.	94, l. 2.	*happiness.* 1691, 1697, and folio, Happiness.
p.	94, l. 4.	*house.* 1691, 1697, and folio, House.
p.	94, l. 9.	*men.* 1691, 1697, and folio, Men.
p.	94, l. 10.	*can.* 1691, 1697, and folio, Can.
p.	94, l. 10.	*affeƈtion.* 1691, 1697, and folio, Affeƈtion.
p.	94, l. 15.	*I'le.* 1691, 1697, and folio, I'll.
p.	94, l. 17.	*wit.* 1691, 1697, and folio, Wit.
p.	94, l. 17.	*choice.* 1691, 1697, and folio, Choice.
p.	94, l. 18.	*juſtice.* 1691, 1697, and folio, Juſtice.
p.	94, l. 19.	*service.* 1691, 1697, and folio, Service.
p.	94, l. 22.	*fault.* 1691, 1697, and folio, Fault.
p.	94, l. 24.	*pardon.* 1691, 1697, and folio, Pardon.
p.	94, l. 24.	*absence.* 1691, 1697, and folio, Absence.
p.	94, l. 27.	*ere.* 1678, 1691, 1697, and folio, e'er.
p.	94, l. 33.	*wit.* 1691, 1697, and folio, Wit.
p.	94, l. 36.	*business.* 1691, 1697, and folio, Business.
p.	94, l. 38.	*face.* 1691, 1697, and folio, Face.
p.	94, l. 40.	*Sir John or my old.* 1691, 1697, and folio, Sir *John*, or my old.
p.	95, l. 3.	*'um.* 1678, 1691, 1697, and folio, 'em.
p.	95, l. 5.	*what.* 1691, 1697, and folio, What.
p.	95, l. 10.	*anger.* 1691, 1697, and folio, Anger.
p.	95, l. 14.	*persons.* 1691, 1697, and folio, Persons.
p.	95, l. 21.	*mercy.* 1691, 1697, and folio, Mercy.

p. 95, l. 29.   *Ungrateful.* 1691, 1697, and folio, ungrateful.
p. 95, l. 32.   *thoughts.* 1691, 1697, and folio, Thoughts.
p. 95, l. 37.   *you'l.* 1691, 1697, and folio, you'll.
p. 95, l. 38.   *tongue.* 1691, 1697, and folio, Tongue.
p. 96, l. 2.   *Door.* 1691, 1697, and folio, *door.*
p. 96, l. 5.   *man.* 1691, 1697, and folio, Man.
p. 96, l. 14.   *word.* 1691, 1697, and folio, Word.
p. 96, l. 21.   *at the Door.* Folio, *at door.*
p. 96, l. 27.   *Warn. Oh, for a gentle.* 1691, 1697, and folio, *Warn. at the door.* Oh, for a gentle.
p. 96, l. 30.   *promise.* 1691, 1697, and folio, Promise.
p. 96, l. 31.   *appointment.* 1691, 1697, and folio, Appointment.
p. 96, l. 32.   *ne're.* 1678, ne'r. 1691, 1697, and folio, ne'er.
p. 96, l. 37.   *Grayes-Inn.* 1691, 1697, and folio, *Gray's*-Inn.
p. 96, l. 38.   *Warn. By this light.* 1691, 1697, and folio, *Warn. at the door.* By this Light.
p. 96, l. 38.   *change.* 1691, 1697, and folio, Change.
p. 96, l. 42.   *then.* 1691, 1697, and folio, than.
p. 97, l. 7.   *e're.* 1678, e'r. 1691, 1697, and folio, e'er.
p. 97, l. 10.   *lye.* 1691, 1697, and folio, lie.
p. 97, l. 14.   *agen.* 1691, 1697, and folio, again.
p. 97, l. 22.   *'tis.* 1691, 1697, and folio, 'Tis.
p. 97, l. 22.   *ear.* 1691, 1697, and folio, Ear.
p. 97, l. 24.   *Maſters order.* 1691, 1697, and folio, Maſter's Order.
p. 97, l. 28.   *meeting.* 1691, 1697, and folio, Meeting.
p. 97, l. 30.   *knowing.* 1691, 1697, and folio, Knowing.
p. 97, l. 32.   *to advise.* 1691, 1697, and folio, To advise.
p. 97, l. 32.   *eye.* 1691, 1697, and folio, Eye.
p. 97, l. 32.   *actions.* 1691, 1697, and folio, Actions.
p. 97, l. 33.   *news.* 1691, 1697, and folio, News.
p. 97, l. 34.   *acknowledgments.* 1691, 1697, and folio, Acknowledgments.
p. 97, l. 35.   *world.* 1691, 1697, and folio, World.
p. 97, l. 37.   *satisfi'd.* 1691, 1697, and folio, satisfied.
p. 97, l. 38.   *truth.* 1691, 1697, and folio, Truth.
p. 97, l. 38.   *friendship.* 1691, 1697, and folio, Friendship.
p. 98, l. 1.   *Landlord disguis'd.* Folio, Landlord, *disguis'd.*
p. 98, l. 2.   *what.* 1691, 1697, and folio, What.
p. 98, l. 5.   *Swallow; they told.* Folio, *Swallow:* they told.
p. 98, l. 6.   *news.* 1691, 1697, and folio, News.
p. 98, l. 6.   *house.* 1691, 1697, and folio, House.
p. 98, l. 8.   *'faith.* 1691, 1697, and folio, 'Faith.
p. 98, l. 17.   *be who.* 1691, 1697, and folio, be hoo.
p. 98, l. 20.   *Grimbard.* 1691, 1697, and folio, Grimbald. The name in the parallel scene of *L'Amant indiscret* is Grimbard.
p. 98, l. 25.   *business.* 1691, 1697, and folio, Business.
p. 98, l. 29.   *bed.* 1691, 1697, and folio, Bed.
p. 98, l. 33.   *orders.* 1691, 1697, and folio, Orders.

p. 98, l. 34.   *regret.* Folio, Regret.
p. 98, l. 36.   *occasions.* 1691, 1697, and folio, Occasions.
p. 98, l. 41.   *man.* 1691, 1697, and folio, Man.
p. 98, l. 42.   *friend.* 1691, 1697, and folio, Friend.
p. 99, l. 6.   *thoughts.* 1691, 1697, and folio, Thoughts.
p. 99, l. 8.   *[aside.* 1691, 1697, and folio, *[Aside.*
p. 99, l. 9.   *generosity.* 1691, 1697, and folio, Generosity.
p. 99, l. 10.   *favours.* 1691, 1697, and folio, Favours.
p. 99, l. 10.   *'um.* 1691, 1697, and folio, 'em.
p. 99, l. 13.   *plot.* 1691, 1697, and folio, Plot.
p. 99, l. 14.   *appointment.* 1691, 1697, and folio, Appointment.
p. 99, l. 19.   *breeding.* 1691, 1697, and folio, Breeding.
p. 99, l. 20.   *company.* 1691, 1697, and folio, Company.
p. 99, l. 22.   *I'le.* 1691, 1697, and folio, I'll.
p. 99, l. 31.   *quarrel.* 1691, 1697, and folio, Quarrel.
p. 99, l. 32.   *I'le.* 1691, 1697, and folio, I'll.
p. 99, l. 33.   *prudence.* 1691, 1697, and folio, Prudence.
p. 99, l. 34.   *o'remaſters.* 1691, 1697, and folio, o'rmaſters.
p. 99, l. 42.   *friendship.* 1691, 1697, and folio, Friendship.
p. 100, l. 2.   *has.* 1691, 1697, and folio, Has.
p. 100, l. 10. *life.* 1691, 1697, and folio, Life.
p. 100, l. 10. *counsel.* 1691, 1697, and folio, Counsel.
p. 100, l. 14. *folly's.* 1691, 1697, and folio, Folly's.
p. 100, l. 14. *sore.* 1691, 1697, and folio, Sore.
p. 100, l. 15. *cure.* 1691, 1697, and folio, Cure.
p. 100, l. 18. *man.* 1691, 1697, and folio, Man.
p. 100, l. 29. *lye.* 1691, 1697, and folio, lie.'
p. 100, l. 32. *marribones.* Folio, Marrow bones.
p. 100, l. 38. *lye?* Folio, Lie?
p. 100, l. 40. *th'occasion.* 1691, 1697, and folio, th'Occasion.
p. 100, l. 41. *lye.* Folio, Lie.
p. 101, l. 2.   *oyl.* Folio, Oil.
p. 101, l. 4.   *anger.* 1691, 1697, and folio, Anger.
p. 101, l. 4.   *I'le.* 1691, 1697, and folio, I'll.
p. 101, l. 7.   *Villain Warner.* 1691, 1697, and folio, Villain, *Warner.*
p. 101, l. 16. *wit to find it out.* Folio, Wit to find it out. *[Aside.*
p. 101, l. 18. *ſtomack.* 1678, 1691, 1697, and folio, Stomach.
p. 101, l. 23. *adieu dear Sir.* 1691, 1697, and folio, adieu, dear Sir.
p. 101, l. 25. *han't.* 1691, 1697, and folio, Han't.
p. 101, l. 25. *matters.* 1691, 1697, and folio, Matters.
p. 101, l. 27. *Sugar-Plums.* Folio, Sugar-Plumbs.
p. 101, l. 27. *firſt.* 1691, 1697, and folio, Firſt.
p. 101, l. 28. *for.* 1691, 1697, and folio, For.
p. 101, l. 30. *reckoning.* 1691, 1697, and folio, Reckoning.
p. 101, l. 34. *'um.* 1691, 1697, and folio, 'em.
p. 101, l. 34. *disguise.* 1691, 1697, and folio, Disguise.
p. 101, l. 36. *counsel.* 1691, 1697, and folio, Counsel.

p. 101, l. 37.   *you.* 1691, 1697, and folio, You.
p, 101, l. 38.   *secret.* 1691, 1697, and folio, Secret.
p. 101, l. 38.   *company.* 1691, 1697, and folio, Company.
p. 101, l. 39.   *man.* 1691, 1697, and folio, Man.
p. 101, l. 41.   *You'l.* 1691, 1697, and folio, You'll.
p. 101, l. 42.   *Well I am.* Folio, Well, I am.
p. 101, l. 43.   *neerer.* 1691, 1697, and folio, nearer.
p. 102, l. 2.   *people.* 1691, 1697, and folio, People.
p. 102, l. 4.   *projeƈt.* 1691, 1697, and folio, Projeƈt.
p. 102, l. 4.   *pate.* 1691, 1697, and folio, Pate.
p. 102, l. 8.   *Fathers.* 1691, 1697, and folio, Father's.
p. 102, l. 9.   *mind.* 1691, 1697, and folio, Mind.
p. 102, l. 12.   *For Secrets.* 1691, 1697, and folio, The couplet is printed in
                  italic.
p. 102, l. 25.   *opinion.* 1691, 1697, and folio, Opinion.
p. 102, l. 28.   *priviledges.* 1691, 1697, and folio, privileges.
p. 102, l. 29.   *My miſtress.* Folio, My Mrs.
p. 103, l. 1.   *man.* 1691, 1697, and folio, Man.
p. 103, l. 6.   *fellows.* 1691, 1697, folio, Fellows.
p. 103, l. 7.   *old English manliness.* 1691, 1697, and folio, Old *English* Man-
                  liness.
p. 103, l. 8.   *condition.* 1691, 1697, and folio, Condition.
p. 103, l. 9.   *shoe.* 1691, 1697, and folio, Shoe.
p. 103, l. 16.   *'tis.* 1691, 1697, and folio, 'Tis.
p. 103, l. 20.   *'um.* 1691, 1697, and folio, 'em.
p. 103, l. 29.   *parts.* 1691, 1697, and folio, Parts.
p. 103, l. 30.   *faith.* 1691, 1697, and folio, Faith.
p. 103, l. 32.   *opinion.* 1691, 1697, and folio, Opinion.
p. 103, l. 33.   *flattery.* 1691, 1697, and folio, Flattery.
p. 103, l. 35.   *creature.* 1691, 1697, and folio, Creature.
p. 103, l. 35.   *world.* 1691, 1697, and folio, World.
p. 103, l. 38.   *Vertuoso.* 1691, 1697, and folio, *Virtuoso.*
p. 104, l. 2.   *you have.* 1691, 1697, and folio, You have.
p. 104, l. 2.   *beaſt.* 1691, 1697, and folio, Beaſt.
p. 104, l. 3.   *old man.* 1691, 1697, and folio, old Man.
p. 104, l. 5.   *brains.* 1691, 1697, and folio, Brains.
p. 104, l. 7.   *pardon.* 1691, 1697, and folio, Pardon.
p. 104, l. 7.   *Gad.* 1691, 1697, and folio, God.
p. 104, l. 10.   *escapes.* 1691, 1697, and folio, Escapes.
p. 104, l. 14.   *fly.* Folio, flie.
p. 104, l. 16.   *a-la-mode.* 1691, 1697, and folio, *A-la-mode.*
p. 104, l. 16.   *conversation.* 1691, 1697, and folio, Conversation.
p. 104, l. 17.   *whiff.* 1691, 1697, and folio, Whiff.
p. 104, l. 17.   *discourse.* 1691, 1697, and folio, Discourse.
p. 104, l. 19.   *in fine.* 1691, 1697, and folio, *in fine.*
p. 104, l. 23.   *so forth.* 1691, 1697, and folio, So forth.
p. 104, l. 23.   *nonsence.* Folio, Non-sence.

p. 104, l. 26.   *at Door.* 1691, 1697, and folio, at door.
p. 104, l. 28.   *Dukes.* Folio, Duke's.
p. 104, l. 29.   *It is.* 1691, 1697, and folio, 'Tis.
p. 104, l. 30.   *Kings.* Folio, King's.
p. 105, l. 5.   *fellow.* 1691, 1697, and folio, Fellow.
p. 105, l. 5.   *fool.* 1691, 1697, and folio, Fool.
p. 105, l. 7.   *wit.* 1691, 1697, and folio, Wit.
p. 105, l. 14.   *you a meer.* 1678, y'ar. 1691, 1697, and folio, y'are.
p. 105, l. 20.   *worlds.* 1691, 1697, and folio, Worlds.
p. 105, l. 24.   *Enter old La.* Folio, *Enter La. Dupe.*
p. 105, l. 30.   *To her Chr.* 1691, 1697, and folio, *To her Christian.*
p. 105, l. 31.   *have you told.* 1678, have you not told.
p. 105, l. 32.   *body.* 1691, 1697, and folio, Body.
p. 105, l. 33.   *foundations.* 1691, 1697, and folio, Foundation.
p. 105, l. 36.   *blessing.* 1691, 1697, Blessing.
p. 105, l. 36.   *endeavours.* 1691, 1697, and folio, Endeavours.
p. 105, l. 38.   *bed.* 1691, 1697, and folio, Bed.
p. 105, l. 39.   *visit.* 1691, 1697, and folio, Visit.
p. 105, l. 40.   *passion.* 1691, 1697, and folio, Passion.
p. 106, l. 1.   *instrument.* 1691, 1697, and folio, Instrument.
p. 106, l. 1.   *concealment.* 1691, 1697, and folio, Concealment.
p. 106, l. 3.   *o're.* 1678, o'r. 1691, 1697, and folio, o'er.
p. 106, l. 3.   *Ladiship.* Folio, Ladyship.
p. 106, l. 13.   *body.* 1691, 1697, and folio, Body.
p. 106, l. 13.   *mind.* 1691, 1697, and folio, Mind.
p. 106, l. 14.   *scruple.* 1691, 1697, and folio, Scruple.
p. 106, l. 17.   *despair.* 1691, 1697, and folio, Despair.
p. 106, l. 18.   *sickness.* 1691, 1697, and folio, Sickness.
p. 106, l. 19.   *shipwrack'd.* 1691, 1697, and folio, Shipwrack'd.
p. 106, l. 22.   *sighs.* 1691, 1697, and folio, Sighs.
p. 106, l. 22.   *groans.* 1691, 1697, and folio, Groans.
p. 106, l. 30.   *obedience.* 1691, 1697, and folio, Obedience.
p. 106, l. 33.   *house.* 1691, 1697, and folio, House.
p. 106, l. 34.   *stoln.* 1691, 1697, and folio, stollen.
p. 106, l. 37.   *I'le.* 1691, 1697, and folio, I'll.
p. 106, l. 38.   *'um.* 1691, 1697, and folio, 'em.
p. 106, l. 41.   *married.* 1691, 1697, and folio, Married.
p. 107, l. 4.   *act.* 1691, 1697, and folio, Act.
p. 107, l. 15.   *Gilberts.* 1691, 1697, and folio, *Gilbert's.*
p. 107, l. 28.   *pretty.* Folio, prety.
p. 107, l. 31.   *bed.* 1691, 1697, and folio, Bed.
p. 107, l. 31.   *voice.* 1691, 1697, and folio, Voce.
p. 107, l. 33.   *reward,* 1691, 1697, and folio, Reward.
p. 107, l. 34.   *life.* 1691, 1697, and folio, Life.
p. 107, l. 35.   *malice.* 1691, 1697, and folio, Malice.
p. 107, l. 39.   *Lechery.* 1691, 1697, and folio, Letchery.
p. 108, l. 1.   *Chymistry.* 1691, 1697, and folio, Chimistry.

p. 108, l. 3.   *hand.* 1691, 1697, and folio, Hand.
p. 108, l. 8.   *finger.* 1691, 1697, and folio, Finger.
p. 108, l. 8.   *hope.* 1691, 1697, and folio, Hope.
p. 108, l. 9.   *blessed.* 1691, 1697, and folio, Blessed.
p. 108, l. 15.   *pardon.* 1691, 1697, and folio, Pardon.
p. 108, l. 15.   *help.* 1691, 1697, and folio, Help.
p. 108, l. 16.   *Heaven.* Folio, Heav'n.
p. 108, l. 18.   *girl.* 1691, 1697, and folio, Girl.
p. 108, l. 19.   *but.* 1691, 1697, and folio, But.
p. 108, l. 22.   *tempters.* 1691, 1697, and folio, Tempters.
p. 108, l. 22.   *wicked act.* 1691, 1697, and folio, Wicked Act.
p. 108, l. 25.   *love.* 1691, 1697, and folio, Love.
p. 108, l. 26.   *ruine.* 1691, 1697, and folio, Ruine.
p. 108, l. 28.   *deeds of darkness.* 1691, 1697, and folio, Deeds of Darkness.
p. 108, l. 29.   *vigour.* 1691, 1697, and folio, Vigour.
p. 108, l. 31.   *advantages.* 1691, 1697, and folio, Advantages.
p. 108, l. 32.   *Heaven.* 1691, 1697, and folio, Heav'n.
p. 108, l. 32.   *good.* 1691, 1697, and folio, Good.
p. 108, l. 32.   *help, lead me.* Folio, help to lead me.
p. 108, l. 34.   *mischief.* 1691, 1697, and folio, Mischief.
p. 108, l. 35.   *old man's humour.* 1691, 1697, and folio, Old Man's Humour.
p. 108, l. 37.   *my old Master.* 1691, 1697, and folio, My Old Master.
p. 108, l. 37.   *Jealousie.* Folio, Jealousy.
p. 108, l. 40.   *angry.* 1691, 1697, and folio, Angry.
p. 108, l. 41.   *friends.* 1691, 1697, and folio, Friends.
p. 108, l. 41.   *quarrel.* 1691, 1697, and folio, Quarrel.
p. 108, l. 42.   *wrath.* 1691, 1697, and folio, Wrath.
p. 108, l. 42.   *here.* 1691, 1697, and folio, Here.
p. 109, l. 1.   *'um.* 1691, 1697, and folio, 'em.
p. 109, l. 2.   *hands.* 1691, 1697, and folio, Hands.
p. 109, l. 3.   *humble.* 1691, 1697, and folio, Humble.
p. 109, l. 4.   *I'le.* 1691, 1697, and folio, I'll.
p. 109, l. 4.   *'um.* 1691, 1697, and folio, 'em.
p. 109, l. 5.   *heart.* 1691, 1697, and folio, Heart.
p. 109, l. 6.   *brains.* 1691, 1697, and folio, Brains.
p. 109, l. 9.   *foul weather.* 1691, 1697, and folio, Foul Weather.
p. 109, l. 11.   *project.* 1691, 1697, and folio, Project.
p. 109, l. 15.   *lines in a sheet.* 1691, 1697, and folio, Lines in a Sheet.
p. 109, l. 16.   *business lyes.* 1691, 1697, and folio, Business lies.
p. 109, l. 17.   *canst.* 1691, 1697, and folio, Canst.
p. 109, l. 20.   *him; just.* 1691, 1697, and folio, him: Just.
p. 109, l. 21.   *when.* 1691, 1697, and folio, When.
p. 109, l. 22.   *faces.* 1691, 1697, and folio, Faces.
p. 109, l. 22.   *by this.* 1691, 1697, and folio, By this.
p. 109, l. 24.   *Mrs. Mill.* Folio, Mrs. Millisent.
p. 109, l. 25.   *old man.* 1691, 1697, and folio, Old Man.
p. 109, l. 26.   *satisfi'd.* 1691, 1697, and folio, satisfy'd.

p. 109, l. 27. *friendship.* 1691, 1697, and folio, Friendship.
p. 109, l. 29. *pardon.* 1691, 1697, and folio, Pardon.
p. 109, l. 29. *'um.* 1691, 1697, and folio, 'em (*ter*).
p. 109, l. 32. *where.* 1691, 1697, and folio, Where.
p. 109, l. 37. *days.* 1691, 1697, and folio, Days.
p. 109, l. 38. *friend.* 1691, 1697, and folio, Friend.
p. 109, l. 41. *lov'd.* 1691, 1697, and folio, Lov'd.
p. 109, l. 41. *occasions.* 1691, 1697, and folio, Occasions.
p. 110, l. 3. *hand.* 1691, 1697, and folio, Hand.
p. 110, l. 4. *what.* 1691, 1697, and folio, What.
p. 110, l. 5. *tongue.* 1691, 1697, and folio, Tongue.
p. 110, l. 6. *Accompt.* 1691, 1697, and folio, Account.
p. 110, l. 10. *to do, it.* 1691, 1697, and folio, to do? It.
p. 110, l. 17. *am I.* 1691, 1697, and folio, Am I.
p. 110, l. 17. *you Rogue.* 1691, 1697, and folio, You Rogue.
p. 110, l. 20. *his way to be.* 1691, 1697, and folio, his way, to be.
p. 110, l. 23. *trick.* 1691, 1697, and folio, Trick.
p. 110, l. 24. *I'le.* 1691, 1697, and folio, I'll.
p. 110, l. 27. *&c.* 1691, 1697, and folio, &c.
p. 110, l. 31. *smoak.* 1691, 1697, and folio, smoke.
p. 110, l. 33. *man.* 1691, 1697, and folio, Man.
p. 110, l. 34. *[Exeunt Sir John.* 1691, 1697, and folio, [*Ex. Sir* John.
p. 110, l. 36. *help.* 1691, 1697, and folio, Help.
p. 110, l. 36. *mistake.* 1691, 1697, and folio, Mistake.
p. 110, l. 39. *Prethee.* 1691, 1697, and folio, Prithee.
p. 110, l. 39. *this indifference.* 1691, 1697, and folio, This Indifference.
p. 110, l. 43. *business.* 1691, 1697, and folio, Business.
p. 111, l. 7. *points.* 1691, 1697, and folio, Point's.
p. 111, l. 13. *why.* 1691, 1697, and folio, Why.
p. 111, l. 16. *people.* 1691, 1697, and folio, People.
p. 111, l. 21. *pity.* 1691, 1697, and folio, Pity.
p. 111, l. 22. *ten.* 1691, 1697, and folio, Ten.
p. 111, l. 24. *agen.* 1691, 1697, and folio, again.
p. 111, l. 25. *morrow.* 1691, 1697, and folio, Morrow.
p. 111, l. 28. *marry?* Folio, *Marry.*
p. 111, l. 31. *married.* 1691, 1697, and folio, Married.
p. 111, l. 37. *heart.* 1691, 1697, and folio, Heart.
p. 111, l. 37. *dead man.* 1691, 1697, and folio, Dead Man.
p. 112, l. 2. *Old man.* 1691, 1697, and folio, Old Man.
p. 112, l. 5. *twenty pieces.* 1691, 1697, and folio, Twenty Pieces.
p. 112, l. 7. *wit.* 1691, 1697, and folio, Wit.
p. 112, l. 10. *masterly Companion.* 1678, masterlie Companion. 1697, Masterly Companion.
p. 112, l. 23. *humour.* 1691, 1697, and folio, Humour.
p. 112, l. 23. *A' kick'd me.* 1678, 1691, 1697, and folio, He kick'd me.
p. 112, l. 24. *money.* 1691, 1697, and folio, Money.
p. 112, l. 26. *Cox nowns.* 1691, 1697, and folio, Coxnowns.

p. 112, l. 31.   *hate.* 1691, 1697, and folio, Hate.

p. 112, l. 38.   *Scander-bag-Rogue.* 1691, 1697, and folio, Scander-bag Rogue.

p. 112, l. 39.   *hark.* Folio, Heark.

p. 112, l. 41.   *doors.* 1691, 1697, and folio, Doors.

p. 113, l. 1.   *Good old Sir.* 1691, 1697, and folio, Good Old Sir.

p. 113, l. 3.   *stomach's.* 1691, 1697, and folio, Stomach's.

p. 113, l. 9.   *she'l.* 1691, 1697, and folio, she'll.

p. 113, l. 10.   *loth.* Folio, loath.

p. 113, l. 22.   *opinion,* 1691, 1697, and folio, Opinion.

p. 113, l. 22.   *wit.* 1691, 1697, and folio, Wit.

p. 113, l. 25.   *happiness.* 1691, 1697, and folio, Happiness.

p. 113, l. 26.   *misery.* 1691, 1697, and folio, Misery.

p. 113, l. 26.   *exploit.* 1691, 1697, and folio, Exploit.

p. 113, l. 27.   *Lawrel.* 1691, 1697, and folio, Laurel.

p. 113, l. 28.   *Serving-men.* 1691, 1697, and folio, Serving-Men.

p. 113, l. 30.   *favour.* 1691, 1697, and folio, Favour.

p. 113, l. 30.   *speech.* 1691, 1697, and folio, Speech.

p. 113, l. 36.   *corner.* 1691, 1697, and folio, Corner.

p. 113, l. 39.   *required.* 1691, 1697, and folio, requir'd.

p. 114, l. 1.   *twenty of them.* 1691, 1697, and folio, *Twenty of 'em.*

p. 114, l. 3.   *unknown.* 1691, 1697, and folio, Unknown.

p. 114, l. 7.   *Outalian-Rogues.* 1691, 1697, and folio, Outalian Rogues.

p. 114, l. 12.   *fig.* 1691, 1697, and folio, Fig.

p. 114, l. 13.   *[Exit Moody.* 1691, 1697, and folio, [*Ex.* Moody.

p. 114, l. 16.   *back-gammon'd.* 1691, 1697, and folio, Back-gammon'd.

p. 114, l. 19.   *misfortune.* 1691, 1697, and folio, Misfortune.

p. 114, l. 19.   *befal'n.* 1691, 1697, and folio, befall'n.

p. 114, l. 24.   *lyes.* 1691, 1697, and folio, lies.

p. 114, l. 27.   *mirth.* 1691, 1697, and folio, Mirth.

p. 114, l. 30.   *projects.* 1691, 1697, and folio, Projects.

p. 114, l. 31.   *Mother-wit.* 1691, 1697, and folio, Mother-Wit.

p. 114, l. 34.   *imagination.* 1691, 1697, and folio, Imagination.

p. 114, l. 35.   *soul.* 1691, 1697, and folio, Soul.

p. 115, l. 2.   *snapt by some young Fellows that lay.* 1691, 1697, and folio, snapt, by some young Fellows, that lay.

p. 115, l. 6.   *very Nick.* 1678, verie Nick.

p. 115, l. 7.   *rascally fellow.* 1678, rascallie fellow. 1691, 1697, folio, Rascally Fellow.

p. 115, l. 9.   *a' god's name.* 1691, 1697, folio, a' God's name.

p. 115, l. 10.   *miracle.* 1691, 1697, and folio, Miracle.

p. 115, l. 12.   *thee man I did.* 1691, 1697, and folio, thee, Man, I did.

p. 115, l. 13.   *familiar.* 1691, 1697, and folio, Familiar.

p. 115, l. 14.   *e're.* 1691, 1697, and folio, e'er.

p. 115, l. 15.   *man, Who's the fool.* 1691, 1697, and folio, *Man, Who's the Fool.*

p. 115, l. 16.   *fool.* 1691, 1697, and folio, Fool (*bis*).

p. 116, l. 19.   *commendations.* 1691, 1697, and folio, Commendations.

412

p. 115, l. 20. *skill.* 1691, 1698, and folio, Skill.

p. 115, l. 21. *ability.* 1691, 1697, and folio, Ability.

p. 115, l. 22. *knock.* 1691, 1697, and folio, Knock.

p. 115, l. 22. *lack-wit, a designing.* 1691, 1697, and folio, Lack-wit, a Designing.

p. 115, l. 23. *hair-brain'd.* 1691, 1697, and folio, Hair-brained.

p. 115, l. 24. *eternal Wind-mil.* 1691, 1697, and folio, Eternal Windml.

p. 115, l. 28. *rascally fellow.* 1678, rascallie. 1691, 1697, and folio, Rascally Fellow.

p. 115, l. 31. *conjurer.* 1691, 1697, and folio, Conjurer.

p. 115, l. 33. *justifications.* 1691, 1697, and folio, Justifications.

p. 115, l. 34. *speak.* 1691, 1697, and folio, Speak.

p. 115, l. 35. *defence.* 1691, 1697, and folio, Defence.

p. 115, l. 36. *luck.* 1691, 1697, and folio, Luck.

p. 115, l. 39. *folly.* 1691, 1697, and folio, Folly.

p. 115, l. 41. *tyranny.* 1691, 1697, and folio, Tyranny.

p. 116, l. 5. *mind.* 1691, 1697, and folio, Mind.

p. 116, l. 5. *courtesie.* 1691, 1697, and folio, Courtesie.

p. 116, l. 9. *kindness.* 1691, 1697, and folio, Kindness.

p. 116, l. 10. *Mistress Christian.* 1691, 1697, and folio, Mrs. Christian.

p. 116, l. 13. *at day of marriage.* 1678, at the day of marriage. 1691, 1697, and folio, at the Day of Marriage.

p. 116, l. 14. *temptation,* 1691, 1697, and folio, Temptation.

p. 116, l. 20. *honour of my wit.* 1691, 1697, and folio, Honour of my Wit.

p. 116, l. 20. *ingag'd.* 1691, 1697, and folio, engag'd.

p. 116, l. 21. *married.* 1691, 1697, and folio, Married.

p. 116, l. 25. *parties.* 1691, 1697, and folio, Parties.

p. 116, l. 30. *cheat is her study.* 1691, 1697, and folio, Cheat is her Study.

p. 116, l. 30. *joy to cosen.* 1691, 1697, and folio, Joy to cozen.

p. 116, l. 31. *lines.* 1691, 1697, and folio, Lines.

p. 116, l. 31. *centre.* 1691, 1697, and folio, Centre.

p. 116, l. 33. *n'ere.* 1691, 1697, and folio, ne'er.

p. 116, l. 34. *womans flesh.* 1691, 1697, and folio, Womans Flesh.

p. 116, l. 34. *night.* 1691, 1697, and folio, Night.

p. 116, l. 34. *find.* 1691, 1697, and folio, found.

p. 116, l. 34. *maidenhead.* 1691, 1697, and folio, Maidenhead.

p. 116, l. 35. *mother.* 1691, 1697, and folio, Mother.

p. 116, l. 38. *bed.* 1691, 1697, and folio, Bed.

p. 116, l. 38. *cram'd.* 1691, 1697, and folio, Cram'd.

p. 116, l. 40. *La-fronds.* 1691, 1697, and folio, *Lafronds.*

p. 116, l. 40. *six-pence.* 1691, 1697, and folio, Six-pence.

p. 117, l. 1. *Cawdels.* 1678, Caudels. 1691, 1697, and folio, Caudles.

p. 117, l. 2. *Glisters.* 1691, 1697, and folio, Clysters.

p. 117, l. 3. *inhumane.* 1691, 1697, and folio, inhuman.

p. 117, l. 19. *wooden Mercury.* 1691, 1697, and folio, Wooden *Mercury.*

p. 117, l. 21. *meat.* 1691, 1697, and folio, Meat.

p. 117, l. 24. *work.* 1691, 1697, and folio, Work.

p. 118, l. 4.   *twinckle.* 1691, 1697, and folio, *twinkle.*
p. 118, l. 6.   *flye.* 1691, 1697, and folio, *fly.*
p. 118, l. 7.   *spye.* 1691, 1697, and folio, *spy.*
p. 118, l. 8.   *daddy.* 1691, 1697, and folio, *Daddy.*
p. 118, l. 9.   *cosen.* 1691, 1697, and folio, cozen.
p. 118, l. 10.   *case.* 1691, 1697, and folio, Case.
p. 118, l. 26.   *Grandham.* 1691, 1697, and folio, Grandam.
p. 118, l. 27.   *spought.* 1691, 1697, and folio, spout.
p. 118, l. 30.   *Mistress Bride.* 1691, 1697, and folio, Mrs. Bride.
p. 118, l. 30.   *stir'd.* 1691, 1697, and folio, stirr'd.
p. 118, l. 32.   *Maiden-heads.* 1691, 1697, and folio, Maidenheads.
p. 118, l. 32.   *lock of her affections.* 1691, 1697, and folio, Lock of her Affections.
p. 118, l. 33.   *e're a man.* 1691, 1697, and folio, e'er a Man.
p. 118, l. 34.   *friends.* 1691, 1697, and folio, Friends.
p. 118, l. 35.   *remedy.* 1691, 1697, and folio, Remedy.
p. 118, l. 35.   *dangers.* 1691, 1697, and folio, Dangers.
p. 118, l. 36.   *business.* 1691, 1697, and folio, Business.
p. 118, l. 37.   *match.* 1691, 1697, and folio, Match.
p. 118, l. 38.   *resolutions.* 1691, 1697, and folio, Resolutions.
p. 118, l. 38.   *battel.* 1691, 1697, and folio, Battel.
p. 119, l. 2.   *life.* 1691, 1697, and folio, Life.
p. 119, l. 2.   *marriage.* 1691, 1697, and folio, Marriage.
p. 119, l. 5.   *whom I prithee.* 1691, 1697, and folio, whom, I prithee.
p. 119, l. 7.   *persons.* 1691, 1697, and folio, Persons.
p. 119, l. 8.   *imply that.* 1691, 1697, and folio, imply, that.
p. 119, l. 11.   *marriage.* 1691, 1697, and folio, Marriage.
p. 119, l. 14.   *mock.* 1691, 1697, and folio, Mock.
p. 119, l. 15.   *matter.* 1691, 1697, and folio, Matter.
p. 119, l. 30.   *tricks.* 1691, 1697, and folio, Tricks.
p. 119, l. 31.   *entayl'd.* 1691, 1697, and folio, entail'd.
p. 119, l. 37.   *cozened.* 1691, 1697, and folio, cozen'd.
p. 119, l. 37.   *twenty to one;.* 1691, 1697, and folio, Twenty to one,.
p. 119, l. 41.   *friend.* 1691, 1697, and folio, Friend.
p. 120, l. 2.   *haunts.* 1691, 1697, and folio, Haunts.
p. 120, l. 23.   *penny.* 1691, 1697, and folio, Penny.
p. 120, l. 24.   *I,.* 1691, 1697, and folio, Ay,.
p. 120, l. 25.   *wise.* 1691, 1697, and folio, Wise.
p. 120, l. 26.   *inveigle.* 1691, 1697, and folio, inveagle.
p. 120, l. 29.   *wind.* 1691, 1697, and folio, Wind.
p. 120, l. 31.   *[Exit Warner.* 1691, 1697, and folio, [*Ex.* Warn.
p. 120, l. 33.   *revenge.* 1691, 1697, and folio, Revenge.
p. 120. l. 39.   *Truly you.* 1691, 1697, and folio, Truly, you.
p. 120, l. 40.   *Condition.* 1691, 1697, and folio, condition.
p. 121, l. 3.   *lye in bed.* 1691, 1697, and folio, lie in Bed.
p. 121, l. 4.   *world.* 1691, 1697, and folio, World.
p. 121, l. 4.   *beards.* 1691, 1697, and folio, Beards.

p. 121, l. 7. *innocency.* 1691, 1697, and folio, Innocency.
p. 121, l. 13. *then to marry.* 1691, 1697, and folio, than to marry.
p. 121, l. 15. *wooing.* 1691, 1697, and folio, Wooing.
p. 121, l. 16. *wooe.* 1691, 1697, and folio, Wooe.
p. 121, l. 17. *cry you.* 1691, 1697, and folio, Cry you.
p. 121, l. 24. *wish.* 1691, 1697, and folio, Wish (*bis*).
p. 121, l. 31. *marry.* 1691, 1697, and folio, Marry.
p. 121, l. 34. *thing.* 1691, 1697, and folio, Thing.
p. 121, l. 34. *world.* 1691, 1697, and folio, World.
p. 121, l. 38. *will not you.* 1691, 1697, and folio, Will not you.
p. 121, l. 39. *Yes, yes, yes.* 1691, 1697, and folio, Yes, Yes, Yes,
p. 121, l. 40. *to night.* 1691, 1697, and folio, to Night.
p. 122, l. 2. *very Melancholy.* 1678, verie Melancholy.
p. 122, l. 5. *Heart.* 1691, 1697, and folio, heart (*bis*).
p. 122, l. 11. *person.* 1691, 1697, and folio, Person.
p. 122, l. 14. *go on, Sir.* 1691, 1697, and folio, Go on, Sir.
p. 122, l. 17. *Divinity.* 1678, Divinitie.
p. 122, l. 20. *whoever.* 1691, 1697, and folio, Whoever.
p. 122, l. 21. *ſtomach.* 1691, 1697, and folio, Stomach.
p. 122, l. 21. *guts.* 1691, 1697, and folio, Guts.
p. 122, l. 22. *person.* 1691, 1697, and folio, Person.
p. 122, l. 23. *and I'll make.* 1668, and make.
p. 122, l. 24. *privy-house.* 1678, Privie-house. 1691, 1697, and folio, Privy-house.
p. 122, l. 30. *ten.* 1691, 1697, and folio, Ten.
p. 122, l. 30. *face.* 1691, 1697, and ʿolio, Face.
p. 122, l. 31. *fiſt.* 1691, 1697, and folio, Fiſt.
p. 122, l. 32. *deny.* 1678, denie.
p. 122, l. 36. *queſtion: come.* 1691, 1697, and folio, Queſtion, Come.
p. 122, l. 41. *Lyes.* 1691, 1697, and folio, Lies.
p. 123, l. 5. *have you forgot.* 1691, 1697, and folio, Have you forgot.
p. 123, l. 8. *are you.* 1691, 1697, and folio, Are you.
p. 123, l. 8. *agen.* 1691, 1697, and folio, again.
p. 123, l. 15. *either be.* 1691, 1697, and folio, Either be.
p. 123, l. 16. *heels.* 1691, 1697, and folio, Heels (*bis*).
p. 123, l. 21. *Murder! Murder!* 1691, 1697, and folio, Murther! Murther!
p. 123, l. 24. *device.* 1691, 1697, and folio, Device.
p. 123, l. 27. *anger.* 1691, 1697, and folio, Anger.
p. 123, l. 28. *patience.* 1691, 1697, and folio, Patience.
p. 123, l. 29. *favour.* 1691, 1697, and folio, Favour.
p. 123, l. 33. *sense and reason.* 1691, 1697, and folio, Sense and Reason.
p. 123, l. 37. *At present I muſt tell you he's mine.* 1691, 1697, and folio, At present, I muſt tell you, he's mine.
p. 123, l. 40. *a Lord!* 1678, 1691, 1697, and folio, ah Lord!
p. 123, l. 41. *fault.* 1691, 1697, and folio, Fault.
p. 124, l. 4. *blew.* 1678, 1691, 1697, and folio, blue.
p. 124, l. 9. *O, ho.* 1691, 1697, and folio, O, oh.

p. 124, l. 15. *discharge.* 1691, 1697, and folio, Discharge.
p. 124, l. 17. *what.* 1691, 1697, and folio, What.
p. 124, l. 17. *bosom.* 1691, 1697, and folio, Bosom.
p. 124, l. 17. *fare you well.* 1691, 1697, and folio, Fare you well.
p. 124, l. 18. [*Exit Sir John.* 1691, 1697, and folio [*Ex. Sir* John.
p. 124, l. 26. *projects.* 1691, 1697, and folio, Projects.
p. 124, l. 26. *bin.* 1691, 1697, and folio, been.
p. 124, l. 27. *pieces.* 1691, 1697, and folio, Pieces.
p. 124, l. 29. *on' you.* 1668, ou' you. 1691, 1697, and folio, an' you.
p. 124, l. 30. *signs and tokens.* 1691, 1697, and folio, Signs and Tokens.
p. 124, l. 36. *tribute.* 1691, 1697, and folio, Tribute.
p. 124, l. 38. *if we are.* 1691, 1697, and folio, If we are.
p. 124, l. 40. *but pray.* 1691, 1697, and folio, But pray.
p. 124, l. 41. *Counsel.* 1678, 1691, 1697, and folio, Council.
p. 124, l. 41. *business.* 1691, 1697, and folio, Business.
p. 124, l. 42. *point.* 1691, 1697, and folio, Point.
p. 124, l. 43. *affairs.* 1691, 1697, and folio, Affairs.
p. 124, l. 43. *world.* 1691, 1697, and folio, World.
p. 125, l. 4. *Wee'l.* 1691, 1697, and folio, We'll. These quartos also print the concluding couplet of the Act in italics.
p. 125, l. 7. *promise.* 1691, 1697, and folio, Promise.
p. 125, l. 8. *night married.* 1691, 1697, and folio, Night Married.
p. 125, l. 11. *ebbs and flows.* 1691, 1697, and folio, Ebbs and Flows.
p. 125, l. 13. *mistake.* 1691, 1697, and folio, Mistake.
p. 125, l. 13. *Mistress's.* 1691, 597, and folio, Mistresses.
p. 125, l. 14. *folly.* 1691, 1697, and folio, Folly.
p. 125, l. 16. *woman.* 1691, 1697, and folio, Woman.
p. 125, l. 16. *consent.* 1691, 1697, and folio, Consent.
p. 125, l. 19. *youth.* 1691, 1697, and folio, Youth.
p. 125, l. 20. *is this the faith.* 1691, 1697, and folio, Is this the Faith.
p. 125, l. *profession.* 1691, 1697, and folio, Profession.
p. 125, l. 22. *example.* 1691, 1697, and folio, Example.
p. 125, l. 24. *women.* 1691, 1697, and folio, Women.
p. 125, l. 26. *Guiny.* 1691, 1697, and folio, *Guinea.*
p. 125, l. 27. *stair-foot.* 1691, 1697, and folio, Stair-foot.
p. 125, l. 29. *promise.* 1691, 1697, and folio, Promise.
p. 125, l. 32. *bed.* 1691, 1697, and folio, Bed.
p. 125, l. 34. *Banquers.* 1678, 1691, 1697, and folio, Bankers.
p. 125, l. 34. *debts.* 1691, 1697, and folio, Debts.
p. 126, l. 5. *that my Mr.* 1691, 1697, and folio, That my Master.
p. 126, l. 8. *design.* 1691, 1697, and folio, Design.
p. 126, l. 10. *Bailifs to arrest.* 1691, 1697, and folio, Bailiffs to Arrest.
p. 126, l. 11. *promise.* 1691, 1697, and folio, Promise.
p. 126, l. 16. [*Ex. Lord.* All the quartos add M. [Millisent] to this stage direction, but obviously Mrs. Millisent enters above here, at one of the proscenium balconies.
p. 126, l. 20. *projection.* 1691, 1697, and folio, Projection.

p. 126, l. 22. *work's.* 1691, 1697, and folio, Work's.
p. 126, l. 25. *wit.* 1691, 1697, and folio, Wit, and so throughout scene.
p. 126, l. 31. *folly.* 1691, 1697, and folio, Folly.
p. 126, l. 32. *point.* 1691, 1697, and folio, Point.
p. 126, l. 32. *actions.* 1691, 1697, and folio, Actions.
p. 126, l. 33. *hairsbreadth.* 1691, 1697, and folio, Hairsbreadth.
p. 126, l. 35. *day.* 1691, 1697, and folio, Day.
p. 126, l. 38. *fate.* 1691, 1697, and folio, Fate.
p. 126, l. 43. *cloaths.* 1691, 1697, and folio, Cloaths.
p. 127, l. 1. *sloven.* 1691, 1697, and folio, Sloven.
p. 127, l. 2. *sings, dances.* 1691, 1697, and folio, Sings, Dances.
p. 127, l. 6. *view.* 1691, 1697, and folio, View.
p. 127, l. 8. *Scritch-Owle.* 1691, 1697, and folio, Scritch Owl.
p. 127, l. 10. *enterprize.* 1691, 1697, and folio, Enterprize.
p. 127, l. 15. *stairs.* 1691, 1697, and folio, Stairs.
p. 127, l. 16. *news.* 1691, 1697, and folio, News.
p. 127, l. 17. *concernment.* 1691, 1697, and folio, Concernment.
p. 127, l. 18. *extreamly.* 1691, 1697, and folio, extremely.
p. 127, l. 19. *years.* 1691, 1697, and folio, Years.
p. 127, l. 20. *days.* 1691, 1697, and folio, Days.
p. 127, l. 23. *thought.* 1691, 1697, and folio, Thought.
p. 127, l. 31. *non-plus'd.* 1691, 1697, and folio, non-pluss'd.
p. 127, l. 32. *consolation.* 1691, 1697, and folio, Consolation.
p. 127, l. 32. *lips.* 1691, 1697, and folio, Lips.
p. 127, l. 35. *premunire.* 1691, 1697, and folio, *Praemunire.*
p. 127, l. 40. *Brown.* 1691, 1697, and folio, brown.
p. 127, l. 41. *five.* 1691, 1697, and folio, Five.
p. 128, l. 2. *covetousness.* 1691, 1697, and folio, Covetousness.
p. 128, l. 5. *cholerick.* 1691, 1697, and folio, Cholerick.
p. 128, l. 7. *'slife.* 1691, 1697, and folio, 'Slife.
p. 128, l. 7. *brains.* 1691, 1697, and folio, Brains.
p. 128, l. 12. *learn't.* 1691, 1697, and folio, learn'd.
p. 128, l. 16. *Land-lord's.* 1691, 1697, and folio, Landlord's.
p. 128, l. 17. *grimmaces.* 1691, 1697, and folio, Grimaces.
p. 128, l. 17. *mouth.* 1691, 1697, and folio, Mouth.
p. 128, l. 19. *Balcone.* 1678, balconie. 1691, 1697, and folio, Balcony.
p. 128, l. 24. *Gramercy.* 1678, Gramercie.
p. 128, l. 28. *Millisent, Rose.* 1691, 1697, and folio, Millisent, *and* Rose.
p. 128, l. 39. *Sea-man.* 1691, 1697, and folio, Seaman.
p. 129, l. 2. *disguises.* 1691, 1697, and folio, Disguises.
p. 129, l. 13. *Song.* In 4to, 1668 an extra leaf in sheet H with the Song, widely spaced so as to occupy both sides of the leaf, has been inserted. Owing to the introduction of this extra leaf there are two leaves paged 57–58. Thus the dialogue continues, p. 56 ends "now for the Song;" catch-word *THE.* p. 57 commences *Mill.* A pretty humour'd Song. . . .
p. 129, l. 15. *slave.* 1691, 1697, and folio, *Slave.*

p. 129, l. 16.   *dart.* 1691, 1697, and folio, *Dart.*
p. 129, l. 17.   *heart.* 1691, 1697, and folio, *Heart.*
p. 129, l. 19.   *joy.* 1691, 1697, and folio, *Joy.*
p. 129, l. 19.   *love.* 1691, 1697, and folio, *Love.*
p. 129, l. 21.   *sorrows and frights.* 1691, 1697, and folio, *Sorrows and Frights.*
p. 129, l. 22.   *heart.* 1691, 1697, and folio, *Heart.*
p. 129, l. 23.   *ne're.* 1691, 1697, and folio, *ne'er.*
p. 129, l. 25.   *top.* 1691, 1697, and folio, *Top.*
p. 129, l. 25.   *happiness.* 1691, 1697, and folio, *Happiness.*
p. 129, l. 27.   *pleasure.* 1691, 1697 and folio, *Pleasure.*
p. 129, l. 28.   *pain.* 1691, 1697, and folio, *Pain.*
p. 129, l. 29.   *vein.* 1691, 1697, and folio, *Vein.*
p. 129, l. 30.   *dream.* 1691, 1697, and folio, *Dream.*
p. 129, l. 30.   *smart.* 1691, 1697, and folio, *Smart.*
p. 129, l. 31.   *heart.* 1691, 1697, and folio, *Heart.*
p. 129, l. 33.   *freedom.* 1691, 1697, and folio, *Freedom.*
p. 129, l. 34.   *smile.* 1691, 1697, and folio, *Smile.*
p. 129, l. 35.   *anger.* 1691, 1697, and folio, *Anger.*
p. 129, l. 36.   *heart.* 1691, 1697, and folio, *Heart.*
p. 129, l. 36.   *recall.* 1691, 1697, and folio, *recal.*
p. 130, l. 2.   *ones heart.* 1691, 1697, and folio, *one's Heart.*
p. 130, l. 5.   *loves.* 1691, 1697, and folio, *Love's.*
p. 130, l. 6.   *desire.* 1691, 1697, and folio, *Desire.*
p. 130, l. 11.   *fruits.* 1691, 1697, and folio, Fruits.
p. 130, l. 21.   *names.* 1691, 1697, and folio, Names.
p. 130, l. 22.   *mans counsel.* 1691, 1697, and folio, Man's Counsel.
p. 130, l. 24.   *Ha!* 1691, 1697, and folio, Hah!
p. 130, l. 24.   *how.* 1691, 1697, and folio, How.
p. 130, l. 26.   *heavenly.* 1691, 1697, and folio, Heavenly.
p. 130, l. 33.   *Bailiffs.* 1691, 1697, and folio, Bayliffs.
p. 130, l. 34.   *plot.* 1691, 1697, and folio, Plot.
p. 130, l. 34.   *dog'd.* 1691, 1697, and folio, dogg'd.
p. 130, l. 37.   *Ex. Millisent, Rose.* 1691, 1697, and folio, [*Ex.* Mill. Rose.
p. 130, l. 38.   *Bailiffs.* 1678, 1691, 1697, and folio, *Bayliffs (bis).*
p. 131, l. 2.   *quarrel.* 1691, 1697, and folio, Quarrel.
p. 131, l. 3.   *Poppits.* 1678, 1691, 1697, and folio, Puppets.
p. 131, l. 10.   *my Mrs.* 1691, 1697, and folio, my Miſtress.
p. 131, l. 11.   *good night.* 1691, 1697, and folio, good Night.
p. 131, l. 16.   *debts.* 1691, 1697, and folio, Debts.
p. 131, l. 23.   *e'ne.* 1691, 1697, and folio, e'en.
p. 131, l. 24.   *Chiding.* 1691, 1697, and folio, chiding.
p. 131, l. 27.   *person.* 1691, 1697, and folio, Person.
p. 131, l. 30.   *Sword-man.* 1691, 1697, and folio, Swordman.
p. 131, l. 34.   *arreſted.* 1691, 1697, and folio, Arreſted.
p. 131, l. 36.   *ingenious.* 1691, 1697, and folio, Ingenious.
p. 131, l. 39.   *you.* 1691, 1697, and folio, You.

p. 132, l. 3. *plot.* 1691, 1697, and folio, Plot.

p. 132, l. 12. *invention.* 1691, 1697, and folio, Invention.

p. 132, l. 12. *child.* 1691, 1697, and folio, Child.

p. 132, l. 13. *Help! Help!* 1691, 1697, and folio, help! help.

p. 132, l. 16. *Hey-tarockit.* 1691, 1697, and folio, Hey-tarock-it.

p. 132, l. 16. *device.* 1691, 1697, and folio, Device.

p. 132, l. 18. *Moody you must know in his younger years.* 1691, 1697, and folio, Moody, you must know, in his younger Years.

p. 132, l. 19. *Towns-man's.* 1691, 1697, and folio, Town-man's.

p. 132, l. 24. *This Child in his Fathers.* 1691, 1697, and folio, This Child, in his Father's.

p. 132, l. 25. *privately.* 1678, privatelie.

p. 132, l. 26. *Bonaventure a Merchant for the East-Indies.* 1691, 1697, and folio, *Bonaventure,* a Merchant, for the East-Indies.

p. 132, l. 27. *memory.* 1678, memorie. 1691, 1697, and folio, Memory.

p. 132, l. 31. *Moguls Country.* 1678, *Mogul's* Countrey. 1691, 1697, and folio, *Mogul's* Country.

p. 132, l. 33. *house.* 1691, 1697, and folio, House.

p. 132, l. 36. *name.* 1691, 1697, and folio, Name (*bis*).

p. 132, l. 41. *dy'd.* 1691, 1697, and folio, died.

p. 133, l. 5. *what a Devil.* 1691, 1697, and folio, what the Devil.

p. 133, l. 11. *Old man.* 1691, 1697, and folio, Old Man (*bis*).

p. 133, l. 13. *arrival.* 1691, 1697, and folio, Arrival.

p. 133, l. 15. *errours.* 1691, 1697, and folio, Errours.

p. 133, l. 19. *lye.* 1691, 1697, and folio, lie.

p. 133, l. 24. *agen before I dye? welcome.* 1691, 1697, and folio, again before I die? Welcome.

p. 133, l. 27. *mouth.* 1691, 1697, and folio, Mouth.

p. 133, l. 37. *carriage.* 1691, 1697, and folio, Carriage.

p. 133, l. 40. *affection.* 1691, 1697, and folio, Affection.

p. 133, l. 40. *dye.* 1691, 1697, and folio, die.

p. 134, l. 5. *flesh and blood.* 1691, 1697, and folio, Flesh and Blood.

p. 134, l. 11. *blood in their veins.* 1691, 1697, and folio, Blood in their Veins.

p. 134, l. 14. *world.* 1691, 1697, and folio, World.

p. 134, l. 15. *Hurricanoes.* 1691, 1697, and folio, Hurricano's.

p. 135, l. 13. *scanderbag.* 1691, 1697, and folio, Scanderbag.

p. 135, l. 15. *Cambridge.* 1691, 1697, and folio, *Cambrige.*

p. 135, l. 19. *withall.* 1678, 1691, 1697, and folio, with.

p. 135, l. 23. *this is.* 1691, 1697, and folio, This.

p. 135, l. 24. *discourse.* 1691, 1697, and folio, Discourse.

p. 135, l. 28. *question.* 1691, 1697, and folio, Question.

p. 135, l. 30. *Turkey.* 1691, 1697, and folio, *Turky.*

p. 135, l. 38. *sence.* 1691, 1697, and folio, sense.

p. 136, l. 5. *East-Indian Apostle.* 1678, 1691, 1697, and folio, *East-India* Apostle.

p. 136, l. 7. *designs.* 1691, 1697, and folio, Designs.

p. 136, l. 13. *stranger.* 1691, 1697, and folio, Stranger.

p. 136, l. 14.   *yesterday.* 1691, 1697, and folio, Yesterday.
p. 136, l. 14.   *story.* 1691, 1697, and folio, Story.
p. 136, l. 17.   *bring me off.* 1691, 1697, and folio, bring me off [*Aside.*
p. 136, l. 20.   *heart.* 1691, 1697, and folio, Heart.
p. 136, l. 21.   *Imposter.* 1691, 1697, and folio, Impostor.
p. 136, l. 24.   *lye.* 1691, 1697, and folio, Lie.
p. 136, l. 34.   *salutations.* 1691, 1697, and folio, Salutations.
p. 136, l. 35.   *what news.* 1691, 1697, and folio, What News.
p. 136, l. 37.   *impudence.* 1691, 1697, and folio, Impudence.
p. 136, l. 38.   *question.* 1691, 1697, and folio, Question.
p. 136, l. 39.   *indiscretion and stupidity.* 1691, 1697, and folio, Indiscretion and Stupidity.
p. 137, l. 2.   *injury.* 1691, 1697, and folio, Injury.
p. 137, l. 9.   *choler.* 1691, 1697, and folio, Choler.
p. 137, l. 13.   *fault.* 1691, 1697, and folio, Fault.
p. 137, l. 13.   *purse.* 1691, 1697, and folio, Purse.
p. 137, l. 13.   *blood.* 1691, 1697, and folio, Blood.
p. 137, l. 19.   *extreamly.* 1678, extreamlie. 1691, 1697, and folio, extremely.
p. 137, l. 24.   *plotting.* 1691, 1697, and folio, Plotting.
p. 137, l. 26.   *house.* 1691, 1697, and folio, House.
p. 137, l. 28.   *Old man.* 1691, 1697, and folio, Old Man.
p. 137, l. 36.   *boldly.* 1678, boldlie.
p. 137, l. 38.   *help of my Landlord.* 1668 misprints, help of my Lordland.
p. 138, l. 7.   *brains.* 1691, 1697, and folio, Brains.
p. 138, l. 12.   *I'le justifie.* 1691, 1697, and folio, I'll justify.
p. 138, l. 21.   *old Lady.* 1691, 1697, and folio, Old Lady.
p. 138, l. 22.   *design.* 1691, 1697, and folio, Design.
p. 138, l. 26.   *on 'em.* [*Exeunt.* 1691, 1697, and folio, omit "[*Exeunt.*"
p. 138, l. 29.   *house.* 1691, 1697, and folio, House.
p. 138, l. 31.   *quarrel.* 1691, 1697, and folio, Quarrel.
p. 138, l. 35.   *revenge.* 1691, 1697, and folio, Revenge.
p. 139, l. 1.   *Non-conformist.* 1691, 1697, and folio, Nonconformist.
p. 139, l. 13.   *Neighbors.* 1691, 1697, and folio, Neighbours.
p. 139, l. 13.   *mumming.* 1691, 1697, and folio, Mumming.
p. 139, l. 18.   *Indian-gowns.* 1691, 1697, and folio, *Indian* Gowns.
p. 139, l. 19.   *masks.* 1691, 1697, and folio, Masks.
p. 139, l. 19.   *you and I will.* 1691, 1697, and folio, You and I will.
p. 139, l. 31.   *why stools.* 1691, 1697, and folio, why Stools.
p. 139, l. 33.   *hoysted.* 1691, 1697, and folio, hoisted.
p. 139, l. 36.   *High-lander's invention.* 1691, 1697, and folio, Highlander's Invention.
p. 139, l. 40.   *A Lou's Touche.* 1678, 1691, 1697, and folio, all read, *A Lon's Touche!* (*Allons touche!*)
p. 140, l. 1.   *health.* 1691, 1697, and folio, Health.
p. 140, l. 2.   *altitudes.* 1691, 1697, and folio, Altitudes.
p. 140, l. 13.   *undone! undone!* 1691, 1697, and folio, Like enough: Undone! Undone! My Daughter's gone.

p. 140, l. 20. *An you will not.* 1691, 1697, and folio, And you will not.

p. 140, l. 30. *wooden breast-work.* 1691, 1697, and folio, Wooden Breast-work.

p. 140, l. 33. *vail'd.* 1691, 1697, and folio, veil'd.

p. 140, l. 39. *joyn'd.* 1691, 1697, and folio, join'd.

p. 140, l. 40. *Sir Martin, & these are.* 1678, 1691, 1697, and folio, Sir Martin, and these are.

p. 141, l. 9. *married.* 1691, 1697, and folio, Married.

p. 141, l. 15. *e'ne.* 1691, 1697, and folio, e'en.

p. 141, l. 16. *fortune.* 1691, 1697, and folio, Fortune.

p. 141, l. 21. *perswaded.* 1691, 1697, and folio, persuaded.

p. 141, l. 28. *consummation.* 1691, 1697, and folio, Consummation.

p. 141, l. 29. *nature.* 1691, 1697, and folio, Nature.

p. 141, l. 31. *married.* 1691, 1697, and folio, Married.

p. 141, l. 35. *Serving-man.* 1691, 1697, and folio, Serving Man.

p. 142, l. 1. *Cawdels.* 1691, 1697, and folio, Cawdles.

p. 142, l. 3. *matrimony.* 1691, 1697, and folio, Matrimony.

p. 142, l. 4. *melancholly.* 1691, 1697, and folio, Melancholly.

p. 142, l. 5. *love.* 1691, 1697, and folio, Love.

p. 142, l. 13. *lov'd.* 1691, 1697, and folio, Lov'd.

p. 142, l. 14. *inclination.* 1691, 1697, and folio, Inclination.

p. 142, l. 15. *now I am afraid you begin.* 1691, 1697, and folio, now, I am afraid, you begin.

p. 142, l. 16. *nights warning.* 1691, 1697, and folio, Night's Warning.

p. 142, l. 17. *love.* 1691, 1697, and folio, Love.

p. 142, l. 20. *quarry.* 1691, 1697, and folio, Quarry.

p. 142, l. 21. *Love's.* 1691, 1697, and folio, print the final couplet in italics.

p. 142, l. 23. *FINIS.* Not in folio.

THE TEMPEST

The text of the comedy, *The Tempest, or The Enchanted Island,* by Davenant and Dryden, was first printed quarto, 1670. Of this date there are two issues, which can be distinguished by the following points. In the first issue, 1670 A, the author's name at the end of the Preface is spelt *Driden;* in the second issue, 1670 B, *Dryden.* Page 2, line 32, *Vall's* in the first issue (a mistake repeated in the folio, 1701) is corrected to *Viall's* in the second issue. Page 3, line 16, 1670 A has *sttar-board*, corrected to *star-board* in 1670 B. In the first issue the pagination of page 7 is misprinted 5.

The Davenant and Dryden comedy was reprinted (but not altogether exactly) in the folio of 1701.

In 1910 the Rowfant Club of Cleveland, Ohio, privately printed for their members one hundred copies of the Davenant and Dryden comedy from the quarto of 1670. This issue, which has no scholarly guarantee, may justly be deemed negligible.

In 1922 the present editor included *The Tempest*, printed from the quarto of 1670, with full annotations in his volume *Shakespeare Adaptations*.

The version of *The Tempest* which appears in all the collected editions of Dryden (save, as has been noted, in the folio of 1701), and which is given by Scott, and again by Saintsbury in his recension of Scott, is none other than the book of Thomas Shadwell's opera, *The Tempest, or The Enchanted Island*, first printed quarto, 1674 (*The Term Catalogues*, Michaelmas (25 November), 1674). It should be noted that in his Variorum *The Tempest*, Furness unwarily presents this libretto (in a mutilated state) for the Davenant and Dryden comedy, and moreover he most inaccurately heads this reprint (p. 389) "Dryden's Version." His comments upon the text, and indeed his shallow and insulse treatment of the whole matter, should be disregarded.

One Frederick W. Kilbourne, the editor of *The Tempest* (1908), in "The Bankside-Restoration Shakespeare" (general editor Appleton Morgan), thinking to give the text of the Davenant and Dryden comedy, not only reprinted Shadwell's libretto from the quarto 1676, but complacently added a note of his own engine and invention to the effect that this represented the play *as revised finally by John Dryden in his Second Edition of* 1676!

Shadwell's libretto was first published quarto 1674, and again 1676 (*bis*), 1690, 1695, 1701, and frequently during the eighteenth century.

The edition of *The Tempest*, 1710 (*price 8d.*), in the collection called "English Plays" (*Neatly and correctly printed, in small volumes fit for the pocket & sold by* T. Johnson, *Bookseller in the* Hague), and advertised under Shakespeare's name "altered by *Davenant & Dryden*," contains, it is true, more of the comedy than most editions supply, although even in this case Shadwell's elaborate scenic directions are freely interpolated throughout, and the text is very faulty, whole lines and speeches having been carelessly dropped.

Since the variants between the Davenant and Dryden comedy, 4to, 1670, and the opera, 4to, 1674, may be esteemed the work of Shadwell I have not conceived it necessary to give full textual notes upon these in an edition of Dryden. In my edition of Shadwell, moreover, I have already furnished an excursus which supplies all these divergences. It will suffice to point out that the alterations which prevail in the Opera were planned upon deliberate and definite lines. For the most part they are excisions of dialogue to allow time for the new songs, dances, and spectacular effects without unduly prolonging the performance. For the Opera, Act II of the Comedy has been wholly rearranged. It is not without interest to note that in the Opera lines of rare beauty have been drastically cut when others could have been equally well spared, and poetic phrase has on several occasions become commonplace, *e.g.* "Absolute *Millan*" of the Comedy, 1670 (and of Shakespeare) in 1674 is "absolute in *Millan*." I have ventured to suggest that here we have another argument in favour of Shadwell's re-handling of the Comedy.

In his alteration of *The Tempest* Dryden evidently follows the First Folio. Thus in I, 11, l. 287, he has "what torment I did find thee in"; the other Folios read "which." It is plain, however, that he consulted the Second and Third Folios, 1632 and 1664. Thus in I, 11, l. 441, the First Folio has "Why speaks my father so ungently?" The Second and Third Folios and Dryden have "urgently." In some instances Dryden does not adhere to any of the Folio readings. In his *Dryden als Shakespeare-Bearbeiter*, Halle a. S., 1882, pp. 9, 10, Max Rosbund gives it as his opinion that it were unsafe to conclude which Folio Dryden employed, but he inclines to think the Third Folio was used. Otto Witt declares himself definitely convinced that Dryden worked on the text of the Third Folio, *The Tempest, or The Enchanted Island. A Comedy by John Dryden*, 1670. *The Sea-Voyage. A Comedy by Beaumont and Fletcher*, 1647. *The Goblins Tragi-Comedy by Sir John Suckling*, 1646, *in ihrem Verhältnis zu Shakspere's "Tempest" und den übrigen Quellen*, Rostock, 1899, pp. 7–10. But as Witt used the Quarto 1701, which is Shadwell's libretto, his arguments are nugatory altogether and fall to the ground.

It should be noted that Dryden was apparently the first to assign to Prospero the speech which commences "Abhor'd Slave," I, 2. All the Folios give this to Miranda, but the responsible editors of Shakespeare have without exception followed Dryden. Theobald well says: "I am persuaded the author never design'd this speech for Miranda," and Capell warmly supports him.

It must not be forgotten that Davenant was collaborating with Dryden, and the two poets may have used Folios of different dates.

p. 152, l. 4. *business.* Folio, 1701, Business.
p. 152, l. 5. *gallantry.* 1701, Gallantry.
p. 152, l. 5. *examen.* 1701, Examen.
p. 152, l. 5. *pomp.* 1701, Pomp.
p. 152, l. 6. *ostentation.* 1701, Ostentation.
p. 152, l. 6. *words.* 1701, Words.
p. 152, l. 6. *talent.* 1701, Talent.
p. 152, l. 8. *gayety.* 1701, Gaiety.
p. 152, l. 9. *Scene.* Quarto, 1670; and folio, 1701. The Hague edition, 12mo, 1710, reads "Sense," which certainly better suits the passage.
p. 152, l. 10. *trappings.* 1701, Trappings.
p. 152, l. 10. *writing.* 1701, Writing.
p. 152, l. 10. *flourishes.* 1701, Flourishes.
p. 152, l. 13. *argument.* 1701, Argument.
p. 152, l. 16. *memory.* 1701, Memory.
p. 152, l. 16. *joyn.* 1701, join.
p. 153, l. 3. *friend.* 1701, Friend.
p. 153, l. 3. *invention.* 1701, Invention.
p. 153, l. 4. *writing.* 1701, Writing.
p. 153, l. 5. *style.* 1701, Style.
p. 153, l. 6. *neerly.* 1701, nearly.
p. 153, l. 7. *fancy.* 1701, Fancy.
p. 153, l. 13. *man.* 1701, Man.
p. 153, l. 13. *corrections.* 1701, Corrections.

p. 153, l. 14.   *writings.* 1701, Writings.
p. 153, l. 15.   *man.* 1701, Man.
p. 153, l. 18.   *name.* 1701, Name.
p. 153, l. 19.   *ingratitude.* 1701, Ingratitude.
p. 153, l. 24.   *reputation.* 1701, Reputation.
p. 153, l. 27.   *imperfections.* 1701, Imperfections.
p. 153, l. 27.   *merit.* 1701, Merit.
p. 153, l. 27.   *name.* 1701, Name.
p. 153, l. 29.   *Driden.* 1670 B, Dryden. 1701, Driden.
p. 154, l. 8.   *subjects.* 1701, *Subjects.*
p. 154, l. 27.   *people.* 1701, *People.*
p. 154, l. 35.   *man.* 1701, *Man.*
p. 154, l. 36.   *e're.* 1701, *e'er.*
p. 154, l. 37.   *man.* 1701, *Man.*
p. 154, l. 39.   *abed.* 1701, *in Bed.*
p. 155, l. 18.   *aiery.* 1701, airy.
p. 157, l. 3.   *The Enchanted Island.* 1701 has, The Tempest, or, The Enchanted Island.
p. 157, l. 19.   *dram.* 1701, Dram.
p. 157, l. 24.   *men.* 1701, Man.
p. 158, l. 3.   *friend.* 1701, Friend.
p. 158, l. 9.   *fate.* 1701, Fate.
p. 158, l. 9.   *hanging.* 1701, Hanging.
p. 158, l. 10.   *destiny.* 1701, Destiny.
p. 158, l. 15.   [*Ex. Stephano.* 1701, [*Exit* Stephano.
p. 158, l. 17.   *man.* 1701, Man.
p. 158, l. 17.   *main-Capstorm.* 1701, Main-Capstorm.
p. 158, l. 19.   *seere-Capstorm.* 1701, Seere-Capstorm.   A misprint for jeer-Capstorm.
p. 158, l. 26.   *turn out all hands.* 1701, turn out, all hands.
p. 158, l. 30.   *Viall's.* 1670 A and 1701, Vall's.
p. 158, l. 32.   *Bulleys.* 1701, Bullies.
p. 159, l. 15.   *star-board.* 1670 A misprints, sttar-board.
p. 159, l. 16.   *neerer.* 1701, nearer.
p. 159, l. 28.   *o're.* 1701, o'er.
p. 159, l. 33.   *noise-maker.* 1701, Noise-maker.
p. 159, l. 37.   *Nut-shell.* 1701, Nut-shel.
p. 160, l. 3.   *crimes.* 1701, Crimes.
p. 160, l. 4.   *shouldest.* 1701, shouldst.
p. 160, l. 8.   *blessing.* 1701, Blessing.
p. 160, l. 10.   *mouths.* 1701, Mouths.
p. 160, l. 11.   *prayers.* 1701, Prayers.
p. 160, l. 14.   *e'ne.* 1701, e'en.
p. 160, l. 15.   *meerly.* 1701, mearly.
p. 160, l. 19.   *water.* 1701, Water.
p. 160, l. 22.   *wills.* 1701, Wills.
p. 160, l. 35.   *walks.* 1701, Walks.

p. 160, l. 40.   *power.* 1701, Power.
p. 161, l. 11.   *ne're.* 1701, ne'er.
p. 161, l. 14.   *spectacle.* 1701, Spectacle.
p. 161, l. 14.   *wrack.* 1701, Wrack.
p. 161, l. 24.   *image.* 1701, Image.
p. 161, l. 30.   *e're.* 1701, e'er.
p. 161, l. 34.   *power.* 1701, Power.
p. 161, l. 39.   *blessing.* 1701, Blessing.
p. 162, l. 6.   *Trunck.* 1701, Trunk.
p. 162, l. 9.   *worldly.* 1701, Worldly.
p. 162, l. 10.   *mind.* 1701, Mind.
p. 162, l. 14.   *cure.* 1701, Cure.
p. 162, l. 14.   *deafness.* 1701, Deafness.
p. 162, l. 19.   *man.* 1701, Man.
p. 162, l. 27.   *people.* 1701, People.
p. 162, l. 36.   *fortitude.* 1701, Fortitude.
p. 162, l. 40.   *Noble man.* 1701, Nobleman.
p. 163, l. 3.   *man.* 1701, Man.
p. 163, l. 5.   *mid-Heaven.* 1701, Mid-Heaven.
p. 163, l. 40.   *odde.* 1701, odd.
p. 163, l. 41.   *arms.* 1701, Arms.
p. 164, l. 5.   *hatches.* 1701, Hatches.
p. 164, l. 12.   *person.* 1701, Person.
p. 164, l. 16.   *mid-season.* 1701, Mid-season.
p. 164, l. 35.   *salt.* 1701, Salt.
p. 165, l. 6.   *sorceries.* 1701, Sorceries.
p. 165, l. 10.   *child.* 1701, Child.
p. 165, l. 11.   *slave.* 1701, Slave.
p. 165, l. 12.   *servant.* 1701, Servant.
p. 165, l. 13.   *spirit.* 1701, Spirit.
p. 165, l. 14.   *earthy.* 1701, Earthy.
p. 165, l. 14.   *commands.* 1701, Commands.
p. 165, l. 18.   *imprison'd.* 1701, Imprison'd.
p. 165, l. 19.   *years.* 1701, Years.
p. 165, l. 21.   *Mill-wheels.* 1701, Mill-Wheels.
p. 165, l. 30.   *breasts.* 1701, Breasts.
p. 165, l. 31.   *ne're.* 1701, ne'er.
p. 165, l. 35.   *peg thee.* 1670 A, peg the.
p. 165, l. 36.   *howld.* 1701, howl'd.
p. 165, l. 39.   *spirit.* 1701, Spirit.
p. 166, l. 1.   *eye-ball.* 1701, Eye-Ball.
p. 166, l. 3.   *child.* 1701, Child.
p. 166, l. 5.   *I'le.* 1701, I'll. And always spelt thus in folio.
p. 166, l. 6.   *answer.* 1701, Answer.
p. 166, l. 7.   *creature.* 1701, Creature.
p. 166, l. 13.   *apparition.* 1701, Apparition.
p. 166, l. 14.   *ear.* 1701, Ear.

p. 166, l. 18.　*e're.* 1701, e'er.
p. 166, l. 20.　*o're.* 1701, o'er.
p. 166, l. 21.　*side-ſtiches.* 1701, Side-ſtiches.
p. 166, l. 25.　*dinner.* 1701, Dinner.
p. 166, l. 41.　*peopl'd.* 1701, Peopl'd.
p. 167, l. 1.　*ne're.* 1701, ne'er.
p. 167, l. 10.　*curse.* 1701, Curse.
p. 167, l. 10.　*red botch.* 1701, Red Botch.
p. 167, l. 13.　*malice.* 1701, Malice.
p. 167, l. 14.　*command.* 1701, Command.
p. 167, l. 15.　*bones.* 1701, Bones.
p. 167, l. 28.　*winds.* 1701, Winds.
p. 167, l. 29.　*waves.* 1701, Waves.
p. 167, l. 36.　*wind.* 1701, Wind.
p. 167, l. 42.　*belly.* 1701, Belly.
p. 168, l. 2.　*magick.* 1701, Magick.
p. 168, l. 3.　*news.* 1701, News.
p. 168, l. 6.　*man.* 1701, Man.
p. 168, l. 10.　*siſter.* 1701, Siſter.
p. 168, l. 38.　*ſtomack.* 1701, Stomach.
p. 168, l. 38.　*rejoyce.* 1701, rejoice.
p. 168, l. 39.　*meal.* 1701, Meal.
p. 169, l. 4.　*head.* 1701, Head.
p. 169, l. 5.　*waves.* 1701, Waves; and thus with initial capital when this
　　　　word occurs throughout the play.
p. 169, l. 5.　*oar'd.* 1701, Oar'd.
p. 169, l. 8.　*death.* 1701, Death; and thus with initial capital when this
　　　　word occurs throughout the play.
p. 169, l. 19.　*crimes.* 1701, Crimes.
p. 169, l. 23.　*Valour.* 1701, valour.
p. 169, l. 27.　*power.* 1701, Power. And always with initial capital in folio.
p. 169, l. 30.　*shipwrackt.* 1701, Shipwreckt.
p. 169, l. 37.　*bounty.* 1701, Bounty.
p. 170, l. 8.　*sins.* 1701, Sins.
p. 170, l. 15.　*breaſts.* 1701, Breaſts.
p. 170, l. 21.　*visions.* 1701, Visions.
p. 170, l. 21.　*o're.* 1701, o'er. And always spelt thus in folio.
p. 170, l. 24.　*in the shape.* 1701, *in shape.*
p. 170, l. 27.　*mortals.* 1701, Mortals.
p. 170, l. 29.　*muſter.* 1701, Muſter.
p. 170, l. 32.　*minds.* 1701, Minds.
p. 170, l. 35.　*virtue.* 1701, Virtue. And always with capital initial in folio.
p. 170, l. 38.　*Murd.* Although both 4to and folio have [*Enter Murther,*
　　　　speech-prefix in 4to is *Murd.*; in folio *Mur.*
p. 171, l. 6.　*spirits.* 1701, Spirits. And always with capital initial in folio.
p. 171, l. 17.　*despair and death.* 1701, Despair and Death.
p. 171, l. 19.　*fruit.* 1701, Fruit.

426

p. 171, l. 19. *birds.* 1701, Birds.
p. 171, l. 22. *conscience.* 1701, Conscience.
p. 171, l. 40. *wrack.* 1701, Wrack.
p. 171, l. 40. *musick.* 1701, Musick. And always with capital initial in folio.
p. 172, l. 12. *knell.* Both quarto 1670 and folio 1701 by some curious error omit the word *knell* and end line *hourly ring his,* but I conceive I am justified in inserting [*knell,*] at this place, and so transferring the comma.
p. 172, l. 25. *soop.* 1701, Soop.
p. 172, l. 32. *prize-Brandy.* 1701, Prize-Brandy.
p. 172, l. 40. *eyes.* 1701, Eyes. In folio "Eye" and "Eyes" are always spelt with capital initial.
p. 173, l. 6. *jade.* 1701, Jade.
p. 173, l. 10. *years.* 1701, Years.
p. 173, l. 11. *agen.* 1701, again.
p. 173, l. 14. *marries.* 1701, Marries.
p. 173, l. 26. *fellow.* 1701, Fellow.
p. 173, l. 32. *subjects.* 1701, Subjects. And always with capital initial in folio.
p. 173, l. 37. *voice.* 1701, Voice. And always with capital initial in folio.
p. 173, l. 43. *people.* 1701, People. And always with capital initial in folio.
p. 174, l. 9. *face.* 1701, Face.
p. 174, l. 15. *bottle.* 1701, *Bottle.*
p. 174, l. 18. *I shall no more.* The folio prints this Song in italic, but the quarto has roman.
p. 174, l. 21. *comfort.* 1701, Comfort.
p. 175, l. 15. *free election.* 1701, free Election.
p. 175, l. 35. *rebellion.* 1701, Rebellion.
p. 175, l. 40. *wood.* 1701, *Wood.*
p. 176, l. 2. *curse.* 1701, Curse.
p. 176, l. 2. *they'l.* 1701, they'll.
p. 176, l. 9. *madness.* 1701, Madness.
p. 176, l. 13. *fool.* 1701, Fool.
p. 176, l. 19. *bring thee Wood.* 1701, bring the Wood.
p. 176, l. 26. *cœlestial.* 1701, Cœlestial.
p. 177, l. 5. *good natur'd.* 1701, good Natur'd.
p. 177, l. 8. *beautiful and bright.* 1701, Beautiful and Bright.
p. 177, l. 10. *her.* 1701, Her.
p. 177, l. 19. *firing.* 1701, Firing.
p. 177, l. 26. *I drink.* 1701, I Drink.
p. 177, l. 27. *worshipful.* 1701, Worshipful.
p. 177, l. 32. *drink her health.* 1701, drink her health.
p. 177, l. 36. *dying.* 1701, Dying.
p. 177, l. 39. *calculation.* 1701, Calculation.
p. 177, l. 41. *face.* 1701, Face.
p. 178, l. 9. *youth.* 1701, Youth.
p. 178, l. 15. *creature.* 1701, Creature. Creature, Creatures, always with capital initial in folio.

p. 178, l. 22.   *enemies.* 1701, Enemies.
p. 178, l. 26.   *courage.* 1701, Courage.
p. 178, l. 30.   *old age.* 1701, Old Age.
p. 178, l. 31.   *conquest.* 1701, Conquest.
p. 178, l. 33.   *fury.* 1701, Fury.
p. 178, l. 33.   *young.* 1701, Young.
p. 178, l. 37.   *beauteous.* 1701, Beauteous.
p. 178, l. 37.   *killing.* 1701, Killing.
p. 178, l. 38.   *charm.* 1701, Charm.
p. 178, l. 39.   *enchantment.* 1701, Enchantment.
p. 178, l. 41.   *fight.* 1701, Fight.
p. 178, l. 43.   *lids.* 1701, Lids.
p. 178, l. 43.   *pierce.* 1701, Pierce.
p. 179, l. 3.   *wake.* 1701, Wake.
p. 179, l. 10.   *fairer.* 1701, Fairer.
p. 179, l. 11.   *delightful.* 1701, Delightful.
p. 179, l. 12.   *necks.* 1701, Necks.
p. 179, l. 13.   *Rain-bow.* 1701, Rain-Bow.
p. 179, l. 16.   *dangerous and fair.* 1701, Dangerous and Fair.
p. 179, l. 25.   *To morrow.* 1701, To Morrow.
p. 179, l. 25.   *news.* 1701, News.
p. 179, l. 27.   *lesson.* 1701, Lesson.
p. 179, l. 32.   *limits.* 1701, Limits.
p. 179, l. 33.   *obedience.* 1701, Obedience.
p. 179, l. 37.   *daughters.* 1701, Daughters.
p. 179, l. 38.   *retire.* 1701, Retire.
p. 179, l. 40.   *bounds.* 1701, Bounds.
p. 179, l. 41.   *path.* 1701, Path.
p. 180, l. 2.   *curled.* 1701, Curled.
p. 180, l. 2.   *rugged.* 1701, Rugged.
p. 180, l. 3.   *dreadful.* 1701, Dreadful.
p. 180, l. 9.   *wild.* 1701, Wild.
p. 180, l. 17.   *pain.* 1701, Pain.
p. 180, l. 18.   *affairs.* 1701, Affairs.
p. 180, l. 21.   *legs.* 1701, Legs.
p. 180, l. 41.   *I'le humble.* 1701, I'll Humble.
p. 180, l. 42.   *pardon.* 1701, Pardon.
p. 181, l. 8.   *poyson.* 1701, Poyson.
p. 181, l. 26.   *shall eat.* 1701, shall Eat.
p. 181, l. 31.   *danger.* 1701, Danger.
p. 181, l. 39.   *dye.* 1701, Die.
p. 182, l. 1.   *my sight.* 1701, My Sight.
p. 182, l. 3.   *beauteous murderer.* 1701, Beauteous Murderer.
p. 182, l. 7.   *fair thing.* 1701, Fair Thing.
p. 182, l. 12.   *disobey'd.* 1701, Disobey'd.
p. 182, l. 12.   *presence.* 1701, Presence.
p. 182, l. 13.   *dye.* 1701, Die.

428

p. 182, l. 14.	*heart.* 1701, Heart.
p. 182, l. 20.	*must die?* 1701. must Die?
p. 182, l. 21.	*for when.* 1701, For when.
p. 182, l. 41.	*command.* 1701, Command.
p. 183, l. 4.	*death.* 1701, Death.
p. 183, l. 7.	*elder.* 1701, Elder.
p. 183, l. 23.	*love.* 1701, Love.
p. 183, l. 29.	*secret.* 1701, Secret.
p. 183, l. 29.	*knowledge.* 1701, Knowledge.
p. 184, l. 9.	*innocence.* 1701, Innocence.
p. 184, l. 16.	*be clear. your Sister.* 1701, be clear, your Sister.
p. 184, l. 39.	*to cure you.* 1701, to Cure you.
p. 184, l. 42.	*promise.* 1701, Promise.
p. 185, l. 7.	*maid.* 1701, Maid.
p. 185, l. 15.	*wildness.* 1701, Wildness.
p. 185, l. 16.	*whelp.* 1701, Whelp.
p. 185, l. 22.	*passion.* 1701, Passion.
p. 185, l. 31.	*feet.* 1701, Feet.
p. 185, l. 35.	*mouth.* 1701, Mouth.
p. 186, l. 3.	*blood.* 1701, Blood.
p. 186, l. 4.	*disease.* 1701, Disease.
p. 186, l. 37.	*open air.* 1701, open Air.
p. 186, l. 40.	*followers.* 1701, Followers.
p. 187, l. 21.	*vengance.* 1701, Vengance.
p. 187, l. 30.	*meat.* 1701, Meat.
p. 187, l. 36.	*service.* 1701, Service.
p. 188, l. 7.	*forth-rights.* 1701, Forth-rights.
p. 188, l. 15.	*Land: well.* 1701, Land: Well.
p. 188, l. 22.	*apparition.* 1701, Apparition.
p. 188, l. 28.	*ore'flowing.* 1701, *o'rflowing.*
p. 188, l. 30.	*bideing.* 1701, *biding.*
p. 188, l. 39.	*heavenly.* 1701, Heavenly.
p. 189, l. 9.	*fruits.* 1701, Fruits.
p. 189, l. 10.	*feast.* 1701, Feast.
p. 189, l. 29.	*marry.* 1701, Marry.
p. 189, l. 31.	*neck.* 1701, Neck.
p. 189, l. 32.	*wrist.* 1701, Wrist.
p. 190, l. 2.	*sucking-Bottle.* 1701, Sucking-Bottle.
p. 190, l. 3.	*God a mighty liquor.* 1701, God A Mighty Liquor.
p. 190, l. 15.	*soul.* 1701, Soul.
p. 190, l. 29.	*season.* 1701, Season.
p. 191, l. 16.	*gulp.* 1701, gulph.
p. 191, l. 19.	*shoe.* 1701, Shoe.
p. 191, l. 24.	*malice.* 1701, Malice.
p. 191, l. 25.	*bin holy-water.* 1701, been Holy-water.
p. 191, l. 28.	*valiant.* 1701, Valiant.
p. 191, l. 33.	*arms.* 1701, Arms.

p. 191, l. 36.   *beginner.* 1701, Beginner.
p. 192, l. 5.   *mouth.* 1701, Mouth.
p. 192, l. 6.   *title.* 1701, Title (*bis*).
p. 192, l. 12.   *war.* 1701, War.
p. 192, l. 15.   *answer.* 1701, Answer.
p. 192, l. 15.   *world.* 1701, World.
p. 192, l. 17.   *first.* 1701, First.
p. 192, l. 24.   *tongues.* 1701, Tongues.
p. 193, l. 13.   *power.* 1701, Power.
p. 193, l. 13.   *foes.* 1701, Foes.
p. 193, l. 20.   *flatteries.* 1701, Flatteries.
p. 193, l. 20.   *frowns.* 1701, Frowns.
p. 193, l. 36.   *further.* 1701, farther.
p. 194, l. 30.   *beauty's.* 1701, Beauty's.
p. 194, l. 30.   *Cancker.* 1701, Cancer.
p. 194, l. 31.   *person.* 1701, Person.
p. 194, l. 31.   *company.* 1701, Company.
p. 194, l. 41.   *mortal.* 1701, Mortal.
p. 195, l. 7.   *ebbe.* 1701, ebb.
p. 195, l. 19.   *powers.* 1701, Powers.
p. 195, l. 23.   *spy.* 1701, Spy.
p. 195, l. 27.   *house.* 1701, House.
p. 195, l. 32.   *fresh-Brook.* 1701, Fresh-Brook.
p. 195, l. 39.   *child.* 1701, Child.
p. 196, l. 6.   *advocate.* 1701, Advocate.
p. 196, l. 19.   *friends.* 1701, Friends.
p. 196, l. 21.   *maid.* 1701, Maid.
p. 196, l. 22.   *corners.* 1701, Corners.
p. 196, l. 29.   *speech.* 1701, Speech.
p. 196, l. 32.   *command.* 1701, Command.
p. 197, l. 4.   *passion.* 1701, Passion.
p. 197, l. 8.   *commands.* 1701, Commands.
p. 197, l. 42.   *stranger.* 1701, Stranger.
p. 198, l. 1.   *birth.* 1701, Birth.
p. 198, l. 6.   *life.* 1701, Life.
p. 198, l. 7.   *mist.* 1701, Mist.
p. 198, l. 7.   *fortunes.* 1701, Fortunes.
p. 198, l. 10.   *free-will.* 1701, Free-will.
p. 198, l. 16.   *youth.* 1701, Youth.
p. 199, l. 2.   *beauty.* 1701, Beauty.
p. 199, l. 10.   *disease.* 1701, Disease.
p. 199, l. 24.   *beauties.* 1701, Beauties.
p. 200, l. 13.   *friendship.* 1701, Friendship.
p. 200, l. 27.   *heavenly.* 1701, Heavenly.
p. 201, l. 1.   *mind.* 1701, Mind.
p. 201, l. 5.   *souls.* 1701, Souls.
p. 201, l. 9.   *fortune.* 1701, Fortune.

p. 201, l. 12.   *joyn'd.* 1701, join'd.
p. 201, l. 12.   *chain of love.* 1701, Chain of Love.
p. 201, l. 17.   *voice.* 1701, Voice.
p. 202, l. 7.   *captivity.* 1701, Captivity.
p. 202, l. 8.   *fool.* 1701, Fool.
p. 202, l. 11.   *o'rebid.* 1701, o'erbid.
p. 202, l. 27.   *conversation.* 1701, Conversation.
p. 203, l. 24.   *jealousie.* 1701, Jealousie.
p. 204, l. 4.   *imprisonment.* 1701, Imprisonment.
p. 204, l. 14.   *dissembler.* 1701, Dissembler.
p. 206, l. 4.   *creature.* 1701, Creature.
p. 206, l. 39.   *ignorance.* 1701, Ignorance.
p. 207, l. 35.   *she should.* 1701, She should.
p. 208, l. 16.   *corner.* 1701, Corner.
p. 209, l. 11.   *person.* 1701, Person.
p. 209, l. 23.   *immortal liquor.* 1701, Immortal Liquor.
p. 209, l. 24.   *water.* 1701, Water.
p. 209, l. 39.   *We want.* 1701 prints in italic.
p. 210, l. 2.   *come, hands.* 1701, Come, hands.
p. 210, l. 6.   *fellow.* 1701, Fellow.
p. 210, l. 7.   *belly.* 1701, Belly.
p. 210, l. 8.   *hectoring.* 1701, Hectoring.
p. 210, l. 9.   *flesh or fish.* 1701, Flesh or Fish.
p. 210, l. 12.   *voyage.* 1701, Voyage.
p. 210, l. 20.   *Your Grace.* 1701 arranges as two lines, commencing the
                 second with For I will . . .
p. 210, l. 30.   *patience good people.* 1701, Patience good People.
p. 210, l. 41.   *lov'st.* 1701, Lov'st.
p. 211, l. 1.   *noble.* 1701, Noble.
p. 211, l. 3.   *Witches.* 1701, Wiches.
p. 211, l. 4.   *Mounsor De-Viles.* 1701, Monsieur *de Viles.*
p. 211, l. 5.   *mark.* 1701, Mark.
p. 211, l. 6.   *tippling.* 1701, Tippling.
p. 211, l. 6.   *serving-men.* 1701, Serving-Men.
p. 211, l. 7.   *homely.* 1701, Homely.
p. 211, l. 8.   *Virtuous.* 1701, Vertuous.
p. 211, l. 15.   *natural.* 1701, Natural.
p. 211, l. 16.   *make love.* 1701, Make Love.
p. 211, l. 17.   *marry'd.* 1701, Marry'd.
p. 211, l. 18.   *great man.* 1701, Great Man.
p. 211, l. 18.   *but make.* 1701, But make.
p. 211, l. 22.   *throat.* 1701, Throat.
p. 211, l. 23.   *give.* 1701, Give.
p. 211, l. 27.   *possession.* 1701, Possession.
p. 211, l. 29.   *skink.* 1701, Skink.
p. 211, l. 29.   *Graces health.* 1701, Grace's Health.
p. 211, l. 31.   *I love thee.* 1701, I Love thee.

p. 212, l. 4.   *chuck.* 1701, Chuck.
p. 212, l. 5.   *words.* 1701, Words.
p. 212, l. 7.   *grace.* 1701, Grace.
p. 212, l. 7.   *correct.* 1701, Correct.
p. 212, l. 9.   *love.* 1701, Love.
p. 212, l. 18.   *do you stand.* 1701, Do you stand.
p. 212, l. 28.   *separation.* 1701, Separation.
p. 213, l. 32.   *his life.* 1701, his Life.
p. 213, l. 33.   *spirit.* 1701, Spirit.
p. 213, l. 37.   *malice.* 1701, Malice.
p. 214, l. 4.   *combat.* 1701, Combat.
p. 214, l. 14.   *fields.* 1701, Fields.
p. 214, l. 14.   *years.* 1701, Years.
p. 214, l. 16.   *Mount Heila.* Only the Hague edition, 1710, here correctly
                 reads, Mount *Heela.*
p. 214, l. 17.   *wings.* 1701, Wings.
p. 214, l. 17.   *flames.* 1701, Flames.
p. 214, l. 18.   *nostrils.* 1701, Nostrils.
p. 214, l. 18.   *smoak.* 1701, Smoak.
p. 214, l. 23.   *pardon.* 1701, Pardon.
p. 214, l. 33.   *mortal mould.* 1701, Mortal Mould.
p. 214, l. 37.   *will.* 1701, Will.
p. 215, l. 2.   *blessing.* 1701, Blessing.
p. 215, l. 28.   *walks.* 1701, Walks.
p. 215, l. 37.   *n'ere.* 1701, ne'er.
p. 215, l. 37.   *years.* 1701, Years.
p. 215, l. 39.   *memory.* 1701, Memory.
p. 216, l. 2.   *had bin here.* 1701, had been here.
p. 216, l. 6.   *shipwrackt.* 1701, Shipwrackt.
p. 216, l. 7.   *vengance.* 1701, Vengance.
p. 216, l. 15.   *blood-thirsty.* 1701, Blood-thirsty.
p. 216, l. 23.   *dye.* 1701, die.
p. 216, l. 28.   *execution.* 1701, Execution.
p. 216, l. 30.   *life.* 1701, Life.
p. 216, l. 36.   *murder.* 1701, Murder.
p. 217, l. 3.   *crueller.* 1701, Crueller.
p. 217, l. 3.   *sentence.* 1701, Sentence.
p. 217, l. 4.   *death.* 1701, Death.
p. 217, l. 6.   *crimes.* 1701, Crimes.
p. 217, l. 7.   *friends.* 1701, Friends.
p. 217, l. 19.   *age.* 1701, Age.
p. 217, l. 22.   *fellows.* 1701, Fellows.
p. 217, l. 30.   *soul has left his body.* 1701, Soul has left his Body.
p. 217, l. 34.   *earth.* 1701, Earth.
p. 217, l. 40.   *precept.* 1701, Precept.
p. 218, l. 6.   *body.* 1701, Body.
p. 218, l. 10.   *I've bin.* 1701, I've been.

p. 218, l. 25.   *fortune.* 1701, Fortune.

p. 219, l. 3.   *I'le never.* 4to, 1670 misprints "I'e." 1701, I'll.

p. 219, l. 4.   *bed.* 1701, Bed.

p. 219, l. 16.   *crimes.* 1701, Crimes.

p. 219, l. 21.   *subjects.* 1701, Subjects.

p. 219, l. 24.   *passions.* 1701, Passions.

p. 219, l. 28.   *In chains a spirit of ætherial mould?* 1701, In Chains a Spirit
      of Ætherial Mould?

p. 219, l. 30.   *pow'r.* 1701, Pow'r.

p. 219, l. 30.   *subjection.* 1701, Subjection.

p. 219, l. 33.   *pardon.* 1701, Pardon.

p. 220, l. 3.   *pardon or reprieve.* 1701, Pardon or Reprieve.

p. 220, l. 5.   *execute.* 1701, Execute.

p. 220, l. 5.   *grace.* 1701, Grace.

p. 220, l. 6.   *prerogative.* 1701, Prerogative.

p. 220, l. 7.   *blood.* 1701, Blood.

p. 220, l. 31.   *salvage.* 1701, Salvage.

p. 220, l. 35.   *aiery.* 1701, airy.

p. 220, l. 41.   *body.* 1701, Body.

p. 220, l. 41.   *soul.* 1701, Soul.

p. 221, l. 4.   *wings.* 1701, Wings.

p. 221, l. 5.   *journey.* 1701, Journey.

p. 221, l. 12.   *circle.* 1701, Circle.

p. 221, l. 19.   *spirit.* 1701, Spirit.

p. 221, l. 22.   *soul.* 1701, Soul.

p. 221, l. 22.   *life's door.* 1701, Life's Door.

p. 221, l. 23.   *Rivers.* 1701, River's.

p. 221, l. 25.   *mouth.* 1701, Mouth.

p. 221, l. 27.   *servant.* 1701, Servant.

p. 221, l. 32.   *air.* 1701, Air.

p. 221, l. 39.   *life.* 1701, Life.

p. 222, l. 4.   *chair.* 1701, *Chair.*

p. 222, l. 10.   *dye.* 1701, Die.

p. 222, l. 15.   *young.* 1701, Young.

p. 222, l. 17.   *breathless sleep.* 1701, Breathless Sleep.

p. 222, l. 21.   *frosty morning.* 1701, Frosty Morning.

p. 222, l. 22.   *mouth.* 1701, Mouth.

p. 222, l. 23.   *soul.* 1701, Soul.

p. 222, l. 27.   *rain'd and snow'd.* 1701, Rain'd and Snow'd.

p. 222, l. 30.   *fought.* 1701, Fought.

p. 222, l. 32.   *dye.* 1701, Die.

p. 222, l. 37.   *live.* 1701, Live.

p. 222, l. 37.   *killing.* 1701, Killing.

p. 222, l. 39.   *crying.* 1701, Crying.

p. 222, l. 41.   *difference.* 1701, Difference.

p. 223, l. 1.   *hurt.* 1701, Hurt.

p. 223, l. 4.   *blood.* 1701, Blood.

p. 223, l. 5.   *I do not love.* 1701, I do not Love.
p. 223, l. 7.   *May live.* 1701, May Live.
p. 223, l. 7.   *blood.* 1701, Blood.
p. 223, l. 12.   *fair and beautiful.* 1701, Fair and Beautiful.
p. 223, l. 16.   *wound.* 1701, Wound.
p. 223, l. 17.   *ſtrength.* 1701, Strength.
p. 223, l. 18.   *blood.* 1701, Bloud.
p. 223, l. 21.   *delight in loving.* 1701, Delight in Loving.
p. 223, l. 25.   *unconſtant.* 1701, inconſtant.
p. 223, l. 28.   *air.* 1701, Air.
p. 223, l. 37.   *life.* 1701, Life.
p. 224, l. 12.   *charity.* 1701, Charity.
p. 224, l. 12.   *pardon.* 1701, Pardon.
p. 224, l. 32.   *denys.* 1701, denies.
p. 225, l. 6.   *errours.* 1701, Errours.
p. 225, l. 7.   *love.* 1701, Love.
p. 225, l. 8.   *friends.* 1701, Friends.
p. 225, l. 26.   *penitence.* 1701, Penitence.
p. 225, l. 28.   *blood.* 1701. Blood.
p. 225, l. 38.   *people.* 1701, People.
p. 226, l. 3.   *compleat.* 1701, complete.
p. 226, l. 12.   *beds.* 1701, Beds.
p. 227, l. 7.   *Sallads without.* 1701, Sallads, without.
p. 227, l. 13.   *hangman.* 1701, Hangman.
p. 227, l. 14.   *friend.* 1701, Friend.
p. 227, l. 15.   *life.* 1701, Life.
p. 227, l. 16.   *mad men.* 1701, Mad Men.
p. 227, l. 27.   *command.* 1701, Command.
p. 227, l. 28.   *power.* 1701, Power.
p. 227, l. 33.   *fool.* 1701, Fool.
p. 227, l. 34.   *world.* 1701, World.
p. 227, l. 39.   *morn.* 1701, Morn.
p. 228, l. 4.   *wing.* 1701, Wing.
p. 228, l. 9.   *conſtitution.* 1701, Conſtitution.
p. 228, l. 12.   *servant.* 1701, Servant.
p. 228, l. 15.   *years.* 1701, Years.
p. 228, l. 23.   *year.* 1701, Year.

AN EVENING'S LOVE

There are two editions of *An Evening's Love*, 4to, 1671. The firſt (A) has "Aćted at the Theater Royal"; the second (B) "Aćted at the Theatre-Royal." This second edition is often miſtaken for the firſt. Mr. Wise, however, *A*

TEXTUAL NOTES

Dryden Library, has pointed out that there are notable differences. In B there are several errors in pagination, but it is largely a page for page reprint of the earlier edition (A). In A the Prologue occupies both sides of one leaf, and the list of *Persons Represented* is given on the recto of the succeeding leaf, the verso remaining blank. In B both the Prologue and list of *Persons Represented* are compressed upon one leaf. In A, Act I, Scene 2, and Act II each commence upon a fresh page; in B such is not the case. Moreover, A being set up from MS., the compositor after the necessary title commenced the letterpress with sig. A. Upon receiving the prefatory matter he employed a series of lower-case letters to register. In the case of B, the compositor commenced with A1 for the title-page and continued with his signatures from A to O. In A each recto has head-line *or, The Mock-Astrologer.* In B each recto has *Or, The Mock-Astrologer.*

The later seventeenth-century quartos are 4to, 1675, and 1691. From the latter of these is taken the text of the folio, 1701, which, however, introduces inferior and unimproved variants, which in one case at least amount to absolute error.

p. 237, l. 5. *noble.* 1691, folio 1701, Noble.
p. 237, l. 7. *Amongst.* The folio commences the Dedication with a preliminary, "May it please your Grace,".
p. 237, l. 8. *opinion.* Folio 1701, *Opinion. sic* throughout.
p. 237, l. 8. *vertue.* 1691, 1701, *Virtue,* and so throughout.
p. 237, l. 8. *obligations.* 1691, 1701, *Obligations.*
p. 237, l. 9. *precedence.* 1701, *Precedence.*
p. 237, l. 11. *men.* 1691, 1701, *Men,* or, *Man,* throughout with capital initial.
p. 237, l. 13. *life.* 1701, *Life* throughout with capital initial, as also "*Lives.*"
p. 237, l. 13. *example.* 1701, *Example* throughout.
p. 237, l. 15. *world.* 1691, 1701, *World* throughout.
p. 237, l. 19. *glory.* 1691, 1701, *Glory.*
p. 237, l. 19. *slave.* 1691, 1701, *Slave.*
p. 237, l. 20. *hand.* 1691, 1701, *Hand.*
p. 237, l. 20. *greatness.* 1691, 1701, *Greatness.*
p. 237, l. 24. *person.* 1701, *Person.*
p. 237, l. 26. *armes.* 1691, 1701, *Arms.*
p. 237, l. 28. *flight.* 1671 misprints *fight.*
p. 237, l. 31. *fortunes.* 1691, 1701, *Fortunes* throughout.
p. 237, l. 32. *loyalty.* 1691, 1701, *Loyalty* throughout.
p. 238, l. 2. *fidelity.* 1701, *Fidelity.*
p. 238, l. 2. *spirits.* 1701, *Spirits.*
p. 238, l. 3. *Soveraign.* 1701, *Sovereign.*
p. 238, l. 6. *dethron'd.* 1701, *Dethron'd.*
p. 238, l. 7. *extoll.* 1701, *extol.*
p. 238, l. 9. *cause.* 1701, Cause.
p. 238, l. 10. *Martyrdome.* 1691, 1701, Martyrdom.
p. 238, l. 10. *chief.* 1701, *Chief.*

p. 238, l. 12.   *conquer'd.* 1701, *Conquer'd.*
p. 238, l. 12.   *that usurping.* 1701, that Usurping.
p. 238, l. 14.   *Enterprize.* 1691, 1701, *enterprize.*
p. 238, l. 20.   *desert.* 1701, *Desert.*
p. 238, l. 20.   *reputation.* 1701, *Reputation.*
p. 238, l. 20.   *valiant.* 1701, *Valiant.*
p. 238, l. 20.   *faithful.* 1701, *Faithful.*
p. 238, l. 22.   *morning.* 1691, 1701, *Morning.*
p. 238, l. 24.   *evening.* 1691, 1701, *Evening.*
p. 238, l. 25.   *day.* 1701, *Day* throughout.
p. 238, l. 25.   *serene.* 1701, *Serene.*
p. 238, l. 25.   *dawn.* 1701, *Dawn.*
p. 238, l. 26.   *prophesie.* 1701, *Prophecy.*
p. 238, l. 27.   *day-light.* 1701, *Day-Light.*
p. 238, l. 27.   *skies.* 1691, 1701, *Skies.*
p. 238, l. 27.   *health.* 1701, *Health.*
p. 238, l. 28.   *body.* 1701, *Body.*
p. 238, l. 28.   *mind.* 1701, *Mind.*
p. 238, l. 28.   *neither.* 1701, *Neither.*
p. 238, l. 29.   *fatigue.* 1701, *Fatiegue.*
p. 238, l. 29.   *exercise.* 1701, *Exercise.*
p. 238, l. 29.   *pains.* 1701, *Pains.*
p. 238, l. 30.   *study.* 1701, *Study.*
p. 238, l. 30.   *extremity.* 1701, *Extremity.*
p. 238, l. 32.   *youthful.* 1701, *Youthful.*
p. 238, l. 33.   *retirements.* 1701, *Retirements.*
p. 238, l. 33.   *honour.* 1701, *Honour.*
p. 238, l. 33.   *poetrie.* 1691, *Poetry.* 1701, *Poetrie.*
p. 238, l. 35.   *applause.* 1701, *Applause.*
p. 238, l. 35.   *business.* 1701, *Business.*
p. 238, l. 36.   *age.* 1691, 1701, *Age.*
p. 238, l. 36.   *shades.* 1701, *Shades.*
p. 238, l. 36.   *reading.* 1701, *Reading.*
p. 238, l. 37.   *imitation.* 1701, *Imitation.*
p. 238, l. 38.   *happiness.* 1701, *Happiness.*
p. 238, l. 39.   *person.* 1701, *Person* throughout.
p. 238, l. 39.   *excellent.* 1701, *Excellent.*
p. 238, l. 40.   *Partner.* 1701, *Part'ner.*
p. 238, l. 42.   *bosome.* 1691, *bosom.* 1701, *Bosom.*
p. 238, l. 42.   *enspir'd.* 1691, *inspir'd.* 1701, *Inspir'd.*
p. 238, l. 43.   *writing.* 1701, *Writing.*
p. 239, l. 1.   *style.* 1701, *Style.*
p. 239, l. 1.   *anticipated.* 1701, *Anticipated.*
p. 239, l. 2.   *envy.* 1691, 1701, *Envy.*
p. 239, l. 3.   *which.* 1701, *Which.*
p. 239, l. 3.   *ashes.* 1701, *Ashes.*
p. 239, l. 4.   *payment.* 1701, *Payment.*

p. 239, l. 5.   *presage.* 1701, *Presage.*
p. 239, l. 6.   *praise.* 1701, *Praise.*
p. 239, l. 7.   *satisfaction.* 1701, *Satisfaction.*
p. 239, l. 7.   *judicious.* 1701, *Judicious.*
p. 239, l. 10.   *adoration.* 1701, *Adoration.*
p. 239, l. 11.   *death.* 1701, *Death.*
p. 239, l. 13.   *consecrated.* 1701, *Consecrated.*
p. 239, l. 13.   *immortality.* 1701. *Immortality.*
p. 239, l. 14.   *praises.* 1701, *Praises.*
p. 239, l. 14.   *celebrated.* 1701, *Celebrated.*
p. 239, l. 14.   *dear.* 1701, *Dear.*
p. 239, l. 14.   *just.* 1701, *Just.*
p. 239, l. 14.   *pious.* 1701, *Pious.*
p. 239, l. 16.   *consideration.* 1701, *Consideration.*
p. 239, l. 16.   *pen.* 1701, *Pen.*
p. 239, l. 18.   *truth.* 1701, *Truth.*
p. 239, l. 18.   *justifie.* 1691, *justify.*
p. 239, l. 19.   *Panegyrick.* 1701, *Penegyrick.*
p. 239, l. 20.   *praises.* 1701, *Praises.*
p. 239, l. 21.   *writes.* 1701, *Writes.*
p. 239, l. 21.   *actions.* 1701, *Actions.*
p. 239, l. 24.   *acknowledgments.* 1701, *Acknowledgments (bis).*
p. 239, l. 25.   *names.* 1701, *Names.*
p. 239, l. 25.   *manes.* 1701, Manes.
p. 239, l. 26.   *favours.* 1701, *Favours.*
p. 239, l. 27.   *publick.* 1701, *Publick.*
p. 239, l. 30.   *vanity.* 1701, *Vanity.*
p. 239, l. 30.   *proud.* 1701, *Proud.*
p. 239, l. 31.   *gracious.* 1701, *Gracious.*
p. 239, l. 33.   *title.* 1691, 1701, *Title.*
p. 239, l. 34.   *reason.* 1701, *Reason.*
p. 239, l. 36.   *present.* 1701, *Present.*
p. 239, l. 38.   *thanks.* 1701, *Thanks.*
p. 239, l. 38.   *written.* 1701, *Written.*
p. 239, l. 39.   *compos'd.* 1701, *Compos'd.*
p. 239, l. 40.   *noble.* 1701, *Noble.*
p. 239, l. 40.   *water-mark.* 1701, *Water-Mark.*
p. 239, l. 41.   *ebb.* 1691, 1701, Ebb.
p. 293, l. 41.   *wit.* 1701, *Wit. sic* throughout.
p. 240, l. 1.   *glory.* 1691, 1701, *Glory.*
p. 240, l. 2.   *honour.* 1691, 1701, *Honour.*
p. 240, l. 2.   *veneration.* 1691, 1701, *Veneration.*
p. 240, l. 3.   *holily.* 1701, *Holily.*
p. 240, l. 3.   *fires.* 1701, *Fires.*
p. 240, l. 4.   *heat.* 1691, 1701, *Heat.*
p. 240, l. 5.   *devotion.* 1691, 1701, *Devotion.*
p. 240, l. 5.   *respect.* 1701, *Respect.*

p. 240, l. 5.   *passion.* 1701, *Passion.*
p. 240, l. 7.   *Your Grace's.* 1701 arranges thus: Your GRACES/Most
                Obliged,/most Humble, and/most Obedient Servant,/*John*
                Dryden./
p. 240, l. 10.   *Preface.* 1701, in roman throughout, proper names being
                italicized.
p. 240, l. 14.   *humour.* 1701, Humour throughout.
p. 240, l. 15.   *contrivance.* 1691, 1701, Contrivance.
p. 240, l. 16.   *Playes.* 1701, Plays.
p. 240, l. 18.   *discourse.* 1701, Discourse.
p. 240, l. 22.   *Opiniatre.* 1701, opiniative.
p. 240, l. 26.   *inferiour.* 1701, inferior.
p. 240, l. 30.   *tastes.* 1701, tasts.
p. 240, l. 31.   *enemies.* 1701, Enemies.
p. 240, l. 32.   *low Comedy.* 1691, 1701, Low Comedy.
p. 240, l. 35.   *satisfi'd.* 1701, satisfy'd.
p. 241, l. 12.   *entertainments.* 1701, Entertainments.
p. 241, l. 13.   *characters.* 1701, Characters.
p. 241, l. 14.   *humours.* 1701, humors.
p. 241, l. 31.   *Empirique.* 1701, Empirick.
p. 241, l. 41.   *translation.* 1701, Translation.
p. 241, l. 42.   *judgement.* 1701, judgment.
p. 242, l. 1.   *play.* 1691, 1701, Play.
p. 242, l. 3.   *people.* 1691, 1701, People.
p. 242, l. 6.   *censures.* 1701, Censures.
p. 242, l. 13.   *humour.* 1701, Humor.
p. 242, l. 14.   *who has.* 1671 misprints *wo has.*
p. 242, l. 18.   *follies.* 1701, Follies.
p. 242, l. 28.   *subjoyns.* 1691, 1701, subjoins.
p. 242, l. 32.   *enemy.* 1701, Enemy.
p. 242, l. 32.   *writings.* 1701, Writings.
p. 242, l. 38.   *extoll.* 1691, 1701, extol.
p. 243, l. 5.   *representation.* 1701, Representation.
p. 243, l. 5.   *observation.* 1701, Observation.
p. 243, l. 10.   *denyes.* 1701, denies.
p. 243, l. 11.   *conceit.* 1701, Conceit.
p. 243, l. 23.   *Playes.* 1701, Plays.
p. 243, l. 29.   *repartie.* 1701, reparty.
p. 243, l. 29.   *soul.* 1701, Soul.
p. 243, l. 29.   *conversation.* 1701, Conversation.
p. 243, l. 43.   *Repartie.* 1691, repartie. 1701, Repartee.
p. 244, l. 11.   *images.* 1701, Images.
p. 244, l. 13.   *books.* 1701, Books.
p. 244, l. 14.   *first Act.* 1691, 1701, First Act.
p. 244, l. 15.   *Satyre.* 1691, 1701, Satyr.
p. 244, l. 33.   *vice.* 1701, Vice.
p. 244, l. 35.   *Chœrea.* 1701, *Chœrae.* Chærea is the correct spelling.

p. 244, l. 42.	*in the Alchemist.* 1701, it the *Alchemist,* misprinting "it" for "in."	
p. 244, l. 43.	*cozenage.* 1701, Cozenage.	
p. 245, l. 10.	*crown'd.* 1701, Crown'd.	
p. 245, l. 16.	*authority.* 1701, Authority.	
p. 245, l. 18.	*Dramatique.* 1701, Dramatick.	
p. 245, l. 22.	*laws of justice.* 1691, 1701, Laws of Justice.	
p. 245, l. 23.	*deterre.* 1691, deterr. 1701, deter.	
p. 245, l. 25.	*Ancient.* 1701, antient.	
p. 245, l. 31.	*art of Poetry.* 1691, 1701, Art of Poetry.	
p. 245, l. 41.	*Comedie.* 1691, 1701, Comedy.	
p. 246, l. 1.	*action.* 1701, Action.	
p. 246, l. 2.	*humane nature.* 1691, humane Nature. 1701, Humane Nature.	
p. 246, l. 11.	*heaven.* 1691, 1701, Heaven.	
p. 246, l. 21.	*Playes.* 1691, 1701, Plays.	
p. 246, l. 23.	*by him.* 1701, by Him.	
p. 246, l. 27.	*theft.* 1701, Theft.	
p. 246, l. 31.	*forreign.* 1701, foreign.	
p. 246, l. 34.	*alwayes.* 1701, always.	
p. 247, l. 16.	*help't in.* 1671, help' in.	
p. 247, l. 22.	*elocution.* 1701, Elocution.	
p. 247, l. 28.	*Chances.* 1701 misprints *Ceanthes.*	
p. 247, l. 37.	*formes.* 1701, forms.	
p. 247, l. 41.	*accidents and designs.* 1701, Accidents and Designs.	
p. 247, l. 43.	*actions and passions.* 1701, Actions and Passions.	
p. 248, l. 2.	*principall.* 1701, principal.	
p. 248, l. 4.	*Judgement.* 1701, Judgment.	
p. 248, l. 5.	*fancy.* 1701, Fancy.	
p. 248, l. 5.	*life.* 1701, Life.	
p. 248, l. 7.	*theft.* 1701, Theft.	
p. 248, l. 14.	*workmanship.* 1691, 1701, Workmanship.	
p. 248, l. 20.	*withall.* 1691, 1701, withal.	
p. 248, l. 22.	*rememberd.* 1701, remembred.	
p. 248, l. 23.	*ages.* 1701, Ages.	
p. 249, l. 10.	*bliss.* 1701, Bliss.	
p. 249, l. 11.	*smackings.* 1691, 1701, smacking.	
p. 249, l. 11.	*kiss.* 1701, Kiss.	
p. 249, l. 15.	*amour.* 1691, 1701, *Amour.*	
p. 249, l. 16.	*work.* 1691, 1701, *Work.*	
p. 249, l. 26.	*pomp and glory.* 1691, 1701, *Pomp and Glory.*	
p. 250, l. 1.	*Persons Represented.* 1701, Dramatis Personæ.	
p. 250, l. 3.	*Wildblood.* 1691, 1701, *Wildbloud.*	
p. 250, l. 5.	*Maskall.* 1701, Maskal.	
p. 250, l. 10.	*Lydall.* 1691, 1701, *Lydal.*	
p. 250, l. 14.	*Bowtell.* 1691, 1701, *Bowtel.*	
p. 251, l. 26.	*How e're.* 1701, Howe'r.	
p. 251, l. 29.	*Embassador's.* 1691, Ambassadour's. 1701, Ambassador's.	

p. 251, l. 31.   *air.* 1691, 1701, Air.
p. 252, l. 1.   *then by laying.* 1691, 1701, than by laying.
p. 252, l. 9.   *dishes.* 1691, 1701, Dishes.
p. 252, l. 18.   *Country.* 1701, Countrey.
p. 252, l. 22.   *world and the flesh.* 1701, World and the Flesh.
p. 252, l. 25.   *drinking and wenching.* 1701, Drinking and Wenching.
p. 252, l. 36.   *dayes.* 1691, Days. 1701, days (throughout.)
p. 252, l. 41.   *Franck.* 1691, 1701, Frank.
p. 253, l. 32.   *father.* 1701, Father.
p. 253, l. 33.   *throats.* 1691, 1701, Throats.
p. 254, l. 10.   *sawcie.* 1691, sawcy. 1701, saucy.
p. 254, l. 17.   *boyes.* 1691, 1701, Boys.
p. 254, l. 36.   *fable.* 1691, 1701, Fable.
p. 254, l. 39.   *language.* 1701, Language.
p. 255, l. 19.   *Vaile.* 1691, Veil. 1701, Vail.
p. 255, l. 27.   *Who shall.* 1701, who shall.
p. 255, l. 29.   *I'le.* 1701, I'll. *sic* throughout.
p. 255, l. 36.   *Secret.* 1701, secret.
p. 256, l. 11.   *newes.* 1701, news.
p. 256, l. 12.   *embarque.* 1701, embark.
p. 256, l. 26.   *heart.* 1701, Heart.
p. 256, l 29.   *feather'd.* 1701, Feather'd.
p. 256, l. 34.   *cur'd.* 1701, Cur'd.
p. 256, l. 36.   *Countries.* 1701, Countreys (*bis*).
p. 257, l. 11.   *servant.* 1701, Servant.
p. 257, l. 14.   *aime.* 1701, aim.
p. 257, l. 22.   *blind-mans-buffe.* 1691, Blind-man's-buff. 1701, Blind-Mans-
                   buff.
p. 257, l. 28.   *libertie.* 1701, liberty.
p. 257, l. 29.   *devotions.* 1701, Devotions.
p. 257, l. 33.   *neighbourhood.* 1691, 1701, Neighbourhood.
p. 257, l. 39.   *fornication and adulterie.* 1691, 1701, Fornication and
                   Adultery.
p. 258, l. 26.   *wit and beauty.* 1701, Wit and Beauty.
p. 258, l. 29.   *Moores.* 1701, *Moors.*
p. 258, l. 30.   *A kind.* 1691, 1701, a kind.
p. 258, l. 30.   *beautie.* 1691, 1701, Beauty.
p. 258, l. 35.   *Nunnerie.* 1691, 1701, Nunnery.
p. 258, l. 37.   *creatures.* 1701, Creatures.
p. 258, l. 39.   *habits.* 1701, Habits.
p. 258, l. 39.   *Apishness.* 1701, apishness.
p. 259, l. 5.   *Palfray.* 1701, Palfry.
p. 259, l. 7.   *horse-play.* 1701, Horse-play.
p. 259, l. 12.   *railly'd.* 1701, rallied.
p. 259, l. 26.   *heart.* 1701, Heart.
p. 259, l. 28.   *zeal and true devotion.* 1691, 1701, Zeal and true Devotion.
p. 259, l. 29.   *divine beauty.* 1691, 1701, Divine Beauty.

p. 259, l. 31.   *ejaculation.* 1691, 1701, Ejaculation.
p. 259, l. 35.   *Marble.* 1701, marble.
p. 259, l. 42.   *law.* 1701, Law.
p. 259, l. 43.   *sun-set.* 1701, Sun-set.
p. 260, l. 16.   *haſt.* 1701, haſte.
p. 260, l. 23.   *knee-deep.* 1701, knee deep.
p. 260, l. 25.   *fingers.* 1701, Fingers.
p. 260, l. 30.   *wing.* 1701, Wing.
p. 260, l. 33.   *bells in the neck.* 1691, 1701, Bells in the Neck.
p. 260, l. 39.   *flyes.* 1701, flies.
p. 261, l. 18.   *sails.* 1691, 1701, Sails.
p. 261, l. 30.   *amour.* 1701, Amour.
p. 262, l. 8.   *brains.* 1701, Brains.
p. 262, l. 8.   *Grates.* 1701 misprints "Gates," but 12mo 1735 correctly, "Grates."
p. 262, l. 10.   *company.* 1701, company.
p. 262, l. 12.   *libertie.* 1701, liberty.
p. 262, l. 18.   *parables.* 1701, Parable. 12mo 1735, Parables.
p. 262, l. 18.   *language.* 1701, Language.
p. 262, l. 19.   *vulgar.* 1701, Vulgar.
p. 262, l. 21.   *water.* 1691, 1701, Water (*bis*).
p. 262, l. 24.   *vices.* 1701, Vices.
p. 262, l. 25.   *Colonie.* 1691, 1701, Colony.
p. 262, l. 31.   *horns.* 1691, 1701, Horns.
p. 262, l. 38.   *eternity.* 1691, 1701, Eternity.
p. 263, l. 2.   *Apoplexie.* 1701, Apoplexy.
p. 263, l. 3.   *heaven.* 1701, Heaven.
p. 263, l. 7.   *12 houses.* 1691, 12 Houses. 1701, 12. Houses.
p. 263, l. 20.   *divine.* 1691, 1701, *Divine.*
p. 263, l. 28.   *barr.* 1691, 1701, *Bar.*
p. 263, l. 30.   *warr.* 1691, 1701, *War.*
p. 263, l. 38.   *gayeties.* 1701, gaieties.
p. 264, l. 4.   *Tantaliz'd.* 1701, tantaliz'd.
p. 264, l. 8.   *Conjur'd.* 1701, conjur'd.
p. 264, l. 24.   *moneth.* 1701, month.
p. 264, l. 27.   *haſt.* 1701, haſte.
p. 264, l. 35.   *ransome.* 1691, 1701, Ransom.
p. 265, l. 12.   *povertie.* 1701, Poverty.
p. 265, l. 14.   *agoe.* 1701, ago.
p. 265, l. 15.   *house.* 1701, House.
p. 265, l. 30.   *Owle.* 1691, 1701, Owl.
p. 265, l. 31.   *complements.* 1701, Compliments.
p. 265, l. 40.   *quality.* 1701, Quality.
p. 265, l. 40.   *dear. Pray when.* 1701 divides this speech, ending one line at "dear," and commencing the next line "Pray when."
p. 266, l. 7.   *quarrell.* 1701, Quarrel.
p. 266, l. 18.   *midnight assignation.* 1691, 1701, Midnight Assignation.

441

p. 266, l. 19.   *voyage beyond sea.* 1701, Voyage beyond Sea.
p. 266, l. 20.   *memory.* 1701, Memory.
p. 266, l. 25.   *impudence.* 1701, Impudence.
p. 266, l. 29.   *purse.* 1701, Purse.
p. 266, l. 30.   *curse.* 1701, Curse.
p. 266, l. 31.   *quest.* 1701, Quest.
p. 266, l. 31.   *lie.* 1691, 1701, Lye.
p. 266, l. 34.   *innocence.* 1701, Innocence.
p. 267, l. 17.   *foretell.* 1701, foretel.
p. 267, l. 23.   *figures.* 1701, Figures.
p. 267, l. 26.   *skie.* 1691, 1701, Sky.
p. 267, l. 29.   *Astrologie.* 1691, 1701, *Astrology.*
p. 267, l. 32.   *tallents.* 1701, Talents.
p. 267, l. 34.   *skilfull.* 1701, skilful.
p. 267, l. 38.   *Chrystal.* 1691, 1701, Crystal.
p. 268, l. 1.   *honour.* 1691, 1701, Honour.
p. 268, l. 10.   *fathers.* 1701, Fathers.
p. 268, l. 15.   *prethee.* 1691, 1701, prithee.
p. 268, l. 15.   *crie.* 1691, 1701, cry.
p. 268, l. 15.   *I'll leave off.* 1671, "I'll leave of."
p. 268, l. 20.   *Girle.* 1691, 1701, Girl.
p. 268, l. 23.   *begone.* 1701, be gone.
p. 268, l. 37.   *starrs.* 1701, Stars.
p. 268, l. 38.   *fellow.* 1701, Fellow.
p. 268, l. 42.   *nature.* 1701, Nature.
p. 269, l. 1.   *fortune in marriage.* 1691, 1701, Fortune in Marriage.
p. 269, l. 3.   *marrying.* 1691, 1701, Marrying.
p. 269, l. 12.   *Astrologie.* 1701, *Astrology.*
p. 269, l. 12.   *study'd.* 1701, studied.
p. 269, l. 19.   *crazie.* 1701, crazy.
p. 269, l. 25.   *Præmunire.* 1691, 1701, *Premunire.*
p. 269, l. 27.   *burre.* 1691, 1701, Burr.
p. 269, l. 29.   *trine.* 1701, Trine.
p. 269, l. 36.   *rogue.* 1701, Rogue.
p. 269, l. 40.   *Trie.* 1701, Try.
p. 270, l. 8.   *School-Boyes questions.* 1691, School boys Questions. 1701, School-Boys-Questions.
p. 270, l. 9.   *Carkass.* 1701, Carkas.
p. 270, l. 34.   *learning.* 1701, Learning.
p. 270, l. 34.   *legs.* 1701, Legs.
p. 270, l. 38.   *Fortune-book.* 1691, 1701, Fortune-Book.
p. 271, l. 5.   *vext.* 1701, vex'd.
p. 271, l. 9.   *dayes.* 1691, 1701, days.
p. 271, l. 11.   *wind.* 1691, 1701, Wind.
p. 271, l. 12.   *trade.* 1701, Trade.
p. 271, l. 14.   *questions.* Questions.
p. 271, l. 15.   *boy.* 1701, Boy.

p. 271, l. 22.   *it will.* 1701, It will.
p. 271, l. 22.   *sins.* 1701, Sins.
p. 271, l. 33.   *'lif.* 1691, 1701, 'slife.
p. 271, l. 33.   *feaſt.* 1691, 1701, Feaſt.
p. 271, l. 33.   *fragments.* 1691, 1701, Fragments.
p. 271, l. 40.   *Embassadors.* 1691, Ambassadour's. 1701, Ambassador's.
p. 272, l. 3.   *al' Angloise.* 1701, *à l'Angloise.*
p. 272, l. 7.   *day and night.* 1701, *Day and Night.*
p. 272, l. 9.   *eyes.* 1701, *Eyes.*
p. 272, l. 17.   *tongue.* 1701, *Tongue.*
p. 272, l. 29.   *oath.* 1701, Oath.
p. 272, l. 30.   *handkerchief.* 1691, 1701, Handkerchief.
p. 273, l. 11.   *valours and magnanimities.* 1701, Valours and Magnanimities.
p. 273, l. 18.   *Gheſts.* 1701, Gueſts.
p. 273, l. 18.   *tumult.* 1701, Tumult.
p. 273, l. 26.   *secret.* 1701, Secret.
p. 273, l. 30.   *Aſtrologie, or Magick.* 1691, *Aſtrology, or Magick.* 1701, *Aſ-trologie or Magick.*
p. 273, l. 33.   *alwayes.* 1701, always.
p. 273, l. 33.   *person.* 1701, Person.
p. 273, l. 34.   *head.* 1701, Head.
p. 273, l. 37.   *drawing-room.* 1691, Drawing-Room. 1701, Drawing-room.
p. 273, l. 40.   *Forreign.* 1701, Foreign.
p. 274, l. 19.   *lazie.* 1701, lazy.
p. 274, l. 26.   *Saints miracle.* 1691, 1701, Saint's Miracle.
p. 274, l. 34.   *What say.* 1701, what say.
p. 274, l. 37.   *grace.* 1701, Grace.
p. 275, l. 3.   *Tallent.* 1701, Talent.
p. 275, l. 9.   *rooking.* 1691, 1701, Rooking.
p. 275, l. 24.   *villifie.* 1691, vilifie. 1701, villify.
p. 275, l. 34.   *Holy-dayes.* 1701, Holidays.
p. 276, l. 1.   *Vaile.* 1691, 1701, Veil.
p. 276, l. 10.   *Coquette's.* 1701, Coquettes.
p. 276, l. 25.   *head.* 1701, Head.
p. 276, l. 27.   *give me.* 1701, Give me.
p. 276, l. 29.   *what will.* 1701, What will.
p. 276, l. 36.   *fie, fie.*   1701, fy, fy.
p. 276, l. 37.   *parn.* 1701, Parn.
p. 277, l. 5.   *commands.* 1701, Commands.
p. 277, l. 10.   *judge.* 1691, 1701, Judge.
p. 277, l. 10.   *merits.* 1701, Merits.
p. 277, l. 22.   *chapter.* 1701, Chapter.
p. 277, l. 30.   *head.* 1691, 1701, Head (*bis*).
p. 277, l. 30.   *horns.* 1691, 1701, Horns (*bis*).
p. 278, l. 4.   *La you there.* 1701, Lau you there.
p. 278, l. 16.   *Heros.* 1701, Hero.
p. 278, l. 17.   *news.* 1701, News.

p. 278, l. 20. *sentence.* 1701, Sentence.
p. 278, l. 25. *glass.* 1691, 1701, Glass.
p. 278, l. 27. *sea.* 1701, Sea.
p. 278, l. 28. *witches horse.* 1691, Witches Horse. 1701, Witch's Horse.
p. 278, l. 29. *bottle of hay.* 1691, 1701, Bottle of Hay.
p. 278, l. 31. *land.* 1701, Land.
p. 278, l. 33. *works in a direct line.* 1701, Works ... line.
p. 278, l. 34. *goe.* 1701, go.
p. 278, l. 37. *honor.* 1701, Honour.
p. 278, l. 40. *fire.* 1701, Fire.
p. 278, l. 40. *enemy.* 1701, Enemy.
p. 279, l. 7. *windbound.* 1701, Windbound.
p. 279, l. 8. *to name.* 1701, to Name.
p. 279, l. 12. *testimony.* 1701, Testimony.
p. 279, l. 14. *eye.* 1691, 1701, Eye.
p. 279, l. 27. *hypocrites.* 1691, 1701, Hypocrites.
p. 279, l. 35. *writing.* 1701, Writing.
p. 279, l. 36. *voice.* 1701, Voice.
p. 279, l. 38. *name.* 1701, Name.
p. 279, l. 43. *schreeks.* 1691, *screeks.* 1701, *skrecks.*
p. 280, l. 3. *night.* 1701, Night.
p. 280, l. 9. *feet.* 1701, Feet.
p. 280, l. 10. *land Devils.* 1691, 1701, Land-Devils.
p. 280, l. 10. *foot Posts.* 1691, 1701, Foot-Posts.
p. 280, l. 14. *assignation.* 1701, Assignation.
p. 280, l. 17. *Magique.* 1701, *Magick.*
p. 280, l. 30. *question.* 1701, Question.
p. 280, l. 34. *arguments.* 1701, Arguments.
p. 280, l. 39. *discusse.* 1701, discuss.
p. 281, l. 5. *Hylegiacalls.* 1691, Hylegyacalls. 1701, Hylegyacals.
p. 281, l. 16. *Torne.* 1701, torn.
p. 281, l. 26. *Aldeboran.* 1701, *Aldebaran.*
p. 281, l. 31. *neighbour.* 1701, Neighbour.
p. 282, l. 7. *worth and vertue.* 1691, 1701, Worth and Vertue.
p. 282, l. 10. *patience.* 1701, Patience.
p. 282, l. 32. *Manners.* 1701, manners.
p. 282, l. 37. *voices.* 1701, *Voices.*
p. 283, l. 7. *give, bestow,.* 1691, 1701, Give, Bestow.
p. 283, l. 15. *prudent.* Prudent.
p. 283, l. 20. *Wolfe.* 1691, 1701, Wolf.
p. 284, l. 3. *Vailes.* 1691, Vails. 1701, Veils.
p. 284, l. 31. *onely.* 1701, only.
p. 284, l. 32. *setled.* 1701, settled.
p. 284, l. 41. *morning-dew.* 1701, Morning-dew.
p. 285, l. 6. *eye, a nose, or a lip.* 1691, 1701, Eye, a Nose, or a Lip.
p. 285, l. 7. *spans.* 1701, Span's.
p. 285, l. 16. *punisher.* 1701, Punisher.

p. 285, l. 19.	*Fresh-Maidenheads.* 1691, fresh Maidenheads. 1701, Fresh Maidenheads.	
p. 285, l. 34.	*Mony.* 1691, 1701, Money.	
p. 285, l. 35.	*money.* 1691, 1701, Money.	
p. 285, l. 41.	*chance.* 1701, Chance.	
p. 286, l. 2.	*ſtake.* 1701, Stake.	
p. 286, l. 4.	*quarters and a sice.* 1691, 1701, Quarters and a Sice.	
p. 286, l. 5.	*sixes.* 1691, 1701, Sixes.	
p. 286, l. 5.	*trey.* 1691, 1701, Trey.	
p. 286, l. 11.	*fives.* 1691, 1701, Fives.	
p. 286, l. 21.	*Afrique.* 1701, *Africk.*	
p. 286, l. 25.	*company.* 1701, Company.	
p. 286, l. 37.	*piſtols.* 1691, 1701, Piſtols.	
p. 286, l. 40.	*acquaintance.* 1701, Acquaintance.	
p. 287, l. 2.	*ſtar.* 1701, Star.	
p. 287, l. 2.	*to night.* 1701, to Night.	
p. 287, l. 16.	*heart and purse.* 1691, Heart, and Purse. 1701, Heart and Purse.	
p. 287, l. 26.	*rascall.* 1701, Rascal.	
p. 288, l. 4.	*quarrel.* 1701, Quarrel.	
p. 288, l. 5.	*ears.* 1701, Ears.	
p. 288, l. 8.	*amour.* 1701, Amour.	
p. 288, l. 16.	*neighbour Princes.* 1701, Neighbour-Princes.	
p. 288, l. 18.	*Chriſtendome.* 1701, *Chriſtendom (bis).*	
p. 288, l. 26.	*oath.* 1701, Oath.	
p. 288, l. 28.	*charity.* 1701, Charity.	
p. 288, l. 31.	*breaches.* 1701, Breaches.	
p. 288, l. 41.	*rebell.* 1701, rebel.	
p. 288, l. 42.	*warr.* 1691, 1701, War.	
p. 289, l. 2.	*example.* 1701, Example.	
p. 289, l. 13.	*Souldier.* 1691, 1701, Soldier.	
p. 289, l. 14.	*Armes.* 1701, Arms.	
p. 289, l. 21.	*enterprise.* 1691, 1701, enterprize.	
p. 289, l. 37.	*syllable.* 1691, 1701, Syllable.	
p. 290, l. 17.	*habit.* 1701, *Habit.*	
p. 290, l. 20.	*triall.* 1691, 1701, trial *(bis).*	
p. 290, l. 34.	*assignation.* 1701, Assignation.	
p. 290, l. 37.	*cleer.* 1701, *clear.*	
p. 290, l. 37.	*Skie.* 1701, *Sky.*	
p. 291, l. 16.	*case.* 1701, *Case.*	
p. 291, l. 17.	*body.* 1701, *Body.*	
p. 291, l. 18.	*cheek.* 1701, *Cheek.*	
p. 291, l. 21.	*kiss.* 1701, *Kiss.*	
p. 291, l. 29.	*Herauld.* 1701, Herald.	
p. 291, l. 32.	*purse of gold.* 1691, 1701, Purse of Gold.	
p. 291, l. 37.	*Banque.* 1691, 1701, bank.	
p. 292, l. 2.	*o're-run.* 1701, over-run.	

p. 292, l. 11.   *red.* 1691, 1701, Red.
p. 292, l. 11.   *black.* 1691, 1701, Black.
p. 292, l. 16.   *guest.* 1691, 1701, Guest.
p. 292, l. 28.   *slave.* 1701, Slave.
p. 292, l. 29.   *downward.* 1701, down ward.
p. 292, l. 30.   *Sowse.* 1701, sowse.
p. 292, l. 37.   *Linnen.* 1701, Linen.
p. 292, l. 40.   *coach and six, sounds.* 1691, Coach and six Horses Sounds.
                 1701, Coach and six Horses, sounds.
p. 293, l. 3.   *Silk-weaver.* 1691, 1701, Silk-Weaver.
p. 293, l. 14.   *Drest.* 1701, Dress'd.
p. 293, l. 19.   *bravery.* 1701, Bravery.
p. 293, l. 24.   *treasure.* 1701, Treasure.
p. 293, l. 25.   *Fairie.* 1691, 1701, Fairy.
p. 293, l. 26.   *Changeling.* 1691, 1701, Changling.
p. 293, l. 30.   *gold.* 1691, 1701, Gold.
p. 293, l. 34.   *world.* 1691, 1701, World.
p. 293, l. 35.   *legs.* 1691, 1701, Legs.
p. 293, l. 36.   *fools.* 1691, 1701, Fools.
p. 294, l. 1.   *throat.* 1701, Throat.
p. 294, l. 2.   *neck.* 1701, Neck.
p. 294, l. 13.   *tools.* 1701, Tools.
p. 294, l. 14.   *box and throw.* 1701, Box and Throw.
p. 294, l. 19.   *fortune.* 1701, Fortune.
p. 294, l. 21.   *lights.* 1701, *Lights.*
p. 294, l. 23.   *The Garden dore opens.* 1691 and 1701 print incorrectly "*The
                 Garden door opens*" as part of the stage direction. 12mo 1735
                 rightly as part of Wildblood's speech, "The Garden Door
                 opens!"
p. 294, l. 25.   *designe.* 1701, design.
p. 294, l. 31.   *Enigma.* 1691, 1701, Ænigma.
p. 294, l. 32.   *bodie or fantome.* 1691, Body or Phantom. 1701, Body or
                 Fantome.
p. 295, l. 1.   *'tis he himself.* 1671 misprints "nimself."
p. 295, l. 5.   *humanitie.* 1691, humanity. 1701, Humanity.
p. 295, l. 8.   *table.* 1701, Table.
p. 295, l. 10.   *spirit of darkness.* 1691, 1701, Spirit of Darkness.
p. 295, l. 11.   *light.* 1701, Light.
p. 295, l. 12.   *command.* 1701, Command.
p. 295, l. 18.   *riddle.* 1701, Riddle.
p. 295, l. 25.   *what can.* 1701, What can.
p. 295, l. 27.   *to put an affront.* 1701, To put an Affront.
p. 295, l. 34.   *fancie.* 1701, fancy.
p. 295, l. 36.   *fallen.* 1701, faln.
p. 296, ll. 3, 4. *valiant, learned.* 1691, 1701, Valiant, Learned.
p. 296, l. 24.   *Law Sute.* 1701, Law-Suit.
p. 296, l. 29.   *Pickerons.* 1691, 1701, Pickeroons.

TEXTUAL NOTES

p. 297, l. 6.   *stollen.* 1691, stolen. 1701, stoln.
p. 297, l. 11. *minute.* 1701, Minute.
p. 297, l. 11. *second.* 1701, Second.
p. 297, l. 14. *evening.* 1691, 1701, Evening.
p. 297, l. 16. *finger.* 1691, 1701, Finger.
p. 297, l. 20. *species.* 1701, Species.
p. 297, l. 21. *appetite.* 1691, 1701, Appetite.
p. 297, l. 29. *Armes.* 1701, Arms.
p. 297, l. 41. *baite.* 1701, bait.
p. 298, l. 19. *Swear.* 1701, swear.
p. 298, l. 21. *Cloathes, Eates.* 1691, Cloaths, eats. 1701, Cloaths, Eats.
p. 298, l. 25. *reliefe.* 1701, relief.
p. 298, l. 28. *newes.* 1701, News.
p. 298, l. 33. *eare.* 1701, Ear.
p. 299, l. 8.   *action.* 1701, Action.
p. 299, l. 9.   *inforc'd.* 1701, enforc'd.
p. 299, l. 10. *fee.* 1691, 1701, Fee.
p. 299, l. 13. *Astrologie.* 1691, 1701, *Astrology (bis).*
p. 299, l. 18. *mediation.* 1691, 1701, Mediation.
p. 299, l. 20. *Holy-day.* 1691, Holyday. 1701, Holiday.
p. 299, l. 28. *tail.* 1701, Tail.
p. 299, l. 37. *ferae naturae.* 1701, *Ferae Naturae.*
p. 299, l. 38. *game.* 1691, 1701, Game.
p. 300, l. 3.   *counsel.* 1701, Counsel.
p. 300, l. 3.   *erre.* 1691, 1701, err.
p. 300, l. 24. *figure.* 1701, Figure.
p. 300, l. 26. *art then.* 1701, Art than.
p. 300, l. 31. *truth.* 1701, Truth.
p. 301, l. 8.   *Clergie.* 1691, 1701, Clergy.
p. 301, l. 22. *memory.* 1701, Memory.
p. 301, l. 23. *street.* 1691, 1701, Street.
p. 301, l. 23. *shop.* 1691, 1701, Shop.
p. 301, l. 34. *immediately.* 1671 misprints, immedeiately.
p. 301, l. 34. *Appartment.* 1691, 1701, Apartment.
p. 301, l. 42. *guild.* 1691, 1701, gild.
p. 302, l. 3.   *nobility.* 1691, 1701, Nobility.
p. 302, l. 4.   *riches.* 1691, 1701, Riches.
p. 302, l. 6.   *destiny.* 1701, Destiny.
p. 302, l. 24. *wayes.* 1701, ways.
p. 303, l. 17. *error.* 1701, Error.
p. 304, l. 15. *fasting.* 1691, 1701, Fasting.
p. 304, l. 30. *Pistolls.* 1691, 1701, Pistols.
p. 304, l. 31. *accomplice.* 1691, 1701, Accomplice.
p. 304, l. 32. *Play.* 1701, play.
p. 304, l. 33. *wind.* 1701, Wind.
p. 304, l. 33. *door.* 1691, 1701, Door.
p. 304, l. 34. *fallen.* 1701, faln.

447

p. 305, l. 4. *grievances.* 1691, 1701, Grievances.
p. 305, l. 24. *humane.* 1701, Humane.
p. 305, l. 25. *inrag'd.* 1701, enrag'd.
p. 305, l. 31. *poverty.* 1701, Poverty (*bis*).
p. 305, l. 35. *throat.* 1691, 1701, Throat.
p. 305, l. 37. *temptations.* 1701, Temptations.
p. 305, l. 41. *flesh and blood.* 1691, flesh and bloud. 1701, Flesh and Blood.
p. 305, l. 42. *confederacie.* 1691, Confederacy. 1701, Confederacy.
p. 306, l. 25. *promises.* 1701, Promises.
p. 306, l. 28. *oathes and proteſtations.* 1691, 1701, Oaths and Proteſtations.
p. 306, l. 31. *leader.* 1701, Leader.
p. 306, l. 31. *whittle.* 1691, 1701, Whittle.
p. 306, l. 32. *Mutton haft.* 1691, 1701, Mutton-Haft.
p. 306, l. 34. *Cizars.* 1691, Scissors. 1701, Scissars.
p. 306, l. 34. *brass chain.* 1701, Brass Chain.
p. 306, l. 36. *dandriffe Comb.* 1691, Dandriff Comb. 1701, Dandriff-Comb.
p. 306, l. 37. *ferret Ribbaning.* 1691, 1701, Ferret Riboning.
p. 306, l. 43. *battel.* 1701, Battle.
p. 306, l. 43. *wing.* 1701, Wing.
p. 307, l. 11. *ſtomack.* 1701, Stomach.
p. 307, l. 31. *Venice-glass.* 1691, *Venice* Glass. 1701, *Venice*-Glass.
p. 307, l. 32. *ground.* 1701, Ground.
p. 308, l. 4. *alliance.* 1701, Alliance.
p. 308, l. 9. *a Treaty of commerce.* 1691, 1701, A Treaty of Commerce.
p. 308, l. 11. *words.* 1701, Words.
p. 308, l. 11. *privateering.* 1691, 1701, Privateering.
p. 308, l. 20. *treacherie.* 1691, 1701, Treachery.
p. 308, l. 21. *nature.* 1701, Nature.
p. 308, l. 28. *extremely.* 1691, 1701, extreamly.
p. 308, l. 33. *ransome.* 1691, 1701, Ransom.
p. 308, l. 35. *prize.* 1691, 1701, Prize.
p. 308, l. 39. *grant.* 1691, 1701, Grant.
p. 309, l. 9. *caſts.* 1691, 1701, Caſts.
p. 309, l. 9. *lip.* 1691, 1701, Lip.
p. 309. l. 10. *fruit.* 1701, Fruit.
p. 309, l. 12. *mignonne.* 1691, 1701, *magnonne.*
p. 309, l. 20. *truth.* 1701, Truth.
p. 309, l. 24. *noble.* 1701, Noble.
p. 309, l. 29. *professions.* 1701, Professions.
p. 309, l. 33. *did not.* 1701, Did not.
p. 309, l. 34. *Melchor's tender and inclination.* 1691, 1701, *Melchor's* tender
　　　　　　　　Love and Inclination.
p. 309, l. 42. *deceiv'd in Melchor.* 1691, 1701, deceiv'd in Don *Melchor.*
p. 310, l. 11. *all.* 1701, All.
p. 310, l. 13. *gravel.* 1691, 1701, Gravel.
p. 310, l. 14. *ſtream.* 1691, 1701, Stream.
p. 310, l. 18. *glory.* 1691, 1701, Glory.

p. 310, l. 29. *a bed.* 1691, a-bed. 1701, a–Bed.
p. 310, l. 34. *devotions.* 1691, 1701, Devotions.
p. 310, l. 35. *me.* 1701, mee.
p. 310, l. 41. *adresses.* 1701, Addresses.
p. 311, l. 1. *ingratitude.* 1691, 1701, Ingratitude.
p. 311, l. 14. *persons.* 1701, Persons.
p. 311, l. 17. *fortunes.* 1701, Fortunes.
p. 311, l. 21. *alarme.* 1691, Alarm. 1701, allarm.
p. 311, l. 25. *key.* 1701, Key.
p. 311, l. 25. *running.* 1671, runing.
p. 311, l. 27. *lights.* 1701, Lights.
p. 311, l. 36. *wit.* 1691, 1701, Wit.
p. 311, l. 36. *counsel.* 1691, 1701, Counsel.
p. 312, l. 5. *Playes.* 1691, 1701, Plays.
p. 312, l. 5. *faces.* 1701, Faces.
p. 312, l. 9. *Must valour.* 1671 superfluously repeats speech-prefix *Mel.*
              before these words.
p. 312, l. 10. *yarely.* 1691, 1701, yarly.
p. 312, l. 12. *limb.* 1701, *Limb.*
p. 312, l. 16. *love.* 1701, Love.
p. 312, l. 17. *wit.* 1691, 1701, Wit.
p. 312, l. 27. *foe.* 1691, 1701, Foe.
p. 312, l. 29. *wall.* 1691, 1701, Wall.
p. 312, l. 35. *Conquerour.* 1701, Conqueror.
p. 313, l. 6. *noise and tumult.* 1701, Noise and Tumult.
p. 313, l. 10. *heavens.* 1701, Heavens.
p. 313, l. 23. *Raskall.* 1691, 1701, Raskal.
p. 313, l. 26. *courage.* 1691, 1701, Courage.
p. 313, l. 26. *temptation.* 1701, Temptation.
p. 313, l. 32. *whedle.* 1691, 1701, wheedle.
p. 313, l. 42. *Allyes.* 1691, 1701, Allies.
p. 314, l. 1. *Corigidore.* 1691, Corigidor. 1701, Corrigidor.
p. 314, l. 9. *light.* 1691, 1701, Light.
p. 314, l. 20. *swarm .*1701, Swarm.
p. 314, l. 25. *con'd.* 1691, 1701, conn'd.
p. 314, l. 31. *ceremony.* 1691, 1701, Ceremony.
p. 314, l. 33. *a God's name.* 1691, a God's Name. 1701, a–God's Name.
p. 314, l. 38. *fellows.* 1701, Fellow.
p. 314, l. 40. *does my.* 1701, does your. 12mo 1735 correctly, "does my . . ."
p. 315, l. 8. *ungratious baggages.* 1691, 1701, ungracious Baggages.
p. 315, l. 31. *flesh and blood.* 1691, 1701, Flesh and Blood.
p. 315, l. 14. *camrade.* 1691, Camrade. 1701, Comrade.
p. 315, l. 17. *clutches.* 1691, 1701, Clutches.
p. 315, l. 24. *Neece Aurelia.* 1691, 1701, Niece Aurelia.
p. 315, l. 38. *you have seen.* 1701, have you seen.
p. 315, l. 40. *rarifie.* 1701, rarify.
p. 315, l. 42. *prodigie.* 1691, Prodigy. 1701, prodigy.

p. 316, l. 8.   *libertie.* 1701, liberty.
p. 316, l. 24.   *cuſtody.* 1691, 1701, Cuſtody.
p. 316, l. 39.   *malefaƈtor.* 1691, 1701, Malefaƈtor.
p. 317, l. 3.   *fire.* 1701, Fire.
p. 317, l. 8.   *years.* 1691, 1701, Years.
p. 317, l. 10.   *hold.* 1701, Hold.
p. 317, l. 19.   *whiffe.* 1701, whiff.
p. 317, l. 22.   *to them within.* 1701 omits *within.*
p. 317, l. 26.   *darkness.* 1691, 1701, Darkness.
p. 317, l. 30.   *are these.* 1701, Are these.
p. 317, l. 33.   *do you.* 1701, Do you.
p. 318, l. 11.   *company.* 1691, 1701, Companv.
p. 318, l. 11.   *nothing.* 1701, Nothing.
p. 318, l. 13.   *band.* 1691, 1701, Band.
p. 318, l. 14.   *bodies.* 1691, 1701, Bodies.
p. 318, l. 15.   *baggage.* 1691, 1701, Baggage.
p. 318, l. 22.   *weeson.* 1691, 1701, Weeson.
p. 318, l. 23.   *briſtles.* 1691, 1701, Briſtles.
p. 318, l. 25.   *ransome.* 1701, Ransome.
p. 318, l. 27.   *sword.* 1691, 1701, Sword.
p. 318, l. 27.   *throat.* 1691, 1701, Throat.
p. 318, l. 38.   *defie.* 1691, 1701, defy.
p. 318, l. 40.   *Cuſtome.* 1691, 1701, Cuſtom.
p. 319, l. 14.   *cozen'd.* 1691, 1701, couzen'd.
p. 319, l. 21.   *Romanes.* 1691, 1701, *Romans.*
p. 319, l. 23.   *fortunes.* 1691, 1701, Fortunes.
p. 319, l. 23.   *courages.* 1691, 1701, Courages.
p. 319, l. 27.   *gratitude, for Don Lopez.* 1701, gratitude for Don *Lopez.*
p. 319, l. 35.   *Starres.* 1701, Stars.
p. 319, l. 41.   *wing.* 1691, 1701, Wing.
p. 320, l. 1.   *bloodshed.* 1691, 1701, Bloodshed.
p. 320, l. 4.   *amour.* 1701, Amour.
p. 320, l. 7.   *trie.* 1701, try.
p. 320, l. 14.   *faith.* 1701, Faith.
p. 320, l. 18.   *singer.* 1701 misprints Finger.
p. 320, l. 18.   *breeches.* 1691, 1701, Breeches.
p. 320, l. 19.   *drawers.* 1691, 1701, Drawers.
p. 320, l. 20.   *smock.* 1691, 1701, Smock.
p. 320, l. 40.   *workes.* 1691, 1701, *works.*
p. 321, l. 10.   *spurre.* 1691, 1701, *spur.*
p. 321, l. 19.   *judgement.* 1701, judgment.
p. 321, l. 20.   *harmony.* 1691, 1701, Harmony.
p. 321, l. 21.   *Chriſtendome.* 1691, 1701, Chriſtendom.
p. 322, l. 3.   *Plate-fleet.* 1691, 1701, Plate-Fleet.
p. 323, l. 4.   *Judgement.* 1691, 1701, *Judgment*
p. 323, l. 6.   *eare.* 1691, 1701, *Ear.*
p. 323, l. 7.   *foe.* 1691, 1701, *Foe.*

p. 323, l. 8.   *jeſts.* 1691, 1701, *Jeſts.*
p. 323, l. 10.   *fearfull.* 1691, fearful. 1701, Fearful.
p. 323, l. 14.   *Monsieur.* 1691, 1701, Mounsieur.
p. 323, l. 16.   *rogue.* 1691, 1701, *Rogue.*
p. 323, l. 17.   *feint.* 1691, 1701, *feign'd.* Sargeaunt, fein'd.
p. 323, l. 18.   *sayes.* 1691, 1701, *says.*
p. 323, l. 21.   *dining.* 1691, 1701, *Dining.*
p. 323, l. 21.   *clock.* 1691, 1701, *Clock.*
p. 323, l. 30.   *prize.* 1691, 1701, *Prize.*
p. 323, l. 32.   *bill.* 1691, 1701, *Bill.*
p. 323, l. 37.   *sums.* 1701, *Summs.*
p. 324, l. 2.   *mercy.* 1701, *Mercy.*
p. 324, l. 4.   *height.* 1701, *heighth.*
p. 324, l. 5.   *FINIS.* 1701 omits.

TYRANNICK LOVE

The First Quarto of *Tyrannick Love* is 1670; the Second Edition, "review'd by the Authour," 1672. These are the authoritative texts. There are also 4tos of 1677, 1686, 1694 and 1695. The Second Edition first adds the concluding paragraph of the Preface, addressed to the critics.

p. 329, l. 1.   *and High-born.* 1686, 1694 and 1695, Folio 1701, (omits).
p 329, l. 10.   *Family.* 1686, 1694 and 1695, Folio 1701, Family.
p. 329, l. 12.   *troublesom.* 1686, troublesome. 1694 and 1695, Folio 1701, troublesom.
p. 329, l. 18.   *applaude.* 1686, 1694 and 1695, Folio 1701, applaud.
p. 329, l. 19.   *joyn.* 1686, 1694 and 1695, Folio 1701, join.
p. 329, l. 21.   *Heroick.* 1686, 1694 and 1695, Folio 1701, Heroic.
p. 329, l. 34.   *joyned.* 1686, joined. 1694 and 1695, Folio 1701, joyned.
p. 330, l. 14.   *was . . . inclination.* 1686, 1694 and 1695, 4to, 1672, and Folio 1701, *were . . . inclinations.*
p. 330, l. 17.   *Examples.* 1686, examples. 1694 and 1695, Folio 1701, *Examples.*
p. 330, l. 19.   *Clergie.* 1686, 1694 and 1695, Folio 1701, *Clergy.*
p. 331, l. 19.   *answered.* 1672, answer'd. 1686, 1694 and 1695, Folio 1701, answer'd.
p. 331, l. 35.   *witness.* 1686, 1694 and 1695, Folio 1701, *Witness.*
p. 332, l. 21.   *Herds-man.* 1672, Herds-man. 1686, 1694 and 1695, Folio 1701, *Herdsman.*
p. 332, l. 24.   *Errour.* 1672, Errour. 1686, 1694 and 1695, Folio 1701, *Error.*
p. 332, l. 41.   *For the little Critiques.* This passage was added in 4to 1672 *et deinceps.* 1686, 1694 and 1695, Folio 1701, *Criticks.*

451

p. 333, l. 9.   *Emperour.* 1686, 1694 and 1695, Folio 1701, Emperor.
p. 333, l. 11.   *XIth.* Thus 1672. 1686, 1694 and 1695, Folio 1701, 11*th.*
p. 333, l. 18.   *raigns.* 1672, raigns. 1686, 1694 and 1695, Folio 1701, *reigns.*
p. 333, l. 21.   *Mad-men.* 1672, Mad-men. 1686, *Mad-men.* 1694 and 1695, mad men. Folio 1701, *mad-men.*
p. 333, l. 25.   *whole.* 1672, whole. 1686, Whole. 1694 and 1695, whole. Folio 1701, *whole.*
p. 333, l. 29.   *sence.* 1672, sence. 1686, Sence. 1694 and 1695, sense. Folio 1701, *sense.*
p. 333, l. 35.   *career.* 1672, career. 1686, 1694 and 1695, Career. Folio 1701, *Career.*
p. 334, l. 11.   *Apollonius.* This character is accidentally omitted in the First Quarto, 1670, but is duly supplied in 1672, and all later editions.
p. 334, l. 13.   *Guyn.* 1672, Guyn. 1686, 1694 and 1695, Folio 1701, *Gwyn.*
p. 334, l. 14.   *Mrs. Hughes.* 1672, *Mrs. Boutell.* 1686, 1694 and 1695, Folio 1701, *Mrs. Bowtell.*
p. 335, l. 28.   *fields.* 1672, fields. 1686, 1694 and 1695, Folio 1701, Fields.
p. 335, l. 32.   *form.* 1672, form. 1686, Form. 1694 and 1695, form. Folio 1701, Form.
p. 336, l. 5.   *Senates succours.* 1672, Senate's succours. 1686, 1694 and 1695, Folio 1701, Senate's Succours.
p. 336, l. 10.   *pow'rs.* 1672, pow'rs. 1686, Pow'rs. 1694 and 1695, powers. Folio 1701, Powers.
p. 336, l. 19.   *I'le.* 1672, I'le. 1686, I'll; and throughout. 1694 and 1695, Folio 1701, I'll.
p. 336, l. 27.   *chear.* 1672, chear. 1686, 1694 and 1695, Folio 1701, cheer.
p. 336, l. 35.   *crowd.* 1672, crowd. 1686, 1694 and 1695, Folio 1701, Crowd.
p. 337, l. 9.   *wounded.* 1672, wounden. 1686, 1694 and 1695, wounden. Folio 1701, wounded.
p. 337, l. 17.   *circumference.* 1672, circumference. 1686, 1694 and 1695, Folio 1701, Circumference.
p. 337, l. 21.   *fields.* 1672, 1686, fields. 1694 and 1695, Folio 1701, Field.
p. 337, l. 32.   *visionary Souldiers.* 1672, visionary Souldiers. 1686, 1694 and 1695, Folio 1701, Visionary Soldiers.
p. 337, l. 40.   *ne're.* 1686, 1694 and 1695, ne'r. Folio 1701, ne'er.
p. 338, l. 11.   *conduct and the care.* 1686, 1694 and 1695, Folio 1701, Conduct and the Care.
p. 338, l. 19.   *envy.* 1686, 1694 and 1695, Folio 1701, Envy.
p. 338, l. 29.   *O're-shading.* 1686, 1694 and 1695, O'r shading. Folio 1701, O'er-shading.
p. 338, l. 30.   *venim.* 1686, 1694 and 1695, venom. Folio 1701, Venom.
p. 340, l. 5.   *extasies.* 1686, 1694 and 1695, Folio 1701, Ecstasies.
p. 340, l. 18.   *applause.* 1686, 1694 and 1695, Folio 1701, Applause.
p. 340, l. 26.   *cryes.* 1686, cries. 1694 and 1695, crys. Folio 1701, Cries.
p. 340, l. 31.   *prophetique.* 1686, 1694 and 1695, Folio 1701, Prophetick.

p. 341, l. 15.   *humanity.* 1672, all humane force; and so the succeeding quartos, and Folio.

p. 341, l. 24.   *leafs.* 1672, leafs. 1686, leaves. 1694 and 1695, Folio 1701, Leaves.

p. 342, l. 16.   *pow'rs divine.* 1686, 1694 and 1695, Folio 1701, Pow'rs Divine.

p. 342, l. 28.   *I owne.* 1686, 1694 and 1695, Folio 1701, I own.

p. 343, l. 14.   *Emp'rour.* 1686, 1694 and 1695, Folio 1701, Emp'ror.

p. 343, l. 29.   *toyls of War.* 1686, 1694 and 1695, toils of War. Folio 1701, Toils of War.

p. 343, l. 36.   *duty.* 1686, 1694 and 1695, Folio 1701, Duty.

p. 343, l. 37.   *conduct.* 1686, 1694 and 1695, Folio 1701, Conduct.

p. 344, l. 13.   *will.* 1686, 1694 and 1695, Folio 1701, Will.

p. 344, l. 21.   *wives.* 1686, 1694 and 1695, Folio 1701, Wives.

p. 344, l. 22.   *love.* 1686, Love. 1694 and 1695, love. Folio 1701, Love.

p. 344, l. 28.   *Pirate.* 1686, Pyrate. 1694 and 1695, Pyrates. Folio 1701, Pyrate.

p. 344, l. 30.   *gain.* 1686, Gain. 1694 and 1695, gain. Folio 1701, Gain.

p. 344, l. 32.   *wreck descrys.* 1686, 1694 and 1695, Folio 1701, Wreck descries.

p. 344, l. 33.   *inrich.* 1686, 1694 and 1695, Folio 1701, enrich.

p. 345, l. 7.   *event.* 1686, 1694 and 1695, Folio 1701, Event.

p. 345, l. 19.   *ground.* 1686, Ground. 1694 and 1695, ground. Folio 1701, Ground.

p. 345, l. 38.   *sum.* 1686, summ. 1694 and 1695, Folio 1701, Sum.

p. 346, l. 8.   *Vertue.* 1686, 1694 and 1695, Folio 1701, Virtue.

p. 347, l. 2.   *should.* 1672, shoud. 1686, 1694 and 1695, Folio 1701, should.

p. 347, l. 3.   *mid-stream's.* 1672, 1686, midstream's. 1694 and 1695, Midstream's. Folio 1701, Mid-stream's.

p. 347, l. 27.   *distils.* 1686, 1694 and 1695, Folio 1701, distills.

p. 347, l. 40.   *meen.* 1686, 1694 and 1695, Folio 1701, Meen.

p. 348, l. 3.   *foe.* 1686, 1694 and 1695, Folio 1701, Foe.

p. 348, l. 30.   *Vertues.* 1686, 1694 and 1695, Folio 1701, Virtues.

p. 348, l. 41.   *acts as duty.* 1686, 1694 and 1695, Folio 1701, Acts as Duty.

p. 349, l. 8.   *Moral virtues.* 1686, Moral Vertues. 1694 and 1695, Folio 1701, Moral Virtues.

p. 349, l. 10.   *virtues are the same.* 1686, 1694 and 1695, Riches are the same. Folio 1701, Precepts are the same.

p. 349, l. 14.   *injuries.* 1686, Injuries. 1694 and 1695, injuries. Folio 1701, Injuries.

p. 349, l. 16.   *deeds.* 1686, 1694 and 1695, Folio 1701, Deeds.

p. 349, l. 26.   *Errour.* 1686, errour. 1694 and 1695, error. Folio 1701, Error.

p. 349, l. 40.   *blood.* 1686, Blood. 1694 and 1695, blood. Folio 1701, Blood.

p. 350, l. 9.   *dy.* 1686, 1694 and 1695, dye. Folio 1701, should Dye.

p. 350, l. 16.   *claims.* 1686, 1694 and 1695, Folio 1701, Claims.

p. 350, l. 39.   *ly'st.* 1686, 1694 and 1695, li'st. Folio 1701, ly'st.

p. 350, l. 43.   *could love.* 1686, 1694 and 1695, could Love. Folio 1701, could love.

p. 352, l. 6.   *Iron heart.* The First Quarto prints "Ironheart." Folio 1701, Iron Heart.

p. 352, l. 8.   *Emperour.* 1686, 1694 and 1695, Folio 1701, Emperor.

p. 352, l. 9.   *doom.* 1686, 1694 and 1695, Folio 1701, Doom.

p. 352, l. 12.   *renown.* 1686, 1694 and 1695, Folio 1701, Renown.

p. 352, l. 34.   *tenth wave.* 1686, 1694 and 1695, tenth Wave. Folio 1701, Tenth Wave.

p. 353, l. 4.   *pray'r.* 1686, 1694 and 1695, Folio 1701, Pray'r.

p. 353, l. 8.   *world.* 1686, 1694 and 1695, Folio 1701, World.

p. 353, l. 9.   *doctrine.* 1686, Doctrine. 1694 and 1695, Doctrin. Folio 1701, Doctrine.

p. 353, l. 10.   *world.* 1686, 1694 and 1695, Folio 1701, World.

p. 353, l. 10.   *Atoms.* 1686, 1694 and 1695, Folio 1701, Atomes.

p. 353, l. 11.   *order.* 1686, 1694 and 1695, Folio 1701, Order.

p. 353, l. 12.   *cause.* 1686, 1694 and 1695, Folio 1701, Cause.

p. 353, l. 12.   *decree.* 1686, 1694 and 1695, Folio 1701, Decree.

p. 353, l. 13.   *workmanship.* 1686, 1694 and 1695, Folio 1701, Workmanship.

p. 353, l. 17.   *news.* 1686, 1694 and 1695, Folio 1701, News.

p. 353, l. 18.   *For what a greater.* This couplet is not in the First Quarto, 1670.

p. 353, l. 22.   *person.* 1686, 1694 and 1695, Folio 1701, Person.

p. 353, l. 22.   *gift.* 1686, 1694 and 1695, Folio 1701, Gift.

p. 353, l. 27.   *fires.* 1686, 1694 and 1695, Folio 1701, Fires.

p. 353, l. 38.   *bonds.* 1686, 1694 and 1695, Folio 1701, Bonds.

p. 353, l. 38.   *piety.* 1686, 1694 and 1695, Folio 1701, Piety.

p. 354, l. 2.   *tides.* 1686, 1694 and 1695, Folio 1701, Tides.

p. 354, l. 25.   *lyes open.* 1686, 1694 and 1695, Folio 1701, lies open.

p. 354, l. 37.   *bonds.* 1686, 1694 and 1695, Folio 1701, Bonds.

p. 354, l. 38.   *yoke.* 1686, 1694 and 1695, Folio 1701, Yoke.

p. 355, l. 4.   *dye.* 1686, 1694 and 1695, die. Folio 1701, Dye.

p. 355, l. 5.   *untye.* 1686, 1694 and 1695, unty. Folio 1701, untye.

p. 355, l. 8.   *Funeral-torch.* 1686, 1694 and 1695, Funeral Torch. Folio 1701, Funeral-Torch.

p. 355, l. 21.   *present.* 1686, 1694 and 1695, Folio 1701, Present.

p. 355, l. 33.   *presents.* 1686, 1694 and 1695, Folio 1701, Presents.

p. 355, l. 40.   *float.* 1672 misprints flout.

p. 356, l. 37.   *dye.* 1686, 1694 and 1695, die. Folio 1701, Die.

p. 357, l. 17.   *But You.* 1686, 1694 and 1695, Folio 1701, But you.

p. 357, l. 25.   *charms.* 1686, Charms. 1694 and 1695, charms. Folio 1701, Charms.

p. 357, l. 33.   *bird.* 1686, Bird. 1694 and 1695, bird. Folio 1701, Bird.

p. 358, l. 2.   *dare dye.* 1686, dare dye. 1694 and 1695, dare die. Folio 1701, dare Die.

p. 358, l. 21.   *bed.* 1686, Bed. 1694 and 1695, bed. Folio 1701, Bed.

p. 358, l. 22.   *disputing hard.* 1686, 1694 and 1695, disputing heard. Folio
1701, Disputing heard.

p. 358, l. 24.   *Gives her hand.* Folio 1701 omits this ſtage-direction.

p. 358, l. 32.   *sacred . . . bond.* 1686, 1694 and 1695, Folio 1701, Sacred
. . . Bond.

p. 359, l. 14.   *bed.* 1686, Folio 1701, Bed.

p. 361, l.   1.   *Moon-shine while.* 1672, *Moon-shine while.* 1686, *Moon-shine,*
while. 1694 and 1695, *Moon shine, while.* Folio 1701, *Moon-*
shine, while.

p. 361, l.   5.   *new-falling.* 1672, *new-falling.* 1686, 1694 and 1695, Folio
1701, *new falling.*

p. 361, l. 15.   *o're.* 1672, *o're.* 1686, 1694 and 1695, Folio 1701, *o'r.*

p. 361, l. 17.   *hiss in the Water.* 1686, 1694 and 1695, Folio 1701, *hiss in the*
water.

p. 361, l. 19.   *lye.* 1686, 1694 and 1695, Folio 1701, *lie.*

p. 361, l. 20.   *battel.* 1686, *Battel.* 1694 and 1695, *Battle.* Folio 1701,
Battel.

p. 361, l. 42.   *source.* 1686, 1694 and 1695, Folio 1701, Source.

p. 362, l.   2.   *whate're.* 1686, what er. 1694 and 1695, what'er. Folio 1701,
whate'er.

p. 362, l.   8.   *Suppliant-like.* 1686, 1694 and 1695, Suppliant like. Folio
1701, Suppliant-like.

p. 362, l. 17.   *e'm.* 1686, 'em. 1694 and 1695, Folio 1701, them.

p. 362, l. 21.   *dreams.* 1686, 1694 and 1695, Folio 1701, *Dreams.*

p. 362, l. 23.   *visions.* 1686, 1694 and 1695, Folio 1701, *Visions.*

p. 362, l. 26.   *Melancholy.* 1686, *melancholy.* 1694 and 1695, Folio 1701,
melancholly.

p. 362, l. 29.   *ſtreams.* 1686, 1694 and 1695, Folio 1701, *Streams.*

p. 362, l. 36.   *objeĉts.* 1686, Objeĉts. 1694 and 1695, objeĉts. Folio 1701,
Objeĉts.

p. 362, l. 37.   *Joy.* 1686, 1694 and 1695, joy. Folio 1701, Joy.

p. 363, l.   7.   *tears.* 1672, *tears.* 1686, 1694 and 1695, Folio 1701, *Tears.*

p. 363, l. 10.   *easie death.* 1686, 1694 and 1695, *easy Death.* Folio 1701,
easie Death.

p. 363 l. 12.   *friend.* 1686, 1694 and 1695, Folio 1701, *Friend.*

p. 363, l. 15.   *year.* 1686, *Year.* 1694 and 1695, Folio 1701, *year.*

p. 363, l. 17.   *Spring-tides.* 1686, 1694 and 1695, Folio 1701, *Spring-Tides.*

p. 363, l. 21.   *Age.* 1686, 1694 and 1695, *age.* Folio 1701, *Age.*

p. 363, l. 30.   *will.* 1686, 1694 and 1695, Folio 1701, Will.

p. 364, l.   2.   *Tempeſts.* 1686, 1694 and 1695, tempeſts. Folio 1701, Tem-
peſts.

p. 364, l. 16.   *Fooles.* 1686, 1694 and 1695, Folio 1701, Fools.

p. 364, l. 33.   *To S. Cath.] But thou.* This follows the folio 1701. All the
quartos incorreĉtly put *To S. Cath.*] before the line "Go
expiate . . ." which is obviously addressed to Damilcar.

p. 364, l. 40.   *Speĉters.* 1686, 1694 and 1695, Folio 1701, Speĉtres.

p. 365, l.   8.   *news.* 1686, 1694 and 1695, Folio 1701, News.

p. 365, l. 36.   *justice.* 1686, 1694 and 1695, Folio 1701, Justice.
p. 366, l. 8.   *choice.* 1686, 1694 and 1695, Folio 1701, Choice.
p. 366, l. 21.   *thred.* 1686, Thred. 1694 and 1695, Thread. Folio 1701, Thred.
p. 366, l. 24.   *child's anger.* 1686, 1694 and 1695, Child's anger. Folio 1701, Child's Anger.
p. 366, l. 39.   *flame.* 1686, 1694 and 1695, Folio 1701, Flame.
p. 366, l. 41.   *crime.* 1686, 1694 and 1695, Folio 1701, Crime.
p. 367, l. 10.   *quarrel.* 1686, 1694 and 1695, Folio 1701, Quarrel.
p. 367, l. 16.   *You'l.* 1686, 1694 and 1695, Folio 1701, You'll.
p. 367, l. 18.   *Free will's a cheat.* 1686, 1694 and 1695, Folio 1701, Free Will's a Cheat.
p. 367, l. 19.   *slavery.* 1686, 1694 and 1695, Slavery.
p. 367, l. 21.   *wyre.* 1686, 1694 and 1695, Folio 1701, Wire.
p. 367, l. 24.   *Lambs.* 1672, lambs. 1686, 1694 and 1695, Folio 1701, Lambs.
p. 367, l. 32.   *Exit Valeria.* The First Quarto, 1670, here has "*Exeunt* Porphyrius *and* Valeria *severally. To* Maximin *enters S.* Catherine. The scene between Maximin and Porphyrius first appears in the Second Quarto, 1672, as "review'd by the Authour."
p. 368, l. 5.   *Mistress.* 1686, Mistris. 1694 and 1695, Folio 1701, Mistress.
p. 368, l. 12.   *beauties.* 1686, Beauties. 1694 and 1695, beauties. Folio 1701, Beauties.
p. 368, l. 15.   *name.* 1686, Name. 1694 and 1695, name. Folio 1701, Name.
p. 368, l. 15.   *quality.* 1686, 1694 and 1695, Folio 1701, Quality.
p. 368, l. 32.   *Embassadour.* 1686, 1694 and 1695, Folio 1701, Ambassadour.
p. 368, l. 36.   *peace.* 1686, 1694 and 1695, Folio 1701, Peace.
p. 368, l. 40.   *breaches.* 1686, 1694 and 1695, Folio 1701, Breaches.
p. 369, l. 22.   *torments.* 1686, 1694 and 1695, Folio 1701, Torments.
p. 369, l. 27.   *ghostly.* 1686, 1694 and 1695, Folio 1701, Ghostly.
p. 369, l. 30.   *appetite.* 1686, 1694 and 1695, Folio 1701, Appetite.
p. 369, l. 32.   *cure, must humour.* 1686, Cure, must Humour. 1694 and 1695, Cure, must humour. Folio 1701, Cure, must Humour.
p. 369, l. 33.   *mind.* 1686, Mind. 1694 and 1695, mind. Folio 1701, Mind.
p. 369, l. 33.   *remedy.* 1686, Remedy. 1694 and 1695, remedy. Folio 1701, Remedy.
p. 369, l. 39.   *joys.* 1686, 1694 and 1695, Joyes. Folio 1701, Joys.
p. 370, l. 9.   *youth and beauty.* 1686, Youth and Beauty, 1694 and 1695, youth and Beauty. Folio 1701, Youth and Beauty.
p. 370, l. 11.   *age, and death's.* 1686, 1694 and 1695, Folio 1701, Age, and Death's.
p. 370, l. 23.   *vitious.* 1686, 1694 and 1695, Folio 1701, vicious.
p. 370, l. 33.   *dwells.* 1694 and 1695, dwels. Folio 1701, dwells.
p. 370, l. 36.   *envy.* 1686, 1694 and 1695, Folio 1701, Envy.
p. 370, l. 40.   *haste.* 1694 and 1695, hast. Folio 1701, haste.
p. 370, l. 41.   *zeal.* 1686, 1694 and 1695, Folio 1701, Zeal.

456

p. 371, l.	2.	*person.* 1686, Person. 1694 and 1695, person. Folio 1701, Person.
p. 371, l.	15.	*courage.* 1686, 1694 and 1695, Folio 1701, Courage.
p. 371, l.	30.	*dangers.* 1686, Dangers. 1694 and 1695, Folio 1701, dangers.
p. 371, l.	38.	*ſtaff.* 1686, 1694 and 1695, Folio 1701, Staff.
p. 371, l.	38.	*tryal.* 1686, 1694 and 1695, Folio 1701, trial.
p. 372, l.	24.	*conflict.* 1686, 1694 and 1695, Folio 1701, Conflict.
p. 372, l.	30.	*breſt.* 1686, 1694 and 1695, Breſt. Folio 1701, Breast.
p. 372, l.	39.	*conqueſt.* 1686, 1694 and 1695, Folio 1701, Conqueſt.
p. 372, l.	42.	*mind.* 1686, Mind. 1694 and 1695, mind. Folio 1701, Mind.
p. 373, l.	1.	*contempt.* 1695 misprints contemp.
p. 373, l.	9.	*Theater.* 1672, 1686, 1694 and 1695, Folio 1701, Theatre.
p. 373, l.	15.	*flight.* 1686, Flight. 1694 and 1695, flight. Folio 1701, Flight.
p. 373, l.	27.	*All-great.* 1672, All great. 1686, 1694 and 1695, Folio 1701, All-great.
p. 373, l.	34.	*blood.* 1686, Blood. 1694 and 1695, blood. Folio 1701, **Blood.**
p. 373, l.	41.	*deed.* 1686, Deed. 1694 and 1695, deed. Folio 1701, Deed.
p. 374, l.	2.	*Traitor.* 1686, 1694 and 1695, Folio 1701, Traytor.
p. 374, l.	33.	*offenders.* 1686, 1694 and 1695, Folio 1701, Offenders.
p. 374, l.	34.	*believers.* 1686, 1694 and 1695, Folio 1701, Believers.
p. 374, l.	41.	*call.* 1686, Call. 1694 and 1695, call. Folio 1701, Call.
p. 375, l.	8.	*beaſt.* 1686, 1694 and 1695, Folio 1701, Beaſt.
p. 375, l.	10.	*Counsellor.* 1686, 1694 and 1695, Counsellour. Folio 1701, Counsellor.
p. 375, l.	18.	*gift.* 1686, Gift. 1694 and 1695, gift. Folio 1701, Gift.
p. 375, l.	23.	*troubles.* 1686, Troubles. 1694 and 1695, troubles. Folio 1701, Troubles.
p. 375, l.	32.	*succession's thy reprieve.* 1686, 1694 and 1695, Folio 1701, Succession's thy Reprieve.
p. 375, l.	35.	*bloody Throne.* 1686, 1694 and 1695, Folio 1701, Bloody Throne.
p. 376, l.	1.	*debts of gratitude.* 1686, 1694 and 1695, Folio 1701, Debts of Gratitude.
p. 376, l.	7.	*great.* 1686, 1694 and 1695, Folio 1701, Great.
p. 376, l.	13.	*Traitors.* 1686, Traytors. 1694 and 1695, Traytor's. Folio 1701, Traitor's.
p. 376, l.	15.	*blood.* 1686, Bloud. 1694 and 1695, Folio 1701, Blood.
p. 376, l.	18.	*adoption.* 1686, 1694 and 1695, Folio 1701, Adoption.
p. 376, l.	23.	*flye.* 1686, flie. 1694 and 1695, Folio 1701, fly.
p. 376, l.	31.	*order.* 1686, 1694 and 1695, Folio 1701, Order.
p. 377, l.	2.	*cheat.* 1686, 1694 and 1695, Folio 1701, Cheat.
p. 377, l.	32.	*Pour'd upon him.* 1686, pour'd upon him. 1694 and 1695, Folio 1701, Pour'd upon him.
p. 378, l.	3.	$\left\{\begin{array}{l}\textit{Besides}\text{——}\\\textit{What is it I can}\ldots\end{array}\right\}$ 1672, $\left.\begin{array}{l}\text{Besides what can}\\\text{I for his safety do?}\end{array}\right\}$

1686, 1694 and 1695, Besides, what can I for his safety do? } Folio 1701, Besides What can I for his Safety do? }

457

p. 378, l. 8.   *terms.* Folio 1701, tearms.

p. 378, l. 28.   *pardon.* 1686, 1694 and 1695, Folio 1701, Pardon.

p. 378, l. 30.   *Then hear.* 1672, Then heere. 1686, 1694 and 1695, Folio 1701, Then here.

p. 378, l. 36.   *gratitude.* 1686, Gratitude. 1694 and 1695, gratitude. Folio 1701, Gratitude.

p. 379, l. 37.   *breast will wear.* 1686, Breast will wear. 1694 and 1695, breast will wear. Folio 1701, Breast will wear.

p. 380, l. 2.   *Holy kiss.* 1686, 1694 and 1695, Folio 1701, Holy Kiss.

p. 380, l. 15.   *He, like a secret Worm.* These four lines are only in the First Quarto, 1670.

p. 381, l. 9.   *Tempest hear.* 1672 misprints, Tempest shear. 1686, 1694 and 1695, Tempests shear. Folio 1701, Tempests hear: which is probably the correct reading.

p. 381, l. 23.   *witness.* 1686, 1694 and 1695, Folio 1701, Witness.

p. 381, l. 35.   *voice and face.* 1686, 1694 and 1695, Folio 1701, Voice and Face.

p. 382, l. 10.   *(Ah) if you knew.* Folio 1701, If you but knew.

p. 382, l. 17.   *I ask you would.* Folio 1701, I ask that you would but some promise give.

p. 382, l. 40.   *to dye.* 1686, 1694 and 1695, to die. Folio 1701, to Die.

p. 383, l. 3.   *hand and foot.* 1686, 1694 and 1695, Folio 1701, Hand and Foot.

p. 383, l. 9.   *hook.* 1686, 1694 and 1695, Folio 1701, Hook.

p. 383, l. 34.   *Sanctuary's.* 1672, Sanctuari's. 1686, 1694 and 1695, Folio 1701, Sanctuary's.

p. 384, l. 16.   *follies.* 1686, 1694 and 1695, Folio 1701, Follies.

p. 384, l. 30.   *toys.* 1686, 1694 and 1695, Folio 1701, Toys.

p. 385, l. 3.   *kind of death.* 1686, 1694 and 1695, Folio 1701, kind of Deaths.

p. 385, l. 11.   *controls.* 1672, controuls. 1686, 1694 and 1695, controlls. Folio 1701, controuls.

p. 385, l. 25.   *immortal birth.* 1686, 1694 and 1695, Folio 1701, Immortal Birth.

p. 385, l. 28.   *and Felicia.* 1672 misprints, *and* Felicio.

p. 385, l. 35.   *confines.* 1686, 1694 and 1695, Folio 1701, Confines.

p. 386, l. 2.   *woman-kind.* 1686, Woman-kind. 1694 and 1695, Woman kind. Folio 1701, Woman-kind.

p. 386, l. 5.   *rage.* 1686, 1694 and 1695, Folio 1701, Rage.

p. 386, l. 30.   *musick.* 1686, 1694 and 1695, Folio 1701, Musick.

p. 386, l. 35.   *sacred.* 1686, 1694 and 1695, Folio 1701, Sacred.

p. 387, l. 5.   *World.* 1686, world. 1694 and 1695, Folio 1701, World.

p. 387, l. 21.   *no tye.* 1686, 1694 and 1695, Folio 1701, no tie.

p. 387, l. 24.   *discords.* 1686, 1694 and 1695, Folio 1701, Discords.

p. 389, l. 4.   *execution.* 1686, 1694 and 1695, Execution. Folio 1701, execution.

p. 389, l. 14.   *Coyn.* 1686, 1694 and 1695, Folio 1701, Coin.

p. 389, l. 24.	{ *Porphyrius kisses . . .* { *Berenice kissing . . .*	These two stages directions are only in the First Quarto, 1670.

p. 389, l. 30. *Cydon her Woman.* 1672 and all subsequent quartos omit *"her Woman."*

p. 389, l. 31. *Scene of Death.* 1686, scene of Death. 1694 and 1695, Folio 1701, Scene of Death.

p. 389, l. 38. *bloody.* 1686, bloudy. 1694 and 1695, Folio 1701, bloody.

p. 390, l. 1. *Partner.* 1686, 1694 and 1695, Folio 1701, Part'ner.

p. 390, l. 4. *tears.* 1686, 1694 and 1695, Folio 1701, Tears.

p. 391, l. 7. *foolish Girl.* 1686, Foolish Girl. 1694 and 1695, Folio 1701, foolish Girl.

p. 391, l. 38. *Gums.* 1686, 1694 and 1695, Gumms. Folio 1701, Gums.

p. 392, l. 15. *Stabbing upward with his Dagger.* Only in the First Quarto, 1670.

p. 392, l. 32. *has not strength.* Folio 1701, has not Pow'r.

p. 392, l. 34. *coward Body.* 1686, Coward Body. 1694 and 1695, Folio 1701, coward Body.

p. 392, l. 39. *Soveraign's.* 1686, 1694 and 1695, Sovereign's. Folio 1701, Sovereigns.

p. 393, l. 1. *breath.* 1686, 1694 and 1695, Folio 1701, Breath.

p. 393, l. 23. *dumb-show.* 1686, dumb Show. 1694 and 1695, Dumb show. Folio 1701, dumb show.

p. 393, l. 32. *memory.* 1686, Memory. 1694 and 1695, memory. Folio 1701, Memory.

p. 394, l. 5. *storms to shore.* 1686, 1694 and 1695, Folio 1701, Storms to Shore.

p. 394, l. 9. *golden Eagles flye.* 1686, 1694 and 1695, Folio 1701, Golden Eagles fly.

p. 394, l. 12. *But to her Gates.* 1672 and all subsequent quartos read: "But to her Gates our peacefull ensignes bear." 1686, 1695 read: "peaceful Ensigns."

p. 395, l. 34. *FINIS.* 4to 1686 and Folio 1701, at the end of the Fifth Act, but other editions after the Epilogue.

EXPLANATORY
NOTES

SECRET-LOVE

p. 2. *Vitiis nemo sine nascitur.* Horace, *Sermonum*, I, iii, 68–9:

>nam vitiis nemo sine nascitur: optimus ille eſt
>qui minimis urgetur.

p. 9. *Cyrus. Artamène, ou, Le Grand Cyrus,* by Madeleine de Scudéry, ten volumes, Paris, 1649–53. Subsequent editions, Paris, 1654, 1656, 1658; Leyde, 1655, 1656. This, the moſt famous of the heroic romances, was originally published under the name of Georges de Scudéry. There is an English translation, London, 1653–4, five volumes, folio. The 12mo reprint, 1690, has: "Artamenes, Or The Grand Cyrus; That Excellent Romance. Written By that Famous Wit of *France, Monsieur* de Scudery, Governor of *Noſtre-Dame.* Englished by F. G. Esq;." The hiſtory of Cleobuline, Queen of Corinth, will be found in Part VII, Book II, of the romance. (London, folio, 1653–4, Vol. II, pp. 108–136.) Further see the note upon the Source of this play.

p. 10. *Plays are like Towns. Voyla Leƈteur, ce que i'auois à vous dire: mais quelque deffence que i'aye employée ie sçay qu'il eſt des ouurages de cette nature, comme d'une Place de guerre: où quelque soin qu'ait apporté l'Ingenieur a la fortifier, il se trouue tousiours quelque Endroit foible, où il n'a point songé, & par où on l'attaque. Mais cela ne me surprendra point: car n'ayant pas oublié que ie suis homme, ie n'ay pas oublié non plus, que ie suis sujet à faillir. Ibrahim ou l'Illuſtre Bassa.* Premiere Partie. Preface. A Paris. Chez Anthoine de Sommauille au Palais. 1641.

> *Behold, Reader, that which I had to say to you, but what defence soever I have imployed, I know that it is of works of this nature, as of a place of war, when notwithſtanding all the care the Engineer hath brought to fortifie it, there is always some weak part found, which he hath not dream'd of, and whereby it is assaulted; but this shall not surprize me; for as I have not forgot that I am a man, no more have I forgot that I am subjeƈt to erre.* Translated by Henry Cogan, London, folio, 1652.

p. 11. *whip'd to appetite.* Cf. "To the Excellent and unknown Author of the ensuing Poem," *Juvenalis Redivivus,* 4to, 1683:

>*But bleſt the teeth that did so kindly bite,*
>*That forc'd even duller Me at length to write;*
>*Stripes in old Letchers oft does raise an Appetite.*

For flagellation scenes in Reſtoration drama see Shadwell's *The Virtuoso,* produced at Dorset Garden in May, 1676, III, the episode of old Snarl and Mrs. Figgup. Also the famous Aquilina and

Antonio scene in *Venice Preserv'd*, III, 1, produced at Dorset Garden, 9 February, 1681–2. There is an allusion to some scandal of this kind in the Introduction, spoken by Haines and Betty Mackarel, to Duffett's skit *The Mock-Tempest*, produced at the Theatre Royal in the winter of 1674:

> Spare 'em not,
> Whom kindness cannot stir, but stripes may move.
> *Bet.* O Mr. *Hains!* I've often felt their Love.

The Epilogue, spoken by Joe Haines, to Lee's *Gloriana; or The Court of Augustus Caesar*, produced at Drury Lane, January, 1676, concludes:

> *We'll deal with you, Gallants, in your own way,*
> *And treat you like those Punks that love for Pay:*
> Cartwright *and I, dress'd like two thundring Whores,*
> *With rods will stand behind the Play-house Doors,*
> *And fish ye up each Day to Pleasures duly,*
> *As* Jenny Cromwell *does, or* Betty Buly.

Cf. also *Epigrams by J. D.* In Francum. XXXIII. *Étude sur la Flagellation au point de vue médical et historique*, Paris, 1899, contains some interesting material; whilst Dr. Eugen Dühren (Iwan Bloch), *Das Geschlechtsleben in England*, Book II, chapter 6, *Die Flagellomanie*, gives amplest details and anecdotes.

p. 11. *A Brother Judgment.* Cf. The Epilogue to *An Evening's Love*:

> First, looking for a Judgment or a Wit,
> Like *Jews*, I saw 'em scatter'd through the Pit.

p. 11. *nick.* Here, to criticize. A very rare use. *O.E.D.* quotes this line.

p. 11. *on Tick.* The earliest date quoted for this phrase is 1642. (British Museum, MSS. Add. 37999.) It came into general use during the reign of Charles II, and this is a very early instance. Cf. Wycherley's *Love in a Wood*, produced at the Theatre Royal in the autumn of 1671, III, 1, where Mrs. Joyner declares that Dapperwit is "a poor wretch that goes on tick for the Paper he writes his *Lampoons* on." Also Buckingham and Rochester's *Satyr* (known as *Timon*):

> Hast thou lost deep to needy *Rogues* on Tick,
> Who ne're cou'd pay, and must be paid next week?

p. 15. *an Ovall face.* The description of Florimel is said to be a portrait of Nell Gwyn.

p. 16. *an out-mouth.* A prettily pouting mouth. J. Cockburn, *Bourignianism Detected*, I, 3, has: "She was Out-mouthed, having Lips and Teeth somewhat big." Here "Out-mouthed" infers a projecting mouth, tending to ugliness.

p. 16. *blub.* Full; swelling. Cf. Shadwell's *A True Widow*, Dorset Garden, 1679, II, where Selfish says to Gatrude: "You have a pretty pouting about the Mouth like me, and fine little Blub-lips." In Otway's

The *Atheist*, Dorset Garden, autumn, 1683, Porcia is said to have
"Plump, red, blub Lips."

p. 16. *constant Maudlin.* Maudlin is here a substantive, a rare (*masculinus*)
use, employed in the sense of a whining lachrymosely sentimental
fellow.

p. 19. *Propriety.* Possession. Cf. Ken *Hymnarium* (1711), *Poetical Works*,
1721, II, 76:

> 'Tis thy Propriety, and not my own.

p. 23. *the slave of love.* This was the name given to Ghanem Ben-Ayoub.
See *Le Livre des Mille Nuits et une Nuit*, tr. Mardrus, Vol. II.

p. 26. *I would have a Lover . . . should hang himself.* Dryden was recollect-
ing *Hudibras*, Part II (1664), canto i, 481 *sqq.*:

> Quoth she, I like this plainness better
> Than false *Mock-Passion, Speech,* or *Letter,*
> Or any feat of *qualm* or *sowning,*
> But *hanging* of your self, or *drowning;*
> Your onely way with me to *break*
> Your mind, is *breaking* of your Neck.

> . . . . . .

and 495 *sqq.*:

> Yet th'are the onely ways to prove
> The unfeign'd *realities* of *Love;*
> For he that hangs, or beats out's brains,
> The *Devils* in him if he feigns.

p. 31. *The Sibylls leaves. Æneid*, III, 443–52:

> insanam vatem aspicies, quae rupe sub ima
> fata canit foliisque notas et nomina mandat.
> quaecumque in foliis descripsit carmina virgo
> digerit in numerum atque antro seclusa relinquit,
> illa manent immota locis neque ab ordine cedunt.
> Verum eadem, verso tenuis cum cardine ventus
> impulit, et teneras turbavit ianua frondes;
> numquam deinde cavo volitantia prendere saxo,
> nec revocare situs aut iungere carmina curat:
> inconsulti abeunt sedemque odere Sibyllae.

There was a Latin saw: *folium recitare Sibyllae.* Cf. Juvenal, VIII,
126:

> Credite me vobis folium recitare Sibyllae.

Upon which Eilhard Lubin glosses: "De re enim certissima Latini
dicere solebant, *Folium Sibyllae.* Sibylla autem Cumæa palmarum
foliis oracula inscribebat." And so in Farquhar's *The Constant
Couple* (Drury Lane, November, 1699), II, Standard says to Wild-
air: "Read, Sir, read; these are the *Sibyl's* Leaves that will unfold
your Destiny."

p. 35.   *knots.* Bows of ribbon. Cf. Etherege, *She Wou'd if She Cou'd*, produced at the Duke's House, Thursday, 6 February, 1667–8, Act III, the New Exchange scene where Ariana at Mistress Gazet's shop says: "We will only fancy a Suit of Knots or two at this Shop, and buy a little Essence, and wait upon Your Ladyship immediately."

p. 35.   *sky.* Blue. Cf. *She Wou'd if She Cou'd*, III, 2, where Sir Jolly talks of "A whole Bevy of Damsels in Sky, and Pink, and Flame-colour'd Taffeta's."

p. 35.   *long patch.* Cf. *Love in a Wood*, III: "*Dapperwit*. Pish, give her but leave to gape, rub her Eyes, and put on her day-Pinner; the long patch under the left eye: awaken the Roses on her cheeks, with some Spanish wool."

p. 39.   *an Hawk that will not plume.* To plume is to pluck the prey, or dismantle it of its feathers. Cf. the hawking scene in *A Woman Killed with Kindness* (4to, 1607), where Sir Charles cries: "Now she hath seiz'd the fowl, and 'gins to plume her."

p. 39.   *truss'd his quarry.* To truss is of a hawk seizing his quarry in the air, and carrying it off. Radcliffe in the *Encyclopaedia Britannica* (1910), X, 143/1, explains: "A hawk is said to 'truss' a bird when she catches it in the air, and comes to the ground with it in her talons."

p. 40.   *noise of Fiddles.* A noise=a band of musicians. Cf. Lyly, *Mother Bombie* (1594), III, 4, Rixula's song:

> Then I wish'd for a noyse
> Of crack-halter boyes,
> On those hempen strings to be twanging.

Also Chapman's *The Blind Beggar of Alexandria* (1598), where Count Hermes as he leads off Elimine says to Bragadino: "Oh that we had a noise of musitions to play to this anticke as we goe."

p. 40.   *watch me as they do Witches.* So in Mrs. Behn's *The Dutch Lover*, produced at Dorset Garden in February, 1672–3, I, 2, Marcel says:
> There is a Knack in Love, a critical Minute:
> And Women must be watcht as Witches are,
> E'er they confess.

One of the tests to which beldames suspected of sorcery were put—a mode particularly favoured by Matthew Hopkins, "Witch-Finder General"—was to tie down the accused in some painful or at least uneasy posture for twenty-four hours, during which time relays of watchers sat round. It was supposed that an imp would come to suck the witch's blood; so any fly, moth, wasp, or other insect seen in the room was her familiar in that shape, and the wretched creature was accordingly convicted of the charge. Numerous confessions are recorded to have been extracted in this manner from old hags by Master Hopkins. Cf. *Hudibras*, Part II, canto iii, 146–8:

> Some for setting above ground,
> Whole days and nights upon their breeches,
> And feeling pain, were hang'd for witches.

Cf. also Mrs. Behn's *The City-Heiress*, produced at Dorset Garden in the spring of 1681–2, Act I, where Sir Anthony advises Charles:

> Watch her close, watch her like a Witch, Boy,
> Till she confess the Devil in her,—Love.

p. 40. *and so inch him, and shove him.* To inch is to drive (in or out) by inches or small degrees. O.E.D. quotes this passage. Cf. also *Cleomenes*, II, 2, where Sosibius says:

> He gets too far into the Soldiers Grace,
> And Inches out my Master.

Cf. *The Ring and the Book*, III, 412–14:

> The brother, Abate Paolo, shrewder mouse,
> Had pricked for comfortable quarters, inched
> Into the core of Rome.

Also 615–18:

> And Pietro who, six months before, had borne
> Word after word of such a piece of news
> Like so much cold steel inched through his breast-blade,
> Now at its entry gave a leap for joy.

The word, although not used quite in the same sense as Dryden, was a favourite with Browning, and it is applied in *The Inn Album* to the slowly spreading shadow of a tree; "The shadow inching round those ferny feet."

p. 41. *Glass Coach.* Coaches with glazed windows were a novelty and greatly admired. The King used such a coach, and de Grammont brought over a new model from France, which began the rage among the mode. In Mrs. Behn's *The Town-Fop; or, Sir Timothy Tawdrey*, 4to, 1677, I, 2, the Nurse rallies Sir Timothy: "You tear it away in Town, and live like Man and Wife with your Jilt, and are every day seen in the Glass Coach, whilst your own natural Lady is hardly worth the Hire of a Hack."

p. 41. *plays booty.* To play booty is to join with confederates in order to trick and victimize another player; to play falsely and seem to lose in order to gain some desired end or object. Thus Mabbe in his translation of *Guzman d'Alfarache*, ed. 1622, I, 222: "Wee are three of vs, let vs all play booty and joyn together to coozen the Cardinall." Cf. Etherege, *The Man of Mode; or, Sir Fopling Flutter*, 4to, 1676, III, 1: *Young Bellair.* What think you of play-it on booty? *Harriet.* What do you mean? *Young Bellair.* Pretend to be in love with one another.

p. 41. *You are my Sultana Queen.* Cf. *The Way of the World*, I, where Witwoud terms the ladies: "Empresses, my Dear——By your What-dee-call-'ems he means Sultana Queens." "Ay, *Roxolana's*," pertly chips in Petulant.

p. 42. *fidg.* To fidge is to move about restlessly: to fidget. Cf. Congreve *The Way of the World*, 4to, 1700, V, where Mrs. Marwood says: "the good Judge, tickl'd with the Proceeding, simpers under a gray Beard, and figes off and on his Cushion as if he had swallow'd *Cantharides*, or sat upon *Cow-Itch*."

p. 43. *that's once.* A phrase expressing determination. Thus in Wycherley's *The Country-Wife*, 4to, 1675, III, 1, Mrs. Pinchwife cries: "Nay, I will go abroad, that's once."

p. 44. *Fifth-rate.* A naval metaphor. *The London Gazette*, 1666, No. 38/4, speaks of "A Fifth Rate Fregat, called the Sweepstakes." The old division of the British Navy was into six rates of vessels, according to the number of guns carried.

p. 44. *Dutch built.* The large flat-bottomed vessels of the Netherlanders. Cf. Andrew Marvell's *The Growth of Popery*, folio, 1677: "Whether (as is imputed) all the Ships taken are Dutch built?"

p. 44. *Pygmalion's Image.* The story of Pygmalion who carved an ivory image of a fair maiden with which he fell in love, and which was at his prayer endowed with life by Aphrodite is told by Ovid, *Metamorphoseon*, X, 243–297, but is more familiar perhaps to modern readers from the play *Pygmalion and Galatea*, by W. S. Gilbert, and from the pictures of Burne Jones.

p. 45. *pumpt for a lye.* Cf. *The Spanish Fryar; or, The Double Discovery*, 4to, 1681, I, where Lorenzo begins to evade and make excuses whilst Gomez interrupts with, "But—no pumping, my dear Colonel."

p. 46. *cry me anon.* As a town-crier.

p. 47. *busk.* See note on *Wild Gallant*, Vol. I, pp. 432–3.

p. 56. *the little Comb.* To comb the wig. Fops affected to do this with grace and fashion. Cf. The Prologue to the Second Part of *The Conquest of Granada by the Spaniards*:

> But, as when Vizard Masque appears in Pit,
> Straight every Man who thinks himself a Wit
> Perks up; and, managing his Comb with grace,
> With his white Wigg sets off his Nut-brown Face.

There are constant allusions to the use of the Comb. Cf. Killigrew's *The Parsons Wedding*, folio 1663 (1664), I, 3: "*Enter* Jack Constant, Will Sadd, Jolly, *and a Footman, they comb their heads, and talk*.

p. 56. *courant slurr.* The fashionable courant or coranto was a dance characterized by a gliding step as distinguished from a leaping step. Cf. Sir John Davies in his *Orchestra; or, A Poeme on Dauncing* (18mo, 1596), stanza 69:

> What shall I name those currant trauases,
> That on a triple *dactile* foot doe runne

Close by the ground with sliding passages,
Wherein that Dauncer greateſt praise hath wonne
Which with beſt order can all orders shunne;
For euery where he wantonly muſt range,
And turne, and wind, with vnexpeƈted change.

A slur is a gliding movement in dancing. Cf. Wycherley's *The Gentleman Dancing-Maſter*, Dorset Garden, March, 1672, Aƈt IV, where Gerard leads Hippolita up and down with "One, two, and a slur." Mrs. Eliza Haywood in *The Female Speƈtator* (1746, Second Edition, colleƈted, 12mo, 1748), IV, 304, has: "She . . . swam round the room as if leading up a courant."

p. 57. *You will not draw in Court.* Heavy penalties were aƈtually attached to this grave breach of etiquette. In England S. James' Park was part of the royal precinƈts, and to draw a weapon there involved serious punishment. This is given as an excuse for his cowardice by Bluffe in *The Old Batchelour*, IV, who sneaks away at the appearance of Sharper, muttering: "My Blood rises at that Fellow so I can't ſtay where he is; and I muſt not draw in the Park."

p. 58. *a man of Garniture and Feather.* "A man of feather," or simply "A Feather," was a beau, a gallant. Cf. Pope's Sir Plume in *The Rape of the Lock*. Cf. the cognate "Plumey." In Mrs. Behn's *The Emperour of the Moon*, 4to, 1687, I, 1, Bellemante cries: "I have been at the Chapel, and seen so many Beaus, such a number of Plumeys." The French *plumet*, although extremely rare, is found as = a fop. In one of the French scenes of *La Precaution inutile*, produced 5 March, 1692, by the Italian comedians, Gaufichon (Aƈt I, 1) says to Leandre: "Je deſtine ma sœur a Monsieur le Doƈteur Balouard, et trente Plumets comme vous ne la détourneroient pas d'un aussi bon rencontre."

p. 59. *Tiffany!* See note, Vol. I. p. 434.

p. 69. *names of Husband and Wife.* One may compare the famous scene between Mirabell and Millamant in *The Way of the World* (IV), when Millamant proteſts, "And d'ee hear, I won't be call'd Names after I'm marry'd: positively I won't be call'd Names." "Names!" cries Mirabell. "Ay," she answers, "as Wife, Spouse, my Dear, Joy, Jewel, Love, Sweet-heart, and the reſt of that nauseous Cant, in which Men and their Wives are so fulsomly familiar . . . but let us be very ſtrange and well-bred: Let us be as ſtrange as if we had been marry'd a great while; and as well-bred as if we were not marri'd at all."

SIR MARTIN MARR-ALL

p. 81. *Regalio's.* An older form of "regalo," a choice entertainment; a present as especially of an elegant repaſt. Often figuratively as here; and so W. de Britaine, *Humane Prudence*, (Third ed. 1686), XI,

53: " I am not much delighted with the Regalio's or Gaiety of the World."

p. 81. *Woodcocks.* The woodcock being a proverbially foolish bird, and hence the term woodcock was often applied to a silly shatter-brained fopling. Cf. in Shadwell's *The Sullen Lovers*, 4to, 1668: *Woodcock*, A Familiar loving Coxcombe.

p. 81. *Lilly.* William Lilly, the famous aſtrologer, 1602–81.

p. 82. *The Swash-Buckler.* Thus S. W. Singer, *Hiſtory of Playing Cards*, 1816, p. 258 (note), speaks of "a lively picture of the swash-buckler manners of the youth of fashion in the reign of Elizabeth."

p. 83. *Durham-yard.* On the riverside by Charing Cross, Strand. It was so named from the palace of the Bishops of Durham from the thirteenth century. Bishop Thomas de Hatfield rebuilt the house in 1345. It ſtood on the site of the buildings now called the Adelphi, and the name is preserved in Durham Street. Durham-yard was one of the general landing-places from the Thames waterway. Cf. Pepys, Sunday, 10 May, 1668: "I took her, and Mrs. Lowther, and old Mrs. Whiſtler, her mother-in-law, by water with great pleasure as far as Chelsey, and so back to Spring Garden at Fox-hall, and there walked, and eat, and drank, and so to water again, and set down the old woman at home at Durham Yard."

p. 84. *old Elizabeth way.* A proverbial phrase for "old-fashioned." It per-ſiſted late. Cf. Swift, *Polite Conversation*, I: "*Lady Smart.* She wears her cloaths as if they were thrown on her with a pitch-fork; and, for the fashion, I believe they were made in the reign of Queen Bess." In Wycherley's *The Gentleman Dancing-Maſter* (Dorset Garden, March, 1672), V, Flirt arranging her menage says to Monsieur: "Then you muſt take the Lease of my House and furnish it as becomes one of my Quality; for don't you think we'll take up with your old Queen Elizabeth furniture as your Wives do."

p. 84. *Piazza's.* An open arcade on the north and eaſt sides of Covent Gar-den Market Place. It was built by Inigo Jones *circa* 1633–4, and for wellnigh a century remained a fashionable promenade. Scene 2, Aɕt IV of Otway's *The Souldier's Fortune* (1680) is the Piazza at midnight. Cf. Brome, *The Covent Garden Weeded* (8vo, 1658), I, i, where Cockbrayne says: "Yond magnificent Peece, the *Piazzo*, will excell that at Venice, by hearsay (I ne're travell'd)."

p. 85. *tows'd.* To towse is to tumble about roughly. Cf. Ramble's couplet, *The London Cuckolds*, V:

> How I'll Mouse her and Touse her and Tumble her till Morning,
> But little dreams the Bridegroom he is to be horning.

p. 85. *what the Lyon's skin.* A saying of Lysander. Plutarch, *Lysander*, VII: Τῶν δ' ἀξιούντων μὴ πολεμεῖν μετὰ δόλου τοὺς ἀφ' Ἡρακλέους γεγονότας καταγελᾶν ἐκέλευεν· Ὅπου γὰρ ἡ λεοντῆ μὴ ἐφικνεῖται, προσραπτέον ἐκεῖ τὴν ἀλωπεκῆν. The Latin Proverb is: Si leonina

pellis non satis est, assuenda vulpina. And in French they say:
Coudre la peau du renard à celle du lion. Cf. Lytton's *Richelieu*
(1839), I, 2:

Richelieu.   What did Plutarch
                Say of the Greek Lysander?
Joseph.   I forget.
Richelieu.   That where the lion's skin fell short, he eked it
                Out with the fox's! A great statesman, Joseph,
                That same Lysander.

p. 86.   *Easter-Term.* The favourite season for country cousins to visit
London. In *The Plain-Dealer*, produced at Drury Lane in the
winter of 1676, I, Manly says of the litigious Widow Blackacre,
"she loves an *Easter*-Term, or any Term, not, as other Country
Ladies do, to come up to be fine, Cuckold their Husbands, and take
their Pleasure; for she has no pleasure, but in vexing others." Cf.
also Dryden's own Epilogue to *Tyrannick Love*, produced at the
Theatre Royal in 1669:

> Nay, what's yet worse, to kill me in the prime
> Of *Easter*-term, in Tart and Cheese-cake Time!

So Rochester's *A Letter from Artemisa*:

> In *Easter*-Term she gets her a new Gown;
> When my young Master's Worship comes to Town:
> From Pedagogue and Mother, just set free.

p. 86.   *Tarts and Cheese-cakes.* One may compare the passage in the well-
known letter published in the *Gentleman's Magazine* of 1745. "I
remember plain *John Dryden*, (before he paid his court with success
to the great,) in one uniform clothing of *Norwich* drugget. I have
ate tarts with him and Madam *Reeve* at the *Mulberry*-garden,
when our author advanced to a sword, and chadreux wig." The
letter represents a tradition, but is in effect a pastiche from Otway's
The Poet's Complaint of his Muse and other originals.

p. 87.   *picque and repicque.* To picque (at Picquet) is to win 30 points on
cards and play, before one's opponent begins to count, entitling the
player to commence his score at 60.
repicque. To win 30 points on cards before beginning to play and
before one's opponent can count, thus entitling the player to com-
mence his score at 90. Cf. Temple, *Letter to Lord Arlington* (1668),
Works (1731), II, 93: "In their Audiences . . . the Cards
commonly run high, and all is Picque and Repicque between
them."

p. 87.   *Capot.* In Picquet "He that wins more than his own Cards reckons
Ten, but he that wins all the Cards reckons Forty, and this is called
a *Capet*." *The Game at Picket*, Cotton, *Compleat Gamester*, Second
Edition, 1680, p. 62.

p. 87.   *want one of up.* Want one point to win the game. "Each Person sets
           his Game with Counters, and if the *set* be not up, deal again; now a
           set is won after this manner, admit that each party is so forward in
           his Game that he wants but four or five to be up, if it so happens,
           that any of the two have a Blank, he wins the *set*." *Ibid.*

p. 90.   *Bug-word.* A Bug-bear word; a word that terrifies and alarms. Cf.
           Duffett's *The Mock-Tempest*, 4to, 1675, III, 1: "I say keep the
           Peace, do you not tremble to use such bug words, if any body
           should hear you it would bring a scandal on the house, and make 'em
           think us whores."

p. 90.   *smoaks.* The *Dictionary of the Canting Crew* has: "Smoke, to Smoke
           or Smell a Design. *It is Smok't*, it is made Public, all have notice."

p. 91.   *claw'd off.* To claw off is to get free from; to get rid of (as an itch by
           clawing the skin). The phrase is not uncommon. Cf. Richardson's
           Clarissa (ed. 1811), VIII, 355: "This . . . is a grief, he declares,
           that he shall never claw off."

p. 95.   *take some pet.* Cotgrave (1611) has: "*Se mescontenter de,* to take the
           pet, or pepper in the nose at."

p. 96.   *Grayes-Inn Walks.* Gray's Inn Walks or Gardens extending north
           from South Square, Gray's Inn, to the King's (now Theobald's)
           Road. They were laid out when Lord Bacon was Treasurer of
           Gray's Inn. Extremely fashionable as a promenade, there are very
           frequent references to this favourite resort. Cf. Pepys, Sunday, 30
           June, 1661: "Hence I to Graye's Inn Walk, all alone, and with
           great pleasure seeing the fine ladies walk there." Also Sunday,
           4 May, 1662: "My wife and I walked to Gray's Inn, to observe
           fashions of the ladies, because of my wife's making some clothes.
           Thence homewards." In *The Feign'd Astrologer*, 4to, 1668, III,
           Endimion says:

> But why baulk'd you *Grays-Inn-Walks,* the *Coffee-houses,* or
>   some sage *Club;*
> There your grand News-mongers conferre.

p. 98.   *Enter to them the Landlord.* One may compare the trick put upon
           Periwinkle by Colonel Fainwell in Mrs. Centlivre's *A Bold Stroke
           for a Wife,* IV, produced at Lincoln's Inn Fields, February, 1717–8.
           The lively Centlivre, no doubt, borrowed from Dryden. In order
           to chouse old Periwinkle Fainwell, disguised as Pillage, a Steward,
           informs him that his Uncle, Sir Toby, is dead, and has left him an
           estate near Coventry.

p. 100.   *Charles Street.* Covent Garden. Built 1637, and then named in com-
           pliment to Charles I. In 1844 renamed Wellington Street. A very
           fashionable quarter for the lodgings of persons of quality.

p. 100.   *silenc'd Minister.* Silenced by the Act of Uniformity, May, 1662,
           when every beneficed clergyman was ordered to use the services of
           the *Book of Common Prayer* under pain of deprivation. Rather than
           conform nearly two thousand ministers went forth from their cures

on Sunday, 24 Auguft, 1662, S. Bartholomew's day. The Conventicle A&t of 1664 made it illegal for more than five persons to assemble for a service not in accordance with Anglican discipline, and the Five Mile A&t, O&tober, 1665, forbade noncomformift minifters to come within that diftance of any city or corporate town. They were silenced, then, from their great exercise of preaching, and no longer able in windy sermons to disseminate "the poisonous principles of schism and rebellion."

p. 101. *Diego Rogue.* Diego, a generic name for a Spaniard, from S. Diego (James) the Patron of Spain, very common in the seventeenth century. Cf. Davenant's *The Play-House to be Let*, III, *The Hiftory of Sr Francis Drake* (Cockpit, 1658), Second Entry, Chorus:

> The Diegos we'll board to rummage their hold;
> And drawing our fteel, they muft draw out their gold.

A little later Diego (as here) came to mean a serving-man from O&tavio's servant, Diego, "*A great Coward and a pleasant Droll*" in Tuke's popular *The Adventures of Five Hours* produced January, 1662–63. In Dryden's *Of Dramatick Poesie* Lisideius remarks that moft of the new French plays are "derived from the *Spanish* Novels. There is scarce one of them without a Veil, and a trufty *Diego*, who drolls much after the rate of the *Adventures*."

p. 103. *You have Reason.* Avoir raison. To be right. Cf. Bedell, *Letters*, VI, 95, 1624: "The King himselfe said aloud that both sides had reason." Also Wycherley's *The Gentleman Dancing-Mafter*, Dorset Garden, March, 1672, 4to, 1673; V, 1: "The Fool has reason, I find, and I am the Coxcomb while I thought him so."

p. 104. *in fine.* Cf. Congreve's *Amendments of Mr. Collier*, 1698, "——*in fine, the Play is a very religious Poem.* Indeed! why then in fine we are tack'd about; then a Play *in fine*, may be a religious Poem it seems: Why then *Sir Martin* with his, *in fine*, here has quite unravel'd his own Plot."

p. 104. *Coxbones.* Cox is a perversion of Cock = God. This persifted until far in the eighteenth century. *The Maunciple's Prologe* (*c.* 1386) has:

> See how he nappeth! see, for cokkes bones,
> As he wol falle from his hors at ones.

Cf. also *The Towneley Myfteries: Herod the Great* (1460): *I Miles.* By cokys dere bonys I make you go wyghtly! (*i.e.* nimbly).

p. 104. *old Madge.* His cudgel. Perhaps conne&ted with the word *Madge* yet in use, and defined as "a leaden hammer, clothed with kersey or woollen cloth, called a madge." *English Mechanic*, 1870, 25 February, 573/1.

p. 104. *on the Pofts.* See note, Vol. I, p. 424, *The Wild Gallant*.

p. 107. *Cabinet of Quintessence.* The modern medicine cheft. Whitelocke speaks of a "cabinet of essences" presented by Bushell, Bacon's servant, to Whitelocke, and by him to Queen Christina.

p. 107. *Gilberts Water.* A popular cordial. William Gilbert (1540–1603) was official physician to Queen Elizabeth. Cf. Dryden, "*To my Honour'd Friend* Dr. Charleton":

> *Gilbert* shall live, till *Lode-stones* cease to draw
> Or *British* Fleets the boundless Ocean awe.

p. 107. *a Lechery.* So Sir Toby in *Twelfth Night*, when half-drunk and asked by Olivia "Cousin, cousin, how have you come so early by this lethargy?" bawls out "Lechery! I defy lechery."

p. 108. *Key-cold.* As cold as a key. Cf. Shakespeare, *Richard III*, I, 2, where Lady Anne says of the corse of Henry VI;

> Poor key-cold figure of a holy king!

Also *The Rape of Lucrece*, 1774–5;

> And then in key-cold Lucrece' bleeding stream
> He falls . . .

The phrase is common, *e.g.* it is found in Dekker's *Seven Deadly Sins of London*. It also occurs in Robert Cawdray's *Treasure or Store-house of Similes*, London, 1600. In a ballad, *Robin Goodfellow* (*Roxburgh Ballads*, II, 84), we have:

> And on the key-cold floor them throw.

p. 108. *swebbing.* To sweb, now North Country dialect, is to swoon. Ray, *North Country Words* (1674), has: "To *Sweb*, to swoon." *A Warning to Faire Women* (1599), II: "Looke in my purse for a peece of ginger: I shall sweb, I shall swound."

p. 110. *smoak.* To smoke, meaning to suspect, to have an inkling of a trick, was in common use from the beginning of the seventeenth until the mid-nineteenth century. Cf. *The Old Batchelour*, III, 1, where Setter says to Lucy masked: "Oh! I begin to smoak ye, thou art some forsaken *Abigail*, we have dallied with heretofore."

p. 112. *Cox nowns.* Cox is a corruption of God. So in *The Merry Wives of Windsor*, IV, 1, when Sir Hugh asks: "William, how many numbers is in nouns?" and William replies: "Two," Mrs. Quickly chips in with: "Truly, I thought there had been one number more, because they say 'Od's nowns'."

p. 112. *Bartlemew.* Warner is going to say "a conceited Bartlemew Cokes," a common term applied to a ninny. Cokes = a fool occurs as early as 1567, and the term largely became general owing to Squire Cokes, the simpleton in *Bartholomew Fair*, first acted in 1614. In Restoration days William Wintershal, who died July, 1679, was especially celebrated in this rôle, and here even the brilliant comedian, James Nokes, fell very far short of him. Cf. *A Letter from Artemisa* by Rochester: "And *Betty Morris* had her

City Cokes." *The Dictionary of the Canting Crew* (*c.* 1700) has: "*Cokes*, the Fool in the Play, or Bartholomew Fair."

p. 112.   *Scander-bag-Rogue.* Cf. *Every Man in his Humour*, acted 1598, I, 3, where Mr. Stephen cries: "horson *scander-bag* rogue." Scanderbag, an old-fashioned intensive term, is a corruption of the name of the famous warrior, George Castriota (1404–67), an Albanian hero, who was for more than a quarter of a century the principal obstacle to the unlimited extension of the Ottoman Empire. He was at first a commander under Amurath II, and owing to his prowess was raised to the rank of Sanjak with the title Iscander Bey (Lord Alexander). In 1443 he renounced Moslemism, and won several battles against the Turk. At the instigation of Pius II he headed a crusade, and defeated Mohammed II with a vast army at Croia. The name Scanderbag is frequently used for a fierce fighter. Cf. Duffett's *The Mock-Tempest*, 4to, 1675, I, 1: "The poor hearts fight as if they were all *Scanderbegs.*"

p. 113.   *Lilly.* The famous Sir Peter Lely, 1618–1680. Lely came to England in 1641. He was knighted by Charles II.

p. 114.   *Mackings.* A diminutive of "mack," which is to be explained as a distortion of "mass." "By Mary" does not seem so satisfactory, since we have "Maskins." Cf. Cotton's *Virgil Travestie*, IV:

> And now this Swabber, by the Maskins,
> Thunders up *Dido's* Gally-Gaskins.

The word is not infrequent. Cf. *Sir John Oldcastle*, 1600, sig. C4: "Now by the macke, a prettie wench indeed." *Every Man in His Humour* (1598), III, iv: "*Cob.* Humour? mack, I thinke it be so, indeed." *The London Prodigal* (1605), II, 2, has: "A by the mackins good syr Lancelot." In rustic parlance this petty oath persisted: Cf. Vanbrugh's *The Relapse, or, Virtue in Danger*, acted at Drury Lane, December, 1696, IV, where the old Nurse on receiving a vail from Young Fashion delightedly mutters to herself: "Gold by mackings!" The *Cheshire Glossary* (1887) gives "By the makkins."

p. 114.   *Cock-sure.* This expression was current early in the sixteenth century. Cf. Latimer's *Sermon on the Ploughers* (1549): "When the devil had once brought Christ to the Crosse he thought all cocksure."

p. 116.   *taking up Linnen.* "To take up" in the sense of "to buy up linen." Cf. *Francion* (1655) translated from du Parc (Charles Sorel), IV, 23: "I must buy me a Cloak lined with plush, or take me up one at the Brokers." Warner's speech has a double meaning. A "Draper" was contemporary slang for a bawd, a bagnio-keeper, and "linen" was the commodity they provided. *Linen-arbour*, a slang term still in use = a bedchamber.

p. 116.   *danc'd in a Net.* To dance in a net is to do something undetected. A favourite phrase with Dryden. Cf. *Mr. Limberham*, II, where Woodall says: "We have carry'd Matters swimmingly: I have

475

danc'd in a Net before my Father, almoſt Check-mated the
Keeper, retir'd to my Chamber undiscover'd." Scott remembering
Dryden wrote: "You muſt not think to dance in a net before old
Jack Hildebrod." *Fortunes of Nigel* (1822), c. XXII.

p. 116. *I find.* In a somewhat unusual sense of to fine =to pay a composition
or consideration for a special privilege. Cf. Mrs. Behn's *The Rover*,
II, 4to, 168, Aἐt IV; where the bawd says: "The Stranger muſt
not be put off, nor *Carlo* neither, who has fin'd again as if for a new
Maidenhead."

p. 116. *mother Temple, Bennet, or Gifford.* Three moſt notorious maquerelles
of the day. Mother Temple receives ample mention in the extra-
ordinary Epilogue, a parody of *Macbeth*, to Duffett's farce, *The
Empress of Morocco*, 4to, 1674, where the Second Witch (aἐted by
Adams) sings:

> *A health, a health to Siſter* T[emple]
> *Her Trade's chief beauty and example,*
> *She'll serve the Gallant, or the Pimp, well.*

p. 116. *Bennet.* Mother Bennet was a bawd of long continuance. On Satur-
day, 22 September, 1660, Pepys notes that Luellin "told me how
the pretty woman that I always loved at the beginning of Cheapside
that sells childs' coats was served by the Lady Bennet (a famous
ſtrumpet), who, by counterfeiting to fall into a swoon upon the
sight of her in her shop, became acquainted with her, and at laſt got
her ends of her to lie with a gentleman that had hired her to pro-
cure that poor soul for him." On Saturday, 30 May, 1668, the
diariſt being in the company of "as very rogues as any in the town
. . . firſt underſtood by their talk the meaning of the company
that lately were called Ballers; Harris telling how it was by a meet-
ing of some young blades, when he was amongſt them, and my
Lady Bennet and her ladies; and their then dancing naked, and all
the roguish things in the world." Wycherley in a ſtrain of com-
pleteſt irony dedicates *The Plain-Dealer* to this procuress, "*To my
Lady B*——," 4to, 1677. *The Tatler*, No. 84, speaks of her as "the
celebrated Mother Bennet." Cf. Radcliffe's *The Ramble*, 1682,
The Poor Whore's Song:

> But if Mother *Bennet* came
> With a Wheedle or a Flam,
> She'd tell you how I cut the Sham.

John Phillips' *Don Quixote*, folio, 1687 (p. 195): He "carry'd her
to much such another House as Mother *Creswel's*, and left her in
the cuſtody of an Aunt of his, not so mean as *Mrs. Buly*, and yet a
little below the Degree of *Madam Bennet.*"

p. 116. *Gifford.* There is a very pertinent allusion to this lady in the Epilogue
to Duffett's farce *The Empress of Morocco*, 4to, 1674, where the
Firſt Witch (William Harris) sings:

A Health, a Health to G[ifford] that Witch,
She needs muſt be in spight of fate Rich
Who sells tough Hen for Quail and Partridg.

In Etherege's *She wou'd if She cou'd*, V, 1, produced in February, 1667–8, 4to, 1668, Freeman cries: "pox on your honourable intrigue, wou'd I were safe at *Giffords.*"

In Sedley's *The Mulberry Garden*, produced at the Theatre Royal, Monday, 18 May, 1668, IV, Modish says: "There's as hard drinking in Gentlemens Houses Now adays, as at Taverns, and as hot service In many a Ladys Chamber, as at *Giffords.*" In Shadwell's *The Miser*, Theatre Royal, January, 1671–2, V, 1, Theodore asserts: "But, Gentlemen, I hate the Name of a Muse, as I do that of a Bawd: Were I a Poet, I would invoke *Creswell* or *Gifford*, before any Muse in Chriſtendom." "Faith," retorts Hazard, "thou art in the right; for they two can supply our Necessities better than all the nine Muses." In Wycherley's *Love in a Wood*, produced at the Theatre Royal in the autumn of 1671, IV, Vincent says to Ranger: "I was going to look you out between the Scenes at the Play-House, the Coffee-house, Tennis-Court, or *Gifford's.*" "Do you want a pretence to go to a Bawdy-house?" retorts his friend.

Gallantry A-la-mode, A Satyrical Poem, 1674, has (p. 8):

At Giffords, Creswels, *and elsewhere*
Where precise Damsel does appear,
Perhaps you'er bin, no greater Cheat
Is shown there Lady spruce *and* neat.

p. 116. *cramm'd Capons*. Eſteemed a great delicacy. So the French Scullion in *The Gentleman Dancing-Maſter* (4to, 1673), I, 2, when summoned to suggeſt a supper for the two ladies at once asks: "En voulez vous de Cram Schiquin."

p. 116. *Chickens in the grease*. Engraissés. So in Shadwell's *The Woman-Captain*, I, 1 (acted 1679; 4to, 1680), among the catalogue of moſt epicurean dainties we have: "Squab Pidgeons, Chickens in the Grease, fat Swans, and Barn-dore Hens."

p. 116. *Shatling*. There are continual references to this famous ordinary. Cf. Pepys, Friday, 15 March, 1667–8: "At noon all of us to Chatelin's, the French house in Covent Garden, to dinner—Brouncker, J. Minnes, W. Pen, T. Harvey, and myself: and there had a dinner coſt us 8s. 6d. a-piece, a damned base dinner, which did not please us at all, but do rather choose the Beare." Yet Chatelin's was very fashionable. On Wednesday, 22 April, 1668, Pepys thought "to have met Mr. Pierce, and his wife and Knepp; but met their servant coming to bring me to Chatelin's, the French house, in Covent Garden, and then with musick and good company, . . . and here mighty merry till ten at night. . . . This night the

Duke of Monmouth and a great many blades were at Chatelin's."
So in a Prologue which appears in *Covent Garden Drollery* (1672),
and later seems to have been spoken before D'Urfey's *The Fool
Turn'd Critick*, 4to, 1678, we have:

> Next these we welcome such as briskly dine
> At *Locket's*, at *Gifford's* or with *Shatiline*.

In Shadwell's *The Miser*, 4to, 1672, I, 1, Theodore bids his
friends go "and bespeak Dinner at *Chatolin's*," and II we find
"Rant, Hazard, Lettice *and* Joyce *at* Chatolin's" when the gentle-
man presently joins them.

p. 116.   *La-fronds.* One of the more fashionable ordinaries of the day. In
Shadwell's *The Sullen Lovers*, produced at the Duke's House,
Saturday, 2 May, 1668; 4to, 1668; II, Stanford says: "One, that
but the other Day could eat but one Meal a Day, and that at a three-
penny Ordinary, now ſtruts in State, and talks of nothing but
Shattelin's and *Lefrond's*." In Sedley's *The Mulberry Garden*, pro-
duced at the King's House, Monday, 18 May, 1668, Act IV,
Modish says: "Leave your *Chaſte Ling*, And *La-Fronds*, dine with
my Lord such a One one day, my Lady what d'you call 'um
another." Cf. The Prologue to Bank's *The Deſtruction of Troy*, 4to,
1678–9:

> the rich Banquet is to come, a Treat
> Cook'd by your Chat'lin *and* La Froon *of* Wit.

p. 116.   *New-River.* The New River was a canal for the supply of water to
London, which had been opened in 1613. For an account of it see
Stow's *Survey of London*, ed. Strype, 1720, Bk. I, pp. 25–6. Cf.
Gould, *A Satyr againſt the Play-House*: (*Poems*, 1689):

> It wou'd be endless to trace all the Vice
> That from the *Play-House* takes immediate Rise·
> It is the unexhauſted *Magazin*
> That ſtocks the Land with Vanity and Sin:
> As the *New-River* does, from *Islington*,
> Through several Pipes supply ev'n half the Town.

p. 118.   *Padders.* One of the commoneſt old slang terms for thieves, robbers.
In Mrs. Behn's *The Roundheads; or, The Good Old Cause*, 4to,
1682, V, 1, Loveless accoſts Ananias as "Mr. *Ananias* the Padder,"
to which the elder retorts: "Bear witness, Gentlemen all, he calls
me Highwayman." Cf. Wycherley's *Epiſtles to the King and Duke*,
1683:

> By Marching World round, all that Hero's gain,
> Is Dirty Boots, and labour for their pain;
> For spoiling of the Roads, and making Padders.

p. 118.   *Domine.* The vocative of *dominus* was used as a term of respect to
several learned professions, and then almoſt entirely addressed to the

clergy, whence *Domine* came exclusively to mean a parson. So in *The Scornful Lady*, II, 1 (1616), Welford replies to Sir Roger's "Good sir, peace be with you," with "Adieu, dear Domine." In Brome's *The Antipodes* (1638), IV, x, Letoy summons Quaylpipe, his curate, with: "You *Domine* where are you?" It may be noted that in *The Country-Wife*, IV, 3, Horner calls the Quack "*Domine Doctor*," but this is an intended exception. Edmund Hickeringill, in his *Priest-craft, its Character and Consequences*, 4to (1705), II, 2, 26, writes: "A little Domine or Curate in the towering and topping Pulpit."

p. 119.   *May-game.* Cf. Fletcher, *The Loyal Subject* (1618), II, 1:

> Pray Heaven we have room enough to march for May-games, Pageants, and bonfires, for your welcome home, sir.

Upon which Dyce writes: "*May-games.* The merry ceremonies of May-day, strewing of primroses, burning of straw on the spokes of a wheel, etc.; perhaps Druidic." Also Fletcher's *The Mad Lover* (not later than 1618), I, 2, where Eumenes says:

> Kill us for telling truth; for my part, general,
> I would not live to see men make a May-game
> Of him I have made a master.

p. 121.   *by my truly.* A mild asseveration. It will not escape notice that Mrs. Christian artfully uses the simplest girlish talk. Cf. Webster's *Westward Hoe*, 4to, 1607, II, 1, where Judith addresses Signior Justiniano, who is disguised as a writing mechanical pedant: "Have you a new pen for me master? for, by my truly, my old one is stark naught, and will cast no ink."

p. 122.   *Pudding-time.* The time when a pudding or puddings are to be had; and so figuratively, at the lucky moment. Heywood, *Proverbs*, II, ix (1546), has: "This geare comth even in puddyng time nightlie." Cf. the old song, *The Vicar of Bray* (c. 1770):

> When George in pudding-time came o'er,
> And moderate men look'd big, sir.

The phrase persisted, and Marryat, *Olla Podrida* (1840), writes: "He came in Pudding-time and was invited to dinner."

p. 122.   *What a Goodier.* What a good year . . . A meaningless expletive which may be taken as corresponding to such phrases as "What the plague . . ." or "What the devil . . ." The origin of "What a good year . . ." is obscure and unexplained. A suggestion which connects it with "What a pox . . ." although ingenious and tempting is not possible. The phrase is common enough, cf. *Much Ado about Nothing* (1599), I, 3, where Conrade greets Don John: "What the good yeere my Lord, why are you thus out of measure sad?"

479

p. 123. *pinking.* To pink = to blink; to half-close the eyes (*Dutch;* pinken, to shut the eyes, wink). Cf. *Roxburgh Ballads* (1681), V, 86:

"When our senses are drown'd, and our eyes they do pink."

p. 127. *premunire. Praemunire facias.* An act in contempt of the royal prerogative, especially the prosecuting in a foreign court a suit cognizable by the law of England. The writ granted for such an offence, and the penalty incurred by it. Hence a predicament, "a fix." The term is very common. Cf. Ravenscroft's *The London Cuckolds*, produced at the Duke's House in the winter of 1681, III, 1, where Engine says: "So, now I have drawn my self into a premunire." In *The Double-Dealer*, 4to, 1694, IV, Lady Plyant cries: "I'm in such a fright; the strangest Quandary and Premunire!"

p. 128. *white pelf.* Silver coins.

p. 128. *Martin Parker.* (Died *circa* 1656.) A royalist and celebrated balladmaker, of whom there is a very ample account in the *D.N.B.* His "when the king enjoyes his owne again" (1643), has been called by Ritson the most famous and most popular air ever heard in this country. Flecknoe in his *Miscellania* (1653) speaks of Parker as inspired by the very spirit of balletting. Parker, indeed, wrote a vast number of ballads, of which the British Museum has a unique collection. He also composed some antic romances.

p. 128. *cholerick as a Cook.* Cf. *The Alchemist*, 4to, 1612; acted in 1610, III, 1:

The place he lives in, still about the fire,
And fume of mettalls, that intoxicate
The braine of man, and make him prone to passion.
Where have you greater atheists, then your cookes?
Or more prophane, or cholerick then your glasse-men?

p. 129. *Sir Martin appears.* This was one of the most famous and popular scenes in the play, and there are numerous references to it in contemporary literature. *E.g.* The Prologue to Shadwell's *The Humourists*, 1670: *As our Sir* Martin *undertakes the Lute.* Also *The Country-Wife*, I, where Harcourt says of Sparkish: "The Rogue will not let us enjoy one another, but ravishes our conversation, though he signifies no more to't, than *Sir Martin Mar-all's* gaping, and auker'd thrumming upon the Lute, does to his Man's Voice, and Musick." Oldham, *A Satyr, In Imitation of the Third of Juvenal* (1682), has:

Commend his Voice and Singing, tho' he bray
Worse than *Sir Martin Marr-all* in the Play.

Also *The Spectator*, 5 (Addison), Tuesday, 6 March, 1711: "I perceived that the Sparrows were to act the part of Singing Birds in a delightful Grove: though upon a nearer Enquiry I found the

EXPLANATORY NOTES

Sparrows put the same Trick upon the Audience that *Sir Martin Mar-all* practised upon his Mistress; for, though they flew in Sight, the Musick proceeded from a Consort of Flagellets and Bird-calls which was planted behind the Scenes."

p. 129. *at the adverse window.* This term as well as *above* denote one of the balconies which were situate directly over the permanent proscenium doors. So in Ravenscroft's *The Citizen turn'd Gentleman,* produced at Dorset Garden in 1672, three of these balconies are employed. "Enter Mr. Jorden, musick" obviously in one balcony from the ensuing dialogue. Then "Cleverwit, in Turk's habit with Betty Trickmore and Lucia appear in the Balcony," number two. A song is sung, and "Young Jorden and Marina in the Balcony against 'em." So in Mrs. Behn's *The Rover; or, The Banish'd Cavaliers,* Part I, produced at Dorset Garden in 1677, "*Enter two Bravoes, and hang up a great Picture of* Angelica's *against the Balcony, and two little ones at each side of the Door,*" whilst a few moments after "*Enter* Angelica *and* Moretta *in the Balcony, and draw a Silk Curtain.*"

p. 129. *Blind Love to this hour.* This song was suggested by a chanson of Voiture. *Les Oeuvres de Monsieur de Voiture.* Quatriesme Edition, Paris, 1654 (p. 61, *Poesies*). Chanson:

> *L'Amour sous la loy*
> *N'a iamais eu d'Amant plus hereux que moy;*
> *Benit soit son flambeau,*
> *Son carquois, son bandeau,*
> *Ie suis amoureux,*
> *Et le Ciel ne voit point d'Amant plus heureux.*

> *Mes iours & mes nuits*
> *Ont bien peu de repos & beaucoup d'ennuis;*
> *Ie me meurs de langeur,*
> *I'ay le feu dans le cœur,*
> *Ie suis amoureux,*
> *Et le Ciel ne voit point d'Amant plus heureux.*

> *Mortels déplaisirs*
> *Qui venez trauerser mes iustes desirs!*
> *Ie ne crains point vos coups;*
> *Car, enfin, malgré vous,*
> *Ie suis amoureux, &c.*

> *A tous ses martyrs,*
> *L'Amour donne en leurs maux de secrets plaisirs,*
> *Ie cheris ma douleur,*
> *Et dedans mon mal-heur,*
> *Ie suis amoureux, &c.*

Les yeux qui m'ont pris,
Payeroient tous mes maux auec vn soûris,
Tous leur traits me sont doux,
Mesme dans leur couroux,
Ie suis amoureux, &c.

Cloris eut des Cieux,
En naissant, la faueur & l'amour des Dieux,
Ie la veux adorer,
Et sans rien esperer
I'en suis amoureux, &c.

Souuent le dépit
Peut bien, pour quelque Temps, changer mon esprit,
Ie maudis sa rigeur,
Mais au fond de mon cœur,
I'en suis amoureux, &c.

Estant dans les fers,
De la belle Cloris, ie chantay ces vers;
Maintenant d'un suiet,
Mille fois plus parfait
Ie suis amoureux, &c.

La seule beauté,
Qui soit digne d'amour, tient ma liberté,
Et ie puis desormais
Dire mieux que iamais,
Ie suis amoureux,
Et le Ciel ne voit point d'Amant plus heureux.

p. 130. *Harmony of the Spheres.* The older aſtrologers imagined that certain celeſtial and concentric globes revolved round the earth and reſpectively carried with them the several heavenly bodies, the moon, sun, planets, and fixed ſtars. The motion of these globes or spheres produced a moſt exquisite music, whence the phrase the "harmony of the spheres," or more frequently "the music of the spheres." Cf. *Twelfth Night*, 1601, III, 1:

I had rather heare you to solicit that
Then Musicke from the Spheares.

p. 131. *Cokes among the Poppits. Bartholomew Fair.* Act V.

p. 132. *Jacobus and a Carolus.* Broad-pieces. After the introduction of the guinea in 1663 the name Broad-piece was applied to the "Unite" or twenty-shilling piece, Jacobus or Carolus, of the preceding reigns, since this was much thinner and broader than the new-milled coinage.

EXPLANATORY NOTES

p. 132. *Hey-tarockit*. Taroc, or tarot, one of a set of playing-cards first used in Italy in the fourteenth century, and also popularly employed in fortune-telling. The expression would seem to be meaningless as are so many to which the exclamation hey! is prefixed.

p. 132. *Dorothy, Daughter to one Draw-water*. Tuesday, 8 October, 1667, Pepys notes: "Away to Cambridge, it being foul, rainy weather, and there did take up at the Rose, for the sake of Mrs. Dorothy Drawwater, the vintner's daughter, which is mentioned in the play of Sir Martin Marrall. Here we had a good chamber, and bespoke a good supper."

p. 133. *spit out of your mouth*. Cf. *Englishmen for My Money*, IV, 1 (4to, 1616), where Frisco puts on Vandal's cloak and cries: "Now look I as like the Dutchman as if I were spit out of his mouth." Also *The London Chanticleers* (4to, 1659), I, 3, where Ditty says: "Look you here; here's one as like you as if it had been spit out of your mouth." The expression is frequent and has persisted to-day in the phrase of "the spit" or "the very spit" of such a one, meaning the exact image and likeness.

p. 135. *smoke for 't*. Pay for it. As in *The Wild Gallant*, I, 1: "some shall smoak for 't." See Vol. I, p. 419.

p. 137. *Stock-fish*. To beat one like a stock-fish is given in John Withals' *Dictionary in English and Latin*, first edition by Wynkyn de Worde (1521), and in Thomas Becon, *Worckes*, London, 1563–4, folio, I, 522. The phrase is old and very frequent.

p. 137. *Poet to Pugenello*. i.e. write the dialogue for marionettes. Pugenello is Ponchinello, Punch. At the conclusion of Shadwell's *The Sullen Lovers; or, The Impertinents*, produced at Lincoln's Inn Fields, Saturday, 2 May, 1668, *enter a Boy in the habit of* Pugenello, *and traverses the Stage, takes his Chair, and sits down, then Dances a Jigg*. Pepys who was present writes: "But a little boy, for a farce, do dance Polichinelli, the best that ever anything was done in the world, by all men's report." The Italian commedia dell' arte made an appearance in England immediately at the Restoration and proved exceedingly popular. As early as 22 October, 1660, the King granted a patent to Giulio Gentileschi to build a theatre for Italian musicians, and here, no doubt, an Italian company performed. With the live actors came the puppets. Friday, 9 May, 1662, Pepys went "to see an Italian puppet play, that is within the rayles there, which is very pretty, the best that ever I saw, and great resort of gallants." On Wednesday, 22 August, 1666, Pepys escorted his wife, Mrs. Knepp, and Mercer "by coach to Moorefields, and there saw *Polichinello*, which pleased me mightily." Exactly a week later he repeated his visit "and showed Batelier, with my wife, *Polichinello*, which I like the more I see it," and on the following Saturday "Sir W. Pen and my wife and Mercer and I to *Polichinello*, but were there horribly frighted to see Young Killigrew come in with a great many more young sparks; but we hid ourselves, so as we think

they did not see us . . . and so, the play being done, we to Isling-
ton, and there eat and drank and mighty merry." *Ponchinello* was
also exhibited at Charing Cross, where it was seen by Pepys on
Wednesday, 20 March, 1666–7, who writes: "To *Polichinelli* at
Charing Cross, which is prettier and prettier, and so full of variety
that it is extraordinary good entertainment." *Ponchinello* was
further one of the annual attractions of Bartholomew Fair. On 15
July, 1669, Sir Henry Herbert warmly wrote to the Earl of Man-
chester then Lord Chamberlain, on behalf of Anthony Devotte,
who was "not in the notion of a player, but totally distinct from that
quality, and makes shewe of puppettes only by virtue of his
Majestie's commission, granted to the Master of Revells under the
great seale, for the authorizing of all publique shewes." Antonio Di
Voto was the master of a puppet-show which played *Ponchinello*,
and on 11 November, 1672, the King issued through the Lord
Chamberlain a particular order to protect him, the royal pleasure
being "That Antonio di Voto Doe sett forth Exercise & Play all
Drolls and Interludes, He not receiving into his Company any per-
son belonging to his Mates or Royal Highnesse Theatres Nor Act
any Play usually acted at any of ye said Theatres Nor takes peeces or
Sceenes out of ye said Theatres." This order is entered in the books
to "Antonio Divoto punchenello."

p. 138.   *a Fool's Handsel.* An old proverb. So in Bartholomew Fair, acted
1614, II, 1, where Justice Overdo in his disguise calls for drink at the
booth, Ursula cries: "Bring him a Six-penny Bottle of Ale: they
say, a Fool's hansel is lucky."

p. 139.   *Possets.* A posset was a draught of hot milk with sugar and spices
curdled by some strong infusion of spirit or wine. Proverbially a
favourite tipple with clerics, it was considered highly invigorating
and customarily drunk on a wedding-night. In *The Scornful Lady*,
II, 1 (1616), Welford, Sir Roger the Curate, Abigail, and Martha
share a fine posset at midnight.

p. 139.   *the Brawls.* Brawl (or brawls), French *le bransle*, was a French dance
resembling a cotillon. The word occurs early in the sixteenth
century. Cf. *Love's Labour Lost*, III, 1: *Moth.* Master will you
win your love with a French brawl? *Armado.* How meanest thou?
brawling in French? *Moth.* No, my complete master: but to jig off
a tune at the tongue's end, canary to it with your feet." (The
canary is a lively Spanish dance.) There are many allusions to
the brawls, and Gray's line (*Letter*, 1750, in *Poems*, ed. 1775)
is well known:

> My grave Lord-Keeper led the brawls.

So in *The House-Warming* (*Ingoldsby Legends*):

> ——a Court where it's thought, in a lord or a duke, a
> Disgrace to fall short in "the Brawls"—(their Cachouca).

Sir John Davies, *Orcheſtra, or A Poeme of Dauncing*, 18mo, 1596, LXII, writes:

Upward and *downeward, forth* and *backe againe,*
To this side and *to that,* and *turning round;*
Whereof a thousand brawles he doth compound,
Which he doth teach vnto the multitude,
And euer with a turne they muſt conclude.

p. 139.   *Jovy. Jovial,* merry. The word is as early as Lydgate. Cf. *The Alchemiſt,* acted 1610, V, 5, where Kaſtril cries:

'Slight thou art not hide-bound! thou art a jovy boy!

Also *The Wild Goose Chase* (1621), III, 1:

In those daies I thought I might be jovy.

p. 139.   *Tony.* A zany; an antic clown. *The Dictionary of the Canting Crew* (*circa* 1700) defines: "*Tony,* a silly Fellow, or Ninny." It has been suggeſted that the term may be derived from Middleton's famous tragedy *The Changeling* (1623), I, 2, where Antonio, disguised as an idiot, gives his name to the play. When he is brought to the asylum, "What is his name?" asks the doctor's man. "His name is Antonio," comes the reply, "Marry, we use but half to him, only Tony." "Tony, Tony, 'tis enough, and a very good name for a fool. What's your name, Tony?"

p. 139.   *Flute-glasses.* A tall slender wine-glass conceived to resemble a flute in shape. Cf. Lovelace's *Lucaſta* (1649):

Elles of Beere, Flutes of Canary,
That well did washe down paſties-mary.

p. 140.   *Cudden.* An entire fool; a dolt. In *The Gentleman Dancing-Maſter,* Dorset Garden, March, 1672, IV, Monsieur cries: "Lord, that people should be such arrant Cuddens, ha, ha, ha!" Cudden was fairly common towards the end of the seventeenth century.

p. 142.   *Quidding.* Apparently "chewing tobacco." Quid in this sense is found in 1727; to quid = to chew tobacco not before 1775, but it may well have been in use more than a century earlier. The clergy were supposed to love the weed. In *The Scornful Lady* (1616), II, 1, Welford asks Sir Roger: "Do you love tobacco?" Answers the Levite:

Surely I love it, but it loves not me,
Yet with your reverence, I will be bold.

Both then smoke luſtily.

THE TEMPEST

p. 152.   *An Imposition.* A task imposed on us.

p. 152.   *Sea-Voyage. The Sea Voyage,* acted at the Globe, was licensed by Sir Henry Herbert, 22 June, 1622. It was first printed in the folio of 1647. After the Restoration it was revived 25 September, 1667, at the Theatre Royal, when Mrs. Knepp acted Aminta. It seems to have been frequently played at this time as a counter-attraction to *The Tempest* at the rival theatre.

In July-August, 1685, there was produced at the Theatre Royal *A Commonwealth of Women,* an alteration of Fletcher's play by Thomas D'Urfey. This proved very successful, and was seen at intervals for more than half a century. At Drury Lane, 21 April, 1746, Macklin, Peg Woffington, and Kitty Clive appeared in D'Urfey's romantic drama.

p. 152.   *Goblins. The Goblins,* acted at Blackfriars, was printed 8vo, 1646. It was revived at the Theatre Royal, 24 January, 1667. "The Goblins are Tamoren and his friends, who, having been defeated in a battle, retreat to a wood, turn thieves, and disguise themselves as Devils" (Genest). The character of Reginella (not Regmella, as Dryden calls her) has considerable charm, but the course of action of the play on the whole is utterly bewildering and confused.

p. 153.   *old Latine Proverb.* Cicero, *Philippic,* XII, 2, 5: "Cuiusvis hominis est errare, nullius nisi insipientis in errore perseverare. Posteriores enim cogitationes, ut aiunt, sapientiores solent esse." The "ut aiunt" shows that the sentiment was proverbial. There is an earlier instance in Euripides, *Hippolytus,* 434, 435.

'Εν βροτοῖς
Αἱ δεύτεραί πως φροντίδες σοφώτεραι.

(in a speech of the Nurse to Phaedra).

Cicero, *Epist. ad Quintum Fratrem,* III, i, 5, 18, says: "Ego vero nullas δευτέρας φροντίδας habere possum in Caesaris rebus."

The Greek proverbial saying Δευτέρων ἀμεινόνων is a little different in meaning, referring originally to the performance of a sacrifice a second time when the first had been under unfavourable auspices. Hence of making a second attempt in the hope of better fortune.

p. 154.   *One of our Women to present a Boy.* The rôle was that of Hippolito, which was probably taken in 1667 by Moll Davis.

p. 157.   *A hoaming Sea.* Hoaming, a very rare word for "tempestuous."

When a strong sudden Flow and Hoaming Seas
Our trembling Fleet with uncouth Furies seize.

The First Book of Virgil's Aeneid, "Made English" by Luke Mil-
bourne, 4to, 1688. "Hoaming" also occurs in Echard's translation
of the *Rudens* (1694): "Now 'tis such a hoaming Sea, we've little
hopes o' Sport."

p. 157.   *Scud.* The light feathery portions of cloud. Here the context requires
them to be travelling in an upper current in a direction opposite to
the lower wind.

p. 157.   *Yaw, yaw.* A corruption of "Yare, yare." Yare signifies eager;
ready; prepared, from the Anglo-Saxon "geáro." Cf. *Measure for
Measure,* IV, 2: "You shall find me yare." Ray gives it as a Suffolk
word, and the "Hear, hear" of Lowestoft boatmen of to-day is
probably a disguised "Yare, yare."

p. 158.   *reef both Top-sails.* The top sails are the first sails to set in getting
a ship under way. They were apparently reefed in the setting.
Reefing is done by gathering up the top part of a sail and tying it to
the yard.

p. 158.   *Capstorm.* A rare form of capstan.

p. 158.   *seere Capstorm. seere-Capstorm is undoubtedly a misprint for the jeer
Capstorm.* Not only does the jeer Capstan do the work described by
Dryden but the misprint is explained by a j being printed upside
down as a long s.

"The Jeer is a piece of hawser which is made fast to the main-
yard and fore-yard of a great ship close to the ties, for small ships
do not use it, and so is reeved through a block which is seized close
to the top, and so comes down and is reeved through another block
at the bottom of the mast close by the deck. Great ships have one
on one side, another on the other side of the ties. The use of this
rope is to help to hoist up the yard, but the chiefest is to succour
the ties and to hold the yard from falling down if the ties should
break."

"The Jeer Capstan. This hath its name from the jeer which is
ever brought to this capstan to be heaved-at by. It serves for many
other uses, as to heave upon the viol, or hold off the cable from the
main capstan." Sir Henry Mainwaring, *Seaman's Dictionary,* 1617.
Printed for the Navy Records Society, 1922, from the original MS.

p. 158.   *Nippers.* Nippers are small ropes (about a fathom and a half or two
fathom long) with a little truck at one end, or some have only a
wale-knot, the use whereof is to hold off the cable from the main
capstan, or the jeer capstan, when the cable is either so slippery or
so great that they cannot strain it, to hold it off, with their hands
only. Sir Henry Mainwaring, *ibid.*

p. 158.   *Vial-block.* Vial or Vial-block, "a large single-sheaved block through
which the messenger passed when the anchor was weighed by the
fore or jeer capstan." Admiral Smyth, *Sailor's Word-Book,* 1867.

"The Violl. When the anchor is in such stiff ground that we
cannot weigh it, or else that the sea goes so high that the main
capstan cannot purchase in the cable, then, for more help, we take

487

a hawser and open one strand, and so put it into nippers (some seven or eight, a fathom distant from each other) and with these nippers we bind fast the hawser to the cable; and so bring this hawser to the jeer capstan and heave upon it, and this will purchase more than the main capstan can. The Violl is fastened together at both ends with an eye and a wale knot, or else two eyes seized together." Sir H. Mainwaring, *ibid.*

p. 158. *a peek.* "The anchor is apeek when the cable has been sufficiently hove in to bring the ship over it." Smyth, *Sailor's Word-Book*, 1867.

p. 159. *Cut the Anchor.* A misprint for "Cat the anchor."

p. 159. *Haul Catt.* "Cat is . . . a . . . strong tackle, or complication of pulleys, to hook and draw the anchor . . . up to the cat head." Falconer, *Marine Dictionary*, 1789.

p. 159. *Haul Aft Misen-sheet.* To haul on a tack (or rope) connected to the clew of the crosjack in setting the sail.

p. 159. *Mackrel-Gale.* A strong breeze such as when mackerel are caught. Cf. Dryden, *The Hind and the Panther*, III, 456:

> The wind was fair, but blew a *mackrel* gale.

p. 159. *Flat in the Fore-sheat.* Means haul in the fore-sheet as taut as possible. The fore-sheet being the lee-clue or corner of the fore-sail and the tack connecting it to the lee-bulwarks. The ship had been running before the wind and it was necessary to haul in the fore-sheet as she came to.

p. 159. *Over-haul your fore-boling.* The fore-bowline is a rope connecting the luff of the fore-sail (or forward edge) to the cathead, or part of the bow, forward of the sail, so that that part of the sail shall be kept well forward as a ship is staying. Thus when the wind is ahead in this manœuvre, the fore-sail is kept aback (with the wind on its fore side) which drives the head of the ship round on the other tack. When the other sails are full, on the new tack, then the bowline is overhauled or let go and the fore-sail hauled round, like the rest of the sails.

p. 159. *Brace in the Lar-board.* Brace in (or up) *to* larboard, to haul the yards sharp up on the port tack so that the ship may sail closer to the wind.

p. 159. *blasphemous, uncharitable Dog.* This is Shakespearean. But why is Trincalo, or in Shakespeare, the Boatswain, blasphemous? Trincalo has certainly said nothing profane, but in Shakespeare, to Gonzalo's remonstrances the Boatswain replies: "What care these roarers for the name of King?" And when he is told to remember whom he has aboard, he answers: "None that I more love than myself." Perhaps this was regarded as blasphemy against the divinity of the monarch who was in the ship.

> There's such divinity doth hedge a king
> That treason can but peep to what it would.

p. 159. *Brace off the fore-yard.* Means ease off the lee braces and take in the slack on the weather braces, so that the yard is not pointing so sharp fore and aft; in consequence of the ship being kept a little more off the wind.

p. 160. *Long-heath, Broom-furs.* The First Folio has: "Long heath, Browne firrs," and this is a passage much discussed by the commentators on Shakespeare. Halliwell considers that "long" refers to the wide expanse of heath. "I have consumed all, plaied away long acre." *Yorkshire Tragedy,* 1608. Broom-furs certainly gives a picture of dryness and stark aridity as opposed to the watery waves. Hanmer read: "ling, heath, broom, furze," and this is accepted by Dyce, W. A. Wright, and others. It seems, however, an unnecessary and somewhat violent change.

p. 160. *Luffe.* Luff is to bring a ship closer *head* to wind, even so that the luffs of the sails begin to shake.

p. 162. *lop, for over-toping.* Shakespeare has "Trash for over-topping." To trash has been explained as to cut down or lop trees and hedges which are overgrown. Also as a hunting term, to keep in check hounds which outdistance the pack.

From this present passage it would appear that the first explanation of "To trash" is the more exact.

p. 163. *mid-Heaven.* Shakespeare has "zenith." Mid-heaven is more strictly an astrological term, being the point of the ecliptic on the meridian. It will be readily remembered that Dryden was an adept in astrological sciences.

p. 164. *Bermoothes.* The Bermudas. In 1610 Sylvester Jourdain published his *Discovery of the Bermudas, otherwise called the Isle of Divels.* There is mention of "the dreadful coast of the Bermudas" in Howe's supplement to Stowe's *Annals.*

p. 165. *blew-ey'd.* Sycorax is termed blue-eyed, because her eyes were dark and sunken, a sign of pregnancy. So in *The Dutchesse of Malfy,* 4to, 1623, II, 1, Bosola says that he suspects that the Duchess is with child because:

> The fins of her eie-lids look most teeming blew,
> She waines i' th' cheeke, and waxes fat i' th' flanke;
> And (contrary to our Italian fashion)
> Weares a loose-bodied gowne.

And in Otway's *Friendship and Fashion,* Dorset Garden, April, 1678, II, Mrs. Goodvile and Lettice rally Victoria. "*Mrs. Goodvile.* Lord, you are paler than you use to be. *Lettice.* Ay, and then that blewness under the eyes. *Mrs. Goodvile.* Besides, you are not so lively as I have known you: pardon me, Cousin. *Lettice.* Well, if there be a fault, Marriage will cure all."

p. 166. *Abhor'd Slave.* It may be noticed that in the First Folio Shakespeare, 1623, this speech, which Dryden assigns to Prospero, is given (improperly, as I am convinced) to Miranda. Theobald well says: "I

489

am persuaded the author never designed the speech for Miranda," and Capell supports him. Several modern authors justly follow Theobald.

p. 167. *red botch.* An inflamed ulcer.

p. 167. *Setebos.* This name is evidently formed from that of *Settaboth,* "A divinity of the Patagonians, described by Master Francis Fletcher in an account of Drake's great voyage."

p. 169. *Blood pursu'd my hand.* Cf. Vergil, *Aeneid,* III, 24–33:

> Accessi, viridemque ab humo convellere silvam
> conatus, ramis tegerem ut frondentibus aras,
> horrendum et dictu video mirabile monstrum.
> Nam quae prima solo ruptis radicibus arbos
> vellitur, huic atro liquuntur sanguine guttae
> et terram tabo maculant. Mihi frigidus horror
> membra quatit, gelidusque coit formidine sanguis.
> Rursus et alterius lentum convellere vimen
> insequor et causas penitus temptare latentes:
> alter et alterius sequitur de cortice sanguis.

p. 171. *trills down.* To trill is to flow in a slender stream, but more constantly and continuously than to trickle.

p. 171. *peid.* Pecked. This rare word which is omitted by the O.E.D. is found in some compound dialect forms. Wood pie (Somerset) = the green woodpecker. Wood pie (Staffordshire, Hants) = woodpecker. Shadwell's operatic version of *The Tempest* has "peck'd" in this passage.

p. 173. *Salvages.* This obsolete form of savage is found in Gower, and persisted for several centuries. Thus in Tate and Brady's version (1696) of the *Psalms,* vii, 2, we have:

> Lest, like a salvage Lion, he
> My helpless Soul devour.

p. 174. *Old Simon the King.* Simon Wadloe, landlord of the Old Devil Tavern, Temple Bar, which was frequented and made famous by Ben Jonson. Wadloe was the original of the popular old song *Old Simon the King,* which was, it may be remembered, the favourite air of Squire Western in *Tom Jones,* IV, 5.

p. 176. *Moon-calf.* An abortion, a monstrosity. Moon-calf, *partus lunaris,* was an old name for a false conception—*mola carnea,* or fœtus imperfectly formed, being supposed to be occasioned by the influence of the moon.

p. 176. *out of the Moon.* There is a French legend that the Man in the Moon is Judas Iscariot. Others say Cain. An English superstition prefers that he should be the man who gathered sticks upon the Sabbath Day, *Numbers* xv, 32–36. A more graceful classical mythology fables that he was Endymion, a shepherd boy of Mount Latmus in

Caria, who was beloved by Selene, the goddess of the moon. Cicero, *Tusculanae Disputationes*, I, 38, 92.

p. 177.   *Pig-nuts*. The tuber of *Bunium flexuosum*; earth-nuts.

p. 187.   *mop and moe*. The First Folio has "mop, and mowe." Antic gestures and grimaces.

p. 188.   *forth-rights*. A forth-right is a straight path or a direct course.

p. 189.   *eight fat Spirits*. In *The Rehearsal*, produced at the Theatre Royal, 7 December, 1671, Buckingham has a bob at these spirits when Bayes (III, 5) cries to his soldiers: "Udzookers, you dance worse than the Angels in *Harry* the Eight, or the fat Spirits in *The Tempest*, I gad."

p. 189.   *going to the door*. That is one of the permanent Proscenium doors.

p. 189.   *Bosens Whistle*. "A silver whistle, suspended from the neck by a lanyard, is the modern Boatswain's badge of office, and it is familiarly termed his 'call.'" Shakespeare a Seaman, *St. James' Magazine*, July, 1862.

p. 189.   *Fuss*. A misprint for "Fubs." Fubs is a term of endearment, usually applied to a small chubby person. Cf. *Sir Courtly Nice*, 4to, 1685, V, where Crack talks of "my *Indian* Fubs of a Sister." Fubs was a nickname given by Charles II to the Duchess of Portsmouth.

p. 190.   *Plashes*. Puddles or marshy pools; standing water.

p. 190.   *she would be loving*. This is the scene referred to by Congreve in *The Way of the World*, produced at Lincoln's Inn Fields, March, 1700, when Fainall says of Sir Wilful: "When he's drunk, he's as loving as the Monster in the Tempest; and much after the same manner." Sycorax (not Caliban) is the Monster to whom allusion is made.

p. 192.   *Blouze*. A vulgar term for a common slatternly woman. In D'Urfey's *Famous History of the Rise and Fall of Massaniello*, Two Parts, acted at Drury Lane in 1699, the name of Massaniello's wife is rather absurdly given as Blowzabella.

p. 192.   *natural*. A loony; a half-witted fool.

p. 192.   *Prize-brandy*. A prize being a legal capture at sea.

p. 196.   *divide the waters*. Cf. the song of Arbaces in Arne's opera *Artaxerxes*, 1762:

> Water parted from the sea
> May increase the river's tide;
> To the bubbling fount may flee,
> Or thro' fertile vallies glide:
> Yet in search of lost repose,
> Doom'd like me, forlorn to roam,
> Still it murmurs as it flows,
> Till it reach its native home.

p. 209.   *skink about*. Serve drink round; pour out liquor. Cf. Shirley's *The Lady of Pleasure*, licensed 15 October, 1635; 4to, 1637; IV, 2: "A drawer is my Ganymede, he shall skink brisk nectar to us."

491

p. 209.   *Rowse.* A full bumper; a draught of liquor. Cf. *Othello*, II, 3, the drinking scene where Cassio enters half tippled, exclaiming "'Fore God, they have given me a rouse already."

p. 209.   *Haunse in Kelder.* Literally Jack-in-the-Cellar, *i.e.* the unborn babe in the womb. This is a favourite expression with Dryden. Cf. *Amboyna*, acted in 1673, IV, 1, where Harman senior remarks at Towerson and Ysabinda's wedding: "You *Englishmen* . . . cannot ſtay for Ceremonies; a good honeſt *Dutchman* would have been plying the glass all this while, and drunk to the hopes of *Hans in Kelder* till 'twas Bedtime."

p. 210.   *drinks like a fish.* The phrase is fairly early and occurs in *The Night-Walker; or, The Little Thief*, licensed 11 May, 1633, as "a play of Fletchers corrected by Sherley," IV, where Toby says: "I can drink like a fish now, like an elephant."

p. 210.   *Brindis.* Italian, *brindisi* and *brendisi*; "a drinking a health to one" (Florio). O.E.D. does not notice this rare word, but includes another form, "Brendice," which Dryden uses in *Amboyna*, I, 1: "I go to fill a Brendice to my noble Captain's Health."

p. 210.   *Up se Dutch.* Up se = Op zijn, in the fashion or manner of. Cf. *The Alchemiſt*, IV, 6:

> I doe not like the dulnesse of your eye:
> It hath a heavy caſt, 'tis upsee Dutch.

p. 211.   *the Witches are of great Families in Lapland.* In mediæval times it was often believed that supernatural powers were the heritage of certain families and even races, descending from one generation to another, and that all Lapp women in particular were born witches. There are many allusions to this traditional superſtition. Cf. Fletcher's *The Chances*, folio 1647, V, where Don John says:

> Sure his devil
> Comes out of Lapland.

Also Mrs. Behn's *The Dutch Lover*, produced at Dorset Garden in 1673, V, where Haunce says: "Do you think I creep in like a *Lapland* Witch through the Keyholes?"

p. 211.   *Wildings.* Wild apples, or any wild fruit. Cf. *The Faerie Queen*, III, vii, 17:

> Oft from the forreſt wildings he did bring,
> Whose sides empurpled were with smyling red.

p. 211.   *Hackney-Devil.* A parody on "hackney-coach." Hackney means plying for common hire.

p. 211.   *Pigs-nye.* Pet; darling. The word is from baby talk. Cf. Massinger's *The Piĉture* (licensed 8 June, 1629), 4to, 1630, II, 1:

> "If thou art,
> As I believe, the pigzney of his heart."

p. 214. *Heila*. A misprint for Hecla. The Hague edition, 1710, reads, "*Hecla*."

p. 221. *Moly*. A fabulous herb of magic power, having a black root and white blossom, and known by this name among the gods, which was given by Hermes to Odysseus as a counter-charm to the enchantments of Circe. *Odyssey*, X, 302–344. Cf. *Comus* (1634):

> And yet more med'cinal is it then that Moly
> That Hermes once to wise Ulysses gave.

p. 221. *trickling Balm*. Cf. Dryden in his translation of the *Georgics*, II, 165–6:

> Balm slowly trickles through the bleeding Veins
> Of happy Shrubs, in *Idumæan* Plains.

The original has:

> Quid tibi odorato referam sudantia ligno
> balsama. . . .

p. 221. *purple Panacea*. Panacea, a name given to a herb vaguely and very variously identified. Phillips, 1706, has: "Panacea . . . the Herb All-heal, or Wound-wort." In some dialects, particularly Cheshire and Yorkshire, All-Heal is known as Self-Heal. Bradley, 1725, speaking of All-Heal, says that the "Flowers are white and very small." Purple here is the Latin *purpureus*, brilliant, beautiful. It may even mean "shining white." Albinovanus has (II, 62) "bracchia purpurea candidiora nive."

p. 221. *vulnerary*. Healing; curative. Latin, *Vulnerarius*. Cf. Pliny, *Historia Naturalis*, XXIII, 4, 40: Oleum oenanthinum "vulnerariis emplastris utile" est.

p. 223. *Hippolito's Sword*. There is an error here. Miranda should have brought Ferdinand's sword. Ariel had said:

> "Anoint the Sword which pierc'd him with this Weapon-Salve,
> And wrap it close from Air till I have time
> To visit him again."

Weapon-salve was supposed to cure a wounded person by being applied to the sword by which the hurt had been inflicted. It was first discovered by Paracelsus. Cf. Davenant's *The Unfortunate Lovers*, 4to, 1649, II, 1:

> "Our medecine we apply,
> Like the weapon-salve, not to ourselves but him
> Who was the sword that made the wound."

Also Mrs. Behn's *The Young King*, 4to, 1683, V, 5:

> "That Balm it was, that like the Weapon-salve
> Heals at a Distance——"

493

Lord Bacon, *Sylva Sylvarum*, sixth edition (1651), p. 217, writes: "It is conftantly Received, and Avouched, that the *Anointing* of the *Weapon*, that maketh the *Wound*, wil heale the *Wound* it selfe. . . . And thus much hath been tried, that the *Ointment* (for *Experiments* sake) hath been wiped off the *Weapon*, without the knowledge of the *Party Hurt*, and presently the *Party Hurt*, hath been in great *Rage of Paine*, till the *Weapon* was *Reannointed*."

One may compare in Scott's *Lay of the Laft Minftrel* the magical cure of William of Deloraine's wound by "The Ladye of Branksome." See also *Bygone Beliefs*, by H. S. Redgrove, chapter V, "The Powder of Sympathy: a Curious Medical Superftition."

p. 227. *She would control the Moon.* Cf. *Paradise Loft*, II, 662–666:

> Nor uglier follow the Night-Hag, when call'd
> In secret, riding through the Air she comes
> Lur'd with the smell of infant blood, to dance
> With *Lapland* Witches, while the labouring Moon
> Eclipses at thir charms.

p. 228. *Saraband.* A slow and ftately Spanish dance in triple time.

p. 229. *The Rhyming Monsieur, and the Spanish Plot.* In the winter of 1667 the vogue of the heroic drama written in couplets was already very great, and in spite of parodies and criticism rhyme long continued to hold its own on the ftage. Howard and Dryden's *The Indian-Queen*, produced at the Theatre Royal in January, 1663–4, and Dryden's sequel *The Indian Emperour*, produced at the same house in the spring of 1665, both had an unprecedented success. In the Prologue to *Aureng-Zebe* (Theatre Royal, 1675), Dryden confesses that

> he Grows weary of his long-lived Miftris Rhyme.

None the less *Aureng-Zebe* drew thronging audiences, as also did Crowne's *The Deftruction of Jerusalem*, a rhyming tragedy in two parts, produced at the Theatre Royal in the spring of 1677. In the Prologue to *Secret Love* (Theatre Royal, 2 March, 1667), Dryden insifts that he has observed in this play

> "The Unities of Action, Place, and Time;
> The scenes unbroken; and a mingled chime
> Of *Johnsons* Humour with *Corneilles* rhyme."

Spanish influence had been very ftrong in the English drama before the closing of the theatres in 1642. Fletcher in particular is indebted to Spanish literature. But immediately after the Reftoration, and for at leaft half a century following, the Spanish playwrights were even more largely drawn upon by English authors. In some cases, it is true, Spanish comedies filtered into England by way of France. But Charles II himself suggefted *Los Empeños de Seis Horas* to Sir Samuel Tuke as "an excellent design" for an English

494

play, and he also handed Moreto's *No Puede Ser* to Crowne. Tuke's *The Adventures of Five Hours*, produced at the Duke's House, 8 January, 1663, won an instant triumph, "and the house by its frequent plaudits did show their sufficient approbation." "It took successively 13 days altogether, no other Play intervening," and was constantly in the bills.

In the original Prologue to *The Wild Gallant*, as produced at the Vere Street Theatre, 5 February, 1662–3, it will be remembered that Dryden introduces two astrologers to foretell the fate of the new play, and after some prognostication the second Astrologer says:

> "But yet the greatest Mischief does remain,
> The twelfth Apartment bears the Lord of Spain;
> Whence I conclude, it is your Author's Lot,
> To be Endanger'd by a Spanish Plot."

p. 229. *Visions bloodier than King Richard's.* This allusion would almost seem to point to a fairly recent revival of Richard III, which was one of the plays assigned as a monopoly to Killigrew's company. In *Covent Garden Drollery*, 1672, p. 13, is a *"Prologue to* Richard *the Third,"* but this gives no indication of the theatre or actors. Contemporary allusions, however, indicate that the tragedy enjoyed some popularity. In Henry Higden's *A Modern Essay On the Thirteenth Satyr of Juvenal*, 4to, 1686, we have:

> Bath'd in cold Sweats he frighted Shrieks
> At visions bloodier than King *Dicks*.

Upon this the author gives a note: *"Vision Dicks.* In the Tragedy of *Richard* the 3rd." In D'Urfey's *A Fool's Preferment*, produced at Dorset Garden in the spring of 1688, Act III, 2, Lyonel, the distracted gentleman, cries out: "A Horse; a Horse; my Kingdom for a Horse."

There was a revival of *Richard III* at Dorset Garden about 1690 with Sandford in the title-rôle; Betterton as Edward IV; Kynaston, Clarence; Williams, Buckingham; Mountfort, Richmond; Smith, Norfolk; Mrs. Betterton, the Duchess of York; Mrs. Knight, Queen Margaret; Mrs. Barry, Queen Elizabeth; and Mrs. Bracegirdle, Lady Anne.

The famous alteration of *Richard III* by Colley Cibber, which was produced at Drury Lane in February, 1699–1700, with Cibber himself as crook-back'd Dick, has kept the stage until the present time.

AN EVENING'S LOVE

p. 232. *Mallem Convivis*. Martial, IX, lxxxii, 4: "Sensus est, Malim mea carmina placere lectoribus atque auditoribus, quam poetis æmulis."

p. 237. *William, Duke of Newcastle*. William Cavendish, 1592–1676, who is perhaps rather remembered by the noble part he played in the Civil Wars, as a great Patron of literature, and owing to the biographical tribute dictated by the affection of his wife, than by his own dramatic works. He wrote four comedies, and tradition says that he gave his translation of *L'Étourdi* to Dryden, who made it into *Sr. Martin Mar-all*. His treatise on horsemanship has attained some celebrity. His lady wrote with fond partiality: "I may justly call him the best lyric and dramatic poet of his age."

p. 237. *Cymon and Lucullus*. In his comparison between Cimon and Lucullus Plutarch says: "We cannot but deem the end of Lucullus happy, as he did not live to see that change in the constitution which fate was preparing for his country in the civil wars. Though the commonwealth was in a sickly state, yet he left it free. In this respect the case of Cimon was particularly similar. For he died while Greece was at the height of her prosperity, and before she was involved in her ruinous troubles. . . . Heaven appears to have favoured both, directing the one what he should do, and warning the other what he should avoid." Langhorne's *Plutarch*, Vol. III, ed. Wrangham (1819), pp. 358–64.

p. 237. *Hannibal*. Who was defeated by Scipio at Zama in 202 B.C.

p. 237. *the last smiles of victory*. The Duke took Howley House, 22 June, 1643; defeated the Fairfaxes at Adwalton Moor, 30 June; captured Bradford, and subjected all Yorkshire, save Wressel Castle and Hull, to lawful authority.

p. 238. *open Martyrdome*. The Duke and Duchess remained in banishment under conditions of grinding poverty for sixteen years. Their English estates and revenues, valued at upwards of £20,000 per annum, were thus left entirely at the mercy of the Parliament men, who levied immense sums on them.

p. 238. *Caius Marius*. "Marius too ambitiously striving like a passioned young man against the weakness and debility of his age, never missed a day but he would be in the field of Mars to exercise himself among the young men, shewing his body disposed and ready to handle all kind of weapons, and to ride horses: albeit that in his later time, he had no great health of body, because he was very heavy and sad." Plutarch, *Caius Marius* (North's translation).

p. 238. *Silius Italicus*. Was consul in A.D. 68, the year Nero perished. Subsequently he was elected proconsul of Asia. Upon retiring from office he spent his time between a mansion near Puteoli, formerly the Academy of Cicero, and his favourite residence, a house in the vicinity of Naples, once occupied by Vergil. *Vide* Martial, VII, 63, and XI, 48:

> Silius haec magni celebrat monumenta Maronis,
> iugera facundi qui Ciceronis habet.
> Heredem dominumque sui tumulive Larisve
> non alium mallet nec Maro, nec Cicero.

The *Bellum Punicum*, a lengthy epic in seventeen books, has met with some very severe judgements, and it must be confessed that Silius too often copies Vergil without taste and without vigour.

p. 238. *Partner of your studies.* The Duchess of Newcastle, Margaret, daughter of Sir Thomas Lucas, died in 1676. This elegant fantast, "Princess of Philosophers," "a wise, wittie, and Learned Lady, which her many Books doe well testifie," published two folio volumes of plays, 1662 and 1668. The Duke contributed songs to these performances, and he wrote five scenes for her comedy in two parts, *The Lady Contemplation,* three Scenes in the first and two in the second part. In *The Publick Wooing,* a comedy, the Duke provided two scenes as well as several speeches. In *Youth's Glory* two scenes and several speeches are from the Duke's pen.

p. 238. *Sulpitia.* In the volume of poems which includes the posthumous elegies of Tibullus, there is also contained a group of short pieces by a lady of high birth and social standing, a niece of Messalla and a daughter of Servius Sulpicius. Nothing is known of her life beyond what may be gathered from the poems, which are addressed to her lover, who according to the fashion of the day is spoken of under a Greek name, Calenus, although he was no doubt a young Roman aristocrat of her own circle.

Of Sulpicia, a poetess of the Flavian period, the works are lost and her name alone remains.

p. 239. *Praesenti tibi maturos.* Horace, *Epistularum,* II, i, 15.

p. 239. *Augustus living.* Suetonius, however, says that Augustus very scrupulously refused even the customary honours and veneration: "Templa quamvis sciret etiam proconsulibus decerni solere: in nulla tamen provincia nisi communi suo Romaeque nomine recepit nam in urbe quidem pertinacissime abstinuit hoc honore. Atque etiam argenteas statuas olim sibi positas conflavit omnes: exque iis aureas cortinas Apollini Palatino dedicavit. . . . Domini appellationem, ut maledictum et opprobrium semper exhorruit." *Augustus Caesar,* LII–LIII. Casaubon glosses: "Hinc orditur de civilitate Augusti memorare, cuius hoc primum documentum ponit, quod honores a civibus supra humanum fastigium non admiserit." Yet Tacitus, of whom Dryden was doubtless thinking, notes it as a fault in Augustus "quod templis coli voluerit."

p. 239. *so pious an Historian. The Life of William Cavendish, Duke of Newcastle,* written by his Duchess, London, folio 1667. The same in Latin, London, folio, 1668.

p. 239.   *manes of Johnson and D'avenant.* Both of whom had been nobly
patronized by the Duke of Newcastle. Langbaine, who calls him
our *English Mecænas,* continues: "He had a more particular kind-
ness for that Great Master of Dramatick Poesy, the Excellent
Johnson and 'twas from him that he attain'd to a perfect Know-
ledge of what was to be accounted True Humour in Comedy."

p. 240.   *Opiniatre.* The folio reads: opiniative, but the earlier form is fuller
flavoured. Among Butler's *Characters* is "An Opiniater." "Is his
own Confident, that maintains more Opinions than he is able to
support. They are all Bastards commonly and unlawfully be-
gotten."

p. 241.   *Zany of a Mountebank.* The zany was the Jack-Pudding or Merry
Andrew whose pranks attracted a crowd round the Dulcimara. In
Butler's *Characters,* "The Mountebank," it is said: "His *Pudding*
is his Setter, that lodges the Rabble for him." Cf. Dryden's Pro-
logue to *The Pilgrim,* 4to, 1700, in reference to "*Quack* Maurus":

> *Our Mountebank has laid a deeper Train,* ⎫
> *His Cant, like* Merry Andrew's *Noble Vein,* ⎬
> *Cat-Calls the Sects, to draw 'em in again.* ⎭

There is a good illustration of a crowd collecting round a mounte-
bank's rostrum in *The Fifth Volume of the Works of Mr. Thomas
Brown,* 1721: "Jo Hayn's Mountebank Speech." Erasmus in the
Moriae Encomium speaks of *circulatores:* "Illic in foro posita mensa,
conscendunt nebulones herbarii, aut praetigiatores, aut aliud quid-
piam simile profitentes, et oratione populum illiciunt." The best
mountebank scene in any English play—and perhaps in any drama
—forms an important episode in *Volpone.*

p. 241.   *habit.* There is a dry bob here at James Nokes and Edward Angel,
the two leading low comedians of the rival theatre, the Duke's.
Dryden had, it is true, adapted the part of Sir Martin Mar-all
"purposely for the Mouth of Mr. *Nokes,*" and this play, *Sr. Martin
Mar-all,* was given at the Duke's House. But it must be remembered
that the Duke of Newcastle directed the choice of theatre in this in-
stance. *Sr. Martin Mar-all* did not in print appear with Dryden's
name until as late as 1691, and at Stationers' Hall, 24 June, 1668, it
was entered as the work of William, Duke of Newcastle. Again
Edward Angel was the original Stephano in *The Tempest,* which
also was a Duke's House play since Dryden had here collaborated
with Davenant. But Dryden was the recognized leading dramatist
of Killigrew's company, and indeed bound to them under contract.
He was, no doubt, a little piqued that *An Evening's Love* did not
prove so extraordinarily successful as *Sr. Martin Mar-all.* In the
famous prologue to *The Conquest of Granada,* Part I, which was
spoken by Nell Gwyn "in a broad-brimm'd hat, and waist-belt,"
he very particularly girds at a ridiculous habit worn by James Nokes.
See the note upon the prologue to *The Conquest of Granada,* I.

Edward Angel was notorious for his approved buffoonery, gag-
ging and grimace, tricks which he recklessly employed often to the
great chagrin of the author of the play. Thus Mrs. Aphra Behn in
the Epistle to the Reader before *The Dutch Lover*, 4to, 1673, in
which comedy he acted Haunce van Ezel, deals him a pretty severe
jobation for his pranks. "My Dutch Lover spoke but little of what
I intended for him, but supplied with a great deal of idle stuff, which
I was wholly unacquainted with until I had heard it first from him;
so that Jack-pudding ever us'd to do: which though I knew before,
I gave him yet the Part, because I knew him so acceptable to most
o' th' lighter Periwigs about the Town, . . . I intended him a habit
much more notably ridiculous, which if ever it be important was
so here."

p. 241. *longing Woman.* Dr. Havelock Ellis in his *Erotic Symbolism* (Vol. V,
Studies in the Psychology of Sex, ed. 1927, p. 211), says: "The old
medical authors abound in narratives describing the longings of
pregnant women for natural and unnatural foods. This affection
was commonly called *pica*, sometimes *citra* or *malatia*." Schurig
devotes the second chapter of his *Chylologia* (1725) to the pica.
"Some women," he tells us, "have been compelled to eat all sorts of
earthy substances, of which sand seems the most common. . . .
Lime, mud, chalk, charcoal, cinders, pitch are also the desired sub-
stances in other cases detailed." Butler in his *Characters*, "A Duke
of Bucks," has: "His Appetite to his Pleasures is diseased and crazy,
like the Pica in a Woman, that longs to eat that, which was never
made for Food, or a Girl in the Green-sickness, that eats Chalk and
Mortar."

p. 242. *Crambe bis cocta.* Erasmus, *Adagia*, "Taedium ex Iteratione," cites
the Greek proverb κράμβη δίσεφθον, which he turns by *crambe re-
cocta*. (*Adagia*, Hannow, folio, 1617, p. 679.) The famous use is of
course *Crambe repetita*, Juvenal VII, 154.

p. 242. *Parcere personis.* Martial, X, xxxiii, 10.

p. 242. ——*In vitium.* Horace, *Ars Poetica*, 282–4.

p. 242. *Neve immunda. Aut immunda crepent.* Horace, *Ars Poetica*, 247–8.

p. 242. *ipse dixit.* Αὐτὸς ἔφα : in the School of Pythagoras, said of the Master.

p. 243. *de Movendo risu.* Quintilian, *De Institutione Oratoria*, VI, iii. Dry-
den, as is his wont, does not quote Quintilian's words, but using his
own phrase and Latinity summarizes none too closely the great
critic. In Chapter III Quintilian discusses at length *urbanitas*,
venustum, *salsum*, *facetum*, *iocum*, *dicacitas*, *ridiculum* and other
terms in all their bearings.

p. 243. *Non displicuisse.* Quintilian, VI, iii, 2.

p. 243. *sunt, enim, longè venustiora.* Quintilian, *eodem capite*.

p. 243. *In omni eius ingenio.* "Utinamque libertus eius Tiro aut alius, quisquis
fuit, qui tris hac de re libros edidit, parcius dictorum numero in-
dulsissent et plus iudicii in eligendis quam in congerendis studii
adhibuissent: minus obiectus calumniantibus foret; qui tamen nunc

quoque, *ut in omni eius ingenio, facilius, quod reiici quam quod adiici possit, invenient.*" Quintilian, *Inst. Orator.*, VI, iii, 5.

The criticism is not of Ovid, but of Cicero. Quintilian has been speaking of a collection of Cicero's witty remarks, extant in his day and supposed to have been compiled by Tiro.

p. 244.   *the Lyar.* Dorante acted by Hart in *The Lyar*, probably produced at the Theatre Royal in Vere Street, 1661; 4to, 1661. This anonymous comedy which is little more than a translation of Pierre Corneille's *Le Menteur* (1642) was revived at Drury Lane in 1684, and printed quarto 1685 as *The Mistaken Beauty; or, The Lyar.* The *Lyar* was seen by Pepys at the Theatre Royal, Bridges Street, on Thursday, 28 November, 1667. He calls it "an old play." *Le Menteur* itself is derived from Alarcon's *La Verdad Sospechosa.*

p. 244.   *I make them happy.* The charge against which Dryden here defends himself was continually being urged. So Jeremy Collier in his *A Short View of the Immorality and Profaness of the English Stage*, 1698, Chapter IV, at length discusses how "*The* Stage Poets *make* Libertines *their* Top-Characters, *and give them* Success *in their* Debauchery." He particularly examines Dryden's argument in this Preface, and roundly avers "*The Defence in the* Preface *to the* Mock-Astrologer *not sufficient*;" "*The* Mock-Astrologer's *Instances from* Ben Johnson *Unserviceable*"; "*The Authority of* Shakespear *against the* Mock-Astrologer" (the character of Falstaff being discussed, and the moral of *The London Prodigal*). These points will be found to have been dealt with in the Introduction.

p. 244.   *Chœrea.* In the *Eunuchus* Chaerea, who has prevailed upon Parmeno to introduce him disguised as the Eunuch slave Dorus into the house of Thais, ravishes the damsel Pamphila. Presently, however, she is discovered to be the sister of Chremes, an Athenian citizen, and her betrothal to her seducer is celebrated.

p. 245.   *Heinsius.* Daniel Heinsius, the famous Dutch humanist, 1580–1665, has a most elaborate commentary upon Horace. In a long note discussing l. 270 of the *Ars Poetica* (*At vestri proavi Plautinos et numeros, et Laudavere sales*) he writes: "Comoedia enim delectat & docet. neq; minus comici διδάσκαλοι & κωμῳδιδάσκαλοι, quam tragici a Graecis dicuntur. Movere autem risum, non constituit comoediam sed aucupium est plebis, & abusus . . . quam homines Menander apud Graecos, apud Latinos Terentius fuerunt. qui ut sapientibus voluptatem potius afferrent; quam risum plebi violenter excuterent, duplici iucunditate utilitatem condierunt; imitatione vitae humane, & inimitabili lepore." Q. Horati Flacci *Opera.* Cum Animadversionibus & Notis Danielis Heinsi. Luguduni Batavorum. Apud Ludovicum Elzevirium. 1612, pp. 78, 79 *sqq.* (notarum).

p. 246.   *Et spes.* Juvenal, VII, 1.

p. 246.   *hulk of Sir Francis Drake.* As is well known, by order of Queen Elizabeth Drake's ship, the Golden Hind, which she had herself visited on 4 April, 1581, was preserved as it were a national monument at Deptford. It became an object of general resort upon a holiday, and gradually it was so adapted and altered that it is said but little of the original remained. As early as Jonson's *Every Man in his Humour*, acted in 1598, I, 3, young Kno'well alludes to "Drakes old ship, at *Detford*." In the Prologue to Shadwell's *The Amorous Bigotte*, 4to, 1690, we have:

> On that foundation then he built, 'tis true,
> But like Drake's Ship, 'tis so repair'd 'tis new.

p. 246.   *El Astrologo fingido.* An excellent "Comedia de Capa y Espada" by Calderon. See the note upon the source of *An Evening's Love.*

p. 246.   *the Feign'd Astrologer.* 4to, 1668. This translation was probably unacted. See the note upon the Source of *An Evening's Love.*

p. 247.   *Terence.* Cicero, *Ad Atticum*, VII, 3, writes: "Secutus sum, non dico Caecilium, mane ut ex portu in Piraeum (malus enim auctor latinitatis est) sed Terentium, cuius fabellae propter elegantiam sermonis putabantur a C. Laelio scribi." Suetonius *Terentii Vita* has: "Non obscura fama est adiutum Terentium in scriptis a Laelio et Scipione, quibuscum familiariter vixit. Eandem ipse auxit: nunquam enim nisi leviter se tutari conatur ut in Prologo Adelphorum. . . . Videtur autem se levius defendisse, quia sciebat Laelio et Scipioni non ingratam esse hanc opinionem; quae tamen magis et usque ad posteriora tempora valuit."

p. 247.   *Hecatommuthi.* "*Gli ecatommithi*, overo Cento Novelle di Giraldi Cinthio." This book was first printed in 1565 at Monreale in Sicily, 2 vols., 8vo.; at Venice in 1566 and 1574. Several of Shakespeare's plots seem to be but secondarily derived from Cinthio as *Measure for Measure* (Decade VIII, Novella 5 of *Gli ecatommithi*), the immediate source of which is Whetstone's *Promos and Cassandra.*

p. 247.   *Beaumont and Fletcher.* The plot of *The Chances* is from *La Señora Cornelia*, which is the fourth Novel of the second Volume of Cervantes' *Novelas ejemplares* (1613).

The Spanish Curate is wholly from stories in a novel translated by Leonard Digges from the Spanish: *Gerardo, the Vnfortunate Spaniard. . . . Written by an ingenious Spanish Gentleman, Don Gonçalo de Cespedes and Meneçes . . . London.* 1622. 4to. This was reprinted in 1653 (1652). The title of the original is: *Poema Tragico Del Espanol Gerardo, y Desengano del amor lasciuo. Por Don Gonzalo de Cespedes y Meneses, vezino y natural de Madrid.* It first appeared at Madrid in 1615 and went through many editions. Though called *Poema* it is a prose romance.

Rule a Wife and Have a Wife. The Perez-Estefania underplot is from *El Casamiento Engañoso*, one of the *Novelas ejemplares* of Cervantes. For the main plot no direct source has been traced, although Hallam suggested the strong probability of some Spanish prototype.

The Little French Lawyer. The story occurs in *Guzman d'Alfarache*, which was written by Mateo Aleman, and first printed in 1599 at Madrid. Hence no doubt Fletcher (who was working with Massinger?) derived it. The earliest known literary form of the story is the Fourth Novella of Massuccio Salernitano, whose *Il Novellino* was first issued at Naples, folio 1476.

p. 250. *Donna Theodosia ... Mrs. Bowtell.* Downes in the *Roscius Anglicanus* assigns Donna Theodosia to Mrs. Hughes. No doubt Mrs. Bowtell succeeded Mrs. Hughes in this rôle. Mrs. Hughes was also the original S. Catherine in *Tyrannick Love*, in which part she was again succeeded by Mrs. Bowtell.

p. 250. *Madrid, in the Year 1665.* The last year of the reign of Philip IV, who passed away just before dawn on Thursday, 25 September.

p. 251. *English Embassador's Retinue.* The English Ambassador was Sir Richard Fanshawe, who had recently negotiated the marriage between Charles II and Catharine of Braganza, and was high in favour at the English court. Fanshawe arrived at Cadiz 24 February (O.S.), 1664, and was received with almost royal honours. An ample and amusing account of his embassy in Spain, where he was to die, is in Lady Fanshawe's *Memoirs.*

p. 252. *Entertainment.* Lady Fanshawe flatly contradicts the usually accepted English idea that Spain is a land of famine, and waxes eloquent over the excellence of their food and wines, and the profuseness of their banquets.

p. 252. *rash.* Rustle. *N.O.D.* quotes this passage. Crockett in *Kit Kennedy* (1899), XXII, speaks of "the strident rash-wish of the sharpening-strake on the scythe."

p. 252. *Tabby-Petticoat.* Tabby is silk taffeta, originally a striped taffeta, but afterwards any watered silk came under this designation.

p. 252. *Pieces of Eight.* A piastre, a coin of varying values in different countries. The Spanish piastre is now synonymous with a dollar and so worth four to five shillings. Cf. Mrs. Behn's *The Rover*, Part I, produced at Dorset Garden, 1677, the scene of which is laid in Spanish Naples, I: "if he part with more than a Piece of Eight—geld him: for which offer he may chance to be beaten, if she be a Whore of the first Rank."

p. 253. *feathers.* A feather was a beau, a gallant. Cf. the cognate "A man of feather," and note to *Secret Love* on that passage. French *plumet* (a rare word)=a fop. In Radcliffe's *The Ramble*, 1682, we have the line "To men of Fringe and Feather known." In Sedley's *The Mulberry Garden*, I, 1 (produced May, 1668; 4to, 1668), Sir Samuel Forecast speaks of fashionable ladies who have "their Chambers cover'd all over with Feathers and Ribands [*i.e.* full of fops and beaus], dancing and playing at Cards with 'um till morning."

p. 254. *Alguazile.* A conftable. So among the *Persons represented in the Play of The Spanish Curate,* Fletcher (and Massinger?), second folio, 1679, we have "Algaziers, whom we call Sergeants." The term is very common in Spanish romances, *e.g. Guzman d'Alfarache,* Brady's translation, ed. 1881, XVI, p. 224: '"Open," cried an alguazil; "open at the summons of juftice." '

p. 254. *Juego de cannas.* Javelin play; djereed. "The flying skirmish of the darted cane," as Dryden terms it in *The Conqueft of Granada,* Part I, I, 1. So Byron, *The Bride of Abydos,* speaks of

> Many an active deed
> With sabre keen, or blunt jereed.

He adds a note: "The jereed is a game of blunt javelins, animated and graceful."

p. 255. *Calle maior.* The Calle Mayor, leading from the Puerta del Sol, which is the heart of the city and the general rendezvous of gallant Madrileños, to the Calle de Bailen.

p. 256. *A Chappel.* Perhaps St. Ginés, a church built about 1358, injured by fire in 1824, and reftored 1874. The Capilla de Santisimo Crifto is famous. The altar is supported by two columns of exquisitely beautiful Semesante, the rareft of Roman marbles. It was no doubt this scene which caused Evelyn to write of *An Evening's Love* as "very profane," and indeed againft this episode the charge is not entirely unwarranted.

p. 259. *old law of pawns. Deuteronomy* xxiv, 10–13. Of pledges. "If the man be poor thou shalt not sleep with his pledge: in any case thou shalt deliver him the pledge again when the sun goeth down, that he may sleep in his own raiment, and bless thee." (*A.V.*)

p. 261. *opiniatre.* Stubborn in one's own conceit; adhering to one opinion. The word is not uncommon in the seventeenth century, and as late as 1716 Lady Bolingbroke wrote of "silly, obftinate, opiniatre friends." Swift's *Works* (1841), II, 530. Pepys uses the form "opiniaftre." Tuesday, 3 July, 1666, he notes that John Vaughan, afterwards Chief Juftice of the Common Pleas, is "moft passionate and opiniaftre."

p. 261. *full sails.* Cf. *The Way of the World,* Act II, the firft entrance of Millamant where Mirabell cries: "Here she comes I' faith full Sail, with her Fan spread and Streamers out, and a Shoal of Fools for Tenders." Congreve has but elaborated Dryden in this famous passage.

p. 262. *a meer Bajazet.* Bajazet I, chief of the Ottoman Turks, who succeeded his father Amurath I in 1389, showed himself a savage and mighty conqueror, but on 28 July, 1402, he was ultimately defeated at Angora in Bithynia by Timur Khan. He was taken captive, and died about nine months later, according to many hiftorians at Antioch in Pisidia. Modern authorities reject the ftory of the iron cage in which Bajazet was imprisoned as a wild beaft, and against the bars of which despairingly he beat out his brains. None the less the legend—if legend it be—was repeated again and again by Western chroniclers and became firmly fixed in the popular imagination. The Byzantine historian Georgios Phrantzes in his *Chronicon* (1468) was the first to relate the strange manner of this incarceration, and it has even been suggested that he misunderstood the Turkish word 'kafes' (a litter or a cage), and that actually Bajazet during the long treks of the Tartar hosts was confined in some kind of covered waggon or large palankeen. The suicide of Bajazet by braining himself against the cage is described (and perhaps originated) by Petrus Perondinus in his *Tamerlanis Vita*, IX (1553): "despondens vita excessit, capite numerosis letibus ferreis caveæ clatris perfracto illisoque cerebro, suo ad id misero funestoque fato compulsus." He has been followed by Pierre de la Primaudaye whose compilations originally published in 1577 were translated into English as *The French Academy*, 1586. Michael Ducas the Byzantine, who wrote before 1462, relates that rumour reported Bajazet to have poisoned himself.

Bajazet plays an important rôle in the First Part of Marlowe's *Tamburlaine the Great*. He is taken prisoner on the field, and presently enter "two Moors drawing Bajazeth in his cage, and his wife following him." He is used as a footstool and otherwise degraded by the conqueror, and towards the end of the drama after a tumultuous speech which commences:

> Now, Bajazet, abridge thy baneful days,
> And beat thy brains out of thy conquer'd head . . .

"He brains himself against the cage"; which example is promptly followed by his wife, Zabina the Turkess.

For a full discussion of the traditions concerning Bajazet and his fate, see J. von Hammer-Purgstall, *Geschichte des Osmanischen Reiches* (Pesth, 1827), Vol. I, Book VIII.

p. 262. *Ægyptian year*. "The Egyptian Year consists of 365 Days, which they divided into twelve Months of 30 days apiece, and five other days (called ἐπαγουμεναί) added at the end of them." *The Elements of Astronomy* . . . By David Gregory, M.D. . . . done into *English*, 1715, Vol. I, p. 245.

p. 263. *Passa-calles*. An early kind of dance tune of Spanish origin. It is thus defined in a *Short Explication of Foreign Words in Musick Books* (1724): "*Passacaglio* or *Passacaille* or *Passagillio* is a kind of Air somewhat like a Chacone, but of a more slow or graver movement."

p. 264. *Conjur'd up a Spirit*. Spirits are not to be evoked with impunity out of any idle curiosity, but should be commanded some task or mission. An old writer says: "The circle is the principal fort and shield of the magician, from which he is not, at the peril of his life, to depart, till he has completely dismissed the spirit, particularly if it be of a fiery or infernal nature. Instances are recorded of many who perished by this means."

p. 264. *Pistols.* The pistole was a gold coin worth about 16s.

p. 268. *Gorget.* Originally a piece of armour for the throat. An article of female dress covering the neck and bosom; a wimple. Cf. Cleveland (1659), *Works,* ed. 1687:

> Pray rectifie my Gorget, smooth my Whisk.

p. 268. *Nostradamusses.* Michel Notre-Dame (1503–66), physician to Henri II of France, and fortune-teller in chief to Catherine de' Medici. His *Centuries,* obscure predictions written in quatrains, were long famous. They were translated into English, and even to-day in France and the Walloon districts of Belgium the peasants consult this book with great assiduity and confidence. In *Le Feint Astrologue,* II, 2, Don Fernard, the mock astrologer, pretends:

> Madame, j'avoueray qu'en mon voyage en France
> Du grand Nostradamus j'acquis la connoissance,
> Avec tant de bonheur, qu'il m'enseigna son Art.

p. 269. *the trine Aspect of the two Infortunes.* The trine aspect is the aspect of two heavenly bodies which are a third part of the zodiac, *i.e.* 120°, distant from each other. An infortune is an unfortunate or malevolent planet. The two infortunes are Saturn and Mars. R. A. Proctor, *The Poetry of Astronomy* (1881), VIII, 278: "Saturn the greater Infortune, as Mars himself is the lesser Infortune." Cf. Massinger's *The City Madam* (1632), II, 2, where Stargaze speaks of "Venus . . . in her joy, and free from the malevolent beams of infortunes."

p. 269. *in Angular houses.* The cardinal houses are *anguli.* Partridge, *Astrological Vade Mecum,* 1679, VII, explains: "The first, tenth, seventh, and fourth [Houses] are called Angles; . . . the Angles are the most powerful." Angles, that is to say Angular houses.

p. 269. *quaerent.* A technical term in astrology. Partridge, *Astrological Vade Mecum,* 1679, IX, p. 48: "First know, that the word Querent signifies no more, but that Man or Woman, who propounds any thing to an Artist by way of inquiry; the word comes from the Latin *Quaero,* and signifies the same with the Greek Ζητέω, to seek or inquire; so the quaesited is no more but the thing sought." Cf. Lilly's *Christian Astrology,* VI, 49: "Significator of the Querent or thing quesited." So in *John Inglesant,* XV, John explains the astrological scheme to his brother: "Venus, the lady of the third, being significator and applying to a friendly trine of Jupiter . . . is a very good argument that the querent should see the quesited speedily and that in perfect health."

p. 269. *the taking Hyleg.* Hyleg is a nativity; the ruling planet of a nativity; apheta. Lilly, *Christian Astrology,* 1647, CIV, "Of the Prorogator of Life, called Hylech, or Hyleg, or Apheta." Cf. *The Bloody Brother* (*Rollo*), 1625, IV, 2, where Norbret discourses

> how that Mars out of the self same house,
> (But another sign) here by a platique aspect
> Looks at the Hilege with a quartile ruling.

p. 269. *rectification for a Nativity*. The correction of an error in a horoscope. Cf. J. Gregory Terrestial Globe (1646) in *Postuma* (1650). "This is called Rectification, or right setting of the Globe."

p. 270. *Centiloquium of Trismegistus*. The mysterious Taauth (Thoth), the Hermes Trismegistus of the ancients, the god of hidden wisdom and keeper of magic secrets, was regarded as the earliest teacher of astrology in Egypt. He is reputed to have laid the foundation of the art in the "Hermetic Books," and to him is due the division of the zodiac into the twelve signs. In classical antiquity many works on the lore of the heavens and on occult sciences in general were universally ascribed to this mythical founder of Egyptian astrology. "Qui tametsi homo, fuit tamen antiquissimus et instructissimus omni genere doctrinae: adeo, ut ei multarum rerum, et artium scientia Trismegisto cognomen imponeret," says Lactantius, *De Falsa Religione*, I. *Centiloquium Hermetis* was printed folio 1493; *Centiloquium Hermetis. Eiusdem de stellis beibenijs*, folio 1519. "Hermes, *his* Centiloquium, *or his hundred Aphorisms Rendred into* English" occupies pp. 290–304 of J. Partridge's "Μικροπαναστρων; Or an Astrological Vade Mecum," London, 12mo, 1679.

p. 270. *Mars in the tenth*. "The mid-heaven, *medium caeli*, or angle of the South, whose line or *cusp* the sun touches at midday or noon, is termed the tenth house in the Astral art, and is the chief or supreme angle of the heavens." Raphael, *A Manual of Astrology*, 1828, pp. 104–106. "The consignificators are Capricorn and Mars, which planet rejoices in this house." Zadkiel, *Hand-Book of Astrology*, 1861, Vol. I, p. 13.

p. 270. *Jupiter configurated*. Associated in a configuration, that is the relative position or "aspects" of the sun, moon, and planets, recognized in Judicial Astrology. Saturn (*infortuna maior*) and Mars (*infortuna minor*) are the malevolent planets. Jupiter (*fortuna maior*) is a benign planet.

p. 270. *Squire Widdrington*. Roger Widdrington was "a squyar of Northombarlonde" of whom the old ballad *Chevy Chase* sings. See Percy's *Reliques*, ed. 1794, Vol. I, p. 14:

> For Wetharryagton my harte was wo
> That ever he slayne shulde be;
> For when both his leggis wear hewyne in to,
> Yet he knyled and fought on hys kne.

Wetharryagton is a corruption of Widdrington.

p. 270.   *Haly, and the spirit Fircu.* Haly, Alis-Ibn-Isa, chief astronomer at
the court of Haroun Alraschid's famous son, Abul Abbas Abdallah
Mamoun, seventh Abasside caliph, 786–835. Haly is alluded to in
the comedy *Albumazar*, II, 3:

> However . . .
> Hali, Albeneza, seem something to dissent.

So in *Love for Love*, II, Sir Sampson addresses the doting old
astrologer Foresight as "my good *Haly*." Cf. the Prologue to *The
Canterbury Tales*, l. 431 (Skeat):

> Old Ypocras, Haly, and Galien.

Oldham in *A Character* has: "*You'd take him for the* Ghost *of
Old* Haly *or* Albumazar, *or the* Spirit Frier *in the* Fortune
Book."
   Fircu is a fantastic name given to a supposed familiar of whom
mention may be found in the old almanacs. In *Love for Love*, II,
Sir Sampson, angrily boasting to Foresight, cries: "I tell you I have
travell'd old *Fircu*, and know the Globe."

p. 271.   *the trade of Lapland.* Fletcher, *The Chances* (folio 1647), V, 3, has:

> Sure, his devil
> Comes out of Lapland, where they sell men winds
> For dead drink and old doublets.

The witches in *Macbeth* traffic in winds, which were considered a
stock-in-trade of northern sorcery. Cf. Bartholomew Anglicus in
R. Steele's *Mediaeval Love* of the Finlanders; "and so to men
that sail by their coasts, and also to men that abide with them from
default of wind, they proffer wind to sailing, and so they sell wind."
"Marry thee! Oons, I'll marry a *Lapland* Witch as soon, and live
upon selling of contrary Winds, and Wrack'd Vessels" bawled Ben
to Miss Prue during their tiff. *Love for Love*, III. *Poor Robin*,
1695, has this quatrain:

> Some Pettifoggers now there be
> That let their conscience out for fee;
> And, like unto a *Lapland* witch,
> Sell their winds dear and so grow rich.

p. 271.   *the drunken Tinker.* This allusion to *The Taming of the Shrew* is of
considerable interest as the poet must have supposed his audience
would readily take the reference. It was one of the plays specifically
allotted to Killigrew, and it was almost certainly revived at the
Theatre Royal, Vere Street. Lacy's adaptation *Sawny the Scot; or,
The Taming of the Shrew*, probably produced in April, 1667, at
the Theatre Royal, where seen by Pepys, entirely omits Christopher

507

Sly. The Prologue to *The London Cuckolds*, produced at the Duke's House in the winter of 1681, has:

> *Then waking (like the Tinker in the Play)*
> *She finds the golden Vision fled away.*

Accordingly the Sly episode must have been familiar in the theatre.

p. 272. *throws down her handkerchief.* The Oriental summons to share the royal bed. Cf. Mrs. Behn's *The False Count*, produced at Dorset Garden in the autumn of 1682, IV: Julia is unveiled. "*Carlos.* Hah! what do I see, by *Mahomet*, she's fair. . . . Receive my Handkerchief. [*Throws it to her.*] *Francisco.* His Handkerchief! bless me, what does he mean? *Guzman.* To do her the honour to lie with her to-night." Cf. Shadwell, *The Scowrers*, produced at Drury Lane late in 1690, I, 1, when upon Sir William demanding a wench Ralph his man replies: "Your provident, prudent, and pious Housekeeper has lodged two who came last Night, for Peace sake, in two several Apartments of your Seraglio, not knowing which of them you would vouchsafe your Handkerchief to." "She has done wisely," answers Sir William, "I will have them both." Also *The Spectator*, LI, (Steele), Saturday, 28 April, 1711: "It is remarkable that the writers of least Learning are best skilled in the luscious Way. The Poetesses of the Age have done Wonders in this kind; and we are obliged to the Lady who writ *Ibrahim* for introducing a preparatory Scene to the very Action, when the Emperor throws his Handkerchief as a Signal for his Mistress to follow him into the most retired Part of the Seraglio. It must be confessed his *Turkish* Majesty went off with a good Air, but, methought, we made but a sad Figure who waited without. This Ingenious Gentlewoman in this piece of Bawdry, refined upon an Author of the same Sex, who, in the *Rover*, makes a Country Squire strip to his Holland Drawers. For *Blunt* is disappointed, and the Emperor is understood to go on to the utmost." *Ibrahim the Thirteenth Emperour of the Turks* (corrected to Twelfth in the Preface, 4to, 1696) by Mrs. Mary Pix was produced at Drury Lane in 1696. The scene of Blunt's disappointment is one of the most prominent episodes in Mrs. Behn's *The Rover*, Part I, produced at the Duke's House in 1677. Blunt was acted by Underhill.

p. 274. *Italians.* "L'Italien, adonné à la sodomie", P. J. Le Roux, *Dictionnaire Comique* (new edition), Amsterdam, 8vo., 1750. Howell, *Paroimiologia*, London, folio, 1659, has: "Tres Italianos, dos bugerones, el otro Atheista."

p. 274. *Argol.* Andrea Argoli, a celebrated astrologer, born in 1570 at Tagliacozzo in the Abruzzi, died at Padua about 1650. His predictions gave rise to such bitter charges of magic that he was obliged to retire to Venice. The Venetian Government recognizing his learning appointed him to the Chair of Mathematics at Padua. He wrote several treatises, the chief of which is *Exactissimae coelestium motuum Ephemerides ad longitudinem Almae Urbis* [*Romae*] *et Tychonis Brahe hypotheses ac deductas e coelo accuratē observationes ab anno* 1641 *ad annum* 1700. 3 vols., 8vo, Patavii, 1648. Hence many little annual almanacks, popularly known as "Argols," were extracted.

p. 274. *Conjunction.* In astrology, an apparent proximity of two planets or other heavenly bodies; the position of these when they are in the same, or nearly the same, direction as viewed from the earth. Charles Pritchard, *Occasional Thoughts of An Astronomer on Nature and Revelation*, 1889, X, 229, says: "The technical phrase 'conjunction' does not necessarily imply any very close proximity."

Opposition. In astrology, the relative position of two heavenly bodies when exactly opposite to each other as seen from the earth's surface, their longitude then differing by 180°. Cf. *The Frankeleyns Tale* (*circa* 1386):

> That now, next at this opposicioun
> Which in the signe shal be of the Leoun.

Trine. In astrology, denoting the aspect of two heavenly bodies which are a third part of the zodiac, *i.e.* 120° distant from each other. Sibly, *Occult Sciences* (1797), I, 143: "A trine aspect △."

Square. An obsolete astrological term denoting quadrate; quartile aspect. Cf. *Paradise Lost*, X, 656–9.

> To the blanc Moone
> Her office they prescrib'd, to th' other five
> Thir planetarie motions and aspects
> In *Sextile*, *Square*, and *Trine*, and *Opposite*,
> Of noxious efficacie.

Sextile. The aspect of two heavenly bodies which are 60° or one-sixth part of the zodiac distant from each other. *Gregory's Astronomy* (1715): "If a Sixth Part of the Zodiac lies between them, they are said to have a Sextile aspect."

p. 275. *and a sharp Sword.* Alluding to the freaks of the Fifth-Monarchy men. These mad fanatics, whose chief teachers were John Rogers, John Simpson, Day, and Feake, feigned to be adepts at explaining the more difficult passages of Scripture, and drew strange new prophecies from *Daniel* and the *Apocalypse*. They pretended to thaumaturgy, and awaited a miracle to establish their claims. Thomas Venner, a raving wine-cooper, in 1656 made a great noise by preaching that "the sword of the Lord was whetted and going forth against the enemies of His people." Thurloe, writing to Henry Cromwell, 15 April, 1656, says: "Fifth-Monarchy men who have their daylye meetings to provoke one another to blood and professe openly that their intention is to trye for it with the sword."

p. 275.   *Boracho's.* Spanish *borracho*, a leathern bottle, whence *borracho* = drunkard, from the large leathern bottles or bags used in Spain to hold wine. Cf. Middleton and Rowley, *The Spanish Gipsy* (4to, 1653), I, 1, when Diego cries to Roderigo: "Art mad?" and he replies: "Not so much with wine . . . I am no borachia." Also *Much Ado About Nothing*, III, 3, Borachio's jest upon his name: "I will, like a true drunkard, utter all to thee." In *The Way of the World*, IV, when Lady Wishfort finds Sir Wilfull drunk she upbraids him with, "Fogh! how you stink of Wine! D'ye think my Niece will ever endure such a *Borachio!* You're an absolute *Borachio.*"

p. 275.   *Begging-box.* The prisoners in debtors' prisons were allowed to beg through the bars of passers-by.

p. 276.   *the Counsellor of the Graces.* This from *Les Précieuses Ridicules*, VII, where Madelon says to Marotte: Vite, venez nous tendre ici dedans le conseiller des grâces. "Par ma foi!" replies the maid. "Je ne sais point quelle bête c'est là; il faut parler chrétien, si vous voulez que je vous entende." "Apportez-nous le miroir, ignorante que vous êtes," Cathos instructs her.

p. 278.   *bottle of hay.* Running water traditionally dissolves all enchantments. The essential idea is probably that which Euripides has expressed in the famous line: Θάλασσα κλύζει πάντα τἀνθρώπων κακά. (*Iphigenia in Tauris*, 1193).

In the *Metamorphoseon* of Apuleius, I, Aristomenes tells how at midnight two witches, Meroe and Panthia, cut the throat of his room-mate Socrates, and how Panthia stops the bleeding wound with a sponge, muttering, "heus tu, spongia, cave in mari nata per flvuium transeas." The next morning Socrates is alive and well, with no trace of a scar, and Aristomenes thinks he has dreamed a nightmare. But whilst they are on their journey they come to a stream whereat Socrates bends down to drink. "nec dum satis extremis labiis summum aquae rorem attigerat, et iugulo eius vulnus dehiscit in profundum patorem et illa spongia de eo repente devolvitur eamque parvus admodum comitatur cruor, denique corpus exanimatum in flumen paene cernuat."

In Marlowe's *Doctor Faustus*, quarto 1604, the Horse-Courser (*i.e.* horse-dealer) buys a horse for forty dollars of Faustus, who warns him, "Ride him not into the water at any hand . . . ride him not into the water, ride him over hedge or ditch, or where thou wilt, but not into the water." A little later, "Re-enter Horse-Courser, all wet, crying, 'Alas! alas! Doctor Fustian quotha! . . . He bade me I should ride him into no water, now I, thinking my horse had had some rare quality that he would not have had me know of, I, like a venturous youth, rid him into the deep pond at the town's end. I was no sooner in the middle of the pond, but my horse vanished away, and I sat upon a bottle of hay, never so near drowning in my life . . . forty dollars, forty dollars for a bottle of

510

hay!' " The episode of the Horse-Courser is reproduced in Mountford's farce *The Life and Death of Dr. Faustus*, 4to, 1697, but produced at least a decade earlier.

p. 279.   *smickering*. To smicker is to look lewdly at; to cast wanton glances. Cf. Davenant's *The Man's the Master*, acted in 1668, III, 1, where Jodelet says to Isabella, "I see I may make love long enough before you smicker at me."

p. 280.   *Tybert and Grimalkin*. Tibert is the name of the cat in the apologue of Reynard the Fox, and hence is generically used for any cat. Grimalkin (probably from *grey* and *Malkin, Matilda*) is an old she-cat. Cats are proverbially connected with witches, and in the Lancashire of 1612 Elizabeth Sothernes, alias Old Dembdike, confessed to the Justice of Peace Roger Nowell that she entertained a spirit "called *Tibb*, in the shape of a black cat."

p. 280.   *wet their feet*. "The cat would lick milk, but she will not wet her feet." Bryan Melbancke, *Philotimus*, 4to, 1583.

p. 281.   *Table of Direction*. A chart of the heavens with the stars duly arranged in their places. Partridge in his *Astrological Vade Mecum*, 1679, gives examples of various tables with their several explanations.

p. 281.   *Hylegiacalls*. Phillips (1706), ed. Hersey, says: "Hylegiacal Places are reckon'd to be five in number, viz. the Ascendant, the mid-Heaven, the 7th House, the 9th and the 11th." The casting of the horoscope is the diagram of the heavens (*thema coeli*) at the nativity with the resultant calculations. The first house (*horoscopus*) begins with the point of the ecliptic that is just rising (*ascendens*). The 7th house signified marriage and course of life; the 9th intellect and disposition (also long journeys); the 11th friends and success.

p. 281.   *Aldeboran*. Oculus Tauri (or Alpha Tauri). A fixed star, reddish of hue, in the constellation of the Bull, near the Hyades. Lockyer, *Heavens* (3rd ed., 1868), speaks of "Aldebaran, the most beautiful star in the constellation of the Bull."

p. 281.   *Cor Scorpii*. Or Antares, a name which means Pro-Mars or Mars' Deputy. It is in the 10th degree of Sagittarius and has a very violent nature. It is said that the axis of the solar system was in line with this star at the outbreak of the Great War of 1914–1918.

p. 282.   *impetus dicendi*. Quintilian, III, viii, 60: "Neque ego negaverim, saepius subsidere in controversiis impetum dicendi prooemio, narratione, argumentis. . . ." Also IX, iv, 35: "Inhibeat enim necesse est hic metus impetum dicendi, et a potioribus avertat."

p. 283.   *Loquere ut te videam*. "At non itidem maior meus Socrates, qui cum decorum adulescentem et diutule tacentem conspicatus foret: 'ut te videam,' inquit, 'aliquid et loquere.' " Apuleius. *Florida*, I, 2. Cf. *Le Dépit Amoureux*, III, 8:

> D'ou vient fort à propos cette sentence expresse
> D'un philosophe: "Parle, afin qu'on te connaisse."

The scene, of course, is borrowed by Dryden from the episode of Albert and the "pédant prodigieusement bavard" Métaphraste, in Molière's comedy. Wycherley has a poem: "*To a Loud, Talkative, Minor* Wit, *who us'd to repeat often, in His Vindication, the* Latin *Saying*, Loquere, ut te videam."

p. 285.   *Black Eyes.* Cf. The Epilogue "Written by a Friend" to Edward Moore's tragedy *The Gameſter*, 8vo, 1753, which commences:

> On every gameſter in th' Arabian nation
> 'Tis said that Mahomet denounc'd damnation:
> But in return for wicked cards and dice,
> He gave 'em black-ey'd girls in Paradise.

p. 285.   *high-running Dice.* A High-runner is a die loaded so as to turn on the high number. Cf. Cotton, *Espernon* (1670), II, v, 235: "False Dice . . . the high and the low runners." Radcliffe, *The Ramble*, 1682, speaks of "Goads, Bars, Flats, High and Low Dyce."

p. 285.   *Raffle.* "A game with 3 Dice, wherein he that throws the greateſt Pair-Royal wins," Blunt's *Glossographia* (1656). Raffle was a very popular game of chance, played with three dice. The winner was the person who threw the three all alike, or, if none did so, the one who threw the higheſt pair.

p. 285.   *Duplets.* Or, Doublet. The same number turning up upon both the dice at a throw.

p. 285.   *chance.* In Hazard, so *The Pardoners Tale* (1386), l. 325 (Skeat):

> Seven is my chaunce, and thyn is cink and treye.

p. 285.   *In and In.* A throw made with four dice, when all fall alike or as two doublets. Cf. Shirley's *The Gameſter*, aċted in 1633, III, where Littleſtock at the tables cries: "A curse upon these reeling dice! that laſt in-and-in was out of my way ten pieces." Also Davenant's *The Man's The Maſter*, aċted in 1668, V: "The devil's in the dice if you throw twice in and in, without any light," mutters Jodelet. The phrase is here figurative, meaning if you come off in triumph. Cotton, *The Compleat Gameſter*, Chapter XXXII, describes the game "Inn and Inn" in some detail.

p. 288.   *Play on tick.* An early inſtance of the phrase. So in Buckingham and Rocheſter's famous *Satyr*, commonly known as *Timon*:

> Haſt thou loſt deep to needy *Rogues* on Tick,
> Who ne're cou'd pay, and muſt be paid next week?

p. 287.   *one Maravedis.* A maravedi was an old Spanish copper coin, the value being about one-sixth part of a penny. The word often occurs in Spanish romances, *e.g. Guzman d'Alfarache*, Brady's translation, ed. 1881, XII, p. 286: "He began counting the money into my hands, by quarters and half-quarters of reals, and even maravedis."

p. 289.   *throw out.* To throw out at hazard is to make a losing caſt. The expression became obsolete in the eighteenth century. Cf. Butler, *A Satyr upon Gaming* (*circa* 1680):

> Although he . . . crucify his Saviour worse,
> Than those Jew-troopers that threw out,
> When they were raffling for His coat.

p. 290. *Mathematicks.* Used here of astrology. There is, of course, a double entendre. Cf. Fletcher's *Rule a Wife and Have a Wife*, acted 1624, II, when Perez suspecting Clara is a go-between asks sardonically:

> What business has she?
> Is she a learned woman i' th' mathematics?
> Can she tell fortunes?

So in post-Augustan Latin *Mathematicus* = an astrologer, and Tacitus has: "Mathematici, genus hominum potentibus infidum, sperantibus fallax, quod in civitate nostra et vetabitur semper et retinebitur." *Histories*, I, 22. Julius Paulus the jurisconsult lays down: "Qui de salute principis . . . mathematico consulit, cum eo qui responderit, capite punitur." V, xxi, 3.

In the time of Constantine the Great the imperial notary, Julius Firmicus Maternus, who later became a Christian, wrote his *Mathematics, De Nativitatibus sive Matheseos,* in eight books, a work which was long considered supremely authoritative on astrology.

p. 290. *Song.* This possibly suggested to Aubrey Beardsley, *The Three Musicians, The Savoy,* No, 1, January, 1896, of which the concluding stanzas run:

> The charming cantatrice reclines
>   And rests a moment where she sees
> Her château's roof that hotly shines
>   Amid the dusky summer trees,
> And fans herself, half shuts her eyes, and smooths the
>   frock about her knees.
>
> The gracious boy is at her feet,
>   And weighs his courage with his chance;
> His fears soon melt in noonday heat,
>   The tourist gives a furious glance,
> Red as his guide-book grows, moves on, and offers up a
>   prayer for France.

p. 292. *Sowse.* To souse is to swoop down violently upon, of birds. Especially of the hawk striking down upon its prey. So "at the souse." Cf. Heywood's *A Woman Killed with Kindness*, 4to, 1607, the hawking-match:

> So; well cast off: aloft, aloft! well flown!
> Oh, how she takes her at the sowse, and strikes her
> Down to the earth, like a swift thunder-clap.

AN EVENING'S LOVE

In Fletcher's *The Chances*, IV, 1, folio, 1647, we have the phrase "Dead, as a fowl at souse," "*i.e.* at the stroke of another bird descending violently upon it," Dyce.

p. 292.   *course Linnen*. This speech is quoted by Betty Goodfield, Act I, *The Woman turn'd Bully*; produced at Dorset Garden in 1675; 4to, 1675.

p. 294.   *I nick him*. To nick in the game of hazard is to win against the other by casting a nick. A nick is a throw which is either the same as the main or has a fixed correspondence to it. Cf. Otway's *The Atheist*, acted at Dorset Garden in 1683, II, where Beaugard's Father says: "I ha' not been robbed, Sir, but I ha' been nicked, Sir, and that's as bad, Sir."

p. 294.   *butters me with forty*. To butter is obsolete slang, meaning "to increase the stakes every throw or every game." *Dictionary Canting Crew* (*c.* 1700): "*Butter*, to double or treble the Bet or Wager to recover all losses."

p. 296.   *Pickerons*. Picarons: brigands; highwaymen. Cf. Howell *Letter* (*c.* 1645), ed. 1650, I, 364: "Your diamond hat-band which the Picaroon snatched from you in the coach."

p. 297.   *Table Diamond*. A diamond cut with a large *table* or front face, with bevelled edges. In *She Stoops to Conquer*, produced at Covent Garden, 15 March, 1773, when Miss Neville asks for her jewels Mrs. Hardcastle puts her off with—"A parcel of old-fashioned rose and table-cut things. They would make you look like the court of King Solomon at a puppet-show."

p. 297.   *erect a Scheme*. To map out, or "set up" a figure of the heavens. "A Figure or Scheme is nothing else but a Delineation of the Heavens in Plane, according to the division of the Sphear." Partridge, *Astrological Vade Mecum*, 1679, VII. Kersey (1715): "*To Erect a Figure*, to divide the 12 Houses a-right." Cf. *Hudibras*, III:

> It is a scheme and face of heaven,
> As th' aspects are dispos'd this even,
> I was contemplating upon.

p. 298.   *Mercury*. Thieves and Thefts belong to the Seventh House. "*Mercury*. Poetically, *Stilbon* by his swift Motion is a Messenger among the Stars . . . and the Author of Thefts, Perjuries and subtil Knavish Tricks. . . . Qualities of Men he governs, are . . . if ill placed troublesome Clerks, Thieves." Partridge, *Astrological Vade Mecum*, 1679, p. 16.

p. 299.   *Dragon's tail*. "The Dragon's-head and Tail are no Stars, but Nodes, or imaginary points in the Heavens, and is no more but the Intersection of the Ecliptick and Orbite of the ☽, to which points when she comes she changes the denomination of her Latitude; . . . the Dragons-head is accounted a Fortune . . . the Dragons-tail is esteemed an Infortune, and doth increase the Evil of the Infortunes, and abateth the good of the fortunate Stars." Partridge,

Aſtrological Vade Mecum, 1679, p. 18. In Fletcher's *Rollo, Duke of Normandy*, 4to, 1640, IV, 2, Norbret the aſtrologer speaks of "*Mars* with the *Dragon's Tail* in the third house." So the French Marquis in Scudéry's *Ibrahim, or, The Illuſtrious Bassa*, Part II, Book I (English translation by Henry Cogan, folio 1652), remarks: "I could say too that *Saturn* regarding *Hecate* with a trine Aspeƈt, and the tail of the Dragon folding itself about the Scorpion prognoſticate no good."

p. 300.   *Albricias*. (Spanish.) A reward to the bearer of good news; largess.

p. 306.   *the Devil take the hindmoſt*. E. B. Tylor, *Primitive Culture* (1870), I, 77, says: "One form of the devil's compaƈt in teaching the black art to a class was to seize one for his fee, letting them all run for their lives, and catching the laſt."

p. 306.   *knives are of little use*. This bob implies that there was very little meat or any food to be had. In Madrid money was lavished on pageants, tourneys and masquerades, but the coinage was debased and viƈtuals heavily taxed. There was general corruption, and a friar preaching at court rebuked Philip to his very face: "Your Majeſty is obliged to appeal to those miniſters, whom you enable to acquire vaſt eſtates, for money necessary to buy food and garments."

p. 306.   *ferret Ribbaning*. Ferret is a ſtout tape moſt commonly made of cotton, but also of silk. Cf. Killigrew's *The Parsons Wedding*, folio 1663 (1664), I, 1: "Your Drum and borrowed scarf shall not prevail, nor shall you win with Charms half-ell-long (hight ferret Ribband) the youth of our Parish."

p. 307.   *Venice-glass*. As being especially brittle. Thus Thomas Gataker, *Marriage Duties Briefly Couched Togither*, 4to, 1620 (p. 41): "the more britle a Venice glasse is, the more gingerly we handle it, and the more tender-edged a knife is the more charily we vse it." Cf. also *On Death* in *Poetical Recreations*, 1688, by Jane Barker (and others), II, 44:

> Life is a Bubble; . . .
> 'Tis far more brittle than a Venice-Glass.

p. 309.   *tender*. Tendre. Mrs. Centlivre in the Preface to *The Man's Bewitched*, 4to, 1710: "'Tis Natural to have a kind of Tender for our own Produƈtions." *Tendre* was a great word with the Précieuses, and "La Carte de Tendre," which may be found in Mlle de Scudéry's *Clélie, histoire romaine*, 1ʳᵉ partie, livre 1, was especially famous.

p. 309.   *languishing caſts*. Ogling. A caſt is a glance with the eye. Cf. *Il Penseroso* (1632): "With a sad Leaden downcaſt caſt." So Sterne, *The Sentimental Journey* (1768), "The Pulse. Paris." "I had given a caſt with my eye into half-a-dozen shops as I came along."

p. 312.   *spoil'd our English Playes*. Alluding to George Digby, Lord Briſtol's, *Better 'tis than it Was*, a translation of Calderon's *Mejor eſtá que eſtaba*; *Worse and Worse*, a translation of *Peor eſtá que eſtaba*;

Elvira, or, the Worst not always True, acted at Lincoln's Inn Fields about 1663, 4to, 1667, an adaptation of *No siempre lo peor es cierlo;* and more particularly to Sir Samuel Tuke's *The Adventures of Five Hours*, produced at Lincoln's Inn Fields, January, 1662–3, folio 1663. The original of Tuke's play is generally said to be Coello's *Empeños de Seis Horas*, but the writer himself definitely states, "It was taken out of Don Pedro Calderon, a celebrated Spanish author." For a full discussion of this difficulty see Martin Hume's *Spanish Influence on English Literature*, pp. 291–5.

p. 312. *yarely.* Briskly; nimbly. A nautical term generally familiar from the shipwreck scene in *The Tempest*. Ray gives yare as a Suffolk word, and the "hear, hear" of Lowestoft boatmen of to-day is perhaps a disguised "yare, yare."

p. 313. *go snip with you.* Or "go snips." To go snip = to go shares. In very common use at the end of the seventeenth century. *O.E.D.* quotes this passage. Bailey (1725), *Erasmus' Colloquies* (1733), 322, has: "The Gamester . . . promises I shall go snips with him in what he shall win."

p. 313. *Wilderness.* A piece of ground in a large garden or park, laid out in a fantastic style as a maze or the like, and generally something secluded. Cf. Miss Braddon, *Wyllard's Weird*, I (1885): "Manifold as were the cares of the hot-houses and ferneries and wildernesses."

p. 314. *Corigidore.* Better, *Corregidor*. (Spanish, *corregidor*). "The chief Justicer, or gouernor of a towne," Minsheu. The name often occurs in Spanish and picaresque romances. Cf. Le Sage, *Asmodeus, or The Devil upon Two Sticks*, trans., 1881, c. xix, p. 297: "It is Signor Don Josepho de Reynaste and Ayala, recorder of the city. . . . It were to be wished . . . that every corregidor would choose him for their pattern." Corregedor is often somewhat loosely used as = a Spanish magistrate.

p. 314. *Rear-mice.* Bats; a word still in use, although now mainly provincial. Sir T. Herbert (1634), *Travels*, 212, has: "Reer-mice, or Bats so large as Goshawks."

p. 314. *Agrippa.* Heinrich Cornelius Agrippa of Nettesheim, born 14 September, 1486, at Cologne; died at Grenoble or Lyons in 1534 or 1535. He has been described as "knight, doctor, and by common reputation, a magician." This remarkable man is certainly one of the most famous names in the annals of occult philosophy. His works were collected in a complete edition at Lyons in 1600. His treatise *De occulta philosophia* was first issued at Antwerp in 1531, although it had been finished some twenty years previously. His rules *Pari die et incremento Lunae* may be read by those curious in such matters in the original, or in a French translation, *La philosophie occulte de Henr. Corn. Agrippa, . . . traduite du latin* [par A. Levasseur], 2 vols., Hague, 1727. There are several French versions under the title *Oeuvres magiques . . . mises en français par*

Pierre d'Aban, Rome, 1744; Liège, 1788; Rome, 1800; Rome, 1744 (*circa* 1830); but all are of the laſt rarity. Rome is, of course, a pseudo-imprint. Oldham, *A Charaĉter*, has: "*I've observ'd all the* Figures *and* Diagrams *in* Agrippa *and* Ptolomy's Centiloquies *there upon ſtriĉt view.*"

p. 315. *one side of the Scene which draws.* The drawing of the scene to represent the opening of a door should be noted.

p. 315. *Baptiſta Porta.* Giovanni Battiſta della Porta, the famous Neapolitan physiciſt, born at Naples in 1538 and died there 1615. His *Magia Naturalis,* in which he treats incidentally of physiognomy, was highly eſteemed. Firſt published at Naples in 1558, the second (and much enlarged) edition followed in 1589. Cf. the Preface to the *Fables,* 1700, where Dryden says of Chaucer: "All his Pilgrims are severally diſtinguish'd from each other: and not only in their Inclinations, but in their very Phisiognomies and Persons. *Baptiſta Porta* could not have describ'd their Natures better, than by the Marks which the Poet gives them."

p. 315. *this very room.* This very place. The scene is a garden, and the word room here is only used as denoting a particular spot, not an interior.

p. 315. *Monſtrum hominis.* Terence, *Eunuchus,* IV, iv, 29 (696).

p. 319. *what do you lack.* The cry of the shopman or prentice at the door or ſtreet-ſtall to attraĉt cuſtomers who are passing.

p. 322. *Plate-fleet.* The fleet which annually brought the produce of the American silver mines to Spain. Cf. Cowley, *Verses on Several Occasions. Adventures of Five Hours* (1663):

> As when our Kings (Lords of the spacious Main)
> Take in juſt wars a rich Plate Fleet of *Spain.*

In *The Loyal Proteſtant,* No. 180, Thursday, 13 July, 1682, is a notice: "We hear that the *Spanish* Plate-Fleet is arrived at the *Havanna,* and will be home in *Auguſt* next."

p. 323. *Like Jews.* In allusion to the dispersion of the Jews over the world. There can hardly be any specific reference to 1 Kings xxii, 17: "I saw all Israel scattered upon the hills, as sheep that have not a shepherd." (*A.V.*)

p. 323. *The Club of jeſts.* No doubt in allusion to "selling bargains," a piece of indecent tomfoolery, which seems to have been much in vogue among the denizens of the pit, and to which Dryden himself in Prologue and Epilogue has several allusions. Thus in the Prologue to *The Prophetess,* an operatic version of Fletcher, produced at Dorset Garden in November, 1690, condoling with the "bright Beauties" whose gallants are away campaigning in Ireland, Dryden bids the fair:

> With your propitious Presence grace our Play,
> And with a Sigh their Empty Seats survey;

517

Then think, on that bare Bench my servant sate,
I see him Ogle still, and hear him Chat;
Selling facetious Bargains, and propounding
That witty Recreation, called Dum-founding.

Sir Samuel Harty in Shadwell's *The Virtuoso*, produced at Dorset
Garden in May, 1676, is greatly given to "selling bargains," and
Dryden in *Mac Flecknoe* does not forget to lash this obscenity:

Where made he love in Prince *Nicander's* vein
Or swept the dust in *Psyche's* humble strain?
Where sold he Bargains, Whip-stich, kiss my Arse,
Promis'd a Play and dwindled to a Farce?

TYRANNICK LOVE

p. 326. *Non jam prima peto. Æneid*, V, 194; 196: Non iam prima peto
Mnestheus neque vincere certo, . . . extremos pudeat rediisse.

p. 329. *former Plays. The Indian Emperour.* This tragedy when published 4to,
1667, was dedicated to the Duchess of Monmouth, who had indeed
sustained a rôle in the play at a Court performance. On Tuesday,
14 January, 1667–68, Pepys notes: "They fell to discourse of the
last night's work at Court, when the ladies and Duke of Monmouth
and others acted 'The Indian Emperour'; wherein they told me
things most remarkable: that not any woman but the Duchesse of
Monmouth and Mrs. Cornwallis did any thing but like fools and
stocks. . . ."

p. 330. *Persons of Honour.* The subject of S. Catharine was, no doubt, chosen
in compliment to Queen Catharine of Braganza.

p. 331. *Maximin.* Caius Julius Verus Maximinus Thrax, the son of a Goth
and an Alanic mother, was Emperor of Rome, 235–8. Of enormous
strength and stature and fiercest bravery he was enrolled by Sep-
timius Severus in the Roman body-guard, and under Alexander
Severus put in command of the newly raised Pannonian troops, who
presently rejecting the timid Alexander invested Maximinus with
the purple at Mainz in March, 235. The newly made emperor took
the field with great vigour against the Germans *trans Rhenum* and
also attacked the Sarmatians and Dacians on the Danube. He openly
despised religion, melted down the statues of the gods and coined
their treasuries, savagely sacking hallowed cities and plundering
temples. There was continual opposition to him at Rome and rival
emperors, the Gordians, and others were set up by the Senate.
Maximinus marched to Italy to punish the offenders, but he could
not at once cross the Isonzo, and his attacks upon Aquileia were re-
pulsed. Deeming his officers guilty of treachery he caused several to

be executed, when a mutiny promptly occurred. He and his son
Maximus were murdered in the camp before Aquileia. Dryden has
confused Maximinus Thrax with Caius Valerius Daja Maxi-
minus for whom see note *infra*.

p. 331. *St. Catharine.* Patroness of education, philosophy, science; of
students, philosophers, theologians; of schools and colleges. A noble
maiden of Alexandria, deeply learned in all philosophy and sciences,
who when only eighteen years of age, what time the Emperor
Maximinus, Caesar of Syria and Egypt, 305–313, was violently
persecuting the Christians, presented herself before him and up-
braided the tyrant for his cruelty, proving how iniquitous was the
worship of idols. Amazed at her wisdom and beauty the Emperor
detained her in the palace whilst he summoned fifty of the most
famous sages and rhetoricians to use all their skill in specious argu-
ments that the maiden might be led to apostatize. But she emerged
from the debate victorious, and many of her adversaries converted
by her eloquence openly declared themselves Christians, only to be
put to a cruel death by the enraged Maximinus. The Saint was cast
into prison, where she was kept eleven days. Meanwhile the Empress,
eager to see so extraordinary a maiden, went with Porphyry, the
commander of the army, to her dungeon, when they in turn yielded
to S. Catharine's burning words and acknowledged Christ. Immedi-
ately they won the martyr's crown. "Postea martyrio coronati
sunt," says the Breviary, 25 November, Matins, Second Nocturn,
Lesson Six. S. Catharine was then condemned to die upon a wheel
furnished with sharp sword-blades and keen razors. But at her
prayer an Angel descended in great glory and broke the instrument
of torture into a thousand pieces. The Emperor in an access of fury
ordered her to be straightway beheaded, which was done, and lo!
Angels bore her body to Mount Sinai as you may see in Luini's
picture.

   S. Catharine is the patroness of Venice and of Goa, where her
feast, 25 November, is celebrated with much pomp and solemnity.
In the ages of faith there was an ever-increasing devotion to this
wonderful Saint, and in England alone sixty-two churches are
dedicated to her. In art she is usually represented with the broken
wheel, whilst Correggio, Titian, Perugino, Parmigiano, Vandyck,
and many others have painted the mystic Marriage of S. Catharine.
It should be remembered that S. Catharine appeared to S. Joan of Arc.

p. 331. *vastus corpore, animo ferus.* Dryden, as not infrequently, is here sum-
marizing rather than quoting. Herodian, VII, writes of Maximin:
"ἦν δὲ καὶ τὴν ὄψιν φοβερώτατος, καὶ μέγιστος τὸ σῶμα." Herodian
is, of course, a Greek historian, and it will be noticed that Dryden
loosely paraphrases in Latin. Julius Capitolinus describes Maxi-
minus as "magnitudine corporis conspicuus, . . . forma virili
decorus, ferus moribus, asper, superbus, contemptor." *Maximini
Duo,* I. Professor Bensly has obliged me with the following note:

"I have now before me *Herodiani Historiae de suis Temporibus libri viii* (Frankfort, 1627) edited by Daniel Pareus, the Greek text and Politian's Latin version in parallel columns. I do not find Dryden's quotation in the actual text; but to each book is prefixed a brief Latin analysis. That to *Liber vii* begins (p. 209):

BREVIARIVM LIBRI SEPTIMI.

MAXIMINVS *Thrax, vasto corpore & crudeli animo praeditus, suscepto imperio statius tyrannidem exercuit.*

The words catch the reader's eye at once. I would suggest that this is Dryden's source. Whether these *breviaria* are Politian's or Pareus's I do not gather. But I *think* this is Dryden's source."

p. 331. *Lazare.* A representation in art, dramatic or pictorial, of a subject which was repulsive in nature such as the picture of a leper.

p. 331. *Sea-marks.* A sea-mark denotes the limit of the flow of the sea. It is often employed figuratively. Cf. Oliver Heywood, *The Best Entail*, 8vo, 1693, in the *Collected Works* (ed. Richard Slater, 1825–7), IV, 473: "Wicked parents are set before you as the sea-marks to avoid, not as land-marks to guide you."

p. 331. *Walls of Aquileia.* "Maximinus fluvium transivit et de proximo Aquileiam obsidere coepit. . . . Timentes milites, quorum affectus in Albano monte erant, medio forte die quum a proelio quiesceretur, et Maximinum et filium eius in tentorio positos occiderunt, eorumque capita praefixa contis Aquileiensibus demonstraverunt." Julius Capitolinus. *Maximini duo*, XXII, XXIII. Affectus = uxores, puerosque.

p. 331. *Atheism or Prophaneness.* Nevertheless these charges were continually being brought against Dryden. Mr. Percy J. Dobell in his *John Dryden, Bibliographical Memoranda* (p. 13) says: "I have a copy of the first edition of *Absalom and Achitophel*, 1681, with contemporary marginal notes, one of which reads 'The Poet an Atheist exceeding Lucretius,' and on the title-page of his copy of *Religio Laici* Narcissus Luttrell has written 'Atheisticall.'" In the Preface to *The Medall* (1682) Dryden complains that he has been dubbed "prophane and saucy Jack, and Atheistick Scribler" by the nonconformist minister who wrote *The Whip* and *A Key*, two poems in answer to *Absalom and Achitophel.* Moreover Dryden himself asserts that Shadwell frequently in print called him an Atheist, although no such passages are among Shadwell's known works to-day. Collier, of course, brings the most rampant accusations of profanity against Dryden, but his witness is so biassed as to be wellnigh negligible.

p. 332. *many accidents.* In particular the alleged delay of Isaac Fuller the painter to deliver according to contract the "new Scene of an Elysium." For the details of his quarrel with and the Chancery suit he brought against the Theatre Royal company see the Theatrical History to this tragedy.

EXPLANATORY NOTES

p. 332. *two Martyrs.* "Quo tempore Maximini uxor, et Porphyrius belli dux, visendae virginis causa carcerem ingressi, et eiusdem praedicatione in Iesum Christum credentes, postea martyrio coronati sunt." *Breviarium Romanum*, Pars Autumnalis, Die 25 Novembris, In II Nocturno, Lectio VI, ad initium.

p. 332. *a French Play.* This *Sainte Catherine*, attributed to a minor dramatist, Desfontaines, is printed in a *Recueil de Tragédies Saintes*, published at Paris by Loyson, 1666. M. Beljame, the eminent critic, justly describes the play as "fort plate et fort ennuyeuse," and from my own reading I am bound to pronounce it truly insipid. The "mistake" Dryden borrowed seems to be a line in Act V, 5, "Fils d'un soldat Goth et d'une femme Alaine." Except as regards the general outlines of the legend the two plays are altogether different.

Desfontaines is believed to have been born at Caen, but practically nothing is known of his career. "Il n'est connu que par ses pièces de théâtre, qui sont toutes au-dessous du médiocre, sous le rapport du plan, de la conduite et de la versification." He lived during the first half of the seventeenth century. Amongst his dozen and a half dramas are *Saint-Alexis, ou l'illustre Olympie*, tragédie, 1644; *Le Martyre de saint Eustache*, tragédie, 1645; *L'illustre Comédien, ou le martyre de saint Genest*, tragédie, 1645. As they were reprinted (*Saint-Alexis*, 12mo, 1666), they undoubtedly attained a certain popularity, but they are mediocre, dull, and uninspired.

p. 332. *Eusebius and Metaphrastes.* Eusebius of Caesarea, *Ecclesiastical History*, Book VIII (A.D. 286–312), gives a very full and terrible account of the persecution, and of the active cruelties of Maximinus. Hence Dryden found his error in confusing two persons, cf. particularly Eusebius, VIII, 13.

Symeon Metaphrastes (Συμεὼν ὁ μεταφράστης), the principal compiler of the legends of Saints in the Menologia of the Byzantine Church. His period is the latter half of the tenth century, and most authorities now identify the Metaphrast with Symeon Magister the Logothete who wrote a Chronicle under Nicephorus Phocas, (963–9). At one time the name of Symeon Metaphrastes was almost a byword for uncritical hagiology, but the latest students have quite restored his reputation as a sound author. His Μαρτύριον τῆς ἁγίας καὶ καλλινίκου μεγαλομάρτυρος τοῦ Χριστοῦ Αἰκατερίνης may be conveniently read pp. 277–302 of Migne, *Patrologia Graeca*, t. CXVI (*Opera omnia Symeonis Logothetae, cognomento Metaphrastae*, III). The narrative is replete with beauties of no mean order. A French translation from Metaphrastes, *La Vie de Saincte Catherine*, will be found under 25 November in the *Histoire de la Vie, Mort, Passion, et Miracles des Saincts*, pp. 500–502, by Viel, Tigeou, Marchant, Lefrere de Laval, and Paschal Robin, Paris, 1610, folio.

p. 332. *a second.* Caius Valerius Daja Maximinus, the Caesar of Syria and Egypt from the year 305. A fanatical idolater and tyrant, he continued the persecution of the Christians in his part of the empire with bitterest severity. Besides sanguinary measures for the destruction of Christians he raised heathen high-priests and magicians to the highest honours. When Constantine and Licinius published the edict for the toleration of Christians at Milan in 312, Maximinus was asked to promulgate it in his part of the empire. In the winter of 312 he marched against Licinius, but in spite of the superiority of his troops he was defeated near Adrianople, 30 April, 313, and fled in haste to Nicomedia. Thence he withdrew to the Taurus, where his position being hopeless he took poison (313). After his death his edicts were cancelled, and decrees favourable to the Christians promulgated throughout the East.

p. 332. *L'Amour Tyrannique.* Tragi-comedie par Monsieur De Scudery. A Paris, Chez Augustin Courbé, Imprimeur & Libraire de Monsieur Frere du Roy, dans la petite Sale du Palais, à la Palme, 1639. Avec Privilege Du Roy. 4to. The play is dedicated to the Duchess d'Aiguillon, and has prefixed an address to the French Academy with a Discourse on Tragedy by De Sillac D'Arbois. This drama in five acts has nothing at all in common with Dryden's tragedy. The scene lies at Amasia, the chief town of Cappadocia—in Asia Minor. The principal characters are Orosmane, King of Cappadocia; his son Tigrane; Tyridate, King of Pontus; Ormene, his queen, daughter to Orosmane; Polyxene, wife of Tigrane; Troilus a Phrygian prince, her brother; Pharnasabe, "iadis Gouuerneur de Tyridate;" Phraate, a general; with various ladies and captains. The scenes are all on a very high note of love and honour, darts and flames, and we have such speeches as this of Polixene:

> Triste, desesperée, interdite, et confuse,
> Honneur, tu veux un don que l'Amour te reffuse:
> La mort, quelque conseil que tu puisses m'offrir,
> Est plus dure a donner, qu'elle n'est a souffrir:
> Et de tous les grands maux, honneur, le mal extreme,
> Est d'en faire endurer, à l'obiet que l'on aime.

There is something fantastically attractive about De Scudery's work, yet it was too unreal to escape oblivion. *L'Amour Tyrannique* was reprinted in volume 7 of *Le Théâtre François,* 12mo, 1737.

p. 333. *Serpit humi tutus.* Horace, *Ars Poetica,* 28. Serpit humi tutus nimium timidusque procellae; of a low grovelling poetic style.

p. 333. *Eludit gyro. Aeneid,* XI, 695. Dryden's mistaken reference, "Virgil, in the sixth of his Aeneids," will be noticed.

p. 333. *your censures.* Opinions.

p. 334. *Porphyrius.* στρατοπεδάρχης δὲ οὗτος ἦν κατὰ χεῖρά τε γενναιότατος, καὶ ἄριστα περὶ πολέμους γεγυμνασμένος. Symeon Metaphrastes. Μαρτύριον . . μεγαλομάρτυρος . . . Αἰκατερίνης. XVI.

p. 334. *Mr. Harris.* William Harris, to be carefully distinguished from the friend of Pepys, the famous Henry Harris of the Duke's Company, as also from Joseph Harris, a player of later date, who wrote three comedies, *The Mistakes; The City Bride;* and *Love's a Lottery.*

p. 334. *S. Catharine.* Αἰκατερινα, νέα τὴν ἡλικίαν, τὴν ὄψιν περικαλλὴς, ἐκ βασιλικοῦ γένους προηγμένη, πᾶσαν ἐπελθοῦσα γραφὴν, τὴν ἔξω τε καὶ τὴν καθ' ἡμᾶς, ὑπό πολλαῖς θεραπαινίσιν εἰς τὴν Ἀλεξάνδρειαν διάγουσα ἦν, ἐν οἴκοις οὕτω βασιλικοῖς ταμιευομένη, Χριστὸν μόνον εἰδυῖα νυμφίον, καὶ τῷ τῆς ψυχῆς αὐτῷ κάλλος τηροῦσα, καὶ μόνῳ τὸν ἔρωτα τῆς καρδίας ἀνάπτουσα. Symeon Metaphrastes. *Op. cit.* III.

p. 334. *Mrs. Hughes.* So the first quarto, 1670. The second quarto, 1672, "The Second Edition, review'd by the Authour," and all subsequent editions give the rôle of S. Catharine to Mrs. Boutell. No doubt Mrs. Hughes relinquished the part very early, it was then taken by and identified with Mrs. Boutell.

p. 334. *Felicia, her Mother.* The name of S. Catharine's mother is traditionally given as Queen Sabinella. Her father was King Costis.

p. 335. *Two, tame, gown'd Princes.* The Senate had appointed two emperors, M. Clodius Pupienus Maximus, who was to exercise the military power *de facto,* and Decimus Caelius Balbinus, who was to direct the civil government in the capital. The Romans, much dissatisfied, raised to the rank of Caesar the elder Gordian's twelve-year-old grandson, afterwards Gordian III, who was then residing in Rome. Broils and fighting inevitably ensued.

p. 336. *Panonian Band.* Pannonia was one of the most important Roman provinces between the Danube and the Alps. It was the regular quarters of seven legions; Tacitus, *Annales,* I, 16, speaks of a mutiny among these troops soon after the death of Augustus, A.D. 14: "Pannonicas legiones seditio incessit:" cf. Velleius Paterculus, II, CX, 2.

p. 337. *Ister's.* Hister, the lower part of the Danube; the upper part, as far as the Axius (Vardar), being Danubius. So Ovid, *Ex Ponto,* I, viii, 11: "Stat vetus urbs, ripae vicina binominis Histri." Vergil, *Georgics,* III, 350: "Turbidus et torquens flaventes Hister arenas."

p. 337. *offer'd us by fits.* The levin flashed forth fitfully to our sight.

p. 337. *shrill and tender.* So in the *Odyssey,* XXIV, 5, the ghosts of the suitors: ταὶ δὲ τρίζουσαι ἔποντο. And *Æneid,* VI, 492-3, of the ghosts of the Greek warriors in Hades: pars tollere vocem Exiguam. In *Julius Caesar,* II, 2, the "ghosts did shriek and squeal about the streets." Tender is here used in the rare and obsolete sense of "thin." So Gower, *Confessio Amantis,* Book VI, 1513-14; III, 52:

> The happes over mannes hed
> Ben honged with a tendre thred.

p. 339. *An execrable superstition.* The "exitiabilis superstitio" of Tacitus, *Annales,* XV, 44.

p. 339.   *murd'rers presence.* Bacon, *Sylva*, 958, has: "It is an usual observa-
tion that if the body of one murdered be brought before the mur-
derer, the wounds will bleed afresh. Some do affirm that the dead
hath opened his eyes." King James I in his *Daemonologie* (1597),
III, 6, speaking of the swimming of witches as one of two tefts (the
firft being the insensible witch-mark), writes: "The other is their
fleeting on the water: for as in a secret murther, if the dead carcase
be at any time thereafter handled by the murtherer, it will gush out
of bloud, as if the blud wer crying to the heauen for reuenge of the
murtherer, God hauing appoynted that secret super-naturall signe,
for tryall of that secrete vnnaturall crime, so it appeares that God
hath appoynted (for a super-naturall signe of the monftruous
impietie of the Witches) that the water shal refuse to receiue them
in her bosom." So Chapman, *The Widdowes Tears*, 4to, 1612, V,
3; where the firft Soldier says: "The Captain will assay an old con-
clusion, often approved, that at the murtherer's sight, the blood re-
vives again, and boils afresh: and every wound has a condemning
voice to cry out guilty gainft the murtherer." There are very many
allusions to this belief: see Shakespeare's *Richard III*, I, ii, 55;
Drayton's *Idea. In Sixtie Three Sonnets* (1594), ed. 1619; 46:

> In making tryall of a Murther wrought,
> If the vile actors of the heynous deed
> Neere the dead Body happily be brought,
> Oft 't'ath been prou'd, the breathlesse Coarse will bleed.

In Richard Whitlock's *Zootomia* (1654) we have: "But at the ap-
proach of whom muft this coarse bleed?" (p. 123; and p. 135). In
A Warning for Faire Women, 4to, 1599, when Browne who has
wellnigh slain John Beane is brought to his dying victim, Mafter
Barnes cries:

> See how his wounds break out afresh in bleeding.

Robert Heath in his *Clarastella*, 12mo, 1650, has a poem, *Bleeding
at the Nose at Clarastella's Approach*, with this couplet:

> So at the Murtherer's approach we see
> The corpse weep at its wounds again.

In Otway's *The Souldiers Fortune*, produced at Dorset Garden
early in 1680; 4to, 1681; at the end of Act IV when Sir David
Dunce would approach Beaugard, whom he is supposed to have
murdered, Lady Dunce fearing the trick will be discovered prevents
him with: "Oh, come not near him, there's such a horrid Anti-
pathy follows all murders, his wounds would ftream afresh should
you but touch him."

It may be remembered that in *Rookwood*, Book III, chapter xii,
Richard Checkley is confronted with the body of Susan Bradley

(Lady Rookwood) in whose murder he was supposed to have been accomplice many years before, and is made to lay his hand on the breast of the corpse swearing his innocence. "I cannot withdraw my hand," he cries, "It sticks to her throat as though 'twere glued by blood. . . . Tear me away, I say: the veins rise; they blacken; they are filling with new blood. I feel them swell; they coil like living things around my fingers. She is alive."

p. 341. *Capaneus.* One of the seven heroes who marched from Argos against Thebes. As he was scaling the walls of the city he was blasted with lightning by Zeus, whom he had dared to defy. See Statius, *Thebaidos*, X, 898 *sqq.*, where Capaneus blasphemes heaven until

> talia dicentem toto Iove fulmen adactum
> corripuit.

See also Euripides, *Phoenissae*, the passage which describes the profane boasting of Capaneus and his destruction (1172–1186), commencing:

> Καπανεὺς δε πῶς εἴποιμ᾽ ἂν ὡς ἐμαίνετο;
> . . . καὶ τοσόνδ᾽ ἐκόμπασε,
> μηδ᾽ ἂν τὸ σεμνὸν πῦρ νιν εἰργαθεῖν Διὸς
> τὸ μὴ οὐ κατ᾽ ἄκρων περγάμων ἑλεῖν πόλιν. . . .

p. 342. *Images.* Dryden here probably intends Maximin to allude to the images of the Lares, according to the old view that the Lares were the deified ancestors of the family. This opinion has been rejected by G. Wissowa, *Religion und Kultus der Römer* (1902). The private Lares were worshipped in the house by the family alone, and the household Lar (*familiaris*) was conceived of as being the central figure of the family devotions. The image of the Lar, made of stone, wood, or metal, sometimes of silver or gold, stood in its special shrine. In later periods the Lares were confounded with the Penates and other deities. Their worship persisted but varied very considerably in character. Thus Alexander Severus had among his household Lares images of Abraham and Alexander the Great, and even introduced a figure of our Blessed Lord. For fuller details see A. de Marchi's *Il Culto privato di Roma antica* (1896–1903).

p. 342. *A Thracian Shepherd.* Maximinus "de vico Thraciae vicino . . . Et in prima quidem pueritia pastor fuit." Julius Capitolinus, *Maximini duo*, I.

p. 343. *My anger.* When enraged, Maximinus "homo natura ferus, sic exarsit ut non hominem sed belluam putares." Julius Capitolinus, *idem*, XVII.

p. 345. *dooming the event.* The event is the Latin *eventus*, the result or final outcome. The gods decreed that in the end Caesar's murder should be avenged by the defeat and deaths of Brutus and Cassius at Philippi, 42 B.C., when Octavianus and Antony gained their great victory.

p. 347.   *in her Tent confers.* Pinturicchio has painted "S. Catharine disputing
with the fifty Philosophers" in a large crowded fresco at the Vatican.

p. 348.   *Cato blush'd to see.* The Floralia celebrated in May (Ovid, *Fasti*, V,
195 *sqq.*) were the occasion of the greatest license. "Nam praeter
verborum licentiam, quibus obscoenitas omnis effunditur; exuuntur
etiam vestibus populo flagitante meretrices; quae tunc mimorum
funguntur officio; et in conspectu populi usque ad satietatem im-
pudicorum luminum cum pudendis motibus detinentur." Lactan-
tius, *De Falsa Religione*, I, 20. When Cato of Utica was once
present at the festival, the spectators hesitated to call upon the
courtezans to strip. Whereupon Cato retired, and was loudly
applauded for his action by all present.

p. 348.   *To follow Vertue, as its own reward.* This old apophthegm is used by
Jonson in his masque, *Pleasure reconcil'd to Virtue* (presented 1618):

> These, these are hours by virtue spar'd,
> Herself, she being her own reward.

Amongst others, Sir Thomas Browne has the same maxim in his
Religio Medici; and Henry More in *Cupid's Conflict* (1647) writes:

> "Virtue is to herself the best reward."

Prior, *Imitations of Horace*, III, 2 (8), 1692:

> On its own worth true majesty is rear'd
> And virtue is her own reward.

Gay, *Epistle of Paul Methuen:*

> Why to true merit should they have regard?
> They know that virtue is its own reward.

In Home's famous tragedy, *Douglas,* produced at Covent Garden,
14 March, 1757; 8vo, 1757: Act III, Glenalvon mocking Lady
Randolph, who has just left him, echoes:

> Amen! and virtue is its own reward!

"Thus, ever, is virtue secure of its reward!" sententiously but with
ludicrous gravity cries Lady Theodosia when she rallies Mrs. Crab-
tree, in Miss Cuthbertson's *Santo Sebastiano, or The Young Pro-
tector* (1806), vol. III, chapter 7. In Vanbrugh's *The Relapse, or,
Virtue in Danger*, produced at Drury Lane on Saturday, 21 Novem-
ber, 1696; 4to, 1697; Berinthia, who is something of a quiz,
banters Worthy: "Virtue is its own Reward: There's a pleasure in
doing good, which sufficiently pays itself." So in Farquhar's *The
Twin-Rivals*, Drury Lane, 14 December, 1702; 4to, 1703; Act I,
Mother Mandrake feigning to refuse a vail from Richmore pro-
tests: "No, no, Sir; Virtue is its own Reward." The latest editors of
Vanbrugh and Farquhar, being singularly uncommunicative con-
cerning their respective authors, did not deem it at all necessary to
note these passages.

p. 348.   *without, regard.* Not looking to any ulterior recompense.

p. 349.   *baptiz'd in fire.* The *Acta Sanctae Catharinae* relate that Maximinus
ordered the converted philosophers to be burned alive. Ἐνταῦθα ὁ
Μαξέντιος οὐκ ἐνεγκὼν τὴν μανίαν, κελεύει αὐτίκα πυρὰν κατὰ
μέσην ἀναφθῆναι τὴν πόλιν, καὶ ταύτῃ τοὺς πεντήκουτα ῥήτορας
ἐμβληθῆναι. Symeon Metaphrastes. *Op. cit.*, XIII.

p. 350.   *there's not a God inhabits there.* This has been parodied in *The Re-
hearsal.*

p. 352.   *the tenth wave.* Cf. Ovid, *Tristia*, I, 11, 50:

> Qui venit hic fluctus, fluctus supereminet omnes;
> Posterior nono est, undecimoque prior.

Commenting upon this Politian says: "Decumanum intelligit fluc-
tum, qui fieri maximus dicitur." In the *Metamorphoseon*, XI, 530,
Ovid again writes:

> Vastius insurgens decimae ruit impetus undae.

Lucan, *Pharsalia*, V, 672–3, has:

> Haec fatum decimus, dictu mirabile, fluctus
> Invalida cum puppe levat.

Seneca, *Agamemnon*, III, 501–2:

> Haec onere sidit. illa convulsum latus
> Summittit undis. fluctus hanc decimus tegit.

Silius Italicus, *Punica*, XIV, 122–4:

> Non aliter Boreas, Rhodopes a vertice praeceps
> Cum sese immisit, decimoque volumine pontum
> Expulit in terras.

Valerius Flaccus, *Argonautica*, II, 54–55:

> Quanta quoties et Palladis arte
> Incassum decimae cecidit tumor arduus undae.

Cf. the Greek, τρικυμία. Further see the *Miscellanea* of Poli-
tian, LXXXVI: "De Fluctu Decimo, seu Decumano, cuius per-
multi poetae meminerunt."

p. 353.   *from wild Atoms wrought.* This teaching is that of Epicurus, who
followed Democritus of Abdera in his atomic theory. The atoms
forming innumerable worlds are the result of τύχη, and not
directed by the νοῦς of Anaxagoras of Clazomenae.

p. 355.   *the Gaules.* Rather the Sabines who threw as well as their gold armlets
their heavy shields upon Tarpeia, crushing her to death. Livy, I, xi.

p. 359.   *Ber. My earthy part——* This beautiful speech of Berenice has been
cruelly parodied in *The Rehearsal*, IV.

p. 359.   *Indian Cave.* No doubt the scene which had already been used for
Ismeron in *The Indian Queen*, III, and for the incantation scene in
The Indian Emperour, II, 1, "the Magician's Cave."

p. 360. *eighty Legions.* Weyer in his *Pseudomonarchia Daemonum* has: "Legio 6666." Scot in his *Discouerie of Witchcraft*, Booke XV, 2, adopts this: "*Note that a legion is* 6666."

p. 360. *Nakar . . . Damilcar.* Certain of the names which Dryden gives his spirits and demons, Damilcar, Melanax, Philidel, Grimbald, seem his own invention. I have not found them in the demonologists.

p. 360. *Sperma Ceti.* Supposed to be aphrodisiacal on account of the false derivation. *Sperma, sperm,* +*ceti,* genitive of *cetus* (κῆτος).

p. 360. *Lignum Aloes.* Cf. *Liber Proverbiorum,* VII, 17, where the harlot says: "Aspersi cubile meum myrrha, et aloe, et cinnamomo." Also *Canticum Canticorum,* IV, 14: "myrrha et aloe cum omnibus primis unguentis."

p. 360. *Sparrows.* The bird was sacred to Venus. "Ob passeris ex natura salacitatem." And in the *Priapeia,* XXV, we have:

Vicinae sine fine prurientes,
Vernis passeribus salaciores.

"Inde Galloprovinciales" says the *Glossarium Eroticum* (1826), "lingua vernacula penem nuncupant *lou passeroun.*" Gaspar Scioppius commenting upon the above lines writes: "Cum Ingolstadii agerem vidi e regione musaei mei passerem coitum vicies repetentem, et inde adeo ad languorem datum, ut avolaturus in terram decideret."

Pigeons were also sacred to Venus, and pigeons' blood was used in confecting love-charms.

p. 360. *Nakar and Damilcar descend.* This incantation scene is parodied in *The Rehearsal,* V. The name Nakar is perhaps an abbreviation of Nakaronkir, "esprit que Mahomet envoie dans leur sommeil aux mussulmans coupables, pour les pousser au repentir" (Collin de Plancy). The incongruity would not have troubled Dryden.

p. 361. *racking.* To rack is said of clouds that drive before the wind. Cf. Bunyan, *Pilgrim's Progress,* I (1678), 1, 32: "I . . . saw the Clouds rack at an unusual rate."

p. 361. *a Gelly of Love!* It will be remembered that the word *jelly* was applied to the alga *Nostoc,* which appears as a jelly-like mass on dry soil after rain, and thus was popularly supposed to be the remains of a fallen "star" or meteor. To this Dryden more than once refers, *e.g.* *Oedipus,* II, 1: "The shooting Stars end all in purple Gellies."

p. 362. *Gemory.* The name is from Weyer's *Pseudomonarchia Daemonum.* "Gomory Dux fortis et potens: apparet ut mulier pulcherrima: ac ducali cingitur corona, in camelo equitans. Bene et vere respondet de praeteritis, praesentibus, futuris, et occultis thesauris ubi lateant. Conciliat amorem mulierum, et maxime puellarum. Imperat legionibus vigintisex." In Collin de Plancy's *Dictionnaire Infernal,* 6me édition, 1863 (p. 307), there is a somewhat fanciful woodengraving by M. L. Breton which represents Gomory riding upon a richly-caparisoned camel.

EXPLANATORY NOTES

p. 362. *A Scene of a Paradise.* The Elysium painted by Isaac Fuller, which is said to have cost £335 10s. See the Theatrical History of the play.

p. 367. *obnoxious to my justice.* "Obnoxious" in the rare sense of "subject to"; answerable, amenable (to authority). So Cleveland in his *Rustick Ramp* (*Works*, ed. 1687): "That Kings are only the Tenants of Heaven, obnoxious to God alone."

p. 368. (*and Lapwing like.*) This bird is so named from his manner of flight. Allusions to its wily method of drawing attention away from its nest are frequent. So Gower, *Confessio Amantis*, II, 329:

> A lappe-winke has lost his feith
> And is the bird falsest of alle.

p. 369. *their Prince commands.* Suetonius tells us that Claudius was the first emperor who purchased the submission of the soldiers with money. "Primus Caesarum fidem militis etiam praemio pigneratus." *Claudius*, X. The Praetorian Guard soon ruled the destinies of Rome. Thus when they became exasperated with Galba they dispatched him, and advanced Otho to the empire. Titus was careful to assume the command of the praetorians, although hitherto nobody above the rank of *eques* had been their prefect. For an example of the power of the praetorians see Spartianus, *Didius Julianus*. Alexander ab Alexandro, VI, writes: Praetoriani "in tantum viribus processere, ut quem vellent, ad spem imperii impellerent, et in principem assumerent, assumptumque mox deturbarent, essentque arbitri totius imperii et moderatores."

p. 369. *An Eagle.* Cf. Dryden's *Heroick Stanzas* (A Poem Upon The Death Of . . . Oliver, Lord Protector), 1659:

> And now 'tis time; for their officious haste,
>   Who would before have born him to the Sky,
> Like eager *Romans* e'er all Rites were past,
>   Did let too soon the sacred Eagle fly.

Dio Cassius, *Historia Romana*, lvi, describing the funeral of Augustus, has (xli, 3): "Καὶ ἡ πυρὰ μεν ἀνηλίσκετο, ἀετὸς δέ τις ἐξ αὐτῆς ἀφεθεὶς ἀνίπτατο ὡς καὶ δὴ τὴν ψυχὴν αὐτοῦ ἐς τὸν οὐρανὸν ἀναφέρων." "Testantur etiam nummi, in quorum una parte est effigies Divi Imperatoris: in altera vero Aquila, cum his verbis: Consecratio. S.C. Itemque effigies ipsorum Imperatorum aquilae insidentium. Quod ex veteri ritu procul dubio ortum, quo Reges et Principes viri post mortem aquilae insidere ab eaque vehi fingebantur pingebanturque." Kirchmann, *De Funeribus Romanorum*, IV, 13. I have used the edition "apud Hackios. Lugd. Batav.," 1672 (p. 568). See further Artemidorus, II, xx.

p. 369. *Erre after bliss.* Err = errare, to wander, to ramble. "We have erred and strayed from thy ways like lost sheep," *Book of Common Prayer*. Dryden's frequent Latinisms should be remarked. So Chaucer, *Troilus and Criseyde*, IV, 302 (*c.* 1379): "O wery goost, that errest to and fro." Sternhold and Hopkins, *Psalms* (1549–62). Psalm cvii, 40:

> And likewise caused them to erre
> Within the wildernesse.

p. 370. *envy.* The odium; unpopularity. (*Envy* is often thus used to translate Latin *invidia*.) Cf. Bacon, *The Historie of the raigne of King Henry VII*, folio, 1622 (p. 100): "This Taxe (called Benevolence) was deuised by Edward the Fourth, for which hee sustained much Enuie."

p. 371. *Ber. Now death draws near.* In Desfontaines *Sainte Catherine*, IV, 4, Valérie (who corresponds to Berenice) has this speech:

> Bien que je cède à cette juste envie
> Mon coeur fait résistance: il aime encore la vie.
> Il s'oppose, il triomphe, et dégénère en soi
> Des aspirations que lui donne la foi,
> Il renonce à sa gloire, il renonce à soi-même,
> Son bonheur l'épouvante, il aime à vivre, il s'aime.
> Ce coeur, ce traitre coeur, toujours irrésolu,
> Laisse prendre à la crainte un pouvoir absolu.

It has been compared to Berenice's lines, but the resemblance is of the slightest, and most certainly adventitious.

p. 373. *witty glosses.* Witty, in an obsolete and somewhat unfavourable sense, artful; wilily ingenious. So Sir T. Herbert, *Travels* (Second Edition), 1638: "As simple as they seeme, they are witty enough in craft, revenge, and villany." J. Beaumont, *Psyche*, XXI, iv; "Witty too in Self delusion."

p. 375. *my Caesar.* Caesar, the heir to the throne; the crown-prince. Thus Spartianus, *Ælius Verus*, 1: "De Ælio Vero dicendum est, qui primus tantum *Caesaris* nomen accepit, adoptione Adriani familiae principum adscriptus." Sextus Aurelius Victor, *De Caesaribus:* Ælius Hadrianus "Deinde, uti solet tranquillis rebus, remissior rus proprium Tibur secessit permissa urbe Lucio Ælio Caesari. . . . Interim Ælio Caesare mortuo . . . ad creandum Caesarem Patres convocat."

p. 376. *adoption* = my adopted Son. This use of abstract nouns is not infrequent with Dryden.

p. 380. *at one door.* One of the permanent proscenium doors.

p. 381. *it is not you I hear.* Cf. Tourneur, *The Revenger's Tragedy*, 4to, 1607; Act II: *Castiza.* Mother, come from that poisonous woman there.

p. 383. *The Wheel.* Metaphrastes, XVIII, says that this instrument was suggested to the Emperor by a Prefect named Chrysasades, who advised thus: "Κέλευσον ὑπὸ περόνη μίᾳ τέσσαρας γενέσθαι τροχὸυς. ἑκάστῳ δὲ τῶν τροχῶν πρηστῆρας ἐμπαγῆναι καὶ ἥλους ὀξεῖς· εἶτα σχοινίοις τὸ μηχάνημα καὶ τροχιλίσκοις πρὸ τῶν αὐτῆς ὀφθαλμῶν ἑλκυσθῆναι."

EXPLANATORY NOTES

p. 383.   *her tender breasts.* "Μέγιστον οὖν κιβώτιον ἐνεγκὼν καὶ μολίβδῳ πρὸς
τὸ ἔδαφος αὐτὸ ἐμπεδώσας, ὡς ἂν πεπηγός τε ᾖ καὶ ἀκίνητον, καὶ
τοῦτο ἀνοίξας, τοὺς τῆς οἰκείας, οἴμοι! συζύγου μαστοὺς, τῇ
ὑποκειμένῃ τῷ πώματι προσηλοῖ τῆς σανίδος ἀκίδι. Ἔπειτα
σφοδρότερον καταφέρεσθαι κελεύει τὸ πῶμα, καὶ μὴ πρότερον
στῆναι, πρὶν ἢ καὶ αὐτοὺς τὸ παράπαν τοὺς μαστοὺς ἀποτέμοι,
τῇ τῆς κολάσεως παραστάσει δριμυτέραν ἐμποιῶν αὐτῇ τῆς
ὀδύνης τὴν αἴσθησιν. Τούτου δὴ γεγονότος, ἐπεὶ ἀποκοπέντας
αὐτοὺς εἶδεν, ἐλεεινῶς ὁ ἀπηνὴς ἐκεῖνος καὶ θηρίων ὠμότερος κοῦφον
ὥσπερ εἰς ὀδύνης λόγον τὸ πρᾶγμα νομίσας ἐπάγει καὶ τὸ
βαρύτερον, καὶ ἀποτμηθῆναι διὰ ξίφους καὶ τὴν κεφαλὴν αὐτῆς
ἀποφαίνεται." Symeon Metaphrastes. *Op. cit.*, XX. It will be
noticed that it is the Empress, Augusta, who is thus tortured, not,
as in Dryden, the mother of the Saint for whom the torment is
intended.

p. 383.   *bearded Tenters.* A tenter is here equivalent to tenter-hook. A tenter
is a wooden framework upon which cloth is stretched after being
milled so that it may dry evenly without shrinking. A tenter-hook
is one of the hooks or bent nails by which the cloth is held in
position. The word is often used out of its technical sense to mean
any sharp iron hook or crotchet. The hook is bearded or barbed,
that is to say jagged, as an arrow or fish-hook.

p. 384.   *Amariel descends.* "Ἡ γὰρ μάρτυς πάντων ὁμοῦ καὶ τοῦ σιδήρου καὶ
τῶν τροχῶν καὶ τῶν δεσμῶν ἐκείνων ἐλέλυτο, ἀγγέλου πρὸς αὐτὴν
ἄνωθεν καταβάντος. Οἱ τρόχοι δὲ, αὐτόματοι κυλισθέντες, πολλοὺς
τῶν ἀπίστων ἀνεῖλον, ὥστε καὶ κράζειν τινὰς τῶν περιεστώτων
ἐπὶ τῷ παραδόξῳ τούτῳ θεάματι· Μέγας ὁ Θεὸς τῶν Χριστιανῶν."
Metaphrastes. *Op. cit.*, XIX.

p. 384.   *Bilbilis.* A town in an elevated position in Hispania Tarraconensis on
the river Salo (Xalon), now Calatayud Vieja. Martial, who was
born at Bilbilis, calls it "Equis et armis nobilem," I, L, 4, and again
"auro Bilbilis et superba ferro," XII, xviii, 9. IV, LV, 10–15,
he even more precisely writes:

> grato non pudeat referre versu,
> saevo Bilbilin optimam metallo,
> quae vincit Chalybasque, Noricosque,
> et ferro Plateam suo sonantem,
> quam fluctu tenui, sed inquieto
> armorum Salo temperator ambit.

Pliny, *Historia Naturalis*, XXXIV (Æris metalla), 14, notes:
"Summa autem differentia in aqua est, cui subinde [ferrum] cana
dens immergitur. Haec alibi atque alibi utilior nobilitavit loca glori-
ferri, sicut Bilbilin in Hispania." Upon this Gabriel Brotier (1779)
glosses: "Manent Bilbilis rudera in monte *Bambola*, prope urbem
Calatayud. Aqua eius temperando ferro celebratissima est amnis
Salo, nunc *Xalon*." Dryden's exceptional accuracy of allusion should
be remarked.

531

p. 395.   *the Bearers.* Valeria had died well "down stage" on the apron. It was the custom in a Restoration theatre at the end of the play for the speaker of the Epilogue to advance and deliver the lines, and the curtain was drawn after the Epilogue. So at the end of Sir Robert Howard's tragedy, *The Vestal Virgin* (first version), acted at the Theatre Royal probably in 1664, "Just as the last Words were spoke, Mr. *Lacy* enter'd, and spoke the Epilogue," which commences:

> *By your leave, Gentlemen——*
> *After a sad and dismal Tragedy,*
> *I do suppose that few expected me.*

p. 395.   *Out of my Calling in a Tragedy.* In the Epilogue "Spoken by Mrs. Ellen" to Sir Robert Howard's *The Great Favourite*, produced at the Theatre Royal, Thursday, 20 February, 1667–8, she says:

> *I know you in your hearts*
> *Hate serious Plays, as I do serious Parts.*

On Wednesday, 22 August, 1667, Pepys went to the Theatre Royal, "and there saw 'The Indian Emperour'; where I find Nell come again, which I am glad of; but was most infinitely displeased with her being put to act the Emperour's daughter; which is a great and serious part, which she do most basely." Again, Monday, 11 November, of the same year, Pepys went "to the King's play-house, and there saw 'The Indian Emperour,' a good play, but not so good as people cry it up, I think, though above all things Nell's ill speaking of a great part made me mad."

p. 395.   *Easter-Term.* See the Theatrical History as to the exact date of the production of this tragedy.

p. 395.   *acting in S. Cathar'n.* There are frequent allusions to this Epilogue which was rapturously applauded by the Town. Worthy of remark is the Epilogue to *Piso's Conspiracy*, a tragedy altered from *Nero*, quarto, 1624, and given at Dorset Garden during the late autumn of 1675 as a counterweight to the success of Lee's *The Tragedy of Nero*, produced at the Theatre Royal in May, 1674. This Epilogue commences:

> *It is a Trick of late grown much in Vogue*
> *When all are kill'd to raise an* Epilogue.
> *This, some Pert Rymer wittily contriv'd*
> *For a Surprize, whil'st the Arch Wag believ'd;* ⎫
> *'Twould please You to see pretty* Miss *reviv'd.* ⎭

A plate illustrating the Epilogue to *Tyrannick Love*, which appeared in vol. II of Buckingham's *Works* (1714), was reproduced by me in my edition of *The Rehearsal* (p. 75), 1914.